U.S. Business Law
Class

충북대학교 인문사회 연구총서

U.S. Business Law Class

KWANG-ROK KIM

PROFESSOR OF LAW
CHUNGBUK NATIONAL UNIVERSITY

충북대학교 출판부

PREFACE

Each time I teach English classes on U.S. laws at Korean universities I am always faced with the daunting problem of providing my students with materials regarding U.S. laws even though there are a lot of books and treaties in relation of U.S. laws. Therefore I am always feeling that "a famine of class materials in a feast of U.S. references" especially when I teach the U.S. business law.

This year, I am teaching "U.S. Business Law" at my school of law at Chungbuk National University as usual ever since the Korea law school system has been launched in Korea in 2009. Frankly speaking I was just asked to open some English classes at a "POSSIBLE" CBNU law school in order to get some more points among universities which applied for authorization of opening law schools during 2007 ~ 2008. At that time I did not pay attention to the specific details on some materials that will be handled in the real classes at the school because opening some English classes was just for use of applying for getting approval of opening a law school.

However I had to teach this "U.S. Business Law" class at my law school since 2011 so I tried to search some suitable materials for the class but it was not easy. Therefore I decided that I should edit class materials for my students, collect U.S. books and treaties regarding U.S. business law, and complete a course material. Then I have compiled some materials from "the LexisNexis Law School Faculty Web site at http://www.lexisnexis.com/lawschool/.," "Introduction to Legal English (Mark E. Wojcik, ILI, 1998)," "The Law of Corporations (Robert W. Hamilton, West Group, 2000)," "Corporations (Emmanuel Law Outlines, Emmanuel Publishing Corp. 1997)," "Understanding Corporate Law (Arthur R. Pinto, Douglas M. Branson, LEXIS Publishing, 1999)" and some other materials into this course material. I know the phrase "though thy beginning was small, yet thy latter end should greatly increase [KJV]" and I am sure all the students and I will fully understand the real meaning of this phrase and improve ourselves for understanding U.S. business law when reading the last page of this course material.

I wish to thank a number of individuals for their help regarding this project and my special thanks to my adorable wife, Kyoung-Shin Park, daughters, Min-Jeong & Dong-Yeon, and my little son Min-Suk for their endless love and efforts. So I wish to dedicate this material to my family. I have been fortunate to teach during past 15 years at universities in Korea as a professor with wonderful students and I definitely know the fortune comes from the bottom of my family's hearts.

January 2015

Kwang Rok Kim

TABLE OF CONTENTS

OLD DOMINION COPPER MINING & SMELTING CO. vs. ALBERT S. BIGELOW

PART I.

BASIC UNDERSTANDING US LAW

CHAPTER 1

US LEGAL SYSTEM[1)]

1.1 INTRODUCTION: GENERAL BACKGROUND

This material, U.S. Business Law Class, is to provide basic legal environments of business corporations in the United States to you, the students of the US Business Law class at Chung buk National University. Therefore, this material will start with basic theories of law and society, U.S. Legal System, Resources of Law, and business ethics which is related to the Corporate Social Responsibility. The purpose of this course is to expose you to the legal environment which business operates in the U.S. and make you understand legal points of U.S. Business entities. For the purpose, we will discuss about business forms and some doctrines applied to the U.S. business forms, focusing on the C-corporation, finances, structures, director's duty, and some significant securities matters such as concept of securities, tender offer, insider trading, and so forth.

1) This Chapter is compiled mainly with materials from the related internet web sites, the LexisNexis Law School Faculty Web site at http://www.lexisnexis.com/ lawschool/., and Mark E. Wojcik, "Introduction to Legal English," International Law Institute (1998).

American Law & Legal education. American Legal Education is unique. It is very different from others. Generally, it is not so concern and single-minded. It is rather normative issue. So every American is arguing what it should be. Law is a hot issue not only of law school but also American life. Discussing law is common attitude for American. Therefore, Law is a kind of state religion.

Historical and Cultural Reason. American always hates their Government. So, they have thought only Law can against government and protect people from the government. There are some events.

Declaration of Independence (1776. 7. 4.) It first stated that Law is more powerful than Government. Law included *Right* and *Freedom* is the only thing that can bond American people.

Federalism. At the very first time, State government had all power. National government could not do something important but only do set out something in constitution. Federalism in the United States is the evolving relationship between U.S. state governments and the federal government of the United States.

There have consistently been battles between State government and Federal government. Since the founding of the country, and particularly with the end of the American Civil War, power shifted away from the states and towards the national government. But, at present, Federal government is stronger than State government.

The Influence of English Law in America. Actually the influence of English law which had virtually ended by the time of the Civil War, is negligible today. However the fundamental Ideas were imported into American Law. First, the concept of supremacy of law, as exemplified in the U.S. by the distinctive principle that even the state is subject to judicial review under constitutional standards. Second, the tradition of precedent, according to which later decisions are based on earlier cases. Third, the notion of trial as contentious proceeding, a contest, often before a jury, in which the adversary parties take the initiative an in which the role of the judge is that of umpire rather than of inquisitor.

There are also some events why federal government has power as stated below.

Marbury V. Madison (1803): Constitution Made by Supreme Court which is National Court. After Thomas Jefferson took office following the presidency of John Adams, Jefferson refused to honor what has become known as the "midnight appointments." Jefferson, instead, appointed his own people to various judge positions. This disagreement between Jefferson and Adams led to the landmark Supreme Court case of Marbury vs. Madison. In this case, Chief Justice John Marshall and his court were instrumental in establishing the idea of "judicial review." The establishment of judicial review is extremely significant in the history of the United States and that of the Supreme Court.

Civil War (1861-1865): Civil War is war of Federalism. Southern States would not protect their people. Civil War Amendments which are 13th, 14th and 15th amendment slim the power of State government. American people would like to say I am the citizen of State before Civil War but I am the citizen of the U.S.A. after Civil War.

New Deal (1930'S): State government did not have a settlement but National government did have a plan to save people from the Great Depression that was in Oct. 1929. That means National government had a power to regulate even state's economy.

Civil Right (1960'S): Equal Right between black and white - Supreme Court allows National government to protect black people. Justice Thurgood Marshall who is black came into the Supreme Court in 1952. Generally speaking, society changes Law but, in this case, Law changed society.

Regan & Gangrich Revolution (1980 and 1990'S): National government gives power back to the State government.

However it is very important to understand the modern American legal system that the civil war amendment of American Constitution is how much influence to the American Legal System. In that civil war amendment of American Constitution, the Thirteenth, Fourteenth, and Fifteenth Amendments were important to the Civil Rights Movement. The Thirteenth Amendment ended slavery in the United States. The Fourteenth Amendment allowed Blacks to have the same rights as Whites. The Fifteenth Amendment allowed Blacks to vote. Although many people were against the amendments at first, the amendments were very helpful for the Civil Rights Movement. Although many were against the amendments, the Thirteenth, Fourteenth, and Fifteenth Amendments played an important part in the Civil Rights Movement. The amendments declared that Blacks were real people and should be treated as equals and not as property. The amendments also gave Blacks the right to vote, making it possible to change things.

Thirteenth Amendment. The Thirteenth Amendment was added to the Constitution in 1865. It made slavery illegal in the United States. Many states passed laws to protect the rights of Blacks, but white people against racial equality, mostly from the South, fought against similar laws when Congress tried to pass them. In addition to the equality issue, some states did not accept the Thirteenth Amendment because they believed freeing the slaves would cause other problems.

Slave owners were used to the slaves' cheap labor and paying others to do the same work would cost more and lower how much money they made. Some slave owners wanted the government to pay for their freed slaves. Workers in the North wanted Blacks to stay in the South because they were afraid Blacks would take their jobs for less pay and poorer working conditions. Many slaves still could not obtain a good job because of discrimination and the lack of a good education. Blacks still did not have the same Civil Rights as Whites.

> *Thirteenth Amendment Section 1.* Neither slavery nor involuntary servitude, except as a punishment for crime whereof the party shall have been duly convicted, shall exist within the United States, or any place subject to their jurisdiction.
>
> *Thirteenth Amendment Section 2.* Congress shall have power to enforce this article by appropriate legislation.

Fourteenth Amendment. Congress passed the Fourteenth Amendment, sometimes called the "Great Amendment," to help protect the rights of the freed slaves. It was added to the Constitution in 1868. It stated that all people who were born in the United States, including African-Americans, are considered natural citizens and have the same rights as all other Americans. It also prohibited any state from making or enforcing any laws that took away or hurt an individual's civil rights. After the Fourteenth Amendment passed, many African-Americans still did not have all the rights Whites had. Many Whites, especially in the South, continued to treat the Blacks unfairly.

Voting was one right many Blacks had taken away. Many Blacks did not vote because some Whites did not want the Blacks to have this power. Voting provided power to change things. These Whites said that Blacks were not smart enough to vote and would not know who to vote for. They purposely did not tell the Blacks when or how to vote and did other things so Blacks could not vote.

> *Fourteenth Amendment Section 1.* All persons born or naturalized in the United States, and subject to the jurisdiction thereof, are citizens of the United States and of the State wherein they reside. No State shall make or enforce any law which shall abridge the privileges or immunities of citizens of the United States; nor shall any State deprive any person of life, liberty, or property, without due process of law; nor deny to any person within its jurisdiction the equal protection of the laws.
>
> *Fourteenth Amendment Section 2.* Representatives shall be apportioned among the several States according to their respective numbers, counting the whole number of persons in each State, excluding Indians not taxed. But when the right to vote at any election for the choice of electors for President and Vice-President of the United States, Representatives in Congress, the Executive and Judicial officers of a State, or the members of the Legislature thereof, is denied to any of the male inhabitants of such State, being twenty-one years of age, and citizens of the United States, or in any way abridged, except for participation in rebellion, or other crime, the basis of representation therein shall be reduced in the proportion which the number of such male citizens shall bear to the whole number of male citizens twenty-one years of age in

such State.

Fourteenth Amendment Section 3. No person shall be a Senator or Representative in Congress, or elector of President and Vice-President, or hold any office, civil or military, under the United States, or under any State, who, having previously taken an oath, as a member of Congress, or as an officer of the United States, or as a member of any State legislature, or as an executive or judicial officer of any State, to support the Constitution of the United States, shall have engaged in insurrection or rebellion against the same, or given aid or comfort to the enemies thereof. But Congress may by a vote of two-thirds of each House, remove such disability.

Fourteenth Amendment Section 4. The validity of the public debt of the United States, authorized by law, including debts incurred for payment of pensions and bounties for services in suppressing insurrection or rebellion, shall not be questioned. But neither the United States nor any State shall assume or pay any debt or obligation incurred in aid of insurrection or rebellion against the United States, or any claim for the loss or emancipation of any slave; but all such debts, obligations and claims shall be held illegal and void.

Fourteenth Amendment Section 5. The Congress shall have power to enforce, by appropriate legislation, the provisions of this article.

Fifteenth Amendment. The Fifteenth Amendment was added to the Constitution in 1870 to protect Blacks' voting rights. It prohibited the national and state governments from refusing citizens the right to vote because of their race, color, or because they were a slave at one time. After the Fifteenth Amendment was passed, a large number of Blacks voted during the late 1860's through the 1880's.

The African-Americans used their voting rights to gain political power and to protect their rights. Soon, southern states started passing laws to make it harder for Blacks to vote. Some states passed laws that required people to pay a poll tax before voting. Others required people to pass a reading or writing test before voting. Since most Blacks had been slaves their whole lives, they had little money to pay a poll tax and did not know how to read or write. Some people were still trying to take away the civil rights of African

Americans.

Fifteenth Amendment Section 1. The right of citizens of the United States to vote shall not be denied or abridged by the United States or by any State on account of race, color, or previous condition of servitude.

Fifteenth Amendment Section 2. The Congress shall have power to enforce this article by appropriate legislation.

WHAT IS FREEDOM? Just imagine that you are the only one in this world. Then, what could you do and what should you do? I guess that you may think you do a lot of things you wished. You feel free from what you are belonging to; for example schools, works, society, regulations, rules and so on. In case of Robinson Crusoeu who is very famous character in the English novel, he just tried to make something to be ordered. Even though he was alone, he loved to make something like regulations. Generally speaking, we, man, always want to escape from society mixed with regulations that restrict our freedom. Then, how come he just tried to rule something around him and to be restricted by what he made as regulations? The answer is very simple. You cannot live alone and you need and want to be a "member" of "society." That is human who cannot live without regulations and laws.

Here, we have two different regulations named State constitutional provision and statue address freedom of speech and civil cause of action for defamation. I am very sure that even if you are human who ought to make laws by instinct, you would have not made those kind laws when you are alone, which means those two regulations can exist in only "society."

In a society, what can you do or what should you do? Of course, you are free just like Jesus who is the only Son of God. But, just think about it. What Jesus did before? Did he do something bad for a society or this world? Did he tried to make the world worse? I am not going to answer to those questions. Instead, let me tell you something that you are definitely, wholly and perfectly free when you have Good in your mind. At least, you should not bother anybody else. Because of that you should do something good for a society and you are not free if you would try to do something bad for a society, or, at least, to other people who live with you in a society.

Then, what should you do to make the world better? I think that you should spread your thought to others, share your opinions and deduct something developed through exchanging minds, ideas, and feelings. Sometimes, you can criticize others in order to extract better ideas and remove really bad influence on a society. But, you should be careful when you express your opinion. You should first think that it will be whether bad or not for the public society. Still more, you should not spoil something in person even though it will not be very bad for a society. Because individual is a kind of small society.

In this instant case, those two regulations look very different. At first sight, Constitution allows us freedom and Code restricts freedom and you may think code should follows the Constitution, not like this. That is right. But, why don't you think the values inside concerned what I mentioned above. Then, you can find out what you should do or what you should not do in our society. In my thought, those two looking different regulations are basically same.

What is freedom? Now, you can tell: Freedom is right to choose to be free or not to be free. Freedom has a contradiction in itself. Choose well for the bright better future society.

1.2 U.S. LEGAL SYSTEM

Question. A salient characteristic of the American judicial system is its cleavage into parallel systems of state and federal courts. How these systems organized and what are the limits of their jurisdiction?

In the United States, laws are made at the federal and state levels. Laws adopted by legislative bodies - Congress and state legislatures - are called "statutes." The federal and state courts enforce statutes. They also create law.

These materials describe some of the basic concepts of our legal system, and the roles played by legislatures and courts.

Federal Statutes. The U.S. Constitution gives Congress to power to enact federal laws ("statutes") on certain subjects.

The Copyright Act is one example of a statute adopted by Congress. Congress's power to enact the Copyright Act stems from Article I, Section 8, of the Constitution, which authorizes Congress to establish laws giving "authors and inventors the exclusive right to their respective writings and discoveries" to encourage progress in the arts and sciences. According to the Constitution, all powers not delegated to Congress are reserved to the states. The "commerce clause" of the Constitution, which concerns interstate commerce, is generally viewed as giving Congress broad power to regulate matters affecting interstate commerce - trademarks used in interstate commerce, for example.

Federal law-making begins when a member of the Senate or the House of Representatives introduces a bill. Most bills are referred to standing committees, for example, the House Committee on the Judiciary, and to subcommittees for study. Bills are later brought before the Senate or House for debate and vote. Differences between the Senate and House versions of a bill are resolved in joint conference committees.

After the House and Senate have approved a uniform version of the bill, the bill is sent to the President. If the President signs the bill, it becomes law. If the President vetoes the bill, it becomes law only if the Senate and House override the veto. This requires the consent of two-thirds of the members of the Senate and House.

State Statutes. State legislatures can pass laws on matters for which they share jurisdiction with Congress. Trademark law is an example of a shared jurisdiction. In other matters, the federal government has taken exclusive jurisdiction. Copyright is an example: The Copyright Act prohibits the states from granting copyright-like protection. States can also pass laws on matters in which the Constitution does not grant jurisdiction to the federal government. State law-making occurs through a process that is similar to the federal process.

Types of Courts. There are several types of courts. The federal and state court systems consist of two levels of courts: Trial courts and appellate courts. Cases are tried in trial courts. Appellate courts review the decisions of the trial courts. The federal court system is divided into 13 judicial circuits. Eleven of the circuits are numbered. Each of the numbered circuits contains more than one state. The Ninth Circuit, for example, covers California, Oregon, Washington, Idaho, Nevada, Arizona, Alaska, and Hawaii. The 12th and 13th circuits are the District of Columbia Circuit and the Federal Circuit. The Federal Circuit handles appeals in patent cases and Claims Court cases.

Each federal circuit has one appellate court. These courts are known as Courts of Appeals or Circuit Courts. The Supreme Court reviews the decisions of the Courts of Appeals. Each federal circuit is divided into judicial districts. A district can be as small as one city or as large as an entire state. The trial courts are known as the United States District Courts.

1.3 JURISDICTION

The Federal Courts have jurisdiction over cases involving federal statutes (the Copyright Act, for example) and other "federal questions." They also have jurisdiction over cases in which the party filing the suit and the party being sued reside in different states. This type of federal jurisdiction is known as "diversity" jurisdiction. Other types of cases must be brought in state court.

CIVIL LAWSUITS.

There are several stages in civil lawsuits, from initiation to trial and then on to stages of appeal. We'll discuss these stages in this section.

Initiation. A civil lawsuit is initiated when the plaintiff files a "complaint" against the defendant alleging that the defendant has wronged the plaintiff in some way recognized by the law. In most civil lawsuits, the plaintiff asks the court to award the plaintiff "damages" (a remedy for the defendant's wrongdoing - usually money) or to order the defendant to do something.

Answer. The defendant responds to the allegations in the complaint by filing an "answer" (a document in which the defendant admits or denies the complaint's allegations and states defenses). The defendant can also file a "counterclaim" against the plaintiff (allegations that the plaintiff has wronged the defendant).

Trial. If the parties do not "settle" the case (reach their own agreement on how to resolve the dispute), the case eventually goes to trial. In most types of civil cases, the Constitution gives the parties a right to a jury trial. The role of the jury is to decide questions of fact. However, in some complex cases, the parties choose to dispense with the jury and have the case decided by the judge.

Appeal. If the losing party in a civil lawsuit is not satisfied with the decision of the trial court, the losing party can appeal the case to the appropriate appellate court.

An Appellate Court's job in reviewing a trial court's decision is to look for "mistakes of law" made by the trial court. Appellate courts do not "second guess" factual issues decided by trial courts. In the U.S. legal system, factual issues are supposed to be resolved by the jury, not by the appellate court. So long as there is adequate factual evidence to support the verdict, an appellate court will not reverse a trial court's decision or "remand" the case (send it back to the trial court for retrial) unless they find that the trial court made a "mistake of law."

Appellate Courts generally issue written opinions explaining how they reached their conclusions on whether to affirm (uphold), reverse, or remand a case. These opinions are important parts of the development of the law because the U.S. legal system is based on "precedent" (reliance on previously decided cases).

In the federal court system, the appeal generally must be filed with the Court of Appeals for the judicial circuit in which the trial was held. A case tried in the United States District Court for the Northern District of California, for example, must be appealed to the Court of Appeals for the Ninth Circuit.

SUPREME COURT REVIEW.

There are two ways to get a case reviewed by the U.S. Supreme Court: by appeal and by certiorari. The losers in certain types of cases - for example, cases involving claims that state statutes are unconstitutional - have a right to appeal to the Supreme Court. For most cases, though, there is no right of appeal to the Supreme Court. However, a party who has lost a case at the federal Court of Appeals level can file a petition for certiorari with the Supreme Court. A petition for certiorari is a document explaining why the Supreme Court should review a case. If the Supreme Court grants certiorari, the appeal proceeds. If the Court denies it, the Court of Appeals' decision stands.

Thousands of petitions for certiorari are filed each year and most are denied. The Supreme Court is likely to grant certiorari on a case only if the case involves a matter of national interest or the Court believes that it must decide the case to resolve conflicts among the Circuit Courts and create uniformity in federal law.

General Procedure of Case. General procedure of case is following the steps as below stated. First, the plaintiff files a summons and a *complaint*[2] with the clerk of court. The plaintiff's attorney will also file an *appearance.*[3]

Second, the summons and complaint will be personally served on the

2) In legal terminology, a complaint is any formal legal document that sets out the facts and legal reasons that the filing party or parties (the plaintiff(s)) believes are sufficient to support a claim against the party or parties against whom the claim is brought (the defendant(s)) that entitles the plaintiff(s) to a remedy, either money damages or injunctive relief. In some jurisdictions, specific types of criminal cases may also be commenced by the filing of a complaint, also sometimes called a criminal complaint or felony complaint.

3) Appearance, from Latin apparere, to appear, is the coming into court of either of the parties to a lawsuit, and/or the formal act by which a defendant submits himself to the jurisdiction of the court.

defendant by a sheriff or a "process server." Other means of service may also be possible under local rule.

Third, the defendant's attorney will file a *general appearance*[4] on behalf of the defendant, unless the defendant denies that court has personal jurisdiction. If the defendant denies that the court has personal jurisdiction, the defendant may file a *special appearance*[5] to challenge the court's exercise jurisdiction.

Fourth, the defendant will file some responsive pleading to the plaintiff's complaint. This may be an answer to the allegations of the complaint, a *motion to dismiss* for lack of personal jurisdiction or subject matter jurisdiction, or a *counter-claim* (or *cross-claim*)[6] to assert the defendant's own claims against the plaintiff.

Fifth, the parties will engage in a period of *discovery*.[7] This may involve the answering of written interrogatories, producing documents and other evidence, taking depositions of parties and witnesses, and admitting facts or the authenticity of documents. A party may move to suppress or exclude certain evidence at this stage.

Sixth, the parties will appear periodically before the judge to report on the status of the case. Eventually the case will be ready for trial unless the case is settled privately between the parties.

Seventh, trial will commence. The trial is call before a jury or a single judge. The trial before a single judge may be called a BENCH TRAIL. If the trial is before a jury, each side will participate in the process of selecting juror(the "*vore dire*").

---

4) A simple and unqualified or unrestricted submission to the jurisdiction of the court.

5) A submission the jurisdiction of the court for some specific purpose only, not for all the purpose of the suit. The special appearance is for the purpose of testing or objecting to the sufficiency of service or the jurisdiction of the court over defendant without submitting to such jurisdiction.

6) Rule of Civil Procedure 13(g). Cross-claim is any claim by one party against a co-party arising out of the transaction or occurrence that is the subject matter of the original action.

7) In criminal proceedings, discovery emphasizes right of defense to obtain access to evidence necessary to prepare its own case (Britton v. State, 44 Wis.2d 109).

Eighth, the trail begins with an opening statement from the plaintiff and, usually, an opening statement from the defendant. The plaintiff will then present its testimony and other evidence in support of its case. The defense may cross-examine the prosecution's witness.

Ninth, when plaintiff has finished presenting its case, the defense will present its own testimony and evidence. Both sides will then make closing arguments and the jury will receive jury instruction to help it reach its verdict. The judge will usually enter a judgment base on the jury's verdict.

Finally, the losing side may decide to appeal to higher court.

CHAPTER 2

US JURY SYSTEM AND SOURCE OF LAW[8)]

2.1 GENERAL INFORMATION ON JURY SYSTEM

The Right to a Jury Trial. The Right to a Jury Trial is a fundamental right provided in the U.S. Constitution and binding on the states through the Fourteenth Amendment. In the words of Sir William Blackstone, the eminent 18th century English legal scholar, the trial by jury is "... the grand bulwark of our liberties ... the most transcendent privilege which any subject can enjoy or wish for." However, Article III, Section 2, clause 3 of the Constitution provides that the "trial of all Crimes, except in Cases of Impeachment, shall be by Jury ..." The Sixth Amendment reinforces this right by stating that "in all criminal prosecutions, the accused shall enjoy the right to a speedy and public trial, by an impartial jury of the State and district wherein the crime shall have been committed ..." The Seventh Amendment preserves the right of trial by jury in civil suits. So, every states

8) This Chapter is compiled mainly with materials from the LexisNexis Law School Faculty Web site at http://www.lexisnexis.com/lawschool/., and Mark E. Wojcik, "Introduction to Legal English," International Law Institute (1998).

of America also guarantees a jury trial in the state court system.[9] The right of the defendant to fair legal process includes having his or her fate determined by "a jury of peers," meaning representative members of the community. However, this right is dependent on those citizens who participate in the process. Jury service provides citizens with one of the few opportunities to actively participate in the workings of their government.

Qualifications for Jury Service.[10] A person is qualified for jury service if he or she is 18 years old or over; if he or she is a citizen of the United States and a resident of Minnesota and the county in which the court is located. A person must also be able to read or speak English and be physically and mentally capable of rendering jury service. However, a person is ineligible for jury service if he or she has not completed sentence or parole after a felony conviction, has already served on a jury within the last four years, or is a judge. Persons cannot be excluded from jury service on the basis of race, national origin, gender, religious belief or income.

An eligible juror may be excused from jury service by the judge or jury commissioner if their ability to perform jury duties is impaired or if performing such duties would be a continuing, extreme hardship to them. Jury service can more easily be deferred or postponed for reasonably short periods of time for reasons such as temporary health problems, vacation plans, employment conflicts, to arrange for child care, or pre-scheduled medical appointments.

Jury Selection. Names of potential jurors are drawn at random from a jury source list compiled from voter registration, drivers license, and state identification lists. The jury source list is intended to represent a fair cross-

---

9) See for the example the Minnesota Constitution, Article I, Section 4. "Trial by Jury: The right of trial by jury shall remain inviolate, and shall extend to all cases at law without regard to the amount in controversy. A jury trial may be waived by the parties in all cases in the manner prescribed by law. The legislature may provide that the agreement of five-sixths of a jury in a civil action or proceeding, after not less than six hours' deliberation, is a sufficient verdict. The legislature may provide for the number of jurors in a civil action or proceeding, provided that a jury have at least six members."

10) This qualifications especially apply to the state of Minnesota.

section of the community. Citizens selected for jury service and qualified to serve form a jury panel. Several types of trial juries may be chosen from the jury panel.

Types of Juries. Citizens may serve on several types of juries in the Minnesota court system. A Grand Jury may be called at the request of the county attorney for the purpose of issuing an indictment or formal charge in limited number of cases (first degree murder, political cases). A grand jury has 16-23 jurors and 12 jurors must agree on finding an indictment. Grand jurors serve for a term of several months. A Petit Jury is used in civil and criminal trials. A criminal jury will consist of twelve persons if the sentence for the crime charged is more than one year of confinement (felony). A jury of six persons will serve if the penalty is one year or less of confinement. All criminal cases require a unanimous jury decision in reaching a verdict. A jury in a civil case consists of six persons. Verdicts in civil cases should be unanimous, except that a civil jury may return a verdict, after six hours of deliberation, with which five of the six jurors agree.

Choosing a Trial Jury. Voir Dire ([vwar deer]) refers to the jury selection process for a particular trial. The goal is to select a fair and impartial jury through the elimination of jurors who may be prejudiced. During *voir dire* examinations, jurors are questioned first by the judge, then by each attorney. If a juror is even distantly related to the complainant or the accused, has previously sued the defendant in an unrelated civil matter, has been otherwise connected with either party in some business transaction, or cannot be fair and impartial for other reasons, he or she may be challenged for bias or "cause." In addition, the respective attorneys may exclude jurors they do not want, without having to show that the jurors are disqualified through cause. The attorney does this through a "peremptory" challenge. However, the number of peremptory challenges available to each attorney is limited.

Role of the Jury. The jury has the responsibility of deciding the facts at issue in a trial. For example, did Bill really drive through a red stoplight and cause the accident? The jurors will listen to the lawyer's opening statements, direct and cross examination of witnesses, and the closing arguments of each side.

They must listen and observe closely the testimony presented. After the judge instructs the jury as to the law and the issues of fact to be reached, they retire to consider the verdict. During deliberations jurors will consider, examine, and weigh all the evidence in the case with the sole power to decide disputed questions of fact and to put their conclusions in a verdict.

In a criminal case, a jury might be sequestered or separated from the public over night and if the case is particularly sensational, the jury may be sequestered for the length of the trial. During a trial, jurors are not to talk to anyone about the case or listen to anyone else talk about the case outside of the courtroom. However, Petit Jury service will usually last for 10-15 court days unless it takes longer to complete a particular trial. Jurors are reimbursed for travel expenses and are paid a small daily rate.

2.2 SOURCES OF LAW

The US government has some special characteristics. Federal republic with a federal government and 50 state governments: Over some matters e.g., treaty making, the federal government has exclusive jurisdiction. In other areas e.g., divorce law, each state makes its own rules. Certain other powers e.g., the power to tax are exercised concurrently by the federal and state governments. A government characterized by separation of powers: The U.S. Constitution and the constitutions of the states divide power among the legislative, judicial, and executive branches. All branches of government, not just the legislature, engage in some form of lawmaking.

Under the characteristic of the US government, sources of law are basically constituted by the primary authority, secondary authorities, and mandatory authority and persuasive authority.

Primary Authority. Primary Authority is the law itself, for example, the U.S. Constitution. There are four types of primary authority:

1. Federal and State Constitutions;
2. Federal and State Statutes;
3. Federal and State Administrative Regulations and Decisions;
4. Federal and State Judicial Decisions so called Case Laws.

Secondary Authority. Secondary Authority is commentary, descriptions, summaries, or statements about the law, such as a treatise about the U.S. Constitution. Although courts may consider some forms of secondary authority when making decisions, the principal objective of legal research is to find the most relevant primary authorities.

Mandatory v. Persuasive Authority. However, Primary Authority may be either Mandatory or Persuasive. Mandatory Authority is primary authority that must be followed by a court. Meanwhile, Persuasive Authority is primary authority that a court may consider but need not follow. Some types of primary authority are mandatory on all courts, state and federal. Other types of primary authority are mandatory only in one state or court.

FEDERAL AND STATE CONSTITUTIONS

U.S. Constitution. Article VI of the Constitution, which is the "Supremacy Clause," provides that it "shall be the supreme law of the Land." When any other type of primary authority conflicts with the U.S. Constitution, a court can declare that authority to be invalid and unenforceable. In the famous case of Marbury v. Madison, the U.S. Supreme Court ruled that the judiciary has the final authority to interpret the Constitution.)

State Constitution. A state constitution is the supreme law within that state and is mandatory on all courts in that state, as long as it does not conflict with the U.S. Constitution, a federal statute, or a federal administrative regulation. In any other state, however, a state constitution is not even persuasive authority.

FEDERAL AND STATE STATUTES

Federal Statute. The Congress of the United States enacts legislation. Although the Supremacy Clause also applies to federal statutes, the Constitution limits and defines Congress' legislative power in Article I, Section 8 by listing there the specific subjects Congress may regulate. Statutes enacted by Congress are mandatory authority on all courts, state and federal, and prevail over all other forms of primary authority except the U.S. Constitution.

State Statute. Every state has a legislature to make laws for that state. Unlike Congress, state legislatures have a general legislative power to enact laws on any subject. A state statute is mandatory authority on all courts in the state, as long as it does not conflict with a higher form of primary authority e.g., a federal statute. In any other state, however, a state statute is not even persuasive authority.

FEDERAL AND STATE ADMINISTRATIVE REGULATIONS AND DECISIONS

Federal Administrative regulations and Decisions. Federal agencies are created by Congress. Some agencies function as the President's cabinet e.g., the Department of State. Other agencies issue regulations to implement and enforce federal statutes. For example, the FDA was created by Congress to implement and enforce the Federal Food and Drug Act.

Federal agency regulations are mandatory authority on all courts, state and federal, and prevail over all other forms of primary authority except federal statutes and the U.S. Constitution. Some agencies not only enact regulations, they also issue decisions. Therefore, the NLRB can adjudicate disputes arising under the National Labor Relations Act. The decisions of federal agencies are usually appealable to the courts.

State Administrative regulations and Decisions. State agencies are created by state legislatures and sometimes by a State Constitution. Some agencies function within the Governor's office. Other agencies issue regulations to implement and enforce state statutes. State agency regulations are mandatory authority on all courts in the state, as long as the regulation does not conflict with a higher form of primary authority e.g., a state statute. Some state agencies not only enact regulations, they also issue decisions in disputes arising under a state regulatory statute. State agency regulations and decisions are not persuasive authority in any other state.

FEDERAL AND STATE JUDICIAL DECISIONS

U.S. Supreme Court Decision. The U.S. Supreme Court is the highest court in the federal judicial system. Article III of the U.S. Constitution lists the types of cases federal courts including, specifically the Supreme Court can adjudicate. When the Supreme Court decides cases interpreting the Constitution, acts of Congress and federal agency regulations, its decisions are mandatory authority on all courts, state and federal.

U.S. Court of Appeals Decision. There are 13 U.S. Courts of Appeal: 11 hear appeals coming from U.S. District Courts, which are trial courts, located in 11 numbered circuits. Namely, the Second Circuit Court of Appeals hears appeals from District Courts sitting in N.Y., Conn., Mass., R.I., Vermont and New Hampshire; 1 hears appeals coming from U.S. District Courts and federal agencies located in the District of Columbia; and 1 hears appeals on certain subjects such as patents coming from U.S. District Courts anywhere in the country. When a U.S. Court of Appeals for a given circuit decides cases interpreting an issue of federal law, its decisions are mandatory authority only on the U.S. District Courts located within that circuit. However, other federal and state courts may regard the decision as persuasive authority.

U.S. District Court Decision. There are over 90 federal judicial districts in the United States and its territories. Some states, such as Connecticut, have only one federal judicial district, but others, such as New York, have as many as four. The U.S. District Courts are the trial courts of the federal judiciary, and their primary role is to resolve issues of fact. However, in the process of managing a case from complaint to final judgment, trial courts often make decisions on matters of law. In most instances, a U.S. District Court decision is not mandatory on any other court, including another U.S. District Court sitting in the same judicial district. However, other federal and state courts may regard the decision as persuasive authority.

State Supreme Court Decision. The highest court in most states is called the Supreme Court, for example, the Connecticut Supreme Court. However, in New York, the lowest courts are called supreme courts, and the highest court is the court of appeals. A state Supreme Court decision on a matter of state law is mandatory authority only on the courts with in that state. However, other state and federal courts construing similar statutes may regard the decision as persuasive authority.

State Appellate Court Decision. Most states have intermediate appellate courts to hear appeals from trial and other specialized courts within the state. A state appellate court decision on a matter of state law is mandatory authority usually only on lower state courts with in the jurisdictional boundaries of that particular appellate court; in some states, the decision may also be mandatory on all lower state courts. Other state and federal courts may regard the decision as persuasive authority.

State Trial Court Decision. Every state has trial courts and lower specialized courts, e.g., family court, to resolve factual disputes. However, trial courts often make decisions on matters of law, although relatively few of those decisions are published. In most instances, a state trial court decision is not mandatory on any other court, including another trial court in the same state. However, other federal and state courts may regard the decision as persuasive authority.

PART II

CORPORATE FORMALITY

CHAPTER 3

COMMERCIAL LAWS WHICH RULE BUSINESS ENTITIES[11)]

3.1 CONCEPT AND SCOPE OF COMMERCIAL LAW

The concept of "commercial law," or "commercial transactions" as it is sometimes called, as a distinct field is relatively recent in the U.S. The Practicing lawyer may still think of law practice as "commercial" to the extent that involves any aspects of business, including even taxation, but the advent of the new Uniform Commercial Code has given a narrower ambit to the term "commercial." The Subjects included are sale of goods, bulk transfers, negotiable instrument, particularly promissory notes, drafts, or bill of exchange, and checks, bank deposits and collections, letter of credit, documents of title, particularly bills of lading and warehouse receipts, investment securities, particularly stocks and bonds, and secured transactions, including assignments of accounts receivable.

Sources of Commercial Law. Commercial law in this sense is largely

11) This Chapter is compiled mainly with materials from Robert W. Hamilton, "The Law of Corporations," West Group (2000); Emmanuel Law Outlines, "Corporations," Emmanuel Publishing Corp. (1997).

a matter of state law because, though Congress has the power to enact legislation concerning interstate commerce, it has been reluctant to exercise that power in this sphere of private. This reluctance is due in part to the success of the National Conference of Commissioners on Uniform States Laws in promoting uniformity through voluntary adoption of uniform laws.

The Negotiable Instrument Law, patterned after the English Bills of Exchange Act, was proposed in 1896 and adopted by all states by 1924.

The Uniform Sales Act, based in part on the English Sale of Goods Act, was recommended in 1906 and eventually adopted by about two thirds of the states.

A succession of uniform laws followed. One of these, the Uniform Bills of Lading Act, was enacted by Congress as the Federal Bills of Lading Act (Pomerene Act) and still governs bills of lading in interstate and foreign commerce.

At the end of the Second World War the Commissioners, together with American Law Institute, undertook a joint project to draft a comprehensive and modern Uniform Commercial Code to replace the older uniform laws. It was proposed in final form in 1957, and by 1967 it had been adopted in almost every state. Louisiana was the sole exception, but later adopted parts of the Codes.

A revision of the provisions on secured transactions was proposed in 1972 and has now been adopted by most states, and a revision of the provisions on investment securities was proposed in 1977 and some other revisions was proposed in 1997 to 2003. The Code has four hundred sections, fills over seven hundred pages with its elaborate comments, took dozens of drafters and advisors over a decade to prepare, and represents the most modern thinking in its field. Although the Code unites in one statue such previously separate fields as sales and negotiable instruments, it omits a number o of subjects that are sometimes regarded as part of commercial law in other countries. Thus courses titled in "Commercial Law" or "Commercial Transactions" have largely replaced separate courses in such as sales and negotiable instruments in U.S. law schools. Several of these, such as insurance, have been omitted because of the difficulty of unification on so grand a scale.

Others, such as bankruptcy and admiralty, or maritime law, have been left out because they are within federal rather than state jurisdiction. Still others, such as corporations and partnerships are not included because the American lawyer sees no close affinity between them and purview of the Code.

Furthermore, even on matters within the Code's area of concern, the lawyer may have to look outside its provisions to federal and state laws on taxation, trade regulation, banking restrictions, and the like.

Uniform Commercial Code. The Uniform Commercial Code (UCC or the Code), first published in 1952, is one of a number of uniform acts that have been promulgated in conjunction with efforts to harmonize the law of sales and other commercial transactions in all 50 states within the United States of America. The goal of harmonizing state law is important because of the prevalence of commercial transactions that extend beyond one state.

The UCC is the longest and most elaborate of the uniform acts. The Code has been a long-term, joint project of the National Conference of Commissioners on Uniform State Laws (NCCUSL) and the American Law Institute (ALI), who began drafting its first version in 1942. Judge Herbert F. Goodrich was the Chairman of the Editorial Board of the original 1952 edition, and the Code itself was drafted by some of the top legal scholars in the United States, including Karl N. Llewellyn, William A. Schnader, Soia Mentschikoff, and Grant Gilmore. The Code, as the product of private organizations, is not itself the law, but only a recommendation of the laws that should be adopted in the states. Once enacted by a state, the UCC is codified into the state's code of statutes. A state may adopt the UCC verbatim as written by ALI and NCCUSL, or a state may adopt the UCC with specific changes. Unless such changes are minor, they can seriously obstruct the Code's express objective of promoting uniformity of law among the various states. Thus persons doing business in different states must check local law.

In one or another of its several revisions, the UCC has been enacted in all of the 50 states, as well as in the District of Columbia, the Commonwealth of Puerto Rico, Guam and the U.S. Virgin Islands. Louisiana has enacted most provisions of the UCC, with the exception of Article 2, preferring to maintain its own civil law tradition for governing the sale of goods.

Uniform Commercial Code (1942-1952) [with National Conference of Commissioners on Uniform State Laws; formerly "Uniform Revised Sales Act" and "Commercial Code"] [Articles 1 to 10: General Provisions, Sales, Commercial Paper, Bank Deposits and Collections, Letters of Credit, Bulk Transfers, Warehouse Receipts, Investment Securities, Secured Transactions, Effective Date and Repealer]. Revisions, Amendments, and Comments to the Uniform Commercial Code (in chronological order):

- Changes and Modifications to the 1952 UCC (1952-1953)
- 1955 Supplement to the 1952 UCC (1954)
- 1958 Supplement to the 1957 UCC (1958)
- Revised Article 9 (Secured Transactions); 1972 Amendments to UCC (1967-1972) [including New Article 11: Effective Date and Transition Provisions]
- Revised Article 8 (Investment Securities); 1977 Amendments to UCC (1975-1977)
- Uniform New Payments Code (1977-1984) [withdrawn and discontinued; formerly "New Payments Code" and "New Uniform Payments Code"; drafted under the supervision of the "3-4-8 Committee" of the Permanent Editorial Board; see also "Current Payment Methods"]
- [New] Article 2A: Leases (1986-1987)
- Permanent Editorial Board Commentaries (ongoing since 1987)
- Current Payment Methods: [New] Article 4A: Funds Transfers (1988-1989); Revised Article 3 (Negotiable Instruments) (1988-1990) [formerly "Commercial Paper"]; Revised Article 4 (Bank Deposits and Collections) (1988-1990)
- Repealer of Article 6 (Bulk Transfers) and Revised Article 6 (Bulk Sales)

(1988-1989)

- Article 2 (Sales) Study Group (1988-1990) [Permanent Editorial Board study; see also "Revised Article 2"]
- Article 9 (Secured Transactions) Study Group (1989-1992) [Permanent Editorial Board study; see also "Revised Article 9"]
- Amendments to Article 2A (Leases) (1990)
- Revised Article 5 (Letters of Credit) (1991-1995)
- Revised Article 2 (Sales) (1992-1999) [see also "Article 2 Study Group"; new Drafting Committee appointed in 1999]
- Revised Article 8 (Investment Securities) (1992-1994)
- Revised Article 9 (Secured Transactions) (1993-1999) [see also "Article 9 Study Group"]
- [New] Article 2B: Software Contracts and Licenses of Information (1995-1999) [formerly "Licenses"; not completed as part of the UCC; promulgated solely by the National Conference of Commissioners on Uniform State Laws as the "Uniform Computer Information Transactions Act"]
- Revised Article 1 (General Provisions) (1996-2001)
- Revised Article 2A (Leases) (1996-1999) [new Drafting Committee appointed in 1999]
- Proposed Amendments to Articles 2 and 2A (Sales and Leases) (1999-2003) [formerly [New] Revised Articles 2 and 2A (Sales and Leases); see also "Revised Article 2" and "Revised Article 2A"]
- Proposed Revisions to Articles 3 (Negotiable Instruments) and 4 (Bank Deposits and Collections) (2000-2002) [formerly "Revised Articles 3, 4, and 4A"]
- Amendments to Article 7 (Documents of Title) (2000-2003)
- Article 9 Review Committee (2008-)

Characteristics of Commercial Laws. Commercial law in the U.S. lacks two of the characteristics that distinguished the law merchant during the middle ages and that have been retained in some civil law countries.

First, the separate commercial courts that once existed in England had declined in influence by the seventeenth century and never took root in the colonies; commercial matters have always been heard by the ordinary law courts in the U.S. To a limited extent the functions of special commercial tribunals are performed by well-established bodies, notably the American Arbitration Association, that offer facilities for commercial arbitration.

Second, the medieval conception of merchants as a distinct class for whom commercial law was specially designed also disappeared from English law before it had a chance to influence American law, and the concepts of "merchant" and "commercial act," found in many civil law countries, are not part of the American legal tradition. For example, bankruptcy is available to all persons and not just to merchants.

The UCC does include a definition of "merchant" in its article on the sale of goods and provides some special rules that apply to such persons because of their expertise, but the Code as a whole applies to both merchants and not-merchants, and with these few exceptions it applies to both alike.

At the same time, American commercial law produced some important developments of its own. In the field of negotiable instruments the almost universal habit of making significant payments by check resulted in an elaborate body of case and statute law that is systemized by the Code. And the flexibility of U.S. commercial law is nowhere more evident than in its recognition and development of new legal devices to secure the extension of credit required for the distribution of goods ranging from automobile to shoes, on both the wholesale and retail level. The most important single contribution of the Code is in consolidating, simplifying, and modernizing the law of such secured transactions in personal property.

However, on the whole, the Code, like the uniform laws that preceded it, represents no drastic upheaval in concepts and doctrines, but rather an effort to order the law and to bring it into harmony with current commercial practices. Nor does it make a complete break with the past, for it provides that the "principles of law and equity, including the law merchant ... shall supplement its provisions" unless they are "displaced by the particular provisions" of the Code.

The drafters of the Code have also tried to allow for future change. In some instances they have purposely failed to provide for a problem in order to leave room for further development on a state-by-state basis; in others the Code provisions expressly admit of change by the development usages. While the Code is intended to be a semi-permanent piece of legislation, it is hoped that it will be flexible enough to accommodate itself to future developments by both courts and legislatures.

3.2 BUSINESS ENTERPRISES LAWS

Scope. By far the most common form for the business enterprises in the U.S. is the individual proprietorship, followed by the corporation and then the partnership, either general or limited. Nevertheless, Business Corporation dominates the economy and employs most of the labor force.

In keeping with the fragmentation of American private law, what is here treated as the law of business enterprises is commonly regarded neither as part of a comprehensive body of commercial law nor as a unit in itself, but rather as such separate field as agency, partnerships, and, most important, corporations. Business enterprises are almost invariably organized under state law (few exceptions such as banking institutions), and incorporation has historically been regarded as founded upon a state grant. Until the beginning of the nineteenth century a corporation could only be formed pursuant to special act of a state legislature, but by the end of the Civil War general state incorporation laws had been widely enacted and by the end of the century use of special legislative charters had been almost entirely abolished.

Sources. After the Civil War when it became an established principle of constitutional law that no state could exclude a corporation incorporated in another state from engaging in interstate commerce within its territory, large corporations began to seek out the most favorable state of incorporation and some of the smaller states tailored their corporation laws to attract them. Delaware has been the most successful and leads all other states by a wide margin as the state of incorporation for large corporations.

Differences among most state corporation laws are not fundamental, however, the American Bar Association's Model Business Corporation Act has been adopted in whole or in significant part by majority states. There has been no substantial demand for federal control over the formation of corporation. Some of the chief statutory differences relate to the rights of shareholders to get money out of the corporation by the declaration of dividends, partial liquidations, and share purchases and redemptions, but the same results can be reached in most states even though procedures may vary. Case law doctrines have contributed to uniformity and, in spite of the large statutory ingredient, the courts have played a major role in such important and expanding areas of corporation law as the fiduciary duties owed by directors, officers, and shareholders. In addition, the corporate papers, such as the charters, by-laws, and resolutions of the shareholders and board of directors, are of great importance.

There is considerably more uniformity in the field of partnerships as a result of the adoption by most states of the Uniform Partnership Act and the Uniform Limited Partnership Act. The law of agency is to be found largely in judicial decisions. In recent decades the activities of business enterprises have been increasingly affected by federal law. Congress, under the commerce power, has regulated the interstate distribution and trading of securities by such statutes as the Securities Act of 1933 and the Securities Exchange Act of 1934, which are administered by the Securities Exchange Commission. Taxation, trade regulation, and the regulation of particular industries have greatly affected business enterprises. The rules and decisions of the agencies that administer these laws are also an important source of law to the lawyer engaged in practice in this field.

Characteristics of Business Enterprises. The corporation, as a business enterprise, is the only one of the three principal forms of business enterprise that has been regarded for most legal purposes as an entity separate and apart from the persons who compose it. It may, of course, deal in property, make contracts, and sue and be sued, all in its corporate name, and one's risk as a shareholder is limited to one's investment.

Most states have a single statute that applies generally to all business corporations regardless of size or distribution of ownership. Nevertheless, corporations vary greatly in structure and one of the current problems of corporation law is how best to take account of the obvious differences between the large publicly held ("public") corporation and the small closely held ("close") corporation. Although the law developed, for the most part, with the economically dominant public corporation in mind, there is now a trend to give special statutory treatment to close corporations, either by provisions scattered throughout the general corporation law or by a special part of that law.

CHAPTER 4

BUSINESS FORMS[12)]

4.1 CORPORATION : PUBLICLY AND CLOSELY HELD

Corporations may usefully be classified as "publicly held" or "closely held." Publicly held corporations are corporations whose shares are widely owned and publicly traded on the national securities exchanges, over the counter, and, increasingly, on the internet. Publicly held corporations are typically managed by professional managers who collectively own a relatively small fraction of the outstanding shares.

Closely held corporations are corporations with relatively few shareholders. There is no public market for their shares. They are typically managed by the shareholders themselves or by persons closely associated with the shareholders. The typical "closely held" corporation has less than ten shareholders. Many may be solely owned by one person, a business form that is called an "incorporated partnership." A corporation owned by several

12) This Chapter is mainly compiled with materials from Robert W. Hamilton, "The Law of Corporations," West Group (2000).

persons may be referred to as an "incorporated partnership." These phrases are potentially misleading, since the entities involved are corporations, not proprietorships or partnerships. In many closely held corporations, the shareholders will have entered into agreements restricting the transferability of shares to ensure that outsiders cannot become shareholders without the consent of the existing shareholders; these agreements also may provide a device by which existing shareholders may have their shares purchased when they die or decide to leave the corporation.

Most publicly held corporations are large and most closely held corporations are small, but size is not the criterion. There exist a few closely held corporations that rival the largest publicly held corporations in size, and there are some publicly traded corporations that consist of little more than a name and hopeful prospects.

This a classification is useful even though there is a Continuum of corporations in terms of diversification of ownership and professional management. There are many "in between" corporations that have some characteristics of public corporations but whose shares are infrequently or "thinly" traded. A corporation with 300 shareholders, for example, may be quite substantial in terms of size and assets, have professional management, and yet there may be only a sporadic or "thin" market for shares. The existence of such corporations does not destroy the basic validity of the distinction between publicly held and closely held, but recognizes the continuum that exists.

In terms of economic activity, publicly held corporations dominate the American (and world) economy. There are roughly 10,000 corporations with securities that are publicly traded on the securities markets in the United States' these corporations account for the great bulk of economic production and activity in the United States. Most of this Nutshell deals with these large economic entities, their ownership, their management, and their effect on American society.

The corporate model on which state corporation statutes and the Model

Business Corporation Act (1984) are based is an idealized model that is not tailored specifically either for the close corporation or for the publicly held corporation, It is a model that is sufficiently broad and generalized that large portions of it are appropriate for both closely held and publicly held corporations.

Many states have supplemented their general corporation statutes with special statutes providing relaxed rules for closely held corporations that elect to take advantage of their provisions. The MBCA (1984), in particular, provide an alternative set of provisions designed especially for closely held corporations.[13)]

Current tax rules favor the use of unincorporated business forms that provide limited liability for their members rather than a closely held corporation. It is therefore probable that greater attention will be paid to these unincorporated forms in the future. However, closely held corporations will remain an important part of corporate law. Profitable closely held businesses that were initially formed as corporations are very likely to continue to retain the corporate form indefinitely.

The income tax rules make conversions from corporate to non-corporate forms generally unattractive. The corporation may also be selected by many new business entities as the initial business form if the owners hope to "go public" in the future. Some persons also may favor the certainty and familiarity of the corporate form over newer, less familiar business forms. However, the central role of the closely held corporation has declined since 1990, and is likely to decline further in coming years.

---

13) RMBCA § 7.32 and § 14.34.

4.2 TRADITIONAL BUSINESS FORMS

As of 1980, there were four principal business forms available for enterprises: the sole proprietorship, the general Partnership, the limited partnership, and the corporation. Only the corporation combined the benefits of limited liability for all participants, centralized management, free transferability of interest, perpetual existence, and a tax structure that tended to minimize taxes for profitable business entities. As a result most businesses elected the corporation as its business form. There were some exceptions, of course. The most important area involved professionals: Lawyers, doctors, architects and several other occupations were prohibited by law from conducting business in corporate form; they traditionally formed general partnerships, but professional corporations and Professional associations permitted some degree of limited liability in many states.

A second area involved start-up enterprises anticipating losses in the early years; for federal income tax reasons they might initially be conducted in the form of proprietorships or general partnerships, Planning to incorporate at a later date when the business became profitable. Commercial real estate ventures often used partnerships or real estate investment trusts rather than corporations, again for tax reasons. But these exceptions only emphasized the central role of the corporation in most areas of economic activity. The following sections discuss briefly each of these traditional alternative forms.

Proprietorships. A proprietorship is a business owned by a single person who has the sole right to manage, is solely entitled to the profits, and is unlimitedly responsible for the debts of the business. A proprietorship is often viewed not as a separate business entity but as an extension of the proprietor himself.

For example, a proprietorship is not a separate entity for federal income tax purposes. Rather, when preparing his federal income tax return, a proprietor prepares a "Schedule C" reflecting the business transactions of the proprietorship, and the net profit or loss shown on Schedule C is transferred directly to his personal income tax return, the Form 1040. Historically, a proprietor, who desired a degree of immunity from personal responsibility for the debts of the proprietorship, could "incorporate his business" by creating a corporation and having all business transactions be executed in the name of the corporation. There was never serious doubt that the shares of a corporation could be entirely owned by a single person.

An "incorporated proprietorship" of this nature was more expensive to operate than a simple proprietorship. However, the "shield of limited liability" provided by the corporate form was a substantial advantage even though it did not protect the proprietor from liability for his personal tortious acts or possibly a failure to exercise oversight responsibility over the acts of employees. In addition, the incorporated proprietorship created some flexibility in planning tax strategies to minimize income taxation that helped to offset the costs of operating a corporation.

GENERAL PARTNERSHIPS

Introduction. A general partnership is the simplest form of business organization involving more than one person. In many ways it is a logical generalization of a proprietorship with more than one member. It is widely used today by a variety of different types of businesses. Originally, the partnership was a common law form of business, but was largely codified by the Uniform Partnership Act (1914), a statute developed by the National Conference of Commissioners on Uniform State Laws ("NCCUSL") and enacted in virtually all states. A revised Uniform Partnership Act was approved in 1994, and has been adopted by somewhat more than half of the states. The description in the following sections is generally based on the 1914 Act with separate discussion of the principal modifications made by the 1994 Act.

Financial Provisions. A general partnership is formed simply by an oral or written agreement of the partners, who share the right to manage and the right to participate in the profits. They also share in partnership losses and are personally responsible for all Partnership obligations. The partnership agreement is usually referred to as the "law" for that partnership since it is binding on all the partners. However, it is not binding on persons who are not partners: They may recover on partnership obligations from any partner without regard to the loss-sharing or other arrangements set forth in the partnership agreement. Profit participations may be allocated by agreement; in the absence of agreement each partner shares equally in profits. If a Partnership suffers losses, they are shared by the partners as they agree, or in the event of a failure to agree, in proportion to their profit sharing ratios.

Each partner is also personally liable on partnership obligations; a partner compelled to satisfy a partnership liability is entitled to indemnification from the partnership, In effect, the partnership must reimburse each partner who personally satisfies a partnership liability. Each partner may be required to make a contribution to the partnership on dissolution to cover his or her share of any losses, including capita] losses of other partners. "Indemnification" and "contribution" are related but different concepts: "Indemnification" relates to the reimbursement of partners who are compelled to pay partnership liabilities in an ongoing partnership, while "contribution" relates to payments needed to settle accounts on the termination of the partnership. It is customary in partnerships to maintain a "capital account" for each partner.

The capital account consists of the original contribution of the partner to the partnership, increased by earnings and profits credited to the account and reduced by losses and distributions to the partner. When a partner withdraws from the partnership he is typically entitled to receive the amount in his capital account. If the account has a negative balance, he may be required to make a contribution to eliminate the negative amount.

If the entire partnership is being wound up and terminated, all capital accounts are reduced to zero by distribution or by contribution, as the case may be. Unrealized gains in the values of partnership assets are normally not credited to the capital account until they are realized or upon the final termination of the partnership. A partner may assign his financial interest in the Partnership. The assignee of such an interest does not become a partner but is entitled to whatever distributions the assigning partner was entitled to. He does not automatically become a partner because the partnership relation is a personal one. The legal phrase that describes this concept is *delectus personae*.

An assignee, of course, may also be admitted to the partnership, in which case he assumes all the rights and duties of a partner. An assignee who is not a partner is not personally liable on partnership obligations and is not required to make a contribution to the partnership on dissolution. The assigning partner remains liable on those obligations. A personal creditor of a partner may surcharge the Partner's interest in the partnership through a device known as a "charging order." By a charging order, Partnership distributions to the debtor partner are diverted to the creditor. The creditor may also be able to foreclose on the interest of the partner and become an assignee of the partner's financial interest. Partnership creditors, of course may proceed directly against partnership assets, Partnership creditors may also enforce their claim against the partners, who are jointly or jointly and severally liable for partnership obligations.

Under the 1914 Act, individual partners are jointly and severally liable for wrongful acts and breaches of trust, and jointly liable for contractual and other obligations. Joint liability may require naming all the partners as defendants. Under the 1994 Act, all liability is joint and several, but a partnership creditor may obtain satisfaction from individual partners only if a judgment is obtained against both the partnership and the specific partners and a writ of execution on the judgment against the partnership has been returned unsatisfied. These rules apply in the absence of a specific guarantee of payment by the partner.

Participation in Management. In a general partnership each partner is also an agent of the partnership for purposes of its business and has a right to participate in management. In the absence of a specific agreement, all partners share equally in management decisions. However, the partners may agree among themselves as to how the partnership business is to be managed; management for example, may be delegated to a committee or to a single partner. Delegation of management authority to a committee is customary in large law and accounting partnerships. An important aspect of partnership law under the 1914 Act is the broad fiduciary duty that exists among the partners. The leading case describing this duty is *Meinhard* case,[14] in which

---

14) *Meinhard v. Salmon*, 249 N.Y. 458, 164 N.E. 545 (N.Y.1928).
Relevant Facts. Walter Salmon leased prime real estate in New York City (located at 42nd Street and 5th Avenue) from Louisa Gerry for a term of twenty years. The leased premises included the Hotel Bristol which Salmon converted from a hotel into shops and office space. In order to raise sufficient capital to convert the property, Salmon entered into a joint venture with Meinhard. Under the terms of their written agreement, Meinhard provided half of the investment funds to complete the re-purposing, and would be entitled to forty percent of net profits during the first five years of their agreement and fifty percent of net profits thereafter until their agreement terminated after twenty years. Salmon had sole authority to manage and operate the building, and they further specified that each would share losses equally, amongst other provisions. During the early years, the joint venture operated at a loss, but over time became quite successful. As the agreement reached its conclusion after almost twenty years, Salmon entered into negotiations with Elbridge T. Gerry, owner of the reversion interest in the property, and eventually entered into a contract to expand operations at the site and combine them with other, surrounding buildings owned by Gerry. Salmon did not tell Meinhard about the new opportunity, or inform him about even the possibility of a new contract concerning the property they had a joint interest in for the preceding twenty years. When Meinhard learned of the new venture, he demanded that the lease be held in trust as an asset of the joint venture, agreeing to assume one half of the guaranty responsibilities of the new agreement. Met with refusal, Meinhard brought suit, and a referee ruled in his favor, awarding him twenty-five percent, or one half of Salmon's interest in the new venture related to the Hotel Bristol Property. On appeal, the Appellate Division affirmed but modified the award, granting Meinhard one half of the new lease in its entirety. Salmon appealed.
Issue. Does a partner in a joint venture violate his duties to his partner when he fails to inform him regarding a new opportunity related to their partnership and instead contracts for the new benefit solely for himself?
Holding. Yes, partners in a joint venture owe each other the highest duties, including both communication and loyalty, and one partner violates those duties when he fails to inform his partner about new opportunities such that both can take advantage of the new venture.
Reasoning. Chief Judge Cardozo delivered the opinion for the majority. He explained that partners owe one another the highest duty, the finest loyalty, a duty that goes beyond ordinary arm's length dealings or traditional business honesty to encompass fiduciary responsibilities and punctilio of honor. Honesty alone, then, is insufficient to comply with the duty owed. Judge Cardozo explained that had Gerry been aware that the current lease belonged to a partnership, he may have approached the partners rather than Salmon alone. Furthermore, while a variety of hypothetical options were left unanswered, Judge Cardozo made clear that at the very least Salmon owed Meinhard the opportunity to compete for participation in the new venture. Judge Cardozo explained that even if Gerry preferred to work with Meinhard rather than Salmon, nothing in that preference- or possibility for successfully extending the existing venture- relieved Salmon of his duty to his co-adventurer. The majority explained that an examination of precedents yielded nothing

Chief Justice Cardozo stated: Joint adventurers, like copartners, owe to one another, while the enterprise continues the duty of the finest loyalty.

Many forms of conduct permissible in a workaday world for those acting at arm's length are forbidden to those bound by fiduciary ties. A trustee is held to something stricter than the morals of the market place. Not honesty alone, but the punctilio of an honor the most sensitive, is then the Standard of behavior. This fiduciary duty has its base in the personal liability of each partner for partnership obligations and the mutual sharing of control inherent in each partnership. The broad fiduciary duty described in *Meinhard* may be appropriate for a small partnership with relatively few members. However, it creates problems in partnerships with large numbers of members, where relationships are less personal than in small partnerships. The 1994 Uniform Partnership Act contains provisions narrowing the scope of this duty and permitting the partnership agreement, within specified limits, to limit this duty further.

A partner may be expelled by the remaining partners. Under the 1914 Act, a power to expel existed only when that power was specifically provided in the partnership agreement. The 1994 Act retains this provision and in addition recognizes an inherent power to expel a partner by the unanimous

---

directly on point, but they analogized the case to one in which a partner sought to extend an expiring lease for his own benefit. In that case, as here, the partner owed his partner information and loyalty, such that he is entitled to the benefit of their bargain. The Court here refused to re-examine the factual findings below, or deviate from the constructive trust created to remedy to wrong. In affirming the order below, the Court determined that Meinhard was entitled to one-half of the lease minus one share (not quite half).

Dissent. Judge Andrews dissented, joined by Judges Kellogg and O'Brien. Judge Andrews saw the case in simple terms, explaining that Salmon and Meinhard had a limited partnership, confined to a single property and terminating after twenty years. The new agreement, covering new properties for a new and expanded term, was far more than a renewal of the existing relationship which the dissenters admitted may have given rise to a duty. In the absence of fraud or unfairness, Judge Andrews concluded that Salmon owed no duty to Meinhard to include him when he created a new venture in anticipation of the planned termination of their limited agreement.

Conclusion. Partners in a joint venture owe each other fiduciary duties, including the duty to present new opportunities to their partners should they arise during the course of the partnership. The fiduciary duties describe encompass more than simple honesty, and requiring the utmost loyalty and certainly the obligation to communicate regarding opportunities that should be available to both partners as a result of their common interests.

vote of the remaining partners in limited circumstances.

A Separate Entity. The 1914 Act defines a partnership as an "association of two or more persons to carry on as co-owners a business for profit." UPA 8 6(1). It was not clear under this statute whether this "association" was an entity in its own right independent of the partners. Early case law tended to treat a partnership as an informal association of individuals and not as a separate entity, but this view gradually changed as many partnerships grew in size and clearly possessed many entity characteristics.

The 1994 Act states explicitly in section 201 that "a partnership is an entity distinct from its partners." Today each partnership has its own federal tax ID number and files its own information tax return; it owns real and personal property in its own name' it can sue and be sued in its own name, and so forth. The notion that a partnership is an entity in its own right leads naturally to distinctions being drawn between "partnership assets" and "personal assets" of each partner and between "partnership liabilities" and "personal liabilities" of each partner. Despite these distinctions, of course, each Partner remained personally responsible for all partnership liabilities to the extent.

Artificial Entities as Partners. The 1914 Act defines "person" as including "partnerships, corporations, and other associations" as well as natural individuals. The 1994 Act adds "joint venture, government, governmental subdivision, agency or instrumentality" to this definition as well, and for good measure also adds "any other legal or commercial entity." Thus, two or more corporations may form a partnership, two or more partnerships may them-selves form another partnership, or one or more individuals or corporations may form a partnership with one or more corporations, partnerships, governmental agencies, or other types of limited liability entities. All of these clearly are partnerships.

Dissolution, Winding Up and Termination. Under the 1914 Act, a general partnership is apparently a fragile form of business: It is "dissolved" automatically when a partner dies or leaves the partnership or when a partner expressly states that he no longer wishes to be a partner. However, the 1914 Act uses the word "dissolution" in a narrow and limited sense. Section 29 of the 1914 Act defines a "dissolution" as "the change in the relation of the partners caused by any partner ceasing to be associated in the carrying on as distinguished from the winding up of the business." In other words, "dissolution" is the mere change in relationship that occurs when a partner dies or leaves the partnership. Despite the "dissolution," the partnership continues to exist for a period of "winding up," i.e. the process of collecting claims, satisfying liabilities, and reducing assets to cash in order to permit a final distribution and settlement of the partnership accounts. Upon the final settlement and the distribution of remaining assets to the partners, the partnership "terminates" and ceases to exist.

Under the 1914 Act, a partner withdrawing from an at-will partnership was able to compel a winding up and termination. However, as a practical matter, the withdrawing partner was usually paid the value of his interest by the partnership and the partnership business continued in the form of a new partnership consisting of the remaining partners and possibly the addition of new partners as well. Under UPA (1914) a partnership was dissolved and reformed every time there was a change in the members of the partnership but the business was continued. The 1994 Act uses the word "dissociation" rather than "dissolution" to refer to the change in relationship that occurs when a partner leaves the partnership. The Act also distinguishes between "events of withdrawal" (which permit a partner to leave the partnership and receive the value of his partnership interest but do not cause winding up and termination), and "events causing dissolution and winding up of the partnership business."

This alternative, rather confusingly, is described in the 1994 Act as the "dissolution and winding up" of the partnership business. Early drafts of the 1994 Act did not use the word "dissolution" at all, but the word was reintroduced in later drafts to refer to the last step of the winding up process.

A partnership dissolution may also be a breach of contract. A partnership may be created by an enforceable contract that states that the partnership is to continue to exist for some stated period; a premature dissolution of that partnership is a breach of that contract. A basic distinction must therefore be made between a "partnership at will" and a "partnership for a term." In a partnership at will, dissolution is usually liability-free; in a partnership for a term, a premature dissolution is a breach of contract and the withdrawing partner may be liable for significant damages.

Revisions Made by the 1994 Act. The 1914 Uniform Partnership Act adequately served the needs of business for many years. However, as the size of many partnerships increased, dissatisfaction increased with respect to the dissolution provisions of that Act, the unlimited personal liability provisions involving joint and joint and several liability, and the broad fiduciary duties contemplated by that Act and uncertainty as to whether those duties could be modified by agreement or waived. This dissatisfaction surfaced in the form of enactment of no uniform amendments in several states. These amendments, of course, destroyed the uniformity of statutory partnership law that had existed for more than sixty years, and led ultimately to the development of a revised Uniform Partnership Act. This new statute was first known as "RUPA" and later renamed the Uniform Partnership Act (1994). The major changes made by the 1994 act include:

- A provision expressly defining a partnership to be an entity in its own right independent of its partners.
- Provisions making clear that a partnership agreement may modify most of the partnership statutory provisions (and adding a list of specific provisions that cannot be modified or can only be modified in limited ways).
- A provision defining, and to some extent limiting, the scope of the fiduciary duty within a partnership.
- A provision making it more difficult for partnership Creditors to seek recovery from partners individually. Liability may be imposed on a

partner only if (1) he or she is named as a defendant along with the partnership and (2) the creditor first seeks exhaustion of partnership assets before seeking a recovery from a partner's personal assets.

- A provision modifying the dissolution provisions to distinguish between "events of withdrawal" and "events causing dissolution and winding up of the "partnership business," and making dear that the dissociation of a partner did not cause a dissolution of the Partnership.
- A provision authorizing partnerships to merge and to convert from a general partnership to a limited partnership.
- A provision authorizing partnerships to make public filings (typically with the Secretary of State) to establish the authority of specific partners to enter into partnership transactions. These filings may be useful, for example, to establish the authority of a partner to convey real property owned by the partnership.
- Provisions authorizing a partner who has dissociated from a partnership to file a public statement announcing that he is no longer associated with the partnership.
- Provisions authorizing the partnership to file a public statement announcing that it is in the process of winding up and dissolution.

The 1994 Act has been adopted by approximately 27 states as this is written. Several states have adopted new partnership statutes that incorporate many provisions of the 1994 Act but depart significantly from the Act in other respects. Modern Partnership law today is therefore an amalgam of the 1914 Act, the 1994 Act, and in many states, some non-uniform provisions. It appears unlikely that partnership law will ever return to the extensive degree of uniformity that existed for many years.

LIMITED PARTNERSHIPS

In General. A limited partnership is a partnership in which there are one or more general partners and one or more limited Partners. The general partners are essentially viewed as having the rights and duties of partners in a partnership without limited partners. They are unlimitedly liable for the debts of the business and have general powers of management. Limited partners, on the other hand, have no personal liability for the debts of the business (except to the extent of their capital contributions) and have only very limited rights to participate in management, If they exceed these limited rights, they become general partners and personally liable for partnership liabilities.

A limited partnership is a creature of statute. A Uniform Limited Partnership Act was promulgated by NCCUSL in 1916 and was widely adopted. A revised Act was approved in 1976 and significant amendments were made in 1983 and1985. Today, all states have limited partnership statutes but there is a considerable degree of diversity among them. A limited partnership is formed by filing a document or certificate with the Secretary of State or with a specified county or city official. A failure to file (or filing in the wrong office) results in the creation of a general partnership rather than a limited Partnership.

In most respects, a limited partnership is governed by the same rules that are applicable to general partnerships. What is unique is the presence of limited partners who are passive investors with very limited power to participate in the management of the firm. Limited partners who do participate in the control of the business or who permit their names to appear in the partnership name may thereby lose their shield of limited liability. A major issue in limited partnership law is the extent to which limited partners may participate in management without loss of the shield of limited liability.

ULPA (1916) simply provided that limited partners who "participated in the control of the business" thereby lost the shield of limited liability. The 1976 Act added a "safe harbor" Consisting of a list of management-related actions that a limited partner might engage in without incurring additional liability. In 1983, the statute was further amended by adding a Provision that states that a creditor may hold a limited partner liable as a general partner only if the creditor dealt with the limited partner "reasonably believing that he was a general partner." The limited partnership has an interesting history. It developed in Europe during the Middle Ages as a device that permitted nobility and churches to participate anonymously in ordinary commerce. It was introduced in the United States at an early time but has never been widely used. During a brief period in the 1960s and 1970s, limited partnerships with publicly traded limited partnership interests were widely used as tax shelters. The curtain came down on these "master limited partnerships" in 1986 with an amendment to the Internal Revenue Code that provided that all businesses that had publicly traded ownership interests must be taxed as a corporation.

Today, traditional limited partnerships are widely used in real estate syndications, particularly for large commercial shopping center and office projects. One significant feature of limited partnership statutes is that they are not free-standing but rely on the general partnership statutes for matters not specifically dealt with in the limited partnership statute. Section 1106 of the current Uniform Limited Partnership Act, for example, Provides, "In any case not provided for in this Act the provisions of the Uniform Partnership Act govern." This "linkage" between the two statutes has created anomalies and practical problems, and as this is written a free-standing revision of BULPA ("ReRULPA") is under consideration by NCCUSL.

Limited Partners with a Corporate General Partner. For many years, a limited partnership was viewed as a device by which passive individual investors could invest in small businesses operated by other individuals. The limited partnership became a distinctly modern business form in the 1970s with the recognition that (1) a corporation (or other limited liability entity) could be the sole general partner in a limited partnership, and (2) limited partners could also be shareholders, directors, or officers of the general partner without losing the shield of limited liability. Limited partnership statutes were amended to make clear that participation by a limited partner in the management of the general partner did not make the limited partner personally liable for partnership obligations. This combination of business forms largely eliminated liability concerns in the limited partnership, so long as the general partner was reasonably financed considering the nature of the business.

In a sense the limited partnership with a corporate general partner is a new business form. Typically, the general partner is 'completely controlled by the limited partners and has a nominal or relatively small equity interest in the enterprise: One per cent for the general partner and 99 percent for the limited partners is a common ratio.

Today, it is unusual to find a limited partnership In which individuals are named as general partners. Basically, there is never any reason to expose any individual to the personal liability that is inherent in the role of general partner. The major advantage of conducting business in the form of a limited partnership with a corporate general partner today is that it combines limited liability for all with favorable federal income tax treatment, discussed below. It also permits trans- actions in ownership interests in the general partner to occur without causing a change in the identity of the general Partner itself.

THE LIMITED LIABILITY PARTNERSHIP

Historically, certain classes of professionals were prohibited from conducting their practices in corporate form. These professionals were viewed as providing individualized services and it was against public policy for them to limit their Personal liability for malpractice or negligence by incorporating. While states varied in determining which services should be viewed as "professional" and subject to this public policy, all states agreed that lawyers, accountants, and medical professionals fell within this category.

Professional partnerships are probably the principal form of general partnership today; many of them have scores or hundreds or thousands, in the case of accounting firms of partners. Many will doubtless be, first, employees of, and, later, Partners in, large law firms that have hundreds of Partners and offices scattered around major cities in the United States and the world. Of course, there also exist many thousands of small businesses that also are general partnerships.

In light of the modern litigious society in which we live today, the major drawback of the general partnership form of business is of course the potential personal liability of Partners for partnership obligations. These problems became evident in Texas during the 1980s during the crisis involving the failure of savings and loan associations, and led to the development of a new partnership business form, the limited liability partnership or "LLP." The principal classes of persons affected were lawyers and accountants. The background that led to this new business form is described in the following excerpt: The LLP is a direct outgrowth of the collapse of real estate and energy prices in the late 1980s, and the concomitant disaster that befell Texas's banks and savings and loan associations. Texas led the nation in bank and savings and loan failures during the 1980s. More than one-third of all the bank failures in the United States occurred in Texas. Ever since the collapse of these financial institutions across the state, the Federal Deposit Insurance Corporation ("FDIC") and the Resolution Trust Corporation ("RTC") (and its predecessor, the Federal Savings and Loan Insurance Corporation ("PSLIC")) have devoted a significant part of their total resources to the recovery of funds lost in the collapse of Texas institutions. Suit was brought against hundreds of shareholders, directors and officers of failed financial institutions.

However, the amounts recovered from the Principal wrongdoers were only a tiny fraction of total losses and attention quickly turned to the roles of the lawyers and accountants who had represented the failed financial institutions before their collapse. "Where were the lawyers?" and "Where were the public accountants?" were cries figuratively heard across the state. Claims against lawyers and accountants for malpractice and breach of duty were attractive because the individual professionals sometimes had been deeply involved in the affairs of their clients. Also, these lawyers and accountants were usually associated with partnerships that had substantial malpractice insurance and numerous wealthy partners. As a result, several highly reputable law firms in Texas found themselves in deep trouble because of their bank and thrift work during the "salad days" of the 1980s. In these cases, individual partners, no matter how innocent or unaware of the transactions in question, were threatened with claims running into the hundreds of millions of dollars. Even the largest malpractice insurance policy covered only a fraction of the claim, and each professional in the partnership was faced with the loss of his personal assets and wealth as well as his interest in the firm. Texas responded to this "crisis" by the enactment of amendments to its partnership statute that authorized general partnerships to limit the liability of innocent partners to their investment in the firm.

In effect, these amendments created another new business form, the "limited liability partnership" or "LLP." The concept was immediately popular not only in Texas but also around the country, and all states quickly adopted statute a authorizing this new business form. The LLP election also appears in the Uniform Partnership Act (1994). A general partnership elects to become an LLP simply by filing a statement with the Secretary of State electing LLP status. It must also change its name so that it contains the phrase "Limited Liability Partnership," "LLP," "Registered Limited Liability Partnership," "RLLP," or acceptable Variations of those phrases or abbreviations. As initially enacted in Texas, the shield of limited liability provided by the LLP election was limited, It provided Protection only against malpractice and negligence claims; it did not provide protection against contract claims that exceeded the available assets of the partnership. Other states adopting LLP statutes, however, quickly extended the shield of limited liability to claims of all types. Statutes also were broadened to make it clear that the limited liability shield provided protection against claims arising from the obligations of indemnification and contribution that exist in all general partnerships. These broader statutes are called "full shield" statutes while the Texas approach is referred to as a "partial shield" statute. In 1997, Texas broadened its statute to cover contract as well as tort claims. The shield of limited liability provided by the LLP statute is not available to partners who themselves commit acts of malpractice or negligence. In many states the protection is also not available to partners who have oversight obligations over those partners, and to partners who are aware of the malpractice or negligence and fail to take steps to prevent it. The statutes of several states, including Texas, also require that LLPs maintain certain minimum levels of assets or insurance. A full broad shield LLP provides limited liability for Partners similar to the limited liability available to shareholders in a corporation or to limited partners in a partnership that do not participate in management. The LLP election is available to all businesses that are general partnerships and is not limited to professional Partnerships. However, it is predominantly used by professional partnerships. Particularly large law and accounting firms.

Following the development of the LLP, many states authorized a similar election for general partners in limited Partnerships. Thus yet another new partnership form was created, the limited liability limited partnership ("LLLP"). An LLLP is a limited partnership in which general partners have the liability protection provided by the LLP election. One of the peculiarities created by the "linkage" problem between the general and limited partnership statutes is that the general partners in an LLLP may have broader protection against liability than the limited partners. This is a result of historical accident and not specific design. In practice, the LLLP is apparently not widely used today; the more common practice in limited partnerships is to have only a single general partner that is itself a corporation that is usually minimally capitalized and has a nominal equity interest in the limited Partnership.

THE LIMITED LIABILITY COMPANY

In the 1970s a new business form, the "limited Liability Company" (an "LLC") was authorized by statute initially in Wyoming, and subsequently in Florida. Once its federal income tax status was established in approximately 1980, all states quickly adopted LLC statutes. In its relatively brief history, the LLC has clearly become the most popular and widely used unincorporated business form that provides limited liability for its members.

An LLC is created by filing a document with the Secretary of State or other state officer. This document, usually called "articles of organization" is a short, summary document similar to modern articles of incorporation. Detailed rules of operation are set forth in an "operating agreement" or in some states "regulations." Operating agreements may be patterned either after a partnership agreement or corporate bylaws. Depending on the complexity of the business and the number of participants, operating agreements may be very short or may be 30 pages or more in length. The LLC combines the corporate benefit of limited liability for all participants with complete flexibility in internal Structure and management. However, it does not involve incorporation in the traditional sense but rather traces its heritage back to the continental tradition of statutory limited liability entities that has taken root in Central and South America. From a liability standpoint, an LLC may be roughly analogized to a limited partnership composed only of limited Partners. However, all of the members may freely participants in management of the business without becoming liable for the business's obligations. This protection is provided simply by a provision in the LLC statute that states that members are not personally liable for the organization's debts.

LLC statutes permit the internal management structure to be modeled either after a corporation or after a general partnership. LLC statutes generally provide that each LLC should elect to be either "member managed" or "manager managed." A member managed LLC is governed by a set of rules similar to a partnership while a manager managed LLC is governed by a set of rules more analogous to a corporation. However, the operating agreement may modify these rules as the members' desire. Originally, the statutes of many states modeled the LLC after a partnership and required at least two members; today the statutes of virtually all states provide that an LLC may have only a single member. A one-member LLC is analogous to an incorporated proprietorship but with none of the required corporate formalities. At the other extreme, member ship interests may also be made readily transferable like shares of stock and may be reflected by certificates, the transfer of which may or may not be restricted by provision in the governing documents. Duration may be perpetual, for a term, or at will. The LLC is, in short, a genuinely novel business form of great flexibility.

Today, a sole proprietor may obtain a significant limited liability shield simply by forming a one-person LLC to operate the business. A proprietor who formed a corporation to operate an "incorporated proprietorship" thirty years ago would in all likelihood today use an LLC rather than a corporation. A one-person LLC has more desirable federal income tax treatment than a corporation while the shield of limited liability is the same. As a result, the LLC has largely supplanted the One-person Corporation for new businesses.

In 1995 NCCUSL approved the Uniform Limited Liability Company Act ("ULLCA"). By this time, however, moat states had developed their own statutes. As a result, ULLCA has not played a central role in developing statutes. Indeed, the ULLCA draws many provisions from the partnership statutes, while many state statutes adopt a more "corporate" approach. A handful of smaller states have adopted ULLCA. In summary, the attractiveness of the LLC as a form of business is that it combines (1) limited liability for all members, (2) flexibility of management structure, and (3) most importantly, a desirable income tax treatment.

4.3 MODERN BUSINESS FORMS

A new business form is adopted by a new venture recently. Today, the principal choices based on the number of owners with the proliferation of business forms are as follows:

(a) If the business has only a single owner, (i) a Proprietorship, (ii) a one person limited liability company, or (iii) a corporation.

(b) If the business has more than one owner but ownership interests are not themselves publicly traded: (i) a general partnership, (ii) a limited partnership, (iii) a limited liability company, (iv) a limited liability partnership, (v) a limited liability limited partnership, or (vi) a corporation.

(c) If ownership interests are or are likely to be publicly traded: a corporation. However, there are a few examples of publicly traded limited liability companies or limited partnerships, but they appear to have no advantage over the corporation form, and their very newness and lack of familiarity by the trading public are disadvantages.

Publicly traded LLCs and LPs are subject to corporate income taxation and are virtually indistinguishable from corporations. If a new business venture is simply launched without a conscious selection of business form being made, a partnership or proprietorship has been created, for better or for worse.

Factors Influencing the Selection of Business Forms. It is not possible to appreciate the issues surrounding the selection of modem business forms without some knowledge of the basic principles of modern federal income taxation. Unfortunately, for many students, the role of federal income taxation in the selection of the business form is a mystery or an enigma. They are not familiar with the broad structure of the Internal Revenue Code which, of course, is a daunting and complex statute that is the subject of separate law school courses.

Indeed, in many business association courses, the role of federal income taxes is ignored simply because it is so complex. It may be enough to know that the current federal income tax regime favors the use of unincorporated business forms for closely held businesses. The corporation is thus the least attractive closely held business form from a purely tax standpoint. All of the unincorporated business forms described above either provide for limited liability of owners or permit limited liability to be obtained by a simple filing procedure.

The differences among them. that may influence the selection of a specific business form include federal and state taxation (both franchise and income), the ease of internal operations, the probability that the business in the future might "go public," the sophistication of the various participants, their estimate whether their relationship with the business is permanent or temporary, and doubtless other factors as well.

FEDERAL TAX REGIMES

There are three basic tax regimes for businesses. They are usually referred to by the subchapter of the Internal Revenue Code dealing with that regime. Subchapter C describes the traditional corporate income tax; Subchapter K describes the tax regime applicable to partnerships and associations taxable as partnerships; and Subchapter S is an alternative tax regime applicable to electing closely held corporations that meet Specific eligibility requirements. Each of these regimes may be briefly described in simplified fashion:

Subchapter C Taxation. The starting point for corporate taxation is that a corporation is a separate taxable entity independent of its shareholders. I.R.C. § 11(a) imposes a separate tax on the income of corporations while § 301 in effect imposes a tax on shareholders who receive distributions of cash or property from corporations, to the extent the corporation has earnings or profits. Thus, the earnings of a C corporation that pays dividends to its shareholders are subject to federal income taxation at two different levels: at the corporate level on the corporation's taxable income and a second time at the shareholders' level on the actual dividends or distributions. This method of taxation is applicable not only to corporations but also to a variety of other associations that are "taxable as a corporation." C corporation taxation is the form of taxation applicable to all publicly held corporations. As indicated previously, there was a brief period in the 1960s and 1970s when "master limited partnerships" were widely sold as a tax-oriented investment. The favorable tax treatment was based on the assumption that the limited partnership would be taxed under subchapter K rather than Subchapter C. The Revenue Act of 1987 effectively ended the tax advantage of publicly traded entities by defining all such entities as corporations for tax purposes. In short, any business entity that has ownership interests that are publicly traded must be taxed as a C corporation. (The Revenue Act of 1987 did "grandfather" a few existing master limited partnerships, and some of these companies may still be in existence.)

Subchapter S Taxation. For many years closely held corporations complained that the double taxation inherent in Subchapter C taxation treated them unfairly and encouraged questionable tax avoidance tactics. In 1957, Congress created a special tax election for qualified closely held Corporations. This election permits many closely held corporations to elect to be taxed in a manner that generally avoids the double taxation of distributions. It permits corporate income to be passed through the corporation and be taxed directly to shareholders, whether or not it is actually distributed to them. While Subchapter S tax treatment is similar to the conduit tax treatment applicable to partnerships and unincorporated entities described below, there are numerous significant technical differences. The S corporation election is also sometimes loosely referred to as a corporation "electing to be taxed as a partnership" or "electing Partnership taxation," those statements are only partially accurate. To be eligible for subchapter S, a corporation must meet the following conditions on the date of election.

(a) It must be a domestic corporation;
(b) It must have no more than 75 shareholders;
(c) Each shareholder must be an individual, a decedent's estate, or certain types of trusts;
(d) No shareholder may be a nonresident alien; and
(e) It may have only one class of stock outstanding (except that classes of common stock differing only in voting rights do not result in the loss of the election).

An S corporation is a true corporation with all attributes of a corporation other than the peculiar tax treatment. Thus, an S corporation has the normal corporate Characteristics of limited liability, centralization of management, perpetual existence, and free transferability of interest.

Subchapter K Taxation. In general terms, Partnerships and "associations taxable as partnerships" are not separate taxable units. Rather, the various tax consequences of their activities are passed through to the owners of the enterprise. The partnership files an information return calculating its business income or loss and then allocates the pro rata share of gains, losses, income, deductions, and so forth, to each individual partner who must include those items in his or her individual income tax return. Under subchapter K allocations need not be strictly in proportion to economic interests. This method of taxation is generically described as "conduit," "pass through," or "partnership-type" taxation. Today it is often referred to as "subchapter K" taxation, or simply as "K" taxation. The rules under subchapter K are much more complex and sophisticated than the rules applicable to C or S corporations.

Impact of Tax Rates. It should be emphasized that as an abstract matter none of the systems of taxation described in the previous section is inherently superior to the others, It all depends on relative tax rates and the detailed rules as to whether income is taxable at the corporate level and, if so, what deductions and credits are available to shareholders at the shareholder level.

Tax minimization strategies change with changes in rates and tax rules. For example, for many years after World War II individual marginal tax rates for wealthy individuals were as high as 80 % while the maximum corporate tax rate was capped at 52 %. Furthermore, the tax rate on long term capital gains was capped at 25 %. This structure of rates strongly encouraged successful businesses (1) to incorporate and take advantage of the C corporation maximum tax rate, (2) to defer paying substantial dividends, (3) to obtain the benefit of assets accumulated in the corporation through transactions that qualified for capital gain treatment, and (4) to provide benefits to shareholder / officers that were tax deductible by the corporation.

During this period, Subchapter K taxation for a profitable business with high-income taxpayers was to be avoided at all costs, since it subjected all the business' income to the very high individual tax rates. Shareholders were much better off if a corporation made no taxable distributions at all. However, reasonable salaries paid to shareholders were deductible by the corporation as an ordinary and necessary business expense, In addition to salaries corporations also provided tax deductible benefits to shareholders, including company vehicles or country club memberships used for business development purposes. Thus some indirect distributions regularly were made to at least some of the shareholders, Shareholders could ultimately sell their shares to third persons to capture the increases in value at the corporate level resulting from limited distributions. The gain from a sale of stock was taxed at a maximum 25 % rate.

The strategy of allowing earnings to accumulate in the corporation and then selling the shares was so common that it became known as the "accumulate and bail-out strategy." An even better tax result was obtained if a shareholder died owning shares of stock, since a special tax rule permits the appreciation in value of the stock to escape taxation entirely. It might be added that shareholders who were not employed by the corporation usually had no method of obtaining distributions from the corporation except at a very substantial cost. Tax rates generally trended downward following World War II reaching their lowest level in 1986. In 1986, individual tax rates were reduced sharply to a maximum rate of 28 % while corporate tax rates were reduced to a maximum rate of 34 %. As a result, the rules of the tax avoidance game changed abruptly, as partnership-type taxation became attractive and C corporation taxation was to be avoided if possible. Current tax rates are higher than they were in 1986; in 1999 the maximum marginal tax rate for individuals is 39.6 % while the maximum corporate tax rate is 35 %. Under these tax rates the most favorable tax regime today for a profitable business is usually subchapter K, followed by Subchapter S, followed by Subchapter C. However, if the participants in the business lack the sophistication to take full advantage of the complexities of subchapter K, S corporation taxation should normally be elected (assuming the entity qualifies).

CHAPTER 5

INCORPORATION[15)]

5.1 FORMATION OF CORPORATION

In General. The process of corporate formation is essentially a very simple one, and much (though not all) of it may be performed By a competent legal secretary, Indeed, one of the great modern innovations in corporate formation is the computer, which permits the mass production of corporate documents with only special name and other minor changes.

A large, publicly held corporation that transacts business in every state may theoretically choose its state of incorporation from among any of the fifty states. As a practical matter, however, most such corporations have selected Delaware as their state of incorporation. The small corporation doing business in only a single state or locality has the same theoretical freedom as the publicly held corporation in this regard, since it is possible to incorporate in any state and qualify to transact business as a foreign corporation in

15) This Chapter is compiled mainly with materials from Robert W. Hamilton, "The Law of Corporations," West Group (2000); Emmanuel Law Outlines, "Corporations," Emmanuel Publishing Corp. (1997).

any other state. However, practical considerations usually dictate that the small corporation be formed in the jurisdiction in which it is solely or principally doing business. There are real costs if any foreign state is selected: The corporation will have to qualify as a foreign corporation in its "home state," it will be subject to two taxing authorities; and it may be subject to suit in a distant state. If there is some reason not to incorporate in the local jurisdiction despite these costs, the alternative usually is Delaware, with its popular statute. As other states have modernized their corporation statutes, the advantages of Delaware as a state of incorporation for small businesses active in other jurisdictions have lessened, and most local businesses today are probably incorporated in the state in which they primarily conduct business.

The Mechanics of Creating a Corporation. The mechanics of creating a corporation vary from state to state, and the specific statute must be consulted for details. Every state requires the filing of a document with a state official, usually the secretary of state, together with the Payment of a filing fee. Depending on the state, the document may be called the "articles of incorporation," the "certificate of incorporation," the "charter" or some other name. Corporate records maintained by the Office of Secretary of State usually are in the form of paper documents. However, computerization of records in this Office offers obvious advantages and many offices now maintain corporate records in electronic form. Some offices maintain both electronic and paper records. The traditional manner of filing articles of incorporation is to mail them in, deliver them by overnight mail service, or deliver them by messenger or courier to the office of the secretary of state. Many state filing offices now also permit electronic filing, often by telefax. This development usually required special legislation since the traditional language of corporation statutes requires submission of an "executed" original as well as a conformed copy, and telefaxed communications do not comply with these requirements.

With further improvements in technology, an electronic filing directly into the computer system maintained by the secretary of state is now practical, and a few states may permit this method of filing. Each filing is reviewed by the office of the secretary of state, which commonly means by a professional staff member within that office. If the document meets the statutory requirements, the corporate existence is usually deemed to relate back to the date and time the document was originally received, any post-filing delays being ignored. In the case of a traditional document, this is the date evidenced by a time stamp placed on the document when it was received or on its envelope. The secretary of state reflects its approval of the filing by an action, traditionally the issuance of a formal "charter" or "certificate of incorporation" which is attached to a duplicate original or copy of the original filing, Increasingly the approval of the filing is evidenced merely by a notation that the document has been accepted for Sling and the issuance of a receipt for the filing fee.

Some 13 states today have additional Sling requirements. Delaware, for example, requires local Sling in the county in which the corporation's registered office is located as well as filing in a state office. Twelve states including Arizona, require that evidence be submitted that the statutory agent has accepted his appointment. In Arizona, the articles of incorporation must be published in a newspaper of general circulation in the county in which the corporation's known place of business is located three consecutive times within 60 days after the articles are filed.[16)]

Georgia and Pennsylvania also require publication of a notice in a local newspaper. Some states may still require recording in every county in which the corporation transacts business. It is generally believed that these publication requirements serve little or no practical benefit; they are retained usually because of the political power of county clerks or newspaper publishers who have come to rely on the fees or charges generated by those requirements.

Local filing or advertising requirements create legal problems if some, but

---

16) Ariz. Kev. Stat. Ann. § 10-055.

not all of them, are complied with before the corporation begins business. Some states have statutes that deal specifically with this question. Delaware, for example, provides that corporate existence begins with the acceptance of the filing by the secretary of state, and the failure to file locally within the specified period increases the filing fee but does not affect the existence of the corporation.[17)]

Some states, however, condition the existence of the corporation on the completion of all filing and advertising requirements. Some six states have a minimum capital requirement. Usually $1,000.00 which must be paid in before the corporation, may begin business.

5.2 INCORPORATORS

The person or persons who execute the articles of incorporation are called "incorporators." Traditionally, three incorporators were required; today all states (except Puerto Rico) require only a single incorporator; a few states still have residency or age requirements for incorporators, but most states now permit an individual to act as incorporator if he or she is of legal age without regard to residency or later Participation in the corporation.

Most states also permit artificial entities such as corporations or trusts to serve as incorporators. The relaxation of the requirements relating to incorporators reflects the minor role they play in the formation of a modem corporation. Depending on the state, incorporators may serve one or more of the following roles:

(1) They execute and deliver the articles of incorporation to the secretary of state;

(2) They or their representatives, receive the charter, Certificate of

17) Del. Code Ann. Tit. 8, § 103(d).

incorporation, notice of acceptance, or fee receipt back from the secretary of state;

(3) They either (i) meet to complete the organization of the corporation or (ii) call the first meeting of the initial board of directors, named in the articles of incorporation, at which the organization of the corporation is completed;

(4) They may voluntarily dissolve the corporation if the corporation has not commenced business and has not issued shares; and

(5) They may amend the articles of incorporation by unanimous consent if the corporation has not commenced business and has not issued any shares.

It is generally believed that there is no risk of liability for actions taken while acting as incorporator of a corporation. Indeed, many attorneys or their secretaries or other law office employees routinely serve as incorporators. The same is not always true of acting as an initial director, however, and many attorneys decline to serve as a director of small corporations they form, or do so only reluctantly.

A "subscriber" is a person who agrees to buy shares in the corporation; in other words, a subscriber is an investor and participant in the venture. At one time many states required that an incorporator also be a subscriber of shares; however, that requirement appears to have disappeared in all states.

5.3 ARTICLES OF INCORPORATION

In General. The document filed with the secretary of state must contain certain mandatory information. While the requirements vary from state to state, the following modest list is typical:[18]

18) It is drawn from § 54 of the 1969 MBCA.

(a) The name of the corporation;

(b) The period of duration, which may be perpetual;

(c) The purpose or purposes of the corporation, which may be generally described as "engaging in any lawful business;"

(d) The number of shares authorized to be issued, including information about the rights and preferences of such shares;

(e) The address of its registered office and the name of its registered agent at that office;

(f) The number of directors and, when required, the names and addresses of the members of the initial board of directors; and

(g) The names and addresses of each incorporator.

Since virtually all modem corporations elect perpetual duration and a purpose of engaging in any lawful business the MBCA (1984) simply provides that every corporation has these attributes unless a shorter duration or narrower Purpose is set forth m the articles of incorporation.

Also, if the corporation has only a single class of shares and elects to be created and organized by a single incorporator the resulting articles of incorporation fits conveniently on a post card. In addition, state statutes provide that a corporation may elect to be governed by certain statutory provisions the election of which must be reflected by an appropriate provision in the articles of incorporation. For example, many statutes provide that a majority in interest of the shareholders shall constitute a quorum of shareholders except that the quorum may be reduced by specific provision in the articles of incorporation to a number smaller than a majority.[19] Many statutes provide that shareholders shall have a preemptive right to acquire new shares or to vote shares cumulatively unless these rights are specifically negated by appropriate provisions in the articles of incorporation. MBCA (1984) Provide "opt in," rather than "opt out," provisions for these rights - i.e., a corporation's shareholders do not have preemptive rights or the right to

---

19) MBCA (1984) § 7.25.

vote cumulatively unless the articles of incorporation specifically provide for them.[20] The statute of each specific state must be consulted to determine the pattern adopted by that state in connection with these rights.

Finally, corporations may elect to place optional provisions relating to internal governance in the articles of incorporation in order to make them more permanent, more difficult to amend, and, hopefully, binding on persons who may not have actual knowledge of them. Such provisions usually may also be placed in the corporation's bylaws. However, many lawyers and judges expect important provisions, or unusual provisions denying customary rights to shareholders or others, to appear in the articles of incorporation. Such provisions are usually repeated in the bylaws to ensure that corporate officers are aware of them.

The Corporate Name. Most statutes set up minimum requirements with respect to the corporate name. The name must contain a word indicating corporations, such as "corporation," "company," or "incorporated," or an abbreviation of one of these words. The name may not contain a word or phrase indicating that it is organized for a purpose that it is not permitted to engage in. As a practical matter, with the development of general purposes clauses, the principal impact of this restriction is to preclude the use of names that suggest a purpose for which corporations may not be organized under the state business corporation act. Thus, "bank," "bank and trust," "certificate of deposit," "title guaranty," or "insurance" may not appear in corporate names in many states since there are special regulatory requirements in statutes relating to formation of corporations for such purposes. These limitations have been relaxed in many states.

The name may not resemble too closely the name of any other corporation formed or qualified to transact business in the state. The precise statutory test varies. Older versions of the MBCA prohibited a name that was the "same or deceptively similar" to any other corporate name, and many state statutes

20) MBCA (1984) § 6.30 and § 7.28(b).

embody this test. Section 4.01 of MBCA (1984) substitutes the test that the name be "distinguishable upon the records of the secretary of state" from any other corporate name. This language was taken from the Delaware statute. The primary purpose of this requirement, however it is phrased, is to make sure that each corporation has a unique name. States that adopt the "same or deceptively similar" standard involve the Secretary of State in making decisions in part on the basis of unfair competition, a policy which, for reasons discussed below, the Secretary of State usually is not be well equipped to enforce.

Some states add another layer to the name availability rules. Texas, for example, Provides that if the name is "similar," as contrasted with the "same or deceptively similar," to any other corporate name, it may be used only if a "letter of consent" is obtained from the owner of the similar name. The purpose of this requirement appears to be the prevention of confusion and unfair competition. Secretaries of State usually maintain lists of corporate names that are in use and therefore not currently available, and check proposed new names against that list. This list is usually stored on a computer to provide instant access, and in some states may be searched by members of the public. This list is usually the sole standard applied by the Secretary of State who typically has neither the staff nor the resources to make an independent investigation of whether the use of the name may constitute unfair competition. It was for this reason that MBCA rephrases the test of name availability as "distinguishable upon the records of the secretary of state."[21]

However, the decision as to name availability, whether the test be "the same," "distinguishable," or "deceptively similar," involves questions of judgment; some Secretaries of State have developed regulations or "house rules" to guide the exercise of discretion or judgment by office employees. As a practical matter, the issue whether or not a specific name is available

21) MBCA (1984) § 4.01.

is rarely litigated. Even if an attorney strongly disagrees with the Secretary of State as to the availability of a name, it is simpler and cheaper to select another name than to litigate over name availability. However, when two corporations or businesses have used similar names in the past, the right to the continued use of such name may have become so valuable as to lead to bitter litigation over whether the use of the name constitutes unfair competition. Secretaries of State are usually directed by statute to accept the results of such litigation in establishing name availability. The discussion so far deals only with "official names," that is the name of the corporation that appears in its articles of incorporation and in the records of the Secretary of State. A corporation, like an individual, may do business under an assumed name so long as the purpose is not fraudulent and does not constitute unfair competition.

Many states have "assumed name statutes" that require a person, whether an individual or a corporation, that is conducting business under an assumed name to file a statement, usually at the county level, disclosing who is actually conducting business under that name. The possible use of an assumed name by a corporation reduces significantly the importance of the name availability determination by the Secretary of State.

A corporation named ABC Corporation, for example, may do business under the name XYZ Corporation upon complying with the assumed name statute, if the state has one. If there happens to be another corporation that has the official name XYZ Corporation, it can enjoin ABC Corporation from using that name as an assumed name only if there is unfair competition, typically name confusion. If the two corporations are not competing against each other because they are in different geographic locations or in totally different businesses, there is probably nothing that the "real" XYZ Corporation can do about it.

As a general proposition, the Secretary of State typically does not know what assumed name a corporation is using or plans to use, in what area of the state the corporation is operating, or even what the nature of the business of the corporation is. As a result the secretary of state is usually not in a position to make reliable judgments about questions of unfair competition. Because of official corporate names are handled on a first-come first-serve basis, many state statutes permit the reservation of a proposed corporate name for a limited time for a nominal fee.[22)]

Many states also authorize the registration of a name by a foreign corporation not transacting business in the state.[23)] A registration of a corporate name allows a foreign corporation with long-term plans to expand into the state to reserve the exclusive use of its name and prevent a local corporation from using the same name as an "official name." A reservation of a name is for a brief period, usually three months, and may not be renewable. On the other hand, a registration of a name may be for a year or more and may be renewed indefinitely without any break, in continuity of protection.

Period of Duration. All business corporation acts now permit a corporation to have perpetual existence. In the past some statutes limited corporations to a fifty year or some other specified life span. These provisions are now obsolete. On the other hand state statutes permit a corporation to elect a limited period of duration. It is probably unwise ever to designate a term less than perpetual. Even if it is contemplated that the corporation will be in business only for a limited period, Plans may change and the articles of incorporation will have to be amended. A failure to amend may result in the corporation having uncertain status after the term expires. Why create a corporate structure that requires someone to remember to file an amendment if it can be avoided?

Capitalization. Articles of incorporation must include information about the types or kinds of securities the corporation is authorized to issue. The required information about types or kinds of securities in articles of incorporation relates to securities the corporation is authorized to issue rather

22) See MBCA § 4.02.

23) See MBCA § 4.03.

than the securities the Corporation actually plans to issue. However, the statutes of several states require disclosure of what securities will actually be issued, either as a part of a tax return or a general information Filing available to the public generally. Minimum capital requirements in state statutes were practically universal twenty-five years ago. These statutes prohibited the corporation from commencing business unless it had received a specified minimum amount of capital and usually imposed personal liability on the directors if they permitted a corporation to commence business without the minimum capital.

The most popular amount was $1,000, but some statutes required $500 or some other amount, and some required some specified percentage of authorized capital. Today all but a handful of states have eliminated such requirements on the theory that any minimum, amount of capitalization is arbitrary and does not provide meaningful protection to creditors. The major problem with these minimum capital provisions was that they took no account of the specific capital needs of the particular business. It made no difference whether a corporation needed $1,000,000 or $100 to start up the contemplated business; both needed an initial capitalization of $1,000. Also, the requirement of $1,000, while perhaps meaningful in the 1950's or 1960's, had become the victim of inflation and was much less significant by the 1990's. The old Model Business Corporation Act eliminated its minimum capitalization requirement in 1969, and the trend is definitely in the direction of eliminating all such requirements. Thus in most states today it is theoretically possible[24)] to form a corporation with a capitalization of one cent.

In states with a minimum capital requirement, the principal enforcement mechanism is to make directors who assent to the corporation commencing business before it has received the required capital liable jointly and severally for that part of the capital not actually received. Usually this liability

24) As it is under the MBCA (1984).

terminates when the required consideration is received. At one time, a few states had *in terrorem* statutes that made the directors personally liable for at corporate obligations incurred before the minimum capital was paid in, even if the shortfall of capital was small and the liabilities incurred were large. None of the remaining states with minimum capital requirements appear to fall within this category.

Registered Office & Agent. Every corporation must maintain a registered office and a registered agent at that office. Some states describe the registered agent as the "statutory agent." The registered office may but need not be the corporation's business office. The primary purpose of a registered office and registered agent is to provide an agent for service of process. The underlying idea is that it should be possible at all times to find a corporation and to have a person upon whom, and a place at which, any notice or process required or permitted by law may be served. A second purpose is to have an office to which tax notices and other official communications from the state may be sent. The original registered office and registered agent is specified in the articles of incorporation; if either is changed thereafter a statement describing the change must be filed with the Secretary of State.

Often a corporation designates its principal business office to be its registered office. In such a case, the registered agent is a corporate officer or employee. The principal disadvantage of this is the possibility that summons, legal documents, or other communications may be mixed in with routine business mail and not receive the attention they deserve. For this reason, many attorneys suggest that they be designated as the registered agent and their office be designated as the registered office. Corporation service companies provide registered offices and registered agents for a modest fee. Corporations that are incorporated in a state in which they do not have a business office, Delaware is the most prominent example, often utilize this service provided by corporations service companies.

Initial Board of Directors. The initial board of directors of the corporation must be named in the articles of incorporation in states in which the initial directors are to complete the formation of the contract. In states where the incorporators perform this function there is usually no requirement that initial directors be named in the articles of incorporation. In states in which the initial board of directors is named in the articles of incorporation, there is no requirement that subsequent changes in membership be reflected by amendments to the articles of incorporation, or in later filings with the secretary of state.

Unlike the registered office and registered agent, the records maintained by the secretary of state do not indicate who the current directors of a corporation are. Where the initial board of directors is named in the articles, it serves as the board only until the first annual meeting of shareholders or until the directors' successors are elected and qualify. The first annual meeting of shareholders may be set immediately after the organizational meeting of the initial board of directors so that elected directors take office almost immediately, It is possible in these states to name in the articles of incorporation persons who are nominal directors That is, directors who have no continuing interest in the business and cease to serve as directors immediately after the organizational meeting.

In this way all disclosure of the identity of the permanent board of directors in the articles of incorporation may be avoided, Whether or not this is desirable depends on the wishes of the clients. Unlike incorporators, directors may sometimes incur liabilities by virtue of their office. Hence, it may be unwise for an attorney or his or her employees to serve as directors, nominal or otherwise, though the risk may be slight as a practical matter if the directorship is for a short period.

Limitation of Directorial Liability. As a result of concern about the liability imposed on directors in the famous case of *Smith v. Van Gorkom*,[25]

---

25) *Smith v. Van Gorkom* 488 A.2d 858, 3 EXC 112 (Del.1985).
Facts. A corporation (Marmon) was attempting a leveraged buy-out of TransUnion. TransUnion's CEO, Van Gorkom proposed a price of $55/share.Van Gorkom and his CFO didn't bother to do any research to see how much the company was worth. Van Gorkom did not even inform TransUnion's legal department about the transaction. $55 a share was only around 60% of what the company was later appraised at. At

the corporation statutes of many states have been amended to permit the shareholders to limit the personal liability of directors for monetary damages for violations of the duty of due care. In 1994, the Model Act was amended to authorize corporations to grant obligatory indemnification of directors with respect to all actions taken by a director except liability for (A) receipt of a financial benefit to which he is not entitled, (B) an intentional infliction of harm on the corporation or its shareholders, (C) a violation of section 8.33 [relating to unlawful distributions], or (D) an intentional violation of

---

the time of the merger, the stock was selling for $37.25 a share, so $55 seemed like a lot. Van Gorkom called an emergency meeting of the board of directors, proposed the merger, and the directors gave him preliminary approval. Van Gorkom did not disclose a number of things at the board meeting where the vote was to be taken, including the fact that there was no basis for the $55 price, and that there had been objections by TransUnion management regarding the merger. Van Gorkom did not provide the directors with copies of the merger agreement. Some shareholders instituted a derivative lawsuit against the directors for *breach of fiduciary duty*.

Procedural History. The Trial Court found that Van Gorkom's actions fell within the *business judgment rule*. The *business judgment rule* says that the courts should not second guess business decisions made by directors. Shareholders appealed.

ISSUE and Holding. Were the directors grossly negligent due to approving the merger without substantial inquiry or procural of expert advice? Yes, they should have made inquiry and breached their duty of care.

RULES. The Business Judgment Rule is a "presumption that in making a business decision, the directors of a corporation acted on an informed basis, in good faith and in the honest belief that the action taken was in the best interests of the company.' ...Thus, the party attacking a board decision as uninformed must rebut the presumption that its business judgment was an informed one." "Under the business judgment rule there is no protection for directors who have made an unintelligent or unadvised judgment."

Analysis. The Court found that the directors breached their *fiduciary duty* by their failure to inform themselves of all information reasonably available to them and relevant to their decision to recommend the merger. The Court also found that there was a failure to disclose all material information such as that which a reasonable stockholder would consider important in deciding whether to approve the merger. Van Gorkom breached his *duty to care* by offering $55 a share because, "the record is devoid of any competent evidence that $55 represented the per share intrinsic value of the Company." Court found that the *business judgment rule* was not a defense because the directors and Van Gorkom did not use any "business judgment" when they came to their decision. The courts will ask: whether there was an adequate decision-making process. In order to hide behind the *business judgment rule*, you have to show that you made an informed decision based on some principle of business. If you randomly pull numbers out of thin air or cast votes without due diligence, then the courts can (and will often) overturn your decisions. The idea behind the *business judgment rule* is people who work in the business have more experience and are better judges of what a corporation should do than a court would be. The courts do not like getting involved in business decisions. However, when businessmen show that they didn't use any of that experience to make a decision, then there is no reason for the courts to defer to them.

Notes. Almost immediately after this decision, Delaware passed a law (DGCL §102(b)(7)) which allows corporations to limit the liability of their directors for breaches of the *duty of care*.

criminal law."[26]

Purposes and Powers. All state statutes now provide that a corporation may be formed for any lawful purpose. Many state statutes still require that the articles of incorporation specify what the Corporation's purpose or purposes are, but usually permit a general statement that the corporation is formed "for lawful business purposes" or "to engage in any lawful business." The use of such clauses has become so common that the MBCA (1984) provides that all corporations have the "purpose of engaging in any lawful business unless a more limited purpose is set forth in the articles of incorporation."

The historical development of purposes clauses is interesting and is typical of basic trends in state corporation law. In the Nineteenth Century, corporations could only be formed for specific purposes, and in some states could only list a single purpose. These provisions were viewed as providing a significant regulatory component: Corporations were viewed with mistrust and permission to do business m corporate form was given only grudgingly. Application of these limiting principles often raised problems of ultra vires and led to a large amount of litigation construing purposes clauses. The first major innovation was a superficially simple one: It permitted a corporation to state multiple purposes while preserving the rule that the Corporation was organized only for whatever purposes were set forth in the articles of incorporation. This, however, opened the proverbial floodgates since there was no limitation on the number of purposes for which a single corporation may be formed. It was theoretically possible for a corporation to list every conceivable business in which a corporation may engage including mining diamonds on the moon.

Purposes clauses therefore became increasingly prolix, increasingly unreadable and often completely uninformative as to what business the corporation actually planned to engage in. The next step permitted a corporation to use a very simple and general clause, e.g., "this corporation

---

26) MBCA (1984), as amended, § 2.02(b)(5).

may engage in any lawful business." Since practically all corporations elected to take advantage of this innovation, the requirement of a purposes clause has been reduced to a formality, and the final step taken in the MBCA to eliminate the clause entirely seems to be natural and sensible. Despite the modern freedom to use "any lawful business" clauses, or to omit the purpose clause entirely, articles of incorporation are sometimes filed with a narrow purposes clause as part of internal corporate planning. Like the limited duration clause, such a provision is apt to create more Problems than benefits since a limited purposes clause does not actually limit the scope of the corporation's activities so that ultra vires conduct may occur.

Modern purposes clauses often specify the principal business or activity of the corporation and couple it with broader language such as, "and to engage in any other lawful business." This provides the reader of the articles of incorporation with information about the nature of the corporation's principal business without restricting the freedom of the corporation to engage in other businesses. It may be necessary to use narrow purposes clauses in corporations that are to engage in businesses subject to specific state or federal regulation that require regulated corporations to have specified purposes. Corporate "purposes" should be distinguished from corporate "powers."

Every state business corporation act contains a list of corporate powers that every corporation organized under that act automatically possesses. In most states this list is broad and not exclusive. The MBCA[27)] is based on the long tradition of powers clauses in state statutes, but it contains additional language in the introductory clause, "and has the same powers as an individual to do all things necessary or convenient to carry out its business and affairs," that is designed to eliminate any historical remnant of doctrines of limited or enumerated powers. The MBCA is also broader

27) MBCA (1984) § 3.02.

than many state statutes in specific areas,[28] authorizing the making of payments or donations or doing of other acts "not inconsistent with law, which furthers the business and affairs of the corporation." This language is independent of the power to make charitable donations,[29] and includes payments for political purposes or to influence elections. A corporation with a narrow purposes clause may nevertheless possess broad powers under the MBCA (1984) or similar state statutes, the broad powers to be exercised m furtherance of narrow purposes.[30]

Where a state statute contains a broad list of powers, it is generally undesirable to include powers clauses m articles of incorporation since the inclusion of certain powers may be construed as negating the existence of non-enumerated ones. Because of peculiar historical problems in some states, however, it may be desirable to refer to certain specific powers in the articles. Where this is felt necessary, the drafting should make clear that the clause relates to powers rather than purposes. A clause that permits a corporation, for example, "to enter into partnerships or joint ventures" states a "power" and not a "purpose." The corporation is utilizing the "Power" to enter into a partnership to achieve a "purpose," e.g., a purpose of buying, selling, and trading in real estate.

5.4 ULTRA VIRES DOCTRINE

In General. The doctrine of ultra vires, literally beyond the scope of the purposes or powers of a corporation, is now largely obsolete in modern corporation law. In an earlier day, however the doctrine had considerable

28) Such as RMBCA § 3.02(15).

29) MBCA § 3.02(13).

30) MBCA § 3.02.

practical importance and was given major attention. Before turning to the vestigial remnants of the doctrine in modern law, a brief description of the scope of the doctrine at common law should be given.

An ultra vires act was one beyond the purposes or powers of a corporation. The earliest view of the matter was that such acts were simply void. A corporation was formed only for limited purposes, the argument ran, and it could do nothing more than it was authorized to do. This early view, however was unworkable and unrealistic. Carried to its logical conclusion it would permit a corporation to accept the benefits of a contract and then refuse to perform its obligations on the ground that the contract was ultra vires, indeed that may have been the view taken early by the English courts. It would also impair the security of title to property in fully executed transactions in which a corporation participated. As a result, even though dicta supporting the view that ultra vires acts were totally void appeared in many cases most courts actually adopted the view that such acts were voidable rather than void.

The doctrine continued to be firmly grounded on the notion that a corporation possessed only limited purposes and powers, but a rather elaborate body of law developed defining when the defense of ultra vires might be asserted.

(a) An ultra vires transaction might be ratified by all the shareholders. Certification could be express or implied, e.g., by the receipt of benefits without objection. Ratification, however, had to be by unanimous consent.

(b) The doctrine of estoppel usually precluded reliance on the defense of ultra vires where the transaction was fully performed by one party. In some cases, however, the corporation was held not to be estopped even where the other party had performed fully because the corporation had not received a "direct" benefit from the transaction. When benefits were classed as "direct" or "indirect" appeared to be erratic.

(c) A fortiori, a transaction which was fully performed by both parties could not be attacked. This principle was generally applied to assure security of land titles.

(d) If the contract was fully executory, the defense of ultra vires might be raised by either party.

(e) If the contract was partially performed, and the Performance was held to be insufficient to bring the doctrine of estoppel into play, a suit in quasi-contract for recovery of benefits conferred was available.

(f) If an agent of the corporation committed a tort within the scope of his or her employment, the corporation could not defend on the ground the act was ultra vires. This conclusion was reached apparently because of the overriding necessity of protecting innocent third parties from corporate abuses over which they had no means of control.

These principles somewhat tamed the doctrine of ultra vires. That doctrine, however, continued to defeat legitimate expectations where the contract was still executory and possessed an unfortunate capacity to be applied m an erratic fashion in other situations as well. As a result, the modern trend has been to eliminate this doctrine from the law of corporations, or at least to sharply restrict its availability.

The Modern Role. Modern developments relating to corporate formation reduce the probability that ultra vires acts will actually occur. Thus, the development of multiple purposes clauses and general clauses permitting corporations to "engage in any lawful business" indirectly limits the role of the doctrine. Further, it is now very simple to amend purposes clauses to broaden them to cover new activities if an ultra vires issue is presented. However, despite these factors, cases involving narrowly drawn purposes clauses still occasionally arise, In order to eliminate the complicated and arbitrary ultra vires rules in these cases, virtually all states have adopted statutes patterned on the following 1950 Model Act provision: No act of a corporation and no conveyance or transfer of real or personal property to or by a corporation shall be invalid by reason of the fact that the corporation was without capacity or power to do such act or to make or receive such conveyance or transfer.[31)]

The MBCA says exactly the same thing in somewhat more elegant language: "The validity of corporate action may not be challenged on the ground that the corporation lacks or lacked power to act."[32)] However, both statutes permit the lack of capacity or power to be asserted in the following types of proceedings:

(1) In a proceeding by the corporation (or by a shareholder in a representative capacity) against the incumbent or former officers or directors of the corporation for exceeding their authority;

(2) In a proceeding by the Attorney General to dissolve the corporation, or to enjoin it from the transaction of unauthorized business; or

(3) In a proceeding by a shareholder against the corporation to enjoin the commission of an ultra vires act or the ultra vires transfer of real or personal property if all parties are before the court and circumstances make such an action equitable.

A limited Purposes clause may be included because one or more of the participants desire to restrict the freedom of a corporation to go into new or different ventures. The possibility of enjoining a corporation from violating such a limited clause is recognized in clause (3), but only "if the circumstances make such an action equitable." However, the Official Comment points out that rights of third persons who may be unaware of the restrictions must be taken into account in assessing equity; in view of the routine and pro forma nature of the modern incorporation process it is unlikely that a third person would be held subject to a limited purposes clause unless he or she was actually aware of it.[33)] The notion that a filing in a public office creates "constructive notice," whatever its merits in other contexts, Probably should not extend to unusual provisions in articles of incorporation and, given the

31) The Model Business Corporation Act (1950) § 7.

32) MBCA (1984) § 3.04(a).

33) See the Official Comment to the RMBCA § 3.04.

modern practice of virtual universal use of general purposes clauses, certainly should not extend to limited purposes clauses.

ULTRA VIRES PROBLEMS IN CONNECTION WITH CORPORATE POWERS

The concept of ultra vires may arise in one other modern context. Modern corporation statutes contain a list of powers that every corporation formed under the statute automatically possesses. Theoretically a corporation may do some act that is beyond its powers as set forth in this list. But the language of the MBCA is so broad that this is unlikely.

However, the language of powers clauses vary and in some states corporations may not be specifically authorized to engage in certain actions even though they appear to be in furtherance of the stated purposes of the corporation. This problem is also declining in importance as the language of statutes is modernized, but the following kinds of activities may create ultra vires problems in some states.

Charitable or Political Contributions. Under early decisions corporations did not have implied power to make donations to charitable, religious, or civic organizations. Most states now generally authorize such contributions though doubt may exist whether power exists to make gifts that are large m comparison to the income or assets of the corporation. A leading Delaware case, *Theodora Holding Corp. v. Henderson,*[34] upholds such gifts so long as they are reasonable in amount given the corporate assets and do not exceed the maximum deduction allowed under the federal income tax law.

Also a distinction may be drawn between gifts to established charities such as universities, hospitals, or the Red Cross, and gifts to organizations or foundations chartered by a controlling shareholder or director. Arguments may also be made that specific charitable gifts directly further the corporation's purpose and should be viewed as business rather than

---

34) *Theodora Holding Corp. v. Henderson,* 257 A.2d 398 (Del.Ch. 1969).

eleemosynary transactions. Direct political contributions by corporations are unlawful and subject to civil and criminal sanctions in many states. In *First National Bank v. Bellotti,*[35] however, the United States Supreme Court held unconstitutional a Massachusetts criminal statute that prohibited corporations from making contributions or expenditures to influence a state referendum.

In *Austin v. Michigan Chamber of Commerce,*[36] the Court recognized

---

35) First National Bank v. Bellotti 22 Ill.435 U.S. 765, 98 S. Ct. 1407, 55 L. Ed. 2d 707, 3 Med. L. Rptr. 2105 (1978).
Brief Fact Summary. The Appellant, the First National Bank of Boston (Appellant) brought suit seeking to have a Massachusetts statute declared unconstitutional because it infringed on the First Amendment constitutional rights of banks and corporations who wanted to spend money to publicize their political views.
Rule of Law. Just because corporations have vast assets at their disposal, they cannot be kept from expressing their own political viewpoints.
Facts. The Appellant wanted to spend money to publicize their views on a proposed constitutional amendment that would have allowed the legislature to impose a gradual tax on the income of individuals in the State of Massachusetts. The Appellant was informed by the attorney general of Massachusetts that they could not do this, because it was in violation of a state criminal statute. The State Supreme Court rejected the Appellant's claims that the statute abridged their freedom of speech and the Supreme Court of the United States (Supreme Court) granted certiorari to consider the question.
Issue & Held. This case considers whether a corporation is deprived of political speech, because of its corporate identity. Reversed.
The court overturned the criminal statute, alleging that because it prohibited protected speech (contribution in furtherance of expressing corporate views), it should be invalidated.
Dissent. Justice Byron White (J. White) dissented, noting that there is a compelling state interest not to allow the corporate domination.
Discussion. A corporation, as an entity, is to be afforded the same freedom of expression of its political views as is an individual.

36) *Austin v. Michigan Chamber of Commerce.* 22 Ill.494 U.S. 652, 110 S. Ct. 1391, 108 L. Ed. 2d 652 (1990).
Brief Fact Summary. This case raises the issue of the constitutionality of a Michigan Statute, which prohibits corporate political expenditures, with the exception of those expenditures made from a segregated fund.
Rule of Law. When a State seeks to regulate corporate political expenditures, it is not in abrogation of the corporation's First Amendment constitutional rights, if the state sets guidelines regarding the origin of the funds.
Facts. The Appellee, the Michigan Chamber of Commerce (Appellee), possessed a segregated political fund, but wished to use money from its general treasury fund to place a political advertisement. The Appellee brought suit in District Court, seeking injunctive relief against Michigan's statutory scheme, arguing that the restriction of expenditures was facially unconstitutional.
Issue. This case considers whether Michigan's restrictions on corporate political expenditures can be constitutionally applied to the Appellee.
Held. The court held that the statutory scheme provided a means for the Appellee to express itself politically and thus there was no abrogation of Appellee's rights in requiring it to follow the statute.

that "narrowly drawn" limitations on corporate political speech were constitutionally permissible. In establishing First Amendment rights for corporations, the Supreme Court appears to be concerned with the rights of the hearer of the speech more than its source. The Model Business Corporation Act codifies the power of corporations to make charitable contributions and other payments or donations in furtherance of the corporation's business and affairs.[37]

Pensions, Bonuses, Stock Option Plans, Job Service Payments, and Other Fringe Benefits. These arrangements obviously serve legitimate business purposes, and it is clear that a corporation in an appropriate case may award these benefits without express statutory authority. Most doubts about the propriety of these financial arrangements arise in either of two contexts: where the compensation appears to be excessive or based on self-dealing, or where arguably there is an absence of consideration. For example, consideration may be lacking where, as a humanitarian gesture, a corporation supplements the modest pension of a retired employee. Or a bonus may be paid to an employee at the end of the year without a prior agreement that a bonus would be paid. Or a voluntary payment may be made to the spouse of a deceased employee.

Technically, the argument about lack of consideration is not based on lack of corporate power but on substantive contract law. In most cases consideration may be found if the court is willing to look for it. For example, a bonus in one year may lead to an inference that a bonus will be paid the following year; a promise to remain in the corporation's employment may be implied; or the payment of an apparently gratuitous pension may yield contemplated benefits to the corporation in the form of improved employee

Dissent. Judge Antonin Scalia (J. Scalia and Judge Anthony Kennedy (J. Kennedy) dissented, arguing that the government should not be allowed to censor the fairness of political speech, by requiring segregated funds. Concurrence. Justice John Paul Stevens (J. Stevens) and Justice William Brennan (J. Brennan) Concurred.

37) MBCA § 3.02(13) and § 3.02(15).

morale and a happier labor force. In the absence of excessive compensation or blatant self-dealing, courts generally strive to uphold rather than strike down compensation arrangements. The MBCA expressly addresses the power of corporations to provide pension and similar benefits to present or former employees.[38)]

The Power to Enter into a Partnership. The statement that it is ultra vires for corporations to enter into partnerships appears in numerous cases. The concern is that the fiduciary duties owed to other partners may conflict with the directors' duties to the shareholders. Because of the prominence of these statements the MBCA specifically authorizes every corporation "to be a promoter, partner, member, associate, or manager of any partnership, joint venture, trust or other enterprise."[39)] The same language appears in the 1969 Model Act. Under such a statute there seems to be no doubt that a corporation has the power to become a partner. Most states have enacted this provision. The major case dealing with the duties of director of a corporation that is a general partner in a limited partnership has toward the limited partners is *In re USACafes.*[40)]

---

38) MBCA § 3.02(12).

39) MBCA (1984) § 3.02(9).

40) *In re USACafes*, 600 A.2d 43 (Del. Ch. 1991).
Brief Fact Summary. Plaintiffs Limited Partners of USACafes, L.P. ("Plaintiffs") brought a class action suit against Defendants USACafes General Partner, Inc and six directors of the General Partner ("Defendants") for breach of fiduciary duty. Plaintiffs claimed that the sale of Plaintiffs' assets to an independent entity, under which Defendants received side payments, breached Defendants' fiduciary duty to Plaintiffs because Defendants consequentially accepted a lower offer price for Plaintiffs' assets.
Rule of Law. Directors of a corporate general partner owe a fiduciary duty to a limited partnership
Facts. Plaintiffs brought a class actions suit on behalf of themselves and all other limited partnership unitholders (except for Defendants) alleging that Defendants breached a fiduciary duty owed Plaintiffs when Defendants sold Plaintiffs' assets to an independent entity, Metsa Acquisition Corp ("Metsa"). Pursuant to the sale, Defendants were to receive certain "side payments," totaling between $15-17 million, including so-called non-compete compensation and loan forgiveness. Plaintiffs argued that because of these side payments, Defendants failed to secure the best offer price from Metsa. In addition, Plaintiffs argued that even if Defendants had secured the best offer, a portion of the personal side payments should have been made directly to the Partnership. Defendants argued that although the General Partners owed a fiduciary duty to the limited partners, the individual directors' fiduciary duties, as directors, were owed to the General Partner and its shareholders, and that Plaintiffs' complaint should consequentially be dismissed for failure to state a claim.

The Power to Acquire Shares of Other Corporations. The power of corporations at common law to acquire shares of other corporations was sharply restricted on the theory that a general power to invest in shares of another corporation constituted an indirect way for corporations to avoid limitations in their own purposes clauses. These restrictions are obsolete, corporations today generally have power to purchase, sell and hold shares or other interests in, or obligations of, other domestic or foreign corporations. This power is now codified in the MBCA; virtually identical language appeared in earlier versions of the Model Act.[41)]

Guaranty of Indebtedness of Another. At common law, it was ultra vires

---

Issue & Held. Whether directors of a corporate general partner owe a fiduciary duty to a limited partnership? Yes, directors of a corporate general partner owe a fiduciary duty to a limited partnership. Although no Corporation law precedence holds that directors have such a duty, common sense requires imposing a fiduciary duty on a director of a corporate general partner of a limited partnership because of the fiduciary duties inherent in the role of a director who sits on the board of an entity that is itself a fiduciary. In fact, two courts have found the sole shareholder and director of a corporate general partner personally liable for breach of fiduciary duty. While these authorities extend the fiduciary duty of the general partner to a controlling shareholder, they support as well, the recognition of such duty in directors of the General Partner who, more directly than a controlling shareholder, are in control of the partnership's property. Analogy to trust law clearly indicates that directors have a fiduciary duty to a limited partnership. The extent of this fiduciary duty need not be determined here. Nonetheless, it surely includes the duty not to use control over a partnership's property to advantage the corporate director at the expense of the partnership. Through their unit ownership and executive positions, the director defendants have dominated and controlled the affairs of USACafes. Among other things, the director defendants have failed to adequately solicit or consider alternative proposals for USACafes, have failed to negotiate in good faith to enhance Unitholders' values, and, instead, have agreed to sell all of its assets to Metsa, at a grossly inadequate price per Unit.

Discussion. This case is noteworthy for its reliance on trust, rather than corporation, law. The Court emphasizes that the trust theory underlying fiduciary duties is consistent with the recognition that a director of a corporate general partner bears a fiduciary duty towards the limited partnership. The Court points to instances in which directors or officers of a corporate trustee have been personally at fault for breach of a fiduciary duty to the beneficiary of the trust and have imposed personal liability on such individuals. Here the court posits a hypothetical situation in self-dealing, in which the board of a corporate general partner forms a new entity and then causes the general partner to sell the assets of the limited partnership to the new entity at an unfairly low price. This, the Court reasons, is a blatant breach of fiduciary duty by the directors. The Court summarizes its position through this hypothetical and states, "Can it be imagined that such persons have not breached a duty to the limited partnership itself? And does it not make perfect sense to say that the gist of the offense is a breach of the equitable duty of loyalty that is placed upon a fiduciary?"

41) MBCA (1984) § 3.02(6).

for a general business corporation to guarantee the indebtedness of another person, e.g., a potential customer, an exception was made for corporations who were formed for the specific purpose of writing surety bonds for a fee. This principle, which has little to commend it as an abstract matter gave rise to a considerable amount of injustice since third persons might readily rely on a corporate guarantee. Fortunately it has been reversed by statutory provision judicial decision; the MBCA, for example, authorizes corporations "to make contracts and guarantees [and] incur liabilities;" virtually identical language appeared in earlier versions of the Model Act.[42]

Loans to Officers or Directors. The MBCA Provides that a corporation may elect directors, appoint officers, employees, and agents "and lend them money and credit."[43] The MBCA recognizes that loans to officers or directors may be beneficial to the corporation, and imposes no special restraints or limitations on them. It was not always so, and it is not so in some states today. The 1969 and earlier versions of the Model Business Corporation Act contained an unqualified prohibition against such loans: they stated that "no loans shall be made by a corporation to its officers or directors." In one form or another, restrictions on loans to officers or directors still appear in the statutes of many states; most of these restrictions are not total prohibitions[44] but permit loans, for example, that are approved by the shareholders or loans that are for the express purpose of permitting the individual to purchase shares of the corporation.

Generally these restrictions have been construed as a "limitation on a specific power granted, not a positive prohibition." In other words, loans that violate these restrictions are ultra vires but not illegal. The1969 version of the Model Act and the statutes of many states also provide that directors who vote for or assent to the making of an improper loan to an officer or director

42) MBCA (1984) § 3.02(7).

43) MBCA (1984) § 3.02(11).

44) See the 1969 Model Business Corporation Act.

are jointly and severally liable for the amount of the loan until it is repaid. It may be argued that this specific provision constitutes the sole remedy for a violation of this restriction on the general powers of a corporation.

As originally approved, the MBCA dealt specifically with loans by a corporation to a director. This section built off the more liberal state statutes, and permitted loans to directors that were (1) approved by a majority of the voting shareholders, (2) approved by the board of directors after a finding that the loan benefits the corporation, or (3) made pursuant to a general plan authorizing loans that was approved by the board of directors after a finding that the plan benefits the corporation.[45]

In 1988, however, the Committee on Corporate Laws adopted a new Model Act provision that dealt systematically with conflict of interest transactions between directors and their corporations. Viewing loans to directors as only a special case of conflict of interest transactions did not require special treatment.[46] There is therefore now no special provision in the MBCA dealing with loans to directors. Restrictions on loans to officers and directors are based on fear that loans to corporate decision-makers are peculiarly subject to abuse; in effect statutes like the 1969 Model Act address this fear by making ultra vires all loans to officers or directors whether or not they are in fact abusive.

MBCA rejects this *per se* rule and treats such loans as merely one type of conflict of interest transaction. The early statutes prohibiting loans to officers or directors sometimes also included a general prohibition, which appears in the 1969 version of the Model Act, against loans "secured by shares of stock of a corporation." Apparently this provision was included to emphasize that from the standpoint of the corporation such a loan was in fact unsecured. However, the desirability of including such a limitation on powers seems questionable and the clause was eliminated from the Model Act in 1969; it

45) MBCA (1984) § 8.32.

46) The Committee repealed the original section 8.32.

also has been eliminated from the statutes of most states.

5.5 COMPLETION OF THE ORGANIZATION OF THE CORPORATION

In General. In addition to preparing and filing the articles of incorporation, the attorney usually handles a number of other routine details in connection with the formation of a corporation. Typically the lawyer:

(1) Prepares the corporate bylaws;

(2) Prepares the call of meeting of the initial board of directors or the incorporators, minutes of this meeting, and waivers of notice or consents if necessary;

(3) Obtains a corporate seal and minute book for the corporation;

(4) Obtains blank certificates for the shares of stock, arrange for their printing or typing, and ensure that they are properly issued;

(5) Arranges for the opening of the corporate bank account;

(6) Prepares the call of meeting of the shareholders, minutes of this meeting and waivers of notice, if necessary;

(7) Prepares employment contracts, voting trusts, Pooling agreements, share transfer restrictions, and other special arrangements which are to be entered into with respect to the corporation and its shares; (8) Obtains taxpayer and employer identification numbers from the Internal Revenue Service and from appropriate state agencies; and

(9) Ensures that the manner in which capital is proposed to be raised is in compliance with the requirements of the federal Securities Act of 1933 and the applicable state blue sky laws; and

(10)If the corporation qualifies for S Corporation tax treatment, discusses with the owners the question whether to make this tax election.

Nature and Purpose of Bylaws. The bylaws of a corporation are a set of rules for governing the internal affairs of the corporation. They are adopted by the corporation and technically are binding only on intra corporate matters. They are often viewed as a contract between the corporation and its officers, directors and Shareholders, and among those individuals themselves. Bylaws are generally not filed with the secretary of state, and are not a matter of public record. They usually may be amended with considerable more facility than the articles of incorporation, In case of conflict between the articles of incorporation and the bylaws, the former, of course, control. It is often optional whether a specific provision is included in the articles of incorporation or m the bylaws. If the provision is unusual or important, maximum legal efficacy is obtained by placing the provision on public record in the articles. On the other hand, corporate officers are much more likely to be conversant with the provisions of the bylaws. For this reason, Procedural matters and mandatory provisions that appear in the articles of incorporation and even in the statute should be repeated in the bylaws. The bylaws should set out what amounts to an operating manual of basic rules for ordinary transactions, sufficiently complete to be relied upon by the directors and officers of the corporation as a checklist in administering the affairs of the corporation.

The Corporate Seal. In most states a formal corporate seal is no longer necessary. A handwritten facsimile seal has the same legal effect as a metal die, and some states have attempted to dispense entirely with the requirement of a seal.[47] Nevertheless, a seal is probably desirable since it helps to delineate corporate transactions from individual transactions. Also, title and abstract companies and attorneys in real estate work are accustomed to corporate conveyances being under seal, and it may be easier to satisfy them if a formal seal is available. No one need fight city hall unnecessarily. The corporate seal is usually affixed to share certificates bonds, debentures, evidences of indebtedness, corporate conveyances of land, certified excerpts from minutes

47) See MBCA (1984) § 3.02(2).

of meetings and important corporate contracts.

Organizational Meetings. Most of the miscellaneous matters relating to the launching of a new corporation are accomplished at a meeting of the initial directors, or in some states, the incorporators. These matters may usually be handled by written unanimous consent if there is no dispute or controversy, thereby dispensing with the requirement of a formal meeting. Typical actions include the acceptance of share subscriptions or contracts to purchase shares, the issuance of shares and the establishment of the consideration for them; the selection and election of permanent directors and officers; the approval of contracts, loans, leases and other business-related matters; approval of the bylaws and the seal; approval of the payment of the expenses of incorporation; adoption of a resolution opening a bank account and designation of the officers authorized to sign checks; and numerous other possible business-related matters. Also, in some circumstances it may be necessary to have a meeting of the shareholders to elect permanent directors; a written unanimous consent may be used in lieu of this formal meeting also.

As a practical matter, the lawyer prepares not only the articles of incorporation and bylaws, but also the various minutes or written consents needed to complete the formation of the corporation. These documents are almost always prepared in advance of the actual formation. It may seem odd to prepare elaborate minutes for a meeting that has not yet taken place, but really it is not; the minutes serve as a script for the actual conduct of the meeting. Of course, if action is being taken by unanimous written consent only signatures are required. In states that require the organizational meeting to be held by initial directors named in the articles of incorporation, attorneys sometimes find it necessary, where the permanent parties in interest do not want their names to appear in the records of the secretary of state, to use nominal initial directors, hold a "meeting" of these initial directors to organize the corporation and issue stock, followed immediately by a "meeting" of shareholders to elect permanent directors, followed immediately by another "meeting" of the permanent directors to conduct other necessary business transactions.

If the permanent directors are willing to serve as the initial directors and be named as such in the articles of incorporation, it is simplest to name the permanent directors also as initial directors, since only a single "meeting" then suffices to complete the formation of the corporation. It was because of scenarios such as these that the draftsmen of the MBCA decided to give each new corporation an option whether to have organizational meetings conducted by incorporators or by initial directors named in the articles of incorporation.

As a practical matter, of course, this decision is made by the attorney forming the corporation as he or she contemplates the desires of the client and the steps needed to complete the formation of the corporation.

Where the unanimous written consent procedure is not available, as may be the case, for example, where one director is absent, the question sometimes arises as to whether it is necessary to actually hold meetings to reflect what the minutes describe, If the corporation is closely held and there is no disagreement about what is to be done, it seems to be a waste of time and silly play-acting to assemble several persons in a single room and actually hold a meeting at which the already-prepared minutes serve as a script.

However, it is generally desirable to actually hold an informal meeting at which the actions referred to in the minutes are quickly approved. Such meetings do have a play-acting atmosphere but the validity of actions taken without a meeting may otherwise be questioned. Such a meeting may take only a minute or so if there is consensus as to what should be done.

5.6 PREINCORPORATION ACTIONS

Introduction. The formation of a new corporation is often not a dean birth. Transactions on behalf of the corporation, or in the corporate name, may occur before the articles of incorporation are filed and the corporate existence begins. Such transactions may be entered into with full knowledge that the corporation is not yet formed, such as subscription agreements or contracts by promoters to ensure that the necessary business assets are available, or inadvertently, resulting from unexpected delays in the formation of the corporation. Preliminary transactions are usually classified under several different headings: promoters' transactions, de facto corporations, and so forth. They are, however, all closely related and often factual situations may be classified under more than one of these headings.

SUBSCRIPTIONS FOR SHARES.

A "subscription" is simply an offer to purchase and pay for a specified number of theretofore unissued shares of a corporation. Subscriptions may be divided into "pre-incorporation subscriptions," that is, subscriptions for shares of a corporation that has not yet been formed, and "post-incorporation subscriptions," that is, subscriptions for unissued shares of an already existing corporation.

Pre-Incorporation Subscriptions. Older texts devote a great deal of attention to pre-incorporation subscriptions as a device by which a new venture may be assured of adequate capitalization before it is launched. Typically, Potential investors would be approached individually to determine whether they would be willing to purchase a specified number of shares; those that agreed to purchase shares signed a simple letter agreement stating that they had subscribed for and agreed to purchase at a specified price a specified number of shares.

At common law, uncertainty existed whether a subscriber might withdraw from his subscription before the corporation came into existence and accepted it. The reason for this uncertainty was that pre-incorporation subscriptions were obtained individually and were usually viewed as independent offers running from each subscriber to the not-yet-formed corporation rather than as a contract among subscribers with the promise of each subscriber supporting the promises of other subscribers.

There was no contract in this situation since one "party" -the corporation- was not in existence and could not be bound so that the other party –the Subscriber- was not bound either. At the same time, there was a strong element of reliance on the part of the promoters of the corporation, and quite possibly also on the part of other subscribers. This problem has largely faded away. Corporation statutes make pre-incorporation subscriptions irrevocable for a limited period.[48] During this period the formation of the corporation can be completed and the subscriptions accepted without regard to technical questions of consideration; until that period has expired the statute makes the pre-incorporation subscription irrevocable by the subscriber. This six-month period is itself a matter of negotiation between promoter and subscriber, and a longer or shorter period of irrevocability may be agreed upon. Also without regard to the period of irrevocability, all the subscribers to shares of a not-yet-formed corporation can agree to the revocation of a subscription by one or more specific Subscribers.

A subscription may be conditioned on the occurrence of certain events, such as obtaining a specified amount of capital, or a specified loan, or a specified lease. The fulfillments of such conditions are conditions precedent to the obligation of the subscribers. The common law developed a rather confusing distinction between conditional subscriptions and "subscriptions on special terms" which constituted a type of condition subsequent. There was little practical difference, however, because failure of the corporation to comply with a "special term" also permitted the subscriber to rescind or withdraw from his or her subscription.

A subscription that is induced by fraud can be rescinded by the subscriber as any other contract. The fraud may be the act of an agent or a promoter of the corporation. After the corporation is formed, its board of directors may call upon the subscribers to make payment on their subscriptions. Under

48) Six months in RMBCA § 6.20(a).

MBCA the board of directors may determine the payment terms of pre-incorporation subscriptions, but calls for payment must be uniform among all subscribers of the same class of shares, "so far as practicable."[49]

Modern distribution techniques for securities permit the meeting of all capital needs of publicly held corporations without resort to subscriptions, indeed, the use of subscriptions in connection with a public offering is unattractive as a practical matter because the subscriptions themselves constitute securities under federal and state securities acts and must be registered. Since the underlying securities themselves also must be registered, the use of subscriptions results in two expensive registrations.

In closely held corporations where it is contemplated that there will be only a few shareholders, a contractual agreement among the contemplated shareholders to form a corporation and purchase specified shares is a binding agreement whether or not it is described as a "subscription agreement." Pre-incorporation contracts have largely supplanted the common law subscription, though the wording in such agreements is usually that each investor "*agrees to purchase and subscribe for*" the securities he or she agreed to purchase. Pre-incorporation agreements are enforceable as multilateral contracts among the subscribers without reference to the special statutory provision relating to pre-incorporation subscriptions described above, which applies when each subscriber commits to a subscription individually and not in consideration of other subscribers' similar commitments. A person who subscribes for or agrees to purchase shares does not become a shareholder until the subscription price has been fully paid, though some states permit shares to be issued for promissory notes for the unpaid portion of the purchase price.

Post-Incorporation Subscriptions. An existing corporation may also seek to raise capital by obtaining commitments from potential investors to purchase shares. Subscriptions of this nature are normally cast in the form of a contract

49) MBCA (1984) § 6.20(b).

between the corporation and the investor, and are enforceable as any other contract by the corporation or the subscriber.[50] It is customary in all modern subscription agreements or agreements to form a corporation to include a representation by purchasers of securities that they are purchasing for investment and not with a view toward resale.

AGREEMENTS TO FORM CORPORATION

A "pre-incorporation agreement" is a contract among proposed shareholders to develop a business to be conducted in the form of a corporation. The contribution of each participant and the number of shares each is to receive are specified in this contract, which is a substitute for the common law Pre-incorporation subscription. Because it is a contract among the participants, it is enforceable in the same manner as any other contract.

A pre-incorporation agreement may be a summary memorandum outlining the main points of an oral agreement or a complete formal document. In a formal document, all aspects of the agreement between shareholders will usually be stated as may understandings as to employment, capitalization voting power, share transfer restrictions, who shall comprise the initial board of directors, or any other matter that is the subject of preliminary agreement. Copies of proposed articles of incorporation, bylaws, and minutes of proposed meetings may be attached as exhibits. The agreement may also designate who are to serve as officers of the corporation, but those designations should be subject to the authority of the board of directors after it is constituted to determine who should serve as officers of the corporation. Pre-incorporation agreements often impose restrictions upon the subsequent transfer of shares issued upon the formation of the corporation pursuant to the agreement.

One important issue with a pre-incorporation agreement is whether it is fully executed by the formation of a corporation as provided in the agreement

50) See MBCA (1984) § 6.20(e).

or whether specific provisions survive the creation of the corporation. If it is desired to have certain provisions of the agreement survive and continue to bind the parties, the agreement should specifically so state since otherwise a court may easily infer that only the provisions actually included in the articles of incorporation, bylaws, and minutes were intended to survive.

If the agreement is to survive it should be specifically assumed by the corporation upon its formation. If the state in question has enacted MBCA, the pre-incorporation agreement may also serve as a Shareholders' agreement if it is appropriately described and executed by all of the shareholders of the corporation.[51] An agreement to form a corporation places the parties to the agreement in the relationship of joint ventures, the object of the venture being the formation of the corporation and the establishment of its business. If the agreement survives, there may be a conceptual difficulty since after the corporation is formed the parties are simultaneously being treated as having the rights of shareholders in the corporation and the rights of joint ventures in an underlying arrangement to form the corporation. To avoid possible conflicts, some courts have taken the position that when the parties adopt the corporate form, with the corporate shield to protect them, they necessarily "cease to be partners and have only the rights, duties and obligations of stockholders."

Other courts, however, have taken the position that the joint venture may continue after the formation of the corporation, at least where the parties' intention to this effect is clear. The question appears to be one of "intention" since there appears to be no reason why both relationships cannot exist simultaneously if that is what the parties desire.

PROMOTERS

In General. A promoter is a person who takes the initiative in developing and organizing a new business venture. A promoter may act either alone or

51) MBCA (1984) § 7.32.

with co-promoters. The term "promoter" is not one of opprobrium; indeed, the promoter is often an aggressive, imaginative entrepreneur who fulfills the essential economic function of taking an idea and creating a profitable business to capitalize on the idea.

The role of a promoter is quite different than the role of an incorporator. The latter basically has the responsibility of signing a document that forms the corporation; the promoter is the person who has the responsibility of assuring that the corporation is an economic success. Obviously, Promoters may also serve as incorporators. The activities of promoters fall into two principal areas.

(1) The promoter must arrange for the necessary capital for the corporation. He or she may invest only personal funds or use personal funds plus loans from banks to obtain the necessary capital. Outside capital may be obtained from a small number of investors, who may be friends or neighbors. If so the promoter must negotiate with the outside investors to determine their share in the forthcoming enterprise, and arrange either by contract or subscription to ensure that the capital will be forthcoming when needed.

(2) The promoter must obtain the necessary assets and personnel so that the Corporation may function. He or she may obtain a lease or an option to purchase needed land, or may enter into a contract to purchase with a view of assigning the contract to the Corporation.

He or she may negotiate construction contracts to build or remodel the necessary buildings. Arrangements must be made to secure the necessary employees which usually will include the promoter as an officer of the new enterprise. The necessary machinery, equipment, or fixtures must be secured, customers must be contacted; arrangements made for advertising; and so forth. Obviously, in this area, the kinds of activities promoters engage in are numerous and varied, depending on the nature of the business being promoted. If the corporation is formed before the promoter commences his activities, subsequent contractual problems are usually minimized since all the necessary steps may thereafter be conducted in the name of the corporation, and there is little chance of confusion between the promoter's individual liability and the corporate liability on the arrangements being negotiated. Thus, actions may be taken in the corporate name and not in the name of the individual promoter. Of course, if a third person requests the personal liability of the promoter as well as the corporation, as may be the case with providers of debt capital, the promoter may execute an obligation individually or separately guaranteeing the corporation's performance.

Often, however, the formation of the corporation turns out to be one of the last steps in the promotional process. The promoter may begin investigation of the profitability of the proposed business, determine that the prospects of success are good, and proceed at once with business negotiations in the areas of capital formation, obtaining business assets, and entering into contracts without actually forming the corporation. In this situation there is greater likelihood of confusion and uncertainty, and most contractual litigation involving promoters arises in connection with not-yet-formed corporations.

Promoters' Contracts. Let us assume that before the corporation is formed the promoter enters into a contract to purchase machinery for the new business being promoted, and consider whether the promoter is personally liable on that contract. In some circumstances personal liability will exist, in other circumstances it will not. There are at least three different situations:

Contracts Executed In The Name Of The Promoter. If the promoter enters into a contract in his or her own name without referring to the corporation with the thought of subsequently assigning the contract to the corporation, personal liability on the part of the promoter clearly exists. The subsequent assignment of the contract to the corporation does not relieve the promoter of personal liability unless the creditor agrees, explicitly or implicitly, to release the promoter and look only to the corporation for performance. The release of a party to a contract when it is assumed by another is called a novation. If the corporation wishes to adopt a contract entered into by the promoter, it typically does so by express resolution adopted by the board of directors.

Contracts Entered In The Name Of The Corporation. The promoter may execute a contract in the corporate name when, in fact the corporation has not yet been formed. Many cases say that such a promoter is personally liable on the theory that a person acting as agent represents that a principal exists, and the promoter is liable because of a misrepresentation.

Other cases rely on the agency principle that a person who purports to act as agent for a nonexistent principal thereby automatically becomes liable for the action. The latter theory is based on contract and the former on tort, though in most cases they should lead to the same result. These cases often give the third person a windfall because presumably that person is not relying on the promoter's credit when entering into a contract in which a corporation is named as the other party; rather he or she is relying on the Corporation's credit or, more likely, on the possibility that the corporation will do well and be able to pay off the obligations. However, virtually all courts in this situation hold the promoter personally liable despite the potential windfall.

If the corporation is thereafter formed and adopts the contract the promoter may argue that the subsequent formation of the corporation corrected any misrepresentation or deception that may have occurred. Or he may argue that the manner of execution of the agreement indicates that the third person was content to accept the liability of the corporation, and that therefore the adoption of the contract by the corporation releases the promoter. In other words, the argument is that the transaction should be construed as a novation. To summarize: if the promoter enters into a contract with a third person in the name of the corporation without disclosing that it is not in existence, the promoter is personally liable on the contract. If the corporation is thereafter created and takes over the contract, the Promoter has a chance of being relieved of liability but there is a substantial chance that a court will conclude that no novation was intended and the promoter remains personally liable.

Contracts Referring To The Fact The Corporation Is Not Yet Formed. In this class of case the contract is executed by the promoter and the third party when both are aware that the corporation has not been formed. The contract itself usually reveals this fact, as for example when it is executed in a name such as "ABC Corporation, a corporation to be formed." Or the promoter may advise the third person that the corporation has not yet been formed when the contract is executed m the corporate name. It may be noted that this situation differs from situation (2) in that both parties are aware that the corporation is not yet in existence and there is no possible misrepresentation as to that fact.

This pattern may be analyzed in several different ways with widely divergent consequences. For example, it may be analyzed as an offer to the corporation which is revocable by either party and will result in a contract only if the corporation is thereafter formed and accepts the offer before it is withdrawn. Or it may be analyzed as an irrevocable option running to the corporation, with the consideration being a promise, express or implied, by the promoter to form the corporation and use best efforts to cause the corporation to adopt the contract. Or, it may be analyzed as a present contract between the third person and the promoter by which the promoter is bound, with the understanding that if the contract is adopted by the corporation the promoter will be released from liability under the contract. It is also possible that a court may conclude that the mere formation of the corporation did not constitute a novation. Which of these various alternatives is the proper one in any specific situation depends on the elusive "intention of the parties." If an attorney is called upon to draft a pre-incorporation agreement it is relatively simple to ascertain the parties' intention and describe it in a written agreement in terms so precise that there can be no cause for misunderstanding.

If the promoter is to be bound until the corporation adopts the contract, and then is to be released from liability a contract that specifically so provides should avoid later disputes. Litigation in this area generally involves agreements in which the intention is not clearly spelled out. The contract may have been negotiated by the parties without legal assistance, or the language chosen may not illuminate the specific problem one way or the other. Or the parties may have been unable to agree on their respective rights in the event of some remote contingency. Rather than forego a lucrative transaction, the parties use language such as "ABC Corporation a corporation to be formed," hoping that the question of the liability of the promoter will not arise, in such situations, the search for intent is truly hopeless, though the courts must resolve the dispute one way or another.

Generalizations about tests which courts use to find "intention" are hazardous. Probably most courts feel that it is likely that the third person intended for someone to be liable. Hence, there is a strong probability that the promoter will initially be held liable, especially where the corporation is never formed. Indeed, many cases state without qualification that the promoter is personally liable in this situation unless there is specific agreement to the contrary. If the third person is to receive payments or partial performance before the corporation is formed, an intention to hold the promoter personally responsible may readily be inferred; presumably the promoter intends to make those payments or render the performance personally until the corporation is formed.

Professor Williston suggested that most persons assume that even if the promoter is initially liable, he or she is nevertheless to be released if the corporation is later formed and adopts the contract. In other words, there is to be a novation. The testimony of the plaintiff in *Bradshaw v. Jones*[52] is representative of this understanding; "I understood that I was working for [Mr. Jones] personally until the railroad was organized; and after the railroad was organized, I was working for the railroad, of course." Not surprisingly, the court concluded that a novation was intended. There are, however, some holdings and a considerable amount of dicta to the contrary. One

52) *Bradshaw v. Jones,* 152 S.W. 695 (Tex. Civ. App.1912).

problem with the Williston approach is that it may encourage promoters to create "straw" corporations to take over contracts even after it is clear that the venture should be abandoned. If the promoters are held liable, they are considered to be partners, and liable for all promotional contracts on a joint and several basis. Where both parties are aware that the corporation has not yet been formed, several cases have held the promoter not personally liable on the contract.

In *Quaker Hill, Inc. v. Parr,*[53] for example, the court concluded that on the facts the third party never intended to rely on the promoters' performance of the contract and therefore should not be able to hold the promoters personally liable. Later cases, however, have held that the burden of proving intention rests on the promoter, and that inferences about intention cannot be based merely on knowledge that formation of a corporation was contemplated. These recent cases demonstrate again the difficulty of prediction of result in this shadowy area, though it is probable in many cases that the third person in fact intended to look only to the corporation for performance of the contract.

Liability of Corporations for Promoters' Contracts. It is quite possible that a promoter will enter into contracts in the name of the corporation that the corporation, after it learns of the existence of the contracts, will decide are not advantageous to it. The corporation is not automatically liable on obligations incurred by its promoters before it is formed. The reason usually given is that the promoter cannot be the corporation's agent since the corporation is not in existence. This Conceptualistic argument can be partially justified on the practical ground that the rule permits subsequent investors in the corporation an opportunity to consider and reject undesirable arrangements agreed to by the promoter. Of particular importance, it permits review and rejection by subsequent investors of contracts entered into between the promoters personally and the corporation.

53) *Quaker Hill, Inc. v. Parr,* 364 P.2d 1056 (Colo.1961). For the full text of this case see *infra* the Appendix I.

The theory on which corporations voluntarily become liable on pre-incorporation contracts negotiated by their promoters has been the subject of a great deal of confusing discussion. Assuming that the arrangement constitutes a contract between the promoter and third person in which it is understood that a corporation will be formed, the corporation "adopts" the contract.

Technically, "ratification" is not the proper word to describe this situation because "ratification" assumes that the corporation was in existence at the time the contract was entered into. Courts nevertheless sometimes use the words "ratification" and "adoption" interchangeably. If the promoter is then relieved from liability, the "adoption" or "ratification" becomes a "novation." In the last analysis, the legal words used are not particularly important. What is necessary is some form of assent by the corporation to the contract after it has been formed. The necessary assent may be express, or it may be implied from the circumstances. If a corporation takes the benefits of a contract made by its promoter, it will usually be concluded that it has assented to the burdens of the contract. For example, if a promoter negotiates a contract by which a third person agrees to become an employee of the corporation for a specified term, and a responsible officer of the corporation permits the employee to render services for the corporation after learning of the terms of the contract, the corporation has probably "adopted" the contract and cannot thereafter fire the employee without cause during the contract period.

Since the corporation becomes liable on the contract only when it assents it has been held that the contract term begins when the assent occurs. This may be of importance for purposes of the statute of limitations or the one-year statute of frauds provision. If the corporation is in existence, it will be responsible for obligations entered into by the promoter on its behalf if the promoter is an authorized agent of the corporation. The issue of authority may be a sensitive one, since either actual or apparent authority will bind the corporation. If the necessary agency relationship does not exist, the corporation may either disaffirm the contract or voluntarily assume it by adoption or ratification.

Promoter's Fiduciary Duties. Co-promoters of a venture owe fiduciary duties to each other, In effect they are treated as partners in a venture to organize the business. Difficult questions may be raised where a promoter enters into self-dealing transactions with the corporation before Outside creditors, investors, or shareholders are brought into the venture. The transaction may involve the receipt of shares of the corporation by the promoter, or the creation of corporate indebtedness in favor of the promoter for services or property. The transaction may be entered into when the promoter is the sole shareholder, or with the approval of the then-shareholders. Later or subsequent creditors, investors, or shareholders may object to the transaction on the ground that the services or property were overvalued or the amount awarded to the promoter was excessive. In m-any cases of this kind the courts have used language of fiduciary duty in reviewing and setting aside transactions to the extent they are believed to be unfair.

The leading case finding a fiduciary duty is *Old Dominion v. Bigelow,*[54] announcing the so-called "Massachusetts rule." Not all courts have agreed, however, involving the same transaction and announcing the "federal rule" that subsequent shareholders or investors may not set aside previously approved promoters' transactions. As a practical matter, the issue in these cases is not so much whether or not a fiduciary duty exists as whether or not there has been full disclosure of the transaction to the subsequent interests. If there has been full disclosure, subsequent creditors, investors, or shareholders may readily protect themselves by refusing to deal with the corporation or by reducing the price at which they acquire shares to reflect the reduction in value caused by the promoter's transaction.

Indeed, the fiduciary duty described above is basically a duty of full disclosure rather than a duty of fair dealing. Cases continue to arise, however,

54) *Old Dominion Copper Mining & Smelting Co. v. Bigelow,* 203 Mass. 159 (Mass.1909). For the full text of this case see *infra* the Appendix I.

in which subsequent investors attack promoter's transactions, and some courts have set them aside on the basis of vague discussion of "fiduciary" duties. Since failure to disclose may constitute a violation of federal or state securities acts, many cases that seventy-five years ago would have been analyzed as "promoter's fraud" cases may now be analyzed as "securities fraud" cases.

Organizational Expenses Incurred By Promoters. Logically, expenses incurred in connection with the organization of a corporation should be treated no differently than other contracts entered into by promoters. For example, if an attorney is employed by promoters to draw up the articles of incorporation, the promoter should be liable for the attorney's fee unless the attorney agrees to look only to the corporation. If the corporation is formed and adopts the contract, it becomes liable for the fee, and whether or not the promoter is released from his or her obligation depends on whether the transaction is deemed a novation.

There are complications, however, organizational expenses such as attorneys' fees are peculiar in that the mere corporate existence is in effect a use of the benefits of the contract by the corporation. Arguably, therefore, by its mere existence the corporation has agreed to pay whatever fee was negotiated by the promoter. The majority view, however, rejects this reasoning and holds that the corporation is not automatically bound. Rather the corporation - since it cannot refuse the Services - can only be compelled to pay a reasonable fee under the circumstances.

Many states have statutes that permit the payment of reasonable charges and expenses of organization of a corporation out of the capital received by it in payment for its shares without impairing capital or rendering such shares not fully paid and non-assessable. See MBCA (1984) § 6.28. It is not clear whether such a provision is necessary in modern corporation statutes; it was retained by the draftsmen of the Model Business Corporation Act (1984) essentially because it could do no harm and might do some good.

The promoter or the attorney may suggest that the attorney take shares in the corporation for organizational expenses and services. There is nothing inherently wrong with this practice: indeed, it somewhat resembles a contingent fee which is based on the success of the business rather than on the outcome of litigation. The value of shares received by an attorney or promoter for services is, of course, taxable income to him or her and may be deducted by the corporation as an expense over a 60 month period.

Promoters naturally expect to be compensated for their efforts, and in view of the nature of their innovative efforts, they may legitimately expect compensation which would be considered generous by a salaried person. A promoter may form a corporation with nominal capital, and then seek outside financial support to make the promotion a success. The subsequent investors will usually purchase shares in the corporation at a higher price than the shares previously issued to the promoter. The investors' interest is thereby diluted and the promoters' interest increased in value. In a sense this increase in value represents partial compensation to the Promoter; it is often a subject of negotiation between promoters and investors. However, both hope that the major portion of the promoter's compensation will result from the fact that the business does well so that the value of everyone's shares will be enhanced.

CHAPTER 6

DE FACTO CORPORATION[55)]

6.1 GENERAL INTRODUCTION

In General. At an earlier time, incorporation was not as simple as it is today. In addition to the basic filing requirement, there might be a requirement that a certain amount of capital be actually paid in and a certificate be filed reflecting that receipt that shares be actually issued, that officers and directors be elected and so forth. These additional requirements greatly increased the likelihood that there might be "premature commencement" of business that corporate obligations might be incurred after some but not all of the necessary corporate steps for formation had been taken. What is the responsibility of directors, officers, or shareholders for these interim obligations?

The procedures required to form a corporation today under most corporation statutes are basically very simple. As a matter of fact, they are so

55) This Chapter is mainly compiled with materials from Emmanuel Law Outlines, "Corporations," Emmanuel Publishing Corp. (1997).

simple and routine that attorneys may become careless and fail to comply with all the requirements that do exist. As a result, premature commencement problems may arise today. Mistakes may range from the trivial, such as using an incorrect address, to the more serious, where the attorney becomes so careless that he or she prepares but fails to file the articles of incorporation at all. Delays in Sling are not uncommon. Perhaps the secretary of state declines to accept the first filing because of some minor defect that the attorney subsequently corrects. In the meantime, the "corporation" has commenced business. Again the issue is whether directors, officers or shareholders have personal liability for the interim debts.

At common law, these problems were usually handled under the "*de facto corporation*" doctrine, though occasionally they appeared as promoters contracts; today many courts still apply common law concepts though they have been largely superseded by a statutory analysis.

A "de facto corporation" according to the common law was not a fully formed corporation, a "de jure corporation", but was nearly as good since it was sufficiently formed to be immune from attack by everyone but the state. The usual test for de facto existence was threefold: there must be a statute under which incorporation was permitted, there must have been a "good faith" or "colorable" attempt to comply with the statute, and there must have been actual user of the corporate privilege. However, the cases arising under this doctrine were confusing, particularly with regard to the second requirement and legal commentators convincingly proved that the traditional tests provide little guidance for the decisions of concrete cases. After examining more than 200 de facto corporation cases arising prior to 1950, for example, the late Professor Frey concluded that the de facto doctrine was "legal conceptualism at its worst." In a later study, considering cases arising between 1960 and 1989, Professor Bradley reaches a similar conclusion.

At common law a "de jure corporation" might exist even though there were some minor defects in its formation. The common law drew a distinction between "mandatory" and "directory" requirements; failure to comply with the latter did not prevent the creation of a de jure corporation. An example of a "directory" requirement was the listing of addresses of directors or incorporators. These problems today are usually resolved by reference to the specific language of the state's incorporation statute. Every state has a statute that provides in substance that the corporate existence begins either upon the filing of the articles of incorporation or their acceptance by the filing authority.[56)] Most statutes add that acceptance of the articles is "conclusive proof that all conditions precedent to incorporation have been complied with except in suits brought by the State.[57)] Thus, if the Secretary of State accepts a filing, a de jure corporation is m existence despite mistakes or omissions in the articles of incorporation.

Another problem that arises under the MBCA[58)] and similar statutes is whether a negative inference should be drawn that the corporate existence has not begun before the articles are accepted for filing. If this inference is accepted, personal liability exists for all pre-acceptance transactions. A few states have addressed this issue by adopting an additional statute that accepts the conclusion that liability exists with respect to transactions that occur during the pre-acceptance period. These statutes are based on section 146 of the 1969 Model Act, which states that "all persons who assume to act as a corporation without authority so to do shall be jointly and severally liable" for all debts and liabilities.

However, even in states in which this statute is m effect, some courts have refused to hold participants personally liable on pre-incorporation transactions. One court construed the phrase "all persons who assume to act" as referring only to active participants in the venture, thereby immunizing inactive participants from liability. [59)]All in all, the predictability of result under this statute was not much greater than under the de facto-de jure test

56) See MBCA (1984) § 2.03(a).

57) See MBCA (1984) § 2.03(b).

58) MBCA (1984) § 2.03(b).

59) *Timberline Equipment Co., Inc. v. Davenport,* 514 P.2d 1109 (Ore. 1973).

of common law.

The committee creating the MBCA took a fresh look at the standard to be applied to shareholder liability for pre-formation transactions, and came up with a somewhat different standard. The MBCA Provides that "all persons purporting to act as or on behalf of a corporation, *knowing there was no incorporation under this Act*, are jointly and severally liable for all liabilities created while so acting."[60]

The basic problem with a simple rule conditioning the existence or nonexistence of a corporation on the acceptance of a filing by the filing office is that it has a substantial capacity for unfairness. Under such a rule, shareholders and promoters may be liable as partners for the pre-acceptance debts of the business. The result is that delay or negligence in filing on the part of A may cause crushing liabilities to be imposed on B who may have bought "shares" in the honest belief that the corporation's articles had been filed and accepted by the filing office. Of course, B might first check with that office, but most investors would not normally think to do so. The standard of the MBCA, "knowing there was no incorporation under this Act," provides considerable protection to B in this situation.[61]

6.2 CORPORATIONS BY ESTOPPEL

In General. Problems of the type discussed in the last section have sometimes been handled in the absence of statute under a related concept, a "corporation by estoppel." This phrase is not meaningful in and of itself. It is necessary to ask who is "estopped," under what circumstances, and for what reason. The classic requirements for equitable estoppel (or "estoppel in pais") are

60) MBCA (1984) § 2.04.

61) MBCA (1984) § 2.04.

(1) there be a false representation to or concealment of a fact from a person ignorant of the truth
(2) with the intention by the person making the representation of causing reliance, and
(3) actual reliance by the innocent party on the basis of the false representation.

"Corporations by estoppel" do not involve these principles. Consider the following situation: A third person deals with what she believes to be a "corporation," relying on its assets and credit. When this "corporation" is unable to meet its obligations to her, she investigates and discovers that no filing had ever been made. She then sues the promoters and shareholders personally on the theory that they are liable as partners.

The defendants, who also were unaware that no filing had been made, defends on the argument that the plaintiff is "estopped" by her prior dealings on a corporate basis (which shows that she was willing to rely solely on the assets and credit of the "corporation") from holding them personally liable. Some courts have accepted this argument. This is certainly not equitable estoppel in the classic sense, since the person who is being "estopped" never made any representation of any kind that was relied on by any other party. Rather, the person who herself relied is the one being estopped.

In effect, courts are applying the label "corporation by estoppel" to reach a desirable result: used in this way "estoppel" is a conclusion, not an explanation. Nevertheless, there is a strong equitable argument for not allowing the plaintiff to recover from the personal assets of the defendants. The plaintiff receives a windfall if, after dealing and relying solely on the "corporation," she is permitted to hold the promoters or shareholders personally liable.

Further, it is harsh, to say the least, to hold the defendants personally liable because of the negligence or neglect of some other person. Particularly where they honestly and reasonably believed that the articles of incorporation had been filed and accepted. For these various reasons, some courts have held that the third person is "estopped" from suing the promoters or shareholders on the theory that there is a "corporation by estoppel." It should be noted that this reasoning has some force even in the situation where the defendants were, or should have been, aware that no filing had been made. The reliance by the plaintiff is unaffected by this fact. However, if an estoppel principle were universally recognized promoters might seriously consider saving the filing fee by not filing anything and routinely conducting business in the corporate name. That proves too much.

The principle of "estoppel" should be limited to situations where (a) the plaintiff dealt with the "corporation" as such, and (b) the defendant believed that the articles of incorporation had been properly filed and was not personally negligent in failing to make sure of that fact. This result is contemplated by the MBCA,[62] and appears to do justice to all parties. Furthermore, it does not seriously -undermine the statutory policy requiring filing of articles of incorporation, since persons knowing that the articles have not been filed would have unlimited liability under all circumstances. Not all the reported courts have agreed that "estoppel" should be applied m these types of cases, though the variations m decisions possibly may be explained by factual variations and variations in statutory wording.

A Unified Conception of "Defective Incorporation." In theory, "corporations de facto" and "corporations by estoppel" are alternative theories. The first relates to the extent to which the incorporator has sought to comply with the incorporation statute, while the second relates to the extent the plaintiffs have dealt with the defendants as a corporation. In fact, however, these two factors are not mutually exclusive.

A recent article, McChesney, Doctrinal Analysis and the Statistical Modeling in Law: The Case of Defective Incorporation suggests that "both factors affect judges' decisions in common-law defective incorporation

62) MBCA (1984) § 2.04.

situations."[63] At the margin, "courts will more likely accord defendants limited liability when they have tried to comply and plaintiffs have treated the firm as a corporation. Evaluated by what they do, not by what they say, judges apply one unitary doctrine-1hat of defective incorporation. The apparent confusion shown by many judges in distinguishing the two doctrines reflects the fact that they are really not two doctrines at all."[64]

---

63) 71 Wash.U.L.Q. 493 (1993).

64) See 71 Wash.U.L.Q, at 530-31.

CHAPTER 7

PIERCING THE CORPORATE VEIL[65)]

7.1 GENERAL INTRODUCTION

In General. Assume for a moment that a corporation has been properly and fully created in accordance with state law so that a "de jure corporation" has been created in the fullest sense of that phrase. The basic question discussed in this Class is whether and to what extent the separate existence of that corporation should be ignored in order to do basic justice or avoid the frustration of some clearly articulated public policy. At first blush, the basic concept that a corporation is a fictitious person or separate legal entity seems to dictate the answer that the separate existence of such a duly formed corporation should never be ignored. The law has not taken this extreme position, however, and courts often refuse to recognize the separate existence of a duly formed corporation.

To put the matter into perspective, however, it should be added that this

65) This Chapter is mainly compiled with materials from Arthur R. Pinto, Douglas M. Branson, "Understanding Corporate Law," LEXIS Publishing (1999); Emmanuel Law Outlines, "Corporations," Emmanuel Publishing Corp. (1997).

is the exceptional case that in most cases courts respect the separate existence of corporations despite arguments that they should not do so. The corporate fiction is a basic assumption that underlies commercial transactions and there must be compelling reasons for a court to ignore that assumption. When the separate existence of the corporation is ignored, courts often use colorful metaphors: "piercing the corporate veil," "alter ego" or "mere instrumentality," to name a few. These phrases shed little light on why the corporate existence is being ignored; they are statements of the conclusion, not reasons.

Shareholder Responsibility for Corporate Indebtedness. A shareholder may become liable for corporate indebtedness in a variety of ways. She may voluntarily guarantee the performance of the corporation's obligation - acting as a surety. She also may become personally liable by executing a document, such as a promissory note, in a way that makes it appear that she is acting as a co-obligor rather than as an agent acting on behalf of the corporation. She may also incur personal liability by failing to describe accurately the name of the corporation when dealing on behalf of the corporation, though case law tends to be generous to shareholders in these cases.

For example, in one case a Mr. Pinson executed a lease in the name "Pinson Air Freight, Inc." when in fact his corporation's name was "Pinson Air Freight of Chattanooga, Inc." The court held the corporation and not Mr. Pinson liable on the lease.[66] These are not true "piercing the corporate veil" cases. In considering cases involving shareholder responsibility for corporate indebtedness, there should also be put aside cases where liability is imposed upon shareholders under conventional theories of contract, agency, or tort law.

In other words, if individual A is personally liable for something individual B did under principles of agency, the same result should be reached if B is a corporation rather than an individual. To argue that the corporate veil is "pierced" in such cases is both unnecessary and confusing.

---

66) *Pinson v. Hartsfield Int'l Comm. Ctr.*, Ltd., 382 S.E.2d 136 (Ga.App.1989).

Where the shareholder is actually acting as a principal in his own name and the corporation is acting as his agent, there is clearly liability on the obligation under simple principles of contract law.

Similarly, if the Shareholder is personally involved in the commission of a tort while acting as an agent for his or her corporation, she is personally liable for the tort because of her own actions and again it is unnecessary to discuss piercing the corporate veil. In this situation, usually both the actor and the corporation are personally liable as joint tort reasons. The balance of this chapter assumes that liability is sought to be imposed on shareholders because of their ownership interest in the corporation and not because of their own conduct or the conduct of their agents.

The question of the status of a corporation usually arises in situations where a liability has clearly been incurred ill the name of a corporation, but the corporation has become insolvent. The creditor, seeking to find a solvent defendant, may sue some or all of the shareholders, arguing that for some reason they should be called upon to pay the corporation's debts. In this situation the creditor may also sue directors, officers, and anyone else in any way connected with the corporation. When the corporation is insolvent and unable to respond in damages, recovery may be sought from the shareholders. The court is then faced with the basic issue of piercing the corporate veil cases: Should the loss be imposed on third persons or on the shareholders; there is a loss and someone must pay. A blind application of the "artificial entity" approach would mean that the creditor always suffers the loss; certainly that result is often reasonable but it is not inevitable.

Most opinions by courts shed little light on the considerations governing how the piercing the corporate veil issue should be resolved. The traditional statement of the piercing corporate veil doctrine, taken from the leading case of *Bartle v. Home Owners Cooperative*,[67] is that: The law permits the

---

67) *Bartle v. Home Owners Cooperative*, 309 N.Y. 103, 127 N.E.2d 832 (1955).
Brief Fact Summary. Plaintiff, trustee in bankruptcy of Westerlea Builders, Inc., attempts to pierce the corporate veil to hold Defendant personally liable for the contract debts of Westerlea, Defendant's wholly

incorporation of a business for the very purpose of escaping personal liability. Generally speaking, the doctrine of "piercing the corporate veil" is invoked "to prevent fraud or to achieve equity." But in the instant case there has been neither fraud, misrepresentation nor illegality. Such statements are unhelpful because they essentially restate the issue by using terms of uncertain content - equity, misrepresentation, fraud, or illegality.

Other tests for piercing the corporate veil also have support in the cases. Some courts have suggested that if the Shareholder has exercised excessive control over the corporation and there is wrongful or inequitable conduct by the corporation, the corporation has become the "instrumentality" of the shareholder and liability is imposed on the shareholder. Other courts have looked to see whether the corporation and Shareholder have such unity of ownership and interest that they are "alter egos" and as a result "the separate existence of the corporation has ceased and recognition of the separate entity might lead to an inequitable result."

Technically, "alter ego" means "other self." The problem with these tests

---

owned subsidiary.

Rule of Law. Because the law permits the incorporation of business to for the purpose of escaping personally liability, the court will only "pierce the corporate veil" to prevent fraud or achieve equity

Facts. Defendant, a cooperative corporation, was organized to provide low income housing for its veteran members. Defendant formed Westerlea to undertake construction to build housing for Defendant's members. Due to financial difficulty, creditors took over Westerlea's construction responsibilities, pursuant to an extension agreement. In October 1952, Westerlea was adjudicated bankrupt. Plaintiff claims Westerlea did not act as an independent corporation. The trial court affirmed the Appellate Division's refusal to pierce the corporate veil finding that Westerlea and Defendant acted as two separate corporations at all times.

Issue & Held. Whether the trial court erred refusal to pierce the corporate veil was proper? Yes. The trial court did not err in refusing to pierce the corporate veil of Westerlea's corporate existence because Westerlea acted as a separate corporation and there was no fraud, misrepresentation or fraud.

Dissent. The corporate veil should be pierced because Westerlea was organized solely to benefit Defendant, not to operate as a separate entity. Westerlea did not have a separate corporate identity because it was Defendant's wholly owned subsidiary that had the same directors and management as Defendant. Westerlea was undercapitalized because Defendant provided Westerlea with small capital and Westerlea maintained insufficient funds to cover the cost of building the homes. Westerlea's purpose was not to profit as a business, but to benefit Defendant's stockholders by providing low cost housing to them.

Discussion. Although Defendant controlled Westerlea's affairs, Westerlea maintained an outward indicia of separate corporate identity at all times. Further, the creditors were not misled, there was no fraud, and Defendant performed no act to cause injury to the creditors of Westerlea by depletion of assets or otherwise.

is that they too rely on words of uncertain content: "excessive control," "wrongful or inequitable conduct," and "unity of ownership and interest." Still other cases utilize a variety of different pejoratives, e.g. "shell," "dummy," or "fiction," rather than analysis; all of this name-calling asserts a conclusion without giving much clue as to the reasons underlying it. As early as 1926, Justice Cardozo complained that the whole problem "is still enveloped in the mists of metaphor" and that the appropriate tests should be "honesty and justice."[68]

7.2 PIERCING THE CORPORATE VEIL IN CONTRACT AND TORT CASES

In General. In the great bulk of cases in which piercing is sought, the corporation has virtually no assets. In these cases, a major consideration in determining whether the shareholders should be liable for losses or injuries suffered by a third party is whether the third party dealt voluntarily with the corporation or whether he or she is an involuntary creditor, typically a tort claimant. The general standards are quite different in these two types of cases.

Contract Case. In a contract case, the third party has usually dealt in some way with the corporation and should be aware that the corporation lacks substance. In the absence of some sort of deception, the creditor thus more or less assumed the risk of loss; if the creditor was concerned that the corporation might not be able to pay the obligation, he should insist that some solvent third person guarantee the performance by the corporation. If such a guarantee is requested and refused, the creditor may either simply forego the transaction or consciously assume the risk that the corporation may not be able to discharge its obligation by entering into the transaction

68) *Berkey v. Third Avenue R. Co.,* 244 N.Y. 602 (N.Y.19267).

anyway. Where a request for a personal guarantee is made and refused, the parties have in effect agreed upon the allocation of risk, at least in the absence of deception, and the court should not interfere with that allocation.

Much the same analysis is true when no request for a guarantee is made, but the creditor simply enters into the transaction without investigation. Everyone assumes a risk when he enters into a transaction without investigation. Thus, in most contracts cases, the loss should be placed on the third person-the result actually reached in the great bulk of the contract cases by not "piercing the corporate veil."

Tort Case. In a tort case, on the other hand, there is usually no element of voluntary dealing, e.g. the plaintiff was trying to get out of the way of the defendant's truck. The question in these cases is whether it is reasonable for owners of a business to transfer a risk of loss or injury to members of the general public through the device of a marginally financed Corporation. This logically should depend on whether the corporation was adequately financed to cover the reasonably foreseeable risks incident to the particular business the corporation is in. If the corporation was not adequately financed in this sense, there is objectionable risk shifting to members of the general public.

In this regard, liability insurance should count as "capitalization" if the risk is an insurable one, since insurance makes funds available to injured tort victims just as much as equity capital does. The issues of public policy raised by tort claims thus bear little relationship to the issues raised by contract claims. This fundamental distinction, however, has not always been perceived by courts, which sometimes indiscriminately cite, and purport to apply, tort precedents in contract cases and vice versa. These general policies do not explain all cases, but they do explain most of them. Some contracts cases involve a naive or unsophisticated plaintiff who is duped into entering into the contract without making an investigation. Some cases of this type impose liability on the presumption that the plaintiff should be entitled to assume that a corporation has a reasonable amount of assets. Some tort cases may involve willful deception of a party to a contract; these cases are usually resolved as fraud cases, not as cases involving piercing the corporate veil.

Another class of piercing case that arises with frequency involves a corporation that conducts its business in a way that will clearly cause injury to creditors. The most common example is when the shareholders regularly make distributions of assets to themselves for their personal use, thereby rendering the corporation unable to meet its obligations to creditors. Since these cases involve direct shareholder enrichment at the expense of creditors, it is not surprising that judicial rhetoric in such cases is strong and plaintiffs usually win. Such transactions should be subject to attack as fraudulent transfers or as fraud on creditors, but in close cases courts may prefer to analyze the situation in terms of the rather vague tests of piercing the corporate veil.

Other types of misconduct by shareholders may be remedied by reliance on piercing the corporate veil theories. For example, the shareholder may mislead a third person regarding the financial status of the corporation so that the third person enters into a transaction believing the corporation has more capital than it actually has. Again this might be attacked as fraud, but shareholder liability may also be imposed on a theory of piercing the corporate veil.

A similar principle may be applied if a shell corporation is substituted - without overt misrepresentation - at the last minute and the other party is tricked into dealing with the shell corporation. Other situations involving manifest unfairness arising from unequal bargaining power but not reaching the level of unconscionability or other types of inequitable, unfair, or fraudulent conduct may also be envisioned. In the absence of any other clearly applicable theory, a court may rely on the piercing the corporate veil doctrine. Several cases involve an oral promise by a shareholder to guarantee payment by the corporation's debt, a guarantee which itself is unenforceable under the statute of frauds. Some courts have held the shareholder liable on his promise on the theory that the "main purpose" exception to the statute of frauds is applicable. Others have imposed liability in part on a piercing the corporate veil theory.

Opinions in many cases accept the basic distinction between contract and tort, and rely on "inadequate capitalization" in holding shareholders liable for corporate tort obligations while talking about "risk assumption" in contracts cases. Cases, in either tort or contract often talk about piercing whenever recognition of the separate corporate existence will lead to "fraud" or an "unfair result" or "cause harm to innocent parties." Many cases, however, are not entirely consistent in following this distinction. Many courts, for example, list "adequate capitalization" as a factor to be considered in contracts cases. Some courts may apply a laundry list of factors to all cases indiscriminately and expressly disavow any distinction between the tests applicable in contract cases and those applicable in tort cases.

The common feature in all piercing cases is that courts agree that piercing is appropriate only when recognition of the separate corporate existence will lead to injustice or an unfair or inequitable result. This is a necessary but not a sufficient condition for imposing liability on shareholders. There has been one empirical study of the actual outcomes of litigated piercing cases.[69)] This study indicates that the corporate veil was pierced in 42 percent of the contracts cases and 31 percent of the tort cases; undercapitalization was a factor in 19 percent of the contracts cases and 13 percent of the tort cases. In this study, the results in 779 contracts cases and 226 tort cases were examined. It is likely that these results were skewed by the fact that liability insurance is often present in tort cases and that insurance usually facilitates a settlement that involves some compensation to the injured plaintiff rather than litigation.

69) Thompson, *Piercing the Corporate Veil: An Empirical Study*, 76 Cornell L. Rev. 1036 (1991).

7.3 INADEQUATE CAPITALIZATION

As indicated above, inadequate capitalization should be relevant primarily in tort cases, though it is often referred to, and sometimes relied upon, in contracts cases as well. The phrase "inadequate capitalization" has more than one possible meaning. A few states require a corporation, before commencing business, to have received some minimum amount of capital usually $1,000, for the issuance of shares. In a sense a corporation in these states that begins business with less than $1,000 is inadequately capitalized, but that is not the usual meaning.

In the piercing area, "inadequate capitalization" usually means a capitalization that is very small in relation to the nature of the risks the business of the corporation necessarily entails. In other words it is based on likely economic needs rather than legal requirements. Thus, while the corporation need not be capitalized so as to ensure that all conceivable liabilities will be discharged, a corporation should be reasonably capitalized in light of the nature and risks of the business. This argument was accepted in the leading California case of *Minton v. Cavaney*,[70] and traces of it appear in opinions in several other jurisdictions. Minton v. Cavaney, like many other cases in this area, also involved another factor: a failure to complete

70) *Minton v. Cavaney*, 364 P.2d 473 (1961).

Case Synopsis. Defendant, the estate of a former director of a defunct corporation, appealed from a judgment of the Superior Court of Los Angeles County (California), which held that the decedent was personally liable for a judgment that was entered against the corporation in a prior wrongful death action.

Facts. Defendant, the estate of a former director of a defunct corporation, appealed from a trial court judgment holding it personally liable for a wrongful death award against the corporation in a prior litigation. Defendant argued that decedent, an attorney, merely accepted director status to accommodate the defunct corporation, and the evidence did not support the determination that the "alter ego" doctrine was applicable.

Discussion. The court disagreed, holding that the trial court was not required to believe the statement that decedent was only a "temporary" director and officer "for accommodation." However, the court reversed the judgment on the grounds that decedent was not a party to the wrongful death action against the corporation, and the judgment in that action was therefore not binding upon him.

Conclusion. The court reversed the trial court's judgment on the grounds that decedent was not a party to the wrongful death action against the corporation, and the judgment in that action was therefore not binding upon him.

the formation of the corporation and the court may have been partially influenced by that factor as well. Whether a corporation is under-capitalized in the sense used here obviously presents a question of fact that turns on the nature of the business of the particular corporation. In a tort case, liability insurance should "count" as equity capital, since it is available to compensate injured members of the general public.

The leading case recognizing this principle is *Radaszewski v. Telecom Corp.*[71)] A corporation engaged in a hazardous business, such as, for example, a truck delivery service, that fails to purchase liability insurance may well thereby subject shareholders to massive personal liability on a piercing theory. There is a serious question as to when the adequacy of capital should be measured. A corporation may be adequately capitalized initially, but then suffer unavoidable economic losses that renders the capital inadequate. Normally, adequacy should be measured at the time of formation of the corporation or perhaps at the time an existing corporation goes into a new capital-intensive or risky line of business.

---

71) *Radaszewski v. Telecom Corp.*, 981 F.2d 305 (8th Cir. 1992).

Brief Fact Summary. Konrad Radaszewski, (Plaintiff), was seriously injured when a truck driven by an employee of Contrux, Inc. struck him while riding his motorcycle. Plaintiff seeks to hold Telecom Corporation, (Defendant), liable for the conduct of an employee of its wholly owned subsidiary, Contrux Inc. Plaintiff appeals the district court ruling in favor of Defendant.

Rule of Law. If a subsidiary is financially responsible, whether by means of insurance or otherwise, the policy behind the second part of the Collet test is met.

Facts. This personal injury suit was brought on behalf of Plaintiff who was injured in an automobile accident by an employee of Contrux, Inc., a subsidiary of Defendant. The district court held that Contrux, Inc. was under capitalized in the accounting sense. Most of the money contributed to it was in the form of loans and Defendant did not pay for all of the stock that was issued to it. However, Contrux, Inc., had $1,000,000 in basic liability coverage plus $10,000,000 in excess coverage. Unfortunately, Contrux, Inc.'s excess liability insurance carrier became insolvent two years after the accident and is now in receivership.

Issue & Held. Whether the corporate veil of Contrux, Inc. can be pierced to bring Defendant into the case. No. Contrux, Inc. had $1,000,000 in basic liability coverage plus $10,000,000 in excess coverage that was sufficient to satisfy federal financial-responsibility requirements and the second element of the Collet test.

Dissent. Liability insurance is only a relevant factor to be considered but does not alone require a verdict for the defendant.

Discussion. Under capitalization of a subsidiary is a proxy under Missouri law for the second element of the tripartite test for piercing the corporate veil first set forth in Collet v. American National Stores, Inc., 708 S.W.2d 273 (Mo.App.1986). The purpose of inquiring as to whether a subsidiary is "properly capitalized," is to determine its financial responsibility. Insurance meets this policy just as well if not better than a healthy balance sheet.

Assuming that an adequately capitalized corporation has suffered Unavoidable losses, the general rule arguably should be that it should not be viewed as being undercapitalized. However, there appears to be scant authority, one way or the other. In any event, courts often simply evaluate the adequacy of capital at the time the transaction or accident occurred. This implicitly assumes that corporations have a duty always to maintain adequate capital for the nature of their operations, and failing to do so risks the imposition of liability on shareholders. A particularly powerful policy argument may be made if assets that might be used for the purchase of insurance or retained in the business to increase the "creditor's cushion" are siphoned off through dividends, salaries or similar Payments. This conduct is sometimes referred to as "stripping" a corporation of its assets, Stripping of assets may create the impression that corporate affairs are being conducted so as to minimize rather than maximize the assets available for tort claimants.

The bounds of this policy argument are totally undefined, and as a result it seldom appears in court opinions. Indeed, it was apparently rejected in the majority opinion in a leading New York case, *Walkovszky v. Carlton.*[72] Its influence, however, should not be underestimated: courts are much more likely to pierce the corporate veil and hold Shareholders liable in tort cases when stripping of assets appears to have occurred.

Conversely adequate capitalization and clear evidence that the corporation "did the best it could" to provide a "cushion" for creditors are likely to protect shareholders against tort claims based on the corporation's acts. The taxicab industry has been an important source of new cases concerning shareholder responsibility for corporate tort liabilities. Particularly in New York City the practice has developed of separately incorporating one or two taxicabs in a large fleet and establishing a separate corporation to operate a central garage, and perhaps yet another corporation to run the dispatching service.

Each operating taxicab company has the minimum required capitalization,

72) *Walkovszky v. Carlton,* 18 NY2d 414 (N.Y. 1966).

usually invested in the taxicab itself, and carries the minimum liability insurance required by state law. A major cost of operating a taxicab in New York City is the cost of the medallion; medallions may be rented or leased. The taxicab while operating on the streets will almost always have a hired driver for at least part of the time. Fired drivers are almost always judgment proof. This is true even in the case of a one taxicab corporation with a single shareholder who also drives the cab. In order to make ends meet, single-owner taxicabs must usually be operated day and night.

In this environment seriously injured victims of such marginal operations are usually limited in recovery to the minimum mandatory liability insurance since the corporation the shareholders, and the hired drivers are all judgment-proof. Not surprisingly, taxicab accident victims have often looked to the assets of shareholders who own a fleet of taxicabs even though they have separately incorporated each vehicle. The theory of "enterprise entity" dictates that the separate existence of each minimally capitalized taxicab corporation should be ignored and the entire fleet of taxicabs should be treated as a single economic entity. The more difficult question is whether a claim may also be made asserted against the personal assets of the shareholders.

In Walkovszky v. Carlton the court refused to hold a shareholder personally liable in the absence of allegations that he or she was conducting business in his or her individual capacity, and "shuttling * * * personal funds in and out of the corporations 'without regard to formality and to suit their immediate convenience.'" However, after the complaint was amended to add this specific allegation, it was upheld on a motion to dismiss and the case thereafter settled. The reluctance of the defendants to go to trial in cases of this character is understandable; most of the litigation arises on a motion to dismiss, and the cases are settled if the complaint survives that motion.

7.4 APPLICATIONS

Failure of Corporate Formalities. Anyone reading cases dealing with shareholder liability for corporate obligations will be struck by the emphasis placed by courts on the failure to follow the requisite corporate formalities as a ground for imposing shareholder liability in both contract and tort cases.

In many opinions, the court describes the failure to follow normal corporate procedures and then concludes that the corporation is the "alter ego" or "instrumentality" of the shareholder or that the "corporate veil should be pierced." There is a substantial risk that the separate existence of a corporation will be ignored if: (a) businesses commenced without completing the organization of the corporation or without issuing shares and receiving the consideration therefor, (b) if shareholders' meetings or directors' meetings are not held, or consents are not signed, (c) if decisions are made by shareholders informally as though they were partners, (d) if shareholders do not sharply distinguish between corporate property and personal property, (e) if personal funds are used for corporate expenses without proper accounting, or (f) if complete corporate and financial records are not maintained.

And this is only a partial list. It is difficult to see, as a matter of logic, why commingling, confusion and informality of the types described in the preceding paragraph have been given the importance that they have. In most cases, these actions are not directly related to the claim advanced by either tort or contract plaintiffs. As a matter of fact, evidence of them is usually first found during discovery long after the transaction giving rise to the particular litigation took place.

To hold shareholders personally liable because of activities that are almost always unrelated to the plaintiffs claim, creates a windfall for the plaintiff. For this reason, some courts have refused to pierce the corporate veil despite considerable evidence of confusion. One arguable justification for piercing the corporate veil in these cases is that the shareholder should not be permitted first to ignore the rules of corporate behavior and then later to claim the advantage of the corporate shield. In the absence of harm to anyone or to the state, however, it is difficult to see why the premise should lead to this conclusion.

The importance given to compliance with corporate formalities as a test for determining whether the corporation's separate existence will be recognized tends to create a trap for unwary shareholders. Shareholders in a small corporation often find managing the business a full-time occupation; formal corporate affairs such as meetings and the like are put off or ignored because there is full agreement in fact by all interested parties regarding what should be done and who should do it. The play-acting aspects of corporate meetings, elections and the like in a closely held corporation may also strike businessmen as rather silly. Insistence by an attorney that formal corporate procedures be followed may be dismissed as a subtle attempt to obtain an additional fee. This attitude invites disaster.

When failure to follow appropriate corporate procedures tends to injure third persons, there is little objection to holding the shareholder liable. Procedures within the corporation may be so undifferentiated that a person may believe he or she is dealing with a shareholder individually rather than with the corporation. Similarly, intermingled personal and corporate assets may disappear into the personal coffers of the shareholder to the detriment of corporate creditors. Corporate assets may be used to pay personal obligations of the shareholders. These factors, however, are present m only a small minority of cases involving failure to follow corporate formalities.

Parent-Subsidiary Cases. Many cases in which shareholder liability has been found concern shareholders that are themselves corporations. In these cases a parent corporation is being held liable for the debts of a subsidiary. They have a somewhat different flavor than cases in which the shareholder defendant is an individual and some cases even suggest that different tests are being applied depending on whether the defendant is an individual or a corporation. When a corporation is the defendant, only another business is being held responsible for the debt; when an individual is the defendant, however, personal liability extending to non-business assets is being imposed. There is the before a widespread belief that piercing may be easier when the shareholder is a corporation rather than an individual.

However, the one empirical study of the actual results reached in litigated cases indicates that this belief may be mistaken; that study indicates that corporate shareholders were held liable in 28 percent of the litigated cases while individual shareholders were held liable in about 40 percent of the litigated cases. Many corporations create subsidiary corporations to operate and manage separate businesses without giving serious thought about limiting liability. However, that is often not true. If the new business involves significant risks, the parent corporation may well decide to form a subsidiary in an effort to assure that its core assets will not be subject to additional risks.

It may be observed that an overly-generous application of the piercing doctrine in parent/subsidiary cases may deter the creation of new businesses if the parent corporation cannot be reasonably assured that the separate corporate entity of the subsidiary will be respected. Corporate shareholders have been held liable for subsidiary obligations in a number of situations: (a) When the subsidiary is being operated in an "unfair manner," e.g., the terms of transactions between parent and subsidiary are set so that profits accumulate in the parent and losses in the subsidiary; (b) When the subsidiary is consistently represented as being a part of the parent, e.g., as a "division" or "local office" rather than as a subsidiary; (c) When the separate corporate formalities of the Subsidiary are not followed; (d) When the subsidiary and parent are operating essentially parts of the same integrated business, and the subsidiary is undercapitalized, and (e) When there is no consistent clear delineation of which transactions are the parent's and which are the subsidiary's.

The maintenance of a consistent delineation between the parent's affairs and the subsidiary's affairs may be somewhat complex as a practical matter. Often the individual acting for the subsidiary is also acting as an agent of the parent in the same or related matters. If the "hat" the agent is wearing is not clear, the argument may be made that she was actually acting on behalf of the parent rather than on behalf of the subsidiary or, quite possible, on behalf of both corporations. These cases may impose liability in terms of agency rather than piercing the corporate veil. In any event it is clear that the probability of parental liability increases significantly whenever there are close relationships, informality of operation, and overlapping of personnel employed by the corporations.

In many instances, ties between parent and subsidiary are inherently very close. Not only does the parent own all the shares of the subsidiary, but the two corporations may be housed in the same plant or offices. They often have common officers, employees, auditors and attorneys. They may file consolidated returns for federal income tax purposes. Such close ties of course are not necessarily inconsistent with the separate existence of the subsidiary. Problems arise from carelessness and casualness. Transactions between parent and subsidiary may not be adequately documented on the theory that "the money goes to the same place anyway."

Common officers and directors may not specify on whose behalf specific action is taken, Independent books and records may not be maintained for each corporation. The parent may not recognize that the subsidiary is theoretically an independent entity with its own board of directors and managers.

Very commonly, the board of directors of the parent may make detailed decisions on behalf of the subsidiary when in theory the decisions should have been made by the board of directors of the subsidiary. Of course, in some cases the failure to delineate between operations of the parent and the subsidiary may actually mislead third persons into believing they are dealing with the parent corporate entity when in fact they are dealing with a subsidiary. Cases, however, tend to impose liability whenever intermingling is present on a wide scale without inquiring specifically whether the plaintiff was actually misled. As a result it is important in every "family" of corporations to maintain the maximum possible degree of separation.

Intermingling of assets on an informal basis is particularly dangerous. Separate accounts may be maintained, but informal transfers or unrecorded "loans" may be made from time to time to meet the day-to-day needs of the subsidiary's business. Such conduct unnecessarily increases the risk that the two corporations will be treated as a single entity.

If funds owned by the parent are needed by the subsidiary, the proper procedure is to establish a formal loan, preferably using a promissory note, and then to transfer the funds to the subsidiary's bank account. The corporate books of both parent and subsidiary then reflect the transaction accurately and the risk that the intermingling of assets will result in the two corporations being treated as one is reduced. Many large corporations with numerous subsidiaries have established centralized cash management plans. Each subsidiary is required to transfer all cash on a daily or overnight basis to a central account managed by the parent. Cash management plans permit the centralized management and investment of funds.

It also permits the parent corporation to obtain a more favorable return than the subsidiaries could obtain individually and eliminates the possibility that funds may be kept in non-interest bearing accounts. Each subsidiary may draw on its funds deposited in this account on a daily basis as needed for its operations. If the cash management plan is properly approved and accurate records of all transfers of cash in both directions are kept, these plans do not involve the kind of intermingling that gives rise to potential liability.[73]

Other common features of a parent/subsidiary "family," are participation in a single employee retirement plan, a centralized accounting and legal staff, and centralized control over the raising of capital. These features also should not give rise to an inference that the separate existence of corporate subsidiaries should be ignored.

The Concept of "Enterprise Entity" "Enterprise entity" refers to the economic unity that is a single business enterprise. Courts are suspicious of

---

73) The leading case so holding is *Fletcher v. Atex, Inc.*, 68 F.3d 1451 (2nd Cir. 1995).

attempts to divide what is essentially a single economic enterprise among several different corporations with the intention of minimizing the assets subject to claims of creditors of each enterprise. Perhaps this is because it is not "playing fair" with creditors who may reasonably believe that a single economic enterprise is the corporate entity; in any event, courts may well "put the enterprise back together" despite the shareholders' attempt to segregate it into separate corporate entities. In this kind of case, a "brother-sister" corporate relationship may be ignored as readily as a parent-subsidiary relationship.

Indeed, an empirical study of litigated cases discovered a number of instances in which brother-sister enterprises were combined into a single unit for liability purposes.

Many large corporations are conglomerates consisting of several essentially discrete and independent businesses. The concept of enterprise entity does not apply to these operations. What is dangerous is taking a single business and separately incorporating its component operations. Of course, if one or more independent businesses are conducted as divisions of the parent corporation and are not separately incorporated, the parent is liable in all events for the debts of those divisions.

Choice of Law and "P.C.V." Until about 1980, the law of "Piercing the corporate veil" appeared to be independent of the state m which the case arose. Courts resolving piercing cases freely cited cases from other jurisdictions without inquiry into whether different states were more liberal or less liberal in imposing, or had different rules about, shareholder liability for corporate obligations. Indeed, the tests and rhetoric used by courts were so vague and amorphous that differences in formulation, even if they had existed, would have had little or no effect on the results reached. Thus, in the few cases in which courts did discuss whether the law of the state of incorporation or the law of the state in which the activities giving rise to the claim should apply, a definitive resolution of this conflicts issue was found to be unnecessary.

In recent years different state policies or philosophies with respect to the imposition of shareholder liability have appeared. Some states now seem clearly to be more "liberal" than others m imposing such liability. Some states have accepted the distinction between tort and contract cases suggested above while others have not. Texas has partially codified its law of piercing the corporate veil by enacting a statute that provides that

(1) in contract cases "actual fraud" for the personal benefit of the shareholder is required for the imposition of liability, and
(2) failure to follow corporate formalities or procedures is never an independent ground for imposing such liability.

A number of states have created a "laundry list" of factors to be considered in piercing the corporate veil cases, and apparently have adopted a mechanical test of piercing the corporate whenever the number of factors favoring piercing exceed the number of factors that do not. The development of such identifiably different principles by specific states means that the conflicts of law issue must be addressed.

Many corporations are of course incorporated in Delaware and conduct their business primarily or entirely in other states. The Delaware position with respect to "veil piercing" has been described as very conservative: Persons seeking to pierce have a "heavy burden, "and the separate existence of corporations will be recognized in the absence of fraud. A plausible argument may be made that the law of the state of incorporation should apply to the piercing issue under the generally accepted rule that "internal affairs" of corporations are to be governed by the law of the state of incorporation. The scope of shareholder liability for corporate obligations plausibly seems to involve "internal affairs." Indeed, Texas has a statute that states explicitly that the responsibility of shareholders for corporate obligations of foreign corporations qualified to transact business in Texas is to be governed by the state of incorporation.

On the other hand, there may be a strong policy in favor of applying the law of the state with the most significant contacts with the litigation, particularly in torts cases. The Restatement of Conflict of Laws sets forth this as the applicable general principle. Consider, for example, a Delaware corporation that is wholly owned by Illinois residents; the corporation's entire business is conducted in Illinois, and a resident of Illinois is injured because of the negligence of the agents of the corporation who are Illinois residents. Certainly a plausible argument may be made that Illinois law rather than Delaware law should be applied since all the important contacts are with Illinois and not with Delaware. If Illinois law would permit "piercing" under the circumstances, it is probably unlikely that an Illinois court would deprive an Illinois resident of a remedy against another Illinois resident merely because the corporation was formed in Delaware and that state has a very conservative piercing rule.

The Federal Law of "P.C.V." An issue that is related to the choice of law issue is whether there is a federal law of piercing the corporate veil that is applicable in suits in which the United States is a party. *Clearfield Trust Co. v. United States* held that federal law should govern questions involving the rights of the United States arising from nationwide federal programs.[74)]

---

74) *Clearfield Trust Co. v. United States*, 318 U.S. 363 (1943).

Brief Fact Summary. The United States issued a check to a recipient. The check was stolen, cashed at J.C. Penney's, which was turned over to Defendant who guaranteed all prior endorsements and collected from the Federal Reserve. Eight months after learning the intended recipient never received the check, the United States informed "interested parties" of the forgery and subsequently sued Defendant to collect the amount of the check.

Rule of Law. When application of the law requires a determination of the rights and obligations of the United States arising from a federal source of law, the Erie doctrine does not apply. Federal courts must interpret federal law to determine the legal and factual issues of the case.

Facts. The United States issued a check to a recipient. The check was presumed to be stolen because the intended recipient never received the check. The check was cashed at a J.C. Penney with the recipient's forged signature. J.C. Penney turned the check over to Clearfield Trust Co., Defendant. Defendant collected the funds owed on the check from the Federal Reserve. The United States informed "interested parties" eight months after it learned that the intended recipient never received the check. The United States then sued Defendant based on its guaranty of all prior endorsements, to recover the amount of the check. The District Court ruled that Pennsylvania law applied and held that the United States was barred from bringing suit due to the eight month delay from learning of the forgery to notifying any parties about the forged check. The United States appealed and the Court of Appeals reversed. Defendant appealed to the Supreme Court.

Issue & Held. Does Pennsylvania law apply to determining the United States' right to recover on a forged check? No. Affirmed. State law and the rule of Erie R. Co. v. Tompkins, 304 U.S. 64, 58 S.Ct. 817, 82 L.Ed.

Federal courts have held, for example, that in a suit to recover over payments from a provider of services under the Medicare Program, a federal law of piercing the corporate veil should be fashioned to determine whether shareholders of the provider are personally liable for such over payments.

Other cases agree with this general approach. In fashioning federal law in this area, courts have generally relied on piercing cases that were in the federal courts because of diversity of citizenship. As a result, the federal law of "piercing" probably does not differ significantly from state law in most respects. Mention should also be made of the Comprehensive Environmental Response, Compensation and Liability Act (CERCLA). This statute imposes broad responsibility for cleaning up toxic waste sites on both present and former "owners" and "operators" of the site.

Early cases were in basic conflict over the relationship between the piercing the corporate veil doctrine and the liability of "owners" and "operators." There were three different approaches.

(1) The "*Actual Control*" test stated that a parent corporation could be held liable as an "operator" of a facility owned by its subsidiary where the parent was "actively involved in the regular operations" of the site.

(2) The "*Authority to Control*" test imposed liability upon the parent

---

1188(1938) does not apply to the rights and obligations of the United States. Rules governing the United States' right to issue commercial paper are founded in the U.S. Constitution. The United States issued the check pursuant to the U.S. Constitution, federal statutes and regulations. Holding that state law governs the United States' right to recover on a forged check would cause great uncertainty and inconsistent rules among the states. Thus, application of federal law is required so that the law governing such issues is uniform. Under federal law and case precedent, prompt notice is not a condition precedent to recovery. However, it may be a defense. The United States, when doing business, must do business the way others do business. The general rule is that if a drawee does not give prompt notice of the forgery, damage is presumed and the drawee is barred from recovering. However, in this situation, the burden should be on Defendant to show damage for the delay in notifying Defendant of the forgery. Although there is evidence tending to show that the forger was likely to be caught if there was no delay, this is not good enough to show an actual injury.

Discussion. This case illustrates that there is still a federal common law in a situation where the United States is a party and the issues involve rights and obligations of the United States that come from federal law. In this case, the Court must use case precedent to interpret the United States' right as drawee to collect on a forged check. The Court's creation of a general rule regarding commercial paper demonstrates the Court's ability to create federal common law when circumstances warrant.

corporation more broadly whenever it had a sufficient ownership interest m the subsidiary that gave it authority to control the operation. In some cases, courts imposed liability under this test only where there was some "nexus" between this authority and the actual operation of the site.

(3) The pure "piercing the corporate veil" test imposed liability on the parent only when the subsidiary's corporate veil could be pierced under traditional, i.e. non-CERCLA, Principles.

The Supreme Court of the United States gave much needed guidance in this area in its opinion in *United States v. Bestfoods.*[75)] This opinion reaffirmed that CEBCLA liability could be imposed on the parent corporation if the corporate veil of its subsidiary could be pierced under applicable state law principles. The opinion then addresses the possibility that a parent corporation might be liable as an "operator" of the site. Such a liability may be imposed, the Court concluded, only if the parent corporation was involved in the operation of the site itself. It was not sufficient that the parent corporation was involved only in the operation of the subsidiary itself. Thus, no parental liability would arise if the parent's activities do not go beyond the normal relationships between parent and subsidiary. If the parent becomes

---

75) *United States v. Bestfoods,* 524 U.S. 51 (S.Ct.1998).

Case Synopsis. Petitioner, federal EPA, sought a writ of certiorari to review a decision of the U.S. Court of Appeals for the Sixth Circuit that partly reversed a decision of the district court that held that respondents, succeeding parent corporations, were liable to pay for the clean up of a hazardous waste site.

Facts. A chemical plant generated industrial waste for many years. The chemical plant significantly polluted the soil and ground water. Respondents, succeeding parent corporations, purchased the chemical plant's assets. Petitioner, federal EPA, filed suit to recover funds for the clean up of the hazardous waste site.

Procedural History. The district court found respondents directly liable to pay clean up costs as operators. The lower appellate court reversed ruling that respondents maintained separate personalities and did not improperly utilize the subsidiary corporate form.

Discussion. The court vacated and remanded holding that a participation-and-control test looking to the parent corporation's supervision over a subsidiary could not be used to identify operation of a facility resulting in direct parental liability. Any parent corporation liability as an operator, stemmed directly from its control over a polluting plant.

Conclusion. The court vacated and remanded for a redetermination of respondents' liability. The court held that any parent corporation liability as an operator, stemmed directly from its control over a polluting plant. The participation-and-control test was inapplicable.

involved in the operation of the site itself, it becomes an "operator" under RERCLA.

Reverse Piercing the Corporate Veil. Most cases involve efforts by a creditor to hold the Shareholder responsible for corporate obligations. In some cases, the shoe is on the other foot. A shareholder argues in a suit against a third party defendant that the separate existence of their own corporation should be ignored. The classic case is *Cargill, Inc. v. Hedge,*[76)] where a farming family created a corporation to own the land and buildings that comprised their farm. When the Hedge family ran into financial difficulty, a creditor obtained a judgment and sought to execute on the land. Minnesota has a statute that provides an exemption from execution of farm property owned by individual farmers. In order to avoid the forced sale of their farm, the Hedges argued that the separate existence of their corporation should be ignored, and they should be entitled to the exemption. Based on the strong Minnesota public policy favoring protection of family farms from execution sale, the Minnesota court applied a "reverse pierce" principle to protect the family, but the court cautioned that this principle should be available only in "carefully limited circumstances."

Other examples of "reverse piercing" exist. Some courts have expressed

---

76) *Cargill, Inc. v. Hedge,* 375 N.W.2d 477 (Minn. 1985).

Case Synopsis. Appellant creditor sought review of a judgment of the Court of Appeals (Minnesota), which affirmed a judgment holding that 80 acres of a farm owned by respondents, husband and wife, were protected by the homestead exemption of Minn. Stat. § 510.02 (1984).

Facts. Respondents owned a farm. They incorporated the farm pursuant to Minn. Stat. § 500.24, subd. 1(c) (1973). The husband purchased farm supplies and services on account from the creditor. The creditor was unaware that the farm was incorporated. The creditor obtained a judgment against the husband and the corporation for the amount of the debt. Respondents filed an action to enjoin the sale of the farm. The trial court held that 80 acres of the farm were exempt from sale pursuant to the homestead exemption of § 510.02. The appellate court affirmed the trial court's judgment.

Discussion. On appeal, the court affirmed the judgment of the appellate court. The court held that the case was a proper one for a reverse pierce of the corporate veil because there was a close identity between respondents and the corporation and public policy favored protection of the homestead. The court determined that creditors were deemed to extend credit with awareness that, should an individual debtor default, a homestead was exempt. Therefore, the court ruled that 80 acres of the farm were protected by the homestead exemption.

Conclusion. The court affirmed the appellate court's judgment holding that 80 acres of respondents' farm were protected by the homestead exemption.

skepticism about the reverse pierce doctrine, arguing in effect that if a person forms a corporation, he should be expected to "take the bitter with the sweet," and not be able to disclaim the corporate existence when it is in his interest to do so. In *Sims v. Western Waste Industries*,[77] the court refused to allow a parent corporation to take advantage of the immunity to direct suit that the Workmen's Compensation statute provided to its wholly owned subsidiary. The court stated, "we are persuaded that the legislature never intended parent corporations, who deliberately chose to establish a subsidiary corporation, to be allowed to assert immunity under the Texas Workers' Compensation Act by reverse piercing of the corporate veil they themselves established. WWI has accepted the benefits of establishing a subsidiary corporation in Texas and will not be allowed to disregard that entity now that it is to their gain to do so." All in all, this doctrine should be viewed to have doubtful validity.

Further Public Policy. Yet another type of piercing the corporate veil case involves the claim that a separate corporate existence should not be recognized because to do so would violate a clearly defined statutory policy. To take an illustrative case, the statutes of several states formerly prohibited branch banking. In other words in these states a banking corporation had to stick to a single location and could not open branches around the state.

Accepting this statutory policy, may a banking corporation own the voting stock of another bank? Or, may a single holding corporation own a majority of, or all, the voting stock of several banks? Answers to questions such as these must be based on an evaluation of the strength of the state policy against branch banking rather than on policies underlying the separate existence of corporations. If the policy is a strong one, the recognition of a separate corporate existence may provide an unacceptable method of circumvention, and the separate corporate fiction must yield to the state policy.

On the other hand, if the policy against branch banking was not a strong one, there was no reason for courts to find a fundamental conflict

---

77) *Sims v. Western Waste Industries,* 918 S.W.2d 682 (Tex.App.1996).

between the statute and the corporate form and hold invalid relationships that conform to the notion of separate corporate existence. Public policy is also the critical question in cases involving family corporations organized to obtain social security or unemployment benefits for owners who would not be eligible for such benefits if the business had continued to be conducted in non-corporate form. Several federal decisions have held that social security benefits may not be denied to a person who "incorporates" his or her business assets and becomes an employee of the corporation for the sole purpose of qualifying for the benefits. Decisions at the state level concerning temporary disability insurance, workmen's compensation, and unemployment compensation, however, are split. A clearer example involves the unemployment compensation statutes that provide for an exemption from the tax for employers having fewer than some designated number of employees.

May a single business be divided into several separate corporate units each employing less than the statutory minimum to obtain the exemption for each? Courts have held, not surprisingly, that the state unemployment commissions may disregard the separate corporations, treat the business as a single unit, and impose the tax on it. Generalization is difficult in such cases. Sometimes assistance may be gained from statutory language that indicates that the policy should be applied to "direct or indirect" relationships. Nevertheless, delicate judgments are required in these cases, for the policies underlying regulatory statutes must be weighed against the policies supporting the concept of the corporate entity.

Taxation and Bankruptcy. Given the broad social and governmental policies involved in the federal income tax laws and the federal bankruptcy act, it is understandable that specialized tests have evolved under these statutes for determining when the separate corporate existence will be disregarded.

Under the Internal Revenue Code of 1954 there is a need to preserve tax revenue and to set aside fictitious transactions that have as their sole purpose the minimization of taxes. A corporation's separate existence generally will be recognized for tax purposes if it is in fact carrying on a bona fide business and is not merely a device created for the purpose of avoiding taxes. The taxpayer, however, must accept any tax disadvantages of the corporate form if he or she has elected to choose that form. Further, even if the corporate form is adopted and carefully followed, the Commissioner has broad powers to disallow deductions or exemptions, or reallocate items of income to clearly reflect income.

Entirely different policies are involved m the bankruptcy area. Bankruptcy courts have considerable flexibility in dealing with controlling or dominant shareholders of bankrupt corporations. The bankruptcy court may:

(1) "Disregard the corporate entity" and hold the shareholder personally liable for the corporation's debts if the shareholder's conduct permits the court to pierce the corporate veil. The effect of this conclusion is that the controlling shareholder may be personally responsible for all corporate obligations; all payments made by the corporation to the shareholder before bankruptcy may also be recovered by the trustee since essentially the corporation and shareholder are treated as a single unit.

(2) Refuse to recognize claims by shareholders against the corporation as bona fide debts provable in bankruptcy. If the claim is based on services or intangible benefits provided to the corporation, the claim may be disallowed in its entirety as fictitious or "not proved."

If it involves infusions of capital or tangible property through loans, the bankruptcy court may consider them as contributions to capital rather than as debt. This treatment of shareholder debt is usually limited to loans made at or shortly after the formation of the corporation when the corporation is inadequately or thinly capitalized, and simply reflects that what in fact was equity capital should be treated as equity capital in bankruptcy proceedings. A number of decisions follow this approach and there are analogous holdings in the tax field. Yet the application of this principle is elusive.

There is no easy way to determine when a corporation is in fact under-capitalized. Most courts have treated the issue on an "all or none" basis and reclassified all the debt as equity even though it is arguable that the court should reclassify only that portion necessary to make the capitalization adequate. As a general matter, the original capitalization of a corporation should be viewed to be adequate if it is able to borrow the balance of the needed capital from independent sources of funds. Similarly, if the shareholder rather than a bank makes the loan under identical circumstances, the transaction should also be viewed as a bona fide loan.

Under the "Deep Rock" doctrine,[78] the bankruptcy court may subordinate claims presented by a controlling shareholder to claims of other creditors or preferred shareholders if the shareholder acted inequitably or unfairly. Examples of inequitable claims include taking unreasonable amounts as salary, manipulation of the affairs of the corporation in disregard of standards of honesty, or selling assets to the corporation at inflated prices. The type of conduct that will result in subordination under the Deep Rock doctrine can only be stated in general terms since the doctrine is based on general principles of equity and fair dealing, It is not necessary to show that the indebtedness was a sham or fiction, since technically what is involved is only "the order of payment of debts" and not an outright rejection of a claim.

The theory is that a person who has acted unfairly in his or her management of the corporation should step aside so that other creditors may be first satisfied. Of course, the assets of a bankrupt estate will be inadequate to satisfy all claims; Subordination therefore usually results in the shareholder receiving nothing on his or her claim. Despite this underlying theory, in at least one case the Deep Rock doctrine was applied when the controversy was between innocent creditors of the bankrupt subsidiary and the equally innocent creditors of the bankrupt parent. The type of conduct that triggers

78) It is named for the Deep Rock Oil Corp., the subsidiary involved in the leading case of *Taylor v. Standard Gas & Electric Co.* 306 U.S. 307 (S.Ct.1939). For the full text of this case, see *infra*, the Appendix I.

these doctrines differs only in degree rather than kind. In a sense these are alternative weapons in the bankruptcy court's arsenal.

Other Generalizations. Three final observations should be made about the confusing and result-oriented doctrines discussed here. First, there is no inherent reason to assume that ignoring the separate corporate existence must be an all-or-nothing affair. Particularly if the dominant question does not involve public statutory policies but merely liability for corporate obligations, a corporation may be viewed as existing for some purposes but not for others. There is some case authority, for example, for piercing the corporate veil to hold shareholders active in the business personally liable, but recognizing the same corporation's separate existence to protect passive investors from the same liabilities.

Second, there is a strong judicial feeling that when a person elects to do business in corporate form he or she must take the bitter with the sweet, and cannot later argue that the separate corporate existence should be ignored when it is to his or her benefit. Except in the rare "reverse pierce" cases the doctrine of piercing the corporate veil is not available for the benefit of shareholders, but only against shareholders. This view is particularly strongly developed in the tax cases.

Finally, where the considerations are not strongly weighted one way or the other, a presumption of separate existence of the corporation should be respected. The fiction of separate corporate existence, in other words, should be the rule not the exception.

PART III

CORPORATIONS

CHAPTER 8

FINANCIAL STRUCTURE[79)]

8.1 INTRODUCTION

In General. A business corporation may obtain money to finance its operations by issuing interests in itself that are generally known as securities. This term is used to describe all types of interests that a corporation may create in itself and offer for sale. There is nothing necessarily secure about a Security; the term here refers to an interest or an investment in a corporation. Securities are of two basic types: debt securities and equity securities.

"Debt securities" are so called because the corporation is considered to be in debt to the person who holds this type of interest; the person has lent the corporation money and eventually the corporation will have to pay it back-with interest.

An "equity security" creates no debt relationship. When a person purchases an equity security, he or she is not lending money to the corporation, but is

79) This Chapter is mainly compiled with materials from Emmanuel Law Outlines, "Corporations," Emmanuel Publishing Corp. (1997).

considered to be acquiring an ownership stake in the business.

8.2 DEBT SECURITIES

In General. A debt security generally is created when the corporation through its Board of Directors decides that it will attempt to borrow money, from individuals, institutions, or the public. Typical sources of borrowed money are the corporation's organizers, or their families, or a bank. If the money is lent to the corporation by such individuals or institutions, the corporation will issue its promissory note, one form of debt security, to the lender. If, on the other hand, the corporation hopes to borrow from members of the general public, it will issue and offer for sale to the public, usually through a broker, debt securities known either as bonds or debentures, which are basically the same except that a bond is secured by particular property of the debtor, while the debenture is unsecured indebtedness. These securities generally are issued in face amounts of $1,000 each. If the bond is sold for more than its face value, it is said to be "sold at a premium." If sold for less than the face value, it is "sold at a discount." Like other evidence of indebtedness, bonds have a maturity date, a specified time when the corporation must pay back the face value of the bond to its holder. The face value is the principal amount owed by the corporation. But a bond costs the corporation more than merely repaying the principal amount for the use of an investor's money.

Mortgage Bond. The corporation will also periodically pay a fixed interest charge, calculated as a percentage of the face value of the bond. Debt securities come in various forms. For instance, mortgage bonds are one type of debt security where the bondholders have a mortgage on the corporation's property. If the corporation fails to pay its obligations, the bondholders may foreclose their mortgage and claim the corporation's property to the extent necessary to satisfy its debt to them.

Debentures. Unlike a mortgage bond, a debenture is a simpler type of debt security; there is no property to which the holder of a debenture has any special claim if the corporation should fail to pay its obligations on the debenture. Debenture holders, and other holders of unsecured debt instruments, are instead considered to be "general creditors" as opposed to "secured creditors" of the corporation. Status as a corporate creditor is one of the important features of a debt security. It means that if the business should fail, the holders of the corporation's bonds may take whatever property secures the bonds. Other creditors[80] then have first claim to the corporation's remaining assets in order to satisfy sums owed to them. The holders of equity securities, which is stock, are left to divide whatever is left, if anything. This preferential claim to corporate assets makes bonds an attractive, if conservative, investment. Therefore, issuing debt securities may be one device whereby a small business can make itself more attractive to outside investors who want steady income and less risk. It also keeps voting control of the corporation in the hands of the organizers, since debt holders, as such, are generally not entitled to vote.

Bond. The corporation could make a bond even more desirable by promising bondholders that the corporation will take certain steps to insure that corporate assets will be retained and available to satisfy payments due to bondholders. For instance, the corporation could agree to limit total corporate debts, reasonably restrict dividend payments to keep a certain amount of funds always on hand, create a special corporate reserve to pay bond obligations, limit issuance of additional bonds, or restrain the corporation from incurring any secured debts that would have a preferential claim to corporate assets above existing bondholders.

Bonds usually pay a fixed amount of interest per year; for example, 8 & 3/4% on a $5,000 bond would entitle its holder to payments of $437.50 each year. The corporation has an obligation to pay this interest regardless

80) Such as note or debenture holders.

of its profits or losses for that year. This is in contrast to dividends on equity securities that may be paid or not as determined by the corporation's Board of Directors even though the corporation has sufficient funds to make a distribution. A corporation may, however, make its obligation to pay any interest conditional on its making a certain profit, and the amount of interest paid could be made dependent on the amount of profits. For instance, in the first case, the corporation would be required to pay the stated interest only to the extent that it had profits with which to make such payments.

In the second instance, the corporation would be obliged to pay a fixed rate of interest, say 8 & 3/4%, and up to an additional 4% of its earnings if it had sufficient earnings to cover the obligatory interest payment and any portion of the additional 4% payment. Whatever the terms of payment, they should be expressed in the bond instrument. This will insure that owners of the bond have notice of these terms and cannot insist on other, more favorable terms. At a predetermined date, the corporation must pay the bondholder the principal amount of the bond, for example, $5,000 on January 1, 2000. When a corporation is profitable it may wish to pay off its bondholders before that date. This may be done with corporate funds or by issuing new bonds at a rate more favorable to the corporation. In order to be able to do this, the corporation must include a "redemption" or "call" provision in the original bond instrument. This provision will state that the corporation has the right to buy back the bond at a certain price, usually a figure in excess of the face value at a set time before the due date of the bond.

Convertible Bond. As an additional feature to attract investors, bonds may be made "convertible;" that is, the holder of the bond is given an option to exchange it for another type of bond or for types of equity securities. Bonds that are convertible must state that they are convertible, what they may be converted into, when and at what price they may be converted, and so forth. Convertibility is considered a desirable investment feature because the bondholder has a relatively safe investment that he or she may convert into a specified different interest if that new interest becomes more attractive.

8.3 EQUITY SECURITIES

In General. The other type of corporate security is an equity security, known as shares or stock in a corporation. Stock is called an equity security because stockholders are considered to be the owners of the corporation. Shares are a function of the wishes of the organizers and of the Articles of Incorporation. A corporation's Articles must state the number of shares and the characteristics of the corporation's stock. When the Articles are approved, the corporation may "issue" all or only a portion of its authorized stock. To issue stock is actually to offer shares of stock for sale. The corporation's Board of Directors may control when and to whom the corporation's shares are offered and sold. When issued shares are actually purchased, they are known as outstanding shares and the purchaser is known as a shareholder or stockholder.

Before the corporation authorizes stock in its Articles, the organizers must decide on the types of stock they feel are appropriate for their corporation. There are several choices. Shares may be with or without "par value." They may have preferences over other classes of shares or may be common shares. These terms and their importance must be understood in the planning of a corporation. Stock may have a par value or may be of "no par value." "Par value" is an arbitrary value per share assigned in the Articles of Incorporation, and does not necessarily reflect the true market value of the stock. Because the law is that par value shares may not be issued and sold by the corporation for less than their par value, it is advisable for the corporation to set a par value lower than the estimated market value of the shares.[81)] Once the stock is sold by a corporation to a shareholder, sales by that shareholder to any other person may occur at whatever price the parties deem appropriate, even if it is less than par.

No Par Value. No par stock allows the Board of Directors or the

81) Section 18 of the Model Act.

shareholders if the Articles of Incorporation have granted them the power to decide, each time shares are issued, what the price per share will be. Since there is no par value attached to the shares, they may be sold without any restriction on sales price. The Board or the shareholders thus has more flexibility to adjust the stocks selling price to reflect the corporation's success or lack of it.[82)] Despite the arbitrary nature of par or stated value in relation to no par stock the concept has some very practical significance. First, and most basically, if stock is sold for less than par or stated value, the purchaser of those shares may be liable, to the corporation or to its creditors, for the difference between what was paid and what should have been paid.

Par Value. The second practical consequence is more subtle. The par or stated value is used to determine the corporation's "capital account." This account, which is really only an entry in the books of the corporation, is determined by multiplying the par or stated value of the corporation's stock by the number of shares outstanding. For example: if the corporation had sold 1000 shares of stock which had a $10 par value, the capital account would be $10,000. If no par shares are issued, the total amount received from their sale is the corporation's "stated capital." However, prior to issuance of no par shares, the Board of Directors may pass a resolution declaring that only a portion of the money received for shares will constitute the corporation's "stated capital" and that the remaining sum will be deemed "capital surplus."

The importance of these accounts is mainly in relation to the payment of dividends. Although Section 45 of the Model Act permits dividends only out of earned surplus retained earnings or out of recent profits, even if there is no accumulated and retained earnings, most states provide for a different formula.

In those situations, the corporation may pay a dividend so long as the capital account is not "impaired" or will not be impaired by virtue of the

82) In a very large corporation, the stock might be traded on a public exchange such as the New York Stock Exchange, in which case the public demand, and not the Board, would determine the selling price of the stock.

distribution. What this means is that a corporation may pay a dividend if the value of its net assets, i.e., its total assets minus its total liabilities, is greater than the amount of its capital account, par value times outstanding shares. If net assets are less than the capital account, no dividend may be paid. To illustrate the point, assume Corporation X has 1000 shares Outstanding at $10 par value. The capital account is $10,000. Assume also that the corporation has $50,000 worth of assets and $25,000 worth of liabilities. Since its net assets ($50,000 - $25,000 = $25,000) exceed the capital account ($25,000 - $10,000 = $15,000), a dividend of up to $15,000 could be declared.

If, alternatively, the corporation's liabilities were $45,000 the net assets would be only $5,000. Since this is less than the amount of the capital account, no dividend at all could be paid. In those states that permit dividends when net assets exceed the capital account, the excess assets could come from retained earnings, which is the basic test under the Model Act for the legality of dividends, or from a capital surplus account, as distinguished from the capital account. We have already discussed the fact that stock may not be issued by the corporation for less than its par or stated value. What happens, however, if it is issued for more than par or stated value? For instance, shares of corporation X have a par value of $1.00 but are sold for $10. From a bookkeeping point of view, $1.00 per share would be recorded in the capital account book, while $9 per share would be recorded in the capital surplus account book. From an operational point of view, the entire $10 per share may be placed in the corporation's bank account and spent, even the $1 per share in the capital account, for corporate purposes. It is only when the net assets fall below the amount in the capital account book that dividends are prohibited.

In addition to distinctions of par and no par value, stock may be divided into different "classes".[83] For instance, it is possible to create one or more

83) Section 16 of the Model Act.

classes of stock whose holders have a preference in receiving dividends over holders of other classes of stock. That is, if the Board of Directors decides to distribute a portion of the corporation's profits to shareholders, the preferred shareholders receive their dividends first, in the order of their preference, and the other shareholders receive their share from the distributable profits remaining after each higher preference has been paid though the holders of debt securities will be entitled to their payments before any shareholder, and regardless of the corporation's financial condition.

Preferred Shares. The payment to preferred shareholders is generally a constant amount, phrased as "a preference of $___ per share" or "a preference of ___% of par value." Thus in a year in which the corporation is very profitable, there may be substantial profits remaining to be distributed to non-preferred shareholders (known as common shareholders). Preferred shares may possess other attractive characteristics in addition to their payment preference. The corporation may create "cumulative" preferred stock, where the corporation is obligated to pay the shareholder a fixed payment each year. If the dividend is not paid in any year due to a lack of income from which to distribute dividends or, even if the income is available to pay a dividend, due to a decision by the Board that it would be better to retain the money for corporate purposes rather than distribute it as a dividend.

It accumulates and the aggregate amount of accumulated unpaid dividends must be paid in full to the holders of cumulative preferred stock before the corporation may pay dividends to the holders of other types of stock with a lower preference.

A variation on cumulative preferred stock is "cumulative to the extent earned" shares. The payments on these shares accumulate only to the extent that the corporation had profits from which it could legally have paid dividends, and the holders of these shares are not entitled to dividends from years in which the corporation had no profits to distribute.

Preferred stock may also be "participating." If it is as established by the Articles of Incorporation, shareholders receive their preferential distributions and then, when all preferences have been paid, are allowed to share with the holders of common stock in the pool of money remaining. This can be very advantageous, since the preferred shareholders get a constant payment and then a second opportunity to share in corporate profits.

It is possible to curtail this benefit by specifying that the common and preferred stockholders divide the profits remaining after the first fixed payment to the preferred shareholders on a 2:1, 3:1, 4:1, and so forth basis, in order to assure the common stockholders the better portion of the remaining profits. Of course, preferred stock need not be participating and would only be made so if the organizers felt it was necessary in order to be able to sell the preferred stock to investors.

Common Stock. Stock that does not possess a dividend preference is known as common stock. Common stock generally is the base of all shareholder power. It typically includes the broadest voting rights and the potential for the largest financial gains, although it is also the least secure of the various investments one may make in a corporation. As with preferred stock, the corporation is not required to distribute its profits to common stockholders, but when the Board of Directors exercises its discretion to distribute profits, the amount available for common stockholders' dividends is determined only after preferred shareholders, if any, have received their distributions.

The common stock dividend is usually phrased in the form of "$___ per share," and is established by the Board rather than by the Articles. The Board of Directors, in its discretion, may vary the amount from time to time, for instance, taking account of the funds available for distribution as opposed to the corporation's need to retain the money.

In addition to the distinctions between preferred and common stock, stock may also be classified according to other characteristics. [84]In the event of a corporate liquidation, when the corporation winds up its operations and distributes its assets, or their value in cash, to its shareholders, one or

84) Section16 of the Model Act.

more classes of stock may be given a preference in the distribution of the corporation's assets or their value.

One class could be granted the exclusive right to receive all the assets. All classes could be allowed to divide them equally, or a class, or classes, could be granted a preference a right to receive a certain value before the holders of any other class of stock receive any payments in liquidation.

Voting Rights. Voting rights may also differ among classes. One class may be given the exclusive right to vote at shareholder meetings for the election of the corporation's Board of Directors. Other classes could be empowered to vote only on extraordinary corporate matters such as merger or dissolution, or all classes could be given equal and complete voting rights. Many corporations do not give voting rights to preferred shareholders. This may be in recognition of the fact that preferred shareholders receive preferential distributions of the corporation's earnings, while the size of distributions to common stockholders depend on the size of the corporation's profit and thus are tied more closely to the skill of the corporation's management. It may seem appropriate, therefore, that the common stockholders are the group responsible for selecting that management.

Classes of stock may also be made "convertible" into stock of another class; that is, the shareholder has the option to swap his or her shares, at a predetermined ratio set in the Articles, for shares of another class of stock or, perhaps, for a bond.[85)]

Classes of stock are also divisible into "series."[86)] Shares of a class may be divided into and issued in a series as provided in the corporation's Articles of Incorporation or as authorized in the Articles with the details established by a resolution of the Board of Directors. Different series could pay dividends at different rates, have different redemption rights, terms, and prices, possess varying provisions for liquidation payments, or be convertible at different

85) Section 18 of the Model Act.

86) Section 16 of the Model Act.

ratios. For instance, Class A preferred stock may have voting rights and exclusive liquidation privileges. There may be Class A Series A, and Class A Series B, which differ in that Series A pays twice the rate of dividends as Series B.

Whatever the organizers' choices as to the types of shares that the corporation will issue, each share certificate representing stock should state the precise characteristics of the stock it represents. This provides each shareholder with clear notice of the rights, duties, and characteristics of the shares he or she owns.

8.4 ISSUING AND SELLING SECURITIES

Issuing Debt or Equity. A small business corporation almost certainly will not utilize all of the securities that have been described. Nevertheless, corporate organizers should consider the characteristics of all types of securities and then select the features most appropriate for their financial needs and anticipated corporate structure.

For instance, if the organizers intend to remain in charge of the corporation, they should arrange to control the stock possessing the power to select the corporation's Board of Directors, which, in turn, is empowered to select the corporation's officers. If there is a need for more investment than the organizers alone can provide, Preferred stock with a good dividend and/or liquidation preference may attract outside investors. Assuming these shares carry no voting rights, they may be issued without diminishing the organizers' control of the corporation's Board. Bonds also may be attractive conservative investments, and holders of debt securities generally have no say in the management of the corporation's affairs. Debt securities can be complicated, however, and for small businesses, they may be very difficult to sell to outsiders. An easier alternative is probably to seek long-term loans from a local bank or an individual. Why should a corporation want to go into debt when it can issue such an attractive variety of equity interests, and thus raise the money it needs through equity financing? Surprisingly, there are certain advantages to debt.

When a corporation pays interest to the holders of its debt securities, it may take a tax deduction in the amount of interest paid, and thereby reduce its taxable income.[87)] On the other hand, it may not take deductions for dividends paid to its shareholders. This favorable aspect of debt securities invites corporations to take advantage of them, particularly when the shareholders are also the lenders. As might be guessed, though, there are restrictions on the tax benefits available through disproportionate debt financing. When the ratio of total debt to total equity exceeds 4:1, for example, when the corporation is $4,000 in debt, which is owed to the shareholders, and has issued only $1,000 in shares, the IRS may regard the debt as a disguised form of stock and attempt to disallow the corporation's tax deductions for "interest" payments. A corporation may try to avoid such a disallowance by maintaining a healthy margin away from the 4:1 borderline.

There is another advantage to debt financing that is known as "leverage." In an economic sense, this means using borrowed money to finance the business. If the company does well, the leveraged financing can significantly increase the rate of return the owners get on their equity investment. Assume a business requires $100,000 to get started and the organizers put in a full $100,000 out of their own pockets. Also, assume the business's operations net a $20,000 profit in the first year. The organizers' rate of return is 20% (they received $20,000 profit on a $100,000 investment).

---

87) Internal Revenue Code Section 163(a). "(a) General rule: There shall be allowed as a deduction all interest paid or accrued within the taxable year on indebtedness." Section 163(a) allows as a deduction all interest paid or accrued within the taxable year on indebtedness. However, for individuals § 163(h)(1) disallows a deduction for personal interest. Under § 163(h)(2)(D), qualified residence interest is not personal interest. Section 163(h)(3)(A) defines qualified residence interest as interest paid or accrued during the taxable year on acquisition indebtedness or home equity indebtedness secured by any qualified residence of the taxpayer. Under § 63(h)(4)(A), "qualified residence" means a taxpayer's principal residence, within the meaning of § 121, and one other residence selected and used by the taxpayer as a residence.

If, in the same situation, they had used leverage, the results are much more dramatic. Assume that instead of putting in the full $100,000 out of their pockets, they put in only $20,000 and were able to borrow the remaining $80,000. They conduct their business with the same total cash input, $100,000, and they make the same profit, $20,000. This time, however, they have an additional expense, the interest on the borrowed money. Assume for simplicity's sake that they borrowed at 10% per year. This would result in an interest charge, tax deductible, of $8,000 (10% of$80,000) per year. When the $8,000 is subtracted from the $20,000, a net profit of $12,000 remains. At first glance, this looks less favorable than the $20,000 earned without borrowing. On closer examination, however, it is clear that the $12,000 was earned on an equity investment by the organizers-of only $20,000. This works out to a 60% rate of return, far higher than the 20% rate in the absence of leverage.

Thus in many cases where the organizers are able to put in the full amount needed, they choose not to. Assume the organizers had $100,000cash. On a leveraged basis as described in the example, they could buy five companies worth $100,000 each or a larger company worth $500,000. In each case, they would put in 20% of the needed cash and borrow the rest. Nevertheless, there are serious drawbacks to leverage. The first is practical. The organizers of a new business cannot always find people or institutions willing to lend them or their business the needed money. If the loans are available, they may be at high interest, carry heavy collateral, and/or require the personal guarantees of the organizers. Any of these factors could put a damper on leveraging.

The second drawback is financial. Just as leverage can increase the rate of return when the company does well, it can be devastating when the company does not do well. Using our original example, assume the corporation makes only $5,000 profit, If the organizers put in the full $100,000, they still have a 5% rate of return, If they borrowed the $80,000 they still must pay the interest of $8,000, which not only wipes out their profit of $5,000 but creates a$3,000 actual as opposed to paper loss.

Selling Securities. When a corporation sells its bonds or stock, it is subject to certain requirements concerning the value it must receive and the type of payment it may accept for their sale. As mentioned previously, par value stock may not be sold by the corporation for less than its par value; however, once a shareholder has purchased stock from the corporation, he or she may sell it to a third party for whatever price he or she wishes. On the other hand, the purchase price of no par stock, when initially sold by the corporation, is generally set by the Board of Directors or the shareholders if the Articles of Incorporation has given them this power and may be adjusted from time to time as with par value stock, once a shareholder purchases no par stock from a corporation, he or she may sell it for whatever price he or she can obtain. No par stock may not be sold by the corporation for less than the stated value assigned to it by the Board. However, since the Board sets that stated value at the time of the sale, this should never be a problem.

Whatever the selling price, the corporation is restricted as to the form of payment it may accept in the sale. For stock or bonds, it may receive only money, property, or services actually rendered to it. "Money" means cash, including a check. "Property" could be tangible physical property, such as land, machinery, a car, etc., or could be intangible property stock in another corporation, patent rights, etc.; however, "property" does not include a promissory note. "Services" refers to services that have already been performed not a promise to perform future services for the corporation generally not pre-incorporation services.

When the corporation receives property or services in exchange for its stock, the Board of Directors has a duty to ascertain the value of the property or services and to determine that the corporation is receiving Some-thing of value at least equal to the par or stated value of the stock that will be issued for it. If the value of the property is less than the aggregate par or stated value, the stock is said to be "watered," and if the corporation should ever be unable to pay its creditors, the holders of watered stock may be liable to the creditors for the corporation's debts to the extent that their shares are watered. [88]

For example, if land worth $25,000 is exchanged for stock having a par or stated value of$100,000, the shareholder receiving that stock could be liable for up to$75,000 in corporate debts. This situation can be avoided if the Board of Directors or the shareholders, if they are responsible for fixing the price of shares, carefully investigates the value of property or services received for the corporation's stock. If the Board determines in good faith and without fraud that the consideration received is equal to the value of the stock, that stock would not be considered "watered" even if it ultimately turns out that the Board was wrong in its valuation.[89]

An additional question concerning corporate finance is that of shareholders' "preemptive rights." A preemptive right gives an existing shareholder the right to purchase new shares of the same class as he or she currently holds or of securities convertible into such shares being issued by the corporation, before such shares are offered to other purchasers.[90] The right allows the shareholder to buy shares from the new issue in proportion to his or her present holdings of that class of corporate stock. For example, Jane Doe holds one-fourth of the common stock of Corporation X. Corporation X is planning to issue 1000 new shares of such stock. Therefore Doe has a right to buy 250 (1/4 of 1000) shares before they may be offered to others. If Doe does not have money to purchase the shares, or does not want more shares of stock, the corporation is then free to offer the shares to others.

Preemptive rights are controlled by statute. Some states require Preemptive rights while some states prohibit them. Other states leave it up to the Articles, with statutory formulations such as "there shall be preemptive rights unless the Articles state the contrary" or "there shall not be preemptive rights unless the Articles state the contrary."

---

88) Section 25 of the Model Act.

89) Section 19 of the Model Act.

90) Section 26(a) of the Model Act.

8.5 DIVIDENDS

A key feature of a business corporation is its ability to issue shares of stock and to distribute corporate earnings and profits to the holders of these shares. Such distributions are known as dividends. Business corporations are authorized to pay dividends, but may do so only pursuant to statutory guidelines.[91)]

Even where it is legally permissible for dividends to be paid, the decision whether to distribute them or to retain profits is within the reasonable discretion of the corporation's Board of Directors. Dividends are not mandatory simply because they are legally possible. There may be other important uses for the corporation's profits which persuade the Board against a distribution. The Board, however, may not unreasonably With-hold dividends from the corporation's shareholders.

Types of Dividends. A corporation may distribute three types of dividends: (1) a cash dividend, which is a payment of money - in cash or by check; (2) a stock or share dividend, which is a distribution of additional shares of stock in the corporation itself - usually a fraction of the stock already held by each shareholder, e.g., for every 10 shares of stock already owned, a dividend of one additional share is declared - which may be of the same or of a different class or series than the stock already owned by the shareholder; or (3) a property dividend, which is one other than a cash or stock dividend and could include a distribution of tangible property such as the corporation's inventory or portions of its land, or it could consist of shares of stock in another corporation. These are known as "in kind" distributions.

Financial Considerations. Regardless of the type of dividend the corporation would like to distribute, it may not distribute dividends if it is insolvent, or, in some jurisdictions, if its net assets are less than its stated capital. In any case, it may not distribute an amount that would render the

91) Section 45 of the Model Act.

corporation insolvent or, in the stricter jurisdictions, reduce its net assets below its stated capital.[92)]

The concept of "insolvency" is relatively simple. "Insolvent" means that the corporation is unable to pay its debts as they become due in the usual course of its business. Therefore, a corporation may not pay dividends if it cannot pay its debts or if the payment of dividends would render it unable to pay its debts.

The concept of "stated capital" is more difficult. It means: (1) the par value of all shares outstanding having a par value, and (2) the value received by the corporation for all shares without par value, except any part there of which the Board of Directors has elected to allocate to the corporation's "capital surplus." For example: Corporation X issues 1000 shares of Class A common stock which the Articles of Incorporation specify shall have a par value of $1.00 each. X also issues 1000 shares of Class B common stock, of no par value, but with respect to which the Board of Directors resolved that 50 cents received from the sale of each share should be allocated to the corporation's stated capital with any remaining money received allocated to capital surplus. Both classes of stock are then sold for$1.00 each. The account books would have entries that look something like this.

	Stated Capital	Capital Surplus
Class A	$1,000	
Class B	$500	$500
	$1,500	$500

Corporation X may take the $2,000 received and use it to finance its business operations; however, it may not pay dividends to its stockholders if it does not have "net assets" worth at least $1,500, or if the payment of dividends would reduce its net assets below the value of $1,500.

92) Section 45 of the Model Act.

Net assets means the value of the corporation's assets, such as property, cash, and so forth, minus the amount of its liabilities. Thus the corporation must have money or property in excess of the sum of its liabilities plus the amount of its stated capital if it wants to pay dividends. If the corporation is successful and makes profits, this requirement should pose no problem. When paying a property or in kind dividend, a corporation is considered to be making a distribution equal to the current value of the property it is distributing. With share dividends, the amount corresponding to the par value of all par value shares, or the stated capital value of no par shares, is the value of the dividend. In either case, the corporation must have net assets sufficient to cover the amount of its stated capital plus the value of the distribution. Also, after a share dividend is distributed, the corporation's capital account is increased by the par or stated capital value of the shares making up the dividend, while one of its surplus accounts is reduced by the same amount.

Any director who is present at a Board of Directors' meeting and who votes to distribute a dividend that violates these restrictions may be liable to the corporation for the portion of the dividend in excess of the amount that properly could have been distributed. A director may avoid this liability if he or she enters his or her dissent to an improper dividend distribution decision in the minutes of the Board meeting, files a written dissent at the end of such meeting, or after the meeting promptly mails a written dissent to the Secretary of the corporation.

This does not allow a director to change his or her vote after the decision has become final, however. A director also will not be held liable if he or she voted for the dividend in good faith, relying in determining the propriety of the dividend on a balance sheet asserted to be correct by the corporation's President, Treasurer, or a Certified Public Accountant. Where directors are subject to liability, they are said to be "jointly and severally liable." This means that any one director who voted for the distribution may be held liable for the entire amount of an improper distribution, or that all directors who voted in favor of it may be held collectively liable. If any director is found liable for an amount greater than his or her pro rata share, however, he or she may sue the other directors to cause them to contribute their portions of the total amount.[93)]

Stock Splits. Since dividends are an important attribute of a business corporation and improper dividends or the improper withholding of dividends can result insubstantial liabilities for corporate directors, it is important for organizers to understand the legalities in this area. It is an area that calls for caution. If any difficult questions arise, especially if there are dissident shareholders, it would be wise to consult an attorney or accountant.

It is also wise to remember that the legalities are only one of many considerations in dividend policy. There are also questions of business judgment: Is a distribution of cash in line with the business needs of the corporation at this time? And practical realities: Do the shareholders expect a distribution now and what action will they take if it is not made? There are, in addition, tax consequences to a distribution or non-distribution of cash dividends. Dividends distributed to shareholders are taxed to those shareholders at their marginal tax rate. This imposes a second tax on corporate earnings.

For example, assume Corporation X had $100,000 of taxable income which, for this example, we will assume is equivalent to its profit for the year. This amount would be taxed at the corporation's normal tax rates, 15% of the first $50,000 25% of the next $25,000, and 34% for amounts over $75,000. This would leave the corporation with $77,750 of post-tax income profit. The Board decides to dis-tribute $25,000 of this amount to its shareholders, Shareholder A receives$ 1,000 of this distribution. Assume A is a 28% taxpayer. This $1,000 will be taxed to the shareholder at 28% leaving A with $720: $1,000 - $280.

This scenario would be repeated for each shareholder, thus reducing the

93) Section 48 of the Model Act.

amount let in his or her hands. Remember, this same pool of money - the corporation's profits from which this distribution came - was first taxed at the corporate level. At the shareholder level, it is taxed a second time. In addition to dividends, a corporation may make another type of distribution to its shareholders through a "stock split" whereby the corporation splits each share of stock into a larger number of shares, usually in order to lower the price per share and thus make its shares more marketable.

For example, Jane Doe holds 10 shares, then selling for $40 each. The corporation decides that it will split its stock at a 4:1 ratio. After the split, Doe has 40 shares, i.e., 4 X 10 worth $10.00 each. The total value of her holdings has not changed, 10 shares at $40 each was worth $400. 40shares at $10 each is still worth $400. Neither has her relative position of ownership changed. Assume there were originally 100 shares outstanding. Her 10 shares represent 10% ownership. If all those shares are split 4 to1, she now owns 40 shares of the 400 outstanding, still a 10% interest.

Because a stock split is only a process whereby the same corporate interests are represented by a greater number of shares, the problems of calculating stated capital and the needs for a reserve of net assets or cash are not present. A corporation generally may split its stock regardless of its financial condition.

8.6 REVIEW ON CORPORATE STRUCTURE

In General. Whenever your fact pattern describes an attempt to remove a director, here's what you should keep in mind: The shareholders, by majority vote, can always remove a director for cause, e.g., fraud, gross incompetence, or a breach of the duty of loyalty. Also, most modem statutes, including the RMBCA, let a majority of the shareholders remove a director even without cause, unless the corporation's charter provides differently. Directors, even by majority vote, cannot remove a fellow director even for cause, unless the charter or bylaws specifically say they can. The court may, under most modem statutes, remove a director for cause, e.g., fraudulent or dishonest conduct, or gross abuse of power.

If your fact pattern involves the removal of an officer, e.g., the president, here's what you should remember: The hoard has the power to remove an officer, with or without cause. That's true even if the officer has an employment contract - the board has power to remove the officer anyway and the officer's only recourse is a suit for damages, not a suit to enjoin the dismissal or to compel reinstatement. Shareholders, even by majority vote, do not have the power to remove an officer.

Election of directors is often tested. The most common issue about election of directors involves fitting board vacancies. Here, the usual rule, and the RMBCA approach, is that the vacancy can be filled either by shareholder vote or board vote. Don't overlook the possibility that a corporation may have cumulative voting. In cumulative voting, a shareholder may aggregate his votes in favor of fewer candidates than there are slots available. For example, A, B and C each own 100 of G Corporation's 300 shares outstanding, and are its 3 directors under annual terms. C dies, and D inherits her shares. The bylaws say that a 90% majority is required for election of new directors. You have to say whether, at the next holders' meeting, D can elect herself as a director, against the wishes of A and B. If G Corporation has cumulative voting, D can do so - she can cast all 300 of her votes in favor of herself, and thus come up with a "100% vote," i.e., 1 vote for each share outstanding, for herself, even if A and B don't vote for her.

You'll sometimes be asked about when shareholders can compel the calling of a special shareholders' meeting. In general, the board is not obligated to call such a meeting, even if a majority of holders requests it, unless the particular action sought to be accomplished must be approved by shareholders. For example, P, majority holder of X Corporation, wants to remove Pres., the corporation's president. P calls for a special meeting of shareholders to consider his motion to fire President. The board refuses. P can't compel the board to hold the special meeting, because shareholders don't have the power to fire officers, and therefore don't have the right to call a special meeting to consider the firing of officers.

Issues involving the corporate structure are often hidden in fact patterns that tell you about the provisions of the corporation's charter and bylaws. Be certain to read these charter and bylaws terms carefully, because they're likely to be implicated in events that you're told about later in the question. If the facts indicate that the board has taken an action which conflicts with the corporation's charter, remember that the charter can only be altered by the shareholders, not the board, so the board's action is probably illegal. For example, X Corporation's charter says that the board consists of 5 members, who will be elected annually. The board unilaterally votes to expand its size to 9, and to stagger terms. This action will be illegal, because only a majority of shareholders, not a board majority, may vary the charter.

Whenever you have to decide the validity of a particular board action, check for failure to comply with notice, quorum and meeting requirements. In particular: A special meeting of the board must normally be preceded by notice to the board members. The notice must specify the subjects and no unlisted subject may be discussed. However, the notice requirement will be deemed waived as to any director who attends the meeting and does not object at the start of the meeting to the lack of notice.

The board may act only if a quorum is present. If the board has a fixed size, a quorum is a majority of that size, even if there are now vacancies. If the board has a variable size, a quorum is a majority of the directors in office at the start of the meeting. Most states let a corporation's charter or bylaws establish a super-majority requirement for a quorum. For example, Corporation's bylaws say that a quorum will consist of 5 out of its 7 directors. This provision will be given effect, so a meeting at which only 4 of 7 are present will be of no effect. Normally, the board may take action only at a meeting. Directors must be present to vote, i.e., they may not vote by proxy.

For example, Paul, one of Corporation's directors, can't come to the board meeting, so he gives his proxy to Steve, and has Steve vote for him at the meeting. Paul won't be deemed present, and his vote won't count.

Look out for the possibility of a telephone meeting: in most states and under the RMBCA, if the director is present for a conference call in which a quorum participates, the director is deemed to be in attendance at the meeting, and his vote. The board may take action only upon a vote of a majority of the directors present at the meeting. So the action doesn't have to be supported by a majority of directors in office, only a majority of those present, assuming that a quorum is present. If the facts indicate that the meeting/quorum/majority-vote requirements weren't met, consider the possibility that the board action is valid anyway, because the directors subsequently ratified it by affirming it or failing to disavow it. For example, No quorum is present when the board purports to approve a contract with a third party. A year later, at a regular meeting, attended by a quorum, a majority of those present vote to approve the transaction. This is a ratification, so the contract is binding as if it had been properly approved the first time. Same result if the board tacitly ratifies, as by accepting benefits under the contract.

Whenever the fact pattern states that an officer acted on behalf of the corporation, consider whether the officer had authority to bind the corporation under any of these 4 doctrines: (1) express actual authority; (2) implied actual authority; (3) apparent authority; and (4) ratification. Look for indications as to whether the officer was expressly authorized to make the contract. An explicit grant of authority usually comes from either the corporation's bylaws, or from a resolution adopted by the board. Usually this form of authority is so easy that you won't find it in your facts.

If the officer had a title within the corporation that would typically include the power to make the deal in question, then the officer had "implied actual authority," i.e., authority that's "inherent in the office." For example, Pete, who is actually the President of Corporation, signs a deal to buy office furniture "Corporation, by Pete, its President." Pete has implied actual authority, because the president of a corporation would typically have authority to make a deal for furniture. Look for situations in which extraordinary action is taken by the corporation's president, without board approval. Such action is probably invalid, since it doesn't fall within any form of authority. For example, X Corporation is a 10-employee business with $1 million in annual revenues. Pres., the president of X Corporation, signs an agreement to pay a $100,000 per year lifetime pension to a retiring vice-president. The board isn't told of the agreement, and thus doesn't authorize it. The contract is probably not enforceable against X Corporation, because it was an extraordinary contract that did not fall within any theory of authority. For instance, the authority isn't "implied actual," because such a deal is too large and unusual to come within the usual powers of the president of a corporation this size.

CHAPTER 9

CORPORATE GOVENANCE[94)]

9.1 INTRODUCTION

In General. Traditionally, powers have been allocated among the shareholders, the directors and the officers of a corporation in a particular way. Even today, most statutes assume that this allocation of powers will be followed. Therefore, we refer to it as the "statutory scheme." However, most modem statutes allow the corporation, if it observes certain formalities, to modify this scheme. The statutory scheme may be summarized as follows:

a. Shareholders: The shareholders act principally through two mechanisms: (1) electing and removing directors, and (2) approving or disapproving fundamental or non-ordinary changes (e.g., mergers).
b. Directors: The directors "manage" the corporation's business. That is, they formulate policy, and appoint officers to carry out that policy.
c. Officers: The Corporation's officers administer the day-to-day affairs of

94) This Chapter is compiled mainly with materials from Robert W. Hamilton, "The Law of Corporations," West Group (2000); Arthur R. Pinto, Douglas M. Branson, "Understanding Corporate Law," LEXIS Publishing (1999); Emmanuel Law Outlines, "Corporations," Emmanuel Publishing Corp. (1997).

the corporation, under the supervision of the board.

Inappropriate structure for very large or very small corporations. For very large or very small corporations, this statutory scheme does not reflect reality. For instance, a small closely-held corporation generally does not have its affairs managed by the board of directors - the shareholders usually exercise control directly. They may happen also to be directors, but they usually do not act as a body of directors, and the controlling Shareholders often disregard any non-shareholder directors.

At the other end of the spectrum, a very large publicly-held company is really run by its officers, and the board of directors frequently serves as little more than a "rubber stamp" to approve decisions made by officers.

Modification of statutory scheme. Modem statutes generally give the corporation the power to modify this traditional statutory scheme where appropriate. This is especially true for closely-held corporations. For instance some statutes allow closely-held corporations to reduce the board to one or two members. But unless a particular modification of the statutory scheme is explicitly authorized by statute, the corporation and its lawyer disregard the statutory scheme at their peril. Much of this chapter is devoted to an explanation of the statutory scheme in detail together with a description of the consequences if the traditional scheme is not actually followed by the corporation.

However, a corporation is basically a three-tiered Creation consisting of shareholders, directors, and officers. Each of these groups possesses unique characteristics that can be important when corporate organizers are shaping their organization's management structure.

9.2 SHAREHOLDERS

Under the statutory scheme, the shareholders do not directly manage the corporation, even though they own it. Instead, they can influence the conduct of the business through a number of indirect methods. There are four main methods by which the shareholders can influence the corporation's affairs:

(1) Elect and remove directors: They have the power to elect[95] and remove directors;

(2) Articles of incorporation and bylaws: They can approve or disapprove of changes to the articles of incorporation or bylaws and thereby influence the allocation of power as among themselves, the directors, and the officers. For instance, the powers and duties of executive officers are usually spelled out in the bylaws, so these powers and duties could be cut back or re-allocated based partly on shareholder-approved bylaw changes.

(3) Fundamental changes: They have the right to approve or disapprove of fundamental changes not in the ordinary course of business, such as a merger, a sale of substantially all of the corporation's assets, or dissolution.

(4) Void or voidable transactions: Finally, some transactions by officers or board of directors are void or voidable unless ratified by a vote of shareholders. For instance many transactions between the corporation and a director or officer are voidable on grounds of self-dealing unless the shareholders ratify the transaction by voting to approve it.

Staggered Terms. The one common exception to annual terms is that in most states, if the articles of incorporation so provide, the directors may have staggered terms. That is, the directors may be initially divided into, say, three "classes" with one class having a three-year term, another a two-year term and the last a one-year term. This classification device is often used today to make it more difficult for a "raider" to replace the board. Shareholders are

95) Directors are normally elected at each annual meeting of shareholders. That is, directors normally serve a one-year term, though of course they can be, and often are, re-elected. See RMBCA § 8.05.

generally given the power to elect directors to fill vacancies on the board, but the board of directors also usually has this power. Therefore, the filling of vacancies is discussed in the treatment of the board of directors. At common law, shareholders had little power to remove a director during his term of office. But modem statutes have dramatically expanded this shareholder power.

However, the shareholders do not have the power to conduct business directly on behalf of the corporation. Shareholders must operate through their control of the board. This means that shareholders cannot bind the corporation by their own direct actions. And this is true even of actions taken by a majority of shareholders. Purportedly in the corporation's name, unless the action is somehow ratified by the board or by an officer with power to bind the corporation to the kind of transaction in question, the action by the shareholders has no effect.

Example: Sam is a majority shareholder of Corporation, but does not sit on the board and is not an officer. He goes to Copy Machine Co. and signs a contract, made out in Corporation's name, to purchase a copy machine. The board learns of this before the machine is delivered, and sends a letter to Copy Machine saying, "We're not bound to take this copier, and we don't want it." Copy Machine can't hold Corporation to the contract, because Sam is merely a shareholder, albeit a majority one, not an officer, and shareholders *quo* shareholders can't bind a corporation.

A corporation "authorizes" the issuance of its stock in its Articles of Incorporation. Its Board of Directors then determines how many shares of stock will be offered for sale. When these shares are purchased they comprise the corporation's "issued and outstanding" stock. For example: in its Articles of Incorporation, Corporation X has been authorized to issue 10,000 shares of stock at $10 par value. It decides that it does not need the full $100,000 which it would receive if all the shares were sold, but that it does need $50,0001o begin business. It is important to keep in mind here that a corporation may sell its stock for more than its par value, although it may not sell it for less. We have equated the par value and sale price in this example merely for convenience. Therefore, the Board of Directors votes to offer for sale only 5,000 of the 10,000 shares. When purchased, these 5,000 shares are the corporation's "issued and outstanding" stock.

Especially in a small corporation, shareholders have a potentially significant role in corporate management-1he election of the corporation's Board of Directors. The Board determines corporate policy and selects the officers who carry out this policy on a day-to-day basis. Shareholder power to remove directors, adopt and revise corporate documents, and to ratify extraordinary corporate events such as merger, consolidation, or dissolution may be reiterated in the corporation's Articles or Bylaws. Shareholders may also be granted additional powers that involve them more intimately in the management of the corporation.

Unless the Articles of Incorporation provide otherwise, each share of stock possesses one vote. Organizers may want to deviate from that arrangement, however, in order to protect or accommodate particular aspects or needs of the corporation. For instance, to prevent an excessive concentration of voting power, the Articles could take the drastic step of providing that no individual may own more than a certain number of shares or a certain percentage of the corporation's voting stock, or that despite the number of shares a stockholder owns, he or she is limited in the number of votes he or she may cast.

In order to implement a restriction of this type effectively, it is advisable that all the shareholders execute a shareholders' agreement containing the limitation and that such restriction also be noted on each of the corporation's share certificates. This will discourage any shareholder from making a transfer that would result in a prohibited accumulation of shares. It would also put any buyer of the shares on notice of the restriction.

Cumulative Voting. Another device used to affect voting rights is "cumulative voting." In all elections for directors, the number of votes a Share-holder gets equals the number of shares she holds, multiplied by the number of directors standing for election. But there are two distinct methods by which these shares can be voted "straight"[96] and "cumulative."[97] Many states statutes require or permit this device when voting for the election of directors while some states prohibit it.[98] This type of voting is basically a protection for minority stockholders and provides each share with as many votes as there are vacancies on the Board to be filled. The shareholder may distribute these votes among candidates as he or she sees fit. This allows the holders of minority share interests to cumulate their votes in their attempt to elect representatives, although not a majority, to the Board. For example, assume Jane Doe owns 10 shares of stock and there are five positions on the Board to be filled. With cumulative voting, Doe would have 50 votes that she may cast however she chooses.

For instance, if Doe owned 10 shares and Mary Smith owned the remaining 15 shares of a 25-share corporation. Smith would, in the absence of cumulative voting, always elect the entire Board. If there were five directors to be elected, she would cast her 15 votes for each of her five choices while Doe casts her 10 for each of her five choices. With cumulative voting, however, Doe would have 50 votes and Smith 75, 15 shares times five directors to be elected. The important feature is that Doe can use her 50 votes however she chooses. Therefore, she might cast 25 each for only two candidates. If she does this, she is assured of electing two Board members because no matter how Smith divides her votes, she cannot mathematically have more than three people with as many or more votes than Doe's two people. If she gave any candidate 26 votes, she would have only 49 left for remaining candidates. If she gave a second candidate 26 votes, she would have only 23 votes left. Doe's two candidates would have to be among the top five vote getters. Of course, Doe could miscalculate and give a greater

96) In "straight" voting, no share may be voted more than once for any given candidate.

97) In "cumulative" voting, by contrast, a voter may vote a single share multiple times for a single candidate once for each director seat that's open. This increases the power of minority shareholders, since a shareholder may cumulate, i.e. lump together, all his votes so as to be sure to elect a single director.

98) Section 33 of the Model Act.

number of candidates fewer votes each, but if she does so she minimizes her choices for representation on the Board. Algebra has produced a formula for maximizing representation. That formula is;

X=(S X N) / D + 1 + 1

Where X equals the number of shares needed to elect a certain number of directors. S equals the total number of shares which will be voting (in person or by proxy) in the election. N equals the number of directors a shareholder wishes to elect D equals the total number of directors to be elected in the particular election. Plugging the numbers in our hypothetical situation into this formula, we see that the number of shares Doe needs to elect two directors is:

X = (25 X 2 / 5 + 1) +1, or X = (50 / 6) +1, or X = 9.3

Since Doe has 10 shares, she can elect her two directors. If she wished to elect three directors, the formula would indicate the impossibility unless Smith misapplied her votes. To elect three directors, a shareholder would need (25 X 3 / 5+1) + 1, or (75/6) + 1, or 13.5 shares more than Doe controls. It is important to remember that cumulative voting, if available at all, is only used for the election of directors and not for other issues that maybe brought before the shareholders for a vote.

VOTING POWER

Classes of Shares. If a corporation has more than one class of stock, its Articles may provide for "class voting." In class voting, each class of shares votes separately and elects representatives to the Board of Directors. For instance: Class A, Class B, and Class C stock are held, respectively, by the three organizers of the corporation. Since each class has the exclusive right to elect one member of the Board, each organizer is assured that he or she will always have a seat on the Board of Directors. This is class voting for directors - to be distinguished from classes of directors. The latter means that some directors have different powers or varying terms of service, or so forth.

Another use of class voting is to allow a certain class to elect proportionately more directors than another class. For instance, the organizers might want to provide Class A stock with rights to elect seven directors out of an 11-person Board, with Class B electing the remaining four directors. This could be true even if there were more Class B shares than Class A. If the organizers want to insure that they retain managerial control(assuming the absence of cumulative voting), all they need do is buy a majority of the Class A stock, thus assuring the election by them of a majority of the Board. Of course, if capital must be raised by the sale of shares to outsiders, the outsiders' willingness to invest in a situation such as we have described would be a consideration. The shares must be made marketable.

Class voting may also operate as a veto if the Articles require unanimity among the classes for shareholder actions. For instance, if a particular action needed a majority of Class A and a majority of Class B shares, the smaller class could stop corporate action even though a majority of the total shares supported the action. This is a drastic method of protecting minority interests and has the disadvantage of possibly paralyzing shareholder action altogether. It is also possible to provide for a class of stock with "contingent" voting rights, that is, shares with voting rights only under special circumstances. A corporation may limit the voting powers of shares of any class. Thus shares could, for instance, be entitled to vote only when the corporation had not paid them dividends, or if sales fell below a specified level. At any given time, however, at least one class of shares must have voting rights so that the corporation's directors may be elected and other shareholder functions may be performed.

Disproportionate voting rights may also be used to allocate corporate power. This may be appropriate, for example, when two or more classes of stock exist and the stockholders have paid different amounts to purchase their shares. The more expensive class of shares might, for instance, be given multiple votes where every share of that class counts as two votes while the other classes enjoy only one vote per share. Or the system could be used to assure that a particular group of shareholders, usually the corporation's organizers, maintain control. The organizers could issue the multiple voting stock to themselves, and sell the other types of shares to outsiders, thereby obtaining disproportionate voting strength.

The outsiders might be less willing to invest under these circumstances and thus the ability to market the shares must be considered by the organizers in making decisions about the attributes of shares. It is also possible to create classes of nonvoting shares. This type of stock might be intended to attract investors and could pay larger, more secure dividends to compensate for its lack of voice in corporate management. Most forms of preferred stock fit this mold. Classes of shares may also be used to equalize voting rights and still reward shareholders who contribute extra money to the corporation. Although voting rights of all shares could be equal, the class of stock issued to a large investor could pay dividends at a more favorable rate, or an investor could be issued another, separate class of nonvoting stock that pays dividends.

In the latter case, the shareholder's economic interest in the corporation would accurately reflect the amount he or she had invested, but his or her ability to control the corporation, through voting power, would not outweigh that of any less affluent organizers. It should be understood here that these examples are intended to be illustrative only. The organizers may create any share structure that fits their needs, is acceptable to investors, and complies with the laws of their jurisdiction.

Quorum and Vote Requirements. Minority shareholders' interests may also be protected by fashioning shareholder quorum and voting requirements to guard against of minority interests. A quorum is the number of shares that must be present at a shareholders' meeting in order for that meeting legally to transact business.

The purpose of a quorum is to prevent a small number of shares from deciding corporate questions m the absence of a more representative number of shares. Usually, it is required that the holders of a majority of the corporation's outstanding shares be represented, whether in person or by proxy, at a shareholders' meeting in order for the meeting to be properly constituted and able to take valid and binding action. If a quorum is not present, any actions taken at the meeting are subject to attack by disgruntled shareholders-who could seek to have a court declare those actions were invalid. However, at both a shareholders' meeting and a board of directors' meeting, no action may be taken without a "quorum."[99]

To protect minority interests, the quorum requirement could be increased to two-thirds or three-fourths or other majority level. Minority shareholders could then purposely absent themselves from, and thus prevent a quorum at, a shareholders' meeting scheduled to vote on matters they opposed. A less drastic method would be to provide that a greater-than-majority vote is required for passage of shareholder motions. This would allow the shareholders to have a quorum, yet would enable minority shareholders to cast enough votes to prevent a matter from passing unless a large majority exists. This type of greater-than-majority vote requirement must be specifically authorized in the corporation's Articles of Incorporation or Bylaws.[100]

Both greater-than-majority quorum and vote requirements have the potential for producing shareholder deadlock. A high quorum is probably the more dangerous, however, since a stubborn shareholder could block all shareholder action by preventing the presence of a quorum and thus the legality of a meeting. A greater-than-majority vote requirement at least allows the shareholders to confront each other, discuss their differences, and pass on to other matters.

Shareholder Agreements. Another method of obtaining shareholder cooperation, one which should not cause shareholder paralysis, is for shareholders to enter into a shareholders' agreement. This is a contract pursuant to which the shareholders bind themselves to do, or refrain from doing, certain things. Among them may be an agreement as to the election of

99) At a board meeting, a quorum is usually a majority of the directors in office, and at a shareholders' meeting, a quorum is usually a majority of the outstanding shares.

100) Section 32 of the Model Act.

directors and, often, a dispute-resolution mechanism.

In addition, there is often a share-transfer restriction, which is intended to allow shareholders to be able to choose their colleagues. Reasonable restrictions on share transfers preserve an established corporate shareholder group and management structure and protect against intrusions by new shareholders and interests with the ambition to take over the corporation. An absolute restriction on the transfer of shares is considered to be against public policy and will not be enforced by the courts, but many non-absolute restrictions have been held to be valid. The most common restriction requires a shareholder wishing to sell his or her stock to offer it first to the existing shareholders in proportion to their current stockholdings and/or to the corporation. If neither the corporation nor the existing shareholders choose to purchase the offered shares, then the selling shareholder could sell this stock to outsiders. To assure representation of each shareholder on the corporation's Board, a shareholders' agreement also generally provides that shareholders will vote to elect certain persons as directors and will continue voting for them as long as they can properly perform their duties to the corporation. In a small corporation this could take the form of the shareholders promising to elect each other to the Board.

Finally, a shareholder's agreement can provide for a dispute-resolution mechanism. This is a valuable device, since it allows shareholders to set a procedure for dispute resolution before a dispute arises and each side seeks a mechanism favorable to themselves. Among the common choices is third-party mediation or giving a third party one share with which to break a tie. Notice of the existence of a shareholders' agreement should be placed on share certificates held by the parties to such an agreement. This puts any potential buyers on notice of restrictions, including transfer restrictions, attached to those shares, and helps to prevent claims that stock is owned by a new shareholder in violation of a share-transfer restriction.

Voting Trusts. "Voting trusts" are another form of control device that consolidates shareholders' voting power in one person or a small group of persons who vote the shares of all the shareholders participating in the trust.[101] Any number of shareholders may form a voting trust by executing a written voting trust agreement, transferring their shares to a voting trustee or trustees, and receiving in return voting trust certificates representing each shareholder's interest in the shares held in trust. The voting trust agreement contains terms that confer upon the trustees the right to vote the shares held by the trust, frequently in a designated manner, such as the names of certain persons to be selected for the corporation's Board of Directors, and usually provides that the shareholders are entitled to continue to receive dividends and other corporate distributions, except stock dividends. The voting trustee keeps a record of the holders of the trust certificates and provides the corporation with a copy of the agreement, including the names and addresses of all the parties to it.

If the terms of the trust do not instruct the trustee(s) how to vote on a particular matter, he or she may vote the shares held by the trust according to his or her own best judgment. Voting trusts are an effective way to concentrate power in a few individuals; however, this result is somewhat at odds with the public policy of encouraging broad participation in corporate control. For these reasons, voting trusts are typically valid only for a specified period of time, often not more than 10 years. After the 10-year period, a voting trust is unenforceable - but the trust may be renewed for successive 10-year periods if the shareholders who participated in the trust sign another voting trust agreement.[102]

Another common use for voting trusts is to protect creditors of a corporation from having management make decisions that put the creditors' loans in jeopardy. Under such a scenario, the creditor demands, as a prerequisite to making a loan, that a majority of the corporation's shares be placed in a trust with a nominee of the creditor named as trustee. The trust

101) Section 34 of the Model Act.

102) Section 34 of the Model Act.

instrument normally leaves general management to the Board, but allows the trustee to act on fundamental financial questions.

FORMALITIES FOR SHAREHOLDER ACTION

In General. We examine now some of the mechanics by which shareholders exercise their right to vote on certain aspects of the corporation's affairs. In particular, we examine: (1) the giving of notice of a shareholders' meeting; (2) the quorum for such a meeting; and (3) the method of voting at such a meeting.

Nearly all states require a corporation to hold an annual meeting of shareholders.[103)] Corporations may also hold a "special" shareholders' meeting; a special meeting is any meeting other than the regularly-scheduled annual meeting.[104)] If the corporation fails to hold an annual meeting, this failure does not make the corporation's subsequent actions invalid.[105)] However, if the annual meeting is not held when scheduled, a shareholder will probably be able to get a court to order that one be held. Meeting will be ordered by court on application of any shareholder if meeting has not been held six months after the end of the corporation's fiscal year or fifteen months after its last annual meeting, whichever comes first.[106)]

The purpose of an annual meeting always includes at least the election of directors. However, the annual meeting may also consider any other relevant issue. According to most statutes, any other issue may be considered even if the issue was not specifically referred to in the notice given to shareholders. Notice of annual meeting "need not include a description of the purpose or purposes for which the meeting is called."[107)] A special meeting is normally called to consider one or a small number of very important matters that

103) See, e.g., RMBCA § 7.01(a).

104) See RMBCA § 7.02(a).

105) See RMBCA 8 7.01(c).

106) See e.g., RMBCA § 7.03(a)(1).

107) See e.g., RMBCA § 7.05(b).

cannot wait until the next annual meeting. Unlike the notice of an annual meeting, the notice of the special meeting must state the particular issues to be raised at the meeting, and no other issues may be considered.[108]

Statutes vary as to who may call a special meeting. Such a meeting may always be called by the board of directors. Also, any person or group who is authorized by the bylaws to call a meeting, e.g., the president, under many bylaws, may do so. Also, some, but by no means all, states allow the holders of a certain percentage of the shares to call a special meeting. The RMBCA goes especially far in this respect: the holders of a mere ten percent of the shares may cause a special meeting to be held.[109] By contrast, Delaware does not allow even a larger percentage of shareholders to call a special meeting; only the board or persons authorized in the bylaws may do so.[110]

Observe that the RMBCA approach gives a raider, i.e., a person attempting a hostile takeover, important powers. If he gains control of a majority of the shares shortly after an annual meeting, he may call a special meeting, remove a majority of the existing directors without cause, and elect his own slate. Under the Delaware approach, by contrast, he probably has to wait until the next annual meeting to gain a majority of the board. But in Delaware, the raider could probably accomplish the same result by use of Delaware's unusual provision allowing action to be taken by a non-unanimous majority of shareholders based on their written consent.

Quorum. Statutes generally require that a quorum be present at the shareholders' meeting equal to a majority of the outstanding shares. However, the percentage required for a quorum may be reduced as provided in the articles of incorporation or bylaws. However, many statutes set a minimum percentage below which not even the articles or bylaws may set the quorum. Many of these require that at least one-third of the shares be present as

108) See RMBCA § 7.05(c) and § 7.02(d).

109) See RMBCA § 7.02(a)(2).

110) See Del. GCL § 211(d).

the minimum allowable quorum, setting this one-third figure.[111] But the RMBCA makes the articles' or bylaws' minimum quorum provision effective no matter how tow it is.[112] Conversely, nearly all states allow the articles or bylaws to set a higher percentage as the quorum. This is frequently used as a control device in closely-held corporations; for instance, the articles might require all shares in a close corporation to be present, as a way of letting the minority shareholder veto action of which he disapproves.

Vote Required for Approval. Once a quorum is present, the traditional rule is that the shareholders will be deemed to have approved of the proposed action only if a majority of the shares actually present vote in favor of the proposed action. Observe that this rule contains two important sub-rules: (1) only a majority of the shares present, not a majority of the total shares eligible to vote, must support the proposal being voted on; and (2) a majority of the shares present must affirmatively vote in favor of the proposal; that is, an abstention is the equivalent of a vote against. The RMBCA changes the traditional rule with respect to (2), by making abstentions the same as votes that are not cast. Provides that action on a matter "is approved if the votes cast ... favoring the action exceed the votes cast opposing the action...."[113] For example, corporation has 1000 shares outstanding. 600 shares are represented at the meeting, a quorum is, of course, 501, assuming that the articles and bylaws do not set a different number. The vote on an action is 280 in favor, 225 opposed and 95 abstaining. Under the traditional approach, the proposal fails, since it needed 301 votes, a majority of the shares present. But under the RMBCA, the action is approved 280-225.[114]

The rules for elections of directors are different from the rules for all other action by shareholders. Most importantly, a minority of shareholders will frequently be able to elect one or more members of the board of directors,

111) See, e.g., Del. GCL § 216.

112) See RMBCA § 7.25(a).

113) See RMBCA § 7.25(c).

114) See Official Comment to RMBCA § 7.25(c).

because of the use of cumulative voting. Cumulative voting does not apply to shareholder approval of matters other than the election of directors.

Also, the standard rule that a majority is enough to constitute approval does not apply to certain issues that are of "fundamental" importance. Most states now allow the articles or bylaws to set a higher percentage as the minimum percentage needed to approve any given transaction, and many corporations have instituted such higher requirements for fundamental transactions like mergers, Indeed, a "super-majority" voting requirement before the corporation can be acquired by another corporation is a common anti-takeover device today. Recall that a quorum of directors is required throughout the directors' meeting. A comparable rule does not apply to shareholders' meetings once a quorum is present at the beginning of the meeting, the quorum is deemed to exist for the rest of the meeting, even if so many shareholders leave the meeting that the total number present would be less than the number needed for the quorum. "Once a share is represented for any purpose at a meeting, it is deemed present for quorum purposes for the remainder of the meeting and for any adjournment of that meeting unless a new record date is or must be set for that adjourned meeting."[115] Thus if a minority block knows that its presence is required for a quorum, and fears that a proposal it opposes will be passed, it should not attend the meeting at all rather than attending and leaving before the vote on the issue.

Written Consent. Just as directors may act by unanimous written consent, so nearly all states allow shareholders to act by unanimous written consent without a meeting. Such a provision is especially useful in closely-held corporations, where the few shareholders are in agreement, and the holders do not want to waste time on a formal meeting.

Furthermore, about a dozen states now allow shareholder approval in the form of written consent by the number of votes needed to approve the

---

115) See e.g., RMBCA § 7.25(b).

action, even if this is non-unanimous.[116] Thus in Delaware for ordinary corporate action requiring approval by a majority of the shares, if the holders of a majority sign a written consent to the action, the action will be binding without a meeting, and the minority shareholders will not have the right to dissent publicly at a meeting. This trend contrasts with the practice as to directors' meetings, where virtually all states require that the directors must either meet or consent unanimously.

Observe that allowing shareholder action to be taken by written majority consent may help a raider. Once the raider acquires a majority of the target's shares, he can carry out shareholder approval of any action needing a mere majority without having to convince the board to hold a special meeting of shareholders.

9.3 DIRECTORS

Directors are the corporation's managers and are elected by the shareholders. They are responsible for determining corporate policy and insuring that such policy is properly carried out by the corporation's officers. Directors' responsibilities may also include determining a corporation's products, services, personnel, prices, salaries, corporate finances, and dividends. In larger corporations, these powers are not usually exercised by the Board except in the most general way. The day-to-day decisions on these issues are typically delegated to officers and managerial employees. In smaller corporations there is often a greater overlap of owner, worker, and manager.

Traditionally, state corporation statutes have provided that the board of directors shall "manage" the affairs of the corporation. These statutes generally view the board not as agents of the stockholders, but as an independent

116) See, e.g., Delaware GCL § 228(a).

institution with responsibility for supervising the corporation's affairs. Thus traditionally and probably even under recently revised statutes, the shareholders cannot order the board of directors to take any particular action. It is the board, not the shareholders, who formulate policy; shareholder control is limited to removing directors or approving or disapproving certain major actions contemplated by the board, e.g., mergers.[117)]

Although older statutes still say that the board of directors shall "manage" the corporation, the reality is that day-to-day management is carried out by the corporation's officers, under the supervision of the board of directors. Some modem statutes now recognize this fact. For instance, the RMBCA says that "All corporate powers shall be exercised by or under the authority of, and the business and affairs of the corporation managed under the direction of, its board of directors...."[118)]

Thus today, the board's main function is to set the policies of the Corporation, and to authorize the making of important contracts. It is also the board which declares dividends; this responsibility is given to it specifically by statute. Beyond this, it is usually up to the board to initiate fundamental changes in the corporation, e.g., mergers or large asset sales, though these must then be submitted to the shareholders for approval.

---

117) See, e.g., *Charlestown Boot & Shoe Co. v. Dunsmore,* 60 N.H. 85 (1880).

Facts. The shareholders of corporation P believed that Osgood needed to be hired to help with two board of directors: Dunsmore and Willard. The shareholders elected to Osgood to "close up its affairs." Dunsmore and Willard did not act in accordance with Osgood and continued to rack up debt for the corporation, because they did not want the business to close.

Issue. Whether P corporation via Osgood has control or Dunsmore and Willard.

Relevant Statute. The business of every such corporation shall be managed by the directors thereof, subject to the by-laws and votes of the corporation, and under their direction by such officers and agents as shall be duly appointed by the directors or by the corporation."

Holding & Analysis. The board of directors, Dunsmore and Willard have control. The statute clearly gives control to the directors, unless the bylaws proscribe otherwise. "The statute does not authorize a corporation to join another officer with the directors, nor compel the directors to act with one who is not a director." The board of directors are to use "ordinary care" in running the corporation. The court argued that it would be unreasonable to hold the board members responsible for managing the business, but then be compelled to act another person who suddenly has greater ability to control the acts of the shareholders.

118) RMBCA § 8.01(b).

This means that shareholders often work in the business and manage it. When a company has more than one shareholder, each of whom wants a say in the company's affairs, problems may arise between majority and minority interests. The result could be that the majority attempts to exclude minority participation on the Board. There are several devices that could assist minority shareholders in thwarting any such effort by the majority. One is a provision, if legally available, for cumulative voting. Another is a shareholders' agreement committing shareholders to elect certain persons to the Board. The first two were discussed in preceding sections of this chapter. A third device is the classification of directors.

The Model Business Corporation Act[119] permits shares to be divided into classes. The Articles of Incorporation could establish these classes based on the right of each class to elect one or more directors. This would mean that if there are three shareholders, three classes of shares would be established, one for each shareholder. Each class would be entitled to elect a specified number of directors. All the other rights and obligations of shareholders could be equivalent and all directors would have the same power and responsibility. This device, however, would guarantee equal or proportional representation for each shareholder.

Corporation X while Mary Smith owned 75 shares and Jeffrey Jones owned the remaining 25 shares. They had decided among themselves that, despite the differences in share ownership, they each would have equal voice on the Board. If they chose the classification method to accomplish their goal, they would draft Articles of Incorporation creating three classes of stock. Each shareholder would obtain stock of a different class from the others and each class would be entitled to elect one director. Thus, carpenter would vote his 100 shares of Class A stock for his choice as director. Smith and Jones would each vote their Class B and Class C stock, respectively, for their choice as directors. Each would have one director and equal representation.

119) Section 16 of the Model Act.

Suppose, in this example, the group had decided that Carpenter, due to his greater number of shares, should have more representation on the Board. The Articles could be drafted to give Class A shareholders the right to elect three directors, while Class B could elect two directors, and Class C one director. This could be designed to maintain on the Board the proportion of interest each shareholder has in the stock of the corporation or to create any representational system the shareholders deem advisable.

Just as minority shareholders may feel the need for protection from the majority, the minority directors, chosen by the minority shareholders, may want some assistance as well. One means of protecting minority interests on the Board is a greater-than-majority quorum and vote requirements - the same device that can be used to protect minority shareholders. With respect to directors, a high quorum will protect a "minority director," a director representing minority shareholding interests, by allowing him or her to block unfavorable decisions by being absent from Board meetings and preventing the presence of the quorum required for the meeting to transact business.

On the other hand, the absence of a director for the purpose of defeating a quorum has negative implications relative to that director's duty to the corporation as a whole. If the organizers choose a high-quorum requirement for Board meetings, it should be coupled with a requirement that directors be given notice of the proposed agenda of each meeting. Thus absences may be strategically planned rather than being indiscriminate. A greater-than-majority vote requirement is another method to protect minority directors. Such a provision could simply state that a three-fifths, two-thirds, three-fourths, and so forth vote was necessary to carry a motion at a Board meeting. If minority directors muster enough votes to prevent that mark from being reached, they may block Board decisions unfavorable to them.

Both high-quorum and high-vote requirements risk a Board of Directors' stalemate that would be detrimental to the corporation, but these provisions are nevertheless an effective way to force directors to be responsive to all the interests represented on the Board. A greater-than-majority vote requirement is probably the safer feature, however, since it at least allows directors to appear and debate issues, giving them the opportunity to decide uncontroversial questions and compromise on others.

It may also be important to preserve an agreed-upon Board composition by preventing a majority faction of shareholders from increasing the number of directors and filling the vacancies with their own selections. To block "packing" the Board, the number of members may be established by a provision in the Articles of Incorporation or Bylaws, which may be made subject to amendment only upon receipt of a higher-than-majority, two-thirds, three-fourths, etc., vote of the shareholders.

Also, whenever the Board has a vacancy caused by the resignation, death or incapacity of a director, the power to fill that position could be vested exclusively in the shareholders acting by a greater-than-majority vote. If directors were elected by classified shares, the vacancy could be filled by the class of shares that elected the previous director. Another safeguard of minority interests is a Bylaw provision that directors may be removed only by a greater-than-majority vote of the shareholders and then only for "cause," that is, for conduct that is detrimental to the best interests of the corporation. This protects against removals for purely personal reasons. However, even purely personal reasons may interfere with the smooth operation of a corporation and so removal without cause may be appropriate.

9.4 OFFICERS

In General. The term "officer" is usually used to describe only the more important executives in the corporation. Typically, the term is used to describe those executives who are appointed directly by the board of directors. Older statutes specify the particular officer-ships that a corporation must have. For instance, many statutes require that there be a president, one or more Vice-presidents, a treasurer, and a secretary. But the modem trend is not to require specific named positions. For instance, both the RMBCA and Delaware leave it up to the board to determine what officers there shall be.[120] Whether or not the statute requires certain named Officers, nearly all statutes allow one person to hold multiple officer-ships simultaneously. In a closely-held corporation, for instance, the president will also commonly be the treasurer. The one exception is that the president and secretary are usually not permitted to be the same person. The reason is that the secretary's principal function is to certify that a person signing a document as chief executive officer is in fact that person; it would make little sense to allow A in his role as secretary to certify that he, A, is in fact the president/CEO, "an imposter would happily certify these facts."

According to the statutory scheme, the corporation's officers serve under and at the will of the board of directors and carry out the day-to-day operations of the corporation. In practice, of course, the officers frequently have much greater power than this implies, especially in large publicly-held corporations. But the important thing to remember is that, as far as most corporate statutes contemplate, the officers are essentially "agents" of the board of directors. A corporation's officers are responsible for carrying out its day-to-day affairs and are selected by the Board of Directors. Some states allow the shareholders of small, closely held corporations to select the corporation's officers directly, instead of requiring officers to be selected by the Board. A device that would protect incumbent officers is greater-than-majority quorum and vote requirements where the Board of Directors votes whether to dismiss an officer. Requiring a greater-than-majority vote would make a hasty dismissal difficult to obtain. However, consider whether the officer may deserve to be banished as soon as possible. Employment contracts with the corporation are further protection for officers. Each officer could be hired by the corporation pursuant to an employment contract specifying

120) See RMBCA, g 8.40(a); Del. GCL § 142(a).

standards of performance, salary, and grounds for dismissal. The contract could not prevent the Board of Directors from dismissing an officer, but if the Board did so without adequate grounds, the officer would be able to sue the corporation for damages and, perhaps, reinstatement.

Right to Hire and Remove. The board of directors has not only the power to appoint officers, but also the power to remove them, with or without cause. This is true even though the officer has an employment contract that is still in force - the board has authority to 6re the officer, but he in tum has the right to suc thc corporation for damages but not the right to specific performance, i.e., the right to be reinstated.

Authority to Act for Corporation. Recall that, under the traditional view, the corporation is managed by the board of directors, not by the officers. Therefore, even when an officer purports to act on behalf of the corporation and to bind the corporation, his action may not be legally sufficient to bind the corporation. Since the officer is an agent of his principal, the corporation, the office's authority to bind his principal is usually analyzed by use of traditional agency principals. The most important concept to keep in mind is that an officer, even the president, will not automatically have authority to bind the corporation to a transaction merely by virtue of his office. Only if one of the doctrines described below applies will the corporation be bound by the act of its officer. For, example, Brown, the treasurer of ABC Corporation, Promises Gray that ABC will guarantee a debt owed by Black to Gray. The mere fact that Brown is ABC Corporation's treasurer does not give him authority to bind ABC. therefore, unless Gray can show that Brown had express authority, implied actual authority, or apparent authority to bind ABC, or that the board subsequently ratified the Brown's action will not cause the corporation to be bound to honor the guarantee, even if Brown honestly believes that he had authority to bind the corporation, and even if Gray honestly believed Brown's statement that he, Brown, had authority.

DOCTRINES

There are four doctrines commonly used to hold that the officer has bound the corporation: (1) express actual authority; (2) implied actual authority; (3) apparent authority; and (4) ratification. We will consider each of these in turn.

Express Actual Authority. Express actual authority is the easiest concept to understand. Usually, this comes into existence by an explicit grant of authority to the officer to act on behalf of the corporation. This explicit grant generally comes from either the corporation's bylaws, or in the form of a resolution adopted by the board of directors. For example, the board adopts a resolution authorizing the Vice President to negotiate and sign a contract to dispose of one of the corporation's surplus plants. This board resolution constitutes a grant of express authority to the when he signs the contract on the corporation's behalf, the corporation will even if it is not usually the case, either generally or in this particular corporation, that vice presidents may sign contracts to sell plants.

Implied Actual Authority. The doctrine of "implied actual authority" is a much fuzzier one. It is often described as "authority which is inherent in the office." There are two common ways in which implied actual authority can come into existence: First, authority may be inherent in the particular post the officer, measured by common understandings of business people. For instance it is today commonly assumed that the president of a corporation has actual sign at least non-extraordinary contracts, e.g., contracts for the corporation to receive supplies that it needs in the ordinary course of its business. Therefore, if president signs such a supply contract on behalf of corporation, the court would probably hold that President had implied actual authority to though the board of directors never specifically authorized him to sign either this particular contract or any similar contract - authority to sign such contracts is simply found to be inherent in the presidency of a corporation.

Second, the board, by its own conduct or inaction, may have implicitly granted the actual authority to the officer in question. presidents in the business world are generally not permitted to sign contracts disposing of surplus plants, the fact that ABC's Corporation's board has allowed Vice President to do so in the past without objection, or the fact that the board has known that Vice President was about to sign the particular contract in question, would be enough to clothe Vice President with implied actual authority to sign the present contract on behalf of ABC.

There has been a lot of litigation about the inherent power of various corporate posts, especially the presidency. Traditionally, the president had little if any authority to bind the corporation merely by virtue of his office. However, this narrow view conflicted with what most non-lawyers thought the president could do. Therefore, the modern trend is to treat the president as having, by mere virtue of his position, at least the authority to bind the corporation in ordinary business transactions. Thus most courts today would probably hold that the president has implied authority, by virtue of his office, to hire and five non-officer-level employees; and the authority to enter into ordinary-course contracts, e.g., contracts to supply the business' ordinary raw materials requirements, or to sell part of the corporation's output. But other kinds of actions would, even under the more expansive modem rule, Probably be found to be "extraordinary" and thus not contracts to sell, lease or mortgage real estate; contracts to sell all of the corporation's assets; contracts to issue and distribute new stock; and agreements to settle important litigation.

There is no generally accepted rule about the inherent authority of the chairman of the board. The scope of this post varies dramatically from corporation to corporation - in some companies this post is held by the chief executive officer, with the president being the chief operating officer, or number two executive; in other cases the chairman is largely an honorary figure, who is not the C.E.O. In general, it is not safe to assume that the chairman has any inherent authority by virtue solely of his position. A vice president or a treasurer probably has little if any authority by virtue of his or her position. However, if a vice president has the appearance of standing close to the top of the corporate hierarchy, e.g., an Executive Vice President, he may under the modern, looser, approach to authority be held to have some limited authority in ordinary-course matters. The secretary has one key element of inherent authority in virtually every jurisdiction: He has inherent authority to certify the records of the corporation, including resolutions of the board of directors. Therefore, a secretary's certificate that a given resolution was duly adopted by the board is binding on the corporation in favor of a third party who relies on the certificate. But the secretary has no other inherent authority to bind the corporation.

For example, Drive-In, a subsidiary of another corporation, wants to induce Bank to make a loan to the parent corporation. Therefore, Dick, Drive-In's secretary, presents Bank with a copy of a resolution of Drive-In's board of directors guaranteeing the loan, together with Dick's certificate that the resolution was duly authorized by the board. Bank makes the loan, and Drive-In goes into bankruptcy. It turns out that the directors never in fact authorized the resolution. *Held*, Drive-In is bound on the guarantee. Dick was Drive-In's secretary. "Generally, it is the duty of the secretary to keep the corporate records and to make proper entries of the actions and resolutions of the directors." Therefore, it was within Dick's authority to certify that a resolution was adopted; statements made by an agent in the course of a transaction that was within the scope of his authority are binding on the principal. Therefore, Drive-In was bound even if its board never in fact adopted the resolution.[121)]

However, suppose that the person receiving a secretary's certification knows that the board action being certified could not possibly have occurred. In this situation, a court would probably not hold the corporation bound by the secretary's certification. Thus on the facts of Drive-In, supra, had Bank known that a majority of Drive-In's directors were out of town when

121) *In re Drive-In Development Corp.*, 371 F.2d 217 (7th Cir. 1966).

the resolution was supposedly enacted, or had Bank been told by one of the directors that the resolution had not been adopted, Bank would have probably lost, notwithstanding the certificate. The reason is that the binding of the corporation to actions certified by the secretary is often based on principles of estoppel, the corporation is "estopped" to deny the correctness of its secretary's certification, and estoppel is an equitable doctrine, the benefits of which will be denied where justice requires. Where the other party has not relied on the certificate, justice would presumably require not applying the estoppel doctrine.

Apparent Authority. A third way in which the officer may bind the corporation is by the doctrine of apparent authority. Under this doctrine, when the actions of a principal (the corporation) give the appearance to as he is acting, the principal is held responsible for creating the impression that the agent had actual authority to act; therefore, the principal may not avoid the transaction. Thus for the third party to successfully invoke the apparent doctrine, he will have to show that: (1) the corporation, by acts other than the officer, indicated to the world that the of6cer had authority to do the act in question; and (2) the plaintiff was aware of those corporate indications and relied on them.

Sometimes, the plaintiff will be able to point to specific, affirmative conduct by the corporation that indicates to the world that the officer has the authority in question. For instance, if the board of directors is aware that Vice President has routinely been signing large contracts to buy raw materials, and the board does not object, a supplier who can show this past pattern of acquiescence, and who can show he was aware of it at the time of his own contract, would probably succeed in arguing that Vice President had apparent authority. But often, the mere post held by the officer, when coupled with industry enough to create apparent authority. This is most likely to happen where the action is by the company's president, and the action is of a sort that presidents are usually permitted to take.

For example, the board of directors of Corporation appoints Smith as president. The chairman's son has long held the post of vice president for Office Supplies, Smith is handed a board resolution expressly denying that Smith has any authority whatsoever to purchase office supplies for Corporation. Nonetheless, Smith, introducing himself to Supplier as president of Corporation, orders office supplies. Supplier does not know of the special limitation on Smith's authority.

Assume as is probably the case that by custom, a person holding the title of president will in most corporations have actual authority to order office supplies. If so, supplier will probably be able to bind corporation to the contract Smith signed with him, on an apparent authority theory. The board of directors, by clothing Smith with the title of "president," has indicated to the world that Smith has the authority usually found in that post. If the board wishes to deny Smith that authority, it must bear the burden of communicating to the world, including to Supplier, that Smith does not have this customary presidential authority, observe that on these facts. Corporation is bound under the apparent authority doctrine even though it is absolutely clear that Smith did not have any kind of actual authority, not even implied actual authority, because of the resolution.

For the apparent authority doctrine to apply, it is not sufficient that the agent himself represents to the third party that he has authority to enter into the transaction. The indications of authority must come from someone else in a position of power at the corporation. Thus if Vice President tells Supplier "I have full authority to contract for the purchase of office supplies," this representation does not create apparent authority, since Supplier should know that Vice President may simply be lying or mistaken about the degree of his authority. If, on the other hand, the board of directors had appointed him with the title Vice President of Supplies and given him a business card with that title, a person who saw and relied on the card would probably succeed in establishing apparent authority.

As we saw in the example involving Smith and the supplies, supra, the mere fact that an officer has been given a common title, e.g., President, will itself be enough to give him apparent authority to do certain transactions. In the case of an officer bearing the title of president, the usual modem rule is that the president has apparent authority "to take actions in the ordinary course of business, but not extraordinary actions." But where is the line between "extraordinary" and "ordinary"? "A useful generalization is that decisions that would make a significant change in the structure of the business enterprise, or the structure of control over the enterprise, are extraordinary corporate actions and therefore normally outside the president's apparent authority." Thus the issuance or re-purchase of shares by the corporation, the taking on of significant debt, the making of significant capital investments, the sale of one of the corporation's significant businesses, or its entry into an important new time of business, would all be "extraordinary," and thus not within the president's apparent authority, in most circumstances.

Observe that a similar "extraordinary vs. ordinary" test is also used to determine whether the president has implied actual authority to take a particular action. But even though a given act by a president will often indicate that he has both implied actual authority, by virtue of his position, and apparent authority, the two doctrines are not the same. Implied actual authority can always be negated by an express board resolution to the contrary; but the board third person who is relying. In the final analysis, it will often be a question of fact for the jury whether, taking into account all the circumstances, the officer had apparent authority to do the act in question. That is, there are many situations that are so close to the blurry line between "extraordinary" and "ordinary course" transactions that it cannot be said as a matter of law that the transaction falls into the one class or the other.

For example, in 1955, P, an individual, brings suit against D Corporation P alleges that in 1920, Yardley, then the president and chairman of D, as well as a substantial stockholder in it, Promised P that if P would leave his existing job to come to work for D, D would pay P a pension of $1500 a year when he reached the age of 60. P was 30 at the time of the promise.

Because P would be forfeiting a pension with his existing employer, Yardley told P, P says, that P would be entitled to the pension even if he was not still working with the company at the age of 60. P in fact works for D Corporation for 25 years, until he is discharged at the age of 55. Yardley is dead by the time of trial, and P is the only source of testimony about the original pension understanding, D defends on the grounds that Yardley did not have authority to bind the corporation to such an arrangement. Held, the question of whether Yardley had apparent authority to make this contract, assuming that its making is proved, is a question of fact for the jury. Since there has been no showing of actual authority, P can win only by showing that Yardley had apparent authority to make this contract. The general rule is that "the president only has [apparent] authority to bind his company by acts arising in the usual and regular course of business but not for contracts of an 'extraordinary' nature." Employment contracts for life are usually regarded as "extraordinary" and therefore beyond the president's apparent authority. On the other hand, the agreement here was not a lifetime employment contract, but merely a contract to pay a pension of at most $1500 dollars, assuming that P worked for D for a reasonable time.

Apparent authority is essentially a question of fact, which depends on "the officer negotiating [the contract] the corporation's usual manner of conducting business, the size of the corporation and the number of its stockholders, the circumstances that give rise to the contract, the reasonableness of the contract, the amounts involved ... to list a few ... of the relevant factors." Here, D had just entered into a new line of business that it had no experience with, and it looked to P as an experienced executive who could help it. Therefore the court cannot say as a matter of law that Yardley as president did not have apparent authority to make the agreement; the case should thus have been heard by the jury, not decided against P by the trial court.[122)]

122) *Lee v. Jenkins Bros.*, 268 F.2d 357 (2d Cir. 1959).

The problem of determining whether an officer has apparent authority can also be thought of in economic terms: Arguably, the court should impose the risk of being wrong on the apparent authority issue on that party, the corporation or the third party, who could avoid a mistake more cheaply, If on particular facts it would be cheaper for the corporation to make sure that third parties know the scope of the officer's actual authority, the corporation should bear the burden, by being bound under the apparent authority doctrine; if, on the other hand, it would be cheaper for the third party to initiate inquiries, it is he who should bear the loss, by not being allowed to use the apparent authority doctrine.

Ratification. Suppose that at the time an officer acts on behalf of the corporation he has neither actual nor apparent authority. The corporation may nonetheless be bound by its subsequent actions, under the doctrine of "ratification." Under this doctrine, if a person with actual authority to enter into the transaction learns of the transaction and either expressly affirms it or even fails to disavow it, the court may find that the corporation is bound.

: In most of the cases where the ratification doctrine is applied, either or both of two special factors is present: (1) the corporation has received benefits under the contract, which it has not returned; or (2) the third party has relied to his detriment on the existence of the contract. However, strictly speaking the mere after-the-fact approval or acquiescence of the board ought to suffice, even without either of these two special factors. Of course, the plaintiff who is claiming ratification must show that the ratifier had full knowledge of the contract. For instance, if the board knows that the president has signed a contract to acquire a company from X, but does not know that the president is receiving a kickback from X or does not know that the contract calls for the corporation to pay a very excessive price, a court would probably not find that the board's mere failure to object constituted ratification.

The above discussion demonstrates that authority is a tricky concept , a third party will often find it hard to be certain that the corporation officer he is dealing with really has authority to bind the corporation to the proposed transaction. However, there is one "bullet-proof way in which a third party can be certain that the corporation will be bound: He should "require the person purporting to act for the corporation to deliver, Prior to the closing of the transaction, a certified copy of a resolution of the board of directors authorizing the transaction in question or directing the named officer to enter into the transaction on behalf of the corporation. The certificate should be executed by the secretary or an assistant secretary of the corporation, the corporate seal should be affixed, and the certificate should recite the date of the meeting, or a statement that the resolution was approved by unanimous written consent, and quote the resolution itself."

The reason that such a certificate is binding on the corporation is that, in all states, the corporation is estopped to deny the correctness of its secretary's certification that a particular resolution was adopted by the board.

SHARING OF RESPONSIBILITY.

It might sound as though Shareholders have very little ability to influence the corporation's affairs, apart from election and removal of directors. However, there are a number of additional ways in which shareholders at least get to share some of the power over corporate operations:

Shareholder resolutions. Shareholders cannot require the directors or officers to take any particular action during the corporation's day-to-day operations. However, shareholders can seek to influence the board by exercising their light to adopt Share-holder resolutions that recommend particular actions to the board. For example, the board of directors of the Hoe Corporation removes X from his post as president. The Ps, who hold a majority of class A stock in the company, seek to put to a shareholder vote a resolution endorsing X and requesting X's reinstatement as president among other actions. Held, for the Ps. It is true that the stockholders do not have the direct power to require the board to reinstate X as president. But they are entitled to vote to pass a resolution recommending that action to the board, if only as a way to signal their desires to the board and, in effect, to warn the directors who will soon be standing for election that this is what the shareholders desire.[123)]

Self-interested transactions. Also, transactions in which the board or officers are personally interested are almost always put to a shareholder vote. Thus incentive compensation plans that cover officers, and arrangements whereby the corporation indemnifies directors or officers against liability, are almost always put to a Share-holder vote. If such a transaction in which directors or officers are personally interested is ratified by the shareholders, this generally does not completely immunize the planned transaction against attack. But individual shareholders who vote for it can't attack the transaction later on; also, approval may make it harder for opposing shareholders to attack the transaction on grounds of general unfairness, by shifting the burden of proof to them from management. But a court will still set aside a transaction involving officers or directors that is fraudulent or "manifestly unfair."

Fundamental changes. Lastly, shareholders are always given the power to approve or disapprove of certain fundamental changes m the corporation. For instance, in most states the following kinds of changes are ineffective without shareholder approval: (1) mergers; (2) sales of all or substantially all of the corporation's assets; (3) amendments of the articles of incorporation; (4) statutory share exchanges, in which all Shareholders are required to exchange

---

123) *Auer v. Dressel,* 118N.B.2d 590 (N.Y. 1954).

Case Synopsis. Appellants, corporation and president, sought review of the order of the Appellate Division of the Supreme Court in the First Judicial Department (New York) that affirmed a supreme court at special term, which granted appellee class-A stockholders' motion for an order under N.Y. Civ. Prac. Act art. 78 requiring appellants to call a special meeting of class-A stockholders.

Facts. Appellees were class-A stockholders of appellant corporation. Appellees brought an action for an order to compel appellant president to comply with a positive duty imposed on him by appellant corporation's bylaws. The bylaws required that the president call a special meeting whenever requested in writing to do so by stockholders owning a majority of the capital stock entitled to vote at such meeting. Appellees had requested such a meeting but appellant president failed to call the meeting. The trial court ordered the meeting and appellants sought review of that order.

Discussion. The court held that the bylaws did not allow any discretion to appellant president as to whether or not to call the meeting when one was demanded. The court held that the purposes for which appellees wished the meeting called were proper. Thus, court held that the order requiring the meeting to be held was proper.

Conclusion. The court affirmed the order that required appellants to call a special meeting of class-A stockholders of the company, holding that since appellees submitted a written request to appellants as required by the bylaws, appellants had no discretion as to whether or not to call a meeting.

their shares for those in another corporation; and (5) dissolution of the corporation. But observe that in most states the power to effect these changes does not reside exclusively in the shareholders. Only if the board of directors first decides to put the matter to a shareholder vote does the vote occur. This is sometimes referred to as the board of directors' "Safekeeping" function.[124)]

9.5 THE BOARD OF DIRECTORS

In General. The board of directors is not legally the agent of the shareholders. So the board can act within its power to run the corporation, even if the majority of the shareholders disapprove.[125)] If the shareholders want to change the board, they may elect different directors at the next annual meeting or try to remove the directors by the calling a special meeting prior to the annual meeting. Generally the statues allow for removal of directors for cause, but they also may provide for removal by the shareholders without cause.[126)] Prior to the statutory enactments on removal, courts found an inherent right to remove directors for cause because shareholders, as owners, had the right to protect the corporation.[127)] However, once elected as directors, directors as fiduciaries to the corporation. Thus they have to serve the best interests of the corporation, including all its shareholders and not merely the interests of those who elect them.

Election of Board Members. As mentioned, members of the board of directors are always elected by the shareholders with the possible exception of the filling of vacancies. Normally, a director's term is one year, and the entire

124) See, e.g., RMBCA § 11.03(b)(1). Shareholders only get to vote if the board submits the proposed merger or share exchange to them.

125) *See People ex rel. Manice v. Powell.* 94 N.E. 634 (N.Y. 1911).

126) RMBCA § 8.08.

127) *See Auer v. Dressel,* 118 N.E.2d. 852 (1957).

board stands for re-election at the annual meeting of shareholders. Before we get into the intricacies of board elections, understand that the stockholder vote to elect directors must satisfy the same basic procedural requirements as a stockholder vote to take any other action, e.g., to approve the sale of the company. Therefore, proper notice of the time and place of the meeting must be given to all Shareholders.[128] A quorum must be present. That is, more than 50% of the shares eligible to rote must be "present," either in person or via a valid proxy.[129] The vote for directors may either be "straight" or "cumulative," depending on the state's corporation statute and the articles of incorporation.

In straight voting, each share may be voted for as many candidates as there are slots on the board, but no share may be voted more than once for any given candidate. Directors are elected by a plurality (not necessarily majority) of the votes cast.[130] Each share has one vote. For example, in a closely-held corporation, A and B are the sole shareholders. A holds 72 shares and B holds 28. The board has three directors. A's candidates are A1, A2 and A3; B's candidates are B1, B2 and B3. If there is straight voting, A cannot cast more than 72 votes for any single candidate, and (most importantly), B cannot cast more than 28 votes for any candidate. Therefore, A's three candidates will receive 72 votes each, B's three candidates will receive 28 votes each, and A's candidates wilt get all the seats on the board.

In cumulative voting, the result in the above example looks pretty unfair to B. Although he has almost one-third of the votes, he has no representation on the board, In fact, even if he had 49 votes to A's 51, he still would not get a board seat under straight voting, since each of A's candidates would receive 51 votes and each of B's would get 49. To remedy this inadequate representation of minority shareholders, the device of cumulative voting was invented. As the name implies, cumulative voting entitles a shareholder to

128) RMBCA § 7.05(a).

129) RMBCA § 7.25(a).

130) *See* RMBCA § 7.28(a).

cumulate or aggregate his votes in favor of fewer candidates than there are slots available, including in the extreme case aggregating all of his votes for just one candidate. The consequences are that a minority shareholder is far more likely to be able to obtain at least one seat on the board. For example, assume the same facts as the above example: A has 72 votes, B has 28 votes and there are three directors to be elected. This time, however, cumulative voting is permitted. B can therefore take his entire "package" of 84 votes, 28 shares x three seats, and put it all on his single favorite candidate, whom we'll call B1. B1 therefore has 84 votes. Now, no matter how A divides up his 216 votes, 72 shares x 3 seats, he cannot come up with three candidates all of whom beat B 1. For instance, if he casts 85votes for A1 and 85 votes for A2, the minimum necessary for A1 and A2 to beat B1, he has used up 170 votes, and has only 46 votes left to put on A3. Therefore, even though B has only 28% of the shares and 28% of the total votes castable in the election, he is assured of at least one seat on a three-seat board by the device of cumulative voting.

Number of Directors. Traditionally, most statutes require that there be at least three directors. But today, many states allow a board to consist of less than three so long as it is equal to the number of shareholders, thus a one-shareholder corporation can have one director and a two-shareholder corporation can have two directors. [131)]A substantial and growing minority of states, in fact, now allows a corporation to have a one or two-member board even if there are more than two Shareholders.[132)] There seems little reason to require that there be more than one or two board members merely because there are, say, three shareholders. For instance, Suppose that A owns all the stock of a corporation, and is the sole director, If he makes a gift of a few shares to each of his children, all of a sudden he would have to expand his board to three, a move that has no business justification. Actually, the

131) California and New York are among these states.

132) *See* Delaware §141(b) and the RMBCA §8.03(a).

number of directors is usually fixed either in the articles of incorporation or in the bylaws. Most statutes leave it up to the corporation whether this should be done in the articles or the bylaws.[133] Observe that if the number is specified in the articles, it may only be changed by shareholder vote; but if it is set in the bylaws, it may usually be changed by the board itself, under the board's general power to amend bylaws.

However, corporation statutes sometimes prevent the board from making very large changes in its size without shareholder approval, even if the bylaws allow the board to change the number of directors. For instance, provides that even if the board has power to change the number of directors, it may increase or decrease the board only by thirty percent or less without shareholder approval. [134]Most statutes allow the articles of incorporation or bylaws to set a minimum and maximum size for the board, rather than a fixed size. When this approach is followed, either the shareholders or the board may adjust the size within the range, but only the shareholders may change the range itself.[135] Observe that the RMBCA's handling of changes in the number of directors leaves some scope for the board to make modest changes, but requires shareholder approval for large changes. This is true whether the corporation uses a fixed or variable number of directors. Thus under the RMBCA scheme the board may usually decide whether to fill one or a small number of vacancies without seeking shareholder approval but may not dramatically expand the power of incumbent directors, by refusing to fill a large number of vacancies, without going back to the shareholders.[136]

Filling of Vacancies. Most statutes allow vacancies on the board to be filled either by the shareholders or by the board, unless the articles of incorporation provide otherwise.[137] Some statutes let the replacement director serve the full

133) *See* e.g., RMBCA § 8.03(a).

134) RMBCA § 8.03(b).

135) RMBCA § 8.03(c) follows this pattern.

136) *See* RMBCA § 8.03(b).

137) *See* e.g., RMBCA § 8.10(a).

unexpired term of his predecessor. Others require him to stand for re-election at the next annual meeting. The two rules differ only where the board is staggered; if A resigns with two and one-half years left on his three-year term, his successor gets to serve the full two and one-half years, whereas under the latter rule he must stand for re-election in six months. The statute requires that the replacement stand for re-election at the next annual meeting.[138)]

Some statutes distinguish between vacancies created by the board is increased a "new" vacancy. States making this distinction usually allow the board to fill old vacancies but not new vacancies. But many states have abolished this distinction; explicitly giving the board the right to fill vacancies "resulting from an increase in the number of directors."[139)]

In many corporations, especially closely-held ones, a key control device is that each separate class of stock is entitled to elect a certain number of directors. For instance, if a closely-held corporation has A and B classes of stock, the B shareholders might be given the light to elect four of nine board members, even though they had only 25% of the total voting power of the corporation.

If a class has the right to elect a specified number of directors, then only that class may vote to fill a vacancy arising from the resignation of one of the directors elected by the class assuming that it is the shareholders, rather than the board, that fill vacancies. [140)]For example, the class A stockholders of the corporation have the exclusive right to elect nine of the eleven members of the board with the common stockholders having the right to elect the remaining two members. A majority of the class A stockholders petition the court to allow a vote for the removal of four of the directors for cause. They also petition for the right to amend the bylaws so that if these four directors are removed for cause, only the class A Shareholders will be permitted to vote

138) RMBCA: § 8.05(d).

139) *See* e.g., RMBCA § 8.10(a).

140) *See* RMBCA § 8.10(b).

to fill the resulting vacancies. Held, for the petitioning class A shareholders. Since the class A shareholders have the exclusive right to elect the four directors now sought to be removed, it is appropriate that they have the sole right to elect any successors.[141)]

A director may normally submit a dated resignation, that is, a resignation that is to take effect at some future time. The key advantage of such a prospective resignation is that the resigning director may participate in the election of his successor always assuming, of course, that the board is authorized, as is usually the case, to fill vacancies.[142)] This is particularly important where, without the vote of the soon-to-resign director, the board would be deadlocked between competing factions.

Any board action normally requires a quorum, and that's true of votes by the board to elect new directors to fill board vacancies. Well, what happens if so many directors resign without 6rst voting for their successors, or otherwise leave the board, that a quorum of the board is no longer possible? Most states have a special rule saying that in this situation, the vacancy can be filled by majority vote of the remaining directors, even though no quorum is present.

Virtually all states provide that a director holds office not only for the term for which he is elected, but until his successor is elected and qualified. A director serving beyond the end of his term is called a holdover director. "Despite the expiration of a director's term, he continues to serve until his successor is elected and qualifies or until there is a decrease in the number of directors."[143)] Without the holdover device, a corporation could become completely deadlocked. For instance, if there were two factions with equal voting power, one faction could refuse to attend an annual meeting or to vote for directors, and the absence of a quorum at the shareholders meeting would prevent any election from taking place; holdover directors would then be the

141) *Auer v. Dressel,* 118 N.E.Zd 590 (N.Y. 1954).

142) *See* RMBCA § 8.10(c).

143) *See,* e.g., RMBCA § 8.05(e).

only directors. Of course, the holdover provision means that in this kind of deadlock situation, the original directors would remain in office forever; the remedy might well be involuntary dissolution of the corporation

Removal of Directors. When may a director be removed? Most statutes allow this to be done by either a shareholder vote or by court order. Most modem statutes provide that directors may be removed by a majority vote of shareholders, either with or without cause. RMBCA says that "The shareholders may remove one or more directors with or without cause unless the articles of incorporation provide that directors may be removed only for cause."[144] Even the minority of jurisdictions whose statutes do not allow Shareholders to remove directors without cause in all circumstances allow it if this right is reserved in the articles of incorporation. However, removal-of-director provisions are generally drafted so as to prevent the majority from understanding the effect of cumulative voting and other minority-protection devices.

To remove a director, it's not necessary that a majority of all shares outstanding be voted against the director, only that a majority of those votes actually cast be against the director. This is an application of the more general rule, that when an action requires shareholder approval, only a majority of shares actually voted, not a majority of shares outstanding, need be voted in favor. Also, keep in mind that a shareholder vote to remove a director requires the same formalities, e.g., a shareholders meeting, as any other shareholder action. In fact some statutes say that there must be a special meeting of shareholders, at which the removal of the director is one of the stated purposes of the meeting.[145]

There are at least two situations in which the Shareholders' power to remove directors without cause has a sharp practical significance. First, when through a friendly or unfriendly takeover, control of the corporation shifts,

---

144) RMBCA § 8.08(a).

145) *See,* e.g., RMBCA § 8.08(d), to this effect.

this right of removal allows the new controlling owner to replace directors with "friendly" directors of his own choosing. Secondly, in a closely-held corporation, the Controlling shareholder(s) will frequently want to make sure that directors he elects remain "friendly" to him; the unrestricted right of removal helps ensure this. Modem statutes also generally say that a court may order a. director removed, but only for cause. For example, RMBCA says that the court may order a director removed as the result of a proceeding commenced either by the corporation or by a 10% shareholder, if the court finds both that: (1) the director "engaged in fraudulent or dishonest conduct, or gross abuse of authority or discretion," and (2) "removal is in the best interest of the corporation."[146)]

Since the shareholders may remove the director without cause, why would a judicial proceeding ever be necessary? There are two situations in which judicial action is the only or better method of removing a director: First, the director may be a shareholder and may possess such voting power that he can block removal by shareholder vote. For instance if the director was elected by cumulative voting and votes he controls were sufficient by themselves to elect him under the cumulative scheme he will be able to block his removal by casting the same number of votes. Second, recall that the director can only be removed if a special shareholders' meeting occurs. If the corporation is publicly-held, and the director refuses to resign when requested to do so, this special meeting will involve considerable delay and expense.[147)] Especially, states generally do not allow the board itself to remove a director.

Procedures for a Directors' Meeting. We now examine the procedural requirements for the holding of a directors' meeting, including (1) frequency of meeting; (2) notice; and (3) quorum. There are two types of board meetings: regular and special. A regular board meeting is one which occurs at a regular interval, e.g., monthly, quarterly or annually. All other meetings

---

146) RMBCA § 8.09.

147) *See* Official Comment to RMBCA § 8.09.

are "special." The frequency for regular meetings is generally specified in the bylaws. The main distinction between regular and special meetings is that a special meeting must normally be preceded by notice to the board members, whereas this is not necessary for a regular meeting. Thus RMBCA provides that a special meeting must be preceded by "at least two days' notice of the date, time and place," unless the articles or bylaws provide for a longer or shorter notice period.[148)]

In any event, a director may waive the required notice in writing. Also, if a director attends the meeting without objecting to the lack of notice, he will generally be held to have thereby waived notice. Attendance constitutes waiver unless the director not only objects upon his arrival but also refrains from voting in favor of, or assenting to, the proposed action at the meeting.[149)] The notice of a special directors' meeting need not specify the business to be transacted at the meeting, and any business may in fact be transacted. This is quite different from the rule governing notices of shareholders' meetings. As a result there is little practical difference between regular and special meetings of directors.

The board of directors may act only if a quorum is present. If the board has a fixed size, a quorum is a majority of that fixed number. This is true even though there are vacancies on the board at the moment. For example, the articles of incorporation of C Corporation provide that it shall have a nine-member board. At the time of a particular directors' meeting, there are two vacancies. A quorum consists of five, not four, board members, since there must be a majority of the total number of seats, not the number of sitting directors. But if the articles set up a variable-she board, a quorum is generally set as a majority of the directors in office at the start of the meeting.[150)]

Some states, but probably still a minority, now allow the articles of

148) RMBCA § 8.22(b).

149) *See,* e.g., RMBCA § 8.23(b).

150) See, e.g., RMBCA § 8.24(a)(2).

incorporation or bylaws to specify a percentage that is less than a majority as the quorum. For instance, both Delaware and the RMBCA allow the articles of incorporation or bylaws to establish any percentage that is one-third or greater as the quorum. [151]Conversely, statutes often permit the articles or bylaws to establish a quorum of more than a majority.[152] Such a provision could be used as a control device in a closely-held corporation. For instance, the bylaws could be amended to provide that all three directors must be present for a quorum; this way, a minority shareholder who controls one seat could actively block corporate action by refusing to attend directors' meetings.

The quorum must be present at the time a vote is taken in order for the vote to constitute the act of the board. Thus even if a quorum is present at the start of a meeting, directors may, by leaving, remove the quorum and thereby prevent further board action. A different rule applies to shareholders' meetings, at which all that counts is that a quorum be present at the start of the meeting. We said just above that the board of directors may not take action unless a quorum is present. There is one exception to this rule: In most states, the board may fill a vacancy even though less than a quorum of directors is present. Carefully-drafted statutes make it clear that this light exists only where the number of directors in office is less than a quorum; other statutes leave open the possibility that a vacancy may be filled if less than a quorum is present at the meeting, even though more than a quorum is in office. For example, Corporation has a board whose fixed size is six directors. A quorum would therefore be four. There are two vacancies at the moment. Under the RMBCA, three directors at a "meeting" may not fill the vacancy, the number of directors in office is not less than a quorum, even though the number of directors at the "meeting" is.[153]

---

151) Delaware § 141(b) and the RMBCA § 8.24(b).

152) *See*, e.g., RMBCA § 8.24(a).

153) *See* RMBCA § 8.10(a)(3) and Official Comment thereto.

But some older statutes might be interpreted to allow the three members to fill the vacancies. Observe that under the RMBCA approach, on these facts a single board member could prevent the board from ever taking action; by staying away, he could prevent there ever being a quorum to fill the vacancies; therefore the vacancies could never be filled, so there could never be a quorum for purposes other than election of directors. Eventually, however, the shareholders could fill the vacancies.

Formalities for Board Action. Normally, the board of directors may take action only at a meeting, not by individual action of the directors, only by vote of a majority of the directors present at the meeting.[154)] However, many modem statutes allow the articles of incorporation to specify a higher percentage than a majority for all or certain board actions. For instance, RMBCA allows a higher number to be required by either the articles of incorporation or the bylaws.[155)] Directors, unlike shareholders, may not vote by proxy. The impact of this requirement is illustrated by the classic case set out in the following example.[156)]

For example, the Minneapolis Agricultural Mechanical Association (MAMA) owns, as its sole valuable asset, some real estate. All the shares of MAMA are owned by King. King borrows money from the State National Bank, and pledges his stock in MAMA with Baldwin, the bank's cashier. King contracts to have MAMA sell the real estate owned by it to Canfield in return for $65,000 in railroad bonds. No board meeting of MAMA is ever held to discuss the sale of the property. However, King causes each board member, at different times and places, to sign a deed to the property as directors. King gives this deed to Canfield, receives the bonds from him, and disappears without paying back the loan to Baldwin or the bank. Baldwin and the bank sue Canfield to obtain a ruling that the deed was not validly conveyed by

154) *See*, e.g., RMBCA § 8.24(c).

155) *See* RMBCA § 8.24(c).

156) *Baldwin v. Canfield,* 1 N.W. 261 (Minn. 1879).

MAMA to Canfield. Held, for Baldwin and the bank.

The members of a corporation's board of directors "have no authority to act, save when assembled at a board meeting. The separate action, individually, of the persons composing such governing body is not the action of the [board.]" Since the deed was never authorized by board action, it was invalid, so Canfield has paid the bond over to King for nothing in return![157]

Clearly, the lawyers for Baldwin and his bank on the one hand, and Canfield on the other, were guilty of sloppiness if not negligence. Since King was the holder of all the shares, and could have controlled the corporation's action, Baldwin and his bank should have gotten a security interest, a mortgage, directly m the real estate, rather than merely accepting a pledge of the corporation's shares. The lawyering for Canfield was even worse. At a bare minimum that lawyer should have gotten a copy of the resolution of the board of directors of MAMA authorizing the sale, together with a certificate from the corporate secretary reciting that the action was taken by a majority of the directors at a meeting for which a proper notice and quorum existed. This certificate and accompanying resolution would have been binding on the corporation even had the meeting not taken place, since the corporate secretary can bind the corporation by his certification that a resolution was duly passed. Why should there be a rule that the directors must act during a duly-convened meeting rather than as separate individuals? The traditional rationale for this requirement is that "the decision-making process is likely to function better when the directors consult with and react to one another. A group discussion of problems is thought to be needed, not just a series of yea or nay responses."

For instance, in Baldwin, had there been a real directors' meeting to discuss the proposed sale by the corporation of its only property, the directors might have insisted that the contract be redrafted to reflect the corporation as seller, and to make sure that the proceeds came to the corporation, so that they could be paid out as dividends to shareholders. The bank, as pledgee

157) *Baldwin v. Canfield,* 1 N.W. 261 (Minn. 1879).

of all the stock, would then have received these dividends to apply against King's debt.

Under modem statutes there are a few exceptions to the general rule that directors may act only by duly-convened meeting. First, nearly all states now provide that directors may act without a meeting if they give their unanimous written consent to the proposed corporate action.[158] Observe that because the written consents must be unanimous, a single director who opposes the action can, in effect, require that a meeting be held to discuss the action. Also, note that under this RMBCA provision,[159] the consent does not become effective until the last director has signed the consent; therefore, the consent method cannot be used as a means of ratifying a purported corporate action that has taken place before all directors have signed, e.g., a conveyance like that in Baldwin. However, the doctrines of ratification and estoppel will, if they apply at all, have a retroactive effect in this situation.

Many states now permit the directors to act by means of a telephone conference call. For instance, RMBCA authorizes the conducting of a meeting by use of "any means of communication by which all directors participating may simultaneously hear each other during the meeting."[160] This is not really an exception to the requirement of the meeting, but rather a re-definition of what constitutes a "meeting," the main purpose of a meeting, that board members be able to simultaneously discuss the proposed matter, is of course carried out when the meeting occurs telephonically. But if less than a quorum were to decide a matter among themselves, and then poll the absent board members by phone one at a time, this would probably not qualify as a telephonic meeting under most statutes, since the element of simultaneous discussions by a quorum would not be present.

In a sense, the related doctrines of ratification, estoppel and acquiescence,

---

158) *See*, e.g., RMBCA § 8.21(a), allowing this unanimous written consent procedure unless the articles of incorporation or bylaws prohibit it.

159) RMBCA § 8.21(a).

160) RMBCA § 8.20(b).

may serve as a substitute for a formal vote of the board at a duly-convened meeting. For instance, suppose that the president of the corporation signs a major contract to buy property without prior board approval. Suppose further that the board members lean of this transaction, but neither vote on it nor disapprove of it in any way. The corporation would probably be estopped from claiming that the transaction is void because it did not receive the required board approval. These cases are usually decided on the theory that the board has impliedly authorized the president to act on its behalf, rather than on the theory that the board has acted without a formal vote, but the result is the same: the transaction is valid just as if the board had formally voted upon it.

Objection by Director. A director may sometimes wish to disassociate herself from action taken by the board, because she feels that the action is unwise, illegal, or a breach of fiduciary duty. It may be quite important for the director to register her dissent, because if she does not do so, she may be personally liable for the board's action even though she remained silent or orally voiced reservations. Therefore, the director in this situation should either submit a formal written dissent or abstention, or should make sure that her oral dissent or abstention is entered in the minutes of the meeting.[161)]

Composition of the Board. Board members of a publicly-held corporation can be thought of as falling into three categories: (1) insiders, executives or employees of the corporation; (2) "quasi-insiders," i.e., People who have some other significant relationship with the Corporation or its chief executive, e.g., the corporation's lawyer or investment banker; and (3) true "outsiders," i.e., those who do not fall into either of the two previous classes. Traditionally, corporate boards were usually dominated by insiders and quasi-insiders. This structure was often criticized on the grounds that it led to a board that merely "rubber stamped" management's decisions, rather than acting as a truly independent force.

---

161) *See* RMBCA § 8.24(d)(2) and (3).

Today, especially among the large publicly held corporations, the trend is to have a majority of true outsiders on the board. For instance, a majority of the boards of most New York Stock Exchange-listed companies is today composed of true outside directors. The ALI's *Principles of Corporate Governance* recommend that even small publicly-held corporations should have at least three directors who are "free of any significant relationship with the corporation's senior executives," i.e., class (3) above.[162]

COMMITTEES

In General. Boards increasingly tend to appoint committees of their members to carry out certain board functions. A committee typically consists of three or more board members and is given authority to take certain specified action on behalf of the board. The two most common kinds of committees are the audit and the compensation committees. Executive and nominating committees are also frequently appointed. There are two main rationales for this increasing use of committees: (1) boards, especially those of large publicly-held corporations, are frequently so large as to be unwieldy, and meet too seldom to stay on top of the corporation's affairs; and (2) some kinds of board actions, e.g., compensation of senior executives, are best handled outside the presence of senior management, and therefore are best handled by a committee composed solely of independent directors.

The RMBCA demonstrates the modem trend of facilitating the use of committees. The RMBCA allows the appointment of committees by the board unless the articles of incorporation or the bylaws specifically prohibit them.[163] With a few exceptions, "each committee may exercise the authority of the board of directors...." [164]However, a majority of the entire sitting hoard must approve the creation of a committee and the appointment of members

162) *See* ALI's *Principles of Corporate Governance* § 3A.01(b).

163) RMBCA § 8.25(a).

164) RMBCA § 8.25(d).

to it.[165] That is it is not enough that a committee is approved by a majority of the directors present at a meeting containing a quorum, the standard for other types of board action. This requirement of an absolute majority reflects the serious authority which can be and often is entrusted to committees.

Under the RMBCA, committees are not allowed to take certain very important types of actions. Some of these off-limits actions include: (1) filling vacancies on the board; (2) amending the articles of incorporation or the bylaws; (3) approving or proposing to shareholders actions that require shareholder approval; and (4) authorizing the issuance or re-purchase of shares.[166] The basic idea behind these limits is to "prohibit delegation of important actions that cannot be overruled or overturned by the board of directors." But even with these limitations, committees can take some very important actions in the name of the board, without separate board approval. For instance, a committee may authorize the corporation to take on tone-term debt or to make a large capital investment; it may set the price at which shares shall be issued, so long as the whole board has approved the issuance; it may appoint or remove senior management, and fix the salary of these executives.[167]

Audit Committee. Probably the most commonly-encountered committee is the audit committee. For example, the New York Stock Exchange now company to have an audit committee composed entirely of independent directors, and probably most non-NYSE middle-sized and large corporations have also appointed such a committee. The audit committee typically meets regularly with the Corporation's outside auditors to review the corporation's financial statements and the audit process. The corporation's outside auditors are usually hired and fired by senior management. Therefore, without an audit committee, there is a real chance that management will try to conceal

165) RMBCA § 8.25(b).

166) RMBCA § 8.25(e).

167) *See* Official Comment to RMBCA § 8.25.

its shortcomings by pressuring the auditors to paint an unduly rosy picture of the corporation's performance. Since audit committee meetings take place outside of the presence of management, the independent directors on the committee can ask the kind of embarrassing questions "Are earnings being properly stated?" "Are there any contingent liabilities which management hasn't told us about?" that directors would probably not ask at a full board meeting.

Nominating Committee. A nominating committee nominates candidates to run for vacancies on the board of directors. Without a nominating committee composed largely of outsiders, the chief executive will tend to nominate either insiders, quasi-insiders, or "outsiders" who are in fact his close friends and whom he expects to be loyal to him. Therefore, if the board is to be more than a rubber stamp for management decisions, it must get a truly independent cadre of outside directors; the nominating committee furnishes a way to do this. For this reason, a nominating committee should have at least a majority of outside director. Probably only a minority of publicly-held corporations have formed nominating committees, but the number is growing rapidly. Regardless of whether it is the CEO or a nominating committee that nominates candidates, these "official" candidates almost always win the election; only in the rare case of a successful "proxy right" does someone not nominated by management or the existing board get elected.

Compensation Committee. Most publicly-held corporations now have a compensation committee composed principally of outside directors. Such a committee sets the salaries and other compensation of the chief executive and other senior management. Again, the theory though not necessarily the practice is that a committee composed of outsiders will be less dominated by the CEO and will thus be more objective and stingier than the full board would be.

Executive Committee. Many companies have an executive committee, which essentially performs the functions of the board between meetings of the full board. Such a committee is especially common where the full board meets only a few times a year. Unlike the three types of committees discussed above, the executive committee is usually composed of insider or quasi-insider members, since they must be available on short notice and be familiar with the daily affairs of the corporation.

PART IV

DUTY OF CARE AND BUSINESS JUDGEMENT RULE

CHAPTER 10

DUTY OF CARE[168)]

10.1 INTRODUCTION TO FIDUCIARY DUTY

In General. The law imposes on certain individuals the responsibility of being a fiduciary. While there is no explicit definition of a fiduciary relationship, it is generally created when one is given power that carries a duty to use that power to benefit another.[169)] The label of a fiduciary is applied to a variety of relationships, such a trustees with the beneficiaries of trusts, or agents and principals, but once it is established, the responsibilities imposed may differ. The often quoted statement by Justice Frankfurter sums this up when he wrote "to say that man is a fiduciary only begins analysis; it gives direction to further inquiry. To whom is he a fiduciary? What obligations does he owe as a fiduciary?"[170)] Much of corporate law is about fiduciary

168) This Chapter is mainly compiled with materials from Arthur R. Pinto, Douglas M. Branson, "Understanding Corporate Law," LEXIS Publishing (1999); Emmanuel Law Outlines, "Corporations," Emmanuel Publishing Corp. (1997).

169) Shepherd, *Law of Fiduciaries* (1981), at 97.

170) *SEC v. Chenery Corp.*, 318 U.S. 80, 85-86 (1943).
Fact Summary. This case was before the Court a second time. The first time, the Court held that a

duties and its parameters. In the corporate context, directors and officers are in a fiduciary relationship to their corporation and to the shareholders. Controlling shareholders may also be characterized as fiduciaries. In the context of publicly held corporation when there is separation of ownership from control, the mechanisms that monitor managers are important in maintaining their accountability to the public shareholders. In those publicly

---

reorganization order of the Securities and Exchange Commission (SEC) could not be sustained on the grounds on which the agency acted. On remand, the SEC reexamined the problem and reached the same result. This case examined whether the Commission's action was proper in light of the principles established in the Court's prior decision.

Rule of Law. Chenery I strongly suggested that the SEC could only create a new principle of law through rulemaking, and this case (Chenery II) flatly rejected that suggestion, holding, "the choice made between proceeding by general rule of by individual, ad hoc litigation is one that lies primarily in the informed discretion of the administrative agency."

Facts. The first time the case was here, the Court emphasized a fundamental rule of administrative law-that a reviewing court may judge the propriety of an agency action solely based upon the grounds invoked by the agency. The first time, the Commission had relied solely on judicial authority which was insufficient to support its decision. This time, the Commission thoroughly reexamined the problem in light of the Holding Company Act (Act), and concluded that the proposed transaction was inconsistent with the standards of the Act. Chenery Corporation argued that the Commission was precluded from doing this in the absence of findings of conscious wrongdoing on the part of the management.

Issue & Held. Was the Commission, which had not previously been confronted with the problem of management trading during reorganization, precluded from utilizing this particular proceeding to announce and apply a new standard of conduct? No. Reversed. The absence of a general rule or regulation regarding management trading did not affect the Commission's duties in relation to the particular proposal before it. The Commission, unlike a court, does have the ability to make new law prospectively through the exercise of its rule-making powers, it has less reason to rely on ad hoc adjudication to formulate new standards of conduct. The function of filling in the gaps of the Act should be performed through quasi-legislative promulgation of rules as much as possible. However, any rigid requirement to that affect would make the administrative process inflexible and incapable of dealing with the many specialized problems which arise. Dissent. The Court by this decision sustained the identical administrative order which it recently held invalid. Since there was no change in the order, no additional evidence in the record, and no amendment of relevant legislation, it was clear there was a change in the attitude of the controlling membership of the Court since the last time the case appeared. Both the Commission and the Court agreed that the purchases at issue were not forbidden by any law, judicial precedent or regulation or rule of the Commission; yet the Court approved the Commission's order that the individuals surrender their shares to the corporation at cost plus 4% interest. The reversal of the position of the Court was due to a fundamental change in its prevailing philosophy to provide deference to administrative authority when confronted with an unfamiliar matter it hadn't dealt with before. Concurrence. None printed.

Discussion. The Commission's conclusion rested squarely in the area where administrative law judges are entitled to the greatest amount of weight by appellate courts, and it was an allowable judgment the Court declined to disturb. The deference given to agency discretion in this case remains a bedrock principle of federal administrative law.

held corporations, in which there is no separation of ownership from control because a shareholder or group of shareholders controls the corporation, the public minority shareholders may need protection from self-dealing by those in control. In the context of closely held corporation, majority owners may use their power to oppress the minority. In all of these contexts, fiduciary duty serves as a limit on the powers of those in positions of control.

10.2 DUTY OF CARE

In General. A director or officer must behave with the level of care that a reasonable person in similar circumstances would use. If the director or officer is found to have breached this duty of care, in a way that causes loss to the corporation, he may be held liable for money damages, which are to be paid to the corporation. Thus, a director's or officer's duty of care is as follows. He must, in handling the corporation's affairs, behave with the level of care that a reasonable person in similar circumstances would use. This sounds like the familiar negligence standard from tort law, and in many ways it is. However, a key rule called the "business judgment" rule in fact makes the duty of care much less burdensome than you might guess. Stated most briefly and generally, the business judgment rule says that courts will not second-guess the wisdom of directors' and officers' business judgments, and will not impose liability for even stupid business decisions so long as the director or officer (1) had no conflict of interest when he made the decision, (2) gathered a reasonable amount of information before deciding, and (3) did not act wholly irrationally.

When the duty of due care is combined with the business judgment rule, what we really have is a scheme that looks quite closely at the process by which the director or officer makes his decision, but then gives very little scrutiny to the substantive wisdom of the decision itself. Thus a director who does not attend board meetings, or who acts without a serious attempt to obtain the available facts is likely to be found to have violated his duty of care. By contrast, a director who tries hard gets most of the available facts, and then makes a decision which is clearly unwise, even when viewed without the benefit of hindsight, probably will not he found to have violated his duty of care, the business judgment rule will protect him as long as his decision was not totally irrational.

Liability for Damages vs. Injunction. If a director or officer violates his duty of care to the corporation, and this violation causes loss to the corporation, the director/officer will be personally liable to pay money damages to the corporation. Often, this will come about procedurally by means of a shareholder's derivative suit, in which a shareholder sues "on behalf of the corporation against the negligent director or officer; if the plaintiff is successful, the director/officer will have to pay damages to the corporation, and the shareholder/plaintiff will share pro rata with all other shareholders by virtue of the corporation's recoupment of its losses. However, there is a quite different context in which the duty of care and the business judgment rule may also be relevant. This is the situation in which the board of directors has approved, but not yet consummated, a transaction, and a shareholder or outsider sues for an injunction to block the proposed transaction. If the court concludes that the directors or officers have not acted with due care, and that shareholders as a whole would be injured, it may block the proposed transaction until it is approved with the required level of diligence.

Courts generally are probably willing to block a proposed transaction, especially in the takeover area, on less of a showing of a violation of due care than they would require before imposing personal liability on directors and officers. This is easy to understand: blocking a transaction that is unfair to shareholders probably will not directly, and certainly not unfairly, hurt the directors and officers who approved it, whereas making them personally liable for potentially huge damages as the result of their service to the corporation may severely hurt them, even bankrupt them.

In general, it is very rare for directors and officers to be found liable for breach of the duty of due care, as distinguished from breach of the duty of loyalty. At least traditionally, most of the cases purporting to impose liability for lack of due care have probably really been cases in which the court believed that the directors were engaged in self-dealing, i.e., they violated their duty of loyalty, but because the proof of self-dealing was not strong enough, the court based its decision upon lack of due care. However, beginning in the 1980s a few cases have found lack of due care even without indications of self-dealing. Therefore, the duty of care is becoming a duty that has some real practical impact upon how corporations are managed.[171)]

The duty of care is imposed on both officers and directors. Essentially the same duty is imposed upon each. However, the duty that is imposed is the duty to behave reasonably "under the circumstances," and the circumstances are obviously somewhat different for an officer than for a director. For instance, an officer will typically have deeper knowledge about the company's affairs than will an outside director, so facts which might not give an outside director cause to investigate might give the officer such cause, making his failure to investigate a violation of due care even though the director's failure would not be. In general, everything we say below applies to both directors and officers unless otherwise noted.

10.3 THE STANDARD OF CARE

The Basic Standard. Virtually all states impose, either by statute or case law, a duty of due care on all officers and directors. The director or officer "must

171) *See* especially the dramatic and instantly-landmark case of *Smith v. Van Gorkom*, in which the Delaware Supreme Court found the directors of a corporation liable for damages because they did not obtain the highest possible price from a takeover bidder, even though the sale price was substantially higher than the stock had ever previously traded, and even though there was no apparent taint of self-dealing.

exercise that degree of skill, diligence and care that a reasonably prudent person would exercise in similar circumstances." The RMBCA spells out this duty in a way that is typical of the law of most states: "A director shall discharge his duties as a director ... : (1) in good faith; (2) with the care an ordinarily prudent person in a like position would exercise under similar circumstances; and (3) in a manner he reasonably believes to be in the best interests of the corporation."[172] An important consequence of this duty of care is that there is no such thing as an "accommodation" or "dummy" director. For example, suppose that X, who knows nothing about business, as a favor to his friend the President of ABC Corporation, accepts a director's post on ABC's board, President assures X that X will only be a "figurehead" who is not expected to have any significant function in ABC's affairs. Despite these assurances, a court will hold that X had a duty of care to ABC, and indirectly to its shareholders and creditors, and that he can be liable for damages if he does not act in accordance with this duty. "[A] Person who accepts a directorship without assuming the responsibilities of a director is courting disaster."

Personal Liability. A director or officer who violates his duty of due care, and who thereby injures the corporation, may be held personally liable for the corporation's damages. This is true even if the director is paid little or nothing for his director's services, and otherwise had little or nothing to gain. In the case of a major corporation, the potential liability can be many times the director's net worth! For this reason, most corporations now pay for directors' and officers' liability insurance. However, the existence of deductibles, co-insurance provisions and other limits means that even with insurance, a director is probably still significantly at risk if he violates his duty of due care.

However, this duty of due care is not as draconian as it might sound. First, under the "business judgment rule", the actual business decisions made by a director or officer will not be second-guessed by the court as long as they are

172) RMBCA § 8.30(a).

rational, made in good faith, and based on reasonable information. Therefore, liability for breach of the duty of due care generally arises only where the director or officer has failed to comply with reasonable procedures for making decisions. Second, even where the director's procedures are inadequate, most courts hold that there is only liability for "gross negligence" or "recklessness." Therefore, most successful claims against directors have come in cases where the director simply fails to do the basic things that directors generally do. Thus a director might be found grossly negligent (and therefore liable) if he does some or all of the following:

(1) fails to attend meetings;

(2) fails to learn anything of substance about the company's business;

(3) fails to read reports financial statements, etc. given to him by the corporation;

(4) fails to obtain help (e.g., advice of counsel) when he sees or ought to see signals that things are going seriously wrong with the business; or

(5) otherwise "neglect[s] to go through the standard motions of diligent behavior."

For example, Mrs. Pritchard is a' director of Pritchard & Baird, a reinsurance broker. Pritchard & Baird goes bankrupt, and its trustees in bankruptcy sue Mrs. Pritchard for Violating her duty of due care as a director. They show that two officers of Pritchard & Baird, Charles and William Pritchard, who are the other two directors, are Mrs. Pritchard's sons, and are the sole other stockholders apart from Mrs. Pritchard, have misappropriated $ 12 million from trust accounts held by the company on behalf of others. During the years the misappropriation took place, Mrs. Pritchard was elderly, alcoholic, and depressed over the death of her husband. She hardly ever attended board meetings, which were in fact rarely held, knew nothing of the corporation's affairs, never read or obtained any financial statements, and in general "did not pay any attention to her duties as a director or to the affairs of the corporation." *Held,* Mrs. Pritchard, and after her death, her estate, breached her duty of due care to the corporation, and is therefore liable for the losses caused by the misappropriations. Directors are not required to conduct a detailed inspection of day-to-day activities. But they must at least become familiar with the fundamentals of the business and must keep informed in a general way about the corporation's activities.

Here Pritchard done even so little as to read the corporation's financial statements at any time, she would have noticed an item called "loans to shareholders" which dwarfed the company's assets, and which would have immediately put her on notice that her sons were effectively stealing trust funds. Had she noticed this, and asked her sons to stop, they probably would have done so, so that her negligence was about for cause of the losses.[173)]

---

173) *Francis v. United Jersey Bank*, 432 A.2d 814 (N.J. 1981).

Fact Summary. Plaintiffs, the trustees in bankruptcy of Pritchard & Baird Intermediaries Corporation ("P&B"), filed suit against Defendant, the executrix of the estate of Lillian Pritchard, for a breach of fiduciary duty as a director of P&B. Lillian Pritchard did not exercise ordinary care in monitoring the finances of P&B when her sons, other members of P&B management, misappropriated funds.

Rule of Law. A director can be personally liable, even to third parties, if they neglect to provide the ordinary care of staying current with corporate affairs as one would normally do in that position, and that neglect is the proximate cause of the damages.

Facts. P&B was a broker between ceding insurance companies and reinsurance companies. They earned a commission on the transactions between the two entities. Typically, brokers in the reinsurance business hold funds from the ceding and reinsuring companies in a separate account and pay each party from that account. The former CEO of P&B, Charles Pritchard, Sr. (the husband of Lillian Pritchard) did not practice this method, but he still ensured that the funds deposited by third parties were never used as personal funds. Charles Pritchard, Sr., eventually stepped down and his two sons controlled the business. Once the sons had control they took out personal loans from the account but never paid back the loans or any interest. This practice of misappropriating funds continued until P&B could no longer meet their obligations, and they went into bankruptcy. During the entire period that the sons controlled P&B, Lillian was the majority shareholder and sat on the Board as a director. During her tenure as director, she never participated in any business matters of P&B. Defendant argued that Lillian was elderly and sick, and therefore should be excused for her absence.

Issue & Held. The issue is whether Lillian Pritchard is personally liable for negligently failing to prevent the misappropriation of P&B funds by her sons. Lillian Pritchard, as a director on the Board, had a duty of care in managing the business. She did not have to know every detail of day-to-day operations, but she needed to have a baseline understanding of the finances and important activities. If she did not understand the activities, then she was obligated to consult counsel for advice. Her absence from the business did not excuse her duties. The court determined that if she did intervene in the dubious financial decisions of her sons, or at least consulted an attorney or expert, it may have prevented her sons from fleecing the company. Therefore, her lack of care was a proximate cause of the damages to the company and the third parties who relied upon the company. Because of the nature of the business (holding assets of third parties), she was liable to the third parties for any damages.

Discussion. The decision makes it impossible for directors to hide their head in the sand to avoid liability. The amount of oversight required will depend on the nature of the business, so it will be very fact-specific.

"No Win" Transactions. Apart from cases involving an almost total failure to go through the motions of being a director, courts have occasion ally found the requisite gross negligence in the fact that the directors approved what was basically a "no win" transaction. That is, if the transaction could at best benefit the corporation slightly if at all, and at worst could damage it greatly, the court may find that the decision was so irrational as to amount to gross negligence. For example, the Ds, who are directors of Guaranty Trust Bank, approve the purchase by Guaranty of bonds owned by Alleghany Corporation Under the purchase arrangement, the seller has the option to buy the bonds back at the sale price within six months. The bonds in fact decline tremendously in value. Alleghany of course does not exercise its repurchase option, and the bank loses money. A stockholder brings a derivative action against the Ds alleging failure to exercise due care. *Held*, for P. The purchase-with-option gave the bank no possibility of profit except for the interest it would derive from the securities while holding them, yet placed on the bank the total risk for any declining value. This arrangement was "so improvident, so risky, so unusual and unnecessary as to be contrary to fundamental conceptions of prudent banking practice." The Ds are therefore liable for the decline in value during the six-month period.[174)]

---

174) *Litwin v. Alten*, 25 N.Y.S.Zd 667 (N.Y. Sup. Ct. 1940).

Case Synopsis. In consolidated actions, plaintiffs filed derivative stockholder suits against defendants for allegedly improper transactions involving a trust company in which plaintiffs owned shares.

Facts. In derivative stockholder action, plaintiffs sued defendants over four allegedly improper transactions. Plaintiffs first claimed defendant officers' stock purchase of a third-party corporation for their personal benefit violated their fiduciary duties.

Discussion. The court held trust company had no interest in third-party corporation; thus, defendant officers had not breached their duty. Plaintiffs also charged defendant officers' bond acquisition on trust company's behalf constituted an improper loan to third-party corporation. The court held that the bonds were purchased negligently but that the applicable statute of limitations prevented recovery against three defendant officers. Plaintiffs also claimed defendant officers negligently extended a loan to a third-party company and then improperly auctioned the loan's collateral due to improper influence from defendant banking firm. The court followed the rule that allowed deference to business decisions, and held defendant directors properly extended the loan using information they possessed and that their auction of the loan's collateral was equitable.

Conclusion. The court entered partial judgment in favor of plaintiffs as to their claim involving the improper purchase of bonds, due to defendant officers' negligence in approving the bond purchase. The court entered judgment in favor of defendants as to plaintiffs' other claims.

Disguised "Self-Dealing" Cases. Cases in which directors are held liable for failing to act with due care are often disguised "self-dealing" cases. That is, the court believes that the directors acted in pursuit of their own ends rather than for the good of the corporation, yet there is not enough evidence of this to make it the basis for the finding of liability; therefore, the court seizes upon lack of due care instead. For instance, in Francis, the court was probably swayed by the fact that D was the mother of the two miscreants, and her refusal to undertake any of the responsibilities of a director may have been motivated in part by her desire to let her sons enrich themselves at the corporation's expense. Similarly, in *Litwin*, the defendant directors were also directors of other related entities that had a major investment in the corporate empire of which Alleghany was a part; if the directors had not voted to have Guaranty Trust buy the bonds, these other business interests might have been hurt by Alleghany's troubles, so the directors may really have been guilty of pursuing the interests of their other investments at the expense of Guaranty Trust's own affairs.

Subjective vs. Objective Standard. The standard of care is basically an objective one. That is, the director will be held to the standard of care that would be exercised by a "reasonable person" in the director's position. Consequently, a director who is simply less smart less able or less innately diligent than an "ordinary" reasonable director will nonetheless have to meet this higher ordinary standard. For example, consider Mrs. Pritchard in the Francis case. Even though she was elderly, alcoholic and depressed over the death of her husband, these factors were not taken into account by the court in determining what level of care was "reasonable" for her. Instead, she was required to conform to the level of directorial skill and diligence that an ordinary "reasonable" director would have shown under the circumstances. Special skills of director: On the other hand, if the director has special skills that go beyond what an ordinary director would have, he uses those skills. For instance if the director is by training an accountant, and he learns of facts which would make a trained accountant suspicious but would not raise the suspicions of an ordinary non-accountant director, he must behave as a reasonable accountant would behave under the circumstances. The rule would be similar for one with special legal, banking or real estate training.

Surrounding Circumstances. The level of care required is that which is reasonable in the circumstances in which the director finds himself. Nature and size of business: These "circumstances" include the nature and size of the particular business. For example, if the corporation is small and its operations relatively simple, the level of attention required of the director is probably somewhat less than if he sits on the board of, say, General Motors. Also, if the business serves as trustee or custodian for the funds of others. Probably a "reasonable" degree of care under the circumstances would include being on the lookout for misappropriation. Thus directors of banks are sometimes said to owe a "higher" standard of care; however, it would be more accurate to say that they owe the same "reasonable" duty of care as any other director, but that in a banking context this duty includes the obligation to be watchful for signs that depositors' accounts are being looted.

Reliance on Experts and Committees. Only rarely can a director, especially a director of a large corporation, directly ascertain the condition of the business. A director of IBM probably has no reasonable way to determine that the company's big supercomputer development program is way behind schedule, that its Singapore branch manager is fixing prices with his counterpart from Hitachi, or that the person overseeing the company pension plan is embezzling Directors normally rely heavily on the expertise and assurances of others, including the company's officers, lawyers, accountants and other persons who are in a better position to know the facts. Generally speaking, the director is entitled to rely on these other people, and is not expected to go behind what they tell him. Thus RMBCA Provides that "a director is entitled to rely on information, opinions, reports, or statements, including financial statements and other financial data," if these are prepared or presented by: (1) officers or employees of the corporation "whom the director reasonably believes to be reliable and competent in the matters preseated"; (2) lawyers, accountants or others as to "matters the director reasonably believes are within the person's professional or expert competence", and (3) a committee of the board "if the director reasonably believes the committee merits confidence."[175)]

On the other hand, it's vital to remember that the reliance must be reasonable. Thus if the director knows facts which indicate that the officer, lawyer, or other third person is tying or is otherwise mistaken, the director cannot bury his head in the sand and continue to rely on this third party's statements. As the RMBCA puts it, "a director is not acting in good faith if he has knowledge concerning the matter in question that makes reliance otherwise permitted ... unwarranted."[176)] For example, X is the director of Corporation, a large construction contractor. There have been persistent rumors that high-level officials of Corporation have bribed foreign officials to get foreign construction contracts, in violation of the federal Foreign Corrupt Practices Act. The board appoints a special board committee to investigate; the committee comes back and reports that there is no substance to these allegations. Ordinarily, X would be permitted to rely on the committee's report, since he "reasonably believes the committee merits confidence."[177)] But if X has actually been told by Y that Y and others have paid $10 million of Corporation's funds to Z to induce Z to give Corporation a contract, X's reliance on the committee is no longer reasonable, because of this actual knowledge. Therefore, X may not hide his head in the sand and say, in effect, "Everything's okay because the committee says so." He must instead explain what he knows, and at least attempt to

175) RMBCA § 8.30(b).

176) RMBCA § 8.30(c).

177) *See* RMBCA § 8.30Cb)(3).

prevent recurrence.

Passive Negligence. In some situations, the duty of due care arises in connection with a specific, affirmative, action by the board of directors. Thus the board may choose to write a certain loan, approve a certain acquisition, or otherwise make an explicit decision to take, or not take, certain action, In this situation, it's not too hard to determine whether the board members have acted with due care. Many if not most situations, however, involve what might be called "passive" negligence, or "nonfeasance." That is, circumstances exist which the board arguably ought to notice and do something about, but instead the board members do nothing. Most commonly, this kind of situation arises when the board fails to detect wrongdoing by officers or employees of the corporation.

No duty to detect wrongdoing: The directors certainly do not have any explicit duty to in fact detect wrongdoing. That is, most courts would probably hold that the board members need not be suspicious sorts who go out of their way searching for evidence of embezzlement, bribery, self-dealing or other misconduct by operating-level managers or employees. For example, the Allis-Chalmers Corporation is a large manufacturing company. The corporation and four of its employees plead guilty to price-fixing and other antitrust charges. The Ps sue the corporation's directors, alleging that they violated their duty of due care by not learning about and preventing these antitrust violations. The Ps point out that some 20 years ago, Allis-Chalmers had entered into various FTC consent decrees regarding price-fixing, as did nine other companies in the same industries. Held, the directors did not violate their duty of due care. Directors "are entitled to rely on the honesty and integrity of their subordinates until something occurs to put them on suspicion that something is wrong... Absent cause for suspicion there is no duty upon the directors to install and operate a corporate system of espionage to ferret out wrongdoing which they have no reason to suspect exists." The 20-year-old consent decrees did not put the board on notice of the real possibility of future price-fixing.[178)]

On the other hand, of course, if the directors are on notice of facts that would make a reasonable person suspicious that wrongdoing is taking place, they must act. For example, D, the president and director of a bank, believes that his bookkeeper is honest. However, there are a number of clues to the contrary which D ignores. For instance, another employee accuses the bookkeeper of being dishonest; several small thefts are reported that might have been committed by the bookkeeper or by someone else; the bookkeeper appears to be living beyond his means, etc. Held, by the Supreme Court, the court below could properly have found that D violated his duty of due care, because he had been put upon his guard and should have at least investigated further. On the other hand, the outside directors were entitled to rely on the president's assurances that the business was operating properly, as well as on the fact that a semi-annual government examination of the bank disclosed no wrongdoing. This comes within the principle, discussed above, that directors may rely on statements by officers or experts if the circumstances make the reliance reasonable.[179)]

---

178) *Graham v. Allis-Chalmers Mfg. Co.,* 188 A.2d 125 (Del. Sup. 1963). In summary, Allis-Chalmers and four of its directors were indicted for price fixing violations of anti-trust laws. Some shareholders instituted a derivative lawsuit against the directors for *breach of fiduciary duty*. The shareholders argued that the directors should have had knowledge of the price fixing and were liable because they didn't have a monitoring system that would have allowed them to uncover the illegal activity.
The Delaware Supreme Court found for the directors. The Delaware Supreme Court found that it was corporate policy at Allis-Chalmers to delegate price-setting authority to the lowest possible levels. While the directors reviewed the general financial goals of the corporation it would not have been practical for the directors to consider in detail the specific problems of the various divisions.
The shareholders argued that the directors should have put into effect a system of watchfulness, which would have brought the illegal activity to their attention. However, the Court found that directors are entitled to rely on the honesty and integrity of their subordinates unless there is something to raise suspicions of wrongdoing. In other words, management need not create a "corporate system of espionage."
This case established the *Graham Standards* which basically impose a duty of inquiry only when there are obvious signs of employee wrongdoing. That's an objective standard and asks whether a reasonable person would have seen the wrongdoing. Alternately, under the standard set by In re Caremark International Inc. Derivative Litigation (698 A.2d 959 (Del. Ch. 1996)), directors are responsible for establishing some sort of monitoring system, but will not be held liable if that system fails.

179) *Bates v. Dresser*, 251 U.S. 524 (1920).

More aggressive duty to put controls into place: In fact, even the traditional view of Graham, that directors have no duty to "ferret out wrongdoing," might not be accepted by every court today. More and more, it is becoming accepted that one of the key functions of a board of directors is to put into place formal control systems to prevent and/or discover wrongdoing, even if there are no concrete grounds to suspect the wrongdoing. For instance, the Securities Exchange Act now requires every publicly-held corporation to "devise and maintain a system of internal accounting controls" to guarantee accurate financial statements and to guard against misappropriation of assets.[180] Most public companies have done this by creating an audit committee that works with the corporation's accountants to install such controls. Similarly, most public companies now have formal mechanisms for making sure that managers and employees comply with applicable legal rules. A modem court might, in contrast to the Graham court, hold that a board member's duty of due care includes the obligation to see that the corporation has those controls needed to discover wrongdoing.

Causation. Even if a director or officer has violated his duty of due care to the corporation, many cases say that he will not be personally liable unless this lack of due care is the legal cause of damage to the corporation. In other words, in many courts the traditional tort notions of cause in fact and proximate cause apply in this context. Cause would have happened anyway. Thus if the loss would have happened anyway even had the directors all behaved with due care, many courts hold that there is no liability.[181]

For instance, in Barnes the corporation was a start-up factory which ran out of money before it got into full production. The judge concluded that most of the delay was probably due to the incompetence of employees, and that there was simply no way to know whether a more attentive set of directors would have, by replacing personnel or other action, been able to make the business a

180) Securities Exchange Act of 1934 § 13(b)(2).

181) *Barnes v. Andrews*, 298 F. 614 (S.D.N.Y. 1924).

success.[182] Therefore, it could not be said that the directors' actions proximately caused the failure, and they were held not liable.

But some states, including Delaware, now reject the requirement of causation when directors are shown to have violated their duty of care. Thus the Delaware Supreme Court held that once P shows that the directors breached their duty of care, that showing overcomes the protection that directors get from the "business judgment" rule.[183] At that point, P has

---

182) Barnes v. Andrews, 298 F. 614 (S.D.N.Y. 1924).

183) *Cede & Co. v. Technicolor. Inc..* 634 A.2d 345 (Del. 1993).
Abstract. An appraisal remedy is one method that can be used to protect minority shareholders. In the event of a merger or acquisition, majority shareholders can force out the minority for a price lower than the stock's true value. However, an appraisal remedy allows minority shareholders who did not vote for the merger to petition the court for an appraisal hearing. The court will then determine the fair value of the minority shares. Delaware has such an appraisal remedy statute. Originally valuation had to be done by the Delaware Block Method, but now courts may use any accepted valuation methods.
Issues & Held. Can the plans and strategies to be used by the acquiring company that were implemented between the dates of the merger agreement and the final merger be included in the valuation of the merged company? Yes, according to the Delaware Supreme Court in Cede & Co. v. Technicolor, IV. Does the holding of the case conflict with the statute? No, as it aligns with the purpose of the statue, protection of minority shareholders.
Analysis. Cede & Co. v. Technicolor is a line of cases that originated when MAF acquired Technicolor in a merger. Cede was a shareholder who brought an action for the appraisal remedy and also sued for fraud and unfair dealing, but lost on the latter actions. In the final case, an important issue was whether the acquiring company's plans that were implemented between the dates of the merger agreement and the final merger could be included in the valuation of the merged company. The Delaware Supreme Court held that Technicolor could be valued using the new management's plans and strategies as a factor.
The appraisal remedy statute states that valuation must be on the date of the merger and cannot include any element of value arising from the merger or expectation surrounding it. However, this may lead to conflict, as new management may have already implemented new plans by the date of the merger. However, the Court worked around this by excluding speculative elements of value arising from the accomplishment or expectation of the merger, but allowing known or provable elements of future value. It could be possible to construe this decision as conflicting with the statute. However, it follows the purpose surrounding the appraisal remedy, the protection of minority shareholders. If the court did not include the new plan of management, the minority would be forced out of an investment that they did not want to exit, and at less than the fair value on the date of the merger, giving the new majority a windfall. Thus, the court's decision allowed the minority to receive the true value of their investment on the date of the merger.
Conclusion. The decision in Cede & Co. v. Technicolor, IV could have many implications. First, the outcome for the minority shareholders will be different based on whether the merger is structured in one step or two, in that minority shareholders have no control whatsoever in a one step merger. Second, determining how speculative new management's plans may or may not be might be difficult. The steps outlined by the court are rather vague and will need to be more defined in the future. Finally, it might discourage two-step mergers, or those using two step mergers may need to make a tender offer in the first step at a substantial premium, or they may wait until the second step has been completed to implement their plans. However, this is not likely because the appraisal remedy is not often used by plaintiffs because of procedural and financial burdens. Also, the benefits of using a two step merger will outweigh any problems caused by this decision.

established a *prima facie* case - even if he can't show that exercise of due care would have avoided the loss - and the burden of proof shifts to the defendants': unless the defendants carry the burden of showing the "entire fairness" of the transaction, they will be liable. The court in Cede expressly rejected the reasoning of Barnes, which required proof of causation.

Joint and Several Liability. When multiple directors are charged with breaching their duty of due care, each will, if she's smart, argue, "Even if I had behaved with due care, the rest of the board would probably not have listened to me, and the loss would have happened anyway." However, at least some courts hold that any board member who violates his duty of due care is jointly and severally liable with all other directors who have done so, as long as the board collectively was a proximate cause of the loss; each director is treated as a probably would not have made a difference.[184)]

10.4 MODERN STATUTORY MODIFICATIONS

Reason for Statutory Modifications. As the number of suits successfully holding directors liable for breach of the duty of due care has multiplied, many states have tried to counteract this trend by modifying their statutes, In general, these states appear to feel that increasing directors' and officers' risk of personal liability does not improve the economic efficiency of business as a whole, and certainly does not improve a state's ability to induce corporations to choose that state as their domicile.

Some Typical Approaches. There are at least four approaches that states have taken to reduce the practical burdens of director liability for money damages for breach of the duty of due. First, Allow shareholders to amend

184) *See* ALI Prin. Corporation Gov., § 7.18, Comment d (taking "no position" on whether the liability should be joint-and-several or, instead, apportioned.)

charter: Some states have allowed the shareholders to amend the corporate charter to eliminate or reduce directors' personal liability for violations of the duty of due care. For instance, Delaware allows the shareholders to modify the corporation's charter to eliminate money damages for breach of the duty of due care, so long as the director has acted in good faith without knowingly violating the law and without obtaining any improper personal benefit.[185)]

Second, looser standard of care: Some states have made the standard of care looser, so only more egregious conduct will give rise to personal liability. For instance, Indiana and Ohio now allow recovery only where the director has intentionally harmed the corporation or acted "recklessly."[186)]

Third, limiting damages: Some states have placed a limit on the amount of money damages that may be recovered against the director or officer. For instance, in Virginia personal liability is generally limited to $100,000, or any lesser sum put in the company's charter by shareholder vote.[187)]

Finally, greater right to indemnify: Many states now allow the corporation to completely indemnify directors and officers for any liability they may have for breach of the duty of due care.

---

185) Delaware GCL § 102(b)(7).

186) See Ind. Code § 23-1-35(1)(e)(2); Ohio Code § 1701.59.

187) Va. Code § 13.1-692.1.

CHAPTER 11

BUSINESS JUDGMENT RULE[188)]

11.1 INTRODUCTION

In General. The "business judgment rule" may be thought of as a "judicial gloss" on what it means for a director to exercise due care. Even if the director's conduct might seem to lack due care when viewed from a general "reasonable person" benefit v. burden tort perspective, the more precise business judgment rule may save the director from liability.

There is no single universally accepted statement of the business judgment rule. The basic idea behind the rule seems to be that business decisions made upon reasonable information and with some rationality do not give rise to directorial liability even if they turn out badly or disastrously from the standpoint of the corporation. In other words, the court will not find an absence of due care merely from the fact that the decision was unwise. For example, the Ds are the directors of American Express Co. They have caused

188) This Chapter is mainly compiled with materials from Arthur R. Pinto, Douglas M. Branson, "Understanding Corporate Law," LEXIS Publishing (1999); Emmanuel Law Outlines, "Corporations," Emmanuel Publishing Corp. (1997).

the corporation to distribute the shares it holds in a separate company, DU, to shareholders as a special dividend. P, an American Express shareholder, brings a derivative suit against the Ds; he alleges that they should have had American Express sell these DLJ shares on the open market instead of distributing them as a dividend. He points out that this technique would have resulted in substantial tax savings to shareholders. Held, for the Ds. P makes no claim that the Ds engaged in fraud or self-dealing. P is merely claiming that a different decision by the board would have been more advantageous. But a complaint alleging merely that some other decision would have been wiser does not state a cause of action, because of the business judgment rule. "More than imprudence or mistaken judgment must be shown." Here, the evidence shows that the directors considered the tax advantages of selling the stock rather than distributing it, but were worried that this path would hurt the corporation's reported earnings; their decision will not give rise to liability so long as it was reached in good faith.[189)]

ALI Definition. The clearest definition of the business judgment rule, and

---

189) *Kamin v. American Express Co.*, 383 N.Y.S.2d 807 (N.Y.Sup.Ct. 1976).

Summary. Plaintiffs, Howard Kamin et al., filed a shareholder derivative suit against Defendant corporation, American Express, and their officers after Defendants allegedly negligently decided to issue a dividend.

Rule of Law. A court will not interfere with the decision of a company's directors unless there is evidence of fraud or dishonest practice.

Facts. Defendant corporation purchased common stock for $29.9 million, and now the stock has a market value of $4 million. The directors decided to declare a special dividend, giving the shares of stock to the shareholders. Plaintiff demanded that Defendants sell the stock on the open market and use the $25.9 million capital gains loss to offset other capital gains. The offset would save Defendant corporation $8 million in taxes. Plaintiffs decided not to pursue Plaintiff's demand, reasoning that the significant loss would adversely affect the value of Defendant's stock. Plaintiff then brought suit, classifying the directors' decision as negligent decision-making.

Issue & Held. The issue is whether Plaintiffs can bring a derivative action challenging the business decision of the directors of the corporation. The court will not overrule a business decision of the directors of a company unless there is evidence of fraud or some other dishonest dealing. The decision to declare a dividend may be an unwise judgment, but it is a judgment that is outside the scrutiny of the court. The only accusation of dishonest dealing was a general assertion that four of the twenty directors had a financial interest in the outcome.

Discussion. This decision is a restatement of the business judgment rule. The courts do not want to invest significant resources into second-guessing business judgments of corporate directors. Going to court for corporate decisions is expensive and can often be avoided through other avenues.

the one that will probably become the leading definition in the future, is given in the ALI's Principles of Corporate Governance. § 4.01(c) "A director or officer who makes a business judgment in good faith fulfills the duty [of care] if the director or officer (1) is not interested in the subject of the business judgment; (2) is informed with respect to the subject of the business judgment to the extent the director or officer reasonably believes to be appropriate under the circumstances; and (3) rationally believes that the business judgment is in the best interests of the corporation." Thus a director who asserts that he is protected by the business judgment rule has to prove three things under the ALI's approach: (1) that he was not "interested" (i.e., that he had no conflict of interest, no personal stake in the outcome that was different from the corporation's stake); (2) that he gathered the reasonably needed information', and (3) that he honestly, and rationally, believed that his decision was in the company's best interest. So, assuming that the director has no conflicts and gathers adequate information, the essence of the business judgment rule is that mere rationality is all that is required - as long as the decision is not entirely crazy or outside the bounds of reason, the fact that, when judged by reference to the facts known to the director, it was very unwise, will not be enough to make the director liable.

Model Act. The RMBCA, by contrast, does not attempt to codify the business judgment rule at all. The RMBCA sets forth the general duty of due care, including the requirement that the director act in a manner "he reasonably believes to be in the best interests of the corporation".[190] The Official Comment says that the elements of the business judgment rule, and its impact on the duty of due care, are left to the courts.[191]

Relation between general duty of care and the business judgment rule: At first blush, the business judgment rule seems in conflict with the general duty of due care described above. Probably the best way to see how the

190) RMBCA § 8.30(a).

191) Official Comment to RMBCA § 8.30.

pieces fit together is this: The duty of due care imposes a fairly stem set of procedural requirements for directors' actions - the director must act in good faith, e.g., not be pursuing his own interests, and he must get all reasonably needed information before deciding. Once these procedural requirements are satisfied, however, the business judgment rule sets out a far more easily satisfied standard with respect to the substance of the business decision: that decision will be upheld so long as it is "rational," a weaker requirement than that the decision be "reasonable".

Note that the interaction between the business judgment rule and the general duty of care is shown on the Plow Chart, "Has the director satisfied her duty of care?" There seem to be three main reasons for limiting directors' liability by use of the business judgment rule: First, a certain amount of innovation and risk-taking is essential if businesses are to grow and prosper. It is generally in the shareholders' interests to have their directors take at least rational risks on the corporation's behalf. Without the business judgment rule, directors would become much more conservative and anti-risk, and the overall economic performance of corporations generally would probably decline. Second, directors, like executives, must constantly engage in a "risk/ return calculus." Judges, especially acting from hindsight, are not very good at making this kind of calculus, they have no training in it, so they may reach inappropriate conclusions if we let them second guess business people. "A reasoned decision at the time made may seem a wild hunch viewed years later against a background of perfect knowledge."[192] Finally, imposing greater director liability would make directors a form of "cost spreaders." But any given director is a poor cost spreader, since he probably serves only a few companies, and cannot incorporate the cost of his mistakes into the price he charges for his services. This is in contrast to the ability of, say, lawyers or accountants to buy malpractice insurance and therefore spread among many clients the cost of law or accounting mistakes.

192) *Joy v. North,* 692 F.2d 880 (2nd Cir. 1982).

Shareholders can spread the risk of business misjudgments far more easily by diversifying their portfolios than directors can spread this risk by serving on multiple boards.[193)] So far, we have been speaking about the principle that rational - though in hindsight unwise - business judgments will not give rise to personal liability on the part of the directors who make them. This is the business judgment "rule." A related principle is that directors' decisions based on rational business judgments are valid and binding upon the corporation, and the courts will not enjoin or set aside these decisions. This latter principle is sometimes called the business judgment "doctrine," to distinguish it from the "rule". Generally we will be talking about the "rule," i.e., we will be talking about personal liability of directors, but we may occasionally be discussing whether the plaintiff can obtain an injunction or undoing of a transaction. The standards for evaluating the directors' judgment seem more or less the same in the "rule" and "doctrine" situations.

193) *See* generally *Joy v. North*, 692 F.2d 880 (2d Cir. 1982).
Synopsis. Plaintiff shareholder challenged an order of the United States District Court for the District of Connecticut that granted summary judgment to defendants, directors and officers, in plaintiff's derivative suit alleging diversity of citizenship, common law breach of trust and fiduciary duty, and violations of the National Bank Act, 12 U.S.C.S. § 84.
Facts. The trial court dismissed certain defendant directors and officers in plaintiff's shareholder derivative action in which plaintiff alleged diversity of citizenship, common law breach of trust and of fiduciary duty, as well as violations of the National Bank Act, 12 U.S.C.S. § 84. A special litigation committee, which included some defendants, submitted a recommendation that there was a limited possibility of liability. The trial court concluded that the business judgment rule limited judicial scrutiny of the committee's recommendations to a determination of the good faith, independence, and thoroughness of the committee and placed the report under seal.}
Discussion. The court reversed the order sealing the report because the good cause asserted therefor was the attorney-client privilege, which had been waived by the submission of the report as a basis for summary judgment. The court disagreed with the committee's report and reversed the trial court, finding that a material issue of fact existed as to the liability of defendants, which precluded summary judgment.
Conclusion. The court reversed the lower court's protective order on a special litigation committee report because it was submitted as evidence in support of a motion to dismiss plaintiff's shareholder derivative suit. The lower court's grant of summary judgment to defendants was reversed.

11.2 REQUIREMENTS FOR APPLICATION OF RULE

Most courts appear to impose three requirements before the director or officer will gain the protection of the business judgment rule: (1) he must not have any private interest in the outcome different from the corporation's interests, i.e., there must be no taint of self-dealing; (2) he must have made the judgment only after gathering the reasonably needed information', and (3) he must have "rationally believed" that his judgment was in the corporation's best interest.[194)]

We now consider each of these requirements in turn. First, the director or officer will lose the protection of the business judgment rule if he has an "interest" in the transaction. Thus if he is a party to the transaction, or is related to a party, or otherwise has some financial stake in the transaction's outcome that is adverse to the corporation's stake, the business judgment rule will not apply. So any taint of self-dealing by the director will be enough to deprive him of the business judgment rule's protection. The rationale behind the business judgment rule is that we want to protect honest, even if mistaken, cases of business misjudgment. But if the director has engaged in self-dealing, he has not really engaged in business judgment, in the sense of judgment on behalf of the corporation, at all instead he has been engaged in pursuing his own objectives. This conduct is not the kind of action we want to protect with a special rule that makes recovery very difficult. For example, X is an officer and director of Printing Corporation He votes to have Printing Corporation purchase most of its paper from Paper Corporation Paper Corporation charges an average of 5% more for the same paper as is available, on substantially the same delivery and credit terms, from Discount Corporation Normally, X's decision to vote to have the purchases made from Paper Corporation would be protected by the business judgment rule, assuming that X acts with reasonable information, and his decision

194) *See* ALI, Prin. Corporation Gov., § 4.01(c).

is not wholly irrational. However, it turns out that X is a secret substantial shareholder in Paper Corporation, who will benefit financially by this large volume of business from Printing Corporation Therefore, X is "interested" in the transaction and he thus will not get the protection of the business judgment rule.

Note that the law governing self-dealing transactions is discussed extensively beginning and is an extremely important body of law. The point we are stressing here is that self-interested transactions, unlike other transactions, don't get any special benefit from the business judgment rule. The requirement that has the greatest practical importance is that the decision must have been an "informed" one in order to be protected by the business judgment rule. That is, the director or officer must have gathered at least a reasonable amount of information about the decision before he made it. As one court has put it, the directors must inform themselves "prior to making a business decision, of all material information reasonably available to them."[195)]

However, even with respect to his duty to become "informed," the business judgment rule is not as tough as it might sound. Most courts would probably hold that a director loses the benefit of the rule only if he was grossly negligent in the amount of information he gathered. In other words, mere "ordinary" negligence in obtaining available information, like mere negligence on the substantive merits of the decision, will not be enough to cause liability. For example, suppose that the directors of X Corporation are asked to approve X's acquisition of Y Corporation The President of X gives the directors ten years of financial information on Y, but director D only reads the last three years of this information. D, as well as his fellow directors, approves the acquisition, it goes forward, and it turns out disastrously because of embezzlements carried out by the founder of Y who is kept on. Had D read the financial statement from seven years previously, he would have discovered in a footnote reason to doubt the honesty of the founder. On these

195) *Aronson v. Lewis*, 473 A.2d 805 (Del. 1984).

facts, a court would probably hold that D gets the benefit of the business judgment rule, thus validating his decision to acquire as long as it was not completely irrational, so long as he was not "grossly negligent" in limiting his reading to the three most recent years. Probably a court would find that while this limited research may have been negligent, it was not "grossly" negligent, in which the court said "we think the concept of gross negligence is ... the proper standard for determining whether a business judgment reached by a board of directors was an informed one."[196] In determining whether the decision was an informed one, the court will generally consider alt of the surrounding circumstances. For example, if the board's decision had to be made in an extremely short time period a smaller amount of information will have to be gathered than if the court had months or years in which to make the decision.

The requirement that the decision be an "informed" one is the key to the most important business judgment rule case to be decided in modem times.[197] Van Gorkom represents a striking exception to the usual rule that if there is no taint of self-interest, and at least some attention paid to directorial responsibilities, the business judgment rule will shield the directors for liability for their decision.

The precise facts of Van Gorkom are of utmost importance, so we consider them in detail. The Ds were the directors of Trans Union Corporation, including its Chairman/CEO, Van Gorkom. Trans Union was publicly-held, and Van Gorkom held a sizeable, but minority, stake. Van Gorkom was near retirement age, and apparently wished to sell his shares prior to retirement. He had his chief financial officer compute the price at which a leveraged buyout could be done; the CFO reported that at $50 per share, the corporation's cash flow would easily support a buyout, but that at $60 a share the cash flow might not be sufficient. Van Gorkom then without

196) *ee*, e.g., Smith v. Van Gorkom, 488 A.2d 858 (Del. 1985). For the full text of this case *see infra* the Appendix I.

197) Smith v. Van Gorkom, 488 A.2d 858 (Del. 1985).

consulting with anyone else in senior management, proposed to his friend Phtzker, a well-known corporate acquirer, to sell him the company for $55 per share. The company's price on the New York Stock Exchange had recently fluctuated between $29 and $38, and in its history had never been higher than $39 1/2. Pritzker agreed to a $55 per share buyout price.

Van Gorkom did not attempt to get any other offers for the company. Nor did he ever commission a formal study of the company's value. Instead, he went to his board of directors and asked them to approve the sale to Pritzker at $55. He did not invite the company's investment bankers to the board meeting. He told the board that Pritzker was demanding an answer within three days. Most members of senior management opposed the deal on the grounds that the price was too low. The board was not shown the proposed merger agreement or any documents concerning the value of the company; it relied solely on Van Gorkom's oral presentation, the chief financial officer's statement that the price offered was in the "low" range of appropriate valuation, and an outside lawyer's advice that the board might be sued if they failed to accept the offer. The board approved the buyout on this basis. The sale went through at $55 per share.

The Delaware Supreme Court, by a three-two vote, held that the directors had been grossly negligent in failing to inform themselves adequately about the transaction that they were approving. The majority seemed especially influenced by the fact that: (1) it was Van Gorkom, not Pritzker, who promoted the deal and named the eventual sale price, and the board never ascertained this; (2) the board had made no real attempts to learn the "intrinsic value" of the company; (3) the board had no written documentation before it and relied completely on oral statements, mostly by Van Gorkom; and (4) the board made its entire decision in a two hour period, with no advance notice that a buyout would be the subject of the meeting, and in circumstances where there was no real crisis or emergency. The board claimed that it had reserved the right to take any higher offer, but the court found that this reservation was illusory, because of tight limits that the Pritzker agreement placed upon the board's ability to accept higher offers from third parties. In any event, the two other bidders who came forward never made a serious offer, apparently in part because of limits placed on other offers by the board's deal with Pritzker.

The two dissenters argued that the directors' decision to approve the merger should have been protected by the business judgment rule. One of them pointed out that the directors were highly sophisticated businessmen who were very well informed about the company's affairs.

The Van Gorkom decision is quite extraordinary. Here we have a buyout done at a price that was 40% above the highest price that the stock had ever traded for in its history. Yet the directors were held grossly negligent for approving the buyout! Perhaps the real key to the decision is that a majority of the court felt that the directors acceded to an autocratic leader, Van Gorkom, rather than making their decision in a collaborative manner. Observe that the stakes for the defendant directors in a case like Van Gorkom are enormous. Had the court finally decided that the buyout was $5 lower than a fully-informed transaction would have been done at, the 20 million shares outstanding would have produced a verdict of $100 million! In reality, the case was settled for $23 million, though this did not come out of the directors' pockets - about half came from directors' liability insurance and the rest from Pritzker, who apparently paid it voluntarily.

Also striking is the fact that the other directors were held jointly and severally liable even though Van Gorkom was clearly the person primarily responsible for the transaction. The explanation is probably that the defendants pursued what turned out to be a poor litigation strategy: the court repeatedly asked them whether there were reasons to treat some directors differently from other directors and they answered "no," preferring to pursue a "one for all and all for one" strategy. Therefore, the court treated them as being jointly and severally liable. The Van Gorkom case seems most significant for the proposition that process is exceptionally important in obtaining the benefits of the business judgment rule. Had the board members reviewed the proposed merger agreement, and obtained an investment banker's opinion that $55 was a "fair" price, the court would probably have found that the decision was an "informed" one, and was therefore protected by the business judgment rule. Thus the actual merits of the decision - whether $55 was an appropriate price - wasn't what really made the difference in Van Gorkom. As Van Gorkom illustrates, directors must do more than merely "go through the motions" in approving major business transactions. Especially in the takeover area, the directors must go out of their way to gather all relevant information, must take whatever time is reasonably available in the circumstances before deciding, and must interrogate management closely rather than merely "rubber stamping" management's recommendations.

The requirement of a "rational" decision: The final requirement for the business judgment rule, according to most courts, is that the director must have "rationally believed" that his business judgment was in the corporation's best interest.[198] That is, the director must actually believe he is acting in the corporation's best interests, and this belief must be at least rational. Observe that the requirement is merely that the belief be "rational," not that it be "reasonable." In other words, so long as the decision is not totally beyond the bounds of reason, it will be sustained even though most people would agree that it was not a good idea.

11.3 EXCEPTIONS TO RULE

Even where these three requirements for the business judgment rule are satisfied, there is at least one kind of situation, and possibly a second, where

198) *See*, e.g., ALI Prin. Corporation Gov., § 4.01(c)(3).

the court will find the rule inapplicable.

Illegality. If the act taken or approved by the director is a violation of a criminal statute, the director will lose the benefit of the business judgment rule. This is true even if the director was pursuing what he saw as the corporation's rather than his own interests, was acting based on full information, and rationally believed that his action would benefit the corporation, the three standard requirements for the rule. Even if there has been no criminal prosecution, if a civil plaintiff can show that the act was a criminal violation, the defendant will lose the benefit of the business judgment rule and his conduct will be evaluated solely based on the general duty of due care. The director is then likely to lose, on the grounds that it is not due care to advocate or permit a violation of the criminal laws. This "illegality" exception to the business judgment rule is especially likely to be invoked if the court concludes that shareholders are among the class meant to be protected by the criminal statute in question.

For example, the Ps, common stockholders in AT&T, bring a shareholders' derivative action against the company's directors. The Ps allege that the Democratic National Committee owes AT&T $1.5 million for services provided by AT&T during the 1968 Democratic National Convention, and that the directors have refused to allow AT&T to attempt to collect this debt. The Ps further claim that the Ds have in effect caused AT&T to violate a federal statute that prohibits campaign spending by corporations. Held, if the Ps can prove that the Ds caused AT&T to violate this rule against federal campaign spending, the Ds will not receive the benefit of the business judgment rule. Directors owe their corporation a fiduciary duty, and the commission of illegal acts breaches that duty even if the illegal acts were committed for the purpose of benefiting the corporation. This is especially true where, as here, shareholders are among the class intended to be protected by the criminal statute since the ban on corporate political spending was intended in part to prevent corporations from in effect spending shareholders' funds for political purposes without their consent.[199)]

Some courts might recognize yet another exception to the business judgment rule: the pursuit by a director of broad social or political goals not related to the corporation's welfare. For instance, if the directors of a computer corporation, whose operations have very little to do with health care, were to donate, year after year, 50% of its net profits to a foundation for cancer research, a court might well hold that this extreme pursuit of social welfare goals at the expense of the corporation's profitability should not be protected by the business judgment rule. This might be the case even if the directors honestly, though mistakenly, believed that such donations were in the corporation's best overall interests, thus perhaps satisfying the "rationally believes" requirement for the business judgment rule.

However, even in this kind of extreme situation, it is not clear that the court would refuse to apply the business judgment rule. Courts tend to give extremely wide latitude to directors' judgments that charitable or social, and perhaps even political, purposes mesh with the corporation's own financial interests. In any event, the corporation will usually be able to dress up its decision into one that is at least rationally related to the corporation's own financial interests.

For example, P, a minority stockholder in the Chicago Cubs baseball team,

---

199) *Miller v. American Telephone & Telegraph Co.*, 507 F.2d 759 (3d Cir. 1974).

Case Synopsis. Appeal from the United States District Court for the Eastern District of Pennsylvania by plaintiff stockholders in a derivative case alleging breach of fiduciary duty by defendants, the corporate officers and directors, and violations of 18 U.S.C.S. § 610.

Facts. Plaintiffs alleged that defendants had violated 18 U.S.C.S §610. Plaintiffs sought permanent relief in the form of an injunction requiring defendants to collect the debt, an injunction against providing further services to the political party until the debt was paid in full, and a surcharge for the benefit of the corporation against the defendant directors in the amount of the debt plus interest from the due date.

Procedural History. A request for a preliminary injunction against the provision of services to the political party was denied by the district court after an evidentiary hearing.

Discussion. On appeal, the court ruled directors had to be restrained from engaging in activities that were against public policy. The business judgment rule did not insulate the corporate directors from liability for breaching §610 prohibiting corporate political contributions.

Conclusion. The court reversed the lower court and remanded the case stating that directors must be restrained from engaging in activities that were against public policy.

brings a stockholders' derivative action against the directors of the team. P alleges that one of the Ds, Philip Wrigley, owner of 80% of the stock, has refused to allow lights to be placed in Wrigley Field, not because he thinks this will benefit the corporation but because he holds the personal social/political opinion that "baseball is a daytime sport" and that the installation of lights will have a bad effect upon the surrounding neighborhood. Held, for Wrigley and the other defendant directors. It is not clear that these motives, even if proven, are contrary to the best interests of the corporation and its stockholders. For instance, if the neighborhood around the park were to deteriorate because of lights, the value of the corporation's property, the park, would deteriorate; also, Patrons might be less willing to come to the park if it were now in a deteriorated, poorer, neighborhood. The fact that all other teams have implemented night baseball is irrelevant, because "it cannot be said that directors, even those of corporations that are losing money, must follow the lead of the other corporations in the field."[200]

---

200) *Shlensky v. Wrieley*, 237 N.E.2d 776 (Ill. App. Ct. 1968). *Brief Fact Summary*. Plaintiff, William Shlensky, filed a derivative action against Defendant director, Phillip Wrigley, to force the installation of lights for night baseball.

Rule of Law. A court will not interfere with an honest business judgment absent a showing of fraud, illegality or conflict of interest.

Facts. Defendant is the director of the Chicago National League Ball Club, which is the company that owns the Chicago Cubs. Although every other major league team had installed lights, Defendant did not install them for the Cubs because he was concerned that night baseball would be detrimental to the surrounding neighborhood. Plaintiff argued that the team was losing money, and that the other Chicago team, the White Sox, had higher attendance during the weekdays because they played at night. Therefore, reasoned Plaintiff, the Cubs would draw more people with weekday night games. Plaintiff asserts that Defendant's first concern should be with the shareholders rather than the neighborhood.

Issue & Held. The issue is whether the court should overrule decisions made by Defendant absent a showing of fraud, illegality or a conflict of interest. The court will not overturn Defendant's decision to not install lights at the ballpark. The court cited some reasons why the light installation could be detrimental, such as lowering the property value of the park itself, a lack of proof on behalf of Plaintiff that financing would be available for lights and would be certain to be offset by increasing revenues. The court cites precedent that asserts that business decisions should not be disturbed just because a defendant can make a reasonable case that the policy chosen by the company may not be the wisest policy available.

Discussion. The court notes that they were not necessarily agreeing with Wrigley's position in refusing to install lights, but that there was some reasons for doing so. The court stated that there was no requirement to show all three factors of illegality, fraud or a conflict of interest, but there was not evidence of any of the above in this case.

11.4 REVIEW ON THE DUTY OF CARE & BUSINESS JUDGMENT RULE

The duty of care, and its sibling, the business judgment rule, are two of the most frequently-tested subjects. Be alert to these issues whenever a fact pattern involves a decision by an officer or the board which could be characterized as unwise. Never consider "duty of care" in the abstract, always discuss it in conjunction with the business judgment rule. In other words, Phrase the initial issue as "did the directors exercise due care?" but then say something like, "If the conditions for the business judgment rule are met, the court will find that the board satisfied its duty of care even though the transaction turned out badly or seems to the court to have been substantively unwise."

Remember the three things a director must do to qualify for the business judgment rule: she must not be "interested," i.e., have & financial stake apart from the corporation's own interest, in the subject matter of the action; she must be reasonably informed about the decision she's making; and she must rationally believe that the judgment she's making is in the best of the corporation. Remember that absent directors are held to the same standard as directors who attended the meeting during which the board approved of a particular action. Thus if the board as a whole violated the duty of due care, i.e., didn't qualify for the business judgment rule, the absent directors will also be liable.

Most frequently-tested aspect of the business judgment rule: the directors don't make an adequate investigation before they commit large sums of money to a project. For example, President, the head of Corporation, wants to sell Corporation to Acquirer. President is worried that the present demand for Corporation's products will be transitory, and believes that the most favorable sale would be one that is accomplished rapidly. Therefore, President urges the Corporation board to approve the sale without debate, and does not fully brief the board on the reasons why Acquirer's offer is the best one that can be gotten. Nor does President or the board have an outsider review the price or other sale terms. The board probably does not qualify for the business judgment rule, because it was not adequately informed. If so the board will be liable for failure to satisfy its duty of care, if its carelessness caused a disadvantageous sale to be made.

A variant is that a report describing the proposed transaction is prepared, but some directors don't read it, these directors don't get the protection of the business judgment rule, because they haven't taken the available steps to make themselves "reasonably informed." Questions sometimes involve board reliance on the opinions of others. Here the rule is that the board is entitled to rely on others where it is reasonable to do so For instance, the board can typically rely on the opinion of the corporation's CPAs, if the latter say that a proposed acquisition is a profitable business that is being sold for a standard multiple of earnings. Also, check whether the directors have acted in good faith, i.e., in a non-self-interested manner. If they are acting so as to further their own business interests at the expense of, say, a minority holder, the directors will not qualify for the business judgment rule. For example, the board refuses to pay out any of $5 million of accumulated earnings as dividends. P, a minority holder, sues to overturn this refusal, and the majority directors defend on the grounds that their dividend policies are protected by the business judgment rule. If P can show that the directors' purpose was to "freeze out" P - by depriving him of income so that he'd sell his shares back to the majority at a low price - the directors won't receive the protection of the business judgment rule.

A fact pattern will rarely fail to meet the "rational belief" requirement for the business judgment rule. Remember that so long as the directors' belief that the action was in the corporation's interest is not wholly irrational, this prong will be deemed satisfied. And this is true even if the action results in financial loss to the corporation. For example, to prevent a minority s/h from acquiring control, Corporation buys shares from 3 other shareholder's at the asking price of $80/share, a price in excess of both book value and market value. As long as the decision was "plausible," the fact that the judge disagrees about the decision's wisdom, or the fact that later events showed that the shares were not worth the price paid, won't prevent the business judgment rule from applying.

PART V

DUTY OF LOYALTY AND SELF-DEALING TRANSACTION

CHAPTER 12

DUTY OF LOYALTY[201]

12.1 INTRODUCTION

In General. The duty of loyalty requires a fiduciary to act for the best interests of the corporation[202] and in good faith. It usually focuses on the

201) This Chapter is mainly compiled with materials from Arthur R. Pinto, Douglas M. Branson, "Understanding Corporate Law," LEXIS Publishing (1999); Emmanuel Law Outlines, "Corporations," Emmanuel Publishing Corp. (1997).

202) *See Dodge v. Ford Motor Co.,* 170 N.W. 668 (Mich. 1919); *Shlensky v. Wrigley*, 237 N.E.2d. 776 (Ill. 1968).

Facts for Dodge v. Ford Motor Co.,. Ford Motor Co. had a surplus of almost $112 million. It declared a dividend of $1.2 million. The Dodge Bros. were major shareholders, and wished to get some money to open a competing business. Ford's Board of Directors refused to issue a larger dividend, claiming that the surplus was needed for expansion and operating cushion.

Procedural Posture. Dodge sued to compel Ford's board to declare a special dividend equal to one-half of its surplus. The lower court awarded the dividend.

Issue & Holding. Whether the refusal of the Ford board of directors to issue such a dividend in this case amounted to a willful abuse of discretion. Yes.

Reasoning. It is well recognized that the power to declare a dividend, and the amount of the dividend, is exclusively within the discretion of the board of directors. However, a board may be compelled to pay a dividend if the failure to do so would be a willful abuse of their discretionary powers, or fraud, or breach of the fiduciary duty. Here, the surplus is so large, that even if Ford were to immediately spend all of the money it planned for expansion, there would still be an obscene surplus.

situation in which the fiduciary, or those associated with her, has a conflict of interest with the corporation and personal interests may be advanced over corporate interests. Generally, the court will scrutinize a conflict of interest transaction to determine if it is fair. The court may not only shift the burden of proof to the directors to show fairness but will inquire as to both the process and substance of the decision. Therefore, in duty of loyalty cases, there is more judicial involvement than in duty of care cases.[203] There are differences because in a duty of care cases the court want to protect business decisions that are intended to enhance corporate gains, while in a duty of loyalty case the directors may be motivated by personal gain.

Conflicts of interest usually involve some form of self-dealing where the fiduciary is in a position to receive a benefit unavailable to other shareholders. The ALI has adopted rules for directors, officers and controlling shareholders when they act with an interest in a matter affecting the corporation. Since the court have used duty of loyalty in both pecuniary and non-pecuniary conflict of interest context, the ALI used the term "duty of fair dealing" in the pecuniary context.[204] Generally, when the duty of loyalty applies, there is a duty of complete candor; the burden of proof shifts to the directors; and, there is greater judicial scrutiny of both the fairness of the process and the substance of the transaction. Under a duty of loyalty analysis, the defendants are not afforded the protection of the business judgment rule with its presumption of a proper decision. Therefore, a plaintiff will often try to characterize the activity of a defendant as a breach of the duty of loyalty in order to take advantage of a more favorable legal landscape.

---

203) *See* Ahmed Bulbulia & Arthur R. Pinto, *Statutory Responses to Interested Directors' Transactions: A Watering Down of Fiduciary Standards?*, 53 Notre Dame L. Rev. 201 (1977).

204) *See* A.L.I. *Corp. Gov. Proj.* PART V (Introductory Note).

12.2 KEY PLAYERS

The duty of loyalty owed to the corporation by its directors, officers and controlling shareholders, which we call "Key Players," has some key concepts. First is the self-dealing transactions. In a transaction where the Key Player and the corporation are on opposite sides, e.g., the Key Player sells property to the corporation, the transaction may be voided by the court, and the Key Player required to pay damages to the corporation, unless the conflict is disclosed in advance. Second is an approval by disinterested holders or directors.

The best way for the Key Player to avoid self-dealing problems is for her to: (1) disclose the conflict transaction in advance, and (2) have a majority of the disinterested directors or disinterested shareholders pre-approve the transaction after this disclosure. Third is fairness or ratification. Alternatively, the Key Player will avoid self-dealing problems if either: (1) the transaction is basically "fair" to the corporation; or (2) disinterested directors or shareholders ratify the transaction after the fact, after receiving full disclosure about it. Fourth is an executive compensation. Decisions about a senior executive's salary, bonuses, stock options or pensions may be overturned if they are clearly "excessive," taking into account the nature of the executive's services. Fifth is a corporate opportunity doctrine. Before a director or senior executive may take for himself an opportunity that is likely to be of interest to the corporation, e.g., Purchase of some property adjacent to the corporation's property, he must first offer that opportunity to the corporation. If he doesn't, he may be required to surrender the opportunity to the corporation after the fact, and/or pay damages. Finally, it is a sale of control. The owner of a controlling block of stock is generally allowed to sell his shares for an above-market "premium," without sharing that premium with other shareholders. However, there are several exceptions.

12.3 FIDUCIARY STATUS

Key Players as Trustees. It is sometimes said that directors, officers and controlling shareholders are in effect "trustees" of the corporation, and have a fiduciary obligation to it. As Justice Cardozo said, in a case involving a joint venture rather than a corporation, but a case which is often cited in connection with the duties of corporate directors and officers: "Joint adventurers ... owe to one another ... the duty of the finest loyalty. Many forms of conduct permissible in a workaday world for those acting at arm's length, are forbidden to those bound by fiduciary ties. A trustee is held to something stricter than the morals of the market place."[205)]

However, the statement that officers, directors and controlling shareholders are in effect trustees of the corporation is only partly accurate. It is true that these Key Players have varying duties to the corporation and its other shareholders that are somewhat similar to the fiduciary duties that a trustee incurs. But there are important differences. For example, a trustee must behave in a prudent manner, whereas the managers of a business enterprise are expected to take risks, sometimes big ones, and often ones that would be inappropriate for a trustee. Similarly, a controlling shareholder may have certain duties to the corporation and to the minority shareholders, but he nonetheless owns his shares and within fairly broad limits is entitled to sell them when and how he wishes, without concern for the minority; again, this is quite different from the position of the trustee, who must put the interests of the beneficiary ahead of his own interests.

Full-Time Employee. There is one situation in which fiduciary responsibilities will be quite strictly enforced in corporate law: any full-time employee of the corporation, including an officer, is an agent of the corporation, and is subject to all the fiduciary rules of agency, including a very strict ban on self-dealing.

---

205) *Meinhard v. Salmon.* 164 N.E. 545 (N.Y. 1928). For the full text of this case see *infra* the Appendix I.

Directors and Controlling Stockholders. By contrast, an outside director, and a controlling shareholder who is not employed by the corporation, are usually held to at least a somewhat more lenient fiduciary standard. This difference is especially noticeable in the corporate opportunity context - a business opportunity that a full-time employee learns about is much more likely to be found to "belong" to the corporation, than is a business opportunity that an outside director or non-employee major shareholder learns about.

CHAPTER 13

SELF-DEALING TRANSACTION[206)]

13.1 INTRODUCTION

The first context in which we need to consider the "duty of loyalty" is the context of the self-dealing transaction. The key aspect of such transactions is that the Key Player, officer, director or controlling shareholder, and the corporation are on opposite sides of the transaction. More precisely, we're especially concerned with transactions in which three conditions are met: (1) the Key Player and the corporation are on opposite sides; (2) the Key Player has helped influence the corporation's decision to enter the transaction; and (3) the Key Player's personal financial interests are at least potentially in conflict with the financial interests of the corporation, to such a degree that there is reason to doubt whether the Key Player is necessarily motivated to act in the corporation's best interests. When we use the term "self-dealing transaction" in this book, we'll be referring to transactions that satisfy all

206) This Chapter is mainly compiled with materials from Arthur R. Pinto, Douglas M. Branson, "Understanding Corporate Law," LEXIS Publishing (1999); Emmanuel Law Outlines, "Corporations," Emmanuel Publishing Corp. (1997).

three of these requirements.

For instance, the paradigmatic illustration of the self-dealing transaction is the sale of property by a director to the corporation, or by the corporation to the director. If the director has influenced the corporation's decision to make the trans-action, there is reason to fear that a sale by the corporation to the director will be at too low a price, and a sale by the director to the corporation will be at too high a price. Observe that the fact that the Key Player happens to be a shareholder in the corporation does not remove this danger of unfairness to the corporation. For even though damage to the corporation will hurt the Key Player qua shareholder the gain to him in his role as independent person will probably be greater than the loss to him as shareholder. This is true even if he is the majority shareholder.

For example, Smith owns 70% of the stock of XYZ Corporation He is also president and one of the three directors. XYZ Corp is in the business of building hotels on property that it acquires. Smith happens to own Black acre, a nice two acre parcel that he and his fellow directors agree is perfect for XYZ to build a hotel on. The board approves XYZ's purchase of the property from Smith at a price of $1 million. There is reason to worry that this price is too high and is thereforc unfair to the corporation. True, if the price is $100,000 too high, Smith will bear $70,000 of this loss, because he owns 70% of the stock. But on the other hand, Smith ends up with $100,000 extra in his pocket, so he is ahead by a net amount of $30,000, and the minority shareholders are behind by $30,000. Since there is reason to think that Smith may have influenced the board's decision even if Smith himself didn't vote on the transaction, the other two directors know that they effectively serve at Smith's pleasure, and that he can decline to reelect them next time, we have all three ingredients for a self-dealing transaction that should be closely scrutinized: (1) a Key Player in a transaction with the corporation; (2) the Key Player possibly influencing the corporation's decision to enter the transaction; and (3) the Key Player's personal financial interests in conflict with those of the corporation. Smith wants to sell high, the corporation wants to buy low. Therefore, a court will probably scrutinize the transaction fairly closely, and will void it if it appears unfair to the corporation.

Historical Rule. Courts have gradually become somewhat more tolerant of self-dealing transactions. Until the late 1800s, courts were completely uncompromising: self-dealing transactions were completely prohibited. For example, it didn't matter that the transaction was "fair" when viewed by an impartial observer, or that the transaction purported to have been approved by a majority of disinterested directors with full knowledge of the facts.

By 1910, most courts had eased that prohibition somewhat: a self-dealing transaction would be allowed to stand if it was both approved by a majority of fully-informed disinterested directors, and was "fair" to the corporation as determined by the court. But a contract in which a majority of the board was interested was voidable even if fair.

Modern View. By 1960, the still more liberal view that generally applies today was in place: a self-dealing transaction found by the court to be fair would be upheld, whether approved by a disinterested board or not. In most states, the rule is at least partly established by statute.

The cases give no clear explanation for this dramatically increased tolerance for at least those self-dealing transactions that are found to be fair. Probably much of this tolerance comes from recognition that there will generally be an economic benefit to the corporation from allowing fair but self-dealing transactions - especially in the case of the close corporation, transactions between a Key Person and the corporation may be the only way a corporation can obtain funds, goods or other things it needs. For example, suppose that Close Corporation is formed by three shareholders, A, B and C. The corporation needs working capital to pursue its business, a service business which so far has no tangible assets. Banks are unwilling to lend to Close. A and B cause a corporation that they control to make an unsecured loan to Close at the prime rate. The transaction is never approved by the sole disinterested director, C, and it is never formally ratified by the stockholders acting as such. In the late 1800s or even 1910, a court would have voided the transaction at C's request, without considering its fairness to Close. But a modem court would probably determine that it was fair to the corporation, since it was not at an excessively high interest rate, and no better terms seemed to be available from other sources, despite the lack of direct approval by disinterested directors or shareholders. The reason is that the transaction has been beneficial to Close, since it enabled it to get funds that it could not otherwise easily obtain.

13.2 STATEMENT OF RULE

Most courts, acting by a combination of statutory interpretation and common-law principles where the statute is silent, seem to divide self-dealing transactions into three categories: (1) Fair transactions; (2) Waste/fraud; and (3) Middle ground.

First is fair transactions. If the transaction is found to be fair to the corporation, considering all the circumstances, nearly all courts will uphold it. This is true whether or not the transaction was ever approved by disinterested directors or ratified by the shareholders. Second is a waste or a fraud. If the transaction is so one-sided that it amounts to "waste" or "fraud" against the corporation, the court will usually void it if a stockholder complains. This is true even though the transaction has been approved by a majority of disinterested directors, acting with full knowledge of the transaction they were approving, or ratified by the shareholders. Third is a middle ground. If the transaction does not fall into either of these categories - the court is not convinced it's perfectly fair, but the unfairness does not amount to waste or fraud - the court's response will probably depend on whether there has been director approval and/or shareholder ratification.

If a majority of disinterested and knowledgeable directors have approved the transaction, the court will probably uphold it; the court will similarly uphold it if it has been ratified by the shareholders. If neither disinterested director approval nor shareholder ratification has occurred, the court will probably invalidate the transaction. The burden of proofs of the Key Player, he must show that the transaction was approved by either: (1) a disinterested and knowledgeable majority of the board without participation by the Key Player; or (2) a majority of the shareholders after full disclosure of the relevant facts.

Thus the most important variable in the modern cases seems to be fairness; clearly-fair transactions are always upheld, clearly-abusive ones waste or fraud are always struck down, and only if the transaction's fairness is ambiguous will the fact of disinterested director approval or shareholder ratification make a difference.

RMBCA

The corporation statutes of 38 states have explicit provisions dealing with transactions between the corporation and a Key Player. Most of these statutes deal solely with contracts between the corporation and a director, not those between a corporation and a non-director officer or controlling shareholder. Probably the most important, and explicit, such statute is RMBCA §§ 8.60-8.63.

These sections were made part of the RMBCA in 1988, replacing a much simpler single provision. Although these new sections have so far not been widely adopted by the states, only Georgia, Mississippi, Montana and Washington had adopted them as of late 1993, they are likely to be influential in the future. Also, the general pattern of these RMBCA provisions - that a self-dealing transaction will be upheld if it is either approved by disinterested directors, ratified by shareholders or found by a court to have been fair - is typical of the approach of most states. Therefore, we consider the RMBCA provisions in some detail, §§ 8.60-8.63 are usually collectively referred to as "Subchapter F" of the RMBCA. The key section of the RMBCA Subchapter F is § 8.61:

Section 8.61 JUDICIAL ACTION

(a) A transaction effected or proposed to be effected by a corporation (or by a subsidiary of the corporation or any other entity in which the corporation has a controlling interest) that is not a director's conflicting interest transaction may not be enjoined, set aside, or give rise to an award of damages or other sanctions, in a proceeding by a shareholder or by or in the right of the corporation, because a director of the corporation, or any person with whom or which he has a personal, economic, or other association, has an interest in the transaction.

(b) A director's conflicting interest transaction may not be enjoined, set aside, or give rise to an award of damages or other sanctions, in a proceeding by a shareholder or by or in the right of the corporation, because the director, or any person with whom or which he has a personal, economic, or other association, has an interest in the transaction, if:

(1) directors' action respecting the transaction was at any time taken in compliance with section 8.62; [or]

(2) shareholders' action respecting the transaction was at any time taken in compliance with section 8.63; [or]

(3) the transaction, judged according to the circumstances at the time of commitment, is established to have been fair to the corporation.

Section 8.60 supplies a set of definitions for Subchapter F; these definitions are too long and convoluted to be reproduced here in full. The key idea is that there are only two ways in which a director will be deemed to have a conflict of interest regarding a transaction which the corporation is entering into:

First, we have "direct" conflicts, i.e., ones where the director or his close relative is a party to or has a large financial interest in the transaction. Such a conflict is deemed to exist if the director "knows at the time of commitment that he or a related person is a party to the transaction or has a beneficial financial interest in or so closely linked to the transaction and of such financial significance to the director or a related person that the interest would reasonably be expected to exert an influence on the director's judgment if he were called upon to vote on the transaction."[207] A "related person" covers principally the director's spouse, child, grandchild, sibling or parent, or any of these people's spouses, or any trust or estate as to which the director is a beneficiary or fiduciary.[208] Note that the above class of "direct" conflicts applies even if the transaction is one that was not, and would not ordinarily have been, brought before the board - in other words, even very minor transactions, e.g., the purchasing of office supplies, are covered by the above class.

Second, we have "indirect" conflicts, i.e., those where the other party in interest is not the director herself, or a close relative, but some business entity associated with the director, or some business associate of the director. Thus a conflict will be deemed to arise where the transaction is brought, or "is of such character and significance to the corporation that it would in the normal course be brought," before the board of directors, and the director knows that the other party to the transaction is either: (A) an entity of which the director is a "director, general partner, agent or employee", (B) an affiliate of one of the entities listed in sub-clause (A); or (C) an individual who is a general partner, principal, or employer of the director.[209] So as to even minor transactions, there is a conflict if the director himself, or his close relative, has a strong enough financial interest that his judgment on whether to approve the transaction could reasonably be expected to be influenced. And a major, board-level, transaction, but not a minor, non-board-level transaction, will present a conflict even if the director's judgment would not be expected to be swayed by his financial interest, if the other party to the transaction is, for instance, the director's employer, his partner, or a company of which the director is a director.

The guts of Subchapter F are set forth in § 8.61 (reproduced above). That section imposes two major rules: Where a transaction is "not a director's

207) RMBCA § 8.60(1)(i).

208) RMBCA § 8.60(3).

209) RMBCA § 8.60(1)(ii).

conflicting interest transaction" the court may not enjoin it or set it aside on account of any interest which the director may have in the transaction. If the transaction is a "director's conflicting interest transaction," the corporation and the director receive a "safe harbor" for the transaction - and the court may thus not set it aside, if: (1) a majority of disinterested directors approved it after disclosure of the conflict to them;[210] or (2) a majority of the votes held by disinterested shareholders are cast in a vote ratifying the action, after disclosure of the conflict;[211] or (3) the transaction "judged according to the circumstances at the time of commitment, is established to have been fair to the corporation."

Here are several aspects of Subchapter F that may not be obvious: First, the definition of "conflicting interest" given in § 8.60 is exclusive. That is, if the transaction does not fall within the definition given there, the transaction is automatically deemed non-conflicting, and the court may not overturn it on grounds of director self-interest.

Example 1: D is a director of X Co. X Co. proposes to enter into a transaction with Smith, who is D's cousin. The transaction comes before the X Co. board for approval. D and Smith are not only cousins but extremely close friends, and D knows that Smith desperately needs the money which would come to him as the result of the proposed transaction. D does not disclose to the X Co. board the fact that Smith is his cousin, or that D wishes the transaction to go forward so as to aid Smith. D has no independent financial interest in the transaction. The board members listen to D's urging that the transaction be approved, and vote for approval. P, a shareholder, now sues the board and Smith, seeking to have the transaction set aside. Under the RMBCA approach, the court must conclude that there is no conflict, and may therefore not even consider overturning the transaction on conflict grounds. The reason is that a cousin is not "related person" under the definitions given in § 8.60(1) and (3), and D had no direct financial

---

210) RMBCA § 8.62.

211) RMBCA § 8.63.

interest of his own in the transaction. Since the transaction is not a "director's conflicting interest transaction" as defined in § 8.60(2), § 8.61(a) requires that the court not enjoin it on account of any conflict arising out of the X-Smith relationship.[212)]

Example 2: D is a director of X Co and Y Co. Y Co, a business machines dealer, proposes to sell several typewriters and copiers to X Co. Due to the relatively small size of this transaction, it would not ordinarily come before the X Co. board. D holds a fairly small shareholding in Y Co, so the transaction is not directly financially significant enough to him that it would be expected to influence his judgment. On these facts, the proposed transaction is not a "director's conflicting interest transaction" because it does not fall within either § 8.60(1)(i) or § 8.60(1)(ii). Therefore, even if D remains silent about the conflict, and the board never votes on it, a court may not set aside the transaction under the RMBCA approach, because it simply does not pose any statutorily-defined conflict.

Second, Subchapter F covers only transactions between the corporation and one of its directors. Transactions between the corporation and a non-director officer or shareholder are not covered by Subchapter P, and are in fact not covered by any provision of the RMBCA having to do with self-dealing. Thus transactions with non-director officers or shareholders under the RMBCA are left entirely to common-law principles, though the court is likely to approach these in almost the same way as a transaction between the corporation and a director.

Third, the disclosure and approval can happen even after the transaction has been challenged by a dissident shareholder or third party. In other words, after-the-deal ratification by the board can suffice. Preapproval is not necessary.[213)] For example, a majority of disinterested directors approve Corporation's purchase of land from Landco, a limited partnership. At

212) This example is suggested by an example given in Official Comment 1 to § 8.61.

213) See Official Comment to RMBCA § 8.62(a).

the time of the approval vote the directors don't know that Bob, one of the directors, is secretly a major partner in Landco. The purchase goes through. Steve, a minority holder in Corporation, then learns of the conflict. He brings a derivative suit to have the transaction unwound. If nothing further happens, and if the court finds that the transaction was "unfair" to Corporation, the court will probably order the transaction unwound or at least order that Bob pay damages to Corporation But if, within a reasonable time after Steve brings suit, the board ratifies the transaction with full disclosure of the nature of the transaction and nature of Bob's ownership interest in the selling partnership, the court will not interfere.

ALI

The ALI's Principles of Corporate Governance also treat the self-dealing problem with great specificity. Here is the key provision:

Section 5.02 TRANSACTIONS WITH THE CORPORATION

(a) General Rule. A director or senior executive who enters into a transaction with the corporation (other than a transaction involving the payment of compensation) fulfills the duty of fair dealing with respect to the transaction if:

(1) Disclosure concerning the conflict of interest and the transaction is made to the corporate decision maker who authorizes in advance or ratifies the transaction; and

(2) Either:

(A) The transaction is fair to the corporation when entered into;

(B) The transaction is authorized in advance, following disclosure concerning the conflict of interest and the transaction, by disinterested directors, or in the case of a senior executive who is not a director by a disinterested superior, who could reasonably have concluded that the transaction was fair to the corporation at the time of such authorization;

(C) The transaction is ratified, following such disclosure, by disinterested directors who could reasonably have concluded that the transaction was fair to the corporation at the time it was entered into, Provided:

(i) a corporate decision maker who is not interested in the transaction acted/or the corporation in the transaction and could reasonably have concluded that the transaction was/ air to the corporation;

(ii) the interested director or senior executive made disclosure to such decision maker pursuant to Subsection (a)(1) to the extent he or she then knew of the material facts;

(iii) the interested director or senior executive did not act unreasonably in failing to seek advance authorization of the transaction by disinterested directors or a disinterested superior; and

(iv) the failure to obtain advance authorization of the transaction by disinterested directors or a disinterested superior did not adversely affect the interests of the corporation m a significant way; or (D) The transaction is authorized in advance or ratified, following such disclosure, by disinterested shareholders, and does not constitute a waste of corporate assets at the time of the shareholder action.

(b) Burden of Proof. A party who challenges a transaction between a director or senior executive and the corporation has the burden of proof, except that if such party establishes that none of Subsections (a)(2)(B), (a)(2)(C), or (a)(2)(D) is satisfied, the director or senior executive has the burden of proving that the transaction was/aw to the corporation.

(c) Ratification of Disclosure or Non-disclosure. The disclosure requirements of § 5.02(a)(1) will be deemed to be satisfied if at any time (but no later than a reasonable time after suit is filed challenging the transaction) the transaction is ratified,

> following such disclosure, by the directors the shareholders, or the corporate decision maker who initially approved the transaction or such decision maker's successor.

Here are a few of the important differences between the ALI's approach and that of the RMBCA. First is a prior disclosure. Perhaps most important, even if the transaction is perfectly fair, under the ALI text it may be avoided by the corporation if the director or executive has not made "disclosure concerning the conflict of interest and the transaction" to the corporation. However, this disclosure may be made after the transaction, so long as it is made "no later than a reasonable time after suit is filed challenging the transaction."[214)]

Second covers "senior executives." The ALI text, unlike the RMBCA, expressly applies to transactions between the corporation and a non-director "senior executive," as well as to transactions involving a director. "Senior executive" is roughly synonymous with what is usually called an "officer." A non-director senior executive has a somewhat easier time to obtain approval than does a director: the non-director executive may have the transaction authorized in advance by a "disinterested superior" rather than by a majority of disinterested directors, which is the only pre-approval route available to the director.[215)]

Third is a Director approval. Whereas the RMBCA, at least on its face, seems to insulate even an unfair transaction against attack if it has been approved by the disinterested board members, the ALI contains its own fairness test for transactions approved by disinterested directors: the transaction must be such that the directors "could reasonably have concluded that the transaction was/air to the corporation at the time of authorization."[216)] In other words, the transaction doesn't have to be one that the court believes actually is fair; but if it is "outside the range of reasonableness" so that no

214) ALI's Principles of Corporate Governance § 5.02(c).

215) *See* ALI's Principles of Corporate Governance § 5.02(a)(2)(B).

216) ALI's Principles of Corporate Governance § 5.02(a)(2)(B).

reasonable observer could believe it to be fair, it will not be upheld.[217)]

Forth is an after-the-fact director ratification. Whereas the RMBCA seems to make it just as easy for the disinterested directors to ratify the transaction after the fact as to approve it in advance, the ALI calls for the court to give closer scrutiny to a ratified-after-the-fact transaction than to an approved-in-advance one. Essentially, after-the-fact ratification works under the ALI only if: (1) the lack of advance approval "did not adversely affect the interests of the corporation in a significant way," a relatively tough standard; and (2) the interested director or senior executive made advance disclosure of the conflict to someone else in the corporation, who then acted on the corporation's behalf in the transaction.[218)]

In summary, the ALI draft makes it considerably easier to attack a conflict-of-interest transaction than does the RMBCA.

Three Paths. Under the RMBCA, the ALI, and the statutes of most states, there are thus three different ways that proponents of a self-dealing transaction can avoid invalidation: (1) by showing that it was approved by a majority of disinterested directors after full disclosure; (2) by showing that it was ratified by shareholders, after full disclosure; and (3) by showing that is was/air when made. We will now consider each of these branches in detail.

13.3 DISCLOSURE PLUS BOARD APPROVAL

The general principle behind the "board approval" branch is simple to state: a transaction may not be avoided by the corporation if it was authorized by a majority of the disinterested directors, after full disclosure of the nature of the conflict and the transaction. However, this formulation raises a number

217) *See* Comment to § 5.02(a)(2)(B).

218) ALI's Principles of Corporate Governance § 5.02(a)(2)(C).

of questions:

WHAT MUST BE DISCLOSED

What information is it that must be disclosed to the disinterested directors? Most courts, and both the RMBCA and the ALI, require disclosure of two major kinds of information: (1) the material facts about the conflict; and (2) the material facts about the transaction.

Conflict. Often the fact that there is a conflict will be obvious to the disinterested directors, e.g., when the contract runs directly between the director and the corporation. But other conflicts will not be obvious, and must therefore be disclosed by the Key Person. This will be tine, for instance, if the other party to the transaction is a corporation in which the Key Person has a significant pecuniary interest. For example, XYZ Corp wants to buy an office building. D, a vice president of XYZ owns all of the stock of Realty Corp, which owns an office building. D has a real estate broker offer the building to XYZ, and the board of XYZ votes to acquire it. The other directors are not aware that D has an interest in Realty Corporation. Even though all material economic facts about the underlying transaction, e.g., the condition and market value of the building, have been disclosed to the other board members, approval by the board of the contract will not insulate the transaction from attack, because D has not disclosed his financial interest in Realty Corp to the board.[219)]

Disclosure of Transaction Apart from disclosure of the facts that cause a conflict the Key Person most also disclose all facts about the underlying transaction that a reasonable observer would consider "material." This obligation goes far beyond the ordinary duty of one party to a contract to disclose essential facts to the other. For instance, if the Key Person knows of facts that are likely to make the proposed contract turn out to the disadvantage of the corporation, he must disclose those facts, where as a third party negotiating at arm's length with the corporation could remain silent.

219) See Illustr. 4 to ALI Prin. Corporation Gov. § 5.02.

When Disclosure Must Be Made. You might think that the requirement of disclosure means that the disclosure must take place before the transaction is entered into. But courts are in fact in disagreement about whether this is required. Some courts will uphold the transaction based on board approval even if the disclosure does not come until after the transaction is entered into, so long as the directors then "ratify" it by formally stating that they have no objection, or perhaps even by simply failing to raise an objection. Thus RMBCA insulates the transaction against judicial review if directors' action respecting the transaction was at any time taken in compliance with other provision[220] providing for approval by disinterested directors.[221] The phrase "at any time" is intended to allow for post-transaction ratification. But other courts, and the ALI's Prin. Corporation Gov., require the disclosure to occur before the transaction, or at least make it tougher for transactions to be ratified after the fact instead of approved beforehand.

WHO IS A "DISINTERESTED" DIRECTOR

The approval must be by a majority of the "disinterested" directors. Who is "disinterested" for this purpose? Most courts would probably agree with the RMBCA, which says that a director is "qualified"[222] if she "does not have either (1) a conflicting interest respecting the transaction, or (2) familial, financial, professional, or employment relationship with a Second director who does have a conflicting interest respecting the transaction which relationship would, in the circumstances, reasonably be expected to exert an influence on the first director's judgment when voting on the transaction."[223]

Dominated Director. Thus a director may be "interested" not only because he or his family has a direct financial interest, but also because he has a close relationship with someone who is a party. For instance, if the chief executive

220) See RMBCA § 8.62.

221) RMBCA § 8.61(b)(1).

222) It is the RMBCA's term for "disinterested".

223) RMBCA § 8.62(d).

of the corporation is a party to the transaction, an "inside director," i.e., a director who is also a full-time employee of the corporation, may well be held to have the sort of relationship with the chief executive that would lead to the director's being found to be "interested." The inside director might be called a "dominated" director here.

Outside Professionals. Even outside directors who serve as professionals, e.g., outside counsel or outside accountant, to the corporation may be found to be "interested" in a transaction in which the CEO is a party. The theory for treating these professionals as "interested" is that they may be afraid they will no longer be engaged by the corporation if they annoy the CEO by voting against the transaction.

Quorum. Often, especially in the case of a close corporation, a majority of the directors will be "interested" in the transaction. For instance, the CEO may be a party to the transaction, and a majority of the directors may be full-time employees who owe their jobs to him. In this situation, there will of course not be enough disinterested directors to constitute a quorum of the board. Therefore, a special rule exists in almost all states to facilitate approval by the disinterested directors: if a majority of the disinterested directors approve the transaction, this constitutes not only approval, but also a quorum. However most statutes require at least two disinterested directors to approve the transaction.[224)]

For example, the board of XYZ Corp has five directors. Two of them propose to enter into a contract with XYZ, and are therefore interested directors. The other three are not interested. One of the three disinterested directors is absent from the board meeting. The other two disinterested directors are sufficient to constitute a quorum for approval purposes, since they represent a majority of the three disinterested directors. If these two approve the transaction, this will constitute the requisite disinterested director approval. If, on the other hand, two of the three disinterested directors were

224) See RMBCA § 8.62(c), and Del. GCL 144(a)(1), both to this effect.

absent the third director's vote approving the transaction would not constitute either a quorum or approval, because there would not be approval by a majority of the total disinterested directors, those present and those absent.

Ideally, the interested director should abstain from either voting or even lobbying the disinterested directors concerning the transaction. However, most statutes provide that participation by the interested director in the consideration or voting does not by itself nullify the approval by the disinterested directors, the interested director's presence and/or vote is simply disregarded, and the sole question is whether a majority of the total disinterested directors has approved the transaction.[225)]

Committee. Under most statutes, approval by disinterested directors may be done at the level of a committee rather than the full board. Usually, this committee may be either one that already exists, e.g., the compensation committee, or one appointed specially to consider the particular transaction. In any event, all that is required for a quorum and for approval is the approval by a majority of the disinterested directors on the committee even if this is less than a majority of the total disinterested directors on the board.

IMMUNIZATION OF UNFAIRNESS

Suppose a majority of disinterested directors, acting after full disclosure of all material facts, approves a transaction that, viewed later by a court is clearly unfair to the corporation. Does the disinterested director approval completely immunize the transaction against attack for self-dealing? Most statutes are written as if the answer were "yes." However, in practice courts often void such transactions if the unfairness is great, despite the disinterested-director approval; frequently, they accomplish this result by finding that the transaction constituted "waste."

ALI. The ALI text gives the court explicit authority to void grossly unfair contracts that have been approved by disinterested directors. The ALI

225) See the last sentence of RMBCA § 8.62(c), to this effect.

provides that a self-dealing transaction approved by disinterested directors must be one that the directors "could reasonably have concluded [was] fair to the corporation at the time of such authorization," so that transactions that no reasonable person would deem to be fair can be struck down.[226)]

Shifting of Burden of Proof. In most states, approval by the disinterested directors does seem to at least shift the burden of proof-, if the transaction has not been approved by disinterested directors, or shareholders, the burden is generally on the Key Player to prove that it was fair; once approved by disinterested directors the burden shifts to the person attacking the transaction to show that it was unfair.

13.4 SHAREHOLDER RATIFICATION

The second main branch for validating a Self-dealing transaction is the ratification by shareholders, following disclosure to them. As in the case of disinterested-director approval, the shareholder ratification will be effective only if it comes after there has been full disclosure to the shareholders of both the conflict and the material acts of the transaction itself.[227)] *In Talbot v.*

---

226) ALI, Principles of Corporate Governance § 5.02(a)(2)(B).

227) *See,* e.g., *Talbot v. James,* 190 S.E.2d 759 (S.C. 1972).

Case Synopsis. Appellants sought review of an order of the Court of Common Pleas for Horry County (South Carolina) reversing a report in which the Master of Equity for Horry County (South Carolina) found that respondent violated his fiduciary duty to appellants as stockholders.

Facts. Appellants, as stockholders, brought an equitable action for an accounting. Respondent director, through a construction company he owned, had entered into a contract with the corporation for construction of respondent apartments. Appellants alleged that by diverting funds to himself, respondent director violated his fiduciary relationship to the corporation and to appellants as stockholders thereof.

Procedural History. The Master of Equity issued a report finding that respondent director violated his fiduciary duty to appellants as stockholders. The trial judge reversed the findings and ordered judgment in favor of respondents.

Discussion. The Supreme Court reversed and remanded, finding that respondent director had contracted with the corporation without making full disclosure to appellants.

Conclusion. The Supreme Court reversed and remanded, finding that respondent had contracted with the corporation without making full disclosure to appellants.

James, 50% shareholder/officer may have disclosed to other shareholders that he would be the building contractor for the corporation's real estate project, but because he did not show that he would charge the corporation a $20,000 fee and $31,000 for his overhead, he did not make full disclosure, and the transaction is voidable by the minority shareholders.

Disinterested Shareholders. Recall that in the case of director authorization, a majority of the disinterested directors must approve. Does a comparable rule apply to shareholder ratification, or may interested shareholders vote and be counted towards a majority? The courts are hopelessly split and confused about this issue - some seem to say that shareholder ratification has no effect unless a majority of the disinterested shareholders approve, whereas others seem to hold that all shareholders may vote and be counted. A court is likely to give a more searching inquiry into the transaction's underlying fairness in those situations where it is not clear that a majority of the disinterested shareholders has approved.

The RMBCA takes a stringent view. The RMBCA requires that a majority of the disinterested shareholders must approve the transaction.[228)] On the other hand, for purposes of determining whether the transaction is approved under general corporate action principles having nothing to do with the conflict, interested shareholder votes may be counted, and are part of the quorum. For example, assume that Parent Corporation owns 60% of Subsidiary Corporation. Parent Corporation wants to merge Subsidiary Corporation into itself. Because Parent Corporation is a party to the transaction the conflict will be deemed ratified by the shareholders only if at least half of the holders of the minority block approve it.[229)] However, for purposes of determining whether the general requirement of shareholder approval for any merger under the RMBCA has occurred, and for determining whether

228) RMBCA § 8.63(a).

229) RMBCA § 8.63(a).

there has been a quorum for that approval, Parent Corporation's votes may be counted.[230)]

13.5 FAIRNESS

The final method of defending a self-dealing transaction against attack is by showing that it is, under all the circumstances, fair to the corporation. In nearly all states, fairness atone will cause the transaction to be upheld, even if there has been no approval by disinterested directors and no ratification by shareholders. "Fairness" is generally determined by the facts as they were known at the time of the transaction.[231)]

In most courts, the transaction will withstand attack if it is proven fair, even though no disclosure whatsoever is made by the Key Player to his fellow executives, directors or shareholders. Thus in the office building example on even if D never disclosed to anyone that he was a controlling shareholder in the firm that owned the building being sold to the corporation, most courts would hold that so long as the pricing terms were in line with what would have been produced by arm's length bargaining, the transaction may not be avoided by the corporation.

However, the ALI text takes a stricter view. Disclosure concerning the conflict and the underlying transaction is an absolute requirement even if the transaction is perfectly fair to the corporation.[232)] But this disclosure need not be made before the transaction; the disclosure may be made anytime up to "a reasonable time after suit is filed challenging the transaction," provided that the transaction is then ratified by the board, the shareholders or the executive

230) See Official Comment 3 to RMBCA § 8.63.

231) See, e.g., RMBCA § 8.61(b)(3) ("judged according to the circumstances at the time of commitment.")

232) ALI Prin. Corporation Gov., § 5.02(a)(1).

who initially approved the transaction without disclosure.[233)]

In most states fairness is really the key element. As we've just seen, if the transaction is fair lack of disinterested-director authorization or shareholder ratification will not make a difference. Conversely, if the transaction is found by the court to be grossly unfair, under most statutes the fact that there was approval by disinterested directors, or ratification by shareholders, will not immunize the transaction.

But some jurisdictions, probably a minority, do allow disinterested-director authorization or shareholder ratification to immunize even an unfair transaction from judicial review. Delaware, for instance, seems to allow such immunization. As the Delaware Supreme Court has stated: "Approval by fully-informed disinterested directors under § 144(a)(1), or disinterested stockholders under § 144(a)(2), Permits invocation of the business judgment rule and limits judicial review to issues of gift or waste, with the burden of proof upon the party attacking the transaction."[234)]

Similarly, the text of the RMBCA as revised in 1988, Purports to forbid judicial review of the fairness of director-authorized or shareholder-ratified transactions. But an Official Comment seems to restore some of the judicial power that the text of the statute takes away. § 8.61(b) states that the court

---

233) ALI Prin. Corporation Gov., § 5.02(c).

234) *Marciano v. Nakash*, 535 A.2d 400 (Del. 1987).

Case Synopsis. Appellants challenged a decision of the Court of Chancery (Delaware), which held that interested director loans made by appellees were not voidable as self-dealing transactions.

Facts. Both parties had entered into a joint venture to market designer jeans. Stock ownership and the composition of the board were shared equally by the parties. Ultimately the board deadlocked over policy issues and a court-approved plan of liquidation followed. Appellees had made loans to the corporation upon which they asserted claims at liquidation. Appellants argued that the debt was voidable under Del. Code Ann. tit. 8, § 144 because it originated in self-dealing transactions.

Discussion. On appeal, appellants argued that the chancery court applied the wrong standard of review for self-dealing transactions and thus its finding of full fairness was erroneous. The court held that relationship alone was not the only factor to determine if an interested director transaction was void. Since the loans were made on favorable terms, the loans were not automatically void under the intrinsic fairness test.

Conclusion. The court affirmed the decision of the chancery court, because although appellees' loans originated in self-dealing transactions, the test of intrinsic fairness supported the validity of the loans in light of the financial circumstances of the corporation.

may not overturn a director-conflict transaction if the action was authorized by disinterested directors after disclosure, or ratified by disinterested shareholders after disclosure.

But Official Comment 2 to § 8.61(b) states that in the case of a director-authorized transaction, the rule just stated is "subject to a critically important predicate condition. The condition - an obvious one - is that the board's action must comply with the care, best interests and good faith criteria prescribed in § 8.30(a) for all directors' actions.. .. If a determination is made that the terms of a director's conflicting interest transaction, judged according to the circumstances at the time of commitment, were manifestly unfavorable to the corporation that determination would be relevant to an allegation that the directors' action was not taken in good faith and therefore did not comply with § 8.30(a)... ."

So the plaintiff who is suing under the RMBCA to overturn a conflict transaction that was approved by the disinterested directors gets a "back door" chance to show unfairness: if he can show that the transaction was so "manifestly unfair" to the corporation that the approval should be found not to have been made in "good faith," then the transaction can be overturned by the court despite the disinterested-director approval. Obviously, this back door will not become available to a plaintiff who merely shows that the transaction was slightly unfair, e.g., the corporation bought property at a price that was, say, 10% too high or sold it a price 10% too low; only substantial and obvious unfairness will do.

DIRECTOR OR SHAREHOLDER APPROVAL

If fairness is what really counts - that is, if fair transactions will be upheld even without director or shareholder approval, and unfair ones will be struck down even with shareholder or director approval - why bother to get approval by disinterested directors or by shareholders? The answer is that in most states, there is still some practical benefit to this kind of approval, a benefit which stems from standards of proof and the burden of proof.

Standards of Proof. First, in most states, the degree of unfairness that must be shown to upset a transaction that has been approved by disinterested directors or shareholders is probably greater than where there has been no approval. Some courts accomplish this by saying that a director-approved or a shareholder-approved transaction will only be overturned if the unfairness is so great that it amounts to fraud or waste. Others appear to look for "gross" unfairness, as opposed to the "ordinary" unfairness that will be enough for invalidation where there has been no approval.

Burden of Proof. Second, the burden of proof shifts in most states when there has been director or shareholder approval. Without such approval, the burden of proof is clearly on the Key Player to show why the transaction is fair. Once there has been disinterested-director approval or shareholder approval, the burden shifts to the person who is attacking the transaction, who must now come forward with evidence of the transaction's unfairness. Most statutes do not expressly document this shift in the burden of proof, but courts seem to make the shift anyway.

The ALI does specifically provide for the shift. "A party who challenges a transaction between a director or senior executive and the corporation has the burden of proof, except that if such party establishes that none of Subsections (a)(2)(B), (a)(2)(C), or (a)(2)(D) [director- authorization, director-ratification and shareholder-approval, respectively] is satisfied, the director or senior executive has the burden of proving that the transaction was fair to the corporation."[235)]

Similarly, the RMBCA in effect provides for a shift of the burden of proof: Without director or shareholder approval, the transaction must be "established to have been fair to the corporation."[236)] But with such approval, the transaction may only be overturned by the court if there is a showing that the terms of the deal, judged according to the circumstances at the time

235) ALI Prin. Corporation Gov. § 5.02(b).

236) RMBCA § 8.61(b)(3).

of commitment, "were manifestly unfavorable to the corporation," and the unfairness is enough to convince the court that directors did not act in good faith when they approved the transaction.[237] This is clearly a tough standard for the plaintiff to meet.

INDIRECT CONFLICTS INVOLVING KEY PLAYER

So far, we've generally assumed that the Key Player is himself directly a party to the transaction in question. But the rules against self-dealing also apply where the conflict of interest is "indirect." That is, self-dealing problems arise where the Key Player has an interest or association with some other entity, and it is that entity that enters into the transaction with the corporation.

Pecuniary Interest. In general, if a Key Player's financial interest in the other entity is such that this interest would reasonably be expected to affect his judgment concerning the transaction, the self-dealing rules apply. For instance, if the Key Player is a significant stockholder of the other corporation, or a partner in a partnership, the transaction involving that other corporation or partnership will be deemed self-dealing, and the rules described above will apply.

The ALI provides that, in general, a Key Player's 10% equity interest in the other entity is the dividing line between an interest that is and is not sufficiently substantial to affect the person's judgment.[238]

13.6 OTHER STANDARDS

Interlocking Directors. Suppose the Key Player does not have a significant ownership interest in the other entity, but is a full time executive or a director

237) *See* Official Comment 2 to RMBCA § 8.61(b).

238) *See* ALI Prin. Corporation Gov., § 1.03(b).

of that other entity. Here, the self-dealing problem is usually thought to be less severe, so the full range of self-dealing rules does not apply. For instance, the fact that a person serves on the board of directors of both companies, the "interlocking directorate" problem, will not by itself usually cause a transaction between the two companies to constitute self-dealing by the director.

For example, RMBCA § 8.60(1)(ii) Provides that a director of a corporation has an indirect interest in the transaction (thus triggering the self-dealing rules) only if he is a director, general partner, agent or employee of the other entity and the transaction:

(1) is brought, or is of such character and significance to the corporation that it would in the normal course be brought, before the board of directors of the corporation for action"; and

(2) the director "knows at the time of commitment" that the other entity is a party to the proposed transaction.

Thus unless the director's own financial interest in the transaction is enough to influence his judgment, the fact that he is, say, a director of the other entity does not create a conflict, unless the transaction is so major to the target corporation that it would normally have to be approved by the target's board. Routine excluded from the indirect-conflict rules.[239)] For example, suppose that the president of Ford Motor Company sits on the board of directors of IBM. Suppose that Ford buys a computer system from IBM. So long as this transaction is sufficiently routine that it would not normally be presented to the IBM board, which is certainly the case, under the RMBCA approach there is no Self-dealing problem on the IBM side of the transaction.

On the other hand, if IBM were to merge with Ford, the kind of transaction that would need board approval on the IBM side, the Ford president would be an interested director, and the self-dealing rules of the

---

239) *See* Official Comment 2(3) to RMBCA § 8.60.

RMBCA would be triggered on the IBM side, so that the transaction would have to be fair, be approved by a majority of the disinterested directors of IBM or be ratified by the IBM shareholders.

REMEDIES FOR VIOLATION

Where there has been a violation of the rule against self-dealing, there are two possible remedies: (1) rescission; and (2) restitution m the form of money damages. The plaintiff will normally be the corporation itself, or a shareholder who has brought a derivative suit in the corporation's name.

Rescission. If it is possible to rescind the transaction, this is normally the appropriate remedy for self-dealing. For instance, in the office building sale hypothetical, if suit were brought by the corporation or a shareholder in a derivative suit, and the closing had not yet occurred, the court would simply order that the contract be cancelled. If there is to be rescission, the corporation must give back any consideration it has received in the transaction. For instance, if the corporation has sold corporate property to a Key Player in what turns out to be an unfair transaction, the corporation may obtain return of the property, but it must then return to the Key Player the price he paid.

Restitutionary Damages. If because of the passage of time or the complexity of the transaction, it is not feasible to rescind it, the appropriate remedy is restitutionary damages. That is, the Key Player will be required to pay back to the corporation any benefit he received beyond what was fair. For instance, in our office building sale hypothetical, if Realty Corp received $1 million for the sale of the building, and the fair market price was only $800,000, D or Realty Corp would have to return to XYZ the $200,000 excess over fair value.

Consequence. Observe that neither rescission nor restitution is a very strong deterrent to self-dealing: In either case, the Key Player who has engaged in the wrongful self-dealing is merely returned to the same position he would have been in had he not done the transaction at all. However, some courts have ordered the self-dealing Key Player to also return any salary he earned during the relevant period, have awarded punitive damages to the corporation, or have ordered the self-dealer to pay the corporation's counsel fees and other litigation expenses.

CHAPTER 14

CORPORATE OPPORTUNITY DOCTRINE[240]

14.1 INTRODUCTION

In General. If an investment opportunity is viewed as belonging to the corporation, that is a corporate opportunity, the corporation should be given the opportunity to invest in it. While this idea seems simple, its application has resulted in differing legal tests to determine which opportunities are corporate opportunities and which opportunities the directors or officers may take advantage of personally. A broad concept of corporate opportunity would limit fiduciaries from taking the investment and could stifle entrepreneurs interested in improving their outside business or developing a new business which could discourage competition.[241] At the same time, a broad rule would encourage fiduciaries to put their time and effort at the disposal of the corporate business. However, there are also different fiduciaries, such as inside and outside directors, that will be

240) This Chapter is compiled mainly with materials from Robert W. Hamilton, "The Law of Corporations," West Group (2000); Emmanuel Law Outlines, "Corporations," Emmanuel Publishing Corp. (1997).

241) See Pat. K. Chew, *Competing Interests in the Corporate Opportunity Doctrine*, 67 N.C. L. Rev. 435 (1989).

affected by whatever rule is established. If a corporate opportunity is found, the issue of whether the corporation in some way rejected or failed to take the opportunity allowing the fiduciary to take it instead can still arise. It may be that the corporation could not afford to undertake the investment or the third party may not have wanted to deal with the corporation.[242] But if it is a corporate opportunity and there are no defenses, courts can order damages or a constructive trust over the investment in favor of the corporation.

14.2 KEY PLAYERS AND CORPORATE OPPORTUNITY

So far in our treatment of the duty of loyalty, we have focused on transactions between the Key Player and the corporation. We turn now to a different type of problem: the Key Player appropriates to himself some business opportunity or property that is found to "belong" to the corporation. Here, there is rarely an issue as to the "fair" price; instead, if the Key Player has taken something that belongs or ought to belong to the corporation this is *per se* wrongful and the corporation may recover. There are three sub-problems: (1) When may a Key Player compete with the corporation?; (2) When may a Key Player make personal use of corporate assets, e.g., by using the company plane to fly on a personal vacation?; and (3) When does a Key Player, by taking advantage of a business opportunity, wrongfully usurp a "corporate opportunity"? Of these three areas, the third is the most difficult and important. We consider each in turn.

Competition with the Corporation. A director or senior executive may not compete with the corporation, where this competition is likely to harm the corporation. For example, Able and Baker are both senior vice presidents

---

242) See *Energy Resources Corporation, Inc. v. Porter*, 438 N.E.2d 391 (Mass. 1982).

of Wannabe's, a large department store in downtown Cleveland. While they are on the Wannabe's payroll, they secretly form a new corporation, Newco, and cause Newco to sign a lease on a vacant building across the street from Wannabe's. They intend to set up a competing department store in this building. They then, still while on the payroll, tell some key suppliers that they'll be opening up a competing department store soon, and that they hope to buy from these suppliers. Able and Baker also tell their plans to two of Wannabe's key executives, Charlie and Devon, saying, "We hope you'll come with us in a month or so after we open the new store." This induces Charlie and Devon to work less hard for Wannabe's, since they figure that they, too, will soon be leaving to join the new store. A court would probably hold that Able and Baker have violated their duty of loyalty to Wannabe's, by effectively competing with Wannabe's while still on the payroll. If so, the court will probably order them to pay money damages to Wannabe's and might - though probably won't - enjoin them from soliciting any further employees from Wannabe's for some period of time.

Seek Approval or Ratification. But as with other types of self-dealing, conduct that would otherwise be prohibited as disloyal competition may be validated by being approved by disinterested directors, or being ratified by the shareholders. With either of these methods, the Key Player must first make full disclosure about the conflict of interest and the competition that he proposes to engage in.[243] Thus had Able and Baker gone to the directors of Wannabe's in the above example, and announced that they wished to own a competing store, and had the disinterested directors approved of this by a majority vote, there would have been no violation of the duty of loyalty.

Preparation To Compete While Still In Corporation's Employment. Executives and directors seldom engage in active competition while still affiliated with

243) See ALI, Prin. Corporation Gov., § 5.06(a)(2) and § 5.06(a)(3).

the corporation. Much more commonly, they prepare, while still on the company's payroll, to engage in later competition. For instance, they may acquire property that will be used in competing, hire employees, negotiate contracts, solicit customers for the soon-to-be-born firm or otherwise pave the way. There are no hard and fixed rules for this situation, but in general courts tend to hold that these activities constitute disloyalty if they occur while the director or executive is still on the original corporation's payroll. A common remedy is for the court to order a return of all salary received during this preparation period.

Competition after End of Employment. A quite different situation is presented where the executive or director first leaves the corporation and only then begins preparing to compete. Assuming that the executive has not signed any "non-compete" agreement, he is not barred from basic competition with his former employer. However, he may not compete by the taking of the former employer's trade secrets. Any of the following acts may be deemed to be a wrongful taking of trade secrets: (1) the systematic solicitation of a large number of the former employer's customers, (2) the solicitation of the former employer's employees to become employees of the new company; and (3) the use of the former employer's secret processes or other methods of doing business.

Additionally, the executive may be barred from competing if he has signed a valid non-competition agreement. However, courts have become increasingly reluctant to enforce broad non-competition agreements, because they do not wish to unduly construct the executive's ability to earn a living. Therefore, non-competition covenants will be enforced only if they are reasonable as to time, area and scope. For instance, suppose a dentist agrees with his employer not to compete by practicing dentistry at any place in New York City for a period of two years following the end of his employment; this would almost certainly be found to be too broad to be enforceable. But a promise not to practice oral surgery for six months in the same small town as the employer, by contrast, would probably be upheld.[244)]

Use of Corporate Assets. A Key Player may not use corporate assets if this use either harms the corporation, or gives the Key Player a financial benefit, including a financial benefit he receives as a stockholder that is not available to other similarly-situated stockholders.[245)] "Corporate assets," for this purpose, consist not only of tangible goods but also intangibles like information. For example, D is the president of Cole Real Estate Corporation, and owns 97% of its shares. She lives rent-free in a house owned by the Corporation, and her sole transportation is two cars owned by the corporation. Held, D has improperly used corporate assets for her personal financial benefit, and has thereby wronged the minority shareholder.[246)]

Approval or Payment. As with other types of self-dealing, approval by disinterested directors, or ratification by shareholders, in each case, only after full disclosure, will help immunize the transaction. Similarly, in the case of use of tangible corporate property, the transaction will not be wrongful if the Key Player pays the/air value for any benefit he has received.[247)]

---

244) See generally, *Karpinski v. Ingrasci*, 268 N.E.2d 751 (1971).

Case Synopsis. Plaintiff employer appealed an order of the Appellate Division of the Supreme Court in the Fourth Judicial Department (New York), which reversed a trial court judgment for the employer and which dismissed the complaint against defendant, a former employee, for breach of a noncompetition agreement.

Facts & Procedural History. The employee was a dentist who was employed by a dental practice. He signed a covenant not to compete. The employer's practice consisted solely of oral surgery. The covenant, however, restricted the employee from practicing both dentistry and oral surgery. When the employee left the practice and opened his own office, the employer sued to enforce the covenant. The trial court gave judgment for the employer. The lower appellate court reversed, finding the restriction against practicing dentistry was too broad.

Discussion. On further review, the court reversed the order of the lower appellate court, holding that an unreasonable restriction in the agreement should be severed and the remainder of the agreement given effect. The court held that the employer was entitled to an injunction barring the former employee from practicing oral surgery in the five specified counties named in the covenant and that it was also entitled to damages actually suffered while the former employee conducted his practice after leaving his employment.

Conclusion. The court reversed the decision.

245) See ALI Prin. Corporation Gov., § 5.04(a).

246) *Cole Real Estate Corporation v. Peoples Bank & Trust Co.*, 310 N.E.2d 275 (Ind. 1974).

247) See ALI Prin. Corporation Gov., § 5.04(a)(1).

KEY PLAYER IN MULTIPLE CORPORATIONS

Special problems arise when a person is a director or controlling shareholder of multiple corporations, and he learns of a business opportunity that may be of interest to more than one of these corporations. If the ordinary rules defining corporate opportunities are applied, the Key Player might find himself in the awkward, even impossible, Position of having to offer the opportunity to multiple corporation.

In general, the few cases that have discussed this problem have been sympathetic to the plight of the shareholder or director in the multiple-corporation context. At least where the director or shareholder learns of the opportunity while wearing his "individual" hat rather than while acting on behalf of the corporation, and the opportunity is not truly essential to any one of the corporations, he probably may offer it to whichever one, or none, that he wishes.

The ALI text similarly makes it easy for a director or controlling shareholder, Provided that he is not a full-time "senior executive," to decline to offer an opportunity to the corporation. So long as the opportunity is offered to the director or shareholder in his individual capacity, and he did not become aware of it in connection with the performance of his corporate duties or through the use of the corporation's information or property, the opportunity is not a "corporate" one and need not be offered to the corporation.[248)]

14.3 LEGAL TESTS FOR CORPORATE OPPORTUNITY

The "Corporate Opportunity" Doctrine. Suppose that a senior executive or director of a corporation learns of an attractive business opportunity. Suppose

248) See ALI Phn. Corporation Gov., §§ 5.05(b)(1), 5.12(b).

further that this business opportunity is not in an area of commerce in which the corporation presently does business. May the executive or director pursue this opportunity on his own, rather than turning it over to the corporation?

The brief, but unhelpful, answer is that the manager may not pursue the opportunity on his own, and must turn it over to the corporation, if the opportunity is one that can be said to "belong" to the corporation. The difficulty is that the rules for distinguishing between opportunities that "belong" to the corporation and those that do not are confusing, and vary substantially from court to court.

Effect of Finding of "Corporate Opportunity." If the manager is found to have taken for himself an opportunity that "belongs" to the corporation, i.e., to have usurped a "corporate opportunity"), the rules are very strict: this taking is *per se* wrongful to the corporation, and the corporation may recover damages equal to the loss it has suffered, or the profits it would have made had it been given the chance to pursue the opportunity.

Often, the court will order any profits made by the manager from the venture to be held in constructive trust for the corporation, and may order the enterprise itself to be turned over to the corporation. For example, D is the president of Hotel Corporation D knows that Hotel Corp is looking for an appropriately zoned two-acre site in the village of Ames on which it can build a hotel. As D knows, the company's search for such a site so far has been notably unsuccessful. D learns through a friend of a good potential site at a fair price. Instead of allowing Hotel Corp to buy the site, he buys it himself, and resells it for a quick profit to a businessman who puts a car dealership on it. The court is likely to find that by buying the land, D has usurped a corporate opportunity, i.e., an opportunity that properly belonged to Hotel Corporation If the court does so conclude, it will order D's profit on the resale to be turned over to Hotel Corporation And, in fact, if Hotel Corp is unable to get another site, D may even be liable to pay a larger sum equal to the profits that Hotel Corp could have made had it been offered the site and built a hotel there.

No Issue of Fairness of Price. Once the court decides that the manager has taken a corporate opportunity, most courts do not recognize any separate issue of "fairness." Thus suppose Manager buys Blackacre which, the court finds, he should have offered to the corporation that employs him. The fact that Manager has paid a fair market price for the property, and the fact that a subsequent increase in value is due to an unforeseen increase in values, or to Manager's own unusual efforts, is irrelevant. Manager will still have to account to the corporation for any profits he has made.

FOUR TESTS

Courts are in disagreement about the proper test for determining whether an opportunity is a "corporate opportunity." There are four tests that are used.

First is the interest or expectancy test. The oldest test, not used as much today as formerly, is the "interest or expectancy" test. As its name implies, this test looks at whether the corporation had an "interest or expectancy" in the opportunity. Courts applying this test also will generally hold the opportunity to be a corporate one if it is "essential" to the corporation.

Example of "Interest." A corporation would be found to have an "interest" in an opportunity if it already has some contract right regarding the opportunity. For instance, if Corporation has a contract to acquire Blackacre, even if the seller can terminate the contract without penalty at any time, Corporation would be held to have an "interest" in Blackacre. Therefore, if the president or a director of corporation were to buy Blackacre instead, this would be the taking of a corporate opportunity belonging to Corporation.

Example of "Expectancy." A corporation has an "expectancy" with respect to an opportunity if its existing business arrangements have led it to reasonably anticipate being able to take advantage of that opportunity. For instance, suppose corporation rents office space in a building at 1865 Palmer Ave, under a lease with two more years to run. Corporation has no "interest" in being able to renew its lease, but most courts would probably hold that it has an "expectancy" of being able to renew. Therefore, if X, a director of Corporation, signs a lease for the space personally, to begin after Corporation's lease expires, he would be found to have taken a corporate opportunity belonging to Corporation under the "expectancy" standard.[249)]

Example of "Essential." An opportunity is "essential" to the corporation if the corporation will suffer serious harm should it not be able to take advantage of that opportunity. For instance, suppose Realty Corp is trying to assemble a one-acre site in the middle of a downtown area, on which it wishes to build a skyscraper; it needs to buy six different small parcels in order to complete this assemblage. If Vice President buys one of these parcels for himself, thus preventing Realty Corp from completing the assemblage and therefore from building the building, he will have taken a corporate opportunity because the parcel he bought was "essential" to Realty Corporation

The "interest or expectancy" test is usually the narrowest of the four tests: Many opportunities that are not found to be within the corporation's "interest or expectancy" nonetheless come within the other tests, and almost anything that comes within the other tests qualifies under the "interest or expectancy" standard.

Second is the "line of business" test. A second, quite popular, test is the "line of business" test. Under this test, an opportunity is a corporate opportunity if it is "closely related to the corporation's existing or prospective activities." A court applying the "line of business" test will probably treat an opportunity as a corporate one even though the activity is not a business that the corporation already engages in, so long as the court feels that the company has some special expertise that equips it to compete in the new area. Thus a "functional relationship" between the types of activity the corporation already engages in and the prospective activity may be enough, even though they are in different industries. Clark suggests that if a company already makes cold medicines, a business that makes contact lens wetting solution would be within its "line of

---

249) *Pike's Peak Co. v. Plunter,* 123 N.W. 19 (Mich. 1909).

business," because "the methods of marketing and distributing the products through drug stores, for example, overlap ... enough to permit significant economies of scale if the businesses were to be combined." Most courts that apply the "line of business" test would probably also find the opportunity to be a corporate one if the "interest or expectancy" test is met. Delaware, for example, appears to treat an opportunity as corporate if either of these two tests is satisfied.

Third is the "fairness" test. A third test, the "fairness" standard, is more amorphous than the "interest or expectancy" or "line of business" tests. Under this standard, the court will measure "the unfairness on the particular facts of a fiduciary taking advantage of an opportunity when the interests of the corporation justly call for protection."[250)] Many of the factors that go to "fairness" are ones that we discuss below in our treatment of "other factors" that influence the decision on whether an opportunity is corporate.

Fourth is the Combine "line of business" and "fairness." Finally, a few courts have adopted a two-step test, which combines the "line of business" and "fairness" tests. Under this approach, even if the opportunity comes within the corporation's "line of business" test, the officer or director will not be liable for usurping it if he can show that his conduct was "fair" to the corporation.[251)]

ALI APPROACH

The ALI's Principles of Corporate Governance are by far the most comprehensive statutory or statute-like treatment of the problems of the corporate opportunity doctrine.[252)] Because of the specificity of the ALI treatment, we reproduce the relevant sections:

Section 5.05 Taking of Corporate Opportunities by Directors or Senior

---

250) *Durfee v. Durfee & Canning, Inc.*, 80 N.E.2d 522 (Mass. 1948).

251) See, e.g., *Miller v. Miller*, 222 N.W.2d 71 (Minn. 1974).

252) By contrast, the RMBCA doesn't deal specifically with the corporate opportunity doctrine at all, and leaves this area to case law.

Executives

(a) General Rule. A director or senior executive may not take advantage of a corporate opportunity unless:

(1) [He or she] first offers the corporate opportunity to the corporation and makes disclosure concerning the conflict of interest and the corporate opportunity;

(2) The corporate opportunity is rejected by the corporation; and

(3) Either:

(A) The rejection of the opportunity is fair to the corporation;

(B) The opportunity is rejected in advance, following such disclosure, by disinterested directors ... in a manner that satisfies the standards of the business judgment rule or

(C) The rejection is authorized in advance or ratified, following such disclosure, by disinterested shareholders, and the rejection is not equivalent to a waste of corporate.

(b) Definition of a Corporate Opportunity. For purposes of this Section, a corporate opportunity means:

(1) Any opportunity to engage in a business activity of which a director or senior executive becomes aware, either:

(A) In connection with the performance of functions as a director or senior executive or under circumstances that should reasonably lead the director or senior executive to believe that the person offering the opportunity expects ft to be offered to the corporation; or

(B) Through the use of corporate information or property, if the resulting opportunity is one that the director or senior executive should reasonably be expected to believe would be of interest to the corporation; or

(2) Any opportunity to engage in a business activity of which a senior executive becomes aware and knows is closely related to a business in which the corporation is engaged or expects to engage.

Section 5.12 Taking of Corporate Opportunities by a Controlling Shareholder

(a) General Rule. A controlling shareholder may not take advantage of a corporate opportunity unless:

(1) The taking of the opportunity is fair to the corporation; or

(2) The taking of the opportunity is authorized in advance or ratified by disinterested shareholders, following disclosure concerning the conflict of interest and the corporate opportunity, and the taking of the opportunity is not equivalent to a waste of corporate.

(b) Definition of a corporate opportunity. For purposes of this section, a corporate opportunity means any opportunity to engage in a business activity that:

(1) Is developed or received by the corporation, or comes to the controlling shareholder primarily by virtue of its relationship to the corporation; or

(2) Is held out to shareholders of the corporation by the controlling shareholder, or by the corporation with the activity that will be within the scope of the business in which the corporation is engaged or expects to engage and will not be within the scope of the controlling shareholder's business.

(c) Burden of Proof. A party who challenges the taking of a corporate opportunity has the burden of proof, except that the controlling shareholder has the burden of proving that the taking of the opportunity is fair to the corporation if the taking of the opportunity was not authorized in advance or ratified by disinterested directors or disinterested shareholders following the disclosure required by Subsection (a)(2).

Following are a few of the especially noteworthy features of the ALI's treatment of corporate opportunity.

If the opportunity is a "corporate opportunity," the insider; director, senior executive or "controlling shareholder," must offer it to the corporation, with full disclosure of its nature before he may take it for himself. If he does not make this offer, he will not be permitted to defend a later suit on the grounds that the corporation was unable for financial or other reasons to take advantage of the opportunity.

The mere fact that the corporation rejects the opportunity does not by itself get the Key Player off the hook. Unless the corporation's rejection is authorized by a majority of disinterested directors, or a majority of disinterested shareholders, in either case, following full disclosure, the Key Player will have to show that the corporate rejection and the overall transaction were fair to the corporation.

On the other hand, if a majority of disinterested directors does authorize the rejection, then the transaction is pretty much immunized against later attack: only if the disinterested directors have violated the business judgment rule, i.e., they have behaved irrationally, may the transaction be attacked, If disinterested shareholders approve the corporation's rejection of the opportunity after full disclosure, only if their action amounts to "waste" may the transaction be attacked.

Senior executive has stricter duty. A "senior executive," i.e., a full-time high-level employee, is held to a somewhat stricter standard than an outside director. Any opportunity of which the senior executive becomes aware, even if this happens outside of the corporation's business, as at a purely social cocktail party, is "corporate" if the executive "knows [that the activity] is closely related to the business in which the corporation is engaged or expects to engage."[253] By contrast, if the outside director learns of the opportunity, and does so while not acting either on behalf of the corporation or by use of corporate information, the opportunity is not a "corporate" one. [254]

A controlling shareholder is treated more like a senior executive than like an outside director. The opportunity is a "corporate" one as to the controlling shareholder if either: (1) she learns of it while acting on the corporation's

253) ALI, Principles of Corporate Governance § 5.05(b)(2).

254) ALI, Principles of Corporate Governance § 5.05(b)(1).

behalf; or (2) or the opportunity is one that is "held out to the [other] shareholders of the corporation" as being "a type of business activity that will be within the scope of the business in which the corporation is engaged or expects to engage and will not be within the scope of the controlling shareholder's business."[255)]

For example, major is the controlling shareholder of newly-formed Corporation, which is to invest in Connecticut real estate. Major also has a separate business that invests in real estate. Major tells his fellow investors, "I'll use my contacts to find good Connecticut real estate investments for Corporation" No matter how Major learns of a particular Connecticut real estate investment, it will be a "corporate" opportunity, because Major has indicated to his fellow shareholders that such opportunities will be for Corporation rather than for any other businesses in which Major is involved.

14.4 OTHER STANDARDS

There are a number of additional factors which courts consider in deciding whether an opportunity is a corporate one. These factors are especially likely to be considered by a court that uses "fairness" as a partial or sole standard:

Capacity in Which Offer Received. Whether the opportunity was offered to the officer or director as an individual or rather as a corporate manager who would convey the offer to the corporation. The case for regarding the opportunity as corporate is obviously stronger in the latter situation than in the former.

How Insider Learned of Opportunity. Whether or not the officer or director teamed of the opportunity while acting in his role as the corporation's agent. Thus if president learns of the opportunity while attending a meeting that

---

255) ALI, Principles of Corporate Governance § 5.12(b)(2).

relates solely to his company's business, the case for finding a corporate opportunity is stronger than where President learns of it while having drinks with a social friend.

Use of Corporate Resources. Whether the officer or director used corporate resources to take advantage of the opportunity. An illustration of the use of corporate resources would be where President takes the company jet to scout out the opportunity. Some corporate plaintiffs have claimed that when the defendant, an employee of the corporation, developed the opportunity while on "company time," i.e., during working hours, this constituted the "use of corporate resources." However, this by itself is unlikely to be a very important factor, especially if the time used is not very substantial.

For example, the three Ds are senior managers at P Corporation They quit to participate in a leveraged buyout of Alvey, a company operating in a related industry. P claims that the buyout of Alvey was a corporate opportunity belonging to P, because the Ds spent company time and other intangible resources, e.g., time of other employees, in putting together the buyout before they quit. Held, for the Ds. It's true that if a defendant is shown to have used corporate assets to acquire the opportunity, he may be "equitably estopped" from denying that the opportunity was a corporate one. But the equitable estoppel doctrine is less likely to be used where only intangible or "soft" corporate assets (e.g., compensated time) are used, than where "hard" assets, e.g., corporate cash, are used. Here, the "company time" and other soft assets used were minimal, especially when compared with the $29.5 million cost of the acquisition. Therefore, it would not be equitable to treat the opportunity as a corporate one.[256)]

Essential to Corporation. Whether the opportunity is essential to the corporation's well-being. The more important the opportunity is to the

256) *Rapistan Corporation v. Michaels*, 511 N.W.2d 918 (Mich. 1994). The directors resigned their positions to pursue a leveraged buy-out of a corporation that had business with considerable overlap with the business of the directors' original corporation. The corporation claims that this LBO opportunity belonged to the corporation. This case is a good one for generating discussion on the proper role of directors and on the factors determining whether an opportunity is corporate.

corporation's well-being, i.e., the worse financial injury the corporation will suffer if it does not have the opportunity, the more likely the opportunity is to be regarded as corporate. For instance, recall our example of Realty Corp, which is trying to complete an assemblage on which to build a single skyscraper. If an executive of Realty snatches away the last lot in the parcel, thus preventing Realty Corp from completing its assemblage, the critical importance to Realty of this last lot makes it very likely that a court will view the lot as an opportunity belonging to Realty.

Reasonable Expectations of Parties. Whether the parties (including the shareholders who do not participate in the taking of the opportunity) had a reasonable expectation that such opportunities would be regarded as corporate ones. The importance of the parties' reasonable expectations can be seen by comparing the following two examples:

Example 1: Smith has been in the commercial real estate business in New York City for many years. His friend Jones has never been in real estate, but has substantial funds to invest. Acting both out of friendship and commercial self-interest, Smith proposes to Jones that they set up SJ. Properties, Inc., to buy two particular buildings in New York City. They do so. Smith then buys a very attractively-priced New York City property on his own. If Jones claims that this third property is a corporate opportunity, he will probably lose, in part because Smith's numerous prior dealings in New York City real estate, Jones' own inexperience, the "friendship" aspect to Smith's invitation to him to join in S.J., all should have given him the reasonable expectation that Smith would not confine all of his subsequent New York City real estate dealings to the SJ. entity.[257)]

257) See *Burg v. Horn.* 380 F.2d 897 (2d Cir. 1967) (from the facts of which this example is very loosely drawn). The Burgs, who bought and sold real estate in Brooklyn, encouraged their good friends, the Horns, to get their feet wet in the real estate business. The Burgs and Horns formed a corporation to buy and sell Brooklyn real estate. The Burgs managed the corporation but also continued to buy and sell properties on their own account. The Horns, evidently suspecting that the best properties went to the Burgs and not to the corporation, sue alleging the usurpation of corporate opportunities. The court held no corporate opportunity, because the directors were not full-time employees of the company and already had prior real estate ventures.

Example 2: Smith, the same Smith as in the prior example, after his years of Successful solo real estate investing in New York City, sells all of his properties to Monster Realty Co., a large, Publicly-owned, real estate investment trust. He goes to work as an executive of Monster, in charge of acquiring additional New York City properties. Here, in the absence of any explicit understanding, the reasonable expectation of Monster, and its public shareholders, is probably that Smith will not buy New York City buildings on his own - he has already wrapped up his prior solo work by selling the entire portfolio of buildings to Monster, and he has taken a supposedly full-time job finding new buildings, so the stockholders could reasonably expect that his full loyalties and efforts at least concerning acquisition of New York City real estate would be for Monster's benefit.

Possible Distinction between Close and Public Corporation. Whether the corporation is closely or publicly held. The case for finding a corporate opportunity is probably stronger in the case of the publicly held corporation; arguing for such a distinction. Such a distinction can be partly justified on the theory that participants in a close corporation have a much greater ability to agree explicitly on what will and will not be deemed a corporate opportunity, so if they remain silent, there is more justification for finding that a particular opportunity was not intended to be corporate, and they find it easier to monitor the behavior of officers and directors than do the stockholders of a publicly held corporation. These differences favor a stricter, more categorical, limit on outside business activities for the officers and directors of a public company. Comparison of Example 1 and Example 2 supra, suggests the sensibleness of defining "corporate opportunity" more broadly in the public corporation.

Distinction between Outside Director and Full-Time Executive. Whether the person taking the opportunity is an outside director or a full-time executive. A full-time executive is commonly understood to owe his entire efforts and loyalties to the corporation that employs him. An outside director, by contrast, often has numerous other business interests, some of which will be, and may properly be, more financially important to him than the corporation that he serves only as a director. Therefore, the outside director should be freer to take an opportunity for himself.

The ALI's Principles of Corporate Governance recognize this distinction:[258)]

(1) Employee: An opportunity is a corporate one if it comes to a full-time employee who knows that the opportunity is "closely related to a business in which the corporation is engaged or expects to engage."

(2) Outside director: If the opportunity comes to an outside director, by contrast, the fact that he knows or should know that the opportunity is closely related to the corporation's present or reasonably anticipated activities is irrelevant; the opportunity is not deemed "corporate" unless the director either:

    (1) learned of the opportunity in connection with performing his duties for the corporation;

    (2) learned of it under circumstances where he should reasonably have believed that it was really being offered to the corporation and not to him personally; or

    (3) learned of it through the use of information or property belonging to the corporation, in which situation a full-time employee will also have to treat the opportunity as "corporate.".

Corporation's Inability to Take Advantage. Whether the corporation had the ability, financial and otherwise, to take advantage of the opportunity. However, this "ability" factor is very controversial. For instance, some courts will not even allow evidence that the corporation would have been financially incapable of taking advantage of the opportunity, on the theory that allowing such evidence would encourage the improper taking of corporate opportunities.[259)]

---

258) ALI, Principles of Corporate Governance § 5.05(b).

259) *See*, e.g., *Klinicki v. Lundgren*, 695 P.2d 906 (Ore. 1985), disallowing evidence of financial inability where the person who took the opportunity did not make full disclosure about it to the corporation. For the full text of this case see *infra* the Appendix I.

WHO IS BOUND

Generally, courts seem to apply the corporate opportunity doctrine only to directors, full-time employees, and controlling shareholders. Thus a shareholder who has only a non-controlling interest, and who is not a director or employee, will generally not be subjected to the doctrine.

There are not many corporate-opportunity cases involving lower-level employees. However, such an employee probably has a similar duty to refrain from usurping a corporate opportunity, under the law of agency, which makes an employee a fiduciary for the employer.[260)] However, when a low-level employee takes a given opportunity for himself, the taking is probably somewhat less likely to be found to be "unfair" to the corporation than where the taking is by, say, an officer. So to the extent that the jurisdiction considers "fairness" in deciding whether something is a corporate opportunity, the low-level employee is likely to have an easier time.

Rejection by Corporation. Even if an opportunity is a "corporate opportunity," the Key Player is not necessarily barred from pursuing it himself. If he offers the corporation the chance to pursue the opportunity, and the corporation rejects the opportunity by a majority vote of disinterested directors or disinterested shareholders, the Key Player may pursue the opportunity himself.[261)]

In order for the Key Player to be allowed to raise the defense that the disinterested directors or shareholders have rejected the opportunity on behalf of the corporation, most courts require that the Key Player have made full disclosure of the nature of the opportunity. Thus if President purports to offer the corporation the chance to pursue the opportunity but understates the potential benefits or overstates the cost to the corporation, rejection by the disinterested directors or disinterested shareholders will probably not be a

260) e are not many corporate-opportunity cases involving lower-level employees. However, such an employee probably has a similar duty to refrain from usurping a corporate opportunity, under the law of agency, which makes an employee a fiduciary for the employer.

261) *See* also ALI Prin. Corporation Gov., § 5.05(a)(3)(B) and (C).

defense.[262)]

The safest path is for the Key Player to offer the opportunity to the corporation before he accepts it himself, and to wait until the disinterested directors or shareholders have rejected it before he acts. But if the Key Player accepts the opportunity himself, and then persuades the disinterested directors or shareholders to ratify his acceptance, and the corporation's rejection, of the opportunity after the fact, this post-facto ratification may still be enough to allow the Key Player to escape liability.

However, courts probably would scrutinize such an after-the-fact ratification more closely on the theory that it is far less likely to manifest a truly voluntary consent than where the opportunity is offered to the corporation in advance, at a time when the corporation may truly benefit from it. In fact, the ALI text has a flat rule against a director's or senior executive's taking a corporate opportunity unless the opportunity has first been disclosed and offered to the corporation and rejected by it. In other words, under the ALI text the director or senior executive may not take a corporate opportunity with no disclosure to the corporation, then receive after-the-fact ratification by disinterested directors or shareholders.

CORPORATION'S INABILITY

A Key Player who takes a corporate opportunity for himself often tries to defend the subsequent lawsuit by contending that the corporation would have been unable to take advantage of the opportunity itself, and has therefore suffered no damage.

This is a troublesome defense, since if the court allows it, the Key Player will have absolutely no incentive to help the corporation overcome its difficulties, he will simply take the opportunity for himself, and count on being able to make a later showing of corporate inability, a showing which is likely to be quite difficult for outsiders to disprove.

262) *See* ALI Prin. Corporation Gov., § 5.05(a)(1).

There are a number of different types of corporate inability that Key Players have raised when sued for usurping a corporate opportunity: (1) the corporation's legal inability (e.g., because of antitrust or other regulatory restraints); (2) the refusal, by the person offering the transaction to deal with the corporation; and (3) the corporation's financial inability to take advantage of the opportunity. Courts are especially reluctant to accept justifications of type (3), since if the opportunity is a good one, there should be a way to overcome financial constraints, e.g., by convincing a bank or other investor to lend money, by taking on a partner, by forming a joint venture, etc.

Courts are in disagreement about whether and when the defense of corporate inability should be accepted. A number of courts take a quite strict view under which if the Key Player does not make full disclosure to the corporation and offer it the opportunity, he is simply not permitted to argue that the corporation could not have taken advantage of the opportunity. This "bright line" rule has the advantage of encouraging full disclosure, and honest efforts by the Key Player to help the corporation take advantage of attractive opportunities.

As noted, this is the approach followed by the ALI's Principles Of corporate Governance: If the Key Player does not offer the opportunity to the corporation, and make full disclosure about it, his taking of that opportunity for himself is flat-out wrongful, even if the corporation would have been totally unable to take advantage itself.

On the other hand, if the Key Player does offer the opportunity to the corporation and the disinterested directors or shareholders reject it, the corporation's financial, legal or other inability to take advantage of the opportunity are to be considered as factors in determining whether they acted "rationally" in rejecting, an additional requirement for the "rejection" defense.[263)] For example, P and Dare directors and major shareholders of Berlinair Inc. an air transport business. P and D learn that BFR, a

263) See Comment to § 5.05(a).

consortium of Berlin travel agents, will be awarding a profitable contract for charter flights. After some early negotiations between Berlinair and BFR, conducted by both P and D, D secretly makes a proposal to BFR on behalf of a new company of which he is the sole owner Air Berlin Charter Co. (ABC). BFR awards the contract to ABC. P brings a derivative suit against D and ABC for diverting a corporate opportunity that belonged to Berlinair. D defends on the grounds that Berlinair did not have the financial ability to undertake the BFR contract, and therefore was not injured by ABC's getting the contract. Held, for P. The court adopts the strict ALI approach, whereby an executive or director has an absolute obligation to offer the opportunity to the corporation with full disclosure, and receive a rejection by the corporation, before he may take the opportunity for himself. Here, the BFR contract was a corporate opportunity of Berlinair, and D did not offer the contract to Bedinair. Therefore, he has breached his duty of loyalty whether or not Berlinail would have been financially able to handle the contract. The stock in ABC must therefore be held in constructive trust for Berlinair, and ABC must account to Berlinair for past profits.[264)]

264) *Klinicki v. Lundgren*, 695 P.2d 906 (Ore. 1985). Other courts take a more lenient view toward the defense of corporate inability. For instance, in *Guth v. Loft, Inc.*, 5 A.2d 503 (Del. 1939), the court apparently treated an opportunity as being a "corporate opportunity" only if the opportunity was one "which the corporation is financially able to undertake." Daniel J. Layton, the concurrent chief justice in *Guth v. Loft, Inc.*, gave the lead judgment for the Delaware Supreme Court. He started off by paying service to the general principle against conflicts of interest. "Corporate officers and directors are not permitted to use their position of trust and confidence to further their private interests. While technically not trustees, they stand in a fiduciary relation to the corporation and its stockholders. A public policy, existing through the years, and derived from a profound knowledge of human characteristics and motives, has established a rule that demands of a corporate officer or director, peremptorily and inexorably, the most scrupulous observance of his duty, not only affirmatively to protect the interest of the corporation committed to his charge, but also to refrain from doing anything that would work injury to the corporation, or to deprive it of profit or advantage which his skill and ability might properly bring to it, or to enable it to make in the reasonable and lawful exercise of its powers."

But then he stated the main p rinciple as this, "On the other hand, it is equally true that, if there is presented to a corporate officer or director a business opportunity which the corporation if financially able to undertake, which is, from its nature, in the line of the corporation's business and is of practical advantage to it, is one in which the corporation has an interest or a reasonable expectancy, and, by embracing the opportunity, the self-interest of the officer or director will be brought into conflict with that of his corporation, the law will not permit him to seize the opportunity for himself." So where a corporation cannot take an opportunity because (1) it lacks finances (2) it is not in the same line

The modem trend is probably toward the strict ALI position, as applied in *Klinicki.* Unless the Key Player has offered the opportunity with full disclosure he may not raise the defense that the corporation could not have taken advantage of the opportunity.

Parent-Subsidiary Problems. Suppose one corporation owns a controlling, but not 100%, interest in another corporation. In this parent-subsidiary context, suppose that the parent decides to take a business opportunity for itself rather than for the subsidiary. Does the corporate opportunity doctrine apply? In brief, the answer is probably "yes" - if the opportunity relates much more closely to the subsidiary's present or contemplated business than to the parent's, the parent probably violates its fiduciary obligation to the subsidiary and the subsidiary's minority shareholders by usurping it for itself. This problem is discussed more fully in the treatment of general parent-subsidiary fiduciary questions.

Remedies. Once the court has determined that a Key Player has usurped what is properly viewed as a corporate opportunity, what remedies are available to the corporation or its shareholders? The usual remedy is quite draconian: the court may order the imposition of a constructive trust, and may order the Key Player to account for all profits earned from the opportunity. If the court imposes a constructive trust, this means that the property is treated as if it belonged to the corporation that owned the opportunity, For instance, in *Klinicki*, the court ordered the shares in ABC to be turned over to Berlinair. The court probably may, but need not, require the corporation to pay the Key Player for the Key Player's direct investment made in creating the opportunity.

Also, the court will usually order the Key Player to account for the profits

---

of business (3) it has not "interest or reasonable expectancy" then a director will be found to have legitimately taken an opportunity for itself. Layton felt that there was no real standard for loyalty and it depends on the facts of the case. The court may enquire and will decide upon the fairness of any transaction. This has been followed in the Delaware General Corporation Law s.144. "The occasions for the determination of honesty, good faith and loyal conduct are many and varied, and no hard and fast rule can be formulated. The standard of loyalty is measured by no fixed scale."

already made from usurpation of the corporate opportunity. Thus in *Klinicki*, D was required to calculate the amount of profits made by ABC, and presumably to turn these profits over to Berlinair in addition to turning over the stock in ABC.

APPENDIX I

SUBSTANTIAL LEADING CASES

SMITH v. VAN GORKOM

Supreme Court of Delaware, 488 A.2d 858 (Del. 1985)
Submitted: June 11, 1984.; Decided: January 29, 1985
Opinion on Denial of Reargument: March 14, 1985.

*863 HORSEY, JUSTICE (FOR THE MAJORITY):

This appeal from the Court of Chancery involves a class action brought by shareholders of the defendant Trans Union Corporation ("Trans Union" or "the Company"), originally seeking rescission of a cash-out merger of Trans Union into the defendant New T Company ("New T"), a wholly-owned subsidiary of the defendant, Marmon Group, Inc. ("Marmon"). Alternate relief in the form of damages is sought against the defendant members of the Board of Directors of Trans Union, *864 New T, and Jay A. Pritzker and Robert A. Pritzker, owners of Marmon.[1)]

Following trial, the former Chancellor granted judgment for the defendant

1) The plaintiff, Alden Smith, originally sought to enjoin the merger; but, following extensive discovery, the Trial Court denied the plaintiff's motion for preliminary injunction by unreported letter opinion dated February 3, 1981. On February 10, 1981, the proposed merger was approved by Trans Union's stockholders at a special meeting and the merger became effective on that date. Thereafter, John W. Gosselin was permitted to intervene as an additional plaintiff; and Smith and Gosselin were certified as representing a class consisting of all persons, other than defendants, who held shares of Trans Union common stock on all relevant dates. At the time of the merger, Smith owned 54,000 shares of Trans Union stock, Gosselin owned 23,600 shares, and members of Gosselin's family owned 20,000 shares.

directors by unreported letter opinion dated July 6, 1982.[2] Judgment was based on two findings: (1) that the Board of Directors had acted in an informed manner so as to be entitled to protection of the business judgment rule in approving the cash-out merger; and (2) that the shareholder vote approving the merger should not be set aside because the stockholders had been "fairly informed" by the Board of Directors before voting thereon. The plaintiffs appeal.

Speaking for the majority of the Court, we conclude that both rulings of the Court of Chancery are clearly erroneous. Therefore, we reverse and direct that judgment be entered in favor of the plaintiffs and against the defendant directors for the fair value of the plaintiffs' stockholdings in Trans Union, in accordance with *Weinberger v. UOP, Inc.,* Del.Supr., 457 A.2d 701 (1983).[3]

We hold: (1) that the Board's decision, reached September 20, 1980, to approve the proposed cash-out merger was not the product of an informed business judgment; (2) that the Board's subsequent efforts to amend the Merger Agreement and take other curative action were ineffectual, both legally and factually; and (3) that the Board did not deal with complete candor with the stockholders by failing to disclose all material facts, which they knew or should have known, before securing the stockholders' approval of the merger.

I.

The nature of this case requires a detailed factual statement. The following facts are essentially uncontradicted:[4]

---

2) Following trial, and before decision by the Trial Court, the parties stipulated to the dismissal, with prejudice, of the Messrs. Pritzker as parties defendant. However, all references to defendants hereinafter are to the defendant directors of Trans Union, unless otherwise noted.

3) plaintiffs and against the defendant directors for the fair value of the plaintiffs' stockholdings in Trans Union, in accordance with *Weinberger v. UOP, Inc.,* Del.Supr., 457 A.2d 701 (1983)

4) More detailed statements of facts, consistent with this factual outline, appear in related portions of this Opinion.

-A-

Trans Union was a publicly-traded, diversified holding company, the principal earnings of which were generated by its railcar leasing business. During the period here involved, the Company had a cash flow of hundreds of millions of dollars annually. However, the Company had difficulty in generating sufficient taxable income to offset increasingly large investment tax credits (ITCs). Accelerated depreciation deductions had decreased available taxable income against which to offset accumulating ITCs. The Company took these deductions, despite their effect on usable ITCs, because the rental price in the railcar leasing market had already impounded the purported tax savings.

In the late 1970's, together with other capital-intensive firms, Trans Union lobbied in Congress to have ITCs refundable in cash to firms which could not fully utilize the credit. During the summer of 1980, defendant Jerome W. Van Gorkom, Trans Union's Chairman and Chief Executive Officer, *865 testified and lobbied in Congress for refundability of ITCs and against further accelerated depreciation. By the end of August, Van Gorkom was convinced that Congress would neither accept the refundability concept nor curtail further accelerated depreciation.

Beginning in the late 1960's, and continuing through the 1970's, Trans Union pursued a program of acquiring small companies in order to increase available taxable income. In July 1980, Trans Union Management prepared the annual revision of the Company's Five Year Forecast. This report was presented to the Board of Directors at its July, 1980 meeting. The report projected an annual income growth of about 20%. The report also concluded that Trans Union would have about $195 million in spare cash between 1980 and 1985, "with the surplus growing rapidly from 1982 onward." The report referred to the ITC situation as a "nagging problem" and, given that problem, the leasing company "would still appear to be constrained to a tax breakeven." The report then listed four alternative uses of the projected 1982-1985 equity surplus: (1) stock repurchase; (2) dividend increases; (3)

a major acquisition program; and (4) combinations of the above. The sale of Trans Union was not among the alternatives. The report emphasized that, despite the overall surplus, the operation of the Company would consume all available equity for the next several years, and concluded: "As a result, we have sufficient time to fully develop our course of action."

-B-

On August 27, 1980, Van Gorkom met with Senior Management of Trans Union. Van Gorkom reported on his lobbying efforts in Washington and his desire to find a solution to the tax credit problem more permanent than a continued program of acquisitions. Various alternatives were suggested and discussed preliminarily, including the sale of Trans Union to a company with a large amount of taxable income.

Donald Romans, Chief Financial Officer of Trans Union, stated that his department had done a "very brief bit of work on the possibility of a leveraged buy-out." This work had been prompted by a media article which Romans had seen regarding a leveraged buy-out by management. The work consisted of a "preliminary study" of the cash which could be generated by the Company if it participated in a leveraged buyout. As Romans stated, this analysis "was very first and rough cut at seeing whether a cash flow would support what might be considered a high price for this type of transaction."

On September 5, at another Senior Management meeting which Van Gorkom attended, Romans again brought up the idea of a leveraged buy-out as a "possible strategic alternative" to the Company's acquisition program. Romans and Bruce S. Chelberg, President and Chief Operating Officer of Trans Union, had been working on the matter in preparation for the meeting. According to Romans: They did not "come up" with a price for the Company. They merely "ran the numbers" at $50 a share and at $60 a share with the "rough form" of their cash figures at the time. Their "figures indicated that $50 would be very easy to do but $60 would be very difficult to do under those figures." This work did not purport to establish a fair price for either the Company or 100% of the stock. It was intended to determine the cash flow needed to service the debt that would "probably" be incurred in a leveraged buyout, based on "rough calculations" without "any benefit of experts to identify what the limits were to that, and so forth." These computations were not considered extensive and no conclusion was reached.

At this meeting, Van Gorkom stated that he would be willing to take $55 per share for his own 75,000 shares. He vetoed the suggestion of a leveraged buy-out by Management, however, as involving a potential conflict of interest for Management. Van Gorkom, a certified public accountant and lawyer, had been an officer of Trans Union *866 for 24 years, its Chief Executive Officer for more than 17 years, and Chairman of its Board for 2 years. It is noteworthy in this connection that he was then approaching 65 years of age and mandatory retirement.

For several days following the September 5 meeting, Van Gorkom pondered the idea of a sale. He had participated in many acquisitions as a manager and director of Trans Union and as a director of other companies. He was familiar with acquisition procedures, valuation methods, and negotiations; and he privately considered the pros and cons of whether Trans Union should seek a privately or publicly-held purchaser.

Van Gorkom decided to meet with Jay A. Pritzker, a well-known corporate takeover specialist and a social acquaintance. However, rather than approaching Pritzker simply to determine his interest in acquiring Trans Union, Van Gorkom assembled a proposed per share price for sale of the Company and a financing structure by which to accomplish the sale. Van Gorkom did so without consulting either his Board or any members of Senior Management except one: Carl Peterson, Trans Union's Controller. Telling Peterson that he wanted no other person on his staff to know what he was doing, but without telling him why, Van Gorkom directed Peterson to calculate the feasibility of a leveraged buy-out at an assumed price per share of $55. Apart from the Company's historic stock market price,[5] and Van Gorkom's long association with Trans Union, the record is devoid of any competent evidence that $55 represented the per share intrinsic value of the Company.

Having thus chosen the $55 figure, based solely on the availability of a leveraged buy-out, Van Gorkom multiplied the price per share by the number of shares outstanding to reach a total value of the Company of $690 million. Van Gorkom told Peterson to use this $690 million figure and to assume a $200 million equity contribution by the buyer. Based on these assumptions, Van Gorkom directed Peterson to determine whether the debt portion of the purchase price could be paid off in five years or less if financed by Trans Union's cash flow as projected in the Five Year Forecast, and by the sale of certain weaker divisions identified in a study done for Trans Union by the Boston Consulting Group ("BCG study"). Peterson reported that, of the purchase price, approximately $50-80 million would remain outstanding after five years. Van Gorkom was disappointed, but decided to meet with Pritzker nevertheless.

Van Gorkom arranged a meeting with Pritzker at the latter's home on Saturday, September 13, 1980. Van Gorkom prefaced his presentation by stating to Pritzker: "Now as far as you are concerned, I can, I think, show how you can pay a substantial premium over the present stock price and pay off most of the loan in the first five years. * * * If you could pay $55 for this Company, here is a way in which I think it can be financed."

Van Gorkom then reviewed with Pritzker his calculations based upon his proposed price of $55 per share. Although Pritzker mentioned $50 as a more attractive figure, no other price was mentioned. However, Van Gorkom stated that to be sure that $55 was the best price obtainable, Trans Union should be free to accept any better offer. Pritzker demurred, stating that his

---

5) The common stock of Trans Union was traded on the New York Stock Exchange. Over the five year period from 1975 through 1979, Trans Union's stock had traded within a range of a high of $39½ and a low of $24¼. Its high and low range for 1980 through September 19 (the last trading day before announcement of the merger) was $38¼-$29½.

organization would serve as a "stalking horse" for an "auction contest" only if Trans Union would permit Pritzker to buy 1,750,000 shares of Trans Union stock at market price which Pritzker could then sell to any higher bidder. After further discussion on this point, Pritzker told Van Gorkom that he would give him a more definite reaction soon. *867 On Monday, September 15, Pritzker advised Van Gorkom that he was interested in the $55 cash-out merger proposal and requested more information on Trans Union. Van Gorkom agreed to meet privately with Pritzker, accompanied by Peterson, Chelberg, and Michael Carpenter, Trans Union's consultant from the Boston Consulting Group. The meetings took place on September 16 and 17. Van Gorkom was "astounded that events were moving with such amazing rapidity."

On Thursday, September 18, Van Gorkom met again with Pritzker. At that time, Van Gorkom knew that Pritzker intended to make a cash-out merger offer at Van Gorkom's proposed $55 per share. Pritzker instructed his attorney, a merger and acquisition specialist, to begin drafting merger documents. There was no further discussion of the $55 price. However, the number of shares of Trans Union's treasury stock to be offered to Pritzker was negotiated down to one million shares; the price was set at $38-75 cents above the per share price at the close of the market on September 19. At this point, Pritzker insisted that the Trans Union Board act on his merger proposal within the next three days, stating to Van Gorkom: "We have to have a decision by no later than Sunday [evening, September 21] before the opening of the English stock exchange on Monday morning." Pritzker's lawyer was then instructed to draft the merger documents, to be reviewed by Van Gorkom's lawyer, "sometimes with discussion and sometimes not, in the haste to get it finished."

On Friday, September 19, Van Gorkom, Chelberg, and Pritzker consulted with Trans Union's lead bank regarding the financing of Pritzker's purchase of Trans Union. The bank indicated that it could form a syndicate of banks that would finance the transaction. On the same day, Van Gorkom retained James

Brennan, Esquire, to advise Trans Union on the legal aspects of the merger. Van Gorkom did not consult with William Browder, a Vice-President and director of Trans Union and former head of its legal department, or with William Moore, then the head of Trans Union's legal staff.

On Friday, September 19, Van Gorkom called a special meeting of the Trans Union Board for noon the following day. He also called a meeting of the Company's Senior Management to convene at 11:00 a.m., prior to the meeting of the Board. No one, except Chelberg and Peterson, was told the purpose of the meetings. Van Gorkom did not invite Trans Union's investment banker, Salomon Brothers or its Chicago-based partner, to attend.

Of those present at the Senior Management meeting on September 20, only Chelberg and Peterson had prior knowledge of Pritzker's offer. Van Gorkom disclosed the offer and described its terms, but he furnished no copies of the proposed Merger Agreement. Romans announced that his department had done a second study which showed that, for a leveraged buy-out, the price range for Trans Union stock was between $55 and $65 per share. Van Gorkom neither saw the study nor asked Romans to make it available for the Board meeting.

Senior Management's reaction to the Pritzker proposal was completely negative. No member of Management, except Chelberg and Peterson, supported the proposal. Romans objected to the price as being too low;[6] he was critical of the timing and suggested that consideration should be given to the adverse tax consequences of an all-cash deal for low-basis shareholders; and he took the position that the agreement to sell Pritzker one million newly-issued shares at market price would inhibit other offers, as would the prohibitions against soliciting bids and furnishing inside information *868 to other bidders. Romans argued that the Pritzker proposal was a "lock up" and amounted to "an agreed merger as opposed to an offer." Nevertheless, Van Gorkom proceeded to

---

6) Van Gorkom asked Romans to express his opinion as to the $55 price. Romans stated that he "thought the price was too low in relation to what he could derive for the company in a cash sale, particularly one which enabled us to realize the values of certain subsidiaries and independent entities."

the Board meeting as scheduled without further delay.

Ten directors served on the Trans Union Board, five inside (defendants Bonser, O'Boyle, Browder, Chelberg, and Van Gorkom) and five outside (defendants Wallis, Johnson, Lanterman, Morgan and Reneker). All directors were present at the meeting, except O'Boyle who was ill. Of the outside directors, four were corporate chief executive officers and one was the former Dean of the University of Chicago Business School. None was an investment banker or trained financial analyst. All members of the Board were well informed about the Company and its operations as a going concern. They were familiar with the current financial condition of the Company, as well as operating and earnings projections reported in the recent Five Year Forecast. The Board generally received regular and detailed reports and was kept abreast of the accumulated investment tax credit and accelerated depreciation problem.

Van Gorkom began the Special Meeting of the Board with a twenty-minute oral presentation. Copies of the proposed Merger Agreement were delivered too late for study before or during the meeting.[7)] He reviewed the Company's ITC and depreciation problems and the efforts theretofore made to solve them. He discussed his initial meeting with Pritzker and his motivation in arranging that meeting. Van Gorkom did not disclose to the Board, however, the methodology by which he alone had arrived at the $55 figure, or the fact that he first proposed the $55 price in his negotiations with Pritzker.

Van Gorkom outlined the terms of the Pritzker offer as follows: Pritzker would pay $55 in cash for all outstanding shares of Trans Union stock upon completion of which Trans Union would be merged into New T Company, a subsidiary wholly-owned by Pritzker and formed to implement the merger; for a period of 90 days, Trans Union could receive, but could not actively solicit, competing offers; the offer had to be acted on by the next evening,

---

7) The record is not clear as to the terms of the Merger Agreement. The Agreement, as originally presented to the Board on September 20, was never produced by defendants despite demands by the plaintiffs. Nor is it clear that the directors were given an opportunity to study the Merger Agreement before voting on it. All that can be said is that Brennan had the Agreement before him during the meeting.

Sunday, September 21; Trans Union could only furnish to competing bidders published information, and not proprietary information; the offer was subject to Pritzker obtaining the necessary financing by October 10, 1980; if the financing contingency were met or waived by Pritzker, Trans Union was required to sell to Pritzker one million newly-issued shares of Trans Union at $38 per share.

Van Gorkom took the position that putting Trans Union "up for auction" through a 90-day market test would validate a decision by the Board that $55 was a fair price. He told the Board that the "free market will have an opportunity to judge whether $55 is a fair price." Van Gorkom framed the decision before the Board not as whether $55 per share was the highest price that could be obtained, but as whether the $55 price was a fair price that the stockholders should be given the opportunity to accept or reject.[8)]

Attorney Brennan advised the members of the Board that they might be sued if they failed to accept the offer and that a fairness opinion was not required as a matter of law.

Romans attended the meeting as chief financial officer of the Company. He told the Board that he had not been involved in the negotiations with Pritzker and knew nothing about the merger proposal until *869 the morning of the meeting; that his studies did not indicate either a fair price for the stock or a valuation of the Company; that he did not see his role as directly addressing the fairness issue; and that he and his people "were trying to search for ways to justify a price in connection with such a [leveraged buy-out] transaction, rather than to say what the shares are worth." Romans testified:

> I told the Board that the study ran the numbers at 50 and 60, and then the subsequent study at 55 and 65, and that was not the same thing as saying that I have a valuation of the company at X dollars. But it was a way — a first step towards reaching that conclusion.

---

8) In Van Gorkom's words: The "real decision" is whether to "let the stockholders decide it" which is "all you are being asked to decide today."

Romans told the Board that, in his opinion, $55 was "in the range of a fair price," but "at the beginning of the range."

Chelberg, Trans Union's President, supported Van Gorkom's presentation and representations. He testified that he "participated to make sure that the Board members collectively were clear on the details of the agreement or offer from Pritzker;" that he "participated in the discussion with Mr. Brennan, inquiring of him about the necessity for valuation opinions in spite of the way in which this particular offer was couched;" and that he was otherwise actively involved in supporting the positions being taken by Van Gorkom before the Board about "the necessity to act immediately on this offer," and about "the adequacy of the $55 and the question of how that would be tested."

The Board meeting of September 20 lasted about two hours. Based solely upon Van Gorkom's oral presentation, Chelberg's supporting representations, Romans' oral statement, Brennan's legal advice, and their knowledge of the market history of the Company's stock,[9)] the directors approved the proposed Merger Agreement. However, the Board later claimed to have attached two conditions to its acceptance: (1) that Trans Union reserved the right to accept any better offer that was made during the market test period; and (2) that Trans Union could share its proprietary information with any other potential bidders. While the Board now claims to have reserved the right to accept any better offer received after the announcement of the Pritzker agreement (even though the minutes of the meeting do not reflect this), it is undisputed that the Board did not reserve the right to actively solicit alternate offers. The Merger Agreement was executed by Van Gorkom during the evening of September 20 at a formal social event that he hosted for the opening of the Chicago Lyric Opera. Neither he nor any other director read the agreement prior to its signing and delivery to Pritzker. * * * On Monday,

---

9) The Trial Court stated the premium relationship of the $55 price to the market history of the Company's stock as follows: * * * the merger price offered to the stockholders of Trans Union represented a premium of 62% over the average of the high and low prices at which Trans Union stock had traded in 1980, a premium of 48% over the last closing price, and a premium of 39% over the highest price at which the stock of Trans Union had traded any time during the prior six years.

September 22, the Company issued a press release announcing that Trans Union had entered into a "definitive" Merger Agreement with an affiliate of the Marmon Group, Inc., a Pritzker holding company. Within 10 days of the public announcement, dissent among Senior Management over the merger had become widespread. Faced with threatened resignations of key officers, Van Gorkom met with Pritzker who agreed to several modifications of the Agreement. Pritzker was willing to do so provided that Van Gorkom could persuade the dissidents to remain on the Company payroll for at least six months after consummation of the merger.

Van Gorkom reconvened the Board on October 8 and secured the directors' approval of the proposed amendments — sight unseen. The Board also authorized the employment of Salomon Brothers, its investment *870 banker, to solicit other offers for Trans Union during the proposed "market test" period.

The next day, October 9, Trans Union issued a press release announcing: (1) that Pritzker had obtained "the financing commitments necessary to consummate" the merger with Trans Union; (2) that Pritzker had acquired one million shares of Trans Union common stock at $38 per share; (3) that Trans Union was now permitted to actively seek other offers and had retained Salomon Brothers for that purpose; and (4) that if a more favorable offer were not received before February 1, 1981, Trans Union's shareholders would thereafter meet to vote on the Pritzker proposal.

It was not until the following day, October 10, that the actual amendments to the Merger Agreement were prepared by Pritzker and delivered to Van Gorkom for execution. As will be seen, the amendments were considerably at variance with Van Gorkom's representations of the amendments to the Board on October 8; and the amendments placed serious constraints on Trans Union's ability to negotiate a better deal and withdraw from the Pritzker agreement. Nevertheless, Van Gorkom proceeded to execute what became the October 10 amendments to the Merger Agreement without conferring further with the Board members and apparently without comprehending the actual implications of the amendments.* * *

Salomon Brothers' efforts over a three-month period from October 21 to January 21 produced only one serious suitor for Trans Union — General Electric Credit Corporation ("GE Credit"), a subsidiary of the General Electric Company. However, GE Credit was unwilling to make an offer for Trans Union unless Trans Union first rescinded its Merger Agreement with Pritzker. When Pritzker refused, GE Credit terminated further discussions with Trans Union in early January.

In the meantime, in early December, the investment firm of Kohlberg, Kravis, Roberts & Co. ("KKR"), the only other concern to make a firm offer for Trans Union, withdrew its offer under circumstances hereinafter detailed.

On December 19, this litigation was commenced and, within four weeks, the plaintiffs had deposed eight of the ten directors of Trans Union, including Van Gorkom, Chelberg and Romans, its Chief Financial Officer. On January 21, Management's Proxy Statement for the February 10 shareholder meeting was mailed to Trans Union's stockholders. On January 26, Trans Union's Board met and, after a lengthy meeting, voted to proceed with the Pritzker merger. The Board also approved for mailing, "on or about January 27," a Supplement to its Proxy Statement. The Supplement purportedly set forth all information relevant to the Pritzker Merger Agreement, which had not been divulged in the first Proxy Statement. * * * On February 10, the stockholders of Trans Union approved the Pritzker merger proposal. Of the outstanding shares, 69.9% were voted in favor of the merger; 7.25% were voted against the merger; and 22.85% were not voted.

II.

We turn to the issue of the application of the business judgment rule to the September 20 meeting of the Board. The Court of Chancery concluded from the evidence that the Board of Directors' approval of the Pritzker merger proposal fell within the protection of the business judgment rule. The Court found that the Board had given sufficient time and attention to the transaction, since the directors had considered the Pritzker proposal on three different occasions, on September 20, and on October 8, 1980 and finally on January 26, 1981. On that basis, the Court reasoned that the Board had acquired, over the four-month period, sufficient information to reach an informed business judgment *871 on the cash-out merger proposal. The Court ruled:

> ... that given the market value of Trans Union's stock, the business acumen of the members of the board of Trans Union, the substantial premium over market offered by the Pritzkers and the ultimate effect on the merger price provided by the prospect of other bids for the stock in question, that the board of directors of Trans Union did not act recklessly or improvidently in determining on a course of action which they believed to be in the best interest of the stockholders of Trans Union.

The Court of Chancery made but one finding; i.e., that the Board's conduct over the entire period from September 20 through January 26, 1981 was not reckless or improvident, but informed. This ultimate conclusion was premised upon three subordinate findings, one explicit and two implied. The Court's explicit finding was that Trans Union's Board was "free to turn down the Pritzker proposal" not only on September 20 but also on October 8, 1980 and on January 26, 1981. The Court's implied, subordinate findings were: (1) that no legally binding agreement was reached by the parties until January 26; and (2) that if a higher offer were to be forthcoming, the market test would have produced it,[10] and Trans Union would have been contractually free to accept such higher offer. However, the Court offered no factual basis or legal support for any of these findings; and the record compels contrary conclusions. This Court's standard of review of the findings of fact

10) We refer to the underlined portion of the Court's ultimate conclusion (previously stated): "that given the market value of Trans Union's stock, the business acumen of the members of the board of Trans Union, the substantial premium over market offered by the Pritzkers *and the ultimate effect on the merger price provided by the prospect of other bids for the stock in question,* that the board of directors of Trans Union did not act recklessly or improvidently...."

reached by the Trial Court following full evidentiary hearing is as stated in *Levitt v. Bouvier,* Del.Supr., 287 A.2d 671, 673 (1972):

> [In an appeal of this nature] this court has the authority to review the entire record and to make its own findings of fact in a proper case. In exercising our power of review, we have the duty to review the sufficiency of the evidence and to test the propriety of the findings below. We do not, however, ignore the findings made by the trial judge. If they are sufficiently supported by the record and are the product of an orderly and logical deductive process, in the exercise of judicial restraint we accept them, even though independently we might have reached opposite conclusions. It is only when the findings below are clearly wrong and the doing of justice requires their overturn that we are free to make contradictory findings of fact.

Applying that standard and governing principles of law to the record and the decision of the Trial Court, we conclude that the Court's ultimate finding that the Board's conduct was not "reckless or imprudent" is contrary to the record and not the product of a logical and deductive reasoning process.

The plaintiffs contend that the Court of Chancery erred as a matter of law by exonerating the defendant directors under the business judgment rule without first determining whether the rule's threshold condition of "due care and prudence" was satisfied. The plaintiffs assert that the Trial Court found the defendant directors to have reached an informed business judgment on the basis of "extraneous considerations and events that occurred after September 20, 1980." The defendants deny that the Trial Court committed legal error in relying upon post-September 20, 1980 events and the directors' later acquired knowledge. The defendants further submit that their decision to accept $55 per share was informed because: (1) they were "highly qualified;" (2) they were "well-informed;" and (3) they deliberated over the "proposal" not once but three times. On *872 essentially this evidence and under our standard of review, the defendants assert that affirmance is required. We must disagree.

Under Delaware law, the business judgment rule is the offspring of the fundamental principle, codified in 8 *Del.C.* § 141(a), that the business and affairs of a Delaware corporation are managed by or under its board of directors.[11] *Pogostin v. Rice,* Del.Supr., 480 A.2d 619, 624 (1984); *Aronson v. Lewis,* Del.Supr., 473 A.2d 805, 811 (1984); *Zapata Corp. v. Maldonado,* Del.Supr., 430 A.2d 779, 782 (1981). In carrying out their managerial roles, directors are charged with an unyielding fiduciary duty to the corporation and its shareholders. *Loft, Inc. v. Guth,* Del.Ch., 2 A.2d 225 (1938), *aff'd,* Del.Supr., 5 A.2d 503 (1939). The business judgment rule exists to protect and promote the full and free exercise of the managerial power granted to Delaware directors. *Zapata Corp. v. Maldonado, supra* at 782. The rule itself "is a presumption that in making a business decision, the directors of a corporation acted on an informed basis, in good faith and in the honest belief that the action taken was in the best interests of the company." *Aronson, supra* at 812. Thus, the party attacking a board decision as uninformed must rebut the presumption that its business judgment was an informed one. *Id.*

The determination of whether a business judgment is an informed one turns on whether the directors have informed themselves "prior to making a business decision, of all material information reasonably available to them." *Id.*[12]

Under the business judgment rule there is no protection for directors who have made "an unintelligent or unadvised judgment." *Mitchell v. Highland-Western Glass,* Del.Ch., 167 A. 831, 833 (1933). A director's duty to inform himself in preparation for a decision derives from the fiduciary capacity in which he serves the corporation and its stockholders. *Lutz v. Boas,* Del.Ch.,

---

11) 8 *Del.C.* § 141 provides, in pertinent part: (a) The business and affairs of every corporation organized under this chapter shall be managed by or under the direction of a board of directors, except as may be otherwise provided in this chapter or in its certificate of incorporation. If any such provision is made in the certificate of incorporation, the powers and duties conferred or imposed upon the board of directors by this chapter shall be exercised or performed to such extent and by such person or persons as shall be provided in the certificate of incorporation.

12) *See Kaplan v. Centex Corporation,* Del.Ch., 284 A.2d 119, 124 (1971), where the Court stated: Application of the [business judgment] rule of necessity depends upon a showing that informed directors did in fact make a business judgment authorizing the transaction under review. And, as the plaintiff argues, the difficulty here is that the evidence does not show that this was done. There were director-committee-officer references to the realignment but none of these singly or cumulative showed that the director judgment was brought to bear with specificity on the transactions.

171 A.2d 381 (1961). *See Weinberger v. UOP, Inc., supra; Guth v. Loft, supra.* Since a director is vested with the responsibility for the management of the affairs of the corporation, he must execute that duty with the recognition that he acts on behalf of others. Such obligation does not tolerate faithlessness or self-dealing. But fulfillment of the fiduciary function requires more than the mere absence of bad faith or fraud. Representation of the financial interests of others imposes on a director an affirmative duty to protect those interests and to proceed with a critical eye in assessing information of the type and under the circumstances present here. *See Lutz v. Boas, supra; Guth v. Loft, supra* at 510. *Compare Donovan v. Cunningham,* 5th Cir., 716 F.2d 1455, 1467 (1983); *Doyle v. Union Insurance Company,* Neb.Supr., 277 N.W.2d 36 (1979); *Continental Securities Co. v. Belmont,* N.Y. App., 99 N.E. 138, 141 (1912).

Thus, a director's duty to exercise an informed business judgment is in *873 the nature of a duty of care, as distinguished from a duty of loyalty. Here, there were no allegations of fraud, bad faith, or self-dealing, or proof thereof. Hence, it is presumed that the directors reached their business judgment in good faith, *Allaun v. Consolidated Oil Co.,* Del. Ch., 147 A. 257 (1929), and considerations of motive are irrelevant to the issue before us.

The standard of care applicable to a director's duty of care has also been recently restated by this Court. In *Aronson, supra,* we stated:

> While the Delaware cases use a variety of terms to describe the applicable standard of care, our analysis satisfies us that under the business judgment rule director liability is predicated upon concepts of gross negligence. (footnote omitted) 473 A.2d at 812.

We again confirm that view. We think the concept of gross negligence is also the proper standard for determining whether a business judgment reached by a board of directors was an informed one.[13)]

13) Compare *Mitchell v. Highland-Western Glass, supra,* where the Court posed the question as whether the board acted "so far without information that they can be said to have passed an unintelligent and unadvised judgment." 167 A. at 833. Compare also *Gimbel v. Signal Companies, Inc.,* 316 A.2d 599, *aff'd per curiam* Del. Supr., 316 A.2d 619 (1974), where the Chancellor, after expressly reiterating the *Highland-Western Glass* standard, framed the question, "Or to put the question in its legal context, did the Signal directors act without the bounds of reason and recklessly in approving the price offer of Burmah?" *Id.*

In the specific context of a proposed merger of domestic corporations, a director has a duty under 8 *Del.C.* 251(b),[14] along with his fellow directors, to act in an informed and deliberate manner in determining whether to approve an agreement of merger before submitting the proposal to the stockholders. Certainly in the merger context, a director may not abdicate that duty by leaving to the shareholders alone the decision to approve or disapprove the agreement. *See Beard v. Elster,* Del.Supr., 160 A.2d 731, 737 (1960). Only an agreement of merger satisfying the requirements of 8 *Del.C.* § 251(b) may be submitted to the shareholders under § 251(c). *See generally Aronson v. Lewis, supra* at 811-13; *see also Pogostin v. Rice, supra.*

It is against those standards that the conduct of the directors of Trans Union must be tested, as a matter of law and as a matter of fact, regarding their exercise of an informed business judgment in voting to approve the Pritzker merger proposal.

III.

The defendants argue that the determination of whether their decision to accept $55 per share for Trans Union represented an informed business judgment requires consideration, not only of that which they knew and

14) 8 *Del.C.* § 251(b) provides in pertinent part:
(b) The board of directors of each corporation which desires to merge or consolidate *shall adopt a resolution approving an agreement of merger* or consolidation. The agreement shall state: (1) the terms and conditions of the merger or consolidation; (2) the mode of carrying the same into effect; (3) such amendments or changes in the certificate of incorporation of the surviving corporation as are desired to be effected by the merger or consolidation, or, if no such amendments or changes are desired, a statement that the certificate of incorporation of one of the constituent corporations shall be the certificate of incorporation of the surviving or resulting corporation; (4) the manner of converting the shares of each of the constituent corporations... and (5) such other details or provisions as are deemed desirable.... The agreement so adopted shall be executed in accordance with section 103 of this title. Any of the terms of the agreement of merger or consolidation may be made dependent upon facts ascertainable outside of such agreement, provided that the manner in which such facts shall operate upon the terms of the agreement is clearly and expressly set forth in the agreement of merger or consolidation. (underlining added for emphasis)

learned on September 20, but also of that which they subsequently learned and did over the following four-month *874 period before the shareholders met to vote on the proposal in February, 1981. The defendants thereby seek to reduce the significance of their action on September 20 and to widen the time frame for determining whether their decision to accept the Pritzker proposal was an informed one. Thus, the defendants contend that what the directors did and learned subsequent to September 20 and through January 26, 1981, was properly taken into account by the Trial Court in determining whether the Board's judgment was an informed one. We disagree with this *post hoc* approach.

The issue of whether the directors reached an informed decision to "sell" the Company on September 20, 1980 must be determined only upon the basis of the information then reasonably available to the directors and relevant to their decision to accept the Pritzker merger proposal. This is not to say that the directors were precluded from altering their original plan of action, had they done so in an informed manner. What we do say is that the question of whether the directors reached an informed business judgment in agreeing to sell the Company, pursuant to the terms of the September 20 Agreement presents, in reality, two questions: (A) whether the directors reached an informed business judgment on September 20, 1980; and (B) if they did not, whether the directors' actions taken subsequent to September 20 were adequate to cure any infirmity in their action taken on September 20. We first consider the directors' September 20 action in terms of their reaching an informed business judgment.

-A-

On the record before us, we must conclude that the Board of Directors did not reach an informed business judgment on September 20, 1980 in voting to "sell" the Company for $55 per share pursuant to the Pritzker cash-out merger proposal. Our reasons, in summary, are as follows:

The directors (1) did not adequately inform themselves as to Van Gorkom's role in forcing the "sale" of the Company and in establishing the per share purchase price; (2) were uninformed as to the intrinsic value of the Company; and (3) given these circumstances, at a minimum, were grossly negligent in approving the "sale" of the Company upon two hours' consideration, without prior notice, and without the exigency of a crisis or emergency.

As has been noted, the Board based its September 20 decision to approve the cash-out merger primarily on Van Gorkom's representations. None of the directors, other than Van Gorkom and Chelberg, had any prior knowledge that the purpose of the meeting was to propose a cash-out merger of Trans Union. No members of Senior Management were present, other than Chelberg, Romans and Peterson; and the latter two had only learned of the proposed sale an hour earlier. Both general counsel Moore and former general counsel Browder attended the meeting, but were equally uninformed as to the purpose of the meeting and the documents to be acted upon.

Without any documents before them concerning the proposed transaction, the members of the Board were required to rely entirely upon Van Gorkom's 20-minute oral presentation of the proposal. No written summary of the terms of the merger was presented; the directors were given no documentation to support the adequacy of $55 price per share for sale of the Company; and the Board had before it nothing more than Van Gorkom's statement of his understanding of the substance of an agreement which he admittedly had never read, nor which any member of the Board had ever seen.

Under 8 *Del.C.* § 141(e),[15] "directors are fully protected in relying in *875 good faith on reports made by officers." *Michelson v. Duncan,* Del.Ch., 386 A.2d 1144, 1156 (1978); *aff'd in part and rev'd in part on other grounds,* Del.

15) Section 141(e) provides in pertinent part: A member of the board of directors ... shall, in the performance of his duties, be fully protected in relying in good faith upon the books of accounts or reports made to the corporation by any of its officers, or by an independent certified public accountant, or by an appraiser selected with reasonable care by the board of directors ..., or in relying in good faith upon other records of the corporation.

Supr., 407 A.2d 211 (1979). *See also Graham v. Allis-Chalmers Mfg. Co.,* Del. Supr., 188 A.2d 125, 130 (1963); *Prince v. Bensinger,* Del. Ch., 244 A.2d 89, 94 (1968). The term "report" has been liberally construed to include reports of informal personal investigations by corporate officers, *Cheff v. Mathes,* Del. Supr., 199 A.2d 548, 556 (1964). However, there is no evidence that any "report," as defined under § 141(e), concerning the Pritzker proposal, was presented to the Board on September 20.[16] Van Gorkom's oral presentation of his understanding of the terms of the proposed Merger Agreement, which he had not seen, and Romans' brief oral statement of his preliminary study regarding the feasibility of a leveraged buy-out of Trans Union do not qualify as § 141(e) "reports" for these reasons: The former lacked substance because Van Gorkom was basically uninformed as to the essential provisions of the very document about which he was talking. Romans' statement was irrelevant to the issues before the Board since it did not purport to be a valuation study. At a minimum for a report to enjoy the status conferred by § 141(e), it must be pertinent to the subject matter upon which a board is called to act, and otherwise be entitled to good faith, not blind, reliance. Considering all of the surrounding circumstances — hastily calling the meeting without prior notice of its subject matter, the proposed sale of the Company without any prior consideration of the issue or necessity therefor, the urgent time constraints imposed by Pritzker, and the total absence of any documentation whatsoever — the directors were duty bound to make reasonable inquiry of Van Gorkom and Romans, and if they had done so, the inadequacy of that upon which they now claim to have relied would have been apparent.

The defendants rely on the following factors to sustain the Trial Court's finding that the Board's decision was an informed one: (1) the magnitude

16) In support of the defendants' argument that their judgment as to the adequacy of $55 per share was an informed one, the directors rely on the BCG study and the Five Year Forecast. However, no one even referred to either of these studies at the September 20 meeting; and it is conceded that these materials do not represent valuation studies. Hence, these documents do not constitute evidence as to whether the directors reached an informed judgment on September 20 that $55 per share was a fair value for sale of the Company.

of the premium or spread between the $55 Pritzker offering price and Trans Union's current market price of $38 per share; (2) the amendment of the Agreement as submitted on September 20 to permit the Board to accept any better offer during the "market test" period; (3) the collective experience and expertise of the Board's "inside" and "outside" directors;[17] and (4) their reliance on Brennan's legal advice that the directors might be sued if they rejected the Pritzker proposal. We discuss each of these grounds *seriatim:*

(1)

A substantial premium may provide one reason to recommend a merger, but in the absence of other sound valuation information, the fact of a premium alone does not provide an adequate basis upon which to assess the fairness of an offering price. Here, the judgment reached as to the adequacy of the premium was based on a comparison between the historically depressed Trans Union market price and the amount of the Pritzker offer. Using market price as a basis for concluding that the premium adequately reflected the true value *876 of the Company was a clearly faulty, indeed fallacious, premise, as the defendants' own evidence demonstrates.

The record is clear that before September 20, Van Gorkom and other members of Trans Union's Board knew that the market had consistently undervalued the worth of Trans Union's stock, despite steady increases in the Company's operating income in the seven years preceding the merger. The Board related this occurrence in large part to Trans Union's inability to use its ITCs as previously noted. Van Gorkom testified that he did not believe the market price accurately reflected Trans Union's true worth; and several of the directors testified that, as a general rule, most chief executives think that the market undervalues their companies' stock. Yet, on September 20, Trans Union's Board apparently believed that the market stock price accurately

17) We reserve for discussion under Part III hereof, the defendants' contention that their judgment, reached on September 20, if not then informed became informed by virtue of their "review" of the Agreement on October 8 and January 26.

reflected the value of the Company for the purpose of determining the adequacy of the premium for its sale.

In the Proxy Statement, however, the directors reversed their position. There, they stated that, although the earnings prospects for Trans Union were "excellent," they found no basis for believing that this would be reflected in future stock prices. With regard to past trading, the Board stated that the prices at which the Company's common stock had traded in recent years did not reflect the "inherent" value of the Company. But having referred to the "inherent" value of Trans Union, the directors ascribed no number to it. Moreover, nowhere did they disclose that they had no basis on which to fix "inherent" worth beyond an impressionistic reaction to the premium over market and an unsubstantiated belief that the value of the assets was "significantly greater" than book value. By their own admission they could not rely on the stock price as an accurate measure of value. Yet, also by their own admission, the Board members assumed that Trans Union's market price was adequate to serve as a basis upon which to assess the adequacy of the premium for purposes of the September 20 meeting.

The parties do not dispute that a publicly-traded stock price is solely a measure of the value of a minority position and, thus, market price represents only the value of a single share. Nevertheless, on September 20, the Board assessed the adequacy of the premium over market, offered by Pritzker, solely by comparing it with Trans Union's current and historical stock price. (*See supra* note 5 at 866.)

Indeed, as of September 20, the Board had no other information on which to base a determination of the intrinsic value of Trans Union as a going concern. As of September 20, the Board had made no evaluation of the Company designed to value the entire enterprise, nor had the Board ever previously considered selling the Company or consenting to a buy-out merger. Thus, the adequacy of a premium is indeterminate unless it is assessed in terms of other competent and sound valuation information that reflects the value of the particular business.

Despite the foregoing facts and circumstances, there was no call by the Board, either on September 20 or thereafter, for any valuation study or documentation of the $55 price per share as a measure of the fair value of the Company in a cash-out context. It is undisputed that the major asset of Trans Union was its cash flow. Yet, at no time did the Board call for a valuation study taking into account that highly significant element of the Company's assets. We do not imply that an outside valuation study is essential to support an informed business judgment; nor do we state that fairness opinions by independent investment bankers are required as a matter of law. Often insiders familiar with the business of a going concern are in a better position than are outsiders to gather relevant information; and under appropriate circumstances, such directors may be fully protected in relying in good faith upon the valuation reports of their management. *877 *See* 8 *Del.C.* § 141(e). *See also Cheff v. Mathes, supra.*

Here, the record establishes that the Board did not request its Chief Financial Officer, Romans, to make any valuation study or review of the proposal to determine the adequacy of $55 per share for sale of the Company. On the record before us: The Board rested on Romans' elicited response that the $55 figure was within a "fair price range" within the context of a leveraged buy-out. No director sought any further information from Romans. No director asked him why he put $55 at the bottom of his range. No director asked Romans for any details as to his study, the reason why it had been undertaken or its depth. No director asked to see the study; and no director asked Romans whether Trans Union's finance department could do a fairness study within the remaining 36-hour[18)] period available under the Pritzker offer.

Had the Board, or any member, made an inquiry of Romans, he

18) Romans' department study was not made available to the Board until circulation of Trans Union's Supplementary Proxy Statement and the Board's meeting of January 26, 1981, on the eve of the shareholder meeting; and, as has been noted, the study has never been produced for inclusion in the record in this case.

presumably would have responded as he testified: that his calculations were rough and preliminary; and, that the study was not designed to determine the fair value of the Company, but rather to assess the feasibility of a leveraged buy-out financed by the Company's projected cash flow, making certain assumptions as to the purchaser's borrowing needs. Romans would have presumably also informed the Board of his view, and the widespread view of Senior Management, that the timing of the offer was wrong and the offer inadequate.

The record also establishes that the Board accepted without scrutiny Van Gorkom's representation as to the fairness of the $55 price per share for sale of the Company — a subject that the Board had never previously considered. The Board thereby failed to discover that Van Gorkom had suggested the $55 price to Pritzker and, most crucially, that Van Gorkom had arrived at the $55 figure based on calculations designed solely to determine the feasibility of a leveraged buy-out.[19)] No questions were raised either as to the tax implications of a cash-out merger or how the price for the one million share option granted Pritzker was calculated.

We do not say that the Board of Directors was not entitled to give some credence to Van Gorkom's representation that $55 was an adequate or fair price. Under § 141(e), the directors were entitled to rely upon their chairman's opinion of value and adequacy, provided that such opinion was reached on a sound basis. Here, the issue is whether the directors informed themselves as to all information that was reasonably available to them. Had they done so, they would have learned of the source and derivation of the

19) As of September 20 the directors did not know: that Van Gorkom had arrived at the $55 figure alone, and subjectively, as the figure to be used by Controller Peterson in creating a feasible structure for a leveraged buy-out by a prospective purchaser; that Van Gorkom had not sought advice, information or assistance from either inside or outside Trans Union directors as to the value of the Company as an entity or the fair price per share for 100% of its stock; that Van Gorkom had not consulted with the Company's investment bankers or other financial analysts; that Van Gorkom had not consulted with or confided in any officer or director of the Company except Chelberg; and that Van Gorkom had deliberately chosen to ignore the advice and opinion of the members of his Senior Management group regarding the adequacy of the $55 price.

$55 price and could not reasonably have relied thereupon in good faith.

None of the directors, Management or outside, were investment bankers or financial analysts. Yet the Board did not consider recessing the meeting until a later hour that day (or requesting an extension of Pritzker's Sunday evening deadline) to give it time to elicit more information as to the sufficiency of the offer, either from *878 inside Management (in particular Romans) or from Trans Union's own investment banker, Salomon Brothers, whose Chicago specialist in merger and acquisitions was known to the Board and familiar with Trans Union's affairs.

Thus, the record compels the conclusion that on September 20 the Board lacked valuation information adequate to reach an informed business judgment as to the fairness of $55 per share for sale of the Company.[20)]

(2)

This brings us to the post-September 20 "market test" upon which the defendants ultimately rely to confirm the reasonableness of their September 20 decision to accept the Pritzker proposal. In this connection, the directors present a two-part argument: (a) that by making a "market test" of Pritzker's $55 per share offer a condition of their September 20 decision to accept his offer, they cannot be found to have acted impulsively or in an uninformed manner on September 20; and (b) that the adequacy of the $17 premium for sale of the Company was conclusively established over the following 90 to 120 days by the most reliable evidence available — the marketplace. Thus, the defendants impliedly contend that the "market test" eliminated the need for the Board to perform any other form of fairness test either on September 20, or thereafter.

Again, the facts of record do not support the defendants' argument. There is no evidence: (a) that the Merger Agreement was effectively amended to

20) For a far more careful and reasoned approach taken by another board of directors faced with the pressures of a hostile tender offer, see *Pogostin v. Rice, supra* at 623-627.

give the Board freedom to put Trans Union up for auction sale to the highest bidder; or (b) that a public auction was in fact permitted to occur. The minutes of the Board meeting make no reference to any of this. Indeed, the record compels the conclusion that the directors had no rational basis for expecting that a market test was attainable, given the terms of the Agreement as executed during the evening of September 20. We rely upon the following facts which are essentially uncontradicted:

The Merger Agreement, specifically identified as that originally presented to the Board on September 20, has never been produced by the defendants, notwithstanding the plaintiffs' several demands for production before as well as during trial. No acceptable explanation of this failure to produce documents has been given to either the Trial Court or this Court. Significantly, neither the defendants nor their counsel have made the affirmative representation that this critical document has been produced. Thus, the Court is deprived of the best evidence on which to judge the merits of the defendants' position as to the care and attention which they gave to the terms of the Agreement on September 20.

Van Gorkom states that the Agreement as submitted incorporated the ingredients for a market test by authorizing Trans Union to receive competing offers over the next 90-day period. However, he concedes that the Agreement barred Trans Union from actively soliciting such offers and from furnishing to interested parties any information about the Company other than that already in the public domain. Whether the original Agreement of September 20 went so far as to authorize Trans Union to receive competitive proposals is arguable. The defendants' unexplained failure to produce and identify the original Merger Agreement permits the logical inference that the instrument would not support their assertions in this regard. *Wilmington Trust Co. v. General Motors Corp.*, Del.Supr., 51 A.2d 584, 593 (1947); II *Wigmore on Evidence* § 291 (3d ed. 1940). It is a well established principle that the production of weak evidence when strong is, or should have been, available can lead only to the conclusion that the strong would have been adverse. *Interstate Circuit v. United States,* 306 U.S. *879 208, 226, 59 S.Ct. 467, 474, 83 L.Ed. 610 (1939); *Deberry v. State,* Del.Supr., 457 A.2d 744, 754 (1983). Van Gorkom, conceding that he never read the Agreement, stated that he was relying upon his understanding that, under corporate law, directors always have an inherent right, as well as a fiduciary duty, to accept a better offer notwithstanding an existing contractual commitment by the Board. (See the discussion *infra,* part III B(3) at p. 55.)

The defendant directors assert that they "insisted" upon including two amendments to the Agreement, thereby permitting a market test: (1) to give Trans Union the right to accept a better offer; and (2) to reserve to Trans Union the right to distribute proprietary information on the Company to alternative bidders. Yet, the defendants concede that they did not seek to amend the Agreement to permit Trans Union to solicit competing offers.

Several of Trans Union's outside directors resolutely maintained that the Agreement as submitted was approved on the understanding that, "if we got a better deal, we had a right to take it." Director Johnson so testified; but he then added, "And if they didn't put that in the agreement, then the management did not carry out the conclusion of the Board. And I just don't know whether they did or not." The only clause in the Agreement as finally executed to which the defendants can point as "keeping the door open" is the following underlined statement found in subparagraph (a) of section 2.03 of the Merger Agreement as executed: The Board of Directors shall recommend to the stockholders of Trans Union that they approve and adopt the Merger Agreement (`the stockholders' approval') and to use its best efforts to obtain the requisite votes therefor. *GL acknowledges that Trans Union directors may have a competing fiduciary obligation to the shareholders under certain circumstances.*

Clearly, this language on its face cannot be construed as incorporating either of the two "conditions" described above: either the right to accept a better offer or the right to distribute proprietary information to third parties. The logical witness for the defendants to call to confirm their construction of this clause of the Agreement would have been Trans Union's outside attorney, James Brennan. The defendants' failure, without explanation, to call this witness again permits the logical inference that his testimony would not have been helpful to them. The further fact that the directors adjourned, rather than recessed, the meeting without incorporating in the Agreement these important "conditions" further weakens the defendants' position. As has been noted, nothing in the Board's Minutes supports these claims. No reference to either of the so-called "conditions" or of Trans Union's reserved right to test the market appears in any notes of the Board meeting or in the Board Resolution accepting the Pritzker offer or in the Minutes of the meeting itself. That evening, in the midst of a formal party which he hosted for the opening of the Chicago Lyric Opera, Van Gorkom executed the Merger Agreement without he or any other member of the Board having read the instruments.

The defendants attempt to downplay the significance of the prohibition against Trans Union's actively soliciting competing offers by arguing that the directors "understood that the entire financial community would know that Trans Union was for sale upon the announcement of the Pritzker offer, and anyone desiring to make a better offer was free to do so." Yet, the press release issued on September 22, with the authorization of the Board, stated that Trans Union had entered into "definitive agreements" with the Pritzkers; and the press release did not even disclose Trans Union's limited right to receive and accept higher offers. Accompanying this press release was a further public announcement that Pritzker had been granted an option to purchase at any time one million shares of *880 Trans Union's capital stock at 75 cents above the then-current price per share. Thus, notwithstanding what several of the outside directors later claimed to have "thought" occurred at the meeting, the record compels the conclusion that Trans Union's Board had no rational basis to conclude on September 20 or in the days immediately following, that the Board's acceptance of Pritzker's offer was conditioned on (1) a "market test" of the offer; and (2) the Board's right to withdraw from the Pritzker Agreement and accept any higher offer received before the shareholder meeting.

(3)

The directors' unfounded reliance on both the premium and the market test as the basis for accepting the Pritzker proposal undermines the defendants' remaining contention that the Board's collective experience and sophistication was a sufficient basis for finding that it reached its September 20 decision with informed, reasonable deliberation.[21)] *Compare Gimbel v. Signal Companies, Inc.,* Del. Ch., 316 A.2d 599 (1974), *aff'd per curiam,* Del. Supr., 316 A.2d 619 (1974). There, the Court of Chancery preliminary enjoined a board's sale of stock of its wholly-owned subsidiary for an alleged grossly inadequate price. It did so based on a finding that the business judgment rule had been pierced for failure of management to give its board "the opportunity to make a reasonable and reasoned decision." 316 A.2d at 615. The Court there reached this result notwithstanding the board's sophistication and experience; the company's need of immediate cash; and the board's need to act promptly due to the impact of an energy crisis on the value of the underlying assets being sold - all of its subsidiary's oil and gas interests. The Court found those factors denoting competence to be outweighed by evidence of gross negligence; that management in effect sprang the deal on the board by negotiating the asset sale without informing the board; that the buyer intended to "force a quick decision" by the board; that the board meeting was called on only one-and-a-half days' notice; that its outside directors were not notified of the meeting's purpose; that during a

21) Trans Union's five "inside" directors had backgrounds in law and accounting, 116 years of collective employment by the Company and 68 years of combined experience on its Board. Trans Union's five "outside" directors included four chief executives of major corporations and an economist who was a former dean of a major school of business and chancellor of a university. The "outside" directors had 78 years of combined experience as chief executive officers of major corporations and 50 years of cumulative experience as directors of Trans Union. Thus, defendants argue that the Board was eminently qualified to reach an informed judgment on the proposed "sale" of Trans Union notwithstanding their lack of any advance notice of the proposal, the shortness of their deliberation, and their determination not to consult with their investment banker or to obtain a fairness opinion.

meeting spanning "a couple of hours" a sale of assets worth $480 million was approved; and that the Board failed to obtain a *current* appraisal of its oil and gas interests. The analogy of *Signal* to the case at bar is significant.

(4)

Part of the defense is based on a claim that the directors relied on legal advice rendered at the September 20 meeting by James Brennan, Esquire, who was present at Van Gorkom's request. Unfortunately, Brennan did not appear and testify at trial even though his firm participated in the defense of this action. There is no contemporaneous evidence of the advice given by Brennan on September 20, only the later deposition and trial testimony of certain directors as to their recollections or understanding of what was said at the meeting. Since counsel did not testify, and the advice attributed to Brennan is hearsay received by the Trial Court over the plaintiffs' objections, we consider it only in the context of the directors' present claims. In fairness to counsel, we make no findings that the advice attributed to him was in fact given. We focus solely on the efficacy of the *881 defendants' claims, made months and years later, in an effort to extricate themselves from liability.

Several defendants testified that Brennan advised them that Delaware law did not require a fairness opinion or an outside valuation of the Company before the Board could act on the Pritzker proposal. If given, the advice was correct. However, that did not end the matter. Unless the directors had before them adequate information regarding the intrinsic value of the Company, upon which a proper exercise of business judgment could be made, mere advice of this type is meaningless; and, given this record of the defendants' failures, it constitutes no defense here.[22] * * * We conclude that Trans Union's Board was grossly negligent in that it failed to act with informed reasonable

22) Nonetheless, we are satisfied that in an appropriate factual context a proper exercise of business judgment may include, as one of its aspects, reasonable reliance upon the advice of counsel. This is wholly outside the statutory protections of 8 *Del.C.* § 141(e) involving reliance upon reports of officers, certain experts and books and records of the company.

deliberation in agreeing to the Pritzker merger proposal on September 20; and we further conclude that the Trial Court erred as a matter of law in failing to address that question before determining whether the directors' later conduct was sufficient to cure its initial error.

A second claim is that counsel advised the Board it would be subject to lawsuits if it rejected the $55 per share offer. It is, of course, a fact of corporate life that today when faced with difficult or sensitive issues, directors often are subject to suit, irrespective of the decisions they make. However, counsel's mere acknowledgement of this circumstance cannot be rationally translated into a justification for a board permitting itself to be stampeded into a patently unadvised act. While suit might result from the rejection of a merger or tender offer, Delaware law makes clear that a board acting within the ambit of the business judgment rule faces no ultimate liability. *Pogostin v. Rice, supra.* Thus, we cannot conclude that the mere threat of litigation, acknowledged by counsel, constitutes either legal advice or any valid basis upon which to pursue an uninformed course. Since we conclude that Brennan's purported advice is of no consequence to the defense of this case, it is unnecessary for us to invoke the adverse inferences which may be attributable to one failing to appear at trial and testify.

-B-

We now examine the Board's post-September 20 conduct for the purpose of determining first, whether it was informed and not grossly negligent; and second, if informed, whether it was sufficient to legally rectify and cure the Board's derelictions of September 20.[23)]

(1)

First, as to the Board meeting of October 8: Its purpose arose in the aftermath

---

23) As will be seen, we do not reach the second question.

of the September 20 meeting: (1) the September 22 press release announcing that Trans Union "had entered into definitive agreements to merge with an affiliate of Marmon Group, Inc.;" and (2) Senior Management's ensuing revolt.

Trans Union's press release stated:

FOR IMMEDIATE RELEASE:

CHICAGO, IL — Trans Union Corporation announced today that it had entered into definitive agreements to merge with an affiliate of The Marmon Group, Inc. in a transaction whereby Trans Union stockholders would receive $55 per share in cash for each Trans Union share held. The Marmon Group, Inc. is controlled by the Pritzker family of Chicago.

The merger is subject to approval by the stockholders of Trans Union at a special meeting expected to be held *882 sometime during December or early January.

Until October 10, 1980, the purchaser has the right to terminate the merger if financing that is satisfactory to the purchaser has not been obtained, but after that date there is no such right.

In a related transaction, Trans Union has agreed to sell to a designee of the purchaser one million newly-issued shares of Trans Union common stock at a cash price of $38 per share. Such shares will be issued only if the merger financing has been committed for no later than October 10, 1980, or if the purchaser elects to waive the merger financing condition. In addition, the New York Stock Exchange will be asked to approve the listing of the new shares pursuant to a listing application which Trans Union intends to file shortly.

Completing of the transaction is also subject to the preparation of a definitive proxy statement and making various filings and obtaining the approvals or consents of government agencies.

The press release made no reference to provisions allegedly reserving to the Board the rights to perform a "market test" and to withdraw from the Pritzker Agreement if Trans Union received a better offer before the shareholder meeting. The defendants also concede that Trans Union never made a subsequent public announcement stating that it had in fact reserved the right to accept alternate offers, the Agreement notwithstanding.

The public announcement of the Pritzker merger resulted in an "en masse" revolt of Trans Union's Senior Management. The head of Trans Union's tank car operations (its most profitable division) informed Van Gorkom that unless the merger were called off, fifteen key personnel would resign.

Instead of reconvening the Board, Van Gorkom again privately met with Pritzker, informed him of the developments, and sought his advice. Pritzker then made the following suggestions for overcoming Management's dissatisfaction: (1) that the Agreement be amended to permit Trans Union to solicit, as well as receive, higher offers; and (2) that the shareholder meeting be postponed from early January to February 10, 1981. In return, Pritzker asked Van Gorkom to obtain a commitment from Senior Management to remain at Trans Union for at least six months after the merger was consummated.

Van Gorkom then advised Senior Management that the Agreement would be amended to give Trans Union the right to solicit competing offers through January, 1981, if they would agree to remain with Trans Union. Senior Management was temporarily mollified; and Van Gorkom then called a special meeting of Trans Union's Board for October 8.

Thus, the primary purpose of the October 8 Board meeting was to amend the Merger Agreement, in a manner agreeable to Pritzker, to permit Trans Union to conduct a "market test."[24)] Van Gorkom understood that the proposed amendments were intended to give the Company an unfettered "right to openly solicit offers down through January 31." Van Gorkom presumably so represented the amendments to Trans Union's Board members on October 8. In a brief session, the directors approved Van Gorkom's oral presentation of the substance of the proposed amendments, *883 the terms of which were not reduced to writing until October 10. But rather than

24) As previously noted, the Board mistakenly thought that it had amended the September 20 draft agreement to include a market test. A secondary purpose of the October 8 meeting was to obtain the Board's approval for Trans Union to employ its investment advisor, Salomon Brothers, for the limited purpose of assisting Management in the solicitation of other offers. Neither Management nor the Board then or thereafter requested Salomon Brothers to submit its opinion as to the fairness of Pritzker's $55 cash-out merger proposal or to value Trans Union as an entity.There is no evidence of record that the October 8 meeting had any other purpose; and we also note that the Minutes of the October 8 Board meeting, including any notice of the meeting, are not part of the voluminous records of this case.

waiting to review the amendments, the Board again approved them sight unseen and adjourned, giving Van Gorkom authority to execute the papers when he received them.[25)]

Thus, the Court of Chancery's finding that the October 8 Board meeting was convened to *reconsider* the Pritzker "proposal" is clearly erroneous. Further, the consequence of the Board's faulty conduct on October 8, in approving amendments to the Agreement which had not even been drafted, will become apparent when the actual amendments to the Agreement are hereafter examined.

The next day, October 9, and before the Agreement was amended, Pritzker moved swiftly to off-set the proposed market test amendment. First, Pritzker informed Trans Union that he had completed arrangements for financing its acquisition and that the parties were thereby mutually bound to a firm purchase and sale arrangement. Second, Pritzker announced the exercise of his option to purchase one million shares of Trans Union's treasury stock at $38 per share — 75 cents above the current market price. Trans Union's Management responded the same day by issuing a press release announcing: (1) that all financing arrangements for Pritzker's acquisition of Trans Union had been completed; and (2) Pritzker's purchase of one million shares of Trans Union's treasury stock at $38 per share.

The next day, October 10, Pritzker delivered to Trans Union the proposed amendments to the September 20 Merger Agreement. Van Gorkom promptly proceeded to countersign all the instruments on behalf of Trans Union without reviewing the instruments to determine if they were consistent with the authority previously granted him by the Board. The amending documents were apparently not approved by Trans Union's Board until a much later date, December 2. The record does not affirmatively establish that Trans Union's

25) We do not suggest that a board must read *in haec verba* every contract or legal document which it approves, but if it is to successfully absolve itself from charges of the type made here, there must be some credible contemporary evidence demonstrating that the directors knew what they were doing, and ensured that their purported action was given effect. That is the consistent failure which cast this Board upon its unredeemable course.

directors ever read the October 10 amendments.[26]

The October 10 amendments to the Merger Agreement did authorize Trans Union to solicit competing offers, but the amendments had more far-reaching effects. The most significant change was in the definition of the third-party "offer" available to Trans Union as a possible basis for withdrawal from its Merger Agreement with Pritzker. Under the October 10 amendments, a better *offer* was no longer sufficient to permit Trans Union's withdrawal. Trans Union was now permitted to terminate the Pritzker Agreement and abandon the merger only if, prior to February 10, 1981, Trans Union had either consummated a merger (or sale of assets) with a third party or had entered into a "definitive" merger agreement more favorable than Pritzker's and for a greater consideration — subject only to stockholder approval. Further, the "extension" of the market test period to February 10, 1981 was circumscribed by other amendments which required Trans Union to file its preliminary proxy statement on the Pritzker merger proposal by December 5, 1980 and use its best efforts to mail the statement to its shareholders by January 5, 1981. Thus, the market test period was effectively reduced, not extended. (*See infra* note 29 at 886.)

In our view, the record compels the conclusion that the directors' conduct on October *884 8 exhibited the same deficiencies as did their conduct on September 20. The Board permitted its Merger Agreement with Pritzker to be amended in a manner it had neither authorized nor intended. The Court of Chancery, in its decision, over-looked the significance of the October 8-10 events and their relevance to the sufficiency of the directors' conduct. The Trial Court's letter opinion ignores: the October 10 amendments; the manner of their adoption; the effect of the October 9 press release and the October 10 amendments on the feasibility of a market test; and the ultimate question as to the reasonableness of the directors' reliance on a market test in

26) There is no evidence of record that Trans Union's directors ever raised any objections, procedural or substantive, to the October 10 amendments or that any of them, including Van Gorkom, understood the opposite result of their intended effect - until it was too late.

recommending that the shareholders approve the Pritzker merger.

We conclude that the Board acted in a grossly negligent manner on October 8; and that Van Gorkom's representations on which the Board based its actions do not constitute "reports" under § 141(e) on which the directors could reasonably have relied. Further, the amended Merger Agreement imposed on Trans Union's acceptance of a third party offer conditions more onerous than those imposed on Trans Union's acceptance of Pritzker's offer on September 20. After October 10, Trans Union could accept from a third party a better offer only if it were incorporated in a definitive agreement between the parties, and not conditioned on financing or on any other contingency.

The October 9 press release, coupled with the October 10 amendments, had the clear effect of locking Trans Union's Board into the Pritzker Agreement. Pritzker had thereby foreclosed Trans Union's Board from negotiating any better "definitive" agreement over the remaining eight weeks before Trans Union was required to clear the Proxy Statement submitting the Pritzker proposal to its shareholders.

(2)

Next, as to the "curative" effects of the Board's post-September 20 conduct, we review in more detail the reaction of Van Gorkom to the KKR proposal and the results of the Board-sponsored "market test."

The KKR proposal was the first and only offer received subsequent to the Pritzker Merger Agreement. The offer resulted primarily from the efforts of Romans and other senior officers to propose an alternative to Pritzker's acquisition of Trans Union. In late September, Romans' group contacted KKR about the possibility of a leveraged buy-out by all members of Management, except Van Gorkom. By early October, Henry R. Kravis of KKR gave Romans written notice of KKR's "interest in making an offer to purchase 100%" of Trans Union's common stock.

Thereafter, and until early December, Romans' group worked with KKR to develop a proposal. It did so with Van Gorkom's knowledge and apparently grudging consent. On December 2, Kravis and Romans hand-delivered to Van Gorkom a formal letter-offer to purchase all of Trans Union's assets and to assume all of its liabilities for an aggregate cash consideration equivalent to $60 per share. The offer was contingent upon completing equity and bank financing of $650 million, which Kravis represented as 80% complete. The KKR letter made reference to discussions with major banks regarding the loan portion of the buy-out cost and stated that KKR was "confident that commitments for the bank financing * * * can be obtained within two or three weeks." The purchasing group was to include certain named key members of Trans Union's Senior Management, excluding Van Gorkom, and a major Canadian company. Kravis stated that they were willing to enter into a "definitive agreement" under terms and conditions "substantially the same" as those contained in Trans Union's agreement with Pritzker. The offer was addressed to Trans Union's Board of Directors and a meeting with the Board, scheduled for that afternoon, was requested.

Van Gorkom's reaction to the KKR proposal was completely negative; he did not view the offer as being firm because of its *885 financing condition. It was pointed out, to no avail, that Pritzker's offer had not only been similarly conditioned, but accepted on an expedited basis. Van Gorkom refused Kravis' request that Trans Union issue a press release announcing KKR's offer, on the ground that it might "chill" any other offer.[27)] Romans and Kravis left with the understanding that their proposal would be presented to Trans Union's Board that afternoon.

Within a matter of hours and shortly before the scheduled Board meeting, Kravis withdrew his letter-offer. He gave as his reason a sudden decision by the Chief Officer of Trans Union's rail car leasing operation to withdraw from the KKR purchasing group. Van Gorkom had spoken to that officer about his participation in the KKR proposal immediately after his meeting with

27) This was inconsistent with Van Gorkom's espousal of the September 22 press release following Trans Union's acceptance of Pritzker's proposal. Van Gorkom had then justified a press release as encouraging rather than chilling later offers.

Romans and Kravis. However, Van Gorkom denied any responsibility for the officer's change of mind.

At the Board meeting later that afternoon, Van Gorkom did not inform the directors of the KKR proposal because he considered it "dead." Van Gorkom did not contact KKR again until January 20, when faced with the realities of this lawsuit, he then attempted to reopen negotiations. KKR declined due to the imminence of the February 10 stockholder meeting.

GE Credit Corporation's interest in Trans Union did not develop until November; and it made no written proposal until mid-January. Even then, its proposal was not in the form of an offer. Had there been time to do so, GE Credit was prepared to offer between $2 and $5 per share above the $55 per share price which Pritzker offered. But GE Credit needed an additional 60 to 90 days; and it was unwilling to make a formal offer without a concession from Pritzker extending the February 10 "deadline" for Trans Union's stockholder meeting. As previously stated, Pritzker refused to grant such extension; and on January 21, GE Credit terminated further negotiations with Trans Union. Its stated reasons, among others, were its "unwillingness to become involved in a bidding contest with Pritzker in the absence of the willingness of [the Pritzker interests] to terminate the proposed $55 cash merger." * * *

In the absence of any explicit finding by the Trial Court as to the reasonableness of Trans Union's directors' reliance on a market test and its feasibility, we may make our own findings based on the record. Our review of the record compels a finding that confirmation of the appropriateness of the Pritzker offer by an unfettered or free market test was virtually meaningless in the face of the terms and time limitations of Trans Union's Merger Agreement with Pritzker as amended October 10, 1980.

(3)

Finally, we turn to the Board's meeting of January 26, 1981. The defendant directors rely upon the action there taken to refute the contention that they did not reach an informed business judgment in approving the Pritzker merger. The defendants contend that the Trial Court correctly concluded that Trans Union's directors were, in effect, as "free to turn down the Pritzker proposal" on January 26, as they were on September 20.

Applying the appropriate standard of review set forth in *Levitt v. Bouvier, supra,* we conclude that the Trial Court's finding in this regard is neither supported by the record nor the product of an orderly and logical deductive process. Without disagreeing with the principle that a business decision by an originally uninformed board of directors may, under appropriate circumstances, be timely cured so as to become informed and deliberate, *Muschel v. Western Union Corporation,* Del. Ch., 310 *886 A.2d 904 (1973),[28)] we find that the record does not permit the defendants to invoke that principle in this case.

The Board's January 26 meeting was the first meeting following the filing of the plaintiffs' suit in mid-December and the last meeting before the previously-noticed shareholder meeting of February 10.[29)] All ten members of the Board and three outside attorneys attended the meeting. At that meeting the following facts, among other aspects of the Merger Agreement, were discussed: (a) The fact that prior to September 20, 1980, no Board member or member of Senior Management, except Chelberg and Peterson, knew that Van Gorkom had discussed a possible merger with Pritzker; (b) The fact that

28) The defendants concede that *Muschel* is only illustrative of the proposition that a board may reconsider a prior decision and that it is otherwise factually distinguishable from this case.

29) This was the meeting which, under the terms of the September 20 Agreement with Pritzker, was scheduled to be held January 10 and was later postponed to February 10 under the October 8-10 amendments. We refer to the document titled "Amendment to Supplemental Agreement" executed by the parties "as of" October 10, 1980. Under new Section 2.03(a) of Article A VI of the "Supplemental Agreement," the parties agreed, in part, as follows: "The solicitation of such offers or proposals [i.e., `other offers that Trans Union might accept in lieu of the Merger Agreement'] by TU... shall not be deemed to constitute a breach of this Supplemental Agreement or the Merger Agreement provided that ... [Trans Union] shall not (1) delay promptly seeking all consents and approvals required hereunder ... [and] shall be deemed [in compliance] if it files its Preliminary Proxy Statement by December 5, 1980, uses its best efforts to mail its Proxy Statement by January 5, 1981 and holds a special meeting of its Stockholders on or prior to February 10, 1981 ...* * * * * *It is the present intention of the Board of Directors of TU to recommend the approval of the Merger Agreement to the Stockholders, unless another offer or proposal is made which in their opinion is more favorable to the Stockholders than the Merger Agreement."

the price of $55 per share had been suggested initially to Pritzker by Van Gorkom; (c) The fact that the Board had not sought an independent fairness opinion; (d) The fact that, at the September 20 Senior Management meeting, Romans and several members of Senior Management indicated both concern that the $55 per share price was inadequate and a belief that a higher price should and could be obtained; (e) The fact that Romans had advised the Board at its meeting on September 20, that he and his department had prepared a study which indicated that the Company had a value in the range of $55 to $65 per share, and that he could not advise the Board that the $55 per share offer made by Pritzker was unfair.

The defendants characterize the Board's Minutes of the January 26 meeting as a "review" of the "entire sequence of events" from Van Gorkom's initiation of the negotiations on September 13 forward. [30)] The defendants also rely on the

---

30) With regard to the Pritzker merger, the recently filed shareholders' suit to enjoin it, and relevant portions of the impending stockholder meeting of February 10, we set forth the Minutes in their entirety:

The Board then reviewed the necessity of issuing a Supplement to the Proxy Statement mailed to stockholders on January 21, 1981, for the special meeting of stockholders scheduled to be held on February 10, 1981, to vote on the proposed $55 cash merger with a subsidiary of GE Corporation. Among other things, the Board noted that subsequent to the printing of the Proxy Statement mailed to stockholders on January 21, 1981, General Electric Company had indicated that it would not be making an offer to acquire the Company. In addition, certain facts had been adduced in connection with pretrial discovery taken in connection with the lawsuit filed by Alden Smith in Delaware Chancery Court. After further discussion and review of a printer's proof copy of a proposed Supplement to the Proxy Statement which had been distributed to Directors the preceding day, upon motion duly made and seconded, the following resolution was unanimously adopted, each Director having been individually polled with respect thereto:

RESOLVED, that the Secretary of the Company be and he hereby is authorized and directed to mail to the stockholders a Supplement to Proxy Statement, substantially in the form of the proposed Supplement to Proxy Statement submitted to the Board at this meeting, with such changes therein and modifications thereof as he shall, with the advice and assistance of counsel, approve as being necessary, desirable, or appropriate.

The Board then reviewed and discussed at great length the entire sequence of events pertaining to the proposed $55 cash merger with a subsidiary of GE Corporation, beginning with the first discussion on September 13, 1980, between the Chairman and Mr. Jay Pritzker relative to a possible merger. Each of the Directors was involved in this discussion as well as counsel who had earlier joined the meeting. Following this review and discussion, such counsel advised the Directors that in light of their discussions, they could (a) continue to recommend to the stockholders that the latter vote in favor of the proposed merger, (b) recommend that the stockholders vote against the merger, or (c) take no position with respect to recommending the proposed merger and simply leave the decision to stockholders. After further discussion, it was moved, seconded, and unanimously voted that the Board of Directors continue to recommend that the stockholders vote in favor of the proposed merger, each Director being individually polled with respect to his vote.

*887 testimony of several of the Board members at trial as confirming the Minutes.[31)] On the basis of this evidence, the defendants argue that whatever information the Board lacked to make a deliberate and informed judgment on September 20, or on October 8, was fully divulged to the entire Board on January 26. Hence, the argument goes, the Board's vote on January 26 to again "approve" the Pritzker merger must be found to have been an informed and deliberate judgment.

On the basis of this evidence, the defendants assert: (1) that the Trial Court was legally correct in widening the time frame for determining whether the defendants' approval of the Pritzker merger represented an informed business judgment to include the entire four-month period during which the Board considered the matter from September 20 through January 26; and (2) that, given this extensive evidence of the Board's further review and deliberations on January 26, this Court must affirm the Trial Court's conclusion that the Board's action was not reckless or improvident.

We cannot agree. We find the Trial Court to have erred, both as a matter of fact and as a matter of law, in relying on the action on January 26 to bring the defendants' conduct within the protection of the business judgment rule. Johnson's testimony and the Board Minutes of January 26 are remarkably consistent. Both clearly indicate recognition that the question of

---

31) In particular, the defendants rely on the testimony of director Johnson on direct examination:

Q. Was there a regular meeting of the board of Trans Union on January 26, 1981? A. Yes.

Q. And what was discussed at that meeting? A. Everything relevant to this transaction.

You see, since the proxy statement of the 19th had been mailed, see, General Electric had advised that they weren't going to make a bid. It was concluded to suggest that the shareholders be advised of that, and that required a supplemental proxy statement, and that required authorization of the board, and that led to a total review from beginning to end of every aspect of the whole transaction and all relevant developments. Since that was occurring and a supplemental statement was going to the shareholders, it also was obvious to me that there should be a review of the board's position again in the light of the whole record. And we went back from the beginning. Everything was examined and reviewed. Counsel were present. And the board was advised that we could recommend the Pritzker deal, we could submit it to the shareholders with no recommendation, or we could recommend against it.

The board voted to issue the supplemental statement to the shareholders. It voted unanimously - and this time we had a unanimous board, where one man was missing before - to recommend the Pritzker deal. Indeed, at that point there was no other deal. And, in truth, there never had been any other deal. And that's what transpired: a total review of the GE situation, KKR and everything else that was relevant.

the alternative courses of action, available to the Board on January 26 with respect to the Pritzker merger, was a legal question, presenting to the Board (*after* its review of the full record developed through pre-trial discovery) *three* options: (1) to "continue to recommend" the Pritzker merger; (2) to "recommend that *888 the stockholders vote against" the Pritzker merger; or (3) to take a noncommittal position on the merger and "simply leave the decision to [the] shareholders."

We must conclude from the foregoing that the Board was mistaken as a matter of law regarding its available courses of action on January 26, 1981. Options (2) and (3) were not viable or legally available to the Board under 8 *Del.C.* § 251(b). The Board could not remain committed to the Pritzker merger and yet recommend that its stockholders vote it down; nor could it take a neutral position and delegate to the stockholders the unadvised decision as to whether to accept or reject the merger. Under § 251(b), the Board had but two options: (1) to proceed with the merger and the stockholder meeting, with the Board's recommendation of approval; *or* (2) to rescind its agreement with Pritzker, withdraw its approval of the merger, and notify its stockholders that the proposed shareholder meeting was cancelled. There is no evidence that the Board gave any consideration to these, its only legally viable alternative courses of action.

But the second course of action would have clearly involved a substantial risk - that the Board would be faced with suit by Pritzker for breach of contract based on its September 20 agreement as amended October 10. As previously noted, under the terms of the October 10 amendment, the Board's only ground for release from its agreement with Pritzker was its entry into a more favorable definitive agreement to sell the Company to a third party. Thus, in reality, the Board was not "free to turn down the Pritzker proposal" as the Trial Court found. Indeed, short of negotiating a better agreement with a third party, the Board's only basis for release from the Pritzker Agreement without liability would have been to establish fundamental wrongdoing by Pritzker. Clearly, the Board was not "free" to withdraw from its agreement with Pritzker on January 26 by simply relying on its self-induced failure to have reached an informed business judgment at the time of its original agreement. *See Wilmington Trust Company v. Coulter,* Del.Supr., 200 A.2d 441, 453 (1964), *aff'g Pennsylvania Company v. Wilmington Trust Company,* Del.Ch., 186 A.2d 751 (1962).

Therefore, the Trial Court's conclusion that the Board reached an informed business judgment on January 26 in determining whether to turn down the Pritzker "proposal" on that day cannot be sustained.[32] The Court's conclusion is not supported by the record; it is contrary to the provisions of § 251(b) and basic principles of contract law; and it is not the product of a logical and deductive reasoning process. * * *

Upon the basis of the foregoing, we hold that the defendants' post-September conduct did not cure the deficiencies of their September 20 conduct; and that, accordingly, the Trial Court erred in according to the defendants the benefits of the business judgment rule.

IV.

Whether the directors of Trans Union should be treated as one or individually in terms of invoking the protection of the business judgment rule and the applicability of 8 *Del.C.* § 141(c) are questions which were not originally addressed by the parties in their briefing of this case. This resulted in a supplemental briefing and a second rehearing en banc on two basic questions: (a) whether one or more of the directors were deprived of the protection of the business judgment rule by evidence of an absence of good faith; and (b)

32) To the extent the Trial Court's ultimate conclusion to invoke the business judgment rule is based on other explicit criteria and supporting evidence (i.e., market value of Trans Union's stock, the business acumen of the Board members, the substantial premium over market and the availability of the market test to confirm the adequacy of the premium), we have previously discussed the insufficiency of such evidence.

whether one or more of the outside directors were *889 entitled to invoke the protection of 8 *Del.C.* § 141(e) by evidence of a reasonable, good faith reliance on "reports," including legal advice, rendered the Board by certain inside directors and the Board's special counsel, Brennan.

The parties' response, including reargument, has led the majority of the Court to conclude: (1) that since all of the defendant directors, outside as well as inside, take a unified position, we are required to treat all of the directors as one as to whether they are entitled to the protection of the business judgment rule; and (2) that considerations of good faith, including the presumption that the directors acted in good faith, are irrelevant in determining the threshold issue of whether the directors as a Board exercised an informed business judgment. For the same reason, we must reject defense counsel's *ad hominem* argument for affirmance: that reversal may result in a multi-million dollar class award against the defendants for having made an allegedly uninformed business judgment in a transaction not involving any personal gain, self-dealing or claim of bad faith. In their brief, the defendants similarly mistake the business judgment rule's application to this case by erroneously invoking presumptions of good faith and "wide discretion":

> This is a case in which plaintiff challenged the exercise of business judgment by an independent Board of Directors. There were no allegations and no proof of fraud, bad faith, or self-dealing by the directors....
>
> The business judgment rule, which was properly applied by the Chancellor, allows directors wide discretion in the matter of valuation and affords room for honest differences of opinion. In order to prevail, plaintiffs had the heavy burden of proving that the merger price was so grossly inadequate as to display itself as a badge of fraud. That is a burden which plaintiffs have not met.

However, plaintiffs have not claimed, nor did the Trial Court decide, that $55 was a grossly inadequate price per share for sale of the Company. That being so, the presumption that a board's judgment as to adequacy of price represents an honest exercise of business judgment (absent proof that the sale price was grossly inadequate) is irrelevant to the threshold question of whether an informed judgment was reached. *Compare Sinclair Oil Corp. v. Levien,* Del.Supr., 280 A.2d 717 (1971); *Kelly v. Bell,* Del.Supr., 266 A.2d 878, 879 (1970); *Cole v. National Cash Credit Association,* Del.Ch., 156 A. 183 (1931); *Allaun v. Consolidated Oil Co., supra; Allen Chemical & Dye Corp. v. Steel & Tube Co. of America,* Del.Ch., 120 A. 486 (1923).

V.

The defendants ultimately rely on the stockholder vote of February 10 for exoneration. The defendants contend that the stockholders' "overwhelming" vote approving the Pritzker Merger Agreement had the legal effect of curing any failure of the Board to reach an informed business judgment in its approval of the merger.

The parties tacitly agree that a discovered failure of the Board to reach an informed business judgment in approving the merger constitutes a voidable, rather than a void, act. Hence, the merger can be sustained, notwithstanding the infirmity of the Board's action, if its approval by majority vote of the shareholders is found to have been based on an informed electorate. *Cf. Michelson v. Duncan,* Del.Supr., 407 A.2d 211 (1979), *aff'g in part and rev'g in part,* Del.Ch., 386 A.2d 1144 (1978). The disagreement between the parties arises over: (1) the Board's burden of disclosing to the shareholders all relevant and material information; and (2) the sufficiency of the evidence as to whether the Board satisfied that burden.

On this issue the Trial Court summarily concluded "that the stockholders of Trans Union were fairly informed as to the pending merger...." The Court provided no *890 supportive reasoning nor did the Court make any reference to the evidence of record.

The plaintiffs contend that the Court committed error by applying an erroneous disclosure standard of "adequacy" rather than "completeness" in determining the sufficiency of the Company's merger proxy materials. The plaintiffs also argue that the Board's proxy statements, both its original statement dated January 19 and its supplemental statement dated January 26, were incomplete in various material respects. Finally, the plaintiffs assert that Management's supplemental statement (mailed "on or about" January 27) was untimely either as a matter of law under 8 *Del.C.* § 251(c), or untimely as a matter of equity and the requirements of complete candor and fair disclosure.

The defendants deny that the Court committed legal or equitable error. On the question of the Board's burden of disclosure, the defendants state that there was no dispute at trial over the standard of disclosure required of the Board; but the defendants concede that the Board was required to disclose "all germane facts" which a reasonable shareholder would have considered important in deciding whether to approve the merger. Thus, the defendants argue that when the Trial Court speaks of finding the Company's shareholders to have been "fairly informed" by Management's proxy materials, the Court is speaking in terms of "complete candor" as required under *Lynch v. Vickers Energy Corp.,* Del.Supr., 383 A.2d 278 (1978).

The settled rule in Delaware is that "where a majority of fully informed stockholders ratify action of even interested directors, an attack on the ratified transaction normally must fail." *Gerlach v. Gillam,* Del.Ch., 139 A.2d 591, 593 (1958). The question of whether shareholders have been fully informed such that their vote can be said to ratify director action, "turns on the fairness and completeness of the proxy materials submitted by the management to the ... shareholders." *Michelson v. Duncan, supra* at 220. As this Court stated in *Gottlieb v. Heyden Chemical Corp.,* Del.Supr., 91 A.2d 57, 59 (1952):

> [T]he entire atmosphere is freshened and a new set of rules invoked where a formal approval has been given by a majority of independent, fully informed stockholders....

In *Lynch v. Vickers Energy Corp., supra,* this Court held that corporate directors owe to their stockholders a fiduciary duty to disclose all facts germane to the transaction at issue in an atmosphere of complete candor. We defined "germane" in the tender offer context as all "information such as a reasonable stockholder would consider important in deciding whether to sell or retain stock." *Id.* at 281. *Accord Weinberger v. UOP, Inc., supra; Michelson v. Duncan, supra; Schreiber v. Pennzoil Corp.*, Del.Ch., 419 A.2d 952 (1980). In reality, "germane" means material facts. Applying this standard to the record before us, we find that Trans Union's stockholders were not fully informed of all facts material to their vote on the Pritzker Merger and that the Trial Court's ruling to the contrary is clearly erroneous. We list the material deficiencies in the proxy materials:

(1) The fact that the Board had no reasonably adequate information indicative of the intrinsic value of the Company, other than a concededly depressed market price, was without question material to the shareholders voting on the merger. *See Weinberger, supra* at 709 (insiders' report that cash-out merger price up to $24 was good investment held material); *Michelson, supra* at 224 (alleged terms and intent of stock option plan held not germane); *Schreiber, supra* at 959 (management fee of $650,000 held germane).

Accordingly, the Board's lack of valuation information should have been disclosed. Instead, the directors cloaked the absence of such information in both the Proxy Statement and the Supplemental *891 Proxy Statement. Through artful drafting, noticeably absent at the September 20 meeting, both documents create the impression that the Board knew the intrinsic worth of the Company. In particular, the Original Proxy Statement contained the following:

> [a]lthough the Board of Directors regards the intrinsic value of the Company's assets to be significantly greater than their book value ..., systematic liquidation of such a large and complex entity as Trans Union is simply not regarded as a feasible method of realizing its inherent value. Therefore, a business combination such as the merger would seem to be the only practicable way in which the stockholders could realize the value of the Company.

The Proxy stated further that "[i]n the view of the Board of Directors ..., the prices at which the Company's common stock has traded in recent years have not reflected the inherent value of the Company." What the Board failed to disclose to its stockholders was that the Board had not made any study of the intrinsic or inherent worth of the Company; nor had the Board even discussed the inherent value of the Company prior to approving the merger on September 20, or at either of the subsequent meetings on October 8 or January 26. Neither in its Original Proxy Statement nor in its Supplemental Proxy did the Board disclose that it had no information before it, beyond the premium-over-market and the price/earnings ratio, on which to determine the fair value of the Company as a whole.

(2) We find false and misleading the Board's characterization of the Romans report in the Supplemental Proxy Statement. The Supplemental Proxy stated:

> At the September 20, 1980 meeting of the Board of Directors of Trans Union, Mr. Romans indicated that while he could not say that $55,00 per share was an unfair price, he had prepared a preliminary report which reflected that the value of the Company was in the range of $55.00 to $65.00 per share.

Nowhere does the Board disclose that Romans stated to the Board that his calculations were made in a "search for ways to justify a price in connection with" a leveraged buy-out transaction, "rather than to say what the shares are worth," and that he stated to the Board that his conclusion thus arrived at "was not the same thing as saying that I have a valuation of the Company at X dollars." Such information would have been material to a reasonable shareholder because it tended to invalidate the fairness of the merger price of $55. Furthermore, defendants again failed to disclose the absence of valuation information, but still made repeated reference to the "substantial premium."

(3) We find misleading the Board's references to the "substantial" premium offered. The Board gave as their primary reason in support of the merger the "substantial premium" shareholders would receive. But the Board did not disclose its failure to assess the premium offered in terms of other relevant valuation techniques, thereby rendering questionable its determination as to

the substantiality of the premium over an admittedly depressed stock market price.

(4) We find the Board's recital in the Supplemental Proxy of certain events preceding the September 20 meeting to be incomplete and misleading. It is beyond dispute that a reasonable stockholder would have considered material the fact that Van Gorkom not only suggested the $55 price to Pritzker, but also that he chose the figure because it made feasible a leveraged buy-out. The directors disclosed that Van Gorkom suggested the $55 price to Pritzker. But the Board misled the shareholders when they described the basis of Van Gorkom's suggestion as follows:

> Such suggestion was based, at least in part, on Mr. Van Gorkom's belief that loans could be obtained from institutional lenders (together with about a $200 million *892 equity contribution) which would justify the payment of such price, ...

Although by January 26, the directors knew the basis of the $55 figure, they did not disclose that Van Gorkom chose the $55 price because that figure would enable Pritzker to both finance the purchase of Trans Union through a leveraged buy-out and, within five years, substantially repay the loan out of the cash flow generated by the Company's operations.

(5) The Board's Supplemental Proxy Statement, mailed on or after January 27, added significant new matter, material to the proposal to be voted on February 10, which was not contained in the Original Proxy Statement. Some of this new matter was information which had only been disclosed to the Board on January 26; much was information known or reasonably available before January 21 but not revealed in the Original Proxy Statement. Yet, the stockholders were not informed of these facts. Included in the "new" matter first disclosed in the Supplemental Proxy Statement were the following: (a) The fact that prior to September 20, 1980, no Board member or member of Senior Management, except Chelberg and Peterson, knew that Van Gorkom had discussed a possible merger with Pritzker; (b) The fact that the sale price of $55 per share had been suggested initially to Pritzker by Van Gorkom; (c) The fact that the Board had not sought an independent fairness opinion;

(d) The fact that Romans and several members of Senior Management had indicated concern at the September 20 Senior Management meeting that the $55 per share price was inadequate and had stated that a higher price should and could be obtained; and (e) The fact that Romans had advised the Board at its meeting on September 20 that he and his department had prepared a study which indicated that the Company had a value in the range of $55 to $65 per share, and that he could not advise the Board that the $55 per share offer which Pritzker made was unfair. * * *

The parties differ over whether the notice requirements of 8 *Del.C.* § 251(c) apply to the mailing date of supplemental proxy material or that of the original proxy material.[33] The Trial Court summarily disposed of the notice issue, stating it was "satisfied that the proxy material furnished to Trans Union stockholders ... fairly presented the question to be voted on at the February 10, 1981 meeting."

The defendants argue that the notice provisions of § 251(c) must be construed as requiring only that stockholders receive notice of the time, place, and purpose of a meeting to consider a merger at least 20 days prior to such meeting; and since the Original Proxy Statement was disseminated more than 20 days before the meeting, the defendants urge affirmance of the Trial Court's ruling as correct as a matter of statutory construction. Apparently, the question has not been addressed by either the Court of Chancery or this Court; and authority in other jurisdictions is limited. *See Electronic Specialty Co. v. Int'l Controls Corp.*, 2d Cir., 409 F.2d 937, 944 (1969) (holding that a tender offeror's September 16, 1968 correction of a previous misstatement, combined with an offer of withdrawal running for eight days until September 24, 1968, was sufficient to cure past violations and eliminate any need

---

33) The pertinent provisions of 8 *Del.C.* § 251(c) provide:

(c) The agreement required by subsection (b) shall be submitted to the stockholders of each constituent corporation at an annual or special meeting thereof for the purpose of acting on the agreement. Due notice of the time, place and purpose of the meeting shall be mailed to each holder of stock, whether voting or non-voting, of the corporation at his address as it appears on the records of the corporation, at least 20 days prior to the date of the meeting....

for rescission); *Nicholson File Co. v. H.K. Porter Co.,* D.R.I., 341 F.Supp. 508, 513-14 (1972), *aff'd,* 1st Cir., 482 F.2d 421 (1973) *893 (permitting correction of a material misstatement by a mailing to stockholders within seven days of a tender offer withdrawal date). Both *Electronic* and *Nicholson* are federal security cases not arising under 8 *Del.C.* § 251(c) and they are otherwise distinguishable from this case on their facts.

Since we have concluded that Management's Supplemental Proxy Statement does not meet the Delaware disclosure standard of "complete candor" under *Lynch v. Vickers, supra,* it is unnecessary for us to address the plaintiffs' legal argument as to the proper construction of § 251(c). However, we do find it advisable to express the view that, in an appropriate case, an otherwise candid proxy statement may be so untimely as to defeat its purpose of meeting the needs of a fully informed electorate.

In this case, the Board's ultimate disclosure as contained in the Supplemental Proxy Statement related either to information readily accessible to all of the directors if they had asked the right questions, or was information already at their disposal. In short, the information disclosed by the Supplemental Proxy Statement was information which the defendant directors knew or should have known at the time the first Proxy Statement was issued. The defendants simply failed in their original duty of knowing, sharing, and disclosing information that was material and reasonably available for their discovery. They compounded that failure by their continued lack of candor in the Supplemental Proxy Statement. While we need not decide the issue here, we are satisfied that, in an appropriate case, a completely candid but belated disclosure of information long known or readily available to a board could raise serious issues of inequitable conduct. *Schnell v. Chris-Craft Industries, Inc.,* Del.Supr., 285 A.2d 437, 439 (1971).

The burden must fall on defendants who claim ratification based on shareholder vote to establish that the shareholder approval resulted from a fully informed electorate. On the record before us, it is clear that the Board failed to meet that burden. *Weinberger v. UOP, Inc., supra* at 703; *Michelson v.*

Duncan, supra. * * *

For the foregoing reasons, we conclude that the director defendants breached their fiduciary duty of candor by their failure to make true and correct disclosures of all information they had, or should have had, material to the transaction submitted for stockholder approval.

VI.

To summarize: we hold that the directors of Trans Union breached their fiduciary duty to their stockholders (1) by their failure to inform themselves of all information reasonably available to them and relevant to their decision to recommend the Pritzker merger; and (2) by their failure to disclose all material information such as a reasonable stockholder would consider important in deciding whether to approve the Pritzker offer.

We hold, therefore, that the Trial Court committed reversible error in applying the business judgment rule in favor of the director defendants in this case.

On remand, the Court of Chancery shall conduct an evidentiary hearing to determine the fair value of the shares represented by the plaintiffs' class, based on the intrinsic value of Trans Union on September 20, 1980. Such valuation shall be made in accordance with *Weinberger v. UOP, Inc., supra* at 712-715. Thereafter, an award of damages may be entered to the extent that the fair value of Trans Union exceeds $55 per share. * * *

REVERSED and REMANDED for proceedings consistent herewith.

MCNEILLY, JUSTICE, DISSENTING:

The majority opinion reads like an advocate's closing address to a hostile jury. And I say that not lightly. Throughout the *894 opinion great emphasis is directed only to the negative, with nothing more than lip service granted the positive aspects of this case. In my opinion Chancellor Marvel (retired) should have been affirmed. The Chancellor's opinion was the product of well reasoned conclusions, based upon a sound deductive process, clearly supported by the evidence and entitled to deference in this appeal. Because of my diametrical opposition to all evidentiary conclusions of the majority, I respectfully dissent. It would serve no useful purpose, particularly at this late date, for me to dissent at great length. I restrain myself from doing so, but feel compelled to at least point out what I consider to be the most glaring deficiencies in the majority opinion. The majority has spoken and has effectively said that Trans Union's Directors have been the victims of a "fast shuffle" by Van Gorkom and Pritzker. That is the beginning of the majority's comedy of errors. The first and most important error made is the majority's assessment of the directors' knowledge of the affairs of Trans Union and their combined ability to act in this situation under the protection of the business judgment rule.

Trans Union's Board of Directors consisted of ten men, five of whom were "inside" directors and five of whom were "outside" directors. The "inside" directors were Van Gorkom, Chelberg, Bonser, William B. Browder, Senior Vice-President-Law, and Thomas P. O'Boyle, Senior Vice-President-Administration. At the time the merger was proposed the inside five directors had collectively been employed by the Company for 116 years and had 68 years of combined experience as directors. The "outside" directors were A.W. Wallis, William B. Johnson, Joseph B. Lanterman, Graham J. Morgan and Robert W. Reneker. With the exception of Wallis, these were all chief executive officers of Chicago based corporations that were at least as large as Trans Union. The five "outside" directors had 78 years of combined experience as chief executive officers, and 53 years cumulative service as Trans Union directors.

The inside directors wear their badge of expertise in the corporate affairs of Trans Union on their sleeves. But what about the outsiders? Dr. Wallis is or was an economist and math statistician, a professor of economics at

Yale University, dean of the graduate school of business at the University of Chicago, and Chancellor of the University of Rochester. Dr. Wallis had been on the Board of Trans Union since 1962. He also was on the Board of Bausch & Lomb, Kodak, Metropolitan Life Insurance Company, Standard Oil and others.

William B. Johnson is a University of Pennsylvania law graduate, President of Railway Express until 1966, Chairman and Chief Executive of I.C. Industries Holding Company, and member of Trans Union's Board since 1968.

Joseph Lanterman, a Certified Public Accountant, is or was President and Chief Executive of American Steel, on the Board of International Harvester, Peoples Energy, Illinois Bell Telephone, Harris Bank and Trust Company, Kemper Insurance Company and a director of Trans Union for four years. Graham Morgan is achemist, was Chairman and Chief Executive Officer of U.S. Gypsum, and in the 17 and 18 years prior to the Trans Union transaction had been involved in 31 or 32 corporate takeovers. Robert Reneker attended University of Chicago and Harvard Business Schools. He was President and Chief Executive of Swift and Company, director of Trans Union since 1971, and member of the Boards of seven other corporations including U.S. Gypsum and the Chicago Tribune.

Directors of this caliber are not ordinarily taken in by a "fast shuffle". I submit they were not taken into this multi-million dollar corporate transaction without being fully informed and aware of the state of the art as it pertained to the entire corporate panoroma of Trans Union. True, even *895 directors such as these, with their business acumen, interest and expertise, can go astray. I do not believe that to be the case here. These men knew Trans Union like the back of their hands and were more than well qualified to make on the spot informed business judgments concerning the affairs of Trans Union including a 100% sale of the corporation. Lest we forget, the corporate world of then and now operates on what is so aptly referred to as "the fast track". These men were at the time an integral part of that world, all professional business men, not intellectual figureheads.

The majority of this Court holds that the Board's decision, reached on September 20, 1980, to approve the merger was not the product of an *informed* business judgment, that the Board's subsequent efforts to amend the Merger Agreement and take other curative action were *legally and factually* ineffectual, and that the Board did *not deal with complete candor* with the stockholders by failing to disclose all material facts, which they knew or should have known, before securing the stockholders' approval of the merger. I disagree.

At the time of the September 20, 1980 meeting the Board was acutely aware of Trans Union and its prospects. The problems created by accumulated investment tax credits and accelerated depreciation were discussed repeatedly at Board meetings, and all of the directors understood the problem thoroughly. Moreover, at the July, 1980 Board meeting the directors had reviewed Trans Union's newly prepared five-year forecast, and at the August, 1980 meeting Van Gorkom presented the results of a comprehensive study of Trans Union made by The Boston Consulting Group. This study was prepared over an 18 month period and consisted of a detailed analysis of all Trans Union subsidiaries, including competitiveness, profitability, cash throw-off, cash consumption, technical competence and future prospects for contribution to Trans Union's combined net income.

At the September 20 meeting Van Gorkom reviewed all aspects of the proposed transaction and repeated the explanation of the Pritzker offer he had earlier given to senior management. Having heard Van Gorkom's explanation of the Pritzker's offer, and Brennan's explanation of the merger documents the directors discussed the matter. Out of this discussion arose an insistence on the part of the directors that two modifications to the offer be made. First, they required that any potential competing bidder be given access to the same information concerning Trans Union that had been provided to the Pritzkers. Second, the merger documents were to be modified to reflect the fact that the directors could accept a better offer and would not be required to recommend the Pritzker offer if a better offer was made. The following language was inserted into the agreement:

> "Within 30 days after the execution of this Agreement, TU shall call a meeting of its stockholders (the `Stockholder's Meeting') for the purpose of approving and adopting the Merger Agreement. The Board of Directors shall recommend to the stockholders of TU that they approve and adopt the Merger Agreement (the `Stockholders' Approval') and shall use its best efforts to obtain the requisite vote therefor; *provided, however, that GL and NTC acknowledge that the Board of Directors of TU may have a competing fiduciary obligation to the Stockholders under certain* circumstances." (Emphasis added)

While the language is not artfully drawn, the evidence is clear that the intention underlying that language was to make specific the right that the directors assumed they had, that is, to accept any offer that they thought was better, and not to recommend the Pritzker offer in the face of a better one. At the conclusion of the meeting, the proposed merger was approved.

At a subsequent meeting on October 8, 1981 the directors, with the consent of the Pritzkers, amended the Merger Agreement so as to establish the right of Trans Union to *solicit* as well as to receive higher bids, *896 although the Pritzkers insisted that their merger proposal be presented to the stockholders at the same time that the proposal of any third party was presented. A second amendment, which became effective on October 10, 1981, further provided that Trans Union might unilaterally terminate the proposed merger with the Pritzker company in the event that prior to February 10, 1981 there existed a definitive agreement with a third party for a merger, consolidation, sale of assets, or purchase or exchange of Trans Union stock which was more favorable for the stockholders of Trans Union than the Pritzker offer and which was conditioned upon receipt of stockholder approval and the absence of an injunction against its consummation.

Following the October 8 board meeting of Trans Union, the investment banking firm of Salomon Brothers was retained by the corporation to search for better offers than that of the Pritzkers, Salomon Brothers being charged with the responsibility of doing "whatever possible to see if there is a superior bid in the marketplace over a bid that is on the table for Trans Union". In undertaking such project, it was agreed that Salomon Brothers would be paid the amount of $500,000 to cover its expenses as well as a fee equal to 3/8ths of 1% of the aggregate fair market value of the consideration to be received by the company in the case of a merger or the like, which meant that in the event Salomon Brothers should find a buyer willing to pay a price of $56.00 a share instead of $55.00, such firm would receive a fee of roughly $2,650,000 plus disbursements.

As the first step in proceeding to carry out its commitment, *Salomon Brothers had a brochure prepared, which set forth Trans Union's financial history, described the company's business in detail and set forth Trans Union's operating and financial projections. Salomon Brothers also prepared a list of over 150 companies which it believed might be suitable merger partners, and while four of such companies, namely, General Electric, Borg-Warner, Bendix, and Genstar, Ltd. showed some interest in such a merger, none made a firm proposal to Trans Union and only General Electric* showed a sustained interest.[1]34) As matters transpired, no firm offer which bettered the Pritzker offer of $55 per share was ever made.

On January 21, 1981 a proxy statement was sent to the shareholders of Trans Union advising them of a February 10, 1981 meeting in which the merger would be voted. On January 26, 1981 the directors held their regular meeting. At this meeting the Board discussed the instant merger as well as

34) [1] Shortly after the announcement of the proposed merger in September senior members of Trans Union's management got in touch with KKR to discuss their possible participation in a leverage buyout scheme. On December 2, 1980 KKR through Henry Kravis actually made a bid of $60.00 per share for Trans Union stock on December 2, 1980 but the offer was withdrawn three hours after it was made because of complications arising out of negotiations with the Reichman family, extremely wealthy Canadians and a change of attitude toward the leveraged buyout scheme, by Jack Kruzenga, the member of senior management of Trans Union who most likely would have been President and Chief Operating Officer of the new company. Kruzenga was the President and Chief Operating Officer of the seven subsidiaries of Trans Union which constituted the backbone of Trans Union as shown through exhaustive studies and analysis of Trans Union's intrinsic value on the market place by the respected investment banking firm of Morgan Stanley. It is interesting to note that at no time during the market test period did any of the 150 corporations contacted by Salomon Brothers complain of the time frame or availability of corporate records in order to make an independent judgment of market value of 100% of Trans Union.

all events, including this litigation, surrounding it. At the conclusion of the meeting the Board unanimously voted to recommend to the stockholders that they approve the merger. Additionally, the directors reviewed and approved a Supplemental Proxy Statement which, among other things, advised the stockholders of what had occurred at the instant meeting and of the fact that General Electric had decided not to make an offer. On February 10, 1981 *897 the stockholders of Trans Union met pursuant to notice and voted overwhelmingly in favor of the Pritzker merger, 89% of the votes cast being in favor of it.

I have no quarrel with the majority's analysis of the business judgment rule. It is the application of that rule to these facts which is wrong. An overview of the entire record, rather than the limited view of bits and pieces which the majority has exploded like popcorn, convinces me that the directors made an informed business judgment which was buttressed by their test of the market.

At the time of the September 20 meeting the 10 members of Trans Union's Board of Directors were highly qualified and well informed about the affairs and prospects of Trans Union. These directors were acutely aware of the historical problems facing Trans Union which were caused by the tax laws. They had discussed these problems *ad nauseam.* In fact, within two months of the September 20 meeting the board had reviewed and discussed an outside study of the company done by The Boston Consulting Group and an internal five year forecast prepared by management. At the September 20 meeting Van Gorkom presented the Pritzker offer, and the board then heard from James Brennan, the company's counsel in this matter, who discussed the legal documents. Following this, the Board directed that certain changes be made in the merger documents. These changes made it clear that the Board was free to accept a better offer than Pritzker's if one was made. The above facts reveal that the Board did not act in a grossly negligent manner in informing themselves of the relevant and available facts before passing on the merger. To the contrary, this record reveals that the directors acted with the utmost care in informing themselves of the relevant and available facts before passing on the merger.

The majority finds that Trans Union stockholders were not fully informed and that the directors breached their fiduciary duty of complete candor to the stockholders required by *Lynch v. Vickers Energy Corp.*, Del.Supr. 383 A.2d 278 (1978) [Lynch I], in that the proxy materials were deficient in five areas.

Here again is exploitation of the negative by the majority without giving credit to the positive. To respond to the conclusions of the majority would merely be unnecessary prolonged argument. But briefly what did the proxy materials disclose? The proxy material informed the shareholders that projections were furnished to potential purchasers and such projections indicated that Trans Union's net income might increase to approximately $153 million in 1985. That projection, what is almost three times the net income of $58,248,000 reported by Trans Union as its net income for December 31, 1979 confirmed the statement in the proxy materials that the "Board of Directors believes that, assuming reasonably favorable economic and financial conditions, the Company's prospects for future earnings growth are excellent." This material was certainly sufficient to place the Company's stockholders on notice that there was a reasonable basis to believe that the prospects for future earnings growth were excellent, and that the value of their stock was more than the stock market value of their shares reflected.

Overall, my review of the record leads me to conclude that the proxy materials adequately complied with Delaware law in informing the shareholders about the proposed transaction and the events surrounding it. The majority suggests that the Supplemental Proxy Statement did not comply with the notice requirement of 8 *Del.C.* § 251(c) that notice of the time, place and purpose of a meeting to consider a merger must be sent to each shareholder of record at least 20 days prior to the date of the meeting. In the instant case an original proxy statement was mailed on January 18, 1981 giving notice of the time, place and purpose of the meeting. A Supplemental Proxy Statement was mailed January 26, 1981 in an effort to advise Trans

Union's *898 shareholders as to what had occurred at the January 26, 1981 meeting, and that General Electric had decided not to make an offer. The shareholder meeting was held February 10, 1981 fifteen days after the Supplemental Proxy Statement had been sent.

All § 251(c) requires is that notice of the time, place and purpose of the meeting be given at least 20 days prior to the meeting. This was accomplished by the proxy statement mailed January 19, 1981. Nothing in § 251(c) prevents the supplementation of proxy materials within 20 days of the meeting. Indeed when additional information, which a reasonable shareholder would consider important in deciding how to vote, comes to light that information must be disclosed to stockholders in sufficient time for the stockholders to consider it. But nothing in § 251(c) requires this additional information to be disclosed at least 20 days prior to the meeting. To reach a contrary result would ignore the current practice and would discourage the supplementation of proxy materials in order to disclose the occurrence of intervening events. In my opinion, fifteen days in the instant case was a sufficient amount of time for the stockholders to receive and consider the information in the supplemental proxy statement.

CHRISTIE, Justice, dissenting: I respectfully dissent.

Considering the standard and scope of our review under *Levitt v. Bouvier,* Del. Supr., 287 A.2d 671, 673 (1972), I believe that the record taken as a whole supports a conclusion that the actions of the defendants are protected by the business judgment rule. *Aronson v. Lewis,* Del.Supr., 473 A.2d 805, 812 (1984); *Pogostin v. Rice,* Del.Supr., 480 A.2d 619, 627 (1984). I also am satisfied that the record supports a conclusion that the defendants acted with the complete candor required by *Lynch v. Vickers Energy Corp.,* Del.Supr., 383 A.2d 278 (1978). Under the circumstances I would affirm the judgment of the Court of Chancery.

ON MOTIONS FOR REARGUMENT

Following this Court's decision, Thomas P. O'Boyle, one of the director defendants, sought, and was granted, leave for change of counsel. Thereafter, the individual director defendants, other than O'Boyle, filed a motion for reargument and director O'Boyle, through newly-appearing counsel, then filed a separate motion for reargument. Plaintiffs have responded to the several motions and this matter has now been duly considered.

The Court, through its majority, finds no merit to either motion and concludes that both motions should be denied. We are not persuaded that any errors of law or fact have been made that merit reargument.

However, defendant O'Boyle's motion requires comment. Although O'Boyle continues to adopt his fellow directors' arguments, O'Boyle now asserts in the alternative that he has standing to take a position different from that of his fellow directors and that legal grounds exist for finding him not liable for the acts or omissions of his fellow directors. Specifically, O'Boyle makes a two-part argument: (1) that his undisputed absence due to illness from both the September 20 and the October 8 meetings of the directors of Trans Union entitles him to be relieved from personal liability for the failure of the other directors to exercise due care at *those* meetings, *see Propp v. Sadacca,* Del.Ch., 175 A.2d 33, 39 (1961), *modified on other grounds, Bennett v. Propp,* Del.Supr., 187 A.2d 405 (1962); and (2) that his attendance and participation in the January 26, 1981 Board meeting does not alter this result given this Court's precise findings of error committed at that meeting.

We reject defendant O'Boyle's new argument as to standing because not timely asserted. Our reasons are several. *One,* in connection with the supplemental briefing of this case in March, 1984, a special opportunity was afforded the individual defendants, *899 including O'Boyle, to present any factual or legal reasons why each or any of them should be individually treated. Thereafter, at argument before the Court on June 11, 1984, the following colloquy took place between this Court and counsel for the individual defendants at the outset of counsel's argument:

COUNSEL: I'll make the argument on behalf of the nine individual defendants against whom the plaintiffs seek more than $100,000,000 in damages. That is the ultimate issue in this case, whether or not nine honest, experienced businessmen should be subject to damages in a case where -

JUSTICE MOORE: Is there a distinction between Chelberg and Van Gorkom vis-a-vis the other defendants?

COUNSEL: No, sir.

JUSTICE MOORE: None whatsoever?

COUNSEL: I think not.

Two, in this Court's Opinion dated January 29, 1985, the Court relied on the individual defendants as having presented a unified defense. We stated:

> The parties' response, including reargument, has led the majority of the Court to conclude: (1) that since all of the defendant directors, outside as well as inside, take a unified position, we are required to treat all of the directors as one as to whether they are entitled to the protection of the business judgment rule...

Three, previously O'Boyle took the position that the Board's action taken January 26, 1981 - in which he fully participated - was determinative of virtually all issues. Now O'Boyle seeks to attribute no significance to his participation in the January 26 meeting. Nor does O'Boyle seek to explain his having given before the directors' meeting of October 8, 1980 his "consent to the transaction of such business as may come before the meeting."[*]

[*] We do not hereby determine that a director's execution of a waiver of notice of meeting and consent to the transaction of business constitutes an endorsement (or approval) by the absent director of any action taken at such a meeting.

It is the view of the majority of the Court that O'Boyle's change of position following this Court's decision on the merits comes too late to be considered. He has clearly waived that right.

The Motions for Reargument of all defendants are denied.

McNEILLY and CHRISTIE, Justices, dissenting: We do not disagree with the ruling as to the defendant O'Boyle, but we would have granted reargument on the other issues raised.

MEINHARD v. SALMON

Court of Appeals of New York, 249 N.Y. 458, 164 N.E. 545 (1928)
Argued December 4, 1928; Decided December 31, 1928

I. OPINION OF THE COURT

CARDOZO, Ch. J.

On April 10, 1902, Louisa M. Gerry leased to the defendant Walter J. Salmon the premises known as the Hotel Bristol at the northwest corner of Forty-second street and Fifth avenue in the city of New York. The lease was for a term of twenty years, commencing May 1, 1902, and ending April 30, 1922. The lessee undertook to change the hotel building for use as shops and offices at a cost of $200,000. Alterations and additions were to be accretions to the land.

Salmon, while in course of treaty with the lessor as to the execution of the lease, was in course of treaty with [*462] Meinhard, the plaintiff, for the necessary funds. The result was a joint venture with terms embodied in a writing. Meinhard was to pay to Salmon half of the moneys requisite to reconstruct, alter, manage and operate the property. Salmon was to pay to Meinhard 40 per cent of the net profits for the first five years of the lease and 50 per cent for the years thereafter. If there were losses, each party was to bear them equally. Salmon, however, was to have sole power to "manage, lease, underlet and operate" the building. There were to be certain pre-emptive rights for each in the contingency of death.

The two were coadventurers, subject to fiduciary duties akin to those of partners (*King v. Barnes,* 109 N. Y. 267). As to this we are all agreed. The heavier weight of duty rested, however, upon Salmon. He was a coadventurer with Meinhard, but he was manager as well. During the early years of the enterprise, the building, reconstructed, was operated at a loss. If the relation had then ended, Meinhard as well as Salmon would have carried a heavy burden. Later the profits became large with the result that for each of the investors there came a rich return. For each, the venture had its phases of fair weather and of foul. The two were in it jointly, for better or for worse.

When the lease was near its end, Elbridge T. Gerry had become the owner of the reversion. He owned much other property in the neighborhood, one lot adjoining the Bristol Building on Fifth avenue and four lots on Forty-second street. He had a plan to lease the entire tract for a long term to some one who would destroy the buildings then existing, and put up another in their place. In the latter part of 1921, he submitted such a project to several capitalists and dealers. He was unable to carry it through with any of them. Then, in January, 1922, with less than four months of the lease to run, he approached the defendant Salmon. The result was a new lease to the Midpoint Realty Company, which is owned and controlled by Salmon, a lease covering the [*463] whole tract, and involving a huge outlay. The term is to be twenty years, but successive covenants for renewal will extend it to a maximum of eighty years at the will of either party. The existing buildings may remain unchanged for seven years. They are then to be torn down, and a new building to cost $3,000,000 is to be placed upon the site. The rental, which under the Bristol lease was only $55,000, is to be from $350,000 to $475,000 for the properties so combined. Salmon personally guaranteed the performance by the lessee of the covenants of the new lease until such time as the new building had been completed and fully paid for.

The lease between Gerry and the Midpoint Realty Company was signed and delivered on January 25, 1922. Salmon had not told Meinhard anything about it. Whatever his motive may have been, he had kept the negotiations to himself. Meinhard was not informed even of the bare existence of a project. The first that he knew of it was in February when the lease was an accomplished fact. He then made demand on the defendants that the lease be held in trust as an asset of the venture, making offer upon the trial to share the personal obligations incidental to the guaranty. The demand was followed by refusal, and later by this suit. A referee gave judgment for the plaintiff, limiting the plaintiff's interest in the lease, however, to 25 per cent. The limitation was on the theory that the plaintiff's equity was to be restricted to one-half of so much of the value of the lease as was contributed or represented by the occupation of the Bristol site. Upon cross-appeals to the Appellate Division, the judgment was modified so as to enlarge the equitable interest to one-half of the whole lease. With this enlargement of plaintiff's interest, there went, of course, a corresponding enlargement of his attendant obligations. The case is now here on an appeal by the defendants.

Joint adventurers, like copartners, owe to one another, while the enterprise continues, the duty of the finest [*464] loyalty. Many forms of conduct permissible in a workaday world for those acting at arm's length, are forbidden to those bound by fiduciary ties. A trustee is held to something stricter than the morals of the market place. Not honesty alone, but the punctilio of an honor the most sensitive, is then the standard of behavior. As to this there has developed a tradition that is unbending and inveterate. Uncompromising rigidity has been the attitude of courts of equity when petitioned to undermine the rule of undivided loyalty by the "disintegrating erosion" of particular exceptions (*Wendt v. Fischer,* 243 N. Y. 439, 444). Only thus has the level of conduct for fiduciaries been kept at a level higher than that trodden by the crowd. It will not consciously be lowered by any judgment of this court.

The owner of the reversion, Mr. Gerry, had vainly striven to find a tenant who would favor his ambitious scheme of demolition and construction. Baffled in the search, he turned to the defendant Salmon in possession of the Bristol, the keystone of the project. He figured to himself beyond a doubt that the man in possession would prove a likely customer. To the eye of an observer, Salmon held the lease as owner in his own right, for himself and no one else. In fact he held it as a fiduciary, for himself and another, sharers in a common venture. If this fact had been proclaimed, if the lease by its terms had run in favor of a partnership, Mr. Gerry, we may fairly assume, would have laid before the partners, and not merely before one of them, his plan of reconstruction. The pre-emptive privilege, or, better, the pre-emptive opportunity, that was thus an incident of the enterprise, Salmon appropriated to himself in secrecy and silence. He might have warned Meinhard that the plan had been submitted, and that either would be free to compete for the award. If he had done this, we do not need to say whether he would have been under a duty, if successful in the competition, to hold the lease so acquired for the [*465] benefit of a venture then about to end, and thus prolong by indirection its responsibilities and duties. The trouble about his conduct is that he excluded his coadventurer from any chance to compete, from any chance to enjoy the opportunity for benefit that had come to him alone by virtue of his agency. This chance, if nothing more, he was under a duty to concede. The price of its denial is an extension of the trust at the option and for the benefit of the one whom he excluded.

No answer is it to say that the chance would have been of little value even if seasonably offered. Such a calculus of probabilities is beyond the science of the chancery. Salmon, the real estate operator, might have been preferred to Meinhard, the woolen merchant. On the other hand, Meinhard might have offered better terms, or reinforced his offer by alliance with the wealth of others. Perhaps he might even have persuaded the lessor to renew the Bristol lease alone, postponing for a time, in return for higher rentals, the improvement of adjoining lots. We know that even under the lease as made the time for the enlargement of the building was delayed for seven years. All these opportunities were cut away from him through another's intervention. He knew that Salmon was the manager. As the time drew near for the expiration of the lease, he would naturally assume from silence, if from nothing else, that the lessor was willing to extend it for a term of years, or at least to let it stand as a lease from year to year. Not impossibly the lessor would have done so, whatever his protestations of unwillingness, if Salmon had not given assent to a project more attractive. At all events, notice of termination, even if not necessary, might seem, not unreasonably, to be something to be looked for, if the business was over and another tenant was to enter. In the absence of such notice, the matter of an extension was one that would naturally be attended to by the manager of the enterprise, and not neglected altogether. At least, there was nothing in the situation to give warning to any one that while the lease was still in being, there [*466] had come to the manager an offer of extension which he had locked within his breast to be utilized by himself alone. The very fact that Salmon was in control with exclusive powers of direction charged him the more obviously with the duty of disclosure, since only through disclosure could opportunity be equalized. If he might cut off renewal by a purchase for his own benefit when four months were to pass before the lease would have an end, he might do so with equal right while there remained as many years (*cf. Mitchell v. Reed,* 61 N. Y. 123, 127). He might steal a march on his comrade under cover of the darkness, and then hold the captured ground. Loyalty and comradeship are not so easily abjured.

Little profit will come from a dissection of the precedents. None precisely similar is cited in the briefs of counsel. What is similar in many, or so it seems to us, is the animating principle. Authority is, of course, abundant that one partner may not appropriate to his own use a renewal of a lease, though its term is to begin at the expiration of the partnership (*Mitchell v. Reed,* 61 N. Y. 123; 84 N. Y. 556). The lease at hand with its many changes is not strictly a renewal. Even so, the standard of loyalty for those in trust relations is without the fixed divisions of a graduated scale. There is indeed a dictum in one of our decisions that a partner, though he may not renew a lease, may purchase the reversion if he acts openly and fairly (*Anderson v. Lemon,* 8 N. Y. 236; cf. White & Tudor, Leading Cases in Equity [9th ed.], vol. 2, p. 642; *Bevan v. Webb,* 1905, 1 Ch. 620; *Griffith v. Owen,* 1907, 1 Ch. 195, 204, 205). It is a dictum, and no more, for on the ground that he had acted slyly he was charged as a trustee. The holding is thus in favor of the conclusion that a purchase as well as a lease will succumb to the infection of secrecy and silence. Against the dictum in that case, moreover, may be set the opinion of DWIGHT, C., in *Mitchell v. Read,* where there is a dictum to the contrary (61 N. Y. at p. 143). [*467] To say that a partner is free without restriction to buy in the reversion of the property where the business is conducted is to say in effect that he may strip the good will of its chief element of value, since good will is largely dependent upon continuity of possession (*Matter of Brown,* 242 N. Y. 1, 7.) Equity refuses to confine within the bounds of classified transactions its precept of a loyalty that is undivided and unselfish. Certain at least it is that a "man obtaining his *locus standi,* and his opportunity for making such arrangements, by the position he occupies as a partner, is bound by his obligation to his co-partners in such dealings not to separate his interest from theirs, but, if he acquires any benefit, to communicate it to them" (*Cassels v. Stewart,* 6 App. Cas. 64, 73). Certain it is also that there may be no abuse of special opportunities growing out of a special trust as manager or agent (*Matter of Biss,* 1903, 2 Ch. 40; *Clegg v. Edmondson,* 8 D. M. & G. 787, 807). If conflicting inferences are possible as to abuse or opportunity, the trier of the facts must make the choice between them. There can be no revision in this court unless the choice is clearly wrong. It is no answer for the fiduciary to say "that he was not bound to risk his money as he did, or to go into the enterprise at all" (*Beatty v. Guggenheim Exploration Co.,* 225 N. Y. 380, 385). "He might have kept out of it altogether, but if he went in, he could not withhold from his employer the benefit of the bargain" (*Beatty v. Guggenheim Exploration Co., supra*). A constructive trust is then the remedial device through which preference of self is made subordinate to loyalty to others (*Beatty* *v. Guggenheim Exploration Co., supra*). Many and varied are its phases and occasions (*Selwyn & Co. v. Waller,* 212 N. Y. 507, 512; *Robinson v. Jewett,* 116 N. Y. 40; cf. *Tournier v. Nat. Prov. & Union Bank,* 1924, 1 K. B. 461).

We have no thought to hold that Salmon was guilty of a conscious purpose to defraud. Very likely he assumed [*468] in all good faith that with the approaching end of the venture he might ignore his coadventurer and take the extension for himself. He had given to the enterprise time and labor as well as money. He had made it a success. Meinhard, who had given money, but neither time nor labor, had already been richly paid. There might seem to be something grasping in his insistence upon more. Such recriminations are not unusual when coadventurers fall out. They are not without their force if conduct is to be judged by the common standards of competitors. That is not to say that they have pertinency here. Salmon had put himself in a position in which thought of self was to be renounced, however hard the abnegation. He was much more than a coadventurer. He was a managing coadventurer (*Clegg v. Edmondson,* 8 D. M. & G. 787, 807). For him and for those like him, the rule of undivided loyalty is relentless and supreme (*Wendt v. Fischer, supra*; *Munson v. Syracuse,* etc., R. R. Co., 103 N. Y. 58, 74). A different question would be here if there were lacking any nexus of relation between the business conducted by the manager and the opportunity brought to him as an incident of management (*Dean v. MacDowell,* 8 Ch. D. 345, 354; *Aas v. Benham,* 1891, 2 Ch. 244, 258; *Latta v. Kilbourn,* 150 U. S. 524). For this problem, as for most, there are distinctions of degree. If Salmon had received from Gerry a proposition to lease a building at a location far removed, he might have held for himself the privilege thus acquired, or so we shall assume. Here the subject-matter of the new lease was an extension and enlargement of the subject-matter of the old one. A managing coadventurer appropriating the benefit of such a lease without warning to his partner might fairly expect to be reproached with conduct that was underhand, or lacking, to say the least, in reasonable candor, if the partner were to surprise him in the act of signing the new instrument. Conduct subject to that reproach does not receive from equity a healing benediction

[*469] A question remains as to the form and extent of the equitable interest to be allotted to the plaintiff. The trust as declared has been held to attach to the lease which was in the name of the defendant corporation. We think it ought to attach at the option of the defendant Salmon to the shares of stock which were owned by him or were under his control. The difference may be important if the lessee shall wish to execute an assignment of the lease, as it ought to be free to do with the consent of the lessor. On the other hand, an equal division of the shares might lead to other hardships. It might take away from Salmon the power of control and management which under the plan of the joint venture he was to have from first to last. The number of shares to be allotted to the plaintiff should, therefore, be reduced to such an extent as may be necessary to preserve to the defendant Salmon the expected measure of dominion. To that end an extra share should be added to his half.

Subject to this adjustment, we agree with the Appellate Division that the plaintiff's equitable interest is to be measured by the value of half of the entire lease, and not merely by half of some undivided part. A single building covers the whole area. Physical division is impracticable along the lines of the Bristol site, the keystone of the whole. Division of interests and burdens is equally impracticable. Salmon, as tenant under the new lease, or as guarantor of the performance of the tenant's obligations, might well protest if Meinhard, claiming an equitable interest, had offered to assume a liability not equal to Salmon's, but only half as great. He might justly insist that the lease must be accepted by his coadventurer in such form as it had been given, and not constructively divided into imaginary fragments. What must be yielded to the one may be demanded by the other. The lease as it has been executed is single and entire. If confusion has resulted from the union of adjoining parcels, the trustee who consented to the [*470] union must bear the inconvenience (*Hart v. Ten Eyck,* 2 Johns. Ch. 62).

Thus far, the case has been considered on the assumption that the interest in the joint venture acquired by the plaintiff in 1902 has been continuously his. The fact is, however, that in 1917 he assigned to his wife all his "right, title and interest in and to" the agreement with his coadventurer. The coadventurer did not object, but thereafter made his payments directly to the wife. There was a reassignment by the wife before this action was begun.

We do not need to determine what the effect of the assignment would have been in 1917 if either coadventurer had then chosen to treat the venture as dissolved. We do not even need to determine what the effect would have been if the enterprise had been a partnership in the strict sense with active duties of agency laid on each of the two adventurers The form of the enterprise made Salmon the sole manager. The only active duty laid upon the other was one wholly ministerial, the duty of contributing his share of the expense. This he could still do with equal readiness, and still was bound to do, after the assignment to his wife. Neither by word nor by act did either partner manifest a choice to view the enterprise as ended. There is no inflex ble rule in such conditions that dissolution shall ensue against the concurring wish of all that the venture shall continue. The effect of the assignment is then a question of intention (*Durkee v. Gunn,* 41 Kan. 496, 500; *Taft v. Buffum,* 14 Pick. 322; cf. 69 A. S. R. 417, and cases there cited).

Partnership Law (Cons. Laws, ch. 39), section 53, subdivision 1, is to the effect that "a conveyance by a partner of his interest in the partnership does not of itself dissolve the partnership, nor, as against the other partners in the absence of agreement, entitle the assignee, during the continuance of the partnership, to interfere in the management or administration of the [*471] partnership business or affairs, or to require any information or account of partnership transactions, or to inspect the partnership books; but it merely entitles the assignee to receive in accordance with his contract the profits to which the assigning partner would otherwise be entitled." This statute, which took effect October 1, 1919, did not indeed revive the enterprise if automatically on the execution of the assignment a dissolution had resulted in 1917. It sums up with precision, however, the effect of the assignment as the parties meant to shape it. We are to interpret their relation in the revealing light of conduct. The rule of the statute, even if it has modified the rule as to partnerships in general (as to this see Pollock, Partnership, p. 99, § 31; Lindley, Partnership [9th ed.], 695; *Marquand v. N. Y. M. Co.*, 17 Johns. 525), is an accurate statement of the rule at common law when applied to these adventurers. The purpose of the assignment, understood by every one concerned, was to lower the plaintiff's tax by taking income out of his return and adding it to the return to be made by his wife. She was the appointee of the profits, to whom checks were to be remitted. Beyond that, the relation was to be the same as it had been. No one dreamed for a moment that the enterprise was to be wound up, or that Meinhard was relieved of his continuing obligation to contribute to its expenses if contribution became needful. Coadventurers and assignee, and most of all the defendant Salmon, as appears by his own letters, went forward on that basis. For more than five years Salmon dealt with Meinhard on the assumption that the enterprise was a subsisting one with mutual rights and duties, or so at least the triers of the facts, weighing the circumstantial evidence, might not unreasonably infer. By tacit, if not express approval, he continued and preserved it. We think it is too late now, when charged as a trustee, to come forward with the claim that it had been disrupted and dissolved. [*472] The judgment should be modified by providing that at the option of the defendant Salmon there may be substituted for a trust attaching to the lease a trust attaching to the shares of stock, with the result that one-half of such shares together with one additional share will in that event be allotted to the defendant Salmon and the other shares to the plaintiff, and as so modified the judgment should be affirmed with costs.

II. Dissenting Opinion: ANDREWS, J.

A tenant's expectancy of the renewal of a lease is a thing, tenuous, yet often having a real value. It represents the probability that a landlord will prefer to relet his premises to one already in possession rather than to strangers. Less tangible than "good will" it is never included in the tenant's assets, yet equity will not permit one standing in a relation of trust and confidence toward the tenant unfairly to take the benefit to himself. At times the principle is rigidly enforced. Given the relation between the parties, a certain result follows. No question as to good faith, or injury, or as to other circumstances is material. Such is the rule as between trustee and cestui (*Keich v. Sanford, Select Cas.* in Ch. 61); as between executor and estate (*Matter of Brown,* 18 Ch. Div. 61); as between guardian and ward (*Milner v. Harewood,* 18 Ves. 259, 274).

At other times some inquiry is allowed as to the facts involved. Fair dealing and a scrupulous regard for honesty is required. But nothing more. It may be stated generally that a partner may not for his own benefit secretly take a renewal of a firm lease to himself. (*Mitchell v. Reed,* 61 N. Y. 123.) Yet under very exceptional circumstances this may not be wholly true. (W. & T. Leading Cas. in Equity [9th ed.], p. 657; *Clegg v. Edmondson,* 8 D. M. & G. 787, 807.) In the case of tenants in common there is still greater liberty. There is said to be a distinction between those holding under a will or through descent and those holding under independent [*473] conveyance. But even in the former situation the bare relationship is not conclusive. (*Matter of Biss,* 1903, 2 Ch. 40). In *Burrell v. Bull* (3 Sand. Ch. 15) there was actual fraud. In short, as we once said, "the elements of actual fraud — of the betrayal by secret action of confidence reposed, or assumed to be reposed, grows in importance as the relation between the parties falls from an express to an implied or a quasi trust, and on to those cases where good faith alone is involved." (*Thayer v. Leggett,* 229 N. Y. 152.)

Where the trustee, or the partner or the tenant in common, takes no new lease but buys the reversion in good faith a somewhat different question arises. Here is no direct appropriation of the expectancy of renewal. Here is no offshoot of the original lease. We so held in *Anderson v. Lemon* (8 N. Y. 236), and although Judge DWIGHT casts some doubt on the rule in *Mitchell v. Reed,* it seems to have the support of authority. (W. & T. Leading

Cas. in Equity, p. 650; Lindley on Partnership [9th ed.], p. 396; *Bevan v. Webb,* 1905, 1 Ch. 620.) The issue then is whether actual fraud, dishonesty, unfairness is present in the transaction. If so, the purchaser may well be held as a trustee. (*Anderson v. Lemon,* cited above.)

With this view of the law I am of the opinion that the issue here is simple. Was the transaction in view of all the circumstances surrounding it unfair and inequitable? I reach this conclusion for two reasons. There was no general partnership, merely a joint venture for a limited object, to end at a fixed time. The new lease, covering additional property, containing many new and unusual terms and conditions, with a possible duration of eighty years, was more nearly the purchase of the reversion than the ordinary renewal with which the authorities are concerned.

The findings of the referee are to the effect that before 1902, Mrs. Louisa M. Gerry was the owner of a plot on [*474] the corner of Fifth avenue and Forty- second street, New York, containing 9,312 square feet. On it had been built the old Bristol Hotel. Walter J. Salmon was in the real estate business, renting, managing and operating buildings. On April 10th of that year Mrs. Gerry leased the property to him for a term extending from May 1, 1902, to April 30, 1922. The property was to be used for offices and business, and the design was that the lessee should so remodel the hotel at his own expense as to fit it for such purposes, all alterations and additions, however, at once to become the property of the lessor. The lease might not be assigned without written consent.

Morton H. Meinhard was a woolen merchant. At some period during the negotiations between Mr. Salmon and Mrs. Gerry, so far as the findings show without the latter's knowledge, he became interested in the transaction. Before the lease was executed he advanced $5,000 toward the cost of the proposed alterations. Finally, on May 19th he and Salmon entered into a written agreement. "During the period of twenty years from the 1st day of May, 1902," the parties agree to share equally in the expense needed "to reconstruct, alter, manage and operate the Bristol Hotel property;" and in all payments required by the lease, and in all losses incurred "during the full term of the lease, i. e., from the first day of May, 1902, to the 1st day of May, 1922." During the same term net profits are to be divided. Mr. Salmon has sole power to "manage, lease, underlet and operate" the premises. If he dies, Mr. Meinhard shall be consulted before any disposition is made of the lease, and if Mr. Salmon's representatives decide to dispose of it, and the decision is theirs, Mr. Meinhard is to be given the first chance to take the unexpired term upon the same conditions they could obtain from others.

The referee finds that this arrangement did not create a partnership between Mr. Salmon and Mr. Meinhard. In this he is clearly right. He is equally right in holding [*475] that while no general partnership existed the two men had entered into a joint adventure and that while the legal title to the lease was in Mr. Salmon, Mr. Meinhard had some sort of an equitable interest therein. Mr. Salmon was to manage the property for their oint benefit. He was bound to use good faith. He could not willfully destroy the lease, the object of the adventure, to the detriment of Mr. Meinhard.

Mr. Salmon went into possession and control of the property. The alterations were made. At first came losses. Then large profits which were duly distributed. At all times Mr. Salmon has acted as manager.

Some time before 1922 Mr. Elbridge T. Gerry became the owner of the reversion. He was already the owner of an adjoining lot on Fifth avenue and of four lots adjoining on Forty-second street, in all 11,587 square feet, covered by five separate buildings. Obviously all this property together was more valuable than the sum of the value of the separate parcels. Some plan to develop the property as a whole seems to have occurred to Mr. Gerry. He arranged that all leases on his five lots should expire on the same day as the Bristol Hotel lease. Then in 1921 he negotiated with various persons and corporations seeking to obtain a desirable tenant who would put up a building to cover the entire tract, for this was the policy he had adopted. These negotiations lasted for some months. They failed. About January 1, 1922, Mr. Gerry's agent approached Mr. Salmon and began to negotiate with him for the lease of the entire tract. Upon this he insisted as he did upon the erection of a new and expensive building covering the whole. He would not consent to the renewal of the Bristol lease on any terms. This effort resulted in a lease to the Midpoint Realty Company, a corporation entirely owned and controlled by Mr. Salmon. For our purposes the paper may be treated as if the agreement was made with Mr. Salmon himself. [*476] In many respects, besides the increase in the land demised, the new lease differs from the old. Instead of an annual rent of $55,000 it is now from $350,000 to $475,000. Instead of a fixed term of twenty years it may now be, at the lessee's option, eighty. Instead of alterations in an existing structure costing about $200,000 a new building is contemplated costing $3,000,000. Of this sum $1,500,000 is to be advanced by the lessor to the les*see,* "but not to its successors or assigns," and is to be repaid in installments. Again no assignment or sale of the lease may be made without the consent of the lessor.

This lease is valuable. In making it Mr. Gerry acted in good faith without any collusion with Mr. Salmon and with no purpose to deprive Mr. Meinhard of any equities he might have. But as to the negotiations leading to it or as to the execution of the lease itself Mr. Meinhard knew nothing. Mr. Salmon acted for himself to acquire the lease for his own benefit.

Under these circumstances the referee has found and the Appellate Division agrees with him, that Mr. Meinhard is entitled to an interest in the second lease, he having promptly elected to assume his share of the liabilities imposed thereby. This conclusion is based upon the proposition that under the original contract between the two men "the enterprise was a joint venture, the relation between the parties was fiduciary and governed by principles applicable to partnerships," therefore, as the new lease is a graft upon the old, Mr. Salmon might not acquire its benefits for himself alone.

Were this a general partnership between Mr. Salmon and Mr. Meinhard I should have little doubt as to the correctness of this result assuming the new lease to be an offshoot of the old. Such a situation involves questions of trust and confidence to a high degree; it involves questions of good will; many other considerations. As has been said, rarely if ever may one partner without the knowledge of the other acquire for himself the renewal of [*477] a lease held by the firm, even if the new lease is to begin after the firm is dissolved. Warning of such an intent, if he is managing partner, may not be sufficient to prevent the application of this rule.

We have here a different situation governed by less drastic principles. I assume that where parties engage in a joint enterprise each owes to the other the duty of the utmost good faith in all that relates to their common venture. Within its scope they stand in a fiduciary relationship. I assume prima facie that even as between joint adventurers one may not secretly obtain a renewal of the lease of property actually used in the joint adventure where the possibility of renewal is expressly or impliedly involved in the enterprise. I assume also that Mr. Meinhard had an equitable interest in the Bristol Hotel lease. Further, that an expectancy of renewal inhered in that lease. Two questions then arise. Under his contract did he share in that expectancy? And if so, did that expectancy mature into a graft of the original lease? To both questions my answer is "no."

The one complaint made is that Mr. Salmon obtained the new lease without informing Mr. Meinhard of his intention. Nothing else. There is no claim of actual fraud. No claim of misrepresentation to any one. Here was no movable property to be acquired by a new tenant at a sacrifice to its owners. No good will, largely dependent on location, built up by the joint efforts of two men. Here was a refusal of the landlord to renew the Bristol lease on any terms; a proposal made by him, not sought by Mr. Salmon, and a choice by him and by the original lessor of the person with whom they wished to deal shown by the covenants against assignment or underletting, and by their ignorance of the arrangement with Mr. Meinhard.

What then was the scope of the adventure into which the two men entered? It is to be remembered that before their contract was signed Mr. Salmon had obtained [*478] the lease of the Bristol property. Very likely the matter had been earlier discussed between them. The $5,000 advance by Mr.

Meinhard indicates that fact. But it has been held that the written contract defines their rights and duties.

Having the lease Mr. Salmon assigns no interest in it to Mr. Meinhard. He is to manage the property. It is for him to decide what alterations shall be made and to fix the rents. But for twenty years from May 1, 1902, Salmon is to make all advances from his own funds and Meinhard is to pay him personally on demand one-half of all expenses incurred and all losses sustained "during the full term of said lease," and during the same period Salmon is to pay him a part of the net profits. There was no joint capital provided.

It seems to me that the venture so inaugurated had in view a limited object and was to end at a limited time. There was no intent to expand it into a far greater undertaking lasting for many years. The design was to exploit a particular lease. Doubtless in it Mr. Meinhard had an equitable interest, but in it alone. This interest terminated when the joint adventure terminated. There was no intent that for the benefit of both any advantage should be taken of the chance of renewal — that the adventure should be continued beyond that date. Mr. Salmon has done all he promised to do in return for Mr. Meinhard's undertaking when he distributed profits up to May 1, 1922. Suppose this lease, non-assignable without the consent of the lessor, had contained a renewal option. Could Mr. Meinhard have exercised it? Could he have insisted that Mr. Salmon do so? Had Mr. Salmon done so could he insist that the agreement to share losses still existed or could Mr. Meinhard have claimed that the joint adventure was still to continue for twenty or eighty years? I do not think so. The adventure by its express terms ended on May 1, 1922. The contract by its language and by its whole import excluded [*479] the idea that the tenant's expectancy was to subsist for the benefit of the plaintiff. On that date whatever there was left of value in the lease reverted to Mr. Salmon, as it would had the lease been for thirty years instead of twenty. Any equity which Mr. Meinhard possessed was in the particular lease itself, not in any possibility of renewal. There was nothing unfair in Mr.

Salmon's conduct.

I might go further were it necessary. Under the circumstances here presented had the lease run to both the parties I doubt whether the taking by one of a renewal without the knowledge of the other would cause interference by a court of equity. An illustration may clarify my thought. A and B enter into a joint venture to resurface a highway between Albany and Schenectady. They rent a parcel of land for the storage of materials. A, unknown to B, agrees with the lessor to rent that parcel and one adjoining it after the venture is finished, for an iron foundry. Is the act unfair? Would any general statements, scattered here and there through opinions dealing with other circumstance, be thought applicable? In other words, the mere fact that the joint venturers rent property together does not call for the strict rule that applies to general partners. Many things may excuse what is there forbidden. Nor here does any possibility of renewal exist as part of the venture. The nature of the undertaking excludes such an idea.

So far I have treated the new lease as if it were a renewal of the old. As already indicated, I do not take that view. Such a renewal could not be obtained. Any expectancy that it might be had vanished. What Mr. Salmon obtained was not a graft springing from the Bristol lease, but something distinct and different — as distinct as if for a building across Fifth avenue. I think also that in the absence of some fraudulent or unfair act the secret purchase of the reversion even by one partner is rightful. Substantially this is such a purchase. Because of the mere label of a transaction we do not place it on one [*480] side of the line or the other. Here is involved the possession of a large and most valuable unit of property for eighty years, the destruction of all existing structures and the erection of a new and expensive building covering the whole. No fraud, no deceit, no calculated secrecy is found. Simply that the arrangement was made without the knowledge of Mr. Meinhard. I think this not enough.

The judgment of the courts below should be reversed and a new trial ordered, with costs in all courts to abide the event.

POUND, CRANE and LEHMAN, JJ., concur with CARDOZO, Ch. J., for modification of the judgment appealed from and affirmance as modified; ANDREWS, J., dissents in opinion in which KELLOGG and O'BRIEN, JJ., concur. Judgment modified, etc.

QUAKER HILL, INC. v. PARR

364 P.2d 1056 (1961).
Supreme Court of Colorado. In Department. September 25, 1961.

Sheldon & Nordmark, Denver, for plaintiff in error.
J. Fred Schneider, Ronald Lee Cooke, Warren O. Martin, Denver, for defendant in error.

DOYLE, Justice.

The plaintiff in error, to which we will refer as Quaker Hill or plaintiff, was plaintiff in the trial court in an action to recover the sum of $14,503.56 from defendants, defendants in error here. Judgment was in favor of the defendants, and Quaker Hill seeks review.

In May, 1958, the plaintiff, a New York corporation with offices in Newark, New York, sold a large quantity of nursery stock to the Denver Memorial Nursery, Inc. A sales contract, together with a promissory note was executed on May 19, 1958, and the Denver Memorial Nursery, Inc. was named as the contracting party in the sales contract and as the maker of the promissory note. The form of the signature on the note was as follows:

"Denver Memorial Nursery, Inc.

E. D. Parr, Pres.

James P. Presba, Sc'y.-Treas."

The contract shows the Denver Memorial Nursery, Inc. as purchaser and is signed:

"E. D. Parr, Pres."

From the evidence it appears that in the year 1958, prior to this transaction, Parr, Presba and others formed a corporation having the name "Denver Memorial Gardens, Inc." Its purpose was to operate a cemetery. In May of 1958 Parr and Presba, while in the course of negotiations with plaintiff to purchase nursery stock, undertook to organize a separate corporation called "Denver Memorial Nursery, Inc." On May 14, 1958, an order was signed by Parr on behalf of Denver Memorial Nursery, Inc. which, to the knowledge of plaintiff, was not yet formed, that fact being noted in the contract. Subsequently another order dated May 16, 1958, together with the mentioned note, was executed and was delivered to the plaintiff, together with a down payment in the amount of $1,000. Under the contract the balance of the purchase price was not due until the end of the year. The nursery stock was shipped immediately and arrived on May 26, 1958. It was temporarily planted with the assistance of plaintiff. After this temporary planting had occurred, a substitute order was sent to Quaker Hill which was similar in all respects to the previous order except that it contained the name "Mountain View Nurseries" instead of "Denver Memorial Nursery, Inc." as the purchaser. During the course of the ensuing winter and spring and prior to the due date of the balance of the purchase price, the nursery stock all died. The contract contained a guarantee providing for replacement of stock which died.

The Denver Memorial Nursery, Inc. was never formed. Because of name confusion, this corporation was called Mountain View Nurseries, Inc. Its articles were executed on May 27, 1958, and were subsequently filed with the Secretary of State. Neither the Denver Memorial Nursery, Inc. nor the Mountain View Nurseries, Inc. ever functioned as going concerns.

The explanation given at the trial for failure to form the corporation prior to entering into the first contract stemmed from insistence of Quaker Hill that the deal be consummated at once because the growing season was rapidly passing. Barker, who was salesman for Quaker Hill at the time of the sale, testified that the transaction was consummated in this form as a result of his insistence.

After Mountain View Nurseries, Inc. was formed, a new note and contract, prepared by the Division Manager of plaintiff and containing the name "Mountain View Nurseries, Inc." as contracting party, was submitted to defendants, signed in the name of Mountain View Nurseries, Inc. and returned to plaintiff. The plaintiff company thereafter used the designation "Mountain View Nurseries" in its communications. The present action seeks to subject defendants to *personal* liability in view of the defunct financial condition of the corporation, based upon the fact that the corporation was not formed at the time the contract was made and on the further ground that the defendants as promoters were individually liable.

In denying plaintiff's claim, the trial court first entered very brief findings, but at the request of plaintiff amended the original findings, the terms of which are hereinafter set forth:

"The Court finds that on or about May 15 through May 19, 1958, the defendants did not represent themselves to be agents of a corporation by the name of 'Denver Memorial Nurseries, Inc.' as suggested in Paragraph 2(a) of the motion but, on the contrary, the defendants, at the suggestion of representatives of the plaintiff agreed to go along with the plaintiff's idea that the name 'Denver Memorial Nurseries, Inc.' be used for the purpose of consummating the order by which certain nursery stock was to be sent to the Denver Memorial Gardens. "The Court finds that on or about May 15 through May 19, 1958, there was no corporation by the name of Denver Memorial Nurseries, Inc.' which fact was well known to the plaintiff and its representatives. "The Court finds that on or about May 15 through May 19, 1958, the defendants were not promoters of a corporation called 'Denver Memorial Nurseries, Inc.' but yielded to the suggestion of the plaintiff that the name of 'Denver Memorial Nurseries, Inc.' be used for the purpose of consummating the order above referred to. "The Court finds that a corporation known as `Denver Memorial Nurseries, Inc.' was never formed. "It is admitted by the defendant, Parr, through his counsel and the Court finds that the defendant, Parr, signed the document marked Exhibit 2, and that following his name appears the word `president.'

* * * * * *

"This question also calls for a conclusion rather than a finding. However, in this respect we find and conclude that the plaintiff intended to contract with a non-existent corporation and well knew that there was no such corporation as `Denver Memorial Nurseries, Inc.' at the time of said contract."

In summary, the facts disclose that Quaker Hill, a New York corporation acting through a local agent, made a sale to a corporation to be formed, and later accepted still another corporation after formation of the latter. The contract imposed no obligation on defendants to form the corporation nor did it name them as obligors on the note or as promisees in the contract. The question is whether under these circumstances personal liability can be imposed.

In urging that the trial court erred and that the cause should be reversed, plaintiff argues:

1. That promoters who enter a contract in the name of a proposed corporation are personally liable in the absence of an agreement that they should not be liable.
2. That the subsequent formation of a corporation and the ratification of the contract does not operate to release the promoters.
3. That the failure of the nursery stock, the subject matter of this contract, is not a defense because the contractual remedy was replacement.
4. That there should be liability on a quantum meruit basis.

The general principle which plaintiff urges as applicable here is that promoters are personally liable on their contracts, though made on behalf of a corporation to be formed. See 13 Am.Jur. 252, Sec. 113, Corporations. See also the section notes in the 1961 cumulative supplement. This doctrine has been recognized and applied in Colorado. See Hersey v. Tully, 8 Colo. App. 110, 44 P. 854; Colorado Land & Water Company v. Adams, 5 Colo. App. 190, 37 P. 39 (concurring opinion). A well recognized exception to this general rule, however, is that if the contract is made on behalf of the corporation and the other party agrees to look to the corporation and not to the promoters for payment, the promoters incur no personal liability.

In the present case, according to the trial court's findings, the plaintiff, acting through its agent, was well aware of the fact that the corporation was not formed and nevertheless urged that the contract be made in the name of the proposed corporation. There is but little evidence indicating intent on the part of the plaintiff to look to the defendants for performance or payment. The single fact supporting plaintiff's theory is the obtaining of an individual balance sheet. On the contrary, the entire transaction contemplated the corporation as the contracting party. Personal liability does not arise under such circumstances. See 41 A.L.R. 2d 477, where the annotation recognizes the noted exception that personal liability does not attach where the contracting party is shown to be looking solely to the corporation for payment and not to the promoters or officers. The early Supreme Court decision in Case Mfg. Co. v. Soxman, 138 U.S. 431, 11 S.Ct. 360, 362, 34 L.Ed. 1019, illustrates the operation of this exception to the general rule. There, as in the present case, an order was signed in the name of a non-existent corporation, the formation of which was contemplated by the parties. Subsequently the corporation was formed. The contention of the individual defendant was similar to that of the defendants here, namely, that the promisee accepted the notes of the corporation to be formed thus manifesting intention to look to that source for its payment. In holding that the question was one of intention of the parties and that the trial court's findings were binding, the Supreme Court declared:

"The second and third assignments of error may be considered together. They present the proposition that the court erred in finding that the notes of the limited liability company of October 20, 1884, were accepted as payment and satisfaction of the original liability under the contract. Here we face the proposition that we are not triers of fact. And, if there were evidence upon which such a finding might properly rest, we should accept the finding as conclusive, and inquire no further into the testimony than we should into its sufficiency to sustain the verdict of a jury."

In the case at bar, the findings of the trial court clearly establish intent on the part of the plaintiff to contract with the corporation and not with the individual defendants.

The curious form of this transaction is undoubtedly explainable on the basis of the long distance dealing, the great rush to complete it, the heavy emphasis on completion of the sale rather than on securing payment or a means of payment. No effort was made to expressly obligate the defendants and this present effort must be regarded as pure afterthought.

Being convinced that the trial court's determination was proper under the circumstances, we conclude that the judgment should be and it is affirmed.

HALL, C. J., and DAY, J., concur.

OLD DOMINION COPPER MINING & SMELTING CO. vs. ALBERT S. BIGELOW

203 Mass. 159
November 18, 19, 1908 - September 14, 1909

Suffolk County
Present: KNOWLTON, C. J., MORTON, HAMMOND, TARING, BRALEY, SHELDON, & RUGG, JJ.

Equity Pleading and Practice, Appeal, Damages, Supplemental answer, Injunction. Conflict of Laws. Corporation, Liability of promoter. Equity Jurisdiction, To compel promoter of corporation to account for secret profit, Laches, Res judicata, Concurrent jurisdiction. Limitations, Statute of. Res Judicata. Constitutional Law, Full faith and credit clause. Joint Tortfeasors. Judgment. Words, "Promoter."

Upon an appeal from the decree of a single justice for the plaintiff in a suit in equity by a corporation against one of its two promoters, to recover damages for a breach of fiduciary duty by the promoters in selling certain property to the plaintiff at a large profit without a disclosure of material facts, the defendant contended that certain facts essential to the plaintiff's case, which were found by the single justice, were not supported by the evidence. The evidence was oral, documentary and in depositions, and this court, after a careful examination of a voluminous record, held that the findings of fact made by the single justice were warranted by the evidence and should stand.

Upon an appeal from the decree of a single justice for the plaintiff in a suit in equity by a corporation against one of its two promoters, to recover damages for a breach of fiduciary duty by the promoters in selling certain property to the plaintiff, to be paid for in shares of the plaintiff, at a large profit without a disclosure of material facts, it appeared that the plaintiff was organized under the laws of the State of New Jersey and that the vote of the plaintiff's directors to purchase the property from the promoters was passed at a meeting of the board of directors which was held in the city of New York, but it also appeared that it was the intention of the parties that the contract should be carried out and consummated by the delivery of deeds and the issuing of certificates of stock in Massachusetts, where it was intended that the offices of the company should be, and where afterwards they were established and where also the contract was in fact carried out. The defendant contended that the contract was governed by the law of New York, and introduced evidence of the law of that State consisting of certain decisions of its courts. The single justice ruled that the rights of the parties arising from the transaction were to be determined according to the law of this Commonwealth. He also found as a fact that the law of New York applicable to the case was the same as that of Massachusetts. Held, that there was no error, and that upon the record and the findings the law of this Commonwealth controlled the rights and obligations of the parties.

A promoter stands in a fiduciary relation to a corporation which he organizes.

In a suit in equity, by a mining corporation organized under the laws of the State of New Jersey, against one of the two promoters who planned and effected its organization, to recover damages for a breach of fiduciary duty by the promoters in selling certain mining property to the plaintiff at a large profit without a disclosure of material facts, it appeared that, at the time of the vote of the plaintiff's directors by which the contract in question was approved, the corporation had been organized and was authorized to do business under the laws of New Jersey, although the whole of its capital stock had not been issued or subscribed for, and that the defendant and the other promoter together owned all the shares of the corporation which then had been issued, that the intrinsic value of the property sold by the promoters to the plaintiff was not more than $1,000,000 although its market value, owing to the skilful manipulation of the promoters, was something less than $2,000,000, and that for this the promoters received stock of the plaintiff of the par value of $3,250,000 and of the actual value of at least that amount, subject to the payment of legitimate expenses of not over $20,000, that it was a part of the plan of organization and was the intention of the promoters that $500,000 of the capital stock should be issued to subscribers at par to provide a working capital, that at a meeting of the directors of the plaintiff, which was held a few days after the first meeting of the stockholders, the defendant became a director and the president of the plaintiff and the other promoter became a director, and it was voted to increase the capital stock and to purchase the property from the promoters for the price above named, paying for it in the new stock, the amount of new stock authorized exceeding that price by $500,000 of par value. At this meeting the votes were passed by a majority of four of the seven directors, the other three not being present. Two months and one week later, another meeting of the directors was held at which all of the seven directors were present, the five in addition to the two promoters being their tools. At this meeting it was voted to issue to the promoters and their nominee the agreed amount of capital stock for the purchase of the property. It then was voted that the treasurer of the company be instructed to issue shares representing $500,000 of par value "to such parties as have subscribed for the same." On the day of this meeting or on the following day, certificates for the shares were issued to the promoters and their nominee in accordance with the votes, and a certificate for the remaining shares of stock of the par value of $500,000 was made out in the name of the treasurer of the company. At the end of the record of the meeting all the directors signed an assent to the acts done, the promoters and their nominee signing for shares of the par value of $3,250,000 and the plaintiff's treasurer signing for shares of the par value of $500,000, which in fact were the property of the plaintiff. All but about $9,000 of the $500,000 of shares in the name of the treasurer were issued to subscribers at par not long after their issue was authorized, and the remaining $9,000 of shares were sold about two years later by direction of the plaintiff's treasurer, their face value being credited on the books as treasury stock and the excess above par for which they were sold being credited to interest account. To none of the subscribers to whom the $500,000 of shares were issued were the terms of the contract with the promoters disclosed before they paid for their shares. Held, that the defendant was liable to account to the plaintiff for the secret profit of the promoters from the sale of their own property to the plaintiff, that there was no such ratification by the stockholders of the contract with the promoters as to deprive the corporation of its remedy, and that the promoters at the time of the transaction did not represent all the shares of capital stock contemplated as a part of the promotion scheme, because they were not the subscribers for the $500,000 of shares to be issued to provide the working capital.

KNOWLTON, C. J., MORTON, & HAMMOND, JJ., dissenting.

There can be no laches so long as there is no knowledge of the wrong complained of and no failure to avail one's self of reasonable opportunities to ascertain the facts.

In a suit in equity founded on a breach of trust where there has been a fiduciary duty on the part of the defendant to disclose the facts on which the cause of action rests, the statute of limitations does not begin to run until the facts have been or ought to have been discovered.

In a suit in equity, by a corporation against one of the two promoters who planned and effected its organization, to recover damages for a breach of fiduciary duty by the promoters in selling certain property to the plaintiff at a large profit without a disclosure of material facts, if the plaintiff proves a case which entitles it to relief, and it appears that the breach of trust on which the liability of the defendant depends was a joint act of the defendant and the other promoter, who is not a party to the suit, for the benefit of both, the division of the profits between the promoters cannot affect the rights of the plaintiff against the defendant, the breach of trust committed by the promoters being in the nature of a tort which makes them liable for the whole damage severally as well as jointly.

In a suit in equity, by a corporation against one of the two promoters who planned and effected its organization, to recover damages for a breach of fiduciary duty by the promoters in selling certain property to the plaintiff at a large profit without a disclosure of material facts, where the plaintiff proves a breach of trust on the part of the promoters which entitles him to relief, and it appears that the situation of the parties and the property is not such as to make it just to order a rescission of the contract of sale, the defendant may be ordered to pay to the plaintiff the amount of the secret profit of the promoters.

In a suit in equity, by a corporation against one of the two promoters who planned and effected its organization, to recover damages for a breach of fiduciary duty by the promoters in selling certain property to the plaintiff in exchange for shares of capital stock of the plaintiff at a large profit without a disclosure of material facts, if the plaintiff proves a case which entitles it to an order for the payment to it of the amount of the secret profit of the promoters, and there is no difficulty in ascertaining the fair market value of the property sold and conveyed by the promoters to the plaintiff or of the shares of the plaintiff's stock received by the promoters in payment, the difference between these two values is the measure of damages, and the test is not the difference between the market value of the shares received by the promoters and the cost to them of the property conveyed by them to the plaintiff.

In a suit in equity, which has been remitted by the full court for a hearing before a single justice upon the question whether the defendant should be allowed to file a supplemental answer setting up as a bar the decree of a court in another jurisdiction rendered, while the suit in this Commonwealth was pending, in a suit by the same plaintiff relating to the same subject matter and in which the issues were identical, the defendant in the suit in this Commonwealth having contributed toward the defense of the suit in which the judgment was rendered and alleging that he was a party or privy thereto, an order of a single justice allowing the defendant to file such a supplemental answer is a matter within the discretion of the single justice, and unless such discretion was exercised wrongly the order must stand. It here was held that in making such an order the single justice could not be said to have erred in permitting the defendant to set up a decree, resting upon the decision of a court of last resort, which was made after the close of the hearing upon the merits in the suit in this Commonwealth.

A decree founded upon a demurrer may be a bar to another suit.

Under art. 4, s.1, of the Constitution of the United States, requiring that full faith and credit shall be given in each State to the public acts, records, and judicial proceedings of every other State, the question whether a defendant in a suit in equity in this Commonwealth, who sets up as a bar to the suit the decree of a United States court in another State, rendered in a suit brought by the same plaintiff in which the same issues were involved, was privy to that suit, is a jurisdictional question to be determined by the law of this Commonwealth, subject to the Constitution of the United States.

Mere participation in the defense to a suit by one not a party to it, because of general or personal interest in the result of the litigation, does not make such participator privy to the suit with a right to set up the judgment or decree therein as a bar to another suit brought against him by the same plaintiff and involving the same issues.

By the settled law of this Commonwealth one of two or more joint tortfeasors, in an action at law or a suit in equity brought against him as severally liable for the joint tort, cannot set up as a bar a judgment or decree in favor of another of the joint tortfeasors in an action or suit brought by the same plaintiff for injury from the same joint tort.

In a suit in equity, brought by a corporation organized under the laws of another State against a citizen of this Commonwealth, after the case had been heard upon the merits and a single justice of this court had made a decree in favor of the plaintiff, from which the defendant had appealed, and while the case was upon the docket of the full court and was about to be reached for argument, the defendant procured in a court of equity, not of the last resort, in the State in which the plaintiff was organized a temporary injunction against the prosecution of the suit in this Commonwealth. Later, the defendant's suit in the other State, in which he obtained such temporary injunction, was decided adversely to him, and he asserted that he intended to prosecute an appeal to the highest court in that State. Thereupon, on a motion by the plaintiff in the suit in this Commonwealth, an interlocutory decree was made by a single justice of this court, restraining the defendant from further prosecuting the suit in the other State "and from commencing or prosecuting any other suit or proceeding either in law or in equity, except in this court, against the plaintiff to prevent it from obtaining the final decision and decree of this court, or in any manner to delay or impede the presentation of said case." The defendant appealed from this interlocutory decree and from refusals of the single justice to vacate or modify it.

Held, that it was manifestly proper that at this stage of the proceedings the defendant should be restrained from attempting to interfere through courts of other jurisdiction with the conclusion of the litigation in this Commonwealth.

Two BILLS IN EQUITY, filed on October 7, 1902, by the Old Dominion Copper Mining and Smelting Company, a corporation organized under the laws of the State of New Jersey, against Albert S. Bigelow of Cohasset, one of the two promoters who planned and effected the organization of the plaintiff, to compel, after rescission by the plaintiff, the restitution of the consideration received by the promoters for certain property alleged to have been sold by them to the plaintiff at a large profit without a disclosure of material facts, or to compel the defendant to account to the plaintiff for such secret profit, and to pay damages for such breach of trust, as described in 188 Mass. 315 -320, the first suit relating to the original issue of thirty thousand shares and the second suit to the original issue of one hundred thousand shares of the capital stock of the plaintiff.

The defendant demurred to the bills, and upon a reservation for determination by this court the demurrers were overruled in a decision reported in 188 Mass. 315.

The cases were heard on the merits by Sheldon, J., who on December 10, 1907, made a decree that the plaintiff should recover from the defendant a sum of money found by the justice to be due to it from him, with interest from a day named, and that execution should issue against the defendant for the total sum with costs. Both the plaintiff and the defendant appealed.

While the cases were on the docket of the full court and were about to be reached for hearing at the March sitting of 1908, the defendant filed a bill in equity in the Court of Chancery of the State of New Jersey, praying for an injunction against the prosecution of the pending suits in this Commonwealth, and upon this bill a temporary injunction was issued by the New Jersey court as described in the opinion. On August 8, 1908, the New Jersey court made a decree dismissing the suit in that State, and the present defendant, as the plaintiff in that suit, announced his intention to prosecute an appeal from the decree. Thereupon, on motion of the plaintiff in the present suits, Braley, J., on August 14, 1908, made in each of the cases the following interlocutory decree:

" It is ordered and decreed that an injunction issue restraining the defendant Albert S. Bigelow, his attorneys, agents, and servants from further prosecuting the action commenced by said Bigelow against the plaintiff in the Court of Chancery in the State of New Jersey, as is in the plaintiff's petition set forth ; and from commencing or prosecuting any other suit or proceeding either in law or in equity, except in this court, against the plaintiff to prevent it from obtaining the final decision and decree of this court, or in any manner to delay or impede the presentation of said case according to the due and orderly course of procedure in this court, or until further order of the court."

On August 26, 1908, the defendant made a motion to vacate the interlocutory decrees of August 14, 1908, and to dissolve the injunction issued thereon. On August 28, 1908, the defendant made another motion to modify the decrees of August 14, 1908, and the injunctions issued thereon. On August 28, 1908, Braley, J., made orders denying both of these motions. In each of the cases the defendant appealed from the decree of August 14, 1908, and from the orders denying the defendant's motions to vacate or modify such decree.

While the appeals from the decrees made by Sheldon, J., were still on the docket of the full court, the defendant made a motion to be allowed to file a supplemental answer setting up as a bar to the plaintiff's claims a judgment of the Circuit Court of the United States for the Southern District of New York entered on July 23, 1908, in a suit in equity entitled Old Dominion Copper Mining J. Smelting Co. v. Frederick Lewisohn & others, executors. The motion was heard at a special sitting of the full court, and on September 4, 1908, this court made an order vacating the decrees and remitting the cases for hearing before a single justice upon the question whether the defendant should be allowed to file the supplemental answer, and, if his motion was allowed, for a further hearing upon the matters set up in this answer, " and for reversal or such modification of the original decree, if any, as ought to be made by reason of these matters," as reported in 199 Mass. 488 .

The cases were heard by Braley, J., upon a motion of the defendant to be allowed in each of the cases to file a supplemental answer setting up the above named judgment as a bar, and to introduce evidence to prove the facts alleged therein. On September 16, 1908, the justice made an order granting the motion. The plaintiff, instead of taking an appeal, asked the justice to report his action to the full court. In accordance with this request he did so.

If his action was reviewable, then, if the allowance of the amendment was wrong, the order was to be reversed; otherwise it was to stand.

A commissioner was appointed to take the evidence relating to the matters set forth in the supplemental answer, and the cases came on to be heard before Hammond, J. On October 9, 1908, he made an order reserving the cases for determination by this court, using in each case the same language, which was as follows:

> "This case came on to be heard upon the evidence relating to the matters set forth in the supplemental answer filed by the defendant September 4, 1908, and evidence introduced on behalf of the defendant and on behalf of the plaintiff, as more fully appears in the commissioner's report thereof ; and after the hearing of said evidence a decree in the form of the original decree in said case was ordered, but the question of whether or not said order should be modified or reversed by reason of said supplemental answer, and the evidence in support thereof, is reserved for the consideration of the full court ; and this case, including the entire record and the commissioner's reports of the evidence, is now reserved for the consideration of the full court as if upon the original appeals from the final decree of December 10, 1901, and for such further modification, if any, as should be made therein by reason of the evidence bearing upon said supplemental answer, and also upon the reservation concerning the order permitting the filing of said supplemental answer, and also upon the appeal of the defendant from the decree entered August 14, 1908, granting an injunction, and also upon the appeals of the defendant from the orders entered August 28, 1908, refusing to modify or vacate said decree of August 14, 1908, and for such final decree and order upon this reservation as justice and equity require. The foregoing is made as a reservation and not as a decree."

The case was argued at the bar in November, 1908, before Knowlton, C. J., Morton, Hammond, Braley, & Rugg, JJ., and afterwards was submitted on briefs to all the justices.

A. Hemenway & J. W. Farley, for the defendant.

L. D. Brandeis & E. F. McClennen, for the plaintiff.

RUGG, J. These are suits in equity, by which the plaintiff seeks to recover secret profits made by the defendant as one of its organizers, in selling to it while under the absolute control and management of himself and his associate, one Lewisohn, certain mining properties belonging to him and Lewisohn. The allegations of the bills are set out at length in 188 Mass. 315, where one of the cases was considered upon demurrer. After the overruling of the demurrer the defendant answered, and the cases were heard before a single justice, who entered decrees in favor of the plaintiff in both cases and filed a report of the facts found by him. Except as to matters immaterial so far as the questions of law are involved, he found that the allegations were sustained. Briefly recapitulated, the facts appearing in the report upon which the plaintiff rests its claim are that in April, 1895, the defendant and Lewisohn formed a device to secure the control of the stock (the par value of which was $500,000) of the Old Dominion Copper Company of Baltimore City, called the Baltimore Company, and the title to certain other neighboring mining properties, called the outside properties, and to cause these properties and the real estate of the Baltimore Company to be transferred to a new corporation (which they should procure to be organized with a much larger capital), for an increased price. Options were secured upon these properties, and the price agreed to be paid by the defendant and Lewisohn to the owners was $1,000,000, divided in the proportion of 547/1000 by the defendant, and 453/1000 by Lewisohn. The outside properties were regarded by all parties as of little or no value and were thrown in as a makeweight in the purchase of the stock of the Baltimore Company. The single justice, while finding that they could not be said to be of no value, was satisfied that their value did not exceed $50,000. No examination to ascertain their value was made by the defendant or Lewisohn, or by any one in behalf of the plaintiff. For the purpose of providing himself with funds to meet in part his financial obligations for the purchase of the properties, the defendant, before taking up the options, organized an underwriting syndicate and another syndicate called the Old Dominion Syndicate. It is not necessary to state the details of these arrangements, further than to say that it is found as a fact that the defendant did not deal fairly with the members of the syndicate in the division of his profits, and did not disclose to the great majority of them the fact of the secret profit. The obligation of purchase was assumed wholly by the defendant and Lewisohn, and the device for the organization of the new corporation was entirely theirs. Although, as first conceived, it was the avowed intention of the defendant and Lewisohn (which the defendant expressed to various members of the syndicate) to form a new corporation with a capital stock of $2,500,000 which should take the property of the Baltimore Company and the outside properties for $2,000,000 of its capital stock and procure a working capital of $500,000 by the sale of the rest of the capital stock to the public for cash at par, they proceeded to organize the plaintiff corporation under the laws of New Jersey, with a capital stock of $3,750,000, divided into one hundred and fifty thousand shares of the par value of $25 each. But it was the intention of the defendant and Lewisohn (as found by the single justice) that "twenty thousand shares of the capital stock of the plaintiff should be issued to new subscribers at par; and this was done in the summer and fall of 1895." This organization was conducted and controlled wholly by the defendant and Lewisohn through themselves and their agents and representatives. Without providing the plaintiff with an independent board of officers or representatives they, as the responsible and only managers of the plaintiff, acting in its name, contracted with themselves as mine owners to sell to it the real estate of the Baltimore Company for $2,500,000 of the capital stock of the plaintiff and the outside properties, of trifling value at best, for $750,000 of such capital stock, and to sell to the general public for working capital the remaining $500,000 of capital stock of the plaintiff at par, without disclosing that they had sold property costing them only $1,000,000 for three and a quarter times its cost.

The first meeting of the stockholders was held on July 7, 1895, at which $1,000, - the lowest amount of capital with which a corporation organized under the laws of New Jersey could begin business, - was paid in by Lewisohn. This money, although deposited to the credit of the plaintiff company upon its organization, was afterwards returned by it to Lewisohn in an accounting with him. A meeting of the directors was held in New York on July 11, 1895, at which the defendant became a director and the president of the plaintiff and Lewisohn a director. Votes were passed to increase the capital stock and two separate votes for the purchase of the mining properties for the prices in stock before indicated. The stock, the market value of which was fully as great as its par value, was issued to the defendant and Lewisohn and one Dumaresq, their nominee, by votes of September 18, 1895, on that or the following day. At the same time a certificate for the remaining twenty thousand shares of stock of the par value of $500,000 was made out in the name of "Thomas Nelson, treasurer," but this stock is found to have belonged to the corporation, and Nelson had no right to act respecting it, as it was taken up by direct subscriptions of the public. The conveyances of the mines by the Baltimore Company and of the outside properties by Lewisohn were not made until December, 1895, or January, 1896. The intrinsic value of the property conveyed by the Baltimore Company is found to have been not more than $1,000,000, although its market value, largely due to the skilful manipulation of the defendant and Lewisohn, and "the ingenious manner in which they created a desire on the part of men interested in mines, as investors or speculators, to be allowed to join in the transaction they were carrying out," was something less than $2,000,000. The report proceeds: " But, taking the most favorable view of the situation possible for the defendant, he and Lewisohn did, by reason of their failure to disclose the real facts as aforesaid, make out of their sale to the plaintiff company a secret profit of fifty thousand shares of its capital stock, of which the defendant's portion was twenty-seven thousand three hundred and fifty shares, and Lewisohn's portion was twenty-two thousand six hundred and fifty shares. If he had fully disclosed the facts to the plaintiff company and secured for it independent advice, it would not have given to him this secret profit; . . . Lewisohn and he were acting in the formation and execution of the scheme together and in concert. Each of them was doing his part to carry out a joint scheme, which was intended to inure to the advantage of both. The control exercised by them over the plaintiff company was a joint control, and was exercised by them for the benefit of both. A proper disclosure of the real facts by either would have frustrated the schemes of both; they both acted together in pursuance of a common design, and for the profit of both." "During all these transactions the full control of the plaintiff company was in the hands of and was exercised by the defendant and Lewisohn, who were its promoters and who themselves determined upon and dictated, under the advice of their counsel, everything that was done by the plaintiff company or in its behalf; it bad no directors, representatives, or advisers other than themselves or their agents; and they did not disclose to it any of the facts which have been stated. This continued to be the case until April, 1902.

"The result of his and Lewisohn's transactions with the plaintiff company was that for the $1,000,000 of their own and their associates' money which they invested, they received, subject to the payment of legitimate expenses of not over $20,000, stock to the par value of $3,250,000, and of the actual value of at least that amount: that is, at the rate of more than three dollars for one. He gave to the members of his syndicate two dollars for one, either wholly in stock or half in cash and half in stock, as they elected. With a few individual exceptions he did not disclose the facts to them. The very great majority of the members of his syndicate did not become aware of the details of what he and Lewisohn had done." The capital stock issued to defendant and Lewisohn was stamped "Issued for property purchased." The law of New Jersey required that such stock be issued only "to the amount of the value" of the property so purchased. Pub. Laws of New Jersey, 1889, p. 414, s. 4; 1893, p. 444, s. 2. The vote of July 11, 1895, to purchase the mining properties was in fact passed by a majority only of the board of directors, for three do not appear to have been present at that time. At the directors' meeting of September 18, 1895, when the votes to issue thirty thousand full paid shares to the defendant and Lewisohn and one hundred thousand like shares to their nominee Dumaresq were passed, seven directors were present, the five aside from Bigelow and Lewisohn being their tools, and at the end of the record of that meeting all the directors signed an assent to the acts done, and Bigelow and Lewisohn, signing for thirty thousand shares of capital stock, Dumaresq signing for one hundred thousand shares of the capital stock, and "Thomas Nelson, Treasurer," signing for twenty thousand shares of capital stock, being the whole number of shares, signified a written approval of the acts of that meeting. The single justice found that the twenty thousand shares were the property of the plaintiff, and that Nelson had no right to attempt to act as their holder.

1. The defendant strenuously contends that certain facts found by the single justice are not supported by the evidence. He first attacks the finding, vital to the plaintiff's case, that the scheme of the defendant and Lewisohn, as framed and executed, contemplated that twenty thousand shares of stock in the plaintiff corporation should be issued to new subscribers at par, and that the defendant and Lewisohn did not agree to take all the stock in the plaintiff corporation in return for the mining properties conveyed to it and $500,000 in cash for a working capital. He argues that the evidence required a finding that Bigelow and Lewisohn agreed as a part of their scheme to take all the capital stock in return for the mines and $500,000 in cash. He also assails the findings, that the property conveyed to the plaintiff by the defendant and Lewisohn for one hundred and thirty thousand of its shares of a par value of $3,250,000 was worth intrinsically not more than $1,000,000, and that its market value, due to the skilful manipulation of the defendant and Lewisohn and their ingenious baiting of the stock market, was less than $2,000,000 ; and he contends that the evidence demonstrates the truth to be that the plaintiff paid no more than it was worth.

The evidence was oral, documentary and in depositions. The rule of practice respecting such a contention as this has been often declared. In an appeal in equity from a final decree, where all the testimony is reported, it is the duty of the appellate court to examine the evidence and decide the case on its merits, both as to the facts and the law; but where the evidence upon disputed issues is partly oral, the findings of fact of a single justice will not be disturbed unless plainly wrong. Jennings v. Vahey, 183 Mass. 47. Lindsey v. Bird, 193 Mass. 200 . It becomes necessary, therefore, to examine the evidence upon this point somewhat in detail.

The offers of the Baltimore Company for the sale of its property to the plaintiff, and of Lewisohn for the sale of the outside properties, were in writing, and the votes of the plaintiff accepting them were spread upon the records of the directors' meeting of July 11, 1895. These provided distinctly for the issue of one hundred and thirty thousand shares of the plaintiff's capital stock in payment for these conveyances. The records of the plaintiff show no vote touching the issue of the remaining twenty thousand shares. If, as claimed by the defendant, it was then contemplated that these shares should be issued to him and Lewisohn at par for cash, it seems probable that a vote to this effect would then have been passed. The only vote respecting the issue of these remaining shares was that of the directors on September 18, 1895, when, after a vote authorizing the issue of a certificate for one hundred thousand shares to Dumaresq (who was the nominee of Bigelow and Lewisohn) and another for thirty thousand shares to Bigelow and Lewisohn, it was voted that the treasurer of the company be " instructed to issue twenty thousand shares ... to such parties as have subscribed for the same." If it was then understood that Bigelow and Lewisohn had agreed to take all the shares, including the twenty thousand for cash at par and were the subscribers therefor, no sufficient reason appears for not saying so in the vote, instead of adopting a phrase suited to express an intent to issue the shares to the general public. Moreover, at this time, as shown by the only subscription list of the plaintiff, the general public had subscribed generously for stock. The language of the vote aptly refers to such subscribers. The only paper, which appears by the evidence to have been signed by subscribers for stock, was dated July 18, 1895, two months before the vote to issue the twenty thousand shares was passed. The certificate for the twenty thousand shares was issued in the name of "Thomas Nelson, Treasurer," he being the treasurer of the plaintiff. It is ingeniously argued that in this matter Nelson was acting as the treasurer of those who had become subscribers to stock and not as treasurer of the plaintiff. But he treated their payments as if made to the treasurer of the plaintiff. If this certificate had been in truth issued to the nominee of Bigelow and Lewisohn in return for their obligation to pay cash for its face value, naturally it would have been issued without any official title attached, as was that to their nominee, Dumaresq. It is a significant coincidence that the form of certificate selected was the same which, in other companies controlled by the defendant, was used when stock was in fact treasury stock. This certificate was subdivided in the autumn of 1895, and nineteen thousand six hundred and fifty shares were issued to various subscribers, who paid for them directly to the plaintiff, and not to Bigelow or Lewisohn. The remaining three hundred and fifty shares, although subscribed for, were not taken by subscribers. They were not taken or paid for by Bigelow or Lewisohn, but about two years later were sold by direction of Nelson, who was still the treasurer of the plaintiff, through brokers, amid their face value credited on the plaintiff's books to treasury stock and the excess above par, for which they were sold, to the interest account. This sum does not appear to have been the equivalent of interest due from the defendant and which should have been paid, if he originally subscribed for the shares, and his name does not appear in connection with them on the plaintiff's books. The transaction respecting the subdivision of this certificate was conducted in substance on the footing of original subscribers, and not of purchasers from Bigelow. The names of those, to whom the shares were issued, appear upon the "Corrected List" of the plaintiff, which was its only record of subscription, and in which the shares taken by each are described as "allotments." If they were subscribers to the defendant and Lewisohn merely for stock held by them, there was no reason why their names should appear on the plaintiff's subscription list. Notices were sent to these subscribers by the treasurer of the plaintiff, and not by Bigelow, and checks were returned payable to the order of the treasurer, and were deposited directly to the credit of the plaintiff, although notices and subscriptions to the syndicate formed by Bigelow to aid him in furnishing the purchase price were sent by and returned to Bigelow. Various written statements of Bigelow, as for instance that they proposed "to open the bag just a little to the public" and that the public were "starving" for the shares, appear inconsistent with the theory that he and Lewisohn were the subscribers for the entire capital stock. These and other circumstances are sufficient to warrant the finding of the single justice. Apparently he credited contemporaneous acts, entries and other writings with their natural inferences rather than the direct oral and other testimony to the contrary given at the trial. It cannot be said that in this he was plainly wrong.

The finding as to the value of the property conveyed by the defendant and Lewisohn to the plaintiff is also supported by testimony and cannot be disturbed. The evidence touching this matter came from various sources. The former owners had operated the mine with some degree of success on a capitalization of $500,000. They had greater experience and a more intimate knowledge respecting it than anyone else, and they seem to have been men accustomed to large business operations and not unfamiliar with mining. They do not appear to have been under any compulsion to sell. The price for which such owners in fact sold their property might well have been regarded as the best test of its value. But the finding was approximately double this sum. Although other circumstances perhaps might have supported a higher valuation, there is no ground for holding this plainly, or even probably, wrong. These are the main facts relied upon by the plaintiff. Other findings are controverted by the defendant. Without discussing them in detail it is enough to say that a careful examination of the voluminous record discloses no reason for doubting their correctness.

2. At the threshold lies the question as to what law determines the character of these transactions and the liability of the defendant therefor. The votes to purchase the real estate of the Baltimore Company and the outside

properties were passed at a meeting of the plaintiff's board of directors held in New York, but they were not New York contracts in the sense that they are to be governed necessarily by the law of New York. As found by the single justice," It was the intention of the parties that these agreements should be carried out and consummated by the delivery of the deeds and the issue of certificates of stock in Massachusetts, where it was intended that the offices of the company should be, and where they were established, in Boston, and where, in fact, they were so carried out. It was intended that the business of the company, outside the actual mining and smelting operations, which were to be conducted in Arizona, should be carried on in Massachusetts; and this was done." Where a contract is made with a purpose by the parties to it that it shall be performed in a particular place, its validity and interpretation are to be determined by the law of the place where it is to be performed. It is made with a view to that law. Pritchard v. Norton, 106 U. S. 124. Hall v. Cordell, 142 U. S. 116. Andrews v. Pond, 13 Pet. 65. Hamlyn v. Talisker Distillery, [1894] A. C. 202. American Halting Co. v. Souther Brewing Co. 194 Mass. 89. The ruling of the single justice that the transaction is to be determined according to the law of this Commonwealth appears to have been right.

But, however that may be, the single justice has found as a fact that the law of New York applicable to the case is the same as that of Massachusetts. The only evidence as to the New York law before the single justice was the following cases decided by the courts of that State:

> Blum v. Whitney, 185 N. Y. 232; Seymour v. Spring Forest Cemetery Association, 144 N. Y. 333; Barr v. New York, Lake Erie J. Western Railroad, 125 N. Y. 263; Brewster v. Hatch, 122 N. Y. 349; Getty v. Devlin, 54 N. Y. 403; Campbell v. Cypress Hills Cemetery, 41 N. Y. 34; Colton Improvement Co. v. Richter, 55 N. Y. Supp. 486; and there were also admitted de bene Old Dominion Copper Mining & Smelting Co. v. Lewisohn, 148 Fed. Rep. 1020; S. C. 136 Fed. Rep. 915; and McCracken v. Robison, 57 Fed. Rep. 375, decided in the United States Circuit Court for the district of New York.

The defendant's attack upon this finding stands upon a somewhat different basis from that upon the other findings of fact, because this rests wholly upon documentary evidence, and the appellate court stands precisely as did the justice, who heard the case, in respect of opportunities to weigh evidence and draw inferences from it. The trial court has not here the advantage of seeing the witnesses and judging of their credibility by personal observation. Hence no special presumption exists in favor of his finding. Harvey-Watts Co. v. Worcester Umbrella Co. 193 Mass. 138 . But the decision must be made upon the evidence which was before the single justice. The cases in the federal courts are not evidence as to the law of New York, for the reason that, this being a question of general law, the federal courts declare the law upon their own views and are not bound by decisions of State courts. Olcott v. Supervisors, 16 Wall. 678, 689. Burgess v. Seligman, 107 U. S. 20, 33, 34. Pleasant Township v. AEtna Ins. Co. 138 U. S. 67, 73. Moreover, the federal cases cited do not purport to declare what is the law of New York. While none of the decisions of the New York courts is based upon facts precisely like those in the case at bar, Brewster v. Hatch, 122 N. Y. 349, and Campbell v. Cypress Hills Cemetery, 41 N. Y. 34, are so nearly akin in essential features, and the statement of legal principles in each is such as to lead to the conclusion that the finding of the single justice was correct.

Blum v. Whitney, 185 N. Y. 232, is relied upon by the defendant as announcing a different doctrine; but it does not so appear to us. Several corporations and their officers there joined in a written contract for the formation of a new corporation with a fixed capitalization and for the transfer of their several properties to it for a definite amount of its stock. The maximum amount that might be paid for the capital stock of a certain other corporation was fixed by implication in the agreement. All the persons contemplated, and none others, became members of the new corporation. These were treated by the court as together constituting the organizers of the corporation. The fact that the maximum price permitted by the agreement was in fact paid for the capital stock of the other corporation and that a great profit was obtained by some of the organizers was regarded not as a fraud upon the corporation but upon the associates in the organization. It was held not to be a case for the application of the law governing promoters. This case cannot be considered as stating a rule in conflict with the finding of the single justice.

In its practical results it is not of much consequence whether the law of the situs, either of Massachusetts or New York, or of the forum, governs, for upon this record and the findings before us, the law of this Commonwealth controls the rights and obligations of the parties.

3. The next inquiry is as to the liability of the defendant. The plaintiff seeks to establish this on the ground that the defendant and Lewisohn framed a scheme, which was an entirety and which as a whole comprised the organization and continued management of the plaintiff by themselves, their agents and representatives, until the completion of the project ; this scheme was the capitalization of the plaintiff for $3,750,000; the sale to it of their property, costing and intrinsically worth $1,000,000, but having in the market a value not over $2,000,000, for $3,250,000 ; the sale to the general public at par for cash of the remaining $500,000 of stock ; and all this without providing the plaintiff with any independent board of officers or advisers to pass upon the wisdom of the purchase and without disclosing the substance of the transaction and their extraordinary profit to the purchasers of its stock for cash at par. This scheme was an entity, one part of it was just as essential as any other part, and one part was the procurement of $500,000 in cash from the unenlightened public as a working capital for the new company.

It has been decided, apparently by a unanimous court, that such a transaction creates a liability on the part of the defendant to account for his profits to the plaintiff in this proceeding. Hayward v. Leeson, 176 Mass. 310. One of the present suits was before the court as reported in 188 Mass. 315, and after an elaborate review of the authorities and examination of the grounds for judgment, it was held that the defendant was liable, notwithstanding the opposing decision on the precise point by the United

States Circuit Court in Old Dominion Copper Mining & Smelting Co. v. Lewisohn, 136 Fed. Rep. 915. Since the decision reported in 188 Mass. 315, the above entitled case against Lewisohn has been considered by the United States Circuit Court of Appeals (148 Fed. Rep. 1020) and by the Supreme Court of the United States (210 U. S. 206) and without dissent a conclusion has been reached contrary to that of this court. The deference due to a decision by the highest court in the land and the intrinsic importance of the question at issue require a reconsideration of our own cases, a re-examination of the authorities and a careful consideration of the principles involved.

The plaintiff seeks to recover a secret profit made by the promoters in the sale of their own property to the corporation, basing its claim on the general and well recognized proposition that a promoter cannot take lawfully a secret profit and will be held to account for it if he does.[1)] Fundamentally the action is to recover profits obtained by a breach of trust. There is a distinct finding by the single justice that the defendant and Lewisohn were the promoters of the plaintiff. This finding is amply justified by the evidence. In their brains it was conceived, by their direction the formalities of its incorporation were carried out, their resources provided its mines, their influence and reputation with those desiring to invest in mines procured its working cash capital. The word "promoter" has no precise and inflexible meaning in this country. In England it is defined by statute. St. 7 & 8 Vict. c. 110, s. 3. See also St. 30 & 31 Vict. c. 131, s. 38. But even there the duties of promoters as fiduciaries to the company are matters of common law cognizance. Erlanger v. New Sombrero Phosphate Co. 3 App. Cas. 1218, 1269. In a comprehensive sense "promoter" includes those who undertake to form a corporation and to

1) Parker v. Nickerson, 112 Mass. 195, 196. Parker v. Nickerson, 137 Mass. 487 , 497. Bagnall v. Carlton, 6 Ch. D. 371. Emma Silverman Mining v.Co. v. Grant, 11 Ch. D. 918, 936. Nant-y-Glo Grave, 12 Ch. D. 738. Lyndney & Wigpool Iron Co. v. Bird, 33 Chandler D. 85. Whaley Bridge Calico Printing Co. v. Green, 5 Q. v. Bacon, 30 Fed. Rep. 538. Yale Gas Stove Co. v. Wilcox, 64 Conn. 101, 119, 120. Hinkley v. Sac Oil Pipe Line Co. 132 Iowa, 396, 402, 403. Fred Macey Co. v. Macey, 143 Mich. 138, 152. Zinc Carbonate Co. v. First National Bank of Shullsburg, 103 Wis. 125. Pietsch v. Milbrath, 123 Wis. 647. Cox v. Coal Oil Investment Co. 61 W. Va. 291, 305.

procure for it the rights, instrumentalities and capital by which it is to carry out the purposes set forth in its charter, and to establish it as fully able to do its business. Their work may begin long before the organization of the corporation, in seeking the opening for a venture and projecting a plan for its development, and may continue after the incorporation by attracting the investment of capital in its securities and providing it with the commercial breath of life. It is now established without exception that a promoter stands in a fiduciary relation to the corporation in which he is interested, and that he is charged with all the duties of good faith which attach to other trusts. In this respect he is held to the high standards which bind directors and other persons occupying fiduciary relations.[2)] That the promoter stands in the relation of a fiduciary to the corporation which he organizes seems to be conceded in Old Dominion Copper Mining & Smelting Co. v. Lewisohn, 210 U. S. 206. The questions to be answered are, whether this rule is applicable, and if it is, whether the plaintiff is in a position to assert its claim.

Notwithstanding this fiduciary relation the promoter may sell property to the company which he is promoting. But in order that the contract may be absolutely binding he must pursue one of four courses : (a) He may provide an independent board of officers in no respect directly or indirectly under his control, and make full disclosure to the corporation through them ; (b) He may make a full disclosure of all material facts to each original subscriber of shares in the corporation ; (c) He may procure a ratification of the contract after disclosing its circumstances by vote of the stockholders of the completely established corporation ; (d) He may be himself the real subscriber of all the shares of the capital stock contemplated as a part of the promotion scheme. The defendant does not contend upon this report that either of the first

2) Dickerman v. Northern Trust Co. 176 U. S. 181, 202. Yeiser v. United States Board 4' Paper Co. 107 Fed. Rep. 340. Chafe v. Berkley, 141 Iowa, 344. Getty v. Devlin, 54 N. Y. 403; S. C. 70 N. Y. 504. Loudenslager v. Woodbury Heights Land Co. 13 Dick. 556, 560. Exter v. Sawyer, 146 Mo. 302, 322. Johnson v. Sheridan Lumber Co. 51 Ore. 35. Camden Land Co. v. Lewis, 101 Maine, 78. Cox v. Coal Oil Investment Co. 61 W. Va. 291, 305. The Telegraph v. Loetscher, 127 Iowa, 383. Hayward v. Leeson, 176 Mass. 310, and cases cited at p. 318.

two courses was followed. He does rest his claim chiefly upon the third and fourth courses. As applied to the facts of this case these two come to the same thing, for the reason that on the findings of the single justice the defendant and his associate were subscribers for only one hundred and thirty thousand shares out of a total one hundred and fifty thousand and in the light most favorable to them they held all the shares which had been issued at the time of the ratification, but not all which it was proposed to issue as a part of the scheme of promotion. The point to be determined, therefore, is whether the promoter is immune from liability if he and his associates are owners of all the issued stock at the time of the act complained of, although intending as a part of their plan the immediate issue of further stock to the public without disclosure, and whether, while a substantial portion of the stock intended to be issued to the public remains unissued, a vote of ratification of the breach of trust will protect him.

A review of the authorities seems to demonstrate that there is a liability of the promoter to the corporation when further original subscribers to capital stock contemplated as an essential part of the scheme of promoters came in after the transaction complained of, even though that transaction is known to all the then stockholders, that is to say, to the promoters and their representatives.

Erlanger v. New Sombrero Phosphate Co. 3 App. Cas. 1218, is one of the most important and thoroughly considered cases, and, as it has been said to be a case often misunderstood (Lord Davey in Salomon v. Salomon, [1897] A. C. 22, 57), it is well to consider it at length. It was first heard by Vice-Chancellor Malins under the name of New Sombrero Phosphate Co. v. Erlanger (5 Ch. D. 73), then by the justices of appeal (5 Ch. D. 102), and finally by the House of Lords, where it was twice argued. The facts were these: Erlanger and his associates, hereafter spoken of as the syndicate, bought of the official liquidator of a broken down company the lease of a phosphate island, for $55,000. The agreement for purchase was signed on September 11, and was subject to the approval of the judge, which was given on September 15, 1871. By its terms the contract was to be completed on November 15, 1871. The syndicate then organized the New Sombrero Phosphate Company under St. 25 & 26 Vict. c. 89 (3 App. Cas. 1264). The articles of association of the new corporation were signed on September 20, 1871, and the company registered on September 20 or 21 (5 Ch. D. 76). On registration the corporation was created under 25 & 26 Vict. c. 89, s. 18 of which provided that upon registration "the subscribers . . . shall thereupon be a body corporate . . . capable forthwith of exercising all the functions of an incorporated company." The signers of the articles of association were tools of the syndicate. The members of the first board of directors were named in the articles of association. Two were out of the country and would not attend meetings; others were an employee of Erlanger, a retired admiral of the English navy, whose shares necessary to qualify him as a director were paid for by Erlanger (5 Ch. D. 107, 108), and the mayor of London; three directors made a quorum, and the last three named attended the meetings. The syndicate anticipated its payments required by its contract and acquired the lease of the island on September 21, 1871. The first meeting of the directors was held on September 29, 1871, at which was produced and approved by resolution an agreement between one Evans (in whose name in behalf of the syndicate the contract for the purchase of the lease from the official liquidator was made), and one Pavy (acting for the new company), dated September 20, whereby Evans sold and Pavy for the company bought the lease of the island for 80,000 in cash and $30,000 in paid up stock. In the discussion of this case in 210 U. S. at p. 216 this contract is stated to have been " provisional on the shares being taken and the company formed," but we do not so understand it as set forth in 5 Ch. D. 75, 76 and 95. It was subject to the new company being registered (which was done on September 20 or 21), and to the contract with the official liquidator being approved by the judge (which was done on September 15) and duly performed (which was done on September 21) and to the confirmation by the company (which was given by vote of the directors on September 29, who were in this regard clothed by the articles of association with all the authority of the corporation itself, 3 App. Cas. 1273, 1274), but it contained no other provisional features. The directors adopted the contract between Evans and Pavy without investigation into its merits, and in ignorance of the profit made by the syndicate except as Evans had such knowledge. After this the public oversubscribed. The stock was issued, $30,000 to the syndicate and $100,000 to the public; and on November 2 $80,000 was paid to the syndicate by the company. 5 Ch. D. 96. Respecting this agreement for sale by the syndicate it is further said in 210 U. S. at p. 217, that "the contract seems to have reached forward to the moment when they [the public] subscribed. As it is put in 2 [1 is meant] Morawetz, Corp. (2d ed.) s. 292, there was really no company till the shares were issued," and on this ground it is stated by the court at p. 216 that the English case "seems to us far from establishing a different doctrine for that jurisdiction." We cannot accede to this interpretation. The company was fully formed the moment it was registered. The subscription for the shares required as a prerequisite to registration under the English statute established the company as fully as the forty shares subscribed and the $1,000 for capital stock, paid into the plaintiff's treasury on or before July 11, 1895, established it. It was enabled to make any contract within the scope of its powers. That is settled by the plain language of 25 & 26 Vict. c. 89, s. 18, quoted above. But it also has been expressly so decided. It was said in Salomon v. Salomon, [1897] A. C. 22, at p. 51: "When the memorandum is duly signed and registered, though there be only seven shares taken, the subscribers are a body corporate ' capable forthwith,' to use the words of the enactment, 'of exercising all the functions of an incorporated company.' Those are strong words. The company attains maturity on its birth. There is no period of minority - no interval of incapacity." This apparently demonstrates the error of the further statement in 1 Morawetz, Corp. (2d ed.) 279, that "Before any shares were issued the existence of the corporation was a fiction." The remark of Lord Cairns (3 App. Cas. at p. 1239) to the effect that the contract for the sale of the island was " provisional on the shares being taken and the company completely formed" was made in connection with the de- fense of laches and not in the discussion as to the liability of the defendants (which he had concluded on an earlier page), and refers only to the fact that the scheme of the defendants to get 80,000 in cash out of the new company under their contract with it was dependent as a practical matter on the shares being taken by the public, and does not and cannot apply to the phraseology of the contract itself, for respecting that it is not correct. The only conditions named in the contract were that the company should be registered and confirm the contract and the contract of the syndicate with the official liquidator be performed. (See 5 Ch. D. 75, 76 and 95.) The distinction which appears to be established between the Erlanger case and the present one, by the decision of the United States Supreme Court, 210 U. S. 206, is that if the promoters organize a company with a capital of $3,750,000 00 and sell to it through their dummy directors property bought by them for this purpose, for $3,250,000, in paid up shares, and then get by public subscription $500,000 for working capital, the transaction is valid. But if promoters, having bought property for $55,000, organize a company with a capital of 130,000, and while they are the only bona fide stockholders by vote of their directors sell to it their property for 110,000, to be paid $80,000 in cash and $30,000 in paid up shares, 100,000 being subscribed in cash by the public, the transaction is void. The only difference between the two cases is that in the Erlanger case the promoters were paid a part of the purchase price in money, the proceeds of public subscription, and received paid up shares, which they took in payment of the balance of the purchase price when the stock was issued to subscribers, while in the present case the whole purchase price was paid in stock, which was issued before any stock was issued to the public although after a substantial public subscription. In other words, the order in which the transaction is carried out, and not its substantial nature, makes the difference between liability and immunity of the promoter. It is true that in the Erlanger case, until after ratification by the company of the contract previously made in its behalf for the purchase of the lease of the island, the mayor of London by acting as a director was liable to take shares of stock and intended to, and did subsequently, take and pay for fifty shares. He and possibly one other (3 App. Cas. 1228) appear to have been the only persons up to that time connected with the company, who subsequently became stockholders, who were not agents of the promoters. But it is also the fact (as stated by Jessel, M. R., in 5 Ch. D. at p. 112) that "Up to this time there was not really a single bona fide shareholder distinct from the promoters," and of course all these assented to the transaction. If this is a vital circumstance, that case is distinguishable in principle from the one at bar and from the case decided by the United States Supreme Court. This appears to us to be a difference upon an immaterial matter. It is of no consequence whether in fact the dummy directors know of the terms of sale and the breach of trust of the promoters. It does not appear in the present case that the nominees of Bigelow and Lewisohn knew any more about the profit the latter were making than did the directors of the New Sombrero Company of the profits of the syndicate. The point is that in both cases the directors were selected with the purpose that they should be the mere instruments of the promoters, and they carried out the will of their masters. Under the English statute the instruments of the promoters in the New Sombrero Company, while its directors, were as fully clothed with all the powers of the corporation and as much the holders of all its stock as were the seven directors of the plaintiff holding in all forty shares of the plaintiff at the time the contract of sale in the present case was made. If the assent of all the stockholders is good in the one case, by the same token it should be equally good in the other; and the breach of trust in the one is equally a breach of trust in the other. This case seems to us an authority in favor of the plaintiff.

In New Sombrero Phosphate Co. v. Erlanger, 5 Ch. D. 73,123, it was said by Baggallay, L. J.: " The syndicate were, in substance, not only the vendors of the property, but also the promoters of the company, and in such a case the syndicate, as promoters, being in a fiduciary relation to the company, it was essential that the public, who were invited to become, and who were expected to become, the shareholders of the company, and to constitute the company, should have the fullest information as to all the surrounding circumstances." See also Jessel, M. R., S. C. at p. 113. In In re British Seamless Paper Box Co. 17 Ch. D. 467, at p. 471, it was said by Jessel, M. R.: "If promoters make an arrangement to get a profit for themselves out of what is apparently paid to the vendors, it is immaterial whether the contract with the vendors is approved of by the directors of the company, who are the promoters, just before the allotment or just after : in both cases it is intended to cheat the future shareholders ; and of course it makes no difference whatever that the persons who, at the time the allotment was made, were in fact the promoters or their nominees, knew of the fraud. You can defraud future allottees as well as present allottees." In the same case on appeal Cotton, L. J., said (17 Ch. D. at p. 479): "The directors stand in a fiduciary relation to the whole company, that is, not only to the existing members but to all whom they intend to bring in." In Broderip v. Salomon, [1895] 2 Ch. 323, at p. 329, it was said by Vaughan Williams, J. (whose conclusion was approved in S. C. sub nomine Salomon v. Salomon, [1897] A. C. 22): " Of course, purchasing at an exorbitant price may be a fraud, even if all the shareholders know of it, if there is an intention to allot further shares at a later period to future allottees." This point was apparently left open in the House of Lords, [1897] A. C. at p. 37. In In re Leeds J. Hanley Theatres of Varieties, [1902] 2 Ch. 809, at p. 823, occurs this language: "At first there were only four directors . . . and the seven necessary signatories of the memorandum of the association.

When it is said that the promoters stood in a fiduciary position towards the company, that does not mean that they stood in such a relation to these directors and these seven signatories. It means that they stood in a fiduciary relation to the future allottees of shares - to the persons who were invited to come and take up the shares of the company." In Gluckstein v. Barnes, [1900] A. C. 240, 257, Lord Robertson says : " The people for whom these gentlemen [the promoters] were bound to act were their coming constituents, the persons out of whose money they proposed to make their gain." In Densmore Oil Co. v. Densmore, 64 Penn. St. 43, at p. 50, it is said : " Where persons form such an association, or begin or start the project of one, from that time they do stand in a confidential relation to each other, and to all others who may subsequently become members or subscribers, and it is not competent, for any of them to purchase property for the purposes of such a company, and then sell it at an advance without a full disclosure of the facts." This language is quoted with approval and applied in Burbank v. Dennis, 101 Cal. 90, 98, and in South Joplin Land Co. v. Case, 104 Mo. 572, 580. To the same point, Pittsburg Mining Co. v. Spooner, 74 Wis. 307, 321-323. In Pietsch v. Milbrath, 123 Wis. 647, at p. 656, it is held that "Persons who act as promoters of a corporation do not necessarily cease to be such when the corporation is organized to do business. . . . So long as there are prospective original subscribers for stock and the promoters and those concerting with them remain in control of the corporation, it is in a position to be deceived. . . . It is deceived in a legal sense when it is rendered helpless by its managers as to protecting those invited to subscribe for its stock, and is then used to aid in defrauding them." This is supported by Fred Macey Co. v. Macey, 143 Mich. 138, 152, a case singularly like the one at bar in its essential features, where relief was granted to the corporation against the promoters although they subscribed for all the capital stock. Other cases which in principle reach the same result are Yeiser v. United States Board 4 Paper Co. 107 Fed. Rep. 340, 348 ; London Trust Co. v. Mackenzie, 62 L. J. Ch. (N. S.) 870 ; Hinkley v. Sac Oil Pipe Line Co. 132 Iowa, 396. It was said in Groel v. United Electric Co. 4 Robbins, 616, 622: "There can be no question that promoters are liable to the corporation for profits secretly made by them in its promotion, and that such liability arises in cases where future allottees of stock are concerned. Knoop v. Bohmrich, 4 Dick. 82. Plaquemines Tropical Fruit Co. v. Buck, 7 Dick. 219. Loudenslager v. Woodbury Heights Land Co. 13 Dick. 556, affirming the principle established in the court of chancery in Woodbury Heights Land Co. v. Loudenslager, 10 Dick. 78." In Central

Trust Co. v. East Tennessee Land Co. 116 Fed. Rep. 743, and Camden Land Co. v. Lewis, 101 Maine, 78, 95, Hayward v. Leeson, 176 Mass. 310 , to this point is cited with approval. St. Louis, Fort Scott & Wichita Railroad v. Tiernan, 37 Kans. 606, and Stewart v. St. Louis, Fort Scott j. Wichita Railroad, 41. Fed. Rep. 736, were both decided on the assumption that the promoters took all the stock, although it appears that later some stock was issued to municipalities through which the tracks of the promoted railroad corporation ran, but whether as a part of the original plan of promotion does not appear, and no weight is attached to this circumstance in the opinions. Numerous other cases which have been cited do not bear upon this point for the reason that in each of them the owners of the property conveyed have owned either the entire capital stock of the corporation or all that it was contemplated to issue. See Foster v. Seymour, .3 Fed. Rep. 65; McCracken v. Robison, 57 Fed. Rep. 375; Barr v. New York, Lake Erie ' Western Railroad, 125 N. Y. 263; Blum v. Whitney, 185 N. Y. 232. In re Ambrose Lake Tin J. Copper Mining Co. 14 Ch. D. 390; Salomon v. Salomon, [1897] A. C. 22; In re British Seamless Paper Box Co. 17 Ch. D. 467; Seymour v. Spring Forest Cemetery Association, 144 N. Y. 333; Hutchinson v. Simpson, 92 App. Div. (N. Y.) 382; Tompkins v. Sperry, 96 Md. 560; Langdon v. Fogg, 18 Fed. Rep. 5, Flagler Engraving Machine Co. v. Flagler, 19 Fed. Rep. 468 ; Insurance Press v. Montauk Fire Detecting Wire Co. 103 App. Div. (N. Y.) 472 ; Higgins v. Lansingh, 154 111. 301; In re Baglan Hall Colliery Co. L. R. 5 Ch. 346. In all these cases it was also true that no shares were ever issued (so far as appears) other than those to the promoters, except that in In re British Seamless Paper Box Co. 17 Ch. D. 467, at a time considerably subsequent to the organization of the corporation, a change in the scheme was made in good faith by which others were brought in as subscribers.

In this respect the question is one of intention of the promoters. If they actually intend at the time the company is brought out to remain its sole owners and that it shall not receive the money of innocent shareholders in the future, then although thereafter the exigencies of the company may be such as to require the issue of additional stock, they may not be responsible. In re British Seamless Paper Box Co. 17 Ch. D. 467, is an illustration of this principle. There it was found that the promoters were and intended to remain the sole proprietors of the property of the company and the sole members of the company. Cotton, L. J., at p. 479, said : " Here it is an established fact that when the company was formed it was intended to be a private company, that is, it was intended to carry it on without calling in the public, or issuing any shares except to the then existing shareholders. Therefore the doctrine that directors may not take a profit for themselves is inapplicable, because all the members knew that they intended to make a profit. It is true that some new members were subsequently taken in. If shortly after this transaction a prospectus had been issued and the public had been invited to come in and take shares, no court would have listened to directors who said that it was not intended to take in fresh members. But this was commenced and carried on entirely as a private company, and a considerable time elapsed before they asked anyone to join them."

In Wills v. Nehalem Coal Co. 52 Ore. 70, a corporation was organized by promoters with a capital of 8150,000. More than half was issued to promoters and their tools in return for property of one of them conveyed at an overvaluation. Afterwards shares were sold to the public without disclosure of the great profit made by promoters. Relief was granted. The contention that the corporation had assented with full knowledge of the facts by all who were the stockholders at the time of the sale was disposed of on the ground that in substance a wrong was done the corporation in diminishing the common fund held for the benefit of all the stockholders by issuing a part of its capital stock for property worth less than its face value. In Richlands Oil Co. v. Morriss, 108 Va. 288, the facts as stated in the opinion were that the promoters, having acquired the control of certain oil leases for an insignificant price, " proceeded to transfer these leases to a company which they organized upon a capitalization of 1,000,000 shares (the par value of each share being $1), and distributed 600,000 of those shares to themselves;

and having perfected the organization of the company by making themselves the president, secretary, treasurer, and directors undertook to market the residue of the shares of stock, amounting to 400,000, without informing the public as to the true condition of affairs." The suit of the corporation was upheld. Upon the point we are now discussing these two cases are indistinguishable in principle from the cases at bar.

This review of decisions seems to establish abundantly the proposition that promoters stand in a fiduciary position toward the corporation, as well when as a part of the scheme of promotion uninformed stockholders are expected to come in after the wrong has been perpetrated, as when at that time there are shareholders to whom no disclosure is made. We find no authority opposed except the Lewisohn cases in the federal courts (210 U. S. 206).

If the question is examined on principle apart from authority, the same result appears clear. The starting point is that a promoter is a fiduciary to the corporation. To use the words of Lord Cairns in Erlanger v. New Sombrero Phosphate Co. 3 App. Cas. 1218, at p. 1236: Promoters " have in their hands the creation and moulding of the company: they have power of defining how, and when, and in what shape, and under what supervision, it shall start into existence and begin business." The corporation is in the hands of the promoter like clay in the hands of the potter. It is to this person, absolutely helpless and incapable of independent initiative or uncontrolled action, that the promoter stands as trustee. It is not necessary to inquire how far he may be trustee also for shareholders or associates. In the present case the inquiry relates wholly to his obligation to the corporation. The fiduciary relation must in reason continue until the promoter has completely established according to his plan the being which he has undertaken to create. His liability must be commensurate with the scheme of promotion on which he has embarked. If the plan contemplates merely the organization of the corporation his duties may end there. But if the scheme is more ambitious and includes beside the incorporation, not only the conveyance to it of property but the procurement of a working capital in cash from the public, then the obligation of faithfulness stretches to the length of the plan. It would be a vain thing for the law to say that the promoter is a trustee subject to all the stringent liabilities which inhere in that character and at the same time say that, at any period during his trusteeship and long before an essential part of it was executed or his general duty as such ended, he could, by changing for a moment the cloak of the promoter for that of director or stockholder, by his own act alone, absolve himself from all past, present or future liability in his capacity as promoter. The plaintiff was fully organized and authorized to do business on July 8 and 11, 1895, when only $1,000 in capital stock had been paid in. It would be an idle ceremony indeed to establish for promoters the obligations of trustees, and at the same time hold that by their tools and with only $1,000 paid in, and that as a mere form (for it was soon after repaid to one of them) they could vote to themselves a wholly unwarranted profit of $1,250,000, kept secret from other initial shareholders, because at that moment they were the only stockholders. By such a course the law would be holding out apples of Sodom to the wronged corporation. Corporations can be formed through irresponsible agents with ease. If these agents can vote away a substantial part of the capital stock for property of comparatively small value, and still with immunity to themselves and their principals receive from the uninformed public cash subscriptions for the rest of the capital stock, the organization and management of corporations might readily become a "system of frauds." Peabody v. Flint, 6 Allen 52, 55. It is answered that the plaintiff has assented to the transaction with full knowledge of the facts. But it has not assented when it stood where it could act independently. The assent to the wrongful act of the promoters was given at the behest and by vote of the promoters themselves, while still occupying the position of protectors to their own creature, while it was bound hand and foot by them and prevented from taking any action except through them as a step in its further exploitation, and while their trust was uncompleted. The corporation although by law fully organized was still in its swaddling clothes, so far as the plans of the promoters were concerned. The value of their stock taken in return for their mining property was dependent in a substantial degree upon the corporation having $500,000 in cash for a working capital. They could not perfect their plans nor reap their contemplated profit, except by retaining their hold upon the corporation until the public had made this contribution. In one sense it is true that the plaintiff was completely organized on July 11 and on September 20, 1895. It was fully competent to be bound by its contracts and ratification of contracts with those dealing with it at arm's length. But it was not free from its wardship to its promoters, whose scheme from the first looked forward to a corporation with treasury filled by subscriptions from the unenlightened public. The corporation was not dealing with these fiduciaries upon an independent ground. The plaintiff, although a legal corporation from July 8, leaned wholly upon its promoters, because they made it so to lean, until long after the events here in controversy. An assent under these conditions can be of no greater effect than the assent of a minor under guardianship to the breaches of trust of his guardian.

The situation is akin to the conveyance of property by a man solvent but in contemplation of insolvency. Such conveyance is not wrong until the contemplated indebtedness is incurred which makes him an insolvent. Then the executed evil intent stretches back and invalidates the original conveyance. Here the conveyance to the corporation with the secret profit, when there are no uninformed subscribers to stock, if nothing more is ever done, is not an actionable tort. But the vicious intent looks forward to the procurement of money from the ignorant public by means of original subscriptions and the execution of this evil intent extends backward to contaminate the sale and its profit.

Stress has sometimes been laid upon the fact that the promoters were paid a part of their purchase price out of the public subscriptions. But there is no difference in principle between such a case and the present, where a substantial part of the value of the stock taken by the defendant and

Lewisohn depended upon the cash subscriptions to be made by the public for the remaining shares not issued to the promoters.

But it is further argued that, the entire capital stock outstanding at the time being' in the hands of the promoters, the sale of the property to the corporation was merely changing the form of title of the promoters from owners of real estate to that of shares of stock, and that, there being then no other shareholders, no wrong was done. It has been decided that where persons own the entire authorized capital stock of the company and take it in payment for the conveyance of their property at a grossly exaggerated price, nobody can be heard to complain. The leading English cases upon this point are In re Gold Co. 11 Ch. D. 701, In re Ambrose Lake Tin & Copper Mining Co. 14 Ch. D. 390, In re British Seamless Paper Box Co. 17 Ch. D. 467, and Salomon v. Salomon, [1897] A. C. 22. But these and many other like cases cited on pages 185 and 186 ante are where the promoters owned all the outstanding capital stock and intended to remain the sole proprietors and did not purpose that there should be, as a part of the promotion plan, a substantial issue of stock for cash to the public. This is pointed out in London Trust Co. v. Mackenzie, 62 L. J. Ch. (N. S.) 870, 875. The distinction is clear between cases of that class and those like the present, where the promoters took for themselves a large number of shares of stock without adequate consideration and without disclosure to the detriment of the corporation and all its future shareholders, at the same time planning that there should be immediate public subscriptions. It is one thing to take all the shares of a corporation in payment for physical property conveyed. It does not much matter to the stockholders in such a case whether the total is one hundred and thirty thousand shares or one hundred and fifty thousand shares. But it is a very different thing to take 130,000/150,000 of capital stock of a corporation whose assets consist of the same physical property, and in addition $500,000 in money subscribed by others. The latter course affects the other stockholders and the corporation itself, and it gives the promoters something appreciably more valuable than what they contribute. It is true that in Salomon v. Salomon and in some other cases there was a part of the authorized capital stock which was not issued, but it was not proposed to be issued as a part of the scheme of promotion and the original shareholders intended to remain the only shareholders. It was to be issued or not in the remote future, as the exigencies of the corporation in the actual conduct of its business might require, but, in any event, it was not to be issued for the purpose of starting the corporation on its course. This circumstance materially affects the question here to be considered. Most, if not all, corporation laws provide in some form for an increase of capital stock. It is of no consequence upon such a point as this, whether the capital stock originally authorized is large but not all issued or whether it is at first small and subsequently an increase is authorized. This seems to be the view taken by the English courts, for it is said by James, L. J., in In re British Seamless Paper Box Co. 17 Ch. D. 467, " If they [the promoters] were intending, although then constituting the whole company, that other people should come in afterwards to whom what had been done would be injurious, the court would feel no difficulty in saying as Lord Langdale did in Society of Practical Knowledge v. Abbott, 2 Beav. 559, that they intended to commit a fraud."

The fundamental reasoning upon which these cases can rest is not that no wrong has been committed, but there is no one to enforce the remedy. All courts recognize the soundness of the doctrine that no man can be on both sides of the same bargain with justice to all interests. The principle that one cannot rightfully sell property, belonging to him in his private right, to himself in a trust capacity is universal.

If this aspect alone is looked at and the corporation is regarded as a distinct person, it cannot be said that the corporation is not wronged by such a breach of duty by promoters. It is only when the corporate personality is disregarded and its component elements as stockholders alone are considered that it can be said that no harm is done on the ground (as was said in Salomon v. Salomon, [1897] A. C. at p. 57) that " the company is bound in a matter intra vires by the unanimous agreement of its members." But looking through the form of the corporation to the stockholders and treating them as the corporation is an exception to the otherwise firmly established universal rule that the corporation is a separate legal entity for all purposes, even though all its stock be held by a single interest and it be to all practical intents merely the instrument of the stockholder. Conley v. Mathieson Alkali Works, 190 U. S. 406. Peterson v. Chicago, Rock Island & Pacific Railway, 205 U. S. 364, 390. We perceive no reason for extending this exception to a case like the present.

The real ground of the decisions of which Salomon v. Salomon is a type is that the corporation is estopped by the circumstance that all persons with financial concern in the matter have assented with knowledge, and thus the lips of everybody are sealed. It is not that no wrong has been done, but that whatever wrong has been done has been condoned. The maxim "Volenti non fit injuria" is invoked. This, however, is setting up confession and avoidance and not a bar to the main cause of action.

The theory upon which corporations are founded is that they are artificial persons, distinct and separate from officers and stockholders. Corporate liabilities do not attach to the latter. The wrong which the defendant and his associate did in this case was in selling property worth intrinsically \$1,000,000 and in the market at most \$2,000,000 for \$3,250,000 without revealing that they were making a secret profit. The wrong was done to the corporation. It affected all its shareholders, present and future alike. It is generally admitted that if there are existing stockholders ignorant of the wrong, redress may be had. But it is had through the corporation or for the benefit of the corporation and not by the stockholder in his own right. The wrong is not done to the shareholders as individuals, nor to the shareholders collectively, it is done to the corporation as an independent being, and thus indirectly the rights of those who are or who may become stockholders are affected. In buying the promoters' mine, the directors of the corporation acted for the corporation, as such, without regard to who were the then stockholders, or even if there were no stockholders. Whoever becomes an originally contemplated shareholder coming in afterwards has as much right to say that the rights of the corporation were not protected and to insist that it should assert its remedy for the wrong done it, as one in at first but not informed. Subsequent subscriptions to original stock as a part of the scheme of promotion do not change the identity of the corporation, but remove an impediment to the enforcement of a remedy for a wrong previously done the corporation. The wrong is not done when the innocent public subscribes, but when the sale was made to the corporation at a grossly exaggerated price with secret profit. The occasion for complaining of this wrong comes when the promoters issue to the public the balance of the stock in order to provide the money necessary to set the corporation on its feet and to give thereby the contemplated value to the stock taken by themselves in payment for their mines. The exemption of the promoter from liability to the corporation for a sale without disclosure when he takes the entire issue of capital stock is an exception to the general rule imposing upon him the liabilities of a trustee. If this exception is to be extended to a case like the present, it leaves nothing of substantial value in the original rule. It might still reach small and grosser forms of want of fidelity to corporations, but would leave unharmed the vastly greater and more refined variety illustrated by the present case. It would point the way to general immunity for the wary.

It is also urged that the maintenance of this suit works an injustice to the defendant in requiring a repayment to the corporation, which will result in a benefit to the thirteen fifteenths of the capital stock taken by the defendant and Lewisohn (who condoned the wrong) as well as to the two fifteenths subscribed for by the innocent public. The size of the repayment which may be required of the defendant is due to the enormous profit taken at the outset. Apart from the unjust profit taken by the promoters, their interest in the plaintiff was only eight seventeenths, or, tested by the cost and intrinsic value of the property conveyed, four seventeenths. The true answer, however, is given by Jessel, M. R., in New Sombrero Phosphate Co. v. Erlanger, 5 Ch. D. 73, at p. 114. "It is said that is not doing justice, and that the suit cannot be maintained in this form, because it will not do justice. But that argument goes too far, because it would apply to a case of the grossest fraud in every instance in which one or more of the actual shareholders of a company took part in that fraud. If the argument were once allowed to prevail, it would only be necessary to corrupt one single shareholder in order to prevent a company from ever setting the contract aside. It may be said you give to the shareholder, who was a party to the fraud, a profit, because he will take it in respect of his shares, and since as between co-conspirators there is no contribution, therefore his brother conspirators, who are made liable for the fraud, cannot make him repay his proportion. But the doctrine of this court has never been to hold its hand and avoid doing justice in favor of the innocent, because it cannot apportion the punishment fully amongst the guilty. A dozen parties to a fraud may be defendants, and one decree or judgment go against all, and if it is a fraud of such a character that none of them can bring an action for contribution, the plaintiff may at his will and pleasure enforce that judgment against any one of them, and perhaps pass over the most guilty of them; still there is no remedy as between those who commit the fraud. It is one of the punishments of fraud that there is no such remedy, and that a guilty party, though not the most guilty, may suffer the greatest amount of punishment. It is one of the deterrents to men to prevent their committing fraud." See also Stockton v. Anderson, 13 Stew. (N. J.) 486.

It is said further that the result reached is harsh from the business man's point of view. A discussion of this aspect of the case involves ethical considerations. Courts are constantly dealing with the various relations of the business world. Legal principles are applied to these transactions, but such principles "have almost always been the fundamental ethical rules of right and wrong."

Robinson v. Mollett, L. R. 7 H. L. 802, 817. Upon its distinctly moral side, there is little to the credit of the defendant and his associate. The offering by the defendant as promoter for public subscription for cash at par a substantial part of the capital stock of a corporation, the rest of whose capital stock had been issued for property conveyed to it under a law which permitted such stock to be issued only for the real value of property, was equivalent to a representation that no fictitious value had been placed upon the property so acquired. But the distinct finding of the single justice is that the real value was less than one third the price for which the defendant and Lewisohn sold it. Nothing can be said in support of a business enterprise carried on by promoters, which involves the purchase by them of mines, costing and intrinsically worth $1,000,000, with money in substantial part solicited from associates on representations that a corporation is to be formed with a capitalization of $2,500,000, of whose stock $2,000,000 is to be issued for the conveyance to it by them of the mines, and the rest for cash ; the actual organization of the corporation under the laws of a State which permitted the issuance of capital stock for property conveyed only to the real value of the property, with a capital stock of $3,750,000, of which $3,250,000 is issued as fully paid for the conveyance of the mines ; the settlement with a very great majority of the associates on the basis of a sale for $2,000,000 of stock as at first represented, the promoters retaining $1,250,000 of shares as a secret profit, intending also to procure from the public subscriptions for $500,000 of stock in cash at par and actually carrying out this purpose, the promoters themselves during all these manipulations having entire control of all executive offices of the corporation. In the absence of compelling authority, we cannot set the seal of judicial approval upon such business policies. See Bigelow v. Old Dominion Copper Mining & Smelting Co. 4 Buch. (N. J.), 71 Atl. Rep. at pp. 176 and 177.

Both on authority outside of our own cases and on principle, it appears to us that the defendant should be held liable. But in this jurisdiction the matter does not stand quite on the basis of an original proposition. In two thoroughly considered opinions in recent years, Hayward v.Leeson, 176 Mass. 310 , and Old Dominion Copper Mining & Smelting Co. v. Bigelow, 188 Mass. 315 , this court has held that liability existed in a case like this. It is not necessary to repeat the arguments of these decisions. There is thus added to considerations which otherwise exist, the force of the doctrine of stare decisis. One or both of these cases have frequently been cited by courts of other jurisdictions and always with approval until Old Dominion Copper Mining J. Smelting Co. v. Lewisohn, 148 Fed. Rep. 1020; S. C. 210 U. S. 206. No arguments have been adduced not considered in those cases, and no points now brought forward were not there discussed. While the rule of stare decisis does not prevent the overruling of those cases, they should not be disturbed unless they now appear to be so clearly wrong as to have no sound support. Mabardy v. McHugh, 202 Mass. 148 . It must appear that the law was "misunderstood or misapplied." 1 Kent Com. 475. There was no misconception of the points involved when these cases were decided, nor any lack of discernment in their application to the affairs of corporations. It does not appear that they have become archaic or inapplicable by reason of business evolution since they were announced. On the contrary, the tendency of custom since the first case was decided has been rather in the direction of more strict accountability of those owing duties to corporations and their stockholders. At all events, we perceive no occasion to relax these principles of accountability for breaches of trust. The mere fact that the Supreme Court of the United States has since decided the question differently is not alone a sufficient consideration for reversing our decisions. It is only when the reasoning of its decision is of convincing power and compels the conclusion that our cases were wrongly decided that it must command our support in other branches of the law than those where it is supreme under the Federal Constitution. With great respect to the decision in 210 U.S. 206, we are constrained to adhere to the law as laid down in the earlier cases in this Commonwealth.

We have discussed the question as if the same legal principles are involved now as were presented upon the demurrer. There are, however, certain aspects of the evidence which seem to us to make it essentially different and materially stronger for the plaintiff. When the votes to purchase the mines of the promoters were passed on July 11, only forty shares of stock had been subscribed for or issued. The votes were passed by the directors alone and there was no vote by the stockholders at this time. It is true that the directors comprised all the stockholders, but on that date they were acting wholly in their capacity as directors, that is, as trustees. They did not attempt, so far as any records show, to shift their character as trustees for that of individual stockholders. They did not pursue the careful course of separation of these dual capacities by calling a stockholders' meeting, which was followed in North-West Transportation Co. v. Beatty, 12 App. Cas. 589, nor did they assent in writing as stockholders. So far as the records show up to this point, there was only a directors' vote for the purchase. Moreover, the records of the plaintiff show that at the opening of this meeting only six of the seven directors were present. Four of these six directors resigned as did also the absent seventh director, their resignations were accepted and their successors were chosen. But of the five newly chosen directors, only two were present and took their seats. Thus there were four directors, a bare quorum and majority, present when the offers for the sale of the mines were presented and the votes for their purchase were passed. These votes to purchase were not consummated until December, 1895, and January, 1896, when the deeds were delivered to the plaintiff. The vote to issue the certificates of stock in payment for the conveyances of mines was passed on September 18, 1895. Under date of July 18, 1895, the only subscription list of the plaintiff was signed. Upon this list appear the names of those outside persons who subscribed for the $500,000 of working capital for the plaintiff. The money was paid by some of the outside stockholders before September 18, and at least as early as September 10, 1895. Stock certificates were made out for the number of shares allotted to each under date of September 18. The rights of all these persons as subscribers had become fixed at least as early as September 10, 1895, before which date the subscriptions were all received, and when notices of their acceptance and demands for payment were sent out. These circumstances amply support the finding of the single justice that issuance of the twenty thousand shares to the public was in the summer or fall of 1895. These stockholders were entitled to have a disclosure made to the corporation through independent officers. There is no pretense that any disclosure was made to these subscribers. On September 18, 1895, the directors of the plaintiff voted to issue the stock as before stated - thirty thousand shares to Bigelow and Lewisohn, one hundred thousand to their nominee Dumaresq, and there was made out the certificate for the remaining twenty thousand shares to " Thomas Nelson, Treasurer," and these four, professing to represent all the stock of the plaintiff, signed the written approval of all previous acts of the directors. This is the first attempt of the stockholders to act respecting this subject. As before pointed out, the certificate to Nelson was wrongfully issued; except as it belonged to outside subscribers, it was treasury stock. There were then other stockholders of the plaintiff who had paid for their stock, although they had not received their certificates, but the plaintiff had their money and they were entitled to be treated as stockholders. Chester Glass Co. v. Dewey, 16 Mass. 94. Chaffin v. Cummings, 37 Maine, 76. Hawes v. Anglo-Saxon Petroleum Co. 101 Mass. 385, 395. Their certificates were dated September 18, 1895, and issued directly. These circumstances show that at the first and only time when there was an effort on the part of the promoters to secure a ratification of their wrongful acts, there were certain shareholders who were not represented and who did not themselves sign in assent and who were in fact ignorant of the wrong done the corporation. Further, they do not show that at any time from the organization of the corporation onward was there a moment when all the stockholders or directors knew of the material facts as to the defendant's relation to the corporation. In this view of the facts, which is supported fully by the evidence, there appears to be no assent by the corporation with knowledge of the facts by all those who at any time constituted all the stockholders, except by assuming the knowledge of Bigelow and Lewisohn on July 11, 1895, when there were only forty shares of stock for which the latter had paid, to be the knowledge of all the stockholders, although there were then seven shareholders as to whose actual knowledge of the scheme there is no evidence, although all were the tools of the defendant and Lewisohn. It is only by treating these subscriptions as a sham that knowledge even of the owners of the forty shares can be found. But these subscriptions were necessary to the organization under the New Jersey law. Hence the rule of Salomon v. Salomon, [1897] A. C. 22, and like cases has no application to these facts, nor does the difficulty meet "the petitioner at the outset that it has assented to the transaction with the full knowledge of the facts," (210 U. S. 211, 212,) unless it is said that in fact knowledge by the plaintiff's dominant stockholders is knowledge by the corporation. But the defendant was committing a breach of trust on his principal, the plaintiff, and where one is committing a wrong in his own interest his knowledge does not bind the corporation, which might in an innocent transaction be affected by his knowledge. Indian Head National Bank v. Clark, 166 Mass. 27. Produce Exchange Trust Co. v. Bieberbach, 176 Mass. 577, 588. These considerations mark the case as different in material respects from that which was stated in Old Dominion Copper Mining & Smelting Co. v. Lewisohn, 210 U. S. 206, and bring it clearly within the well recognized rule of promoters' liability, laid down in the numerous and undisputed cases, before cited. The Supreme Court of the United States has never passed upon these facts nor upon such a case as is thus presented. We know of no authority which countenances a different decision upon them than that here reached. The conflict between the federal courts and this court in this respect appears to be not upon the merits of the case as disclosed upon the present record. See Bigelow v. Old Dominion Copper Mining & Smelting Co. 4 Buch. (N. J.), 71 Atl. Rep. 153, 175.

But there is still another aspect in which the case differs from that presented in the federal court and in our previous decision. The defendant held out to subscribers of his syndicate, before the incorporation of the plaintiff, that its capital stock was to be $2,500,000 and that they would get for one share in the Baltimore Company two in the new company and that the rest would be sold to furnish the working capital. The right of these parties to become stockholders in the plaintiff company was fixed before its first meeting of stockholders was held, because they had signed the syndicate agreement and had made two payments on account of their subscriptions. They were sharers thus in the profit of $1,000,000 above the costs of mines. But they were also entitled to disclosure of the secret profit of $1,250,000 more taken by the defendant and Lewisohn and it is found that most of them were ignorant of it. Respecting any sale to the plaintiff in which they had agreed to become shareowners on any other basis than that of two for one, they were entitled to disclosure. This is quite aside from any rights they may have had against Bigelow for not treating them fairly on the division of profits. It stands on different ground. In that relation they were sharers in promoters' profits and they received what they expected. But they had also agreed to be subscribers to stock of the plaintiff. In that character they were not promoters, but stockholders and entitled to all their rights. That they knew there was to be a sale for $2,000,000 and a profit of two for one was no reasonable ground for expectation that the defendant would take a large additional secret profit. As to this secret profit, the members of the syndicate had the same rights as the outside public, that is, they were entitled to a disclosure to an independent and impartial board of officers who should be in a position to act for the interests of the corporation as opposed to those of the promoters. In this regard the case is like Arnold v. Searing, 3 Buch. (N. J.) 262. where the defendants were held liable.

4. It is argued that, even though the ratification in writing be disregarded, still the acts of the stockholders of the plaintiff after some of them knew of the fact that there was some profit to Bigelow and Lewisohn beyond that accruing to all the other members of the syndicate has amounted to a ratification. The complete answer to this argument is that the single justice has found that until shortly before the bringing of these suits neither the stockholders nor the company had gained any knowledge as to the facts upon which the claim is now based, that the very great majority of the stockholders never knew or assented to the operations by which the secret profit was

obtained and did not have knowledge of or access to the books or records of the corporation. The votes of ratification of 1899 and 1901 being passed under these conditions do not bind the plaintiff.

5. Several other objections are made to the granting of relief to the plaintiff. It is urged that the plaintiff ought not to recover because, a large majority of its stock being held by a Maine corporation, an agreement has been entered into by that corporation and certain trustees by which it was attempted to provide for the conduct of these suits and sequestrate the proceeds to holders of negotiable certificates. But this agreement is one to which the plaintiff is not a party, and it was made long after these suits were instituted. If it is illegal, it may be set aside in appropriate proceedings, but the rights of the plaintiff for the benefit of all its stockholders cannot be refused enforcement on such ground.

6. The defence of laches cannot prevail. It is found as a fact that as soon as the defendant and his associates released their absolute control of the plaintiff, the action was seasonably begun. The plaintiff is held to the exercise of diligence after the discovery of the facts, but there can be no laches so long as there is no knowledge of the wrong complained of and no failure to avail one's self of reasonable opportunities to ascertain the facts. So long as the plaintiff was wholly in the power of the defendant, it could not be charged with knowledge. Mere lapse of time is no bar to relief under these circumstances. Lydney Wigpool Iron Ore Co. v. Bird, 33 Ch. D. 85. Lagunas Nitrate Co. v. Lagunas Syndicate, [1899] 2 Ch. D. 392, 433. Twin-Lick Oil Co. v. Marbury, 91 U. S. 587.

7. Nor is the statute of limitations a bar. The time limited by the statute does not begin to run against a breach of trust, where there is a fiduciary duty to disclose the facts on which the cause of action rests, until the facts have or ought to have been discovered. Atlantic National Bank v. Harris, 118 Mass. 147. R. L. c. 202, s. 11. The ground of the defendant's liability is his breach of trust as a promoter.

8. It follows from what has been said as to the nature of the wrong done

by the defendant that he is liable in solido. The act of the defendant and Lewisohn was a joint act for the benefit of both. Their subdivision of the profits made cannot affect the right of the plaintiff. The breach of trust, which they as promoters committed, was in the nature of a tort. This renders them liable severally as well as jointly and for the whole damage. Hayward v. Leeson, 176 Mass. 310, 324, and cases cited. 188 Mass. at p. 329. Feneff v. Boston J. Maine Railroad, 196 Mass. 575, 581. Gluckstin v. Barnes, [1900] A. C. 240. Bigelow v. Old Dominion Copper Mining & Smelting Co. 4 Buch. (N. J.), 71 Atl. Rep. 153, 176.

9. As to the character of relief which can be afforded, it is said first that rescission is the only remedy open to the petitioner. The single justice has found that the situation of the parties and the properties is not such as to make it just at this time to order a rescission. The evidence justifies this finding. It was decided in this case at its earlier stage, 188 Mass. 315, 329, that rescission is not the only remedy. Hayward v. Leeson, 176 Mass. 310, 321. Parker v. Nickerson, 137 Mass. 487 . We are not disposed to question the correctness of the decision upon this point. When one has committed a breach of trust, there is no occasion to be over-solicitous to see that the faithless fiduciary should not make reparation for the wrong done. In re Olympia, [1898] 2 Ch. 153, 169. Lyndney Wigpool Iron Ore Co. v. Bird, 33 Ch. D. 85, 94. The essence of the suit is that a secret profit was taken by the promoters. The obvious remedy is a return of the secret profit. The difficulty of ascertaining the amount of that profit, which troubled the court in In re Cape Breton Co. 29 Ch. D. 795 does not exist here. See Bentinck v. Fenn, 12 App. Cas. 652; Gluckstein v. Barnes, [1900] A. C. 240; In re Leeds & Hanley Theatres of Varieties, [1902] 2 Ch. 809; Yale Gas Stove Co. v. Wilcox, 64 Conn. 101.

10. The plaintiff has also appealed from the decrees in its favor. It presses its appeals on the ground that it is entitled to recover the difference between the market value of the shares received by the defendant and Lewisohn and the cost to them of the property conveyed to it. This is the measure of

recovery where there is a fiduciary relation at the time of the purchase. But there is no finding here that such relation existed at the time the defendant and Lewisohn purchased the property. There is no evidence which requires such a finding. The corporation was not organized until a considerable period after the options had been secured. The defendant and Lewisohn were, during all this time, free to do as they chose with their purchase so far as the plaintiff was concerned. This has been before decided, 188 Mass. 321. The plaintiff contends in the alternative that its measure of damage is the difference between the intrinsic value of the property conveyed and the value of the stock issued therefor. Market value is the standard commonly applied where property has such value. It is only in cases where the value of property cannot be fairly ascertained by the application of this test that resort is had to any other. The single justice appears to have experienced no difficulty in determining that value of these mines. There are no exceptional circumstances which call for the application of any other than the ordinary rule.

11. Since the decision of this case on demurrer, reported in 188 Mass. 315, and the entry of the decrees by the single justice after a full hearing upon the facts, the defendant has been permitted to file a supplementary answer. Old Dominion Copper Mining j. Smelting Co. v. Bigelow, 199 Mass. 488. He there sets up, as a bar to the plaintiff's claim, a judgment of the Circuit Court of the United States for the Southern District of New York, entered on July 23, 1908, in favor of the defendants in a suit like one of the present suits in all particulars, except that it was prosecuted against the executors of the will of Lewisohn, the defendants' demurrer to the plaintiff's bill being sustained and the final decree being entered, whereby the claim against Lewisohn was held to be without foundation, and he contends that the matter is thereby res judicata as to himself. The supplemental answer further avers that the issues were the same as those here involved, and that the present defendant was a privy to the judgment in that case, and participated in the defense, and acted with Lewisohn's executors throughout

the entire pendency of the suit. The Lewisohn suit was heard in the Circuit Court of the United States and on appeal in the United States Circuit Court of Appeals, and afterwards upon certiorari in the Supreme Court of the United States. 210 U. S. 206. On these supplemental answers a hearing was had before a single justice, who reserved questions arising thereon for the consideration of this court upon the pleadings and all the evidence.

One of the two suits before us seeks to set aside the conveyance of the outside properties and secure the return of the thirty thousand shares of capital stock issued therefor, and the other to recover damages resulting from the conveyance to the plaintiff of the mines and other real estate of the Baltimore Company for the excessive valuation of one hundred thousand such shares. In other respects the two bills are alike. Two suits (the bills in which have the same allegations as these, mutatis mutandis), were brought against the executors of Lewisohn in the United States Circuit Court for the Southern District of New York. The one relating to the outside properties and the issue of the thirty thousand shares was decided ultimately by the United States Supreme Court, and a final decree was entered dismissing the suit.

In the other suit respecting the issue of one hundred thousand shares for the mines and other real estate of the Baltimore Company, no decree has been entered, and it appears to be still pending. Separate offers of sale were presented and separate votes were passed by the directors of the plaintiff for the purchase of the outside properties for thirty thousand shares of its full paid non-assessable capital stock and for the purchase of the property of the Baltimore Company for one hundred thousand like shares. Separate votes were also passed to issue the thirty thousand shares to the defendant and Lewisohn and to issue the one hundred thousand shares to Dumaresq. Probably the defense of res judicata cannot apply to the suit respecting one hundred thousand shares, for the suit touching those shares against Lewisohn's executors has never gone to judgment and is still pending. The res at issue iii that suit, which appears to be somewhat different from that involved in the other, has therefore never become judicata. This circumstance is noted in passing. In some aspects of the case it may be important and perhaps decisive. In view of the ground, upon which this opinion is based, however, it makes no difference in the result and we do not further advert to it.

It appears that the fundamental questions in the suit in the federal court were precisely the same as those raised in the present suit relating to the thirty thousand shares and passed upon in 188 Mass. 315 . The present defendant was not a party to the suit in the federal court, but there is evidence that be participated in the defense of it.

The plaintiff objects that the order of the single justice allowing the defendant to file the supplemental answers was erroneous. This order was made in the exercise of judicial discretion, and unless such discretion was wrongly exercised it must stand. The facts averred in these answers could not have been pleaded when the original answers were filed, for the events they set up have occurred since. It is urged that the decree in favor of the executors of Lewisohn was entered in the United States Circuit Court before the trial upon the merits in this court, and might have been pleaded in bar notwithstanding the proceedings in the Supreme Court of the United States upon a writ of certiorari. But even if this be the law, the single justice cannot be said to have erred in permitting the defendant to set up a decree, which rests upon a decision of the court of last resort made after the close of the hearing upon the merits in the present suits. The decree in the federal court, although founded upon a demurrer, may under proper circumstances be a bar to another suit, as well as one founded upon a hearing of evidence. Yates v. Utica Bank, 206 U. S. 181, 183. Northern Pacific Railway v. Slaght, 205 U. S. 122, and cases cited at 130. In the view that we take of the case, it is not necessary to discuss other objections urged by the plaintiff to the force of this decree or the similarity of the issues in the two sets of suits.

12. The most important and difficult question is whether the contention of the defendant is sound that the decree of the federal court is a complete

bar to the present suits. His argument is that under the law of New York the decree of the Circuit Court of the United States is a bar to the maintenance of another suit for the same cause of action by the same plaintiff against him, and that, under art. 4, s. 1, of the Constitution of the United States, the effect given by the law of New York to the decree must be given by this court, in order that it receive the constitutionally required full faith and credit. The constitutional provision is as applicable to a decree of the Circuit Court in the Southern District of New York as to a decree in the State courts. Deposit Bank v. Frankfort, 191 U. S. 499, 515. Central National Bank v. Stevens, 169 U. S. 432, 460. The general effect of the decree (except as to matters of law or practice arising under the statutes of the United States, which have no bearing in the present case) is governed by the law of the State of New York where the federal court was sitting. Hancock National Bank v. Farnum, 176 U. S. 640, 645, citing Crescent City Live Stock Co. v. Butchers' Union, 120 U. S. 141, 147; Metcalf v. Watertown, 153 U. S. 671, 676; Pittsburgh, Cincinnati, Chicago & St. Louis Railroad v. Long Island Loan & Trust Co. 172 U. S. 493.

But before we reach the consideration of the effect of the decree and the interpretation that should be given to it under the laws of New York, there is a preliminary and fundamental question as to the precise meaning of the full faith and credit clause of the Federal Constitution as applied to the circumstances of this case.

An analysis of the defendant's contention shows that his defense of estoppel by res judicata rests upon the ground that he was either a party or privy to the New York judgment. It is not and cannot be urged that the New York suit was a proceeding in rem as to the plaintiff's cause of action. It was a personal suit. Except in proceedings in rem, there is no such thing known to the law as an adjudication of a cause of action, which can be availed of as res judicata by any others than by parties and their privies. The doctrine of stare decisis stands on a wholly different ground. The contention is that, even though the court was convinced that its former decision upon the merits was erroneous and desired to correct the mistake by deciding the later case differently, the decision against the plaintiff would prevent such correction of error. The fact that a party has fully litigated his cause of action in one suit and has been defeated is of no avail in another suit, to which a stranger to the first suit is a party, involving precisely the same issues. This principle is illustrated by many cases. Keokuk & Western Railroad v. Missouri, 152 U. S. 301. Crescent City Live Stock Co. v. Butchers' Union Slaughter-House Co. 120 U. S. 141, 155. Moore v. Albany, 98 N. Y. 396. Trimmer v. Rochester, 130 N. Y. 401. Stone v. New York, 138 N. Y. 124. Wallace v. Straus, 113 N. Y. 238. Collins v. Hydorn, 135 N. Y. 320. Groth v. Washburn, 39 Hun, 324. Furlong v. Banta, 80 Hun, 248.

The defendant can prevail on his supplementary answers only upon the ground that he was either a party or privy to the judgment rendered in the United States Circuit Court. The defendant Bigelow was not a party to that suit, and he does not assert that he was. The extent of his contention is that he was in privity with the executors of Lewisohn, and therefore entitled to the benefit of the judgment in their favor.

The first matter for determination is this: Does the full faith and credit clause require the courts of all other States to give effect to the law of any particular State, where a judgment may be entered, as to who are privies to such judgment, or does it permit or require the courts of the State where a third person sets up the defense that he is privy to a judgment entered in the courts of another State to decide that question according to its own law? Hence it becomes necessary to inquire what has been decided by the Supreme Court of the United States, whose decisions upon this as a federal question are binding upon all State courts.

It was said in Smithsonian Institution v. St. John. 214 U. S. 19, at pp. 28 and 29: "Without doubt the constitutional requirement, art. IV. s. 1, that ' full faith and credit shall be given in each State to the public acts, records and judicial proceedings of every other State,' implies that the public acts of every State shall be given the same effect by the courts of another State that they have by law and usage at home. This is clearly the logical result of the principles announced as early as 1813 in Mills v. Duryee, 7 Cranch, 481, and steadily adhered to ever since. Hancock National Bank v. Farnum, 176 U. S. 640, 642." But the broad language of this decision, as well as the comprehensive phrase of the Constitution itself and of the act of Congress in pursuance thereof are to be read and interpreted in the light of the thing intended to be accomplished, and " of some established principles, which they were not intended to overthrow." Huntington v. Attrill, 146 U. S. 657, 685. Many cases have arisen in which this phase of the subject has been discussed. It has been generally held that, no matter how clear may be the language of the statute, nor how decisive the decisions of the courts, of the sister State, as to the scope and effect of judgments upon residents of other States, yet in certain aspects such judgments may and ought to be narrowly scrutinized and the constitutional injunction given a reasonable interpretation. It was said in Public Works v. Columbia College, 17 Wall. 521 at p. 528: "The clause of the Federal Constitution which requires full faith and credit to be given in each State to the records and judicial proceedings of every other State, applies to the records and proceedings of courts only so far as they have jurisdiction. Whenever they want jurisdiction the records are not entitled to credit." This was a case where three of five partners appeared in an action against the copartnership, the other two members being non-residents not served with process and not appearing, and under the law of New York a judgment could be rendered under these circumstances against the copartnership. But it was held that the absent partners were not bound by a judgment so entered. In D'Arcy v. Ketchum, 11 How. 165, a judgment was entered against a non-resident defendant, who had not appeared or been served with process, in accordance with a statute of New York, permitting such course where joint debtors were sued and one only appeared. This statute had been adjudged valid by the courts of New York. It was admitted that the defendant was a joint debtor with the person served in New York, yet it was held that the Constitution and act of Congress did not purport to give effect to State judgments as binding upon non-resident defendants not served with process and not appearing. See Goldey v. Morning News, 156 U. S. 518, 521.

It was said, in the recent case of Brown v. Fletcher, 210 U. S. 82, 88, that "the constitutional question does not preclude the courts of a State in which the judgment of a sister State is presented from inquiry as to the jurisdiction of the court by which the judgment is rendered. See the elaborate opinion by Mr. Justice Bradley, speaking for the court, in Thompson v. Whitman, 18 Wall. 457. That opinion has been followed in many cases.... Even record recitals of jurisdictional facts do not preclude oral testimony as to the existence of those facts." Old Wayne Life Association v. McDonough, 204 U. S. 8, 15. These principles are illustrated in application to a variety of facts: for example, as to whether attachment of property gives power to enter a judgment of effect beyond the property attached, Pennoyer v. Neff, 95 U. S. 714, 730; as to the limits of jurisdiction of parish courts in the settlement of estates, Simmons v. Saul, 138 U. S. 439, 448; as to whether the return of service is sufficient to confer jurisdiction, Knowles v. Gaslight ‘ Coke Co. 19 Wall. 58 ; as to whether the judgment is responsive to the issues tendered, Reynolds v. Stockton, 140 U. S. 254, 265; as to whether an attorney had authority to appear, Cooper v. Newell, 173 U. S. 555, 566, Hall v. Lanning, 91 U. S. 160; as to whether the cause of action was such as to give the State court jurisdiction to render a judgment entitled, according to settled principles of public and international law, to enforcement by other courts, Wisconsin v. Pelican Ins. Co. 127 U. S. 265 ; as to whether judgment rendered upon appearance by prothonotary, authorized by statute of the State where judgment was entered, was within the terms of a power of attorney, Grover & Baker Sewing Machine Co. v. Radcliffe, 137 U. S. 287, 295 ; as to validity of decree of foreign court respecting devolution of real estate within another State, Clarke v. Clarke, 178 U. S. 186, 195 ; as to effect of decree for future payment of alimony, Lynde v. Lynde, 181 U. S. 183 ; as to whether divorce obtained by the court having jurisdiction of persons of both parties must be recognized in their domiciliary state, Andrews v. Andrews, 188 U. S. 14, German Savings & Loan Society v. Dormitzer, 192 U. S. 125, 128 ; as to effect of foreign divorces obtained ex parte, Bell v. Bell, 181 U. S. 175, Streitwolf v. Streitwolf, 181 U. S. 179, Atherton v. Atherton, 181 U. S. 155, Haddock v. Haddock, 201 U. S. 562 ; as to whether one was "holder" of note within the meaning of a warrant of attorney authorizing confession of judgment, National Exchange Bank v. Wiley, 195 U. S. 257, 269 ; as to whether determination of domicil of deceased person by appointment of personal representatives foreclosed similar inquiry in other States, Thormann v. Frame, 176 U. S. 350 ; as to whether service on public officer impliedly authorized to receive service for a foreign corporation, in respect of business transacted by it in one State, was also impliedly authorized to the same extent as to business not there transacted, Old Wayne Life Association v. McDonough, 204 U. S. 8, 22; as to whether a corporation is really doing business in the State in which service is made, within the rule that it is essential to jurisdiction over a foreign corporation having neither property nor agent in the State that it be doing business there, Commercial Mutual Accident Co. v. Davis, 213 U. S. 245 and cases cited at 255, Caledonian Coal Co. v. Baker, 196 U. S. 432 ; as to whether administration could be granted upon the estate of a living person, Scott v. McNeal, 154 U. S. 34 ; as to the sufficiency' of service by publication, Smith v. Woolfolk, 115 U. S. 143 and cases cited, Clark v. Wells, 203 U. S. 164, 171; as to whether in fact hearing had been granted to one alleged to be an alien enemy, Windsor v. McVeigh, 93 U. S. 274; as to judgment of foreclosure against alien enemy, Lasere v. Rochereau, 17 Wall. 437 ; as to sufficiency of scire facias to keep alive a judgment, Owens v. Henry, 161 U. S. 642 ; as to legality of constructive service, Brooklyn v. Insurance Co. 99 U. S. 362, Freeman v. Alderson, 119 U. S. 185, Empire v. Darlington, 101 U. S. 87, Pana v. Bowler, 107 U. S. 529; as to validity of statute imposing personal liability for local assessment upon non-resident landowner, Dewey v. Des Moines, 173 U. S. 193 ; as to sufficiency of any steps necessary to confer jurisdiction,

Howard v. De Cordova, 177 U. S. 609 ; as to validity of statute authorizing collection of execution for unpaid balance due on stock subscriptions from foreign stockholders in a corporation, Wilson v. Seligman, 144 U. S. 41; as to whether recital of settlement of cause in a judgment rested on an unfulfilled promissory agreement, Jacobs v. Marks, 182 U. S. 583 ; as to whether the State court having once rendered final judgment could without notice reopen case and enter a different judgment, Wetmore v. Karrick, 205 U. S. 141, 149. In all these cases it was held that judgments of the courts of sister States, valid there, might be refused recognition elsewhere without doing violence to the federal Constitution. This review of some of the decisions of the Supreme Court of the United States shows how full and complete is the inquiry permitted into the circumstances by which it is contended that the judgment of the court of the sister State binds the person as to whom it is invoked. Such judgments do not stand upon the same footing as domestic judgments. They may be attacked collaterally. Huntington v. Attrill, 146 U. S. 657, 685. There is nothing in the Federal Constitution or laws to prevent the most searching investigation, "into the jurisdiction of the court in which the judgment is rendered, over the subject matter, or the parties affected by it, or into the facts necessary to give such jurisdiction." Fuller, C. J., in Thormann v. Frame, 176 U. S. 350.

The present contention is that the judgment in favor of the executors of Lewisohn avails the defendant because they were privies respecting the subject matter of the suit. We do not find it to be the law of New York that in a suit in New York the defendant would be entitled to prevail on any other ground. The underlying question is one of jurisdiction. The defendant was not a party to the suit against Lewisohn. He was not served with process. No attempt was made by himself or by the plaintiff to join him as a party. Indeed, the bill in the Lewisohn suit alleges that Bigelow cannot be made a party by reason of residence outside the jurisdiction, and this fact is not controverted. It follows that the United States Circuit Court for the District of New York acquired no jurisdiction to render a judgment binding upon or in favor of Bigelow, unless he was a privy with Lewisohn.

It has been several times said that a judgment concludes, and may be invoked by, one who is a privy. Minneapolis Association v. Canfield, 121 U. S. 295, 308. Mitchell v. First National Bank of Chicago, 180 U. S. 471, 480, and cases cited. These are general statements, however, and we do not find that the precise point has ever been decided as to the effect which must be given to the judgment in the courts of one State touching privies, non-resident in the first State, and domiciled in the one where the question arises. Strong arguments can be conceived to support the proposition that except as to property rights arising by succession only those can be bound as privies, who are domiciled within the State where the judgment is rendered. But we do not pursue this inquiry. For the purposes of this discussion we assume without deciding that such a judgment binds privies of this description. Whether or not he was a privy is fundamental to the jurisdiction of the United States Circuit Court to enter a judgment, which as to Bigelow was capable of becoming res judicata.

At the outset it is to be observed that the domicil of the defendant is in this Commonwealth, and that domicil generally determines the particular territorial jurisprudence to which every individual is subjected. Grover & Baker Sewing Machine Co. v. Radcliffe, 137 U. S. 287, 298.

The foundation of the doctrine of res judicata is that there has been a judicial inquiry into the subject matter, in which the person to be affected by the judgment has had an opportunity by representative to be heard fully. The inquiry as to jurisdiction is in its last analysis, whether one was in such relation to the action in the sister State as to be bound by its judgment. Ordinarily, the question of jurisdiction is whether one was in law a party to the judgment. Whether a court has jurisdiction of a person depends upon whether he was really a party to it. The cases we have reviewed show that this is to be determined by the courts of the government where it arises according to its jurisprudence, subject to the duty imposed by the Constitution of the United States. The law of the State whose courts entered the judgment does not control. Where it is not contended that one was a party, it is equally an inquiry as to jurisdiction to determine whether he was a privy to one who was a party. By parity of reasoning, whether one is a privy to a judgment rendered in a sister or foreign State must also be determined by the law of the sovereignty where the question arises.

Privity was not a matter in issue in the suit, judgment in which is pleaded, nor can it be determined by an inspection of the judgment roll. It must be decided by evidence outside the record. It is not to be settled according to the law of the State where the judgment is rendered. This plainly appears from D'Arcy v. Ketchum, 11 How. 165. The substance of the New York statute, there decided not to be entitled to full faith and credit when followed by the courts in entering judgment, was that, in cases of joint debtors, all non-residents should be privies with any domestic fellow or joint debtor duly served with process and bound by the judgment. See to substantially the same effect Harris v. Hardeman, 14 How. 334; Ewer v. Coffin, 1 Cush. 23; Stone v. Wainwright, 147 Mass. 201; Phelps v. Brewer, 9 Cush. 390. The same principle is illustrated in Hall v. Lanning, 91 U. S. 160, and Public Forks v. Columbia College, 17 Wall. 521, where, by statute or usage, all partners were treated as so much in privity that appearance and defense by one bound all his copartners. Yet such a statute or usage was held not entitled to full faith and credit in the sister State.

We understand these federal cases in principle to cover the question before us, and to decide in substance that legislation or judicial determination of one State, that its domestic judgments shall bind non-residents decided by it to be privies, have no extraterritorial force, and are not entitled to recognition under the full faith and credit clause of the Federal Constitution. The same conclusion follows from the cases above cited, which permit inquiry into the extent of the powers of an agent to subject his principal to the jurisdiction of a foreign court.

But whether or not we interpret these decisions aright, as being decisive against this contention of the defendant, it seems to us that on reason it must be the law that the ascertainment of those non-residents not served with process nor appearing, who are bound by the judgment of a sister State as privies, must be by the courts of the jurisdiction where the question arises, and not by those of the State in which the judgment is rendered. This rests primarily upon the considerations touching the constitutional provision and the reason for its enactment. Its purpose was not to enlarge or change the jurisdiction of the courts of the several States. It was a recognized principle of international law, at the time the Constitution was adopted, that where parties had once fairly litigated a dispute in the courts of any civilized government, the same question ought not to be tried anew. But such judgments were commonly regarded as prima facie evidence of the matter decided and might be re-examined under some circumstances, the whole subject resting in comity and not in obligation. Bissell v. Briggs, 9 Mass. 462. Hilton v. Guyot, 159 U. S. 113, 181. In this regard the several colonies before the Declaration of Independence were as to each other foreign nations. Differences of practice grew up, as to the way in which judgments of foreign courts should be proved, and the precise weight to be attached to them. It was in this state of the law that the Constitution was adopted. Diversity of practice was turned into uniformity by the Constitution, which prescribed the effect to be given to judgments of courts, and empowered Congress to legislate further as to forms of proof. But it was not intended to enlarge the jurisdiction of the courts of the several States, or confer any new power upon them. It has simply made certain and of universal application between the several States that which before rested only in comity, and does still as to judgments of courts of foreign nations. It was intended merely to be regulative. It "establishes a rule of evidence rather than of jurisdiction." Anglo-American Provision Co. v. Davis Provision Co. (No. 1) 191 U. S. 373. Cole v. Cunningham, 133 U. S. 107, 112. Bissell v. Briggs, 9 Mass. 462, 467. "Judgments recovered in one State of the Union, when proved in the courts of another government, whether State or national, within the United States, differ from judgments recovered in a foreign country in no other respect than in not being re-examinable on their merits, nor impeachable for fraud in obtaining them, if rendered by a court having jurisdiction of the cause and of the parties." Wisconsin v. Pelican Ins. Co. 127 U. S. 265, 292. Hanley v. Donoghue, 116 U. S. 1, 4. Hilton v. Guyot, 159 U. S. 113, 185. Union 4. Planters' Bank v. Memphis, 49 C. C. A. 455, 465, and cases cited. This is further illustrated by what was said by Mr. Justice Gray, in Lynde v. Lynde, 181 U. S. 183, at pp. 186, 187: "By the Constitution and the act of Congress, requiring the faith and credit to be given to a judgment of the court of another State that it has in the State where it was rendered, it was long ago declared by this court : ' The judgment is made a debt of record, not examinable upon its merits ; but it does not carry with it, into another State, the efficacy of a judgment upon property or persons, to be enforced by execution. To give it the force of a judgment in another State, it must be made a judgment there; and can only be executed in the latter as its laws may permit.' "

In other words, the question whether the plaintiff can try its case here against Bigelow after failing against the estate of Lewisohn arises after full faith and credit have been given to the New York decree, and is not included in giving it full faith and credit. The decree does not have the effect contended for by the defendant proprio vigore. Whether it should bar the plaintiff from another suit is a question of public policy. Such a question must be decided according to the law of the State where it arises.

This conclusion is strongly supported by the argument of convenience. It is a principle of the common law that a judgment binds the parties and their privies. But there is no generally prevailing definition of privity which can be automatically applied to all cases. Who are privies requires careful examination into the circumstances of each case as it arises. Its determination is often difficult for a court possessed of plenary jurisdiction. But if the question who are privies is to be decided as a fact under the law of a foreign jurisdiction upon such evidence as the parties may be able to produce, complication is multiplied. The present case furnishes a capital illustration of the evil workings of such a rule. The courts of authority in New York seem not to have decided the precise question we now have to pass upon. Eminent lawyers have been called by both parties to testify as experts. But no two of them agree in their definition of privies, although several think that the executors of Lewisohn and the defendant were privies. There is great diversity in the details of the views expressed by those called by the defendant as to the exact grounds upon which they say the plaintiff would be barred in the courts of New York in a suit against Bigelow. We cannot conceive that it was the intent of the framers of the Constitution to put parties to the expense, inconvenience and unsatisfactory method of resorting to this class of testimony in order to establish their rights, when courts exist in every State, which could with much less difficulty determine the question according to the law of the forum. There is nothing inconsistent with this result in Whitman v. Oxford National Bank, 176 U. S. 559, and Hancock National Bank v. Farnum, 176 U. S. 640. These cases decided that the liability imposed upon stockholders in Kansas corporations, by the Constitution and laws of that State, were contractual in their nature, and were enforceable in the courts of other jurisdictions. These decisions in effect hold that the laws of a sovereign power, as to the rights and liabilities arising out of the relations between a domestic corporation and its stockholders, are binding upon the latter as contracts, because they assented to be so bound by voluntarily becoming such stockholders. Bernheimer v. Converse, 206 U. S. 516, 529. Tilt v. Kelsey, 207 U. S. 43, 47, simply decided in substance that a judgment in rem by a court having jurisdiction thereof binds everybody interested in it. Laing v. Rigney, 160 U. S. 531, held that on the facts shown the State court had jurisdiction of all persons sought to be charged. None of these decisions are apposite to the point now under discussion.

We are, therefore, of opinion that whether Bigelow was in such privity with the executors of Lewisohn, respecting the litigation in New York, as to be able to invoke, in his own defense, the judgment there rendered, is a jurisdictional question to be determined by the law of this Commonwealth, subject to the Federal Constitution.

It remains to inquire whether, according to the law of this Commonwealth, the Circuit Court for the District of New York had such jurisdiction of the defendant as to enable him to invoke its judgment as a bar in the present suit, on the ground of res judicata. This in turn depends upon the question whether the defendant was a privy with the defendants in the Lewisohn suit, or in such relation to it that he can plead the judgment in favor of the Lewisohn estate, as an estoppel against the plaintiff. The evidence shows that he knew of the suit, and through his counsel gave such assistance in the preparation of the briefs for the arguments of that suit as might have been expected. But, as he was not a party, this fact is not of much importance. It is treated by most of the expert witnesses called by the defendant as to the New York law as of no consequence. Privity depends upon the relation of the parties to the subject matter, rather than their activity in a suit relating to it after the event. Participation in the defense because of general or personal interest in the result of the litigation does not make one privy to the judgment. Stryker v. Goodnow, 123 U. S. 527, 540. People v. Knickerbocker Ins. Co. 106 N. Y. 619.

The liability of the defendant, as has been pointed out, according to the law of this Commonwealth, is one arising ex delicto. The wrong committed was a tort, in which the defendant and Lewisohn acted in concert. The finding of the single justice, supported by the evidence is, in substance, that they were joint tortfeasors. The inquiry then is, whether one of several joint tortfeasors can plead a judgment in favor of his joint tortfeasor against a plaintiff claiming to have been injured by their joint act as an estoppel in a suit by the same plaintiff against himself.

This can hardly be regarded as an open question in this Commonwealth. In Sprague v. Oakes, 19 Pick. 455, which was an action for trespass quare clausum fregit, it was said, respecting such a defense, "The defendant was neither a party nor privy to that judgment, was not bound by it, nor could he take advantage of it." This case has never been overruled or questioned, and must be regarded as stating the law of this Commonwealth. There are other authorities to the same point. Lansing v. Montgomery, 2 Johns. 382. Marsh v. Berry, 7 Cowen, 344. Moore v. Tracy, 7 Wend. 229. Gittleman v. Feltman, 122 App. Div. (N. Y.) 385. Atlantic Dock Co. v. Mayor & Aldermen of New York, 53 N. Y. 64. Tyng v. Clarke, 9 Hun, 269. Calkins v. Allerton, 3 Barb. 171, 174. Goble v. Dillon, 86 Ind. 327. Thompson v. Chicago, St. Paul & Kansas City Railroad, 71 Minn. 89. Three States Lumber Co. v. Blanks, 118 Tenn. 627.

The reason upon which these decisions rest is that there can be no estoppel arising out of a judgment, unless the same parties have had their day in court touching the matter litigated, and unless the judgment is equally available to both parties. It requires no discussion to demonstrate that a judgment in the Lewisohn suit against the defendants would not have fixed liability upon the present defendant. Hence there can be no estoppel under our law or under the general principles of jurisprudence, because it is not mutual. Brigham v. Fayerweather, 140 Mass. 411, 415. Dallinger v. Richardson, 176 Mass. 77, 83. Worcester v. Green, 2 Pick. 425, 429. Biddle & Smart Co. v. Burnham, 91 Maine, 578. Moore v. Albany, 98 N. Y. 396. "Estoppels to be good must be mutual." Litchfield v. Goodnow,123 U. S. 549, 552. Nelson v. Brown, 144 N. Y. 384, 390. Bigelow could not have appeared as of right and made a defense in that suit. No judgment can be regarded as res judicata as to any matter where the rights in the subject matter arise out of mutuality, and not by succession, unless the party could, as matter of right, appear and defend, even though he may have had knowledge of the suit. Otherwise, he might be bound by a judgment as to which he had never had the opportunity to be heard, which is opposed to the first principles of justice. Brabrook v. Boston Five Cents Savings Bank, 104 Mass. 228, 233. There is no privity between joint wrongdoers, because all are jointly and severally liable. Corey v. Havener, 182 Mass. 250 . Feneff v. Boston & Maine Railroad, 196 Mass. 575, 581. Pinkerton v. Randolph, 200 Mass. 24 , 28. There is no right of contribution between joint wrongdoers, where they are in pari delicto with each other. Churchill v. Holt, 127 Mass. 165. They are equally culpable, and the wrong complained of results from their joint effort. The right of recovery over by a municipality against a person, whose wrong created a defect in the highway (Holyoke v. Hadley Co. 174 Mass. 424) is no exception to this rule, because the tort committed by each of the wrongdoers is diverse in character, and rests upon a different basis of liability, and there is a right of indemnity in favor of the municipality. Lowell v. Glidden, 159 Mass. 317, 319. We are aware of no instance of joint participation in a common tortious enterprise where there is any right of contribution. One comprehensive definition of privies is such persons as are " privies in estate - as donor and donee, lessor and lessee and joint tenants; or privies in blood- as heir and ancestor; or privies in representation - as executor and testator or administrator and intestate; or privies in law-where the law without privity in blood or estate casts land upon another, as by escheat." Buckingham v. Ludlum, 10 Stew. 137, 141. Douglass v. Howland, 24 Wend. 35, 53. Joint tortfeasors come within none of the classes thus described. The definition in 1 Greenl. Ev. s. 535, adopted by the Supreme Court of the United States, in Litchfield v. Goodnow, 123 U. S. 549, 551, namely, " Mutual or successive relationship to the same rights of property" equally fails to include joint tortfeasors. If we turn to the law of privity as illustrated in actions against partnership and joint debtors, the soundness of this conclusion is confirmed. It has been repeatedly decided that an administrator of a decedent in one jurisdiction is not in privity with an administrator of the same estate appointed in another jurisdiction, and that a judgment against one such administrator is not res judicata to the other. Ingersoll v. Coram, 211 U. S. 335, and cases cited. Johnson v. Powers, 139 U. S. 156. In Chase v. Henry, 166 Mass. 577 , it was held that discharge in insolvency in this Commonwealth did not bar the debt of a copartnership, one member of which was a non-resident, although two were residents and the copartnership had a regular place of business here. It has been several times held that judgment against one surviving partner upon a claim against the partnership was not admissible in evidence against the executors of a deceased partner, although the existence of the partnership was not disputed. Buckingham v. Ludlum, 10 Stew. 137. Moores' Appeals, 34 Penn. St. 411. Sturges v. Beach, 1 Conn. 507. Larison v. Hager, 44 Fed. Rep. 49. The converse, which is exactly parallel to the present case, namely, that a judgment in favor of one partner or joint and several debtor will not avail his associate in liability, has often been decided. Townsend v. Riddle, 2 N. H. 448. McLelland v. Ridgeway, 12 Ala. 482. State Bank v. Robinson, 13 Ark. 214, 221. Detroit v. Houghton, 42 Mich. 459, 460. It is difficult to conceive of persons more closely identified with their common business than joint debtors and partners, and if judgments against one do not bind his associate, we do not see how persons occupying the less intimate relation to each other, which Bigelow and Lewisohn did, can be bound as privies. See also Williams v. Bankhead, 19 Wall. 563, 570.

Apart from authority and on principle the same result seems necessary. Joint tortfeasors act in unison respecting a common wrongful enterprise. It is one of the penalties, which the common law (differing in this respect from the civil law) inflicts upon those who jointly engage in intentional violation of the rights of others, that each shall be left to bear the natural results of his conduct. Courts will not lend their aid in adjusting the conflicting claims of wrongdoers touching their own turpitude.

An injured party is given the right to pursue his remedy, either singly or together, against those who thus cause injury, and may proceed to judgment against all in separate actions. He is barred only by a satisfaction. An inevitable corollary of these generally undisputed propositions and one consonant with a fundamental sense of justice is that a party has a right to try his case against everybody who has done him a wrong by immediate and direct culpable action. He is not precluded by a failure against one alleged joint wrongdoer from attempting to pursue another. He is entitled to his day in court against a particular adversary. We believe there are no exceptions to this rule stated in this form. The cases where judgment in favor of an active agent or servant avails a passive principal or master (Portland Gold Mining

Co. v. Stratton's Independence, 158 Fed. Rep. 63 and cases cited), or where the relation of indemnitor and indemnitee exists (Port Jervis v. First National Bank of Port Jervis, 96 N. Y. 550) do not constitute exceptions to this rule, but stand on a different ground.

For another reason the New York judgment in favor of Lewisohn seems not to be a bar. The joint actor with the defendant was not the defendant in the New York suit, but it was prosecuted against his executors. If it be assumed that there was a kind of privity between the two who acted in concert, that privity was broken by the death of one. There is no privity between Lewisohn's executors and Bigelow. Ela v. Edwards, 13 Allen 48. Merrill v. New England Ins. Co. 103 Mass. 245, 249. Thomson v. American Surety Co. 170 N. Y. 109. It cannot be said that the plaintiff has elected to pursue his remedy against the estate of Lewisohn to the exclusion of his rights against Bigelow. As between joint tortfeasors the doctrine of election has no application, and moreover the plaintiff sought the New York forum voluntarily only in the sense of being compelled to go there that a court might acquire jurisdiction of those defendants.

The determination that the relation between Lewisohn and Bigelow was that of joint tortfeasors respecting a cause of action arising ex delicto disposes also of the argument pressed by the defendant, that Lewisohn was trustee, agent or representative of Bigelow to such an extent that he was in privity with him. See Bigelow v. Old Dominion Copper Mining & Smelting Co. 4 Buch. (N. J.), 71 Atl. Rep. 153, 176.

The conclusion is, therefore, that the matters set up in the supplemental answers do not preclude the plaintiff from continuing the prosecution of the present suits.

Both parties have introduced a large amount of evidence as to the law of New York touching the effect which would by its courts be accorded to the judgment against the plaintiff in the Lewisohn litigation in a suit like the present pending in its courts against the defendant. In the view which we take of this case that question has become wholly immaterial, and we do not pass upon it.

13. The defendant has briefly argued that a decision for the plaintiff in these suits involves a denial to him of due process of law, the equal protection of the laws, and an impairment of the obligation of contracts. It does not seem necessary to discuss these arguments further than to say that they do not appear to us to have any application to the issues here pending.

14. The present cases were upon the calendar of the full court for argument at its January sitting, 1908. Upon motion of the defendant based upon representations as to the need of delay to enable him to prepare a brief, they were assigned as the first cases for argument at the March sitting of this court, 1908. A few days before the coming in of the court at that sitting, the present defendant applied to the Court of Chancery in the State of New Jersey, where the plaintiff is domiciled, and secured a temporary injunction against its prosecution of these suits. The suit in New Jersey was decided adversely to the plaintiff by the chancellor, in whose elaborate opinion one of the vice-chancellors concurred, on August 8, 1908. Bigelow v. Old Dominion Copper Mining & Smelting Co. 4 Buch. (N. J.), 71 Atl. Rep. 153. This decision was not by the court of last resort, and the present defendant, the plaintiff there, asserted that he intended to prosecute an appeal to the highest court in the State of New Jersey. Thereupon, on motion, an interlocutory decree was entered by a single justice of this court, restraining the defendant, " his attorneys, agents and servants from further prosecuting the action commenced by said Bigelow against the plaintiff in the Court of Chancery in the State of New Jersey . . . ; and from commencing or prosecuting any other suit or proceeding either in law or in equity, except in this court, against the plaintiff to prevent it from obtaining the final decision and decree of this court or in any manner to delay or impede the presentation of said case." These suits were then pending before the full court under R. L. c. 159, s. 19. This statute, however, does not prevent the entering by a single justice of decrees respecting interlocutory matters which may call for a speedy hearing and decision, but in no wise affecting the questions covered by the

final decree. R. L. c. 159, s.s. 17, 21, 22. Parker v. Nickerson, 137 Mass. 487 , 491. The defendant appealed from this interlocutory decree and from a refusal of the single justice to modify or vacate it.

It is a general principle of chancery jurisprudence that, as between courts of co-ordinate and concurrent jurisdiction, the court which first obtains possession of a transaction shall dispose of it without interference from other courts. Riggs v. Johnson Co. 6 Wall. 166, 196. Home Ins. Co. v. Howell, 9 C. E. Green, 238. The jurisdiction of courts of equity to restrain a citizen suitor from prosecuting litigation in another State is well settled. Cunningham v. Butler, 142 Mass. 47 ; S. C. sub nomine Cole v. Cunningham, 133 U. S. 107. The present suits were begun October 7, 1902. This court plainly had jurisdiction of the subject matter and the parties. The defendant made no contest in these respects, but proceeded to hearing upon the merits and accepted the jurisdiction of the court up to the point of argument before the full bench. It was manifestly proper that at this stage of the proceedings, in view of his conduct of the suits theretofore, he should be restrained from attempting to interfere in courts of other jurisdiction with the conclusion of this litigation. It is hardly necessary to say that the interlocutory decree does not purport to restrain him from enforcing whatever rights he may have to a writ of error from the Supreme Court of the United States to the final judgments which may be entered in this court. His full rights under the Federal Constitution are preserved. The decrees are to be so modified as to include the costs of these appeals, and as modified are affirmed. So ordered.[3)]

KNOWLTON, C. J. This is an important case. The decrees from which the appeal was taken to this court call for the payment of considerably more than two million dollars. The questions of law involved are far-reaching. As I do not agree to the opinion of the majority of the court, I deem it my duty to state the reasons for my dissent.

---

3) The case was taken to the Supreme Court of the United States by writ of error.

The fundamental question is, what right and power has a corporation to bind itself, acting through its stockholders in confirmation of the doings of its directors, in the transaction of business, after it has been completely organized under the law of the State of New Jersey, and after the amount of the capital required to authorize it to do business under the statute has been paid in, but before the whole of its capital stock has been issued or subscribed for. The plaintiff corporation was established under the laws of the State of New Jersey. Its rights and powers, and the rights of its stockholders, depend upon the law of that State. Unless it has suffered a wrong as a corporation of that State it has no standing here.

To organize a corporation under the laws of New Jersey, articles of association in writing must be signed by not less than three persons, stating the name of the company, the place or places where its business is to be conducted, the object for which it is to be formed, " the total amount of the capital stock of such company, which shall not be less than two thousand dollars, the amount with which they will commence business, which shall not be less than one thousand dollars, and the number of shares into which the same is divided, and the par value of each share." It must also contain a statement of the names and residences of the stockholders and the number of shares held by each, with the " period at which such company' shall commence and terminate, not exceeding fifty years." Gen. Sts. of New Jersey, 912-946, s.s. 10-189. The certificate must be proved and acknowledged, and then recorded as deeds of real estate are required to be recorded. It must also be filed in the office of the secretary of state. When this has been done, the company is a corporation from the time of the commencement of the period fixed in the certificate.

The report of the single justice, with the evidence, shows that the plaintiff corporation was organized in all respects in compliance with the statute, that the requisite amount of capital to qualify it to commence business was paid in in cash, and that the corporation was legally authorized to do any business within the purposes of its organization. Although but a small part of its authorized capital had been paid in or subscribed for, it was permitted by law to exercise all the powers of a corporation and to perform all its contemplated functions for fifty years, if it could obtain money or credit sufficient for the purpose. It then made contracts with the defendant Bigelow and his associate Lewisohn, who were the promoters of it, and who therefore stood in fiduciary relations to it, which contracts would be voidable as fraudulent for that reason, unless there was a full and fair disclosure of the facts to the corporation, as represented either by an independent board of directors who were in a position properly to protect its rights, or by its existing stockholders who were the owners of it. The directors were selected by the defendant and Lewisohn, and they were not impartial and independent officers, qualified properly to represent the corporation in matters where its interests might be adverse to those of the promoters. Indeed, as stockholders, they were then the representatives of the promoters. The capital which they paid in under their subscriptions was paid with money furnished by the promoters, and the beneficial interest in all the stock of the company, as it was then organized, was in the defendant and Lewisohn, who were the real owners of the entire corporation. Under these contracts, and in payment for property conveyed to the corporation, thirty thousand shares of stock were issued to the defendant and Lewisohn and taken in their names, and one hundred thousand shares were issued to Philip E. Dumaresq, " who took them as the nominee and for the benefit and subject to the orders of the defendant and Lewisohn." These shares "were held for and controlled by the defendant and Lewisohn." Twenty thousand shares more, which made up the total authorized capital of the company, were found by the judge to have been still the property of the corporation itself, and they were intended to be issued to independent subscribers for a working capital. They then stood in the name of Thomas Nelson, treasurer. More than two months after the original contracts were made, and while the ownership of the stock was as above stated, all the directors of the corporation signed, in the record book, a statement approving of the previous action of the board in making these contracts, and a similar statement was signed by the defendant and Lewisohn and Dumaresq as stockholders, and by Nelson as a stock-holding treasurer.

Upon these findings the defendant and Lewisohn were the owners of all the authorized capital stock of the corporation, except the twenty thousand shares in the treasury, which belonged to the corporation, and through the corporation they owned that also. As stockholders, they knew all the facts affecting the validity or propriety of the contracts which they had made with the company. At that time they had no interest adverse to that of the corporation, for they were the sole owners of the corporation. One question is whether this ratification with full knowledge, by all the stockholders, was binding upon the corporation. Another question is whether the contracts were valid when originally made, having been agreed to with full knowledge by the only persons beneficially interested in the corporation. More specifically, the broad question is whether a corporation, which has full power to make every other kind of a contract within the purposes of its organization, is powerless to make a contract, or through its stockholders to ratify a contract, with one standing in a fiduciary relation to it.

There is no question of fraud upon the corporation; for all of the owners of it were fully informed in regard to the transactions, and approved of them. Under such circumstances there can be no fraud. After a corporation is fully organized, the stockholders for the time being own and control it. In a broad sense, they are the corporation, although the corporation as a separate entity may exercise its powers as an individual, under their direction and for their benefit. The power of a corporation through its stockholders, choosing proper agents, to deal formally with those in a fiduciary relation to it is established beyond the possibility of question. It matters not that the fiduciaries are themselves stockholders, if the other stockholders are not misled. And it matters not whether they constitute all of the stockholders, or only a part of them, if all the stockholders know all the facts and consent to the transaction.

The only question that seems to me debatable, on this branch of the case, is whether the power of the corporation, or of its stockholders, to act in matters of this kind is taken away by the fact that its stock is not all issued, and that a part of it is retained to be issued to obtain working capital, or for other purposes. On principle, it is difficult to see how this can affect its right under the law to do business of this kind, as it may do business of every other kind.

It is suggested that to make contracts with one in a fiduciary relation may be detrimental to the interests of the corporation, and constitute a fraud upon persons subsequently subscribing for stock not then issued, even if the existing stockholders know all the facts and are content. But it is to be noticed that, under the law of New Jersey, the organization of a corporation does not necessarily give any indication or suggestion as to the value of its stock. It does not indicate that more than $1,000 of capital has been actually paid in, if that sum is fixed in the articles of association as the amount necessary to qualify it to do business. As to the balance of the shares, it does not show whether much, or little, or nothing at all has been paid upon them. It does not indicate that contracts have or have not been made with the corporation, and if they have been made, whether they are advantageous or disadvantageous to it. Under this system, everybody is bound to know that, apart from the general facts of organization which appear of record, one buying stock or subscribing for it must ascertain by inquiry if he would know whether it is of large value or of no value. Evidently the statute was intended to give very broad latitude to organizers of corporations, and to give corporations full powers to contract, while only a small amount of stock has been issued, which may be owned by a very few persons.

Promoters, as well as directors, stand in a fiduciary relation to a corporation. They do not stand in such a relation directly to particular stockholders, or to a particular class of stockholders. Their relation to stockholders is only as the stockholders claim through the corporation by virtue of their ownership of it. Through the corporation, promoters and directors stand in this relation to those who own stock while their fiduciary relation to the corporation continues. They are never in such a relation to those who become stockholders after their relation to the corporation has ended. Their fiduciary relation to the corporation extends through it to all the owners of it. The stockholders for the time being are all the owners of it. These stockholders can sell its property, or wind it up, or control it as they please. No one else has any interest in it, and the directors or promoters have no relations, as such, to anyone else. If additional stock is issued after their relations to the corporation are terminated, they are not and they never were in fiduciary relations to the takers of this new stock. In this respect there is no difference between directors and promoters. All this is said in reference to corporations which are regularly and completely organized, and are authorized to do business and fully to exercise their powers and franchises under the law, notwithstanding that a part of their authorized capital has not been taken. Of course, if a corporation is merely in an inchoate condition, and has not acquired the power to exercise its franchises, a different rule would apply.

So too, promoters may enter into arrangements with underwriters or syndicates or single persons who expect to take stock, and may thus assume obligations. In the present cases I do not intimate that the defendant might not be held liable to some of the persons who arranged with him to take a part in the enterprise.

But whatever may be thought of the conduct of promoters who make contracts with a corporation while they are the sole owners of it, and whether it be held that their fiduciary relations extend to future stockholders or only to those who are the owners while this relation exists, the question before us is whether, under the law of New Jersey, a corporation is powerless to bind itself as to such contracts, when they are entered into with the assent of the existing stockholders, all of whom have full knowledge of the facts. On principle, I think that a corporation organized in that State is not so crippled. Let us consider the authorities.

In re Ambrose Lake Tin & Copper Mining Co. 14 Ch. D. 390, was a case in which a sale of property was made to a corporation by the promoters of it, which would have been voidable for fraud if the promoters had not been the owners of its stock. It was held that, inasmuch as the vendors were themselves the stockholders of the company and knew all the facts, there was no fraud upon the corporation. In this case the judges thought that one of the purposes of these promoters was to obtain profit from future purchasers of the stock who were ignorant of the transaction; but under the circumstances the corporation could not avoid the contract. In North- West Transportation Co. v. Beatty, 12 App. Cas. 589, a contract of purchase of property by a corporation was entered into by directors with one of their number. It was held that the vendor was entitled to exercise his voting power as a stockholder to ratify the contract. He controlled a majority of the votes through ownership of his stock, acquired in a manner authorized by the constitution of the company. It was held that his exercise of his power could not be deemed oppressive for this reason. Sir Richard Baggallay, in delivering the unanimous opinion of the Privy Council, said, " Unless some provision to the contrary is to be found in the charter or other instrument by which the company is incorporated, the resolution of a majority of the shareholders, duly convened, upon any question with which the company is legally competent to deal, is binding upon the minority, and consequently upon the company, and every shareholder has a perfect right to vote upon any such question, although he may have a personal interest in the subject matter opposed to, or different from, the general or particular interests of the company." Referring to dealings with a director acting in a fiduciary capacity, he said: "Any such dealing or engagement may, however, be affirmed or adopted by the company, provided such affirmance or adoption is not brought about by unfair or improper means, and is not illegal or fraudulent or oppressive towards those shareholders who oppose it." In this case ratification was by only a small majority of the stockholders.

Salomon v. Salomon, [1897] A. C. 22, was a case in which the proprietor of a business organized a corporation with a capital stock of forty thousand shares, of the par value of one pound each. He, his wife, his daughter and his four sons took one share each. With only seven shares taken, he sold out his business to the corporation for a price which might be found to be much more than it was worth. He then took twenty thousand shares more of the stock; the remaining nineteen thousand nine hundred and ninety-three shares never were issued. The company soon became insolvent, and a receiver, in the interest of creditors, sought to hold this organizer and promoter for fraud upon the corporation. It was held upon these facts that there was no fraud and no liability. Lord Chancellor Halsbury quoted from the headnote in Erlanger v. New Sombrero Phosphate Co. 3 App. Cas.1218, and then said, " But if every member of the company - every shareholder - knows exactly what is the true state of the facts (which for this purpose must be assumed to be the case here) Vaughan Williams, J.'s conclusion seems to me to be inevitable, for no case of fraud upon the company could here be established." He said this in a case in which only seven shares of stock out of an authorized capital of forty thousand shares had been issued when the contract with the promoter was made. This case seems to me fully to cover the case at bar, in which the only fraud proved was the constructive fraud of a sale to a corporation from one in a fiduciary relation to it.

Other cases establish the proposition that it makes no difference that not all the stock of the company has been issued, if the holders of all outstanding stock agree. In St. Louis, Fort Scott & Wichita Railroad v. Tiernan, 37 Kans. 606, and Stewart v. St. Louis, Fort Scott & Wichita Railroad, 41 Fed. Rep. 736, a part of the stock, although not a large amount, was issued to municipalities after the transaction to which the stockholders agreed. In Hutchinson v. Simpson, 92 App. Div. (N. Y.) 382, a large amount of stock was held in the treasury for other corporate uses. The same was true in Blum v. Whitney, 185 N. Y. 232, which in its reasoning and the authorities cited is a very strong case for the defendant. Only a part of the authorized stock had been issued when the contract was made in In re British Seamless Box Co. 17 Ch. D. 467, and more was issued about a year and a quarter afterwards. Tompkins v. Sperry, 96 Md. 560, is an important case supporting the proposition that stockholders may bind the corporation in transactions of this kind which are voidable for constructive fraud. Except as I shall state hereafter, I know of no case which holds that it makes any difference that not all the stock has been issued, if the corporation is completely organized and authorized to go on with its ordinary business. There are dicta of some English judges, indicating that such a transaction, when it is expected that a prospectus will be issued under the English practice inviting subscriptions for stock from the public, would be fraudulent as against future stockholders. These are in opinions in which the judges hold that there is no fraud upon the corporation as there was knowledge and consent of the stockholders, and they seem to assume that the corporation is not fully organized and qualified to do business. But they are without discussion or seeming consideration of the question when a corporation and its stockholders become competent to make binding contracts as to such matters. Other cases which support the defendant's position are Foster v. Seymour, 23 Fed. Rep. 65, McCracken v. Robison, 57 Fed. Rep. 375, and Barr v. New York, Lake Erie & Western Railroad, 125 N. Y. 263.

This court, in Hayward v. Leeson, 176 Mass. 310 , in dealing with a corporation established under the laws of Tennessee, held that the receivers of the company might maintain a suit for fraud against promoters, notwithstanding that the stockholders, at the time of the transaction, knew all the facts and agreed to the contract. The particulars of the statute of Tennessee, as to the organization of corporations, do not appear in the report of the case. When the present suits came before the court upon a demurrer, Hayward v. Leeson was followed and held to govern them. 188 Mass. 315. The precise questions which were then before us have been considered by the Circuit Court of the United States and the United States Circuit Court of Appeals in the second circuit, in a suit brought by this plaintiff against Lewisohn's heirs, and upon a demurrer to averments of fact against Lewisohn substantially identical with those against the defendant in the present suits, there was a decision for the defendants. Old Dominion Copper Mining &

Smelting Co. v. Lewisohn, 136 Fed. Rep. 915; S. C. 148 Fed. Rep. 1020. As appears by the record before us, five judges of the federal courts in that circuit, at different stages of the proceeding, agreed in their view of the law of the case. The suit was then carried to the Supreme Court of the United States, and the justices of that court were unanimous in sustaining the defendant's demurrer. Upon the averments of the bill, they treated Bigelow and Lewisohn as the real owners of the corporation when the contracts were made, through their appointees, who took the stock which they paid for. The judge who wrote the opinion sat as Chief Justice with those other members of this court who took part in the decision of Hayward v. Leeson. The view expressed in the opinion of the Supreme Court of the United States is at variance with a part of the reasoning and with the decision in Hayward v. Leeson. This latest decision must be treated as establishing the law for the federal courts. The cases cited show that the law is settled in the same way in some of the State courts.

In addition to the deference that a unanimous opinion of the justices of the Supreme Court of the United States should receive in any other court, it is for me a very important consideration that, upon questions which will often be litigated in the federal tribunals by reason of the diverse citizenship of the parties, the law ought to be the same in the State courts as in the federal courts. It would be unfortunate if, in this large class of cases, the rights of a suitor should depend upon whether he is finally held subject to the jurisdiction of a federal court or to that of a State court.

It seems to me that the great weight of authority, upon the turning point of this case, is in favor of the defendant. I do not regard the case of Erlanger v. New Sombrero Phosphate Co. 3 App. Cas. 1218 (5 Ch. D. 73), relied on by the plaintiff, as having any bearing upon the question on which the present case turns, namely, when is a corporation so far organized that its stockholders, acting with full knowledge, can bind it? No such question arose in that case, and there was no occasion to consider such a question. So far as appears, the question was never thought of. The court was dealing with a fraud upon a corporation whose stockholders were ignorant of the facts that constituted the fraud, and took no action in regard to the matter. It seems to me that the dicta of certain English judges relied on by the majority of the court overlook the fact that the fiduciary relation of promoters of a corporation is of no practical consequence if the promoters are the sole owners of the corporation, and if, at - the time of the transaction in question, the corporation is legally organized and qualified to do every kind of business, although this fact is generally recognized by the English courts. I also think that the judges uttering the dicta were influenced by the statutory provision in the English law for the issuing of a prospectus to the public, inviting subscriptions to the stock, after the corporation is organized in other particulars. There is no such provision in the statute of New Jersey.

It is also to be remembered that the dicta were uttered in connection with decisions that the corporation was bound by the knowledge and action of all its existing stockholders, notwithstanding that only a part of the authorized stock had been taken. One or two of the dicta are in other cases in which no question in regard to action by all the stockholders with knowledge arose. In Pietsch v. Milbrath, 123 Wis. 647, 651, it appears that the plaintiffs took their stock upon grossly false representations as to the organization of the corporation, and they were allowed a remedy. Yeiser v. United States Board '' Paper Co. 107 Fed. Rep. 340, 348, was a case of gross, active fraud, and some stockholders who were ignorant of the facts were brought in before the transaction in question was consummated. Of course, this decision is of no effect as against the later adjudication in 210 U. S. 206, covering the precise question before us. Neither of these two cases seems to me important in reference to the question on which the present decision depends. I think the corporation in the present case is bound by the knowledge and consent of its stockholders.

The defendant relies upon the independent defense that the decision against the plaintiff, upon the same averments of fact in the suit against the other of the two joint actors, is a bar to the present claim, as res judicata.

Evidence was introduced to prove the law of New York, where the decree was entered. The defendant called thirteen witnesses of the greatest eminence and distinction, who testified as experts in law that, in their opinion, under the law of New York, the decree would be a bar to these suits if they were brought against this defendant in the courts of that State. Many of these witnesses had had a long judicial experience. Three of them had sat in the Court of Appeals, two of them for long terms, and one as_a Chief Judge. Several others had served a long time in the Supreme Court of New York, sitting in the general term and in the appellate division. Others had held other high positions in their profession, and all of them were lawyers whose opinions are entitled to great weight. The plaintiff called two eminent lawyers who expressed a contrary opinion. Many decisions of the courts of New York were also put in evidence. The defendant contended that, if the decree is a bar under the law of New York, it is equally so when pleaded in Massachusetts.

If it were necessary to consider this branch of the defense, it perhaps would be a grave question whether the defense was or was not made out. But as to that I express no opinion, preferring to rest this opinion on the other ground.

I am authorized to say that Mr. Justice Morton concurs in this opinion.

HAMMOND, J. Upon the questions (1) whether the facts found by the single justice are supported by the evidence and should stand, (2) whether "the transaction is to be determined by the law of Massachusetts," (3) whether the plaintiff has been guilty of laches, (4) what shall be the nature of the relief (if there is any relief), (5) what effect shall be given to the judgment rendered in the Lewisohn case by the Circuit Court of the United States for the Southern District of New York, (6) whether a decision for the plaintiff in these suits involves a denial to the defendant of due process of law, or the equal protection of the laws, and (7) whether the interlocutory order entered by a single justice enjoining the defendant from further prosecuting his suit against the plaintiff elsewhere except in this court should stand, I agree with the majority of the court.

But upon the question on the merits, namely, whether upon the facts found the defendant is answerable to the plaintiff, I agree with the dissenting opinion filed by the Chief Justice; and for the reasons stated therein I think that the bills should be dismissed.

FLETCHER v. ATEX, INC.

68 F.3d 1451 (1995), United States Court of Appeals, Second Circuit.
Argued May 26, 1995; Decided October 5, 1995.

Steven J. Phillips, Levy Phillips & Konigsberg, New York City (Alani Golanski, Levy Phillips & Konigsberg, New York City, on the brief), for Plaintiffs-Appellants.
Thomas E. Reidy, Nixon, Hargrave, Devans & Doyle, Rochester, New York (Henry J. DePippo, Flor M. Ferrer-Colón, Nixon, Hargrave, Devans & Doyle, Rochester, New York, on the brief), for Defendant-Appellee.
Before: KEARSE, CALABRESI, and CABRANES, Circuit Judges.

JOSÉ A. CABRANES, Circuit Judge:

This is a consolidated appeal from a final judgment of the United States District Court for the Southern District of New York (Morris E. Lasker, *Judge*), granting defendant-appellee Eastman Kodak Company's motion for summary judgment and dismissing all claims against it in two actions, *Fletcher v. Atex, Inc.*, 92 Civ. 8758 and *Hermanson v. 805 Middlesex Corp., Inc.*, 94 Civ. 1272. *Fletcher v. Atex, Inc.*, 861 F.Supp. 242 (S.D.N.Y.1994). The plaintiffs-appellants filed suit against Atex, Inc. ("Atex") and its parent, Eastman Kodak Company ("Kodak"), to recover for repetitive stress injuries that they claim were caused by their use of computer keyboards manufactured by Atex. Plaintiffs-appellants argue that the district court erred in granting summary judgment in favor of Kodak on the ground that Kodak could be held liable for the plaintiffs' alleged injuries. They contend that summary judgment was inappropriate because genuine issues of material fact existed regarding Kodak's liability as a defendant under each of the plaintiffs' four theories of liability, which we describe below.

I. BACKGROUND

The *Fletcher* and *Hermanson* plaintiffs filed their respective complaints on December 4, 1992, and February 25, 1994, seeking recovery from Atex and Kodak, among others, for repetitive stress injuries that they claim were caused by their use of Atex computer keyboards. From 1981 until December 1992, Atex was a wholly-owned subsidiary of Kodak. In 1987, Atex's name was changed to Electronic Pre-Press Systems, Inc., ("EPPS"), but its name was changed back to Atex in 1990. In December 1992, Atex sold substantially all of its assets to an independent third party and again changed its name to 805 Middlesex Corp., which holds the proceeds from the sale. Kodak continues to be the sole shareholder of 805 Middlesex Corp. After extensive discovery, Kodak moved for summary judgment in *Fletcher* on April 21, 1994, and in *Hermanson* on April 28, 1994. The plaintiffs opposed Kodak's motion, arguing that genuine issues of material fact existed as to Kodak's liability under any number of theories, including (1) that Atex was merely Kodak's alter ego or instrumentality; (2) that Atex was Kodak's agent in the manufacture and marketing of the keyboards; (3) that Kodak was the "apparent manufacturer" of the Atex keyboards; and (4) that Kodak acted in tortious concert with Atex in manufacturing and marketing the allegedly defective keyboards.

In support of their first theory, the plaintiffs argued that Kodak "dominated and controlled" Atex by maintaining significant overlap between the boards of directors of the two companies, "siphoning" off funds from Atex through use of a cash management system, requiring Kodak's approval for major expenditures, stock sales, and real estate acquisitions, participating in negotiations involving the sale of Atex to a third party, and including references to Atex as a "division" of Kodak and to the "merger" between Atex and Kodak in Atex's promotional literature and Kodak's Annual Report. Second, the plaintiffs claimed that, at the very least, the references to Atex in the promotional literature raised a question of material fact regarding Kodak's intent to confer authority on Atex to act as its agent in the manufacturing and marketing of computer keyboards. In support of their third theory, the plaintiffs maintained that the use of Kodak's name in Atex's advertising, promotional, and packaging materials provided assurances to consumers that the Kodak name stood behind Atex's products, and Kodak could thus be held liable as the "apparent manufacturer" of the keyboards. Finally, they argued that the fact that Kodak was generally aware of the danger of repetitive stress injuries and the fact that Kodak had tested the ergonomics of three Atex keyboards in 1990 presented evidence of concerted tortious action between Atex and Kodak. The *Fletcher* and *Hermanson* actions were consolidated before the district court for the purposes of summary judgment proceedings.

On August 17, 1994, the district court rejected each of the plaintiffs' theories of Kodak's liability and granted Kodak's motion for summary judgment in both actions. In its opinion, the court referred to, but did not rely upon, an identical suit filed against Atex and Kodak in New York state court, *King v. Eastman Kodak Co.,* No. 23439/92 (N.Y.Sup. Ct. June 9, 1994), in which Kodak's motion for summary judgment was granted on similar grounds. *Fletcher,* 861 F.Supp. at 243. First, the district court found that Kodak and Atex observed all corporate formalities and maintained separate corporate existences. It held that Atex's participation in Kodak's cash management system and Kodak's control over Atex's major expenditures and asset sales were insufficient to raise an issue of material fact regarding Kodak's liability under an alter ego theory. *Id.* at 244-45. Second, it held that the representations in various advertisements, promotional literature, and annual reports were similarly insufficient as a matter of law to find Kodak liable under an agency theory. *Id.* at 247. Third, the court held that Kodak was entitled to summary judgment on the plaintiffs' apparent manufacturer theory because the company was not involved in the sale or distribution of the keyboards. *Id.* at 245-46. Finally, the court found that the plaintiffs' concerted action theory failed as a matter of law because they offered no evidence indicating that Kodak and Atex had agreed to commit a tortious act. *Id.* at 246. This appeal followed.

II. DISCUSSION

A. The Summary Judgment Standard

We review a district court's grant of summary judgment *de novo* to determine whether there is a genuine issue of material fact and whether the moving party is entitled to judgment as a matter of law. *Healy v. Rich Prods. Corp.*, 981 F.2d 68, 72 (2d Cir. 1992). Summary judgment shall be granted "if the pleadings, depositions, answers to interrogatories, and admissions on file, together with the affidavits ... show that there is no genuine issue as to any material fact and that the moving party is entitled to a judgment as a matter of law." FED.R.CIV. P. 56(c). "[T]he mere existence of *some* alleged factual dispute between the parties will not defeat an otherwise properly supported motion for summary judgment; the requirement is that there be no *genuine* issue of *material* fact." *Anderson v. Liberty Lobby, Inc.*, 477 U.S. 242, 247-48, 106 S.Ct. 2505, 2509-10, 91 L.Ed.2d 202 (1986) (emphasis in original). While the court must view the inferences to be drawn from the facts in the light most favorable to the party opposing the motion, *Matsushita Elec. Indus. Co. v. Zenith Radio Corp.*, 475 U.S. 574, 587, 106 S.Ct. 1348, 1356, 89 L.Ed.2d 538 (1986), a party may not "rely on mere speculation or conjecture as to the true nature of the facts to overcome a motion for summary judgment." *Knight v. U.S. Fire Ins. Co.*, 804 F.2d 9, 12 (2d Cir.1986), *cert. denied,* 480 U.S. 932, 107 S.Ct. 1570, 94 L.Ed.2d 762 (1987). The non-moving party may defeat the summary judgment motion by producing sufficient specific facts to establish that there is a genuine issue of material fact for trial. *Celotex Corp. v. Catrett,* 477 U.S. 317, 322, 106 S.Ct. 2548, 2552, 91 L.Ed.2d 265 (1986). Finally, "'mere conclusory allegations or denials'" in legal memoranda or oral argument are not evidence and cannot by themselves create a genuine issue of material fact where none would otherwise exist. *Quinn v. Syracuse Model Neighborhood Corp.*, 613 F.2d 438, 445 (2d Cir.1980) (quoting *SEC v. Research Automation Corp.*, 585 F.2d 31, 33 (2d Cir.1978)).

B. Theories of Liability

Plaintiffs argue that the district court should have denied Kodak's motion for summary judgment on the ground that genuine issues of material fact existed regarding each of the plaintiffs' four theories of liability. We consider the plaintiffs' arguments on each of these theories in turn.

1. Alter Ego Liability

The plaintiffs claim that the district court erred in granting Kodak's motion for summary judgment on their alter ego theory of liability. The plaintiffs offer two arguments in this regard. First, they contend that the district court was estopped from granting Kodak's motion for summary judgment because the New York state court found in *King v. Eastman* that issues of material fact existed regarding Kodak's domination of Atex. Second, they argue that even if collateral estoppel does not apply in the instant case, genuine issues of material fact remain that preclude a grant of summary judgment in favor of Kodak.

The district court correctly noted that "[u]nder New York choice of law principles, `[t]he law of the state of incorporation determines when the corporate form will be disregarded and liability will be imposed on shareholders.'" *Fletcher,* 861 F.Supp. at 244 (quoting *Kalb, Voorhis & Co. v. American Fin. Corp.,* 8 F.3d 130, 132 (2d Cir.1993)). Because Atex was a Delaware corporation, Delaware law determines whether the corporate veil can be pierced in this instance.

Delaware law permits a court to pierce the corporate veil of a company "where there is fraud or where [it] is in fact a mere instrumentality or alter ego of its owner." *Geyer v. Ingersoll Publications Co.,* 621 A.2d 784, 793 (Del.Ch.1992). Although the Delaware Supreme Court has never explicitly adopted an alter ego theory of parent liability for its subsidiaries, lower Delaware courts have applied the doctrine on several occasions, as has the United States District Court for the District of Delaware. *See Geyer,* 621 A.2d at 793; *Mabon, Nugent & Co. v. Texas Am. Energy Corp.,* No. CIV.A. 8578,

1990 WL 44267, at *5, (Del.Ch. Apr. 12, 1990); *Harper v. Delaware Valley Broadcasters, Inc.*, 743 F.Supp. 1076, 1085 (D.Del.1990), *aff'd*, 932 F.2d 959 (3d Cir.1991). Thus, under an alter ego theory, there is no requirement of a showing of fraud. *Id.* at 1085. To prevail on an alter ego claim under Delaware law, a plaintiff must show (1) that the parent and the subsidiary "operated as a single economic entity" and (2) that an "overall element of injustice or unfairness ... [is] present." *Id.* (internal quotation marks omitted); *see also Mabon,* 1990 WL 44267, at *5; *Harco Nat'l Ins. Co. v. Green Farms, Inc.,* No. CIV.A. 1331, 1989 WL 110537, at *5, (Del Ch. Sept. 19, 1989).

In the New York state action of *King v. Eastman,* the court granted Kodak's motion for summary judgment, relying on an erroneous interpretation of Delaware's alter ego doctrine. The court noted that although the plaintiffs had raised "ample questions of fact regarding the first element of the piercing theory — domination," they made "no showing that Kodak used whatever dominance it had over Atex to perpetrate a fraud or other wrong that proximately cause[d] injury to them." This was an error; under Delaware law, the alter ego theory of liability does not require any showing of fraud.

a. Collateral Estoppel

Although the plaintiffs acknowledge that the New York state court erred in its interpretation of Delaware law, they argue that the court's treatment of the question of Kodak's domination over Atex should preclude all further litigation of that issue. We disagree and hold that the New York court's findings in *King v. Eastman* regarding Kodak's domination over Atex do not have collateral estoppel effect under New York law.

The doctrine of collateral estoppel "precludes a party from relitigating in a subsequent action or proceeding an issue clearly raised in a prior action or proceeding and decided against that party ... whether or not the tribunals or causes of action are the same." *Ryan v. New York Tel. Co.,* 62 N.Y.2d 494, 500, 478 N.Y.S.2d 823, 826, 467 N.E.2d 487, 490 (1984) (citing *Ripley v. Storer,* 309 N.Y. 506, 517, 132 N.E.2d 87 (1956)). Under New York law, two conditions must be met to preclude relitigation in the second action: (1) "the issue must have been material to the first action or proceeding and essential to the decision rendered therein" and (2) "the party against whom collateral estoppel is asserted [must have been] afforded a full and fair opportunity in the prior administrative proceeding to contest the decision now said to be controlling...." 62 N.Y.2d at 500-01, 478 N.Y.S.2d at 826, 467 N.E.2d at 490. Neither condition was met in this case.

First, the state court's finding of "ample questions of fact" regarding Kodak's domination of Atex was not essential to its judgment in *King.* The state court did not decide the summary judgment motion based on its finding of factual disputes between the parties. To the contrary, it *granted* summary judgment to Kodak on the plaintiffs' alter ego theory of liability based on its erroneous interpretation of Delaware law. Since the court's finding of domination was not essential to the judgment, its conclusions should not be accorded preclusive effect in the present action.

The plaintiffs counter that the state court's finding of a factual dispute on the issue of domination should be given preclusive effect, even though it was not essential to the judgment, because it was fully litigated by the parties and fully considered by the court. They rely on *Malloy v. Trombley,* 50 N.Y.2d 46, 427 N.Y.S.2d 969, 405 N.E.2d 213 (1980), which held that a court's alternative holding, while not essential to the judgment, could be given conclusive effect. However, the *Malloy* court carefully limited its holding: "[W]ithout intending to enunciate any broad rule, we hold in this instance that the rule of issue preclusion is applicable notwithstanding that in a precise sense the issue precluded was the subject of only an alternative determination by the trial court." 50 N.Y.2d at 52, 427 N.Y.S.2d at 973, 405 N.E.2d at 216. In *Malloy,* the trial court articulated a viable alternative ground to *support* its conclusion, a ground that the Court of Appeals noted had "validating authenticity" because it was likely expressed by the trial court to provide another basis for affirmance in case the other ground was rejected on appeal. 50 N.Y.2d at 52, 427 N.Y.S.2d at 972, 405 N.E.2d at 215. Here, the trial court's finding of a factual dispute on the issue of domination was not an alternative holding at all. It was *at odds* with the court's conclusion that summary judgment was appropriate and certainly did not provide "validating authenticity" for the court's holding.

Second, the court's finding of a factual dispute cannot have collateral estoppel effect because Kodak did not have a "full and fair opportunity" to litigate the question that the plaintiffs are asserting against it. Under New York law, a party has not had a full and fair opportunity to litigate an issue if it has had no opportunity to appeal the adverse finding. *People v. Medina,* 208 A.D.2d 771, 617 N.Y.S.2d 491, 493 (2d Dep't 1994); *see also Pinkney v. Keane,* 737 F.Supp. 187, 195 (E.D.N.Y.) ("Under New York law, a party who has obtained a final judgment in its favor is not normally precluded from relitigating a subsidiary issue that was decided against it."), *aff'd,* 920 F.2d 1090 (2d Cir. 1990), *cert. denied,* 501 U.S. 1217, 111 S.Ct. 2824, 115 L.Ed.2d 995 (1991). Kodak was in precisely this situation. It *could not* appeal the trial court's finding of a material factual dispute, because the final judgment — that is, the grant of summary judgment — was in Kodak's favor.

In sum, the collateral estoppel doctrine does not bar the relitigation of the question of Kodak's domination over its subsidiary, Atex, because the state court's finding was not essential to its judgment and because Kodak did not have a full and fair opportunity to litigate the issue.

b. Summary Judgment on the Alter Ego Theory

To prevail on an alter ego theory of liability, a plaintiff must show that the two corporations "'operated as a single economic entity such that it would be inequitable ... to uphold a legal distinction between them.'" *Harper,* 743 F.Supp. at 1085 (quoting *Mabon,* 1990 WL 44267, at *5). Among the factors to be considered in determining whether a subsidiary and parent operate as a "single economic entity" are:

"[W]hether the corporation was adequately capitalized for the corporate undertaking;

whether the corporation was solvent; whether dividends were paid, corporate records kept, officers and directors functioned properly, and other corporate formalities were observed; whether the dominant shareholder siphoned corporate funds; and whether, in general, the corporation simply functioned as a facade for the dominant shareholder." *Harco,* 1989 WL 110537, at *4 (quoting *United States v. Golden Acres, Inc.,* 702 F.Supp. 1097, 1104 (D.Del.1988)). As noted above, a showing of fraud or wrongdoing is not necessary under an alter ego theory, but the plaintiff must demonstrate an overall element of injustice or unfairness. *Harco,* 1989 WL 110537, at *5.

A plaintiff seeking to persuade a Delaware court to disregard the corporate structure faces "a difficult task." *Harco,* 1989 WL 110537, at *4. Courts have made it clear that "[t]he legal entity of a corporation will not be disturbed until sufficient reason appears." *Id.* Although the question of domination is generally one of fact, courts have granted motions to dismiss as well as motions for summary judgment in favor of defendant parent companies where there has been a lack of sufficient evidence to place the alter ego issue in dispute. *See, e.g., Akzona, Inc. v. Du Pont,* 607 F.Supp. 227, 237 (D.Del. 1984) (rejecting plaintiffs' alter ego theory of liability on a motion to dismiss); *Nelson v. International Paint Co.,* 734 F.2d 1084, 1092 (5th Cir.1984) ("[I]n the lack of sufficient evidence to place the alter ego issue in dispute, a corporate defendant may be entitled to summary judgment."); *see also Japan Petroleum Co. (Nigeria) v. Ashland Oil Inc.,* 456 F.Supp. 831, 838, 846 (D.Del.1978) (finding that subsidiary was not instrumentality of parent on a motion for summary judgment).

Kodak has shown that Atex followed corporate formalities, and the plaintiffs have offered no evidence to the contrary. Significantly, the plaintiffs have not challenged Kodak's assertions that Atex's board of directors held regular meetings, that minutes from those meetings were routinely prepared and maintained in corporate minute books, that appropriate financial records and other files were maintained by Atex, that Atex filed its own tax returns and paid its own taxes, and that Atex had its own employees and management executives who were responsible for the corporation's day-to-day business. The plaintiffs' primary arguments regarding domination concern (1) the defendant's use of a cash management system; (2) Kodak's exertion of control over Atex's major expenditures, stock sales, and the sale of Atex's assets to a third party; (3) Kodak's "dominating presence" on Atex's board of directors; (4) descriptions of the relationship between Atex and Kodak in the corporations' advertising, promotional literature, and annual reports; and (5) Atex's assignment of one of its former officer's mortgage to Kodak in order to close Atex's asset-purchase agreement with a third party. The plaintiffs argue that each of these raises a genuine issue of material fact about Kodak's domination of Atex, and that the district court therefore erred in granting summary judgment to Kodak on the plaintiffs' alter ego theory. We find that the district court correctly held that, in light of the undisputed factors of independence cited by Kodak, "the elements identified by the plaintiffs ... [were] insufficient as a matter of law to establish the degree of domination necessary to disregard Atex's corporate identity." *Fletcher,* 861 F.Supp. at 245.

First, the district court correctly held that "Atex's participation in Kodak's cash management system is consistent with sound business practice and does not show undue domination or control." *Id.* at 244. The parties do not dispute the mechanics of Kodak's cash management system. Essentially, all of Kodak's domestic subsidiaries participate in the system and maintain zero-balance bank accounts. All funds transferred from the subsidiary accounts are recorded as credits to the subsidiary, and when a subsidiary is in need of funds, a transfer is made. At all times, a strict accounting is kept of each subsidiary's funds. Courts have generally declined to find alter ego liability based on a parent corporation's use of a cash management system. *See, e.g., In re Acushnet River & New Bedford Harbor Proceedings,* 675 F.Supp. 22, 34 (D.Mass.1987) (Without "considerably more," "a centralized cash management system ... where the accounting records always reflect the indebtedness of one entity to another, is not the equivalent of intermingling funds" and is insufficient to justify disregarding the corporate form.); *United States v. Bliss,* 108 F.R.D. 127, 132 (E.D.Mo.1985) (cash management system indicative of the "usual parent-subsidiary relationship"); *Japan Petrol.,* 456 F.Supp. at 846 (finding segregation of subsidiary's accounts within parent's cash management system to be "a function of administrative convenience and economy, rather than a manifestation of control"). The plaintiffs offer no facts to support their speculation that Kodak's centralized cash management system was actually a "complete commingling" of funds or a means by which Kodak sought to "siphon[] all of Atex's revenues into its own account."

Second, the district court correctly concluded that it could find no domination based on the plaintiffs' evidence that Kodak's approval was required for Atex's real estate leases, major capital expenditures, negotiations for a sale of minority stock ownership to IBM, or the fact that Kodak played a significant role in the ultimate sale of Atex's assets to a third party. Again, the parties do not dispute that Kodak required Atex to seek its approval and/or participation for the above transactions. However, this evidence, viewed in the light most favorable to the plaintiffs, does not raise an issue of material fact about whether the two corporations constituted "a single economic entity." Indeed, this type of conduct is typical of a majority shareholder or parent corporation. *See Phoenix Canada Oil Co. v. Texaco,* 842 F.2d 1466, 1476 (3d Cir.1988) (declining to pierce the corporate veil where subsidiary required to secure approval from parent for "large investments and acquisitions or disposals of major assets"), *cert. denied,* 488 U.S. 908, 109 S.Ct. 259, 102 L.Ed.2d 247 (1988); *Akzona,* 607 F.Supp. at 237 (same, where parent approval required for expenditures exceeding $850,000); *Japan Petrol.,* 456 F.Supp. at 843 (finding no parent liability where parent approval required for expenditures exceeding $250,000). In *Akzona,* the Delaware district court noted that a parent's "general executive responsibilities" for its subsidiary's operations included approval over major policy decisions and guaranteeing bank loans, and that that type of oversight was insufficient to demonstrate domination and control. *Akzona,* 607 F.Supp. at 238 (internal quotation marks omitted). Similarly, the district court in the instant case properly found that the presence of Kodak employees at periodic meetings with Atex's chief financial officer and comptroller to be "entirely appropriate." *Fletcher,* 861 F.Supp. at 245 (citing *Akzona,* 607 F.Supp. at 238); *see Acushnet,* 675 F.Supp. at 34 ("The quarterly and annual reports made [to the parent] do not represent an untoward intrusion by the owner into the corporate enterprise. The right of shareholders to remain informed is similarly recognized in many public and closely held corporations.").

The plaintiffs' third argument, that Kodak dominated the Atex board of directors, also fails. Although a number of Kodak employees have sat on the Atex board, it is undisputed that between 1981 and 1988, only one director of Atex was also a director of Kodak. Between 1989 and 1992, Atex and Kodak had no directors in common. Parents and subsidiaries frequently have overlapping boards of directors while maintaining separate business operations. In *Japan Petroleum,* the Delaware district court held that the fact that a parent and a subsidiary have common officers and directors does not necessarily demonstrate that the parent corporation dominates the activities of the subsidiary. 456 F.Supp. at 841; *see Scott-Douglas Corp. v. Greyhound Corp.,* 304 A.2d 309, 314 (Del.Super.Ct.1973) (same). Since the overlap is negligible here, we find this evidence to be entirely insufficient to raise a question of fact on the issue of domination.

Fourth, the district court properly rejected the plaintiffs' argument that the descriptions of the relationship between Atex and Kodak and the presence of the Kodak logo in Atex's promotional literature justify piercing the corporate veil. *Fletcher,* 861 F.Supp. at 245. The plaintiffs point to several statements in both Kodak's and Atex's literature to evidence Kodak's domination of its subsidiary. For example, plaintiffs refer to (1) a promotional pamphlet produced by EPPS (a/k/a Atex) describing Atex as a business unit of EPPS and noting that EPPS was an "agent" of Kodak; (2) a document produced by Atex entitled "An Introduction to Atex Systems," which describes a "merger" between Kodak and Atex; (3) a statement in Kodak's 1985 and 1986 annual reports describing Atex as a "recent acquisition[]" and a "subsidiar[y] ... combined in a new division"; and (4) a statement in an Atex/EPPS document, "Setting Up TPE 6000 on the Sun 3 Workstation," describing Atex as "an unincorporated division of Electronic Pre-Press Systems, Inc., a Kodak company." They also refer generally to the fact that Atex's paperwork and packaging materials frequently displayed the Kodak logo.

It is clear from the record that Atex never merged with Kodak or operated as a Kodak division. The plaintiffs offer no evidence to the contrary, apart from these statements in Atex and Kodak documents that they claim are indicative of the true relationship between the two companies. Viewed in the light most favorable to the plaintiffs, these statements and the use of the Kodak logo are not evidence that the two companies operated as a "single economic entity." *See Coleman v. Corning Glass Works,* 619 F.Supp. 950, 956 (W.D.N.Y.1985) (upholding corporate form despite "loose language" in annual report about "merger" and parent's reference to subsidiary as a "division"), *aff'd,* 818 F.2d 874 (1987); *Japan Petrol.,* 456 F.Supp. at 846 (noting that representations made by parent in its annual reports that subsidiary serves as an agent "may result from public relations motives or an attempt at simplification"); *American Trading & Prod. Corp. v. Fischbach & Moore, Inc.,* 311 F.Supp. 412, 416 (N.D.Ill.1970) ("boastful" advertising and consideration of subsidiaries as "family" do not prove that corporate identities were ignored).

Fifth, the plaintiffs contend that Atex's assignment of its former CEO's mortgage to Kodak in order to close the sale of Atex's assets to a third party is evidence of Kodak's domination of Atex. We reject this argument as well. The evidence is undisputed that Kodak paid Atex the book value of the note and entered into a formal repayment agreement with the former CEO. Formal contracts were executed, and the two companies observed all corporate formalities.

Finally, even if the plaintiffs did raise a factual question about Kodak's domination of Atex, summary judgment would still be appropriate because the plaintiffs offer no evidence on the second prong of the alter ego analysis. The plaintiffs have failed to present evidence of an "overall element of injustice or unfairness" that would result from respecting the two companies' corporate separateness. *See Harper,* 743 F.Supp. at 1085 (holding that plaintiff cannot prevail on alter ego theory "because he has failed to allege any unfairness or injustice which would justify the court in disregarding the [companies'] separate legal existences"). In the instant case, the plaintiffs offer nothing more than the bare assertion that Kodak "exploited" Atex "to generate profits but not to safeguard safety." There is no indication that Kodak sought to defraud creditors and consumers or to siphon funds from its subsidiary. The plaintiffs' conclusory assertions, without more, are not evidence, *see Quinn,* 613 F.2d at 445, and are completely inadequate to support a finding that it would be unjust to respect Atex's corporate form. For all of the foregoing reasons, the district court's order entering summary judgment on the plaintiffs' alter ego theory of liability is affirmed.

2. Agency Liability

The plaintiffs next contend that a genuine issue of fact was raised as to whether Kodak could be held liable on an agency theory — that is, whether Kodak, as principal, could be liable for the tortious acts of Atex, its agent. The plaintiffs rely on statements in Atex/ EPPS literature to support their theory: (1) the statement in the Atex document "Setting Up TPE 6000 on the Sun 3 Workstation" that "Atex is an unincorporated division of Electronic Pre-Press Systems, Inc., a Kodak company"; and (2) the statements in the EPPS promotional pamphlet that "EPPS serves as Kodak's primary agent to supply electronic pre-press products" and that "Atex is the largest of the EPPS business units." In granting Kodak's motion for summary judgment, the district court rejected the plaintiffs' agency theory of liability, finding that there was no evidence that Kodak authorized the statements. *Fletcher,* 861 F.Supp. at 247.

The plaintiffs contend that the fact that Kodak permitted the use of its logo on these documents raises a question of fact as to whether Kodak authorized or appeared to authorize the references to Atex/EPPS as its agent. First, the plaintiffs' argument fails under a theory of actual authority. The Restatement (Second) of Agency states: "Authority is the power of the agent to affect the legal relations of the principal by acts done in accordance with the principal's manifestations of consent to him." RESTATEMENT (SECOND) OF AGENCY § 7 (1958). "Manifestation of consent" is "the expression of the will to another as distinguished from the undisclosed purpose or intention." *Id.* cmt. b; *see also Greene v. Hellman,* 51 N.Y.2d 197, 203-04, 433 N.Y.S.2d 75, 79, 412 N.E.2d 1301, 1305 (1980). A close reading of the record reveals no evidence that Kodak conferred actual authority upon Atex to act on its behalf. The plaintiffs have offered no evidence that either document was produced by Kodak; in fact, it appears that Atex and EPPS published and disseminated the documents at issue. The presence of a parent's logo on documents created and distributed by a subsidiary, standing alone, does not confer authority upon the subsidiary to act as an agent.

For similar reasons, plaintiffs' arguments fail under a theory of apparent authority. New York's Court of Appeals has made it clear that "apparent authority is dependent upon verbal or other acts *by a principal* which reasonably give an appearance of authority to conduct the transaction." *Greene,* 51 N.Y.2d at 204, 433 N.Y.S.2d at 80, 412 N.E.2d at 1306 (emphasis added) (citing RESTATEMENT (SECOND) OF AGENCY § 8 cmts. a, c). "Key to the creation of apparent authority," the court continued, "is that the third person, accepting the appearance of authority as true, has relied upon it." *Id.* The plaintiffs offer no evidence that Kodak authorized or gave the appearance of having authorized the statements in the Atex/EPPS documents. Atex's/EPPS's use of the Kodak logo is not a "verbal or other act[] by a *principal,"* but rather, an act by the purported agent. Furthermore, the record contains no evidence that the plaintiffs relied on the documents at issue. If there were evidence that the plaintiffs relied on these documents and if there were evidence that Kodak uttered or authorized them, then there would be an issue of material fact as to the existence of apparent authority.

However, there is neither. We affirm the district court's order granting summary judgment to the defendant on the plaintiffs' agency theory of liability.

3. Apparent Manufacturer

The plaintiffs' third theory of liability is that Kodak should be held liable as the "apparent manufacturer" of the Atex keyboards. RESTATEMENT (SECOND) OF TORTS § 400 (1965). The apparent manufacturer doctrine is set forth in the Restatement as follows: "One who puts out as his own product a chattel manufactured by another is subject to the same liability as though he were its manufacturer." *Id.* This theory of liability is well-established under New York law. *See Commissioners of State Ins. Fund v. City Chem. Corp.,* 290 N.Y. 64, 69, 48 N.E.2d 262 (1943); *Markel v. Spencer,* 5 A.D.2d 400, 171 N.Y.S.2d 770, 780 (4th Dep't 1958), *aff'd,* 5 N.Y.2d 958, 184 N.Y.S.2d 835, 157 N.E.2d 713 (1959).

The district court held that Kodak could not be held liable under the apparent manufacturer doctrine because "[t]here is no indication in the Restatement [and in New York case law] that Section 400 was intended to apply to a party which is not a seller of chattel, or is [not] otherwise involved in the chain of distribution of a product." *Fletcher,* 861 F.Supp. at 245. In support of its holding, the district court cited the New York state court ruling in *King v. Eastman,* which held that Kodak was not liable under this section because, *inter alia,* it was not involved in the sale or distribution of the allegedly defective keyboards. *Id.* at 246. The *King* court relied on two federal court opinions, which similarly limited the application of § 400. *See Torres v. Goodyear Tire and Rubber Co.,* 867 F.2d 1234, 1236 (9th Cir. 1989) (parent not liable under § 400 for subsidiary's product where it was not manufacturer or seller); *Affiliated FM Ins. Co. v. Trane Co.,* 831 F.2d 153, 156 (7th Cir.1987) (parent not liable under § 400 in the absence of evidence that it was involved in manufacture, sale, or installation of product); *see also Nelson,* 734 F.2d at 1087-88 (section 400 does not apply to one who allows manufacturer to use its name but was not itself a manufacturer nor a distributor of the product).

Kodak argues that the district court's conclusion is supportable on three different theories. First, § 400 cannot apply because Kodak was neither the seller nor the distributor of the allegedly defective keyboards. Second, even if § 400 liability could reach a party who did not sell or distribute the products in question, it does not apply to Kodak in this instance because the Kodak logo was not affixed to the keyboards or their packages, only to promotional and advertising materials. Finally, even if § 400 can apply when a defendant's name appears only on promotional and packaging materials, the materials submitted here do not suggest that Kodak, rather than Atex, manufactured the keyboards. We agree.

First, New York courts have only applied the apparent manufacturer doctrine to sellers of a product or parties otherwise involved in the chain of distribution. The commentary to the Restatement states:

> The words "one who puts out a chattel" include anyone who supplies it to others for their own use or for the use of third persons, *either by sale or lease or by gift or loan.*

RESTATEMENT (SECOND) OF TORTS § 400 cmt. a (emphasis added). Although no New York court, with the exception of the *King* court, has explicitly declined to apply § 400 where a parent arguably represents itself as the manufacturer of a product without participating in its sale or distribution, no New York court has ever extended liability under the doctrine to anyone other than sellers of products manufactured by third parties. *See Willson v. Faxon, Williams & Faxon,* 208 N.Y. 108, 113, 101 N.E. 799 (1913) (finding seller of laxatives could be held liable under apparent manufacturer doctrine where seller purchased tablets from manufacturer and affixed its own label to the product); *State Ins. Fund,* 290 N.Y. at 69, 48 N.E.2d 262 (finding chemical vendor could be held liable under earlier version of § 400 where vendor purchased chemicals from a distributor, removed distributor's label, and affixed its own); *Markel,* 171 N.Y.S.2d at 780 (finding defendant Ford Motor Company liable for malfunctioning brake pedal arm that it sold as a component part of a Ford automobile); *Schwartz v. Macrose Lumber & Trim Co.,* 50 Misc.2d 547, 270 N.Y.S.2d 875, 889 (Sup.Ct.

Queens County 1966) (finding vendor liable under apparent manufacturer doctrine for defective nail in box sold by vendor under vendor's name), *rev'd on other grounds,* 29 A.D.2d 781, 287 N.Y.S.2d 706 (2d Dep't 1968).

In support of their argument for § 400 liability, the plaintiffs draw our attention to several cases in other jurisdictions. All of these cases are distinguishable. Although they hold that participation in the chain of distribution is not essential to liability under the apparent manufacturer doctrine, each involved a licensing agreement in which the defendant allowed the use of its name in exchange for control over (or involvement in) the manufacture of the product. *See Kasel v. Remington Arms Co.,* 24 Cal.App.3d 711, 718, 724, 101 Cal.Rptr. 314 (2d Dist.1972) (licensor who retains "right to inspect and control the quality" of product could be liable as an "integral component[] of the ... enterprise responsible for placing ... products on the market"); *City of Hartford v. Assoc. Constr. Co.,* 34 Conn.Sup. 204, 384 A.2d 390, 393, 396 (1978) (licensor who "retained and exercised rights of control as to the quality and the methods and manner of application of the product" could be held liable under § 400); *Connelly v. Uniroyal, Inc.,* 75 Ill.2d 393, 408, 411, 27 Ill.Dec. 343, 389 N.E.2d 155 (1979) (licensor who remained involved with "the goods and manufacturing operations" of product liable under § 400 as an "integral part of the marketing enterprise"), *cert. denied,* 444 U.S. 1060, 100 S.Ct. 992, 62 L.Ed.2d 738 (1980). In the instant case, the plaintiffs have not produced any evidence that Kodak developed, designed, sold or distributed the allegedly defective keyboards. Contending otherwise, the plaintiffs point to the fact that Atex, in response to an interrogatory, listed Kodak among over thirty companies that were "involved in the design, manufacture, sale, marketing, leasing and/or installation of Atex keyboards." This interrogatory, however, was amended to delete Kodak from the list, and defendant's attorney submitted an affirmation attesting that the inclusion of Kodak was in error. Plaintiffs have submitted no other evidence of Kodak's actual participation in the manufacturing or distribution process; nor have they submitted any evidence of a licensing agreement between Kodak and Atex.

Second, even assuming that New York law permits a party that did not sell or distribute a product to be held liable under the apparent manufacturer doctrine, the plaintiffs offer no evidence that Kodak held itself out as the manufacturer of the Atex keyboard. *See* RESTATEMENT (SECOND) OF TORTS § 400. There is no question that the keyboards prominently display the name of Atex, the true manufacturer, and the plaintiffs do not dispute the defendant's assertion that the Kodak logo was not affixed to the Atex keyboards or their packages. Under these circumstances, it is difficult to understand how any defendant could be held liable on an apparent manufacturer theory. Indeed, the cases cited by the plaintiffs only extend § 400 liability to defendants who placed their names directly on the product or the product packaging at issue. *See Willson,* 208 N.Y. at 110, 113, 101 N.E. 799 (defendant could be held liable where vial containing tablets causing plaintiff's injuries labeled with defendant's name); *State Ins. Fund,* 290 N.Y. at 69, 48 N.E.2d 262 (defendant could be held liable where inscription on label of product bore defendant's name); *Markel,* 171 N.Y.S.2d at 780 (defendant liable for defective component part where vehicle marked with defendant's name); *Schwartz,* 270 N.Y.S.2d at 889 (defendant liable where plaintiff injured by nail packaged in box labeled with defendant's name); *Forry v. Gulf Oil Corp.,* 428 Pa. 334, 344, 237 A.2d 593 (1968) (defendant could be held liable where tire embossed with its name); *Carney v. Sears, Roebuck & Co.,* 309 F.2d 300, 304 (4th Cir.1962) (defendant could be held liable where its name appeared on defective product's label as well as in advertising).

Third, even if apparent manufacturer liability could extend to a defendant whose name appears only on promotional and advertising materials, rather than on the product itself, the materials offered by the plaintiffs do not suggest that Kodak manufactured the Atex keyboards. Many of the documents that the plaintiffs rely on make reference only to Atex computer *software,* such as the Atex "Color Imaging System" and the "PC Custom Display Software User Manual." Furthermore, Atex is repeatedly identified as the manufacturer of the Atex computer systems in all the documents identified by the plaintiffs. Under these circumstances, the plaintiffs' argument — that the presence of the Kodak logo on these documents is sufficient to raise an issue of material fact as to whether Kodak represented itself as the manufacturer of the keyboards — must fail.

For these reasons, we affirm the district court's order granting summary judgment for the defendant-appellee on the plaintiffs' apparent manufacturer theory of liability.

4. Concerted Tortious Action

The plaintiffs' final theory of liability is that Kodak acted in tortious concert with Atex in designing and marketing the allegedly defective keyboards. The plaintiffs present alternative arguments for Kodak's liability under the so-called concerted action doctrine. First, they argue that "the evidence of Kodak's direct participation in the marketing of the defective keyboard equipment" raises an issue of material fact regarding Kodak's acting in concert with Atex. In the alternative, they argue that Kodak could be liable under a separate theory of concerted action under which liability may be premised upon "concerted action by substantial assistance."

Section 876 of the Restatement (Second) of Torts provides that:

> For harm resulting to a third person from the tortious conduct of another, one is subject to liability if he (a) does a tortious act in concert with the other or pursuant to a common design with him, or (b) knows that the other's conduct constitutes a breach of duty and gives substantial assistance or encouragement to the other so to conduct himself....

It remains an open question under New York law whether concerted action liability can be premised on a showing of concerted action by "substantial assistance or encouragement." Although the New York Court of Appeals has referred to both the traditional "common design" approach as well as the "substantial assistance" theory of concerted action, *see Bichler v. Eli Lilly & Co.*, 55 N.Y.2d 571, 580-81, 450 N.Y.S.2d 776, 780, 436 N.E.2d

182, 186 (1982), no cases have ever applied the "substantial assistance" approach. We find it unnecessary to decide this question of New York law at this time, because the plaintiffs' claim fails as a matter of law under either theory.

Under the first theory of concerted action, New York law "provides for joint and several liability on the part of all defendants having an understanding, express or tacit, to participate in a common plan or design to commit a tortious act." *Rastelli v. Goodyear Tire & Rubber Co.,* 79 N.Y.2d 289, 295, 582 N.Y.S.2d 373, 375, 591 N.E.2d 222, 224 (1992) (internal quotation marks omitted). The Court of Appeals has held that "[i]t is essential that each defendant charged with acting in concert have acted tortiously and that one of the defendants committed an act in pursuance of the agreement which constitutes a tort." *Id.* The plaintiffs argue that various statements in the Atex/EPPS literature and the use of the Kodak logo on certain documents packaged with Atex products, as well as the fact that Atex's interrogatory answer initially listed Kodak among the companies "involved in the design, manufacture, sale, marketing, leasing and/or installation of Atex keyboards," demonstrate Kodak's "full collaboration" in the marketing of the keyboards. In addition, the plaintiffs present various reports and documents on ergonomics[1] and repetitive stress injuries that Kodak created for the use of its own employees as evidence that "Kodak was fully aware of both the hazards associated with keyboard use and the means of reducing or eliminating those hazards." Finally, they rely on the Kodak Design Resource Center's evaluation of the ergonomics of three Atex keyboards in 1990 as evidence that "Kodak was a full participant with Atex in the deliberations about whether to warn users of the Kodak/Atex equipment, exactly what

1) Ergonomics is the study of the design of requirements of work in relation to the physical and psychological capabilities and limitations of people.... The aim of the discipline is to prevent the development of occupational disorders and to reduce the potential for fatigue, error, or unsafe acts through the evaluation and design of facilities, environments, jobs, tasks, tools, equipment, processes, and training methods to match the capabilities of specific workers." See 57 Fed.Reg. 34192, 34199 app. A (Aug. 3, 1992) (OSHA advance notice of proposed rulemaking on ergonomics safety).

such warnings should state, and what would be the risks of not issuing such warnings."

As the district court correctly held, "none of this tends to show that Kodak and Atex had `an understanding ... to participate in a common plan or design to commit a tortious act.'" *Fletcher,* 861 F.Supp. at 246 (alteration in original) (quoting *Rastelli,* 79 N.Y.2d at 295, 582 N.Y.S.2d at 375, 591 N.E.2d at 224). As noted above, the defendant's attorney submitted an affirmation attesting that the answer to the interrogatory was an error, and the plaintiffs have offered no additional evidence that Kodak actually participated in the design or manufacture of the Atex keyboards. The documents offered by the plaintiffs do not suggest any "agreement" between Kodak and Atex to act "jointly and tortiously." They merely refer to general statements about the "merger" between Atex and Kodak and the "marriage" between the two companies.

Furthermore, none of the evidence demonstrates that Kodak's actions were tortious. The fact that Kodak prepared guidelines for its employees to use in relation to their own computer workstations does not constitute tortious conduct with regard to the keyboards developed and sold by Atex. There is no allegation that Kodak's internal guidelines were ever used in conjunction with the design or manufacture of the Atex keyboards. Likewise, while it is undisputed that Atex retained Kodak's Design Resource Center to evaluate the ergonomics of various Atex keyboards in 1990, nothing contradicts the evidence in the record that this evaluation occurred only after all of the keyboards at issue had been designed, developed, and manufactured. Furthermore, the plaintiffs have offered no shred of evidence to support their speculation that "Kodak was a full participant with Atex in the deliberations about whether to warn users of the Kodak/Atex equipment." Nothing contradicts the defendant's evidence that Atex retained Kodak as an "independent organization" solely to conduct a single evaluation of three Atex keyboards. Finally, there is no allegation that Kodak's laboratory performed the tests on the Atex equipment negligently or provided Atex with false information about its evaluation of Atex's keyboards.

In their second argument, the plaintiffs contend that even if there was no agreement between the parties to act tortiously, Kodak may be liable under the concerted action theory by providing "substantial assistance or encouragement" to Atex in furtherance of its tortious conduct. A "substantial assistance" claim based on § 876 of the Restatement (Second) of Torts requires evidence that (1) the defendant knows that the other's conduct constitutes a breach of duty and (2) the defendant gives substantial assistance or encouragement to the other's conduct. RESTATEMENT (SECOND) OF TORTS § 876(b).

We find that, viewed in the light most favorable to the plaintiffs, Kodak's general awareness of the hazards of repetitive stress injuries and the Kodak laboratory's evaluation of the Atex keyboards in 1990 are insufficient to raise a question of material fact regarding Kodak's knowledge of or substantial assistance in Atex's allegedly tortious conduct. Kodak's knowledge about repetitive stress injuries generally cannot be construed as knowledge of the alleged defective design of the Atex keyboard or Atex's alleged failure to warn keyboard users of the hazards of repetitive stress injuries. Furthermore, the plaintiffs have offered no evidence to contradict the defendant's assertions that Kodak's one-time evaluation of the keyboards in 1990 occurred years after the keyboards in question were designed and distributed. Finally, the plaintiffs present no evidence to suggest that Kodak was involved - either before or after the 1990 evaluation-in the decision to include warnings about repetitive stress disorders or user guidelines with Atex keyboards. Thus, we find that summary judgment on this claim was also appropriate.

III. CONCLUSION

To summarize: We affirm the district court's order granting summary judgment for the defendant on each of the plaintiffs' four theories of liability.

1. We agree with the district court's conclusion that the defendant was entitled to summary judgment on the plaintiffs' alter ego theory of liability. The collateral estoppel doctrine does not preclude relitigation of the question of Kodak's domination over Atex because the state court's finding of material facts in dispute was not essential to its judgment and because the defendant did not have a full and fair opportunity to litigate the issue. The elements identified by the plaintiffs were insufficient to raise a material issue of fact regarding domination, and further, the plaintiffs failed to offer evidence of injustice that would justify disregarding Atex's corporate form.
2. We affirm the district court's conclusion that the defendant was entitled to summary judgment on the plaintiffs' agency theory of liability because the plaintiffs offered no evidence that Kodak authorized or appeared to authorize Atex to act on its behalf in the manufacturing and marketing of keyboards or that the plaintiffs relied on the documents in question.
3. We agree with the district court's conclusion that the defendant was entitled to summary judgment on the plaintiffs' apparent manufacturer theory of liability on the ground that, under New York law, a parent cannot be liable as an apparent manufacturer where it was not the seller or the distributor of the product.
4. Finally, we agree with the district court's conclusion that the defendant was entitled to summary judgment on the plaintiffs' concerted tortious action theory. We also affirm the court's finding that the plaintiffs offered no evidence that Kodak and Atex had an agreement to commit a tortious act. Finally, we find that there was no evidence to support the plaintiffs' theory that Kodak provided "substantial assistance or encouragement" to Atex in furtherance of its allegedly tortious conduct.

TAYLOR v. STANDARD GAS & ELEC. CO.

306 U.S. 307 (1939)
Argued Jan. 5, 1939; Decided Feb. 27, 1939.

[306 U.S. 307, 308] Mr. Jason L. Honigman, of Detroit, Mich. (Messrs. A. W. Sempliner, of Detroit, Mich., Travis I. Milsten, of Tulsa, Okl., and Milton J. Miller, of Detroit, Mich., of counsel), for petitioners.

Messrs. Nathan A. Gibson, of Tulsa, Okl., R. M. Campbell, of Chicago, Ill., Wilbur J. Holleman, of Tulsa, Okl., A. Louis Flynn, of Chicago, Ill., and Jacob K. Javits and Selig J. Levitan, both of New York City, for respondent Standard Gas & Electric Co.

Messrs. James F. Oates, Jr., of Chicago, Ill., William P. Sidley, Paul V. Harper, John Dern, and Gordon W. Winks, all of Chicago, Ill., for respondent Reorganization Committee.

Mr. George S. Ramsey, of Tulsa, Okl. (Messrs. Villard Martin and Garrett Logan, both of Tulsa, Okl., of counsel), for respondent H. W. Creis, trustee.

Mr. W. F. Semple, of Tulsa, Okl., for respondent debtor corporation.

Mr. Justice ROBERTS delivered the opinion of the Court.

The question presented is whether the District Court abused its discretion in approving the compromise of a claim by a parent against a subsidiary corporation and a plan of reorganization based upon the compromise, in proceedings under Section 77B of the Bankruptcy Act.[1] The Circuit Court of Appeals, by a divided court, approved the District Court's order.[2]

The petitioners are a committee for the protection of preferred

1) U.S.C.A. Tit. 11, Sec. 207.

2) Taylor et al. v. Standard Gas & Electric Co. et al., 10 Cir., 96 F. 2d 693.

stockholders. The respondents are the trustee of the debtor, Deep Rock Oil Corporation (a Delaware corporation whose business was that of producing, refining, and selling gasoline, oil, and other petroleum products, from lands located in Oklahoma, Kansas, Texas, and Arkansas), a reorganization committee, representing note-holders and certain holders of preferred stock, and Standard Gas and Electric Company, which owns practically all of the common stock of the debtor, claiming as a creditor.

The debtor was organized in 1919 to take over the properties then being operated by one C. B. Shaffer.[3)] Standard Gas & Electric Company, hereinafter called Standard, then had investments in various utility properties but had never been interested in oil. Byllesby & Company, hereinafter called Byllesby, an investment banking corporation which controlled Standard, entered into a contract with Shaffer whereby he was to organize the debtor corporation and to be paid by that corporation for his properties $15,580,000 made up of cash, a note, and preferred and common stock of the company. Byllesby agreed to purchase $11,000,000 par value of first mortgage bonds of an authorized issue of $15,000,000, $5, 000,000 par value of preferred stock, and 120,000 shares of common stock, par $1, for $15,200,000 in cash, to be applied by the company to the cash payments to be made to Shaffer and for working capital. Shaffer received for the properties turned over by him 80,000 shares of common stock, 50,000 shares of $100ar preferred stock, $9,500,000 in cash and a note of Byllesby and Standard for $1,000,000. In fact $12,000, 000 of the first mortgage bonds were underwritten by a syndicate formed by Byllesby and sold to the public. The result of the above transactions was to leave Deep Rock with approximately $6,700,000 of cash. Shortly thereafter the remaining $3,000,000 of bonds were pledged to secure Deep Rock's notes for $2,000,000. From its organization Deep Rock was, most of the time, 'two jumps ahead of the wolf', as one of Standard's

3) The corporate name was Shaffer Oil & Refining Company. This was changed in 1931 to Deep Rock Oil Corporation. The company will be referred to by the latter name.

officers testified. The common stock went into a voting trust which gave Standard and Shaffer equal control. Shaffer undertook the management of the properties and business. After two years Standard became dissatisfied with Shaffer's management and he severed his connection with the company selling his common stock to Standard and surrendering to Deep Rock 50,000 shares of preferred stock which was cancelled.

Thenceforward the debtor was under the complete control and domination of Standard through ownership of the common stock. Standard's officers, directors, and agents always constituted a majority of the Board. The remaining directors were operating officers or employes of Deep Rock who had been employed on behalf of Deep Rock by Standard or the Byllesby Management Corporation, hereafter called Management Corporation, a wholly owned subsidiary of Standard, or were under the complete control of Standard. A majority of Deep Rock's officers were officers or directors of Standard or of the Management Corporation, or of both. The officers of the debtor, who were chosen for their technical or business experience in the oil industry, although allowed some discretion in the matter of development and operation of the oil properties, reported to and were always subject to the direction of officers and directors of Standard. All of the fiscal affairs of the debtor were wholly controlled by Standard, which was its banker and its only source of financial aid.

Deep Rock was placed in the hands of a receiver in March 1933 and the present proceeding under Section 77B of the Bankruptcy Act was instituted in June 1934. Standard filed a claim as a creditor in the receivership and in the bankruptcy proceedings, which the receivers and the trustee resisted. The claim was referred to a master, before whom trial lasted many months. All the witnesses were officers, directors or agents of Standard, or its affiliates, and officers of the debtor. All the documentary evidence came from the books and records of Standard and Deep Rock. The basis of claim was an open account which embraced transactions between Standard and Deep Rock from the latter's organization in 1919 to the receivership in 1933. The account consists of thousands of items of debit and credit. The book entries were made under the direction of Standard's auditing department, which supervised the auditing department of Deep Rock, and it is not surprising, therefore, that the books of the two companies agree with respect to all items.

The account contains debits to Deep Rock in excess of $52,000,000 and credits of approximately $43,000,000 leaving a balance shown to be due Standard of $9,342,642.37, which was the amount of the claim presented. Cash payments by Standard to Deep Rock, or to others for its account, as shown by the books, total $31,804,145.04. Management and supervision fees paid or credited to Management Corporation amount to $1,219,034.83. Interest charges by Standard to Deep Rock on open account balances total $ 4,819,222.07. Rental charges upon a lease to Deep Rock of oil properties owned by a Standard subsidiary but claimed by petitioners to belong, in equity, to Deep Rock, amount to $4,525,000. Debits by Standard to Deep Rock of the amounts of dividends declared by Deep Rock to Standard, but not paid, reach the sum of $3,502,653. In addition there are hundreds of debits and credits representing other inter- company items.

Two preferred stockholders were permitted to intervene in the proceedings and they joined in the trustee's objections to the claim. Many transactions entered in the account were attacked as fraudulent and it was asserted that as Standard had made Deep Rock its mere agent or instrumentality it could not transmute itself from the status of the proprietor of Deep Rock's business to that of creditor. The hearings before the master were closed, but before he made any report, and as a result of negotiations initiated by the reorganization committee organized at the instance of Byllesby, representing approximately eighty-two per cent. of the noteholders and sixty per cent. of the preferred stockholders of Deep Rock, Standard proposed a compromise of its claim.

The court referred the proposal to the master who reported favorably. The trustee and his counsel also recommended the approval of the compromise, which involved the allowance of Standard's claim at $5,000,000. In contemplation of the approval of this compromise a reorganization of Deep Rock was proposed by the reorganization committee. The plan was based upon the trustee's appraisal of the debtor's assets at $16,800,000, of which $7,300,000 represented net current assets, mainly cash, and the remainder comprised fixed assets valued at $9,500,000. It provided that upon approval of the compromise of Standard's claim, the reorganization would be effected by the formation of a new company which would take over the debtor's assets and would issue $10,000,000 par value of fifteen year six per cent. income debentures which were to go to the holders of the debtor's unpaid notes of like amount; 25,000 shares of $7 cumulative preferred stock and 520,000 shares of no par common stock, of which the entire preferred stock and 390,000 shares of common should go to Standard on account of its claim, 80,000 shares of common to the noteholders, and 50,000 shares of common to the preferred stockholders of the old company. Standard's claim to the extent of $3,500,000 was to stand on a parity with the debtor's notes.

In the District Court the petitioners insisted that as the testimony before the master had been closed he should be required to pass upon the provability of Standard's claim and no reorganization plan should be considered until the validity of the claim had been adjudicated. The court, without passing on this demand, refused to approve the compromise or the plan of reorganization. Referring to the 50,000 shares of preferred stock outstanding, the judge stated that somebody had received the money represented by this stock from the public; that the plan in effect wiped out preferred stockholders and that he could not approve any plan which had this effect. In the course of the hearing he stated: 'The evidence is overwhelming that Standard ran this company; they officered it; they capitalized it; it is just a child in their hands, and if there ever was a case the law is clear on, it is nothing but an instrumentality, according to the admissions.' He indicated, however, that he would approve a plan according Standard a parity with the noteholders for a smaller proportion of its claim allowing the balance on a parity with the preferred stockholders, and suggested that the parties negotiate further in an effort to reach a fair result.

Months later the reorganization committee presented an amended plan which, as modified by the Court, contemplated the compromise of Standard's claim at $5,000,000, as before, and the organization of a new company which should issue $10,000,000 par value of debentures and 520,000 shares of common stock. These securities were to be distributed as follows: The new issue of debentures was to go to the holders of the old notes. In lieu of interest on the old notes accumulated to January 1, 1937, totaling $2,300,000, the noteholders were to receive $ 1,200,000 in cash and 40,000 shares of common stock; interest accruing subsequent to January 1, 1937, was to be paid in cash. The old preferred stockholders were to receive 100,000 shares of common stock and Standard was to receive for its claim 380,000 shares of common stock. Thus there was allocated to Standard approximately seventy-three per cent., to the old preferred stockholders nineteen per cent., and to the noteholders eight per cent. of the common stock. The District Court permitted the petitioners to intervene and, over their objections, approved the compromise and the plan. A majority of the Circuit Court of Appeals examined the record only to the extent of determining that it was possible that Standard might establish its claim in whole or in part, and concluded that the District Court had not exceeded the bounds of reasonable discretion in granting its approval. One judge thought that the instrumentality rule was applicable; that, under the rule, Standard had no provable claim; and that it was an abuse of discretion to approve the compromise and the reorganization plan. We agree with the conclusion of the dissenting judge, but for different reasons.

The petitioner insist that the appraisal upon which the plan was based was inordinately low and that, for this reason alone, the plan should not have been approved. The appraisal was supported by substantial evidence and the values shown by it were approved and adopted by the District Court and by the Circuit Court of Appeals. We accept the concurrent findings of the two courts that the value of the debtor's assets does not exceed $17,000,000.

As the debentures to be issued to the noteholders, plus the cash they are to get, total $11,200,000, the equity remaining in the property is not over $5,800,000. Standard's share of this equity will be seventy-three per cent., or $4,234,000, and will give it complete control of the new company. The preferred stockholders will receive nineteen per cent. or $1,020,000,- a minority interest without representation on the board of directors. The question is whether, within the bounds of reason and fairness, such a plan can be justified. We think the history of Standard's dealings with Deep Rock requires a negative answer.

Without going into the minutiae of the transactions between the two companies, enough may be stated to expose the reasons for our decision. As has been stated, Standard came into complete control of Deep Rock in 1921. From the outset Deep Rock was insufficiently capitalized, was topheavy with debt and was in parlous financial condition. Standard so managed its affairs as always to have a stranglehold upon it. At organization Deep Rock had cash working capital of only about $6, 600,000 and a mortgage indebtedness of $12,000,000, the interest and sinking fund requirements of which were nearly $2,000,000 a year. Its assets at that time were appraised at about $16,000,000. Shortly thereafter it created a further note issue of $2,000,000. Upon the acquirement of Shaffer's interest, in 1921, Standard caused Deep Rock to issue short term notes of a par of $3,500,000. Deep Rock also, between 1921 and 1924, borrowed substantial sums on promissory notes some of which were discounted or subsequently taken up by Standard. So inadequate was Deep Rock's capitalization that, in the period from organization to 1926, the balance due on open account to Standard grew to more than $14,800,000. Standard determined to place some of this indebtedness of Deep Rock with the public. In order to do so it had to improve Deep Rock's balance sheet. This it did by purchasing 80,000 shares of preferred stock for which it credited Deep Rock $7,223,333.33. It then bought $7,500,000 face value two year six per cent. notes for $7,273,750, which were sold to the public through a syndicate organized by Byllesby.

Deep Rock's requirements of additional capital persisted and, by the spring of 1928, the open account and a note which Deep Rock had given Standard for advances totaled over $11,000,000. As the two year notes held by the public were maturing, Standard found it necessary to make a new offering. There still remained nearly $2,000,000 of first mortgage bonds outstanding which had to be retired to make an unsecured note issue salable. Standard, therefore, determined that Deep Rock's balance sheet must again be put in such shape that notes could be sold. It accordingly purchased common stock from Deep Rock to the amount of the then open balance and commuted 90,000 shares of the preferred stock, which it held, into common. It caused Deep Rock to issue $10,000,000 of six per cent. notes which were sold by a syndicate organized by Byllesby and applied the proceeds to the redemption of the two year notes and the outstanding mortgage bonds. This financing, however, merely changed the character of Deep Rock's funded indebtedness and gave it no new working capital. This $ 10,000,000 note issue is the one now outstanding. As before, Deep Rock's resources were wholly insufficient for its business and the open account began again to build up so that between February 1928 and February 1933, the date of receivership, the account had grown to $9,342,642.37.

No dividends were paid on preferred stock until 1926. In that and the following year existing arrearages were paid by Standard, for Deep Rock's account, in the amount of $1,435,813. Between 1928 and 1931 Standard advanced Deep Rock, for payment of preferred dividends, $1,106,706. During the period between 1926 and 1929 Deep Rock declared dividends on its common stock in a total of $3,064,685.50. Of these dividends $1,946, 672 was charged by Standard, as owner of common stock, against Deep Rock in the open account. Standard took new common stock for dividends to the amount of $1,015,437.50 and advanced Deep Rock cash to pay dividends to outside holders of common stock in the sum of $102,576. Against the total of $2,645,095 advanced by Standard to pay Deep Rock's dividends, Standard credited payments received from Deep Rock in the open account in the sum of $927,500.

These dividends were declared in the face of the fact that Deep Rock had not the cash available to pay them and was, at the time, borrowing in large amounts from or through Standard.

About 1922 Standard decided that, in view of the unsatisfactory progress of Deep Rock, earnings must be increased by the acquisition of additional oil properties and by the erection of a modern gasoline cracking plant. Upon recommendation of the operating officials, Standard decided that Deep Rock should purchase the so-called Bradstreet properties, the price of which was $650,000. Of this amount $500,000 was advanced by Standard for account of Deep Rock and $150,000 paid by notes of Deep Rock. Title to the property was taken in the name of J. C. Kennedy, an employe of Deep Rock, as trustee. Kennedy never executed any declaration of trust. Deep Rock charged against him not only the original purchase price of the Bradstreet properties but the moneys thereafter expended in their development and in the acquisition of additional leases, amounting, to October 1, 1925, to $1,033,294.32, much of which represented advances by Standard.

In 1922 Deep Rock conveyed a small portion of its land to R. J. Graf, a Standard official, as trustee. Upon this land Deep Rock erected a new cracking plant at a total cost of $861,297.79. This expenditure was charged to R. J. Graf, trustee. Again part or all of the sums so expended were advanced by Standard to Deep Rock and charged against the latter.

In 1922 Standard had caused a company to be formed in Delaware known as Deep Rock Oil and Refining Company, intending that it should take title to the Bradstreet properties and the cracking plant. The purpose, as Standard's officers now state, was to keep these assets from going into direct ownership of Deep Rock and thus coming under the lien of its mortgage, so that they could be used as the basis of additional financing. The records of the Refining Company show that its capital stock was issued against the transfer by Kennedy and Graf as trustees of the Bradstreet and cracking properties but there are no corporate records of Deep Rock or of

Standard concerning any actual transfer and no book entries of Deep Rock or Standard were made concerning the supposed transfer until December 1925, as of October 1, 1925. At that time, by direction of one Brahancy, the chief accounting officer of Standard, entries were made in Standard's books and those of Deep Rock to evidence the following transaction: Standard assumed the advances made by Deep Rock for improvement of the Bradstreet properties and the cracking plant totaling $1,894,592.11 by crediting Deep Rock with that sum and Refining Company gave its note to Standard in that amount. Deep Rock also credited Kennedy, Trustee, with the $650,000 paid for the Bradstreet properties and Standard assumed this charge. The entire capital stock of Refining Company, evidencing equity ownership in the Bradstreet properties and the cracking plant, was transferred to Standard. Thus, on the face of things, Standard, through ownership of the capital stock of Refining Company, owned and controlled the Bradstreet properties and the cracking plant and put itself in such a position that, without its continued cooperation, Deep Rock could not function. As at October 1, 1925, but in fact somewhat later, at the dictation of Standard's officials, a lease was executed by the Refining Company to Deep Rock covering the properties in question whereby Deep Rock should, for the first three months, pay $75,000 per month and, for the ensuing four and three-quarters years, pay $50,000 a month to Refining Company as rental. Such rental as was paid by Deep Rock was at once declared by Refining Company as a dividend to Standard and such as was not paid was debited to Deep Rock by Standard in the open account. Under this lease, which expired October 1, 1930, Deep Rock paid, or became obligated to Standard in the total of, $3,075,000. During the term of the lease the operations of the leased properties showed a net loss of $30,401.40. The lease further provided that Deep Rock, at its own cost, should make all improvements and additions to the leased property, should make good all depreciation and return the property in the same condition as when leased. Additions to the cracking plant cost Deep Rock, during the term, $264,680. 51; and there were charged against

Deep Rock in alleged fulfilment of its obligations under the lease, taxes of Refining Company and other items amounting to $192,415.91. Meantime, in two letters written bankers in connection with the sale of notes of Deep Rock, the president of Deep Rock, who was also president of Standard, made statements, and warranted their truth, to the effect that Deep Rock owned these leased properties. In spite of the losses entailed upon Deep Rock by the lease arrangement, Standard dictated its renewal for another term of five years commencing October 1, 1930, and from that date to the receivership Deep Rock paid, or was debited by Standard with, $1,450,000, as rental and suffered, in the operation of the properties leased, a total loss of.$1, 584,458.05. During the combined terms of the two leases Deep Rock was charged in the open account for Standard's subsidiary management corporation in payment of managerial, engineering, and financial advice, $1,020,000.

Immediately after the last and presently outstanding note issue was sold to the public Standard's annual report, for the first time, disclosed its claim to the ownership of the Refining Company properties. At the date of the receivership Standard claimed it owned the Refining Company's properties through stock ownership, and held its note in the amount of $1, 894,592.11. The trustee in bankruptcy attacked this transaction as fraudulent and asserted Deep Rock's ownership of all the property represented by the Refining Company's stock free of any indebtedness to Standard in respect of it.

During the whole period from 1919 to the receivership, Standard charged Deep Rock interest at the rate of seven per cent. per annum compounded monthly on the balance shown by the open account. During the entire period the Management Corporation charged Deep Rock with round annual sums for management and supervision of Deep Rock's affairs which totaled $1,219,034.83, all of which Standard assumed and charged into the open account.

It is impossible within the compass of this opinion to detail the numerous other transactions evidenced by the books of the two companies many of which were to the benefit of Standard and to the detriment of Deep Rock. All of them were accomplished through the complete control and domination of Standard and without the participation of the preferred stockholders who had no voice or vote in the management of Deep Rock's affairs.[4] The suggested basis of compromise of Standard's claim needs comment. As has been said, when, in 1928, it became necessary to refinance Deep Rock's note obligations, Standard had to wipe out the enormous and threatening credit balance in its favor on Deep Rock's books. It, therefore, took common stock in payment of the balance. It is said that the compromise figure is reached by disregarding all transactions prior to February 24, 1928, when Standard commuted its then claim, starting fresh from that date, and considering only the items in the account thenceforward to the date of receivership. It is asserted that, during the period in question, Standard paid out, for account of Deep Rock, in cash, $ 6,850,971.50 and credited Deep Rock against these expenditures $4,475,803. 59, leaving a balance of cash advanced of $2,375,167.91, as to which there can be no question; the Bradstreet properties and the cracking plant are to be returned to Deep Rock's ownership by transfer of the stock of the Refining Company and its note now held by Standard. It is asserted that in consideration of this transfer Deep Rock ought to assume the original cost of the Bradstreet properties advanced by Standard ($650,000), plus the amount of the disbursements by Deep Rock upon those properties which Standard had credited to Deep Rock when it took over the Refining Company stock ($1,894,592.11), less rentals charged by the Refining Company to Deep Rock prior to February 24, 1928, which rentals had been absorbed in the settlement by Standard of February 24, 1928 ($1,475,000). This leaves Deep Rock owing on the Bradstreet and cracking plant accounts $1,585,485. 18. Simple interest at five per cent. is to be allowed on each of the two sums so ascertained. This brings the claim

4) At no time did the charter confer voting power on preferred stockholders, except in case and so long only as the company should be in default in payment of dividends on the preferred for a period of more than six months. At no time did Standard have less than a majority of the voting stock outstanding.

to approximately $5,000,000. It is said that this computation of the claim eliminates debits to Deep Rock made since 1928 for the fees of Management Corporation, for dividends on preferred and common stock held by Standard, and for every other questionable item; and that there can be no just criticism of the recognition of Standard's claim in the amount represented by the compromise offer.

Petitioners invoke the so-called instrumentality rule,-under which, they say, Deep Rock is to be regarded as a department or agent of Standard,- to preclude the allowance of Standard's claim in any amount. The rule was much discussed in the opinion below. It is not, properly speaking, a rule, but a convenient way of designating the application, in particular circumstances, of the broader equitable principle that the doctrine of corporate entity, recognized generally and for most purposes, will not be regarded when so to do would work fraud or injustice. This principle has been applied in appropriate circumstances to give minority stockholders redress against wrongful injury to their interests by a majority stockholder.[5] It must be apparent that the preferred stockholders of Deep Rock assert such injury by Standard as the basis of their attack on the decree below. We need not stop to discuss the remedy which would be available to them if Section 77B of the Bankruptcy Act had not been adopted for we think that, by that section, the court, in approving a plan, was authorized and required, as a court of equity, to recognize the rights and the status of the preferred stockholders arising out of Standard's wrongful and injurious conduct in the mismanagement of Deep Rock's affairs.

The Section contains a provision new in bankruptcy legislation with respect to the standing of stockholders in corporate reorganization. Subsection (b) provides: 'A plan of reorganization ... (2) may include provisions modifying or altering the rights of stockholders generally, or of any class of them, either through the issuance of new securities of any character or

5) Compare Southern Pacific Co. v. Bogert, 250 U.S. 483, 39 S.Ct. 533.

otherwise; ....' In the present case there remains an equity after satisfaction of the creditors in which only the preferred stockholders and Standard can have an interest. Equity requires the award to preferred stockholders of a superior position in the reorganized company. The District Judge, we think, properly exercised his discretion in refusing to approve the first offer of compromise and concomitant plan because it partly subordinated preferred stockholders to Standard. The same considerations which moved him to reject that plan required the rejection of the new offer and the amended plan.

Deep Rock finds itself bankrupt not only because of the enormous sums it owes Standard but because of the abuses in management due to the paramount interest of interlocking officers and directors in the preservation of Standard's position, as at once proprietor and creditor of Deep Rock. It is impossible to recast Deep Rock's history and experience so as even to approximate what would be its financial condition at this day had it been adequately capitalized and independently managed and had its fiscal affairs been conducted with an eye single to its own interests. In order to remain in undisturbed possession and to prevent the preferred stockholders having a vote and a voice in the management, Standard has caused Deep Rock to pay preferred dividends in large amounts. Whatever may be the fact as to the legality of such dividends judged by the balance sheets and earnings statements of Deep Rock, it is evident that they would not have been paid over a long course of years by a company on the precipice of bankruptcy and in dire need of cash working capital. This is only one of the aspects in which Standard's management and control has operated to the detriment of Deep Rock's financial condition and ability to function. Others are apparent from what has been said and from a study of the record. If a reorganization is effected the amount at which Standard's claim is allowed is not important if it is to be represented by stock in the new company, provided the stock to be awarded it is subordinated to that awarded preferred stockholders. No plan ought to be approved which does not accord the preferred stockholders a right of participation in the equity in the Company's assets prior to that of Standard, and at least equal voice with Standard in the management. Anything less would be to remand them to precisely the status which has inflicted serious detriment on them in the past. REVERSED.

Mr. Justice FRANKFURTER took no part in the consideration or decision of this case.

WALKOVSZKY v. CARLTON

18 NY2d 414 (N.Y. 1966), Court of Appeals of New York
Argued September 26, 1966; Decided November 29, 1966

OPINION OF THE COURT

Fuld, J. This case involves what appears to be a rather common practice in the taxicab industry of vesting the ownership of a taxi fleet in many corporations, each owning only one or two cabs.

The complaint alleges that the plaintiff was severely injured four years ago in New York City when he was run down by a taxicab owned by the defendant Seon Cab Corporation and negligently operated at the time by the defendant Marchese. The individual defendant, Carlton, is claimed to be a stockholder of 10 corporations, including Seon, each of which has but two cabs registered in its name, and it is implied that only the minimum automobile liability insurance required by law (in the amount of $10,000) is carried on any one cab. Although seemingly independent of one another, these corporations are alleged to be "operated * * * as a single entity, unit and enterprise" with regard to financing, supplies, repairs, employees and garaging, and all are named as defendants.[1] The plaintiff asserts that he is also

1) The corporate owner of a garage is also included as a defendant.

entitled to hold their stockholders personally liable for the damages sought because the multiple corporate structure constitutes an unlawful attempt "to defraud members of the general public" who might be injured by the cabs. [*417] The defendant Carlton has moved, pursuant to CPLR 3211(a)7, to dismiss the complaint on the ground that as to him it "fails to state a cause of action". The court at Special Term granted the motion but the Appellate Division, by a divided vote, reversed, holding that a valid cause of action was sufficiently stated. The defendant Carlton appeals to us, from the nonfinal order, by leave of the Appellate Division on a certified question.

The law permits the incorporation of a business for the very purpose of enabling its proprietors to escape personal liability (*see, e.g., Bartle v. Home Owners Co-op.,* 309 N. Y. 103, 106) but, manifestly, the privilege is not without its limits. Broadly speaking, the courts will disregard the corporate form, or, to use accepted terminology, "pierce the corporate veil", whenever necessary "to prevent fraud or to achieve equity". (*International Aircraft Trading Co. v. Manufacturers Trust Co.,* 297 N. Y. 285, 292.) In determining whether liability should be extended to reach assets beyond those belonging to the corporation, we are guided, as Judge Cardozo noted, by "general rules of agency". (*Berkey v. Third Ave. Ry. Co.,* 244 N. Y. 84, 95.) In other words, whenever anyone uses control of the corporation to further his own rather than the corporation's business, he will be liable for the corporation's acts "upon the principle of respondeat superior applicable even where the agent is a natural person". (*Rapid Tr. Subway Constr. Co. v. City of New York,* 259 N. Y. 472, 488.) Such liability, moreover, extends not only to the corporation's commercial dealings (*see, e.g., Natelson v. A. B. L. Holding Co.,* 260 N. Y. 233; *Quaid v. Ratkowsky,* 224 N. Y. 624; *Luckenbach S. S. Co. v. Grace & Co.,* 267 F. 676, 681, cert. den. 254 U. S. 644; *Weisser v. Mursam Shoe Corp.,* 127 F. 2d 344) but to its negligent acts as well. (*See Berkey v. Third Ave. Ry. Co.,* 244 N. Y. 84, *supra*; *Gerard v. Simpson,* 252 App. Div. 340, mot. for lv. to app. den. 276 N. Y. 687; *Mangan v. Terminal Transp. System,* 247 App. Div. 853 mot. for lv. to app. den. 272 N. Y. 676.)

In the Mangan case (247 App. Div. 853, mot. for lv. to app. den. 272 N. Y. 676, *supra*), the plaintiff was injured as a result of the negligent operation of a cab owned and operated by one of four corporations affiliated with the defendant Terminal. Although the defendant was not a stockholder of any of the operating [*418] companies, both the defendant and the operating companies were owned, for the most part, by the same parties. The defendant's name (Terminal) was conspicuously displayed on the sides of all of the taxis used in the enterprise and, in point of fact, the defendant actually serviced, inspected, repaired and dispatched them. These facts were deemed to provide sufficient cause for piercing the corporate veil of the operating company — the nominal owner of the cab which injured the plaintiff - and holding the defendant liable. The operating companies were simply instrumentalities for carrying on the business of the defendant without imposing upon it financial and other liabilities incident to the actual ownership and operation of the cabs. (*See, also, Callas v. Independent Taxi Owners Assn.,* 66 F. 2d 192 [D. C. Ct. App.], cert. den. 290 U. S. 669; *Association of Independent Taxi Operators v. Kern,* 178 Md. 252; *P. & S. Taxi & Baggage Co. v. Cameron,* 183 Okla. 226; cf. *Black & White v. Love,* 236 Ark. 529; *Economy Cabs v. Kirkland,* 127 Fla. 867, adhered to on rearg. 129 Fla. 309.)

In the case before us, the plaintiff has explicitly alleged that none of the corporations "had a separate existence of their own" and, as indicated above, all are named as defendants. However, it is one thing to assert that a corporation is a fragment of a larger corporate combine which actually conducts the business. (*See* Berle, The Theory of Enterprise Entity, 47 Col. L. Rev. 343, 348-350.) It is quite another to claim that the corporation is a "dummy" for its individual stockholders who are in reality carrying on the business in their personal capacities for purely personal rather than corporate ends. (*See African Metals Corp. v. Bullowa,* 288 N. Y. 78, 85.) Either circumstance would justify treating the corporation as an agent and piercing the corporate veil to reach the principal but a different result would follow in each case. In the first, only a larger corporate entity would be held financially responsible (*see, e.g., Mangan v. Terminal Transp. System,* 247 App. Div. 853, mot. for lv. to app. den. 272 N. Y. 676, *supra*; *Luckenbach S. S. Co. v. Grace & Co.,* 267 F. 2d 676, 881, cert. den. 254 U. S. 644, *supra.*; cf. *Gerard v. Simpson,* 252 App. Div. 340, mot. for lv. to app. den. 276 N. Y. 687, *supra.*) while, in the other, the stockholder would be personally liable. (See, e.g., *Natelson v. A. B. L. Holding Co.,* 260 N. Y. 233, *supra*; [*419] *Quaid v. Ratkowsky,* 224 N. Y. 624, *supra*; *Weisser v. Mursam Shoe Corp.,* 127 F. 2d 344, *supra.*;.) Either the stockholder is conducting the business in his individual capacity or he is not. If he is, he will be liable; if he is not, then, it does not matter — insofar as his personal liability is concerned — that the enterprise is actually being carried on by a larger "enterprise entity". (*See* Berle, The Theory of Enterprise Entity, 47 Col. L. Rev. 343.)

At this stage in the present litigation, we are concerned only with the pleadings and, since CPLR 3014 permits causes of action to be stated "alternatively or hypothetically", it is possible for the plaintiff to allege both theories as the basis for his demand for judgment. In ascertaining whether he has done so, we must consider the entire pleading, educing therefrom " 'whatever can be implied from its statements by fair and reasonable intendment.' " (*Condon v. Associated Hosp. Serv.,* 287 N. Y. 411, 414; *see,* also, *Kober v. Kober,* 16 N Y 2d 191, 193-194; *Dulberg v. Mock,* 1 N Y 2d 54, 56.) Reading the complaint in this case most favorably and liberally, we do not believe that there can be gathered from its averments the allegations required to spell out a valid cause of action against the defendant Carlton.

The individual defendant is charged with having "organized, managed, dominated and controlled" a fragmented corporate entity but there are no allegations that he was conducting business in his individual capacity. Had the taxicab fleet been owned by a single corporation, it would be readily apparent that the plaintiff would face formidable barriers in attempting to establish personal liability on the part of the corporation's stockholders. The fact that the fleet ownership has been deliberately split up among many corporations does not ease the plaintiff's burden in that respect. The corporate form may not be disregarded merely because the assets of the corporation, together with the mandatory insurance coverage of the vehicle which struck the plaintiff, are insufficient to assure him the recovery sought. If Carlton were to be held individually liable on those facts alone, the decision would apply equally to the thousands of cabs which are owned by their individual drivers who conduct their businesses through corporations organized pursuant to section 401 of the Business Corporation Law and carry the minimum insurance required by subdivision 1 (par. [a]) of section 370 of the Vehicle and Traffic Law. These [*420] taxi owner- operators are entitled to form such corporations (*cf. Elenkrieg v. Siebrecht,* 238 N. Y. 254), and we agree with the court at Special Term that, if the insurance coverage required by statute "is inadequate for the protection of the public, the remedy lies not with the courts but with the Legislature." It may very well be sound policy to require that certain corporations must take out liability insurance which will afford adequate compensation to their potential tort victims. However, the responsibility for imposing conditions on the privilege of incorporation has been committed by the Constitution to the Legislature (N. Y. Const., art. X, §1) and it may not be fairly implied, from any statute, that the Legislature intended, without the slightest discussion or debate, to require of taxi corporations that they carry automobile liability insurance over and above that mandated by the Vehicle and Traffic Law.[2]

This is not to say that it is impossible for the plaintiff to state a valid cause of action against the defendant Carlton. However, the simple fact is that the plaintiff has just not done so here. While the complaint alleges that the separate corporations were undercapitalized and that their assets have been intermingled, it is barren of any "sufficiently particular[ized] statements"

---

2) There is no merit to the contention that the ownership and operation of the taxi fleet "constituted a breach of hack owners regulations as promulgated by [the] Police Department of the City of New York". Those regulations are clearly applicable to individual owner-operators and fleet owners alike. They were not intended to prevent either incorporation of a single-vehicle taxi business or multiple incorporation of a taxi fleet.

(CPLR 3013; see 3 Weinstein-Korn- Miller, N. Y. Civ. Prac., par. 3013.01 *et. seq.*, p. 30-142 *et. seq.*) that the defendant Carlton and his associates are actually doing business in their individual capacities, shuttling their personal funds in and out of the corporations "without regard to formality and to suit their immediate convenience." (*Weisser v. Mursam Shoe Corp.,* 127 F. 2d 344, 345, *supra.*.) Such a "perversion of the privilege to do business in a corporate form" (*Berkey v. Third Ave. Ry. Co.,* 244 N. Y. 84, 95, *supra.*;) would justify imposing personal liability on the individual stockholders. (*See African Metals Corp. v. Bullowa,* 288 N. Y. 78, *supra.*;.) Nothing of the sort has in fact been charged, and it cannot reasonably or logically be inferred from the happenstance that the business of Seon [*421] Cab Corporation may actually be carried on by a larger corporate entity composed of many corporations which, under general principles of agency, would be liable to each other's creditors in contract and in tort.[3)]

In point of fact, the principle relied upon in the complaint to sustain the imposition of personal liability is not agency but fraud. Such a cause of action cannot withstand analysis. If it is not fraudulent for the owner-operator of a single cab corporation to take out only the minimum required liability insurance, the enterprise does not become either illicit or fraudulent merely because it consists of many such corporations. The plaintiff's injuries are the same regardless of whether the cab which strikes him is owned by a single corporation or part of a fleet with ownership fragmented among many corporations. Whatever rights he may be able to assert against parties other than the registered owner of the vehicle come into being not because he has been defrauded but because, under the principle of respondeat superior, he is entitled to hold the whole enterprise responsible for the acts of its agents.

3) In his affidavit in opposition to the motion to dismiss, the plaintiff's counsel claimed that corporate assets had been "milked out" of, and "siphoned off" from the enterprise. Quite apart from the fact that these allegations are far too vague and conclusory, the charge is premature. If the plaintiff succeeds in his action and becomes a judgment creditor of the corporation, he may then sue and attempt to hold the individual defendants accountable for any dividends and property that were wrongfully distributed (Business Corporation Law, §§ 510, 719, 720).

In sum, then, the complaint falls short of adequately stating a cause of action against the defendant Carlton in his individual capacity. The order of the Appellate Division should be reversed, with costs in this court and in the Appellate Division, the certified question answered in the negative and the order of the Supreme Court, Richmond County, reinstated, with leave to serve an amended complaint.

KEATING, J. (DISSENTING).

The defendant Carlton, the shareholder here sought to be held for the negligence of the driver of a taxicab, was a principal shareholder and organizer of the defendant corporation which owned the taxicab. The corporation was one of 10 organized by the defendant, each containing [*422] two cabs and each cab having the "minimum liability" insurance coverage mandated by section 370 of the Vehicle and Traffic Law. The sole assets of these operating corporations are the vehicles themselves and they are apparently subject to mortgages. [4)] From their inception these corporations were intentionally undercapitalized for the purpose of avoiding responsibility for acts which were bound to arise as a result of the operation of a large taxi fleet having cars out on the street 24 hours a day and engaged in public transportation. And during the course of the corporations' existence all income was continually drained out of the corporations for the same purpose. The issue presented by this action is whether the policy of this State, which affords those desiring to engage in a business enterprise the privilege of limited liability through the use of the corporate device, is so strong that it will permit that privilege to continue no matter how much it is abused, no matter how irresponsibly the corporation is operated, no matter what the cost to the public. I do not believe that it is.

Under the circumstances of this case the shareholders should all be held

---

4) It appears that the medallions, which are of considerable value, are judgment proof. (Administrative Code of City of New York, § 436-2.0.)

individually liable to this plaintiff for the injuries he suffered. (*See Mull v. Colt Co.,* 31 F. R. D. 154, 156; *Teller v. Clear Serv. Co.,* 9 Misc 2d 495.) At least, the matter should not be disposed of on the pleadings by a dismissal of the complaint. "If a corporation is organized and carries on business without substantial capital in such a way that the corporation is likely to have no sufficient assets available to meet its debts, it is inequitable that shareholders should set up such a flimsy organization to escape personal liability. The attempt to do corporate business without providing any sufficient basis of financial responsibility to creditors is an abuse of the separate entity and will be ineffectual to exempt the shareholders from corporate debts. It is coming to be recognized as the policy of law that shareholders should in good faith put at the risk of the business unincumbered capital reasonably adequate for its prospective liabilities. If capital is illusory or trifling compared with the business to be done and the risks [*423] of loss, this is a ground for denying the separate entity privilege." (Ballantine, Corporations [rev. ed., 1946], § 129, pp. 302-303.)

In *Minton v. Cavaney* (56 Cal. 2d 576) the Supreme Court of California had occasion to discuss this problem in a negligence case. The corporation of which the defendant was an organizer, director and officer operated a public swimming pool. One afternoon the plaintiffs' daughter drowned in the pool as a result of the alleged negligence of the corporation.

Justice Roger Traynor, speaking for the court, outlined the applicable law in this area. "The figurative terminology 'alter ego' and 'disregard of the corporate entity' ", he wrote, "is generally used to refer to the various situations that are an abuse of the corporate privilege * * * The equitable owners of a corporation, for example, are personally liable when they treat the assets of the corporation as their own and add or withdraw capital from the corporation at will * * * ; when they hold themselves out as being personally liable for the debts of the corporation * * * ; *or when they provide inadequate capitalization and actively participate in the conduct of corporate affairs*". (56 Cal. 2d, p. 579; italics supplied.)

Examining the facts of the case in light of the legal principles just enumerated, he found that "[it was] undisputed that there was no attempt to provide adequate capitalization. [The corporation] never had any substantial assets. It leased the pool that it operated, and the lease was forfeited for failure to pay the rent. Its capital was 'trifling compared with the business to be done and the risks of loss' ". (56 Cal. 2d, p. 580.) It seems obvious that one of "the risks of loss" referred to was the possibility of drownings due to the negligence of the corporation. And the defendant's failure to provide such assets or any fund for recovery resulted in his being held personally liable.

In *Anderson v. Abbott* (321 U. S. 349) the defendant shareholders had organized a holding company and transferred to that company shares which they held in various national banks in return for shares in the holding company. The holding company did not have sufficient assets to meet the double liability requirements of the governing Federal statutes which provided that the owners of shares in national [*424] banks were personally liable for corporate obligations "to the extent of the amount of their stock therein, at the par value thereof, in addition to the amount invested in such shares" (U. S. Code, tit. 12, former § 63).

The court had found that these transfers were made in good faith, that other defendant shareholders who had purchased shares in the holding company had done so in good faith and that the organization of such a holding company was entirely legal. Despite this finding, the Supreme Court, speaking through Mr. Justice Douglas, pierced the corporate veil of the holding company and held all the shareholders, even those who had no part in the organization of the corporation, individually responsible for the corporate obligations as mandated by the statute.

"Limited liability", he wrote, "is the rule, not the exception; and on that assumption large undertakings are rested, vast enterprises are launched, and huge sums of capital attracted. But there are occasions when the limited liability sought to be obtained through the corporation will be qualified or denied. Mr. Justice Cardozo stated that a surrender of that principle of limited liability would be made 'when the sacrifice is essential to the end that some accepted public policy may be defended or upheld.' * * * The cases of fraud make up part of that exception * * * But they do not exhaust it. *An obvious inadequacy of capital, measured by the nature and magnitude of the corporate undertaking, has frequently been an important factor in cases denying stockholders their defense of limited liability* * * * *That rule has been invoked even in absence of a legislative policy which undercapitalization would defeat.* It becomes more important in a case such as the present one where the statutory policy of double liability will be defeated if impecunious bank-stock holding companies are allowed to be interposed as non-conductors of liability. *It has often been held that the interposition of a corporation will not be allowed to defeat a legislative policy, whether that was the aim or only the result of the arrangement* * * * 'the courts will not permit themselves to be blinded or deceived by mere forms of law 'but will deal' with the substance of the transaction involved as if the corporate agency did not exist and as the justice of the case may require.' " (321 U. S., pp. 362-363; emphasis added.) [*425]

The policy of this State has always been to provide and facilitate recovery for those injured through the negligence of others. The automobile, by its very nature, is capable of causing severe and costly injuries when not operated in a proper manner. The great increase in the number of automobile accidents combined with the frequent financial irresponsibility of the individual driving the car led to the adoption of section 388 of the Vehicle and Traffic Law which had the effect of imposing upon the owner of the vehicle the responsibility for its negligent operation. It is upon this very statute that the cause of action against both the corporation and the individual defendant is predicated.

In addition the Legislature, still concerned with the financial irresponsibility of those who owned and operated motor vehicles, enacted a statute requiring minimum liability coverage for all owners of automobiles. The important public policy represented by both these statutes is outlined in section 310 of the Vehicle and Traffic Law. That section provides that: "The legislature is concerned over the rising toll of motor vehicle accidents and the suffering and loss thereby inflicted. The legislature determines that it is a matter of grave concern that motorists shall be financially able to respond in damages for their negligent acts, so that innocent victims of motor vehicle accidents may be recompensed for the injury and financial loss inflicted upon them."

The defendant Carlton claims that, because the minimum amount of insurance required by the statute was obtained, the corporate veil cannot and should not be pierced despite the fact that the assets of the corporation which owned the cab were "trifling compared with the business to be done and the risks of loss" which were certain to be encountered. I do not agree.

The Legislature in requiring minimum liability insurance of $10,000, no doubt, intended to provide at least some small fund for recovery against those individuals and corporations who just did not have and were not able to raise or accumulate assets sufficient to satisfy the claims of those who were injured as a result of their negligence. It certainly could not have intended to shield those individuals who organized corporations, with the specific intent of avoiding responsibility to the public, where the operation of the corporate enterprise yielded profits sufficient to purchase additional insurance. Moreover, it is reasonable [*426] to assume that the Legislature believed that those individuals and corporations having substantial assets would take out insurance far in excess of the minimum in order to protect those assets from depletion. Given the costs of hospital care and treatment and the nature of injuries sustained in auto collisions, it would be unreasonable to assume that the Legislature believed that the minimum provided in the statute would in and of itself be sufficient to recompense "innocent victims of motor vehicle accidents * * * for the injury and financial loss inflicted upon them".

The defendant, however, argues that the failure of the Legislature to increase the minimum insurance requirements indicates legislative acquiescence in this scheme to avoid liability and responsibility to the public. In the absence of a clear legislative statement, approval of a scheme having such serious consequences is not to be so lightly inferred. The defendant contends that the court will be encroaching upon the legislative domain by ignoring the corporate veil and holding the individual shareholder. This argument was answered by Mr. Justice Douglas in *Anderson v. Abbott* (*supra*.;, pp. 366-367) where he wrote that: "In the field in which we are presently concerned, judicial power hardly oversteps the bounds when it refuses to lend its aid to a promotional project which would circumvent or undermine a legislative policy. To deny it that function would be to make it impotent in situations where historically it has made some of its most notable contributions. If the judicial power is helpless to protect a legislative program from schemes for easy avoidance, then indeed it has become a handy implement of high finance. *Judicial interference to cripple or defeat a legislative policy is one thing; judicial interference with the plans of those whose corporate or other devices would circumvent that policy is quite another.* Once the purpose or effect of the scheme is clear, once the legislative policy is plain, we would indeed forsake a great tradition to say we were helpless to fashion the instruments for appropriate relief." (Emphasis added.)

The defendant contends that a decision holding him personally liable would discourage people from engaging in corporate enterprise. [*427] What I would merely hold is that a participating shareholder of a corporation vested with a public interest, organized with capital insufficient to meet liabilities which are certain to arise in the ordinary course of the corporation's business, may be held personally responsible for such liabilities. Where corporate income is not sufficient to cover the cost of insurance premiums above the statutory minimum or where initially adequate finances dwindle under the pressure of competition, bad times or extraordinary and unexpected liability, obviously the shareholder will not be held liable (Henn, Corporations, p. 208, n.7). The only types of corporate enterprises that will be discouraged as a result of a decision allowing the individual shareholder to be sued will be those such as the one in question, designed solely to abuse the corporate privilege at the expense of the public interest.

For these reasons I would vote to affirm the order of the Appellate

Division. Chief Judge Desmond and Judges Van Voorhis, Burke and Scileppi concur with Judge Fuld; Judge Keating dissents and votes to affirm in an opinion in which Judge Bergan concurs.

Order reversed, etc.

KLINICKI v. LUNDGREN

Supreme Court of Oregon, In Banc., 695 P.2d 906 (1985); 298 Or. 662
Argued and Submitted September 5, 1984; Decided February 20, 1985.

Brad Littlefield, of Goldsmith, Siegel, Engel & Littlefield, Portland, and Lloyd B. Egenes, of O'Gara, Friedman, Egenes & Burke, San Francisco, Cal., argued the cause and filed a petition and response for petitioner on review/respondent on review F.R. Klinicki. Janet A. Metcalf, of English & Metcalf, Portland, argued the cause and filed a petition and response for petitioner on review/respondent on review Air Berlin Charter Co.

JONES, Justice.

The factual and legal background of this complicated litigation was succinctly set forth by Chief Judge Joseph in the Court of Appeals opinion as follows:

"In January, 1977, plaintiff Klinicki conceived the idea of engaging in the air transportation business in Berlin, West Germany. He discussed the idea with his friend, defendant Lundgren. At that time, both men were furloughed Pan American pilots stationed in West Germany. They decided to enter the air transportation business, planning to begin operations with an air taxi service and later to expand into other service, such as regularly scheduled flights or chater flights. In April, 1977, they incorporated Berlinair, Inc., as a closely held Oregon corporation. Plaintiff was a vice-president and a director. Lundgren was the corporation's president and a director. Each man owned 33 percent of the company stock. Lelco, Inc., a corporation owned by Lundgren and members of his family, owned 33 percent of the stock. The corporation's attorney owned the remaining one percent of the stock. Berlinair obtained the necessary governmental *909 licenses, purchased an aircraft and in November, 1977, began passenger service.

"As president, Lundgren was responsible, in part, for developing and promoting Berlinair's transportation business. Plaintiff was in charge of operations and maintenance. In November, 1977, plaintiff and Lundgren, as representatives of Berlinair, met with representatives of the Berliner Flug Ring (BFR), a consortium of Berlin travel agents that contracts for charter flights to take sallow German tourists to sunnier climes. The BFR contract was considered a lucrative business opportunity by those familiar with the air transportation business, and plaintiff and defendant had contemplated pursuing the contract when they formed Berlinair. After the initial meeting, all subsequent contacts with BFR were made by Lundgren or other Berlinair employes acting under his directions.

"During the early stages of negotiations, Lundgren believed that Berlinair could not obtain the contract because BFR was then satisfied with its carrier. In early June, 1978, however, Lundgren learned that there was a good chance that the BFR contract might be available. He informed a BFR representative that he would make a proposal on behalf of a new company. On July 7, 1978, he incorporated Air Berlin Charter Company (ABC) and was its sole owner. On August 20, 1978, ABC presented BFR with a contract proposal, and after a series of discussions it was awarded the contract on September 1, 1978. Lundgren effectively concealed from plaintiff his negotiations with BFR and his diversion of the BFR contract to ABC, even though he used Berlinair working time, staff, money and facilities.

"Plaintiff, as a minority stockholder in Berlinair, brought a derivative action against ABC for usurping a corporate opportunity of Berlinair. He also brought an individual claim against Lundgren for compensatory and punitive damages based on breach of fiduciary duty.[1)]

---

1) The named plaintiff in the complaint is F.R. Klinicki. The named defendants are Kim Lundgren, Berlinair, Inc., an Oregon corporation, and Air Berlin Charter Company, an Oregon corporation. The complaint set forth four causes of suit summarized as follows:

(A) The first cause of suit was brought by plaintiff as a derivative stockholders suit in his own behalf and on behalf of all other stockholders of Berlinair, Inc. "and in the right of Berlinair, Inc. and for its

"The trial court found that ABC, acting through Lundgren, had wrongfully diverted the BFR contract, which was a corporate opportunity of Berlinair. The court imposed a constructive trust on ABC in favor of Berlinair, ordered an accounting by ABC and enjoined ABC from transferring its assets. The trial court also found that Lundgren, as an officer and director of Berlinair, had breached his fiduciary duties of good faith, fair dealing and full disclosure owed to plaintiff individually and to Berlinair. The court did not award plaintiff any actual damages on the breach of fiduciary duty claim. All the issues were *910 tried to the court, except that a jury was empaneled to try the punitive damages issue. It returned a verdict in favor of plaintiff and assessed punitive damages against Lundgren in the amount of $750,000. Lundgren then moved to dismiss plaintiff's claim for punitive damages. The court granted the motion to dismiss and, *sua sponte,* entered judgment in favor of Lundgren notwithstanding the verdict on the punitive damages claim." *Klinicki v. Lundgren,* 67 Or. App. 160, 162-63, 678 P.2d 1250, 1251-52 (1984) (footnote omitted).

ABC appealed to the Court of Appeals contending that it did not usurp a corporate opportunity of Berlinair. Plaintiff cross-appealed from the trial court's dismissal of the punitive damages claim and from the entry of judgment in favor of Lundgren notwithstanding the verdict on that issue. The Court of Appeals affirmed the trial court on all issues.

---

benefit" seeking a constructive trust against Lundgren and ABC jointly and severally, an accounting by all defendants and an injunction and attorney fees.

(B) The second cause of suit involves a personal claim by Klinicki requesting the court to require Lundgren to purchase the stock of plaintiff in Berlinair after the BFR corporate opportunity held by ABC is restored to Berlinair, Inc.

(C) The third cause of suit — Count I — is an individual claim of Klinicki for an accounting from Lundgren and ABC.

(D) The third cause of suit — Count II — is plaintiff's individual claim for unjust enrichment against Lundgren.

(E) The third cause of suit — Count III — is a personal claim by plaintiff against Lundgren for breach of implied covenant of good faith and fair dealing to plaintiff. For the third cause of suit plaintiff sought a constructive trust and accounting decree against Lundgren and ABC covering any "monies, funds, assets, facilities and properties received and acquired as a result of Lundgren's breach of fiduciary duty."

(F) The fourth cause of action is an individual suit by Klinicki solely against Lundgren for breach of fiduciary duty seeking general damages of $50,000 and $1 million in punitive damages.

I. THE APPEAL BY AIR BERLIN CHARTER CO. (ABC)

ABC petitions for review to this court contending that the concealment and diversion of the BFR contract was not a usurpation of a corporate opportunity, because Berlinair did not have the financial ability to undertake that contract. ABC argues that proof of financial ability is a necessary part of a corporate opportunity case and that plaintiff had the burden of proof on that issue and did not carry that burden.

There is no dispute that the corporate opportunity doctrine precludes corporate fiduciaries from diverting to themselves business opportunities in which the corporation has an expectancy, property interest or right, or which in fairness should otherwise belong to the corporation. *See* Henn & Alexander, Laws of Corporations 632-37, § 237 (3rd ed. 1983). The doctrine follows from a corporate fiduciary's duty of undivided loyalty to the corporation.[2] ABC agrees that, unless Berlinair's financial inability to undertake the contract makes a difference, the BFR contract was a corporate opportunity of Berlinair.[3]

---

2) * * [Officers and directors] must devote themselves to the corporate affairs with a view to promote the common interests and not their own, and they cannot, either directly or indirectly, utilize their position to obtain any personal profit or advantage other than that enjoyed also by their fellow shareholders [citations omitted]. In short, there is demanded of the officer or director of a corporation that he furnish to it his undivided loyalty; if there is presented to him a business opportunity which is within the scope of its own activities and of present or potential advantage to it, the law will not permit him to seize the opportunity for himself; if he does so, the corporation may elect to claim all of the benefits of the transaction. Nor is it material that his dealings may not have caused a loss or been harmful to the corporation; the test of his liability is whether he has unjustly gained enrichment. *Bailey v. Jacobs,* 325 Pa. 187, 194, 189 A. 320, 324 [(1937)].' * * * see generally Fletcher, Cyclopedia Corporations § 861.1 (rev. ed. 1965); * * * Note, 'Corporate Opportunity', 74 Harv.L.Rev. 765 (1961)." *Seaboard Industries, Inc. v. Monaco,* 442 Pa. 256, 261-62, 276 A.2d 305, 309 (1971).

The Corporate Directors' Guidebook (pp 1599-1600) defines the duty of loyalty:

"I. Duty of Loyalty. By assuming his office, the corporate director commits allegiance to the enterprise and acknowledges that the best interests of the corporation and its shareholders must prevail over any individual interest of his own. The basic principle to be observed is that the director should not use his corporate position to make a personal profit or gain to his personal advantage. * * *"

This definition reflects the fiduciary duties which generally attach to directors of close corporations. *See, e.g., Delaney v. Georgia-Pacific Corp.,* 278 Or. 305, 564 P.2d 277 (1977); *Baker v. Commercial Body Builders,* 264 Or. 614, 507 P.2d 387 (1973).

3) ABC asserts in its brief that the single issue in the corporate opportunity portion of this appeal is the financial

We first address the issue, resolved by the Court of Appeals in Berlinair's favor, of the relevance of a corporation's financial ability to undertake a business opportunity to proving a diversion of corporate opportunity *911 claim. This is an issue of first impression in Oregon.

The Court of Appeals held that a corporation's financial ability to undertake a business opportunity is not a factor in determining the existence of a corporate opportunity unless the defendant demonstrates that the corporation is technically or de facto insolvent. Without defining these terms, the Court of Appeals specifically placed the burden of proof[4] as to this issue on the fiduciary by saying: "To avoid liability for usurping a corporate opportunity on the basis that the corporation was insolvent, the fiduciary must prove insolvency." 67 Or. App. at 165, 678 P.2d at 1254. The Court of Appeals then concluded "that ABC usurped a corporate opportunity belonging to Berlinair when, acting through Lundgren, the BFR contract was diverted" because nothing in Lundgren's testimony or otherwise in the record suggested that Berlinair was insolvent or was no longer a viable corporate entity. 67 Or. App. at 166, 678 P.2d at 1254. Accordingly, the Court of Appeals held that the constructive trust, injunction, duty to account and other relief granted by the trial court against ABC were appropriate remedies.

One commentator, Daniel Walker, in *Legal Handles Used to Open or Close the Corporate Opportunity Door,* 56 NW UL Rev 608 (1961), wrote that few areas of the law are as plagued with platitudes as the fiduciary responsibility of corporate officers and directors. He noted that the Supreme Court of the

---

ability of Berlinair to undertake the BFR contract. It makes no point of the fact that the trial court found Kim Lundgren usurped the corporate opportunity for himself, yet ABC was controlled and owned by Kim Lundgren, his father, Leonard Lundgren, and their attorney.

4) This case was tried before the effective date of the Oregon Evidence Code. The code now provides:
"OEC 305. Allocation of the burden of persuasion. A party has the burden of persuasion as to each fact the existence or nonexistence of which the law declares essential to the claim for relief or defense the party is asserting."
"OEC 307. Allocation of the burden or producing evidence. (1) The burden or producing evidence as to a particular issue is on the party against whom a finding on the issue would be required in the absence of further evidence. (2) The burden of producing evidence as to a particular issue is initially on the party with the burden of persuasion as to that issue."

United States, seemingly caught up in its enthusiasm for such platitudes, strings together a whole series of them quoting from *Pepper v. Litton,* 308 U.S. 295, 311, 60 S.Ct. 238, 247, 84 L.Ed. 281, 291-92 (1939):

> "'He who is in such a fiduciary position cannot serve himself first and his *cestuis* second.... He cannot by the intervention of a corporate entity violate the ancient precept against serving two masters * * *. He cannot utilize his inside information and his strategic position for his own preferment. He cannot violate rules of fair play by doing indirectly through the corporation what he could not do directly. He cannot use his power for his personal advantage and to the detriment of the stockholders.... [His power] may not be exercised for the aggrandizement, preference, or advantage of the fiduciary to the exclusion or detriment of the *cestuis*.'" Walker, 56 NW UL Rev at 608 n 1.

Walker then commented:

> "One aspect of corporate fiduciary responsibility that has particularly troubled the courts in their search for a rule of thumb is that relating to so-called corporate opportunities. *What are the legal rules to be applied in determining when a corporate official, given an opportunity to make a profitable acquisition (business, lease, land, stock, whatever), can take it for himself rather than turning it over to the corporation?* * * *
>
> "The answer given by many courts may start with a bow to the fiduciary concept (*e.g.,* 'Of course, those having fiduciary duty must never place themselves in a situation of divided loyalties'), but it frequently ends up with an amorphous test which may help the court state the result but rarely helps anyone find the result: 'The officer is free to take an opportunity providing the corporation does not have an interest or expectancy *912 [whatever that is] in the opportunity.' It is just as helpful, and as unhelpful, to say as some courts do that if the opportunity 'belongs' to the corporation or if the officer is under a 'duty' to negotiate the opportunity for the corporation, the official cannot have it. The problem is, when does it 'belong' to the corporation and under what circumstances does the 'duty' arise? * * *" 56 NW UL Rev at 608-09 (emphasis added; brackets in original; footnote omitted).

Before proceeding further our initial task must be to define what is meant by "corporate opportunity," and to determine when, if ever, a corporate fiduciary may take personal advantage of such an opportunity. Our resolution of this case will be limited to announcing a rule to be applied when allegations of usurpation of a corporate opportunity are made against a director of a close corporation. The determination of a rule to apply to similar situations arising between a director and a publicly held corporation presents problems and concepts which may not necessarily require us to apply an identical rule in that similar but distinguishable context.

As we mentioned at the outset, this issue is a matter of first impression in this state. While courts universally stress the high standard of fiduciary duty owed by directors and officers to their corporation, there are distinct schools of thought on the circumstances in which business opportunities may be taken for personal advantage. One group of jurisdictions severely restricts the corporate official's freedom to take advantage of opportunities by saying that the ability to undertake the opportunity is irrelevant and usurpation is essentially prohibited; other jurisdictions use a test which gives relatively wide latitude to the corporate official on the theory that financial ability to undertake a corporate opportunity is a prerequisite to the existence of a corporate opportunity.

A rigid rule was applied in *Irving Trust Co. v. Deutsch,* 73 F.2d 121 (2nd Cir.1934). In that case a syndicate made up of directors of Acoustic Products Co. purchased for themselves from another corporation the rights to manufacture under certain radio patents which were concededly essential to Acoustic. They justified this on the ground that Acoustic was not financially able to purchase the patents on which the defendants later made very substantial profits. The court refused to inquire whether the conclusion of financial inability was justified. Referring to the facts which raised a question whether Acoustic actually did lack the funds or credit necessary to make the acquisition, the court said:

"* * * Nevertheless, they [the facts in the case concerning whether Acoustic lacked funds to carry out of contract] tend to show the wisdom of a rigid rule forbidding directors of a solvent corporation to take over for their own profit a corporate contract on the plea of the corporation's financial inability to perform. If the directors are uncertain whether the corporation can make the necessary outlays, they need not embark it upon the venture; if they do, they may not substitute themselves for the corporation any place along the line and divert possible benefits into their own pockets. * * *" 73 F.2d at 124.

An oft-cited Harvard Law Review note discussed executive appropriation of corporate opportunities and the *Irving Trust* case as follows:

"Where an opportunity is within the corporation's line of business, the executive seems normally required to offer it for consideration by the board of directors and to await rejection — should it be forthcoming — before seizing it himself. There are, however, some exceptions to this disclosure requirement, all of which rest immediately on the proposition that the circumstances clearly evidence corporate inability * * * to seize the opportunity * * *. [An] exception to the requirement of tender arises where the corporation is insolvent and nearly defunct. [*Jasper v. Appalachian Gas Co.,* 152 Ky. 68, 153 S.W. 50 (1913).] The problem with this exception is the difficulty of its extension to cases where the *913 corporation is in serious financial difficulty or lacks liquid assets but may still be a going concern. [In *Hannerty v. Standard Theatre Co.,* 109 Mo. 297, 19 S.W. 82 (1891), a finding of absence of corporate opportunity was based on the financial inability of the corporation. *But see Irving Trust Co. v. Deutsch,* 73 F.2d 121 (2d Cir. 1934), and *Electronic Dev. Co. v. Robson,* 148 Neb. 526, 28 N.W.2d 130 (1947), where mere financial inability was held inadequate to exonerate an executive who appropriated an opportunity.] In neither case will it ordinarily be entirely clear that, given knowledge of the opportunity, the corporation will be unable to secure needed financing with reasonable rapidity. The very existence of a prospective profitmaking venture may generate additional financial backing and may convince creditors to be less importunate in their demands. Every major executive, including the one who has discovered the opportunity, would seem obligated to make a genuine effort to enable the corporation to secure the anticipated profit. * * *

"Fearing that anything less than a prophylactic rule would discourage executives from expending their full efforts to obtain financing for the corporation, at least one court has articulated the rule that the executive is precluded from appropriating the opportunity where the corporation is allegedly unable to obtain the required funds.

[Citing *Irving Trust Co. v. Deutsch,* supra.] * * *" Note, *Corporate Opportunity,* 74 (Vol. I) Harv.L.Rev. 765, 772-73 (1961) (brackets contain text of footnotes; other footnotes omitted).

In 1962, Professor Victor Brudney wrote in the Michigan Law Review:

"* * * [A] question of corporate opportunity * * * may be analogized to the situation in which the corporation is apparently unable to exploit a potential opportunity because of lack of funds, because of some legal obstacle, or because the person offering the opportunity is purportedly unwilling to deal with it, and the insider takes advantage of the corporate opportunity for his own benefit. Despite frequent pious platitudes to the contrary, neither legislatures nor courts have seen fit to deprive the insider in all, or indeed in most, such circumstances of the temptation to choose between his interest and the interest of the recognized beneficiaries by prescribing a universal rule denying him the fruits of such extraneous activities when they have not demonstrably harmed the corporation or its other security holders.[5] * * *" Brudney, *Insider Securities Dealings During Corporate Crises,* 61 (Vol. I) Mich.L.Rev. 1, 25 (1962).

He then noted the *Irving Trust* case, saying with apparent approval:

"* * * However, from time to time a court will require an insider to account for his profits even in the absence of a showing of harm, on the theory that although the corporation might be unable itself to exploit a particular opportunity, the insider should be denied the right to exploit it and the concomitant temptation to inhibit the corporation from making every effort to do so." 61 Mich.L.Rev. at 25-26 (footnotes omitted).

Representing a more relaxed view of a corporate official's responsibility, in *Guth v. Loft, Inc.,* 23 Del. Ch. 255, 272-73, 5 A.2d 503, 511 (1939), the Supreme Court of Delaware said:

---

5) "See Carrington & McElroy, *The Doctrine of Corporate Opportunity,* 14 Bus.Law. 957 (1959); Fuller, *Restrictions Imposed by Directorship Status on Personal Business Activities of Directors,* 26 Wash.L.Rev. 189 (1941); Ramsey, *Directors Power to Compete with His Corporation,* 18 Ind.L.J. 293 (1943); Walker, *Legal Handles Used to Open or Close the Corporate Opportunity Door,* 56 NW.U.L.Rev. 608 (1961); Comment, 31 Calif.L.Rev. 188 (1943); Note, 39 Colum.L.Rev. 219 (1939); Note, *Corporate Opportunity,* 74 Harv. L.Rev. 765 (1961); Note, 54 Harv.L.Rev. 1191 (1941); Note, *Statutory Sanctions for Conduct of Corporate Directors,* 26 Iowa L.Rev. 334 (1941); Note, 84 U.Pa.L.Rev. 1008 (1936); Note, 2 U.Chi.L.Rev. 323 (1935); Note, 44 Yale L.J. 527 (1935)."

"* * * [I]f there is presented to a corporate officer or director a business *914 opportunity *which the corporation is financially able to undertake,* is, from its nature, in the line of the corporation's business and is of practical advantage to it, is one in which the corporation has an interest or a reasonable expectancy, and, by embracing the opportunity, the self-interest of the officer or director will be brought into conflict with that of his corporation, the law will not permit him to seize the opportunity for himself. * * *" (Emphasis added.)

The language in *Guth* implies that financial ability to undertake a corporate opportunity is not only relevant, but perhaps a condition precedent to the existence of a corporate opportunity. But the language in *Guth* was dictum because that famous case, involving the creation of the PepsiCola enterprise, did not involve the issue of financial ability to undertake the opportunity. The court may have thought that a lack of funds short of insolvency was relevant because it discussed Guth's defense in this area, finding that "Loft's net asset position at that time was amply sufficient to finance the enterprise."[6] But other language in *Guth* raises the question whether the terms "ability to undertake" and "ability to take advantage of" have broader concerns than mere financial capacity or incapacity:

"* * * Where a corporation is engaged in a certain business, and an opportunity is presented to it embracing an activity as to which it has *fundamental knowledge, practical experience and ability to pursue, which, logically and naturally is adaptable to its business*

6) In *Guth v. Loft, Inc.*, 23 Del. Ch. 255, 270, 5 A.2d 503, 510 (1939), the court held that determination of the issue of breach of duty should be made from a consideration of all the circumstances of the transactions, noting the accepted rule that corporate officers and directors are not permitted to use their position of trust and confidence to further their private interests:

"* * * The standard of loyalty is measured by no fixed scale.

"If an officer or director of a corporation, in violation of his duty as such, acquires gain or advantage for himself, the law charges the interest so acquired with a trust for the benefit of the corporation, at its election, while it denies to the betrayer all benefit and profit. The rule, inveterate and uncompromising in its rigidity, does not rest upon the narrow ground of injury or damage to the corporation resulting from a betrayal of confidence, but upon a broader foundation of a wise public policy that, for the purpose of removing all temptation, extinguishes all possibility of profit flowing from a breach of the confidence imposed by the fiduciary relation. Given the relation between the parties, a certain result follows; and a constructive trust is the remedial device through which precedence of self is compelled to give way to the stern demands of loyalty. [Citations omitted.]"

> *having regard for its financial position, and is one that is consonant with its reasonable needs and aspirations for expansion,* it may be properly said that the opportunity is in the line of the corporation's business." 23 Del. Ch. at 279, 5 A.2d at 514 (emphasis added).

On the other end of the legal spectrum from *Irving Trust Co. v. Deutsch, supra,* are two Minnesota cases: *Miller v. Miller,* 301 Minn. 207, 222 N.W.2d 71, 77 A.L.R.3d 941 (1974), and *A.C. Peters v. St. Cloud Enterprises, Inc.,* 301 Minn. 261, 222 N.W.2d 83 (1974). In *Miller,* the Minnesota Supreme Court stated a two-step test to be applied in corporate opportunity cases. The first step, the "line of business" part of the test, was described as follows:

> "* * * The threshold question to be answered is whether a business opportunity presented is also a `corporate' opportunity, i.e., whether the business opportunity is of sufficient importance and is so closely related to the existing or prospective activity of the corporation as to warrant judicial sanctions against its personal acquisition by a managing officer or director of the corporation. This question, necessarily one of fact, can best be resolved, we believe, by resort to a flexible application of the `line of business' test set forth in *Guth v. Loft, Inc., supra.* The inquiry of the factfinder should be directed to all facts and circumstances relevant to the question, the most significant being: Whether the business opportunity presented is one in which the complaining corporation has an interest or an expectancy growing out of *915 an existing contractual right; the relationship of the opportunity to the corporation's business purposes and current activities - whether essential, necessary, or merely desirable to its reasonable needs and aspirations -; whether within or without its corporate powers, the opportunity embraces areas adaptable to its business and into which the corporation might easily, naturally, or logically expand; the competitive nature of the opportunity - whether prospectively harmful or unfair -; *whether the corporation, by reason of insolvency or lack of resources, has the financial ability to acquire the opportunity;* and whether the opportunity includes activities as to which the corporation has a fundamental knowledge, practical experience, facilities, equipment, personnel, and the ability to pursue. The fact that the opportunity is not within the scope of the corporation's powers, while a factor to be considered, should not be determinative, especially where the corporate fiduciary dominates the board of directors or is the majority shareholder."

301 Minn. at 224-25, 222 N.W.2d at 81 (emphasis added).

In other words, the court found that financial ability is a prerequisite to establishing a corporate opportunity. The court went on to hold that, where the facts were in dispute, the burden of proof on the financial issue rests upon the "party attacking the acquisition":

> "If the facts are undisputed that the business opportunity presented bears no logical or reasonable relation to the existing or prospective business activities of the corporation *or that it lacks either the financial or fundamental practical or technical ability to pursue it,* then such opportunity would have to be found to be noncorporate as a matter of law. If the facts are disputed or reasonable minds functioning judicially could disagree as to whether the opportunity is closely associated with the existing or prospective activities of the corporation or its financial or technical ability to pursue it, *the question is one of fact with the burden of proof resting upon the party attacking the acquisition."* 301 Minn. at 225, 222 N.W.2d at 81 (emphasis added).

The companion case of *A.C. Petters v. St. Cloud Enterprises, Inc., supra,* applied the rule of *Miller v. Miller, supra. See also Ellzey v. Fyr-Pruf, Inc.* 376 So.2d 1328 (Miss. 1979). Counsel for defendant, relying on *Miller,* contends there is no corporate opportunity if there is no capacity to take advantage of the corporate opportunity. We reject this argument. By the same token, we reject plaintiff's contention, relying on *Irving Trust,* that financial ability is totally irrelevant in an unlawful taking of a corporate opportunity.

In this opinion we previously quoted from an article written by Professor Victor Brudney in 1962 when he was advocating a strict view on usurpation of corporate opportunities in closely held corporations, Brudney, *Insider Securities Dealings During Corporate Crises, supra.* Almost 20 years later, this same noted authority on Corporation Law, joined by Professor Robert Charles Clark, wrote in the Harvard Law Review that the law of corporate opportunities is still among the least satisfactory limbs of doctrine in the corpus of corporate law. After criticizing the Minnesota court's approach in *Miller* as adding "only a new layer of confusion to an already murky area of law, without forwarding the analysis in any significant fashion," the authors assert that "[n]ot only are the common formulations vague, but the courts have articulated no theory that could serve as a blueprint for constructing meaningful rules." Brudney and Clark, *A New Look at Corporate Opportunities,* 94 Harv.L.Rev. 997, 998 (1981). In that article, Professors Brudney and Clark argue that a principled doctrine should distinguish between publicly held corporations and close corporations. They suggest that in the former case a categorical ban on diversions is usually appropriate, but that separate rules should be developed for fulltime *916 executives, outside directors and parent companies. They assert, however, that in cases involving close corporations, a more flexible, selective approach should govern in light of the essentially contractual nature of the close corporate venture. They reason:

"* * * Investors in public corporations are usually passive and widely scattered contributors of money to be managed by pre-selected officers to whom they effectively delegate full decisionmaking power over operating matters. In contrast, investors in private ventures are fairly small in number and tend to know one another. They make more conscious choices when selecting managers from among themselves. They are likely to be active participants rather than merely passive contributors of funds. And they can consent in a more meaningful way to diversions of corporate assets by fellow participants, either when they form or join enterprises, or on the occasion of the diversion. Accordingly, such investors have less need of categorical strictures on such diversions." 94 Harv L Rev at 1003 (footnotes omitted).

The authors then suggest guidelines for the taking of business opportunities by participants in closely held corporations:

"(1) If the disputed opportunity is functionally related to the corporation's business, then, whether or not it is 'necessary' or of 'special value,' individual participants may not take it.

"(2) If the corporation has an 'interest' or 'expectancy' in the opportunity, individual participants may not take it.

"(3) If the participants consent in advance or contemporaneously to diversion of the new project, an individual participant may take it, even though the taking would otherwise run afoul of (1) or (2); provided, however, that nothing less than express contemporaneous consent will permit the taking of functionally related opportunities whose acceptance is `necessary' to prevent loss or injury to the corporation." 94 Harv L Rev at 1011 (footnote omitted).

They conclude that the burden should be on the diverter to prove that the particular diversion was originally consented to by the venturers. Brudney and Clark then address the specific issue in this case — the relevance of corporate incapacity to undertake a corporate opportunity to usurpation of a corporate opportunity by a fiduciary:

"Our proposed principles * * * leave no room for some of the other variables that frequently appear in the opinions. There is a substantial body of case law that permits officers to divert corporate opportunities when some showing is made that the corporation is unable to take the opportunity because of limitations in its charter or contracts, external legal constraints, *its inability to finance the acquisition,*[7)] or the unwillingness of the persons offering the opportunity to deal with the corporation.

"As courts have pointed out on several occasions, if financial disabilities or third party refusals to deal with the corporation are accepted as tests, the inevitable result will be to permit the diversion. This is true because courts must resolve the legal issues on the basis of a set of facts largely within the control of the diverter. *Thus, for example, when managers argue that the corporation could not have financed an offered bargain, the capacity of outsiders to show that the corporation could have raised the money is limited.* * * *" 94 Harv. L.Rev. at 1020-21 (footnotes omitted).

The authors conclude:

"There is no reason to allow the diverters to exploit opportunities that they claim the corporation is unable to exploit, *917 if the claimed inability may be feasibly eliminated. To permit claims of disability to become the subject of judicial controversy when they can only be disproven by outsiders with great difficulty and at considerable

7) *"City of Miami Beach v. Smith,* 551 F.2d 1370 (5th Cir.1977); *Presidio Mining Co. v. Overton,* 261 F. 933 (9th Cir.1919), *aff'd,* 270 F. 388 (9th Cir.), *cert. denied,* 256 U.S. 694, 41 S.Ct. 535, 65 L.Ed. 1175 (1921); *Rankin v. Frebank Co.,* 47 Cal. App.3d 75, 121 Cal. Rptr. 348 (1975); *Katz Corp. v. T.H. Canty & Co.,* 168 Conn. 201, 362 A.2d 975 (1975); *A.C. Petters Co. v. St. Cloud Enterprises, Inc.,* 301 Minn. 261, 222 N.W.2d 83 (1974) (per curiam); *Gauger v. Hintz,* 262 Wis. 333, 55 N.W.2d 426 (1952)."

expense is to tempt participants to actions whose impropriety is visible but rarely subject to effective challenge. Availability of the defense of corporate incapacity reduces the incentive to solve corporate financing and other problems.

"The argument against the defense of incapacity or disability may be less forceful for close corporations than for public corporations because of the greater familiarity of the participants with the affairs of the firm, their better access to relevant information, and the relative manageability of the problems. But the arguments against the defense are not without power in the close corporation context as well, as several courts have noted. Moreover, *the possibility of obtaining consent to non-pro rata participation in a venture that the corporation appears unable to exploit should remove the seeming harshness of a rule that does not allow the defense of corporate incapacity.* Indeed, rejection by the other participants of a request to assist in curing the incapacity might occur in circumstances that imply consent to the requesting person's taking the opportunity." 94 Harv.L.Rev. at 1022 (emphasis added).

On April 13, 1984, the American Law Institute published its "Tentative Draft No. 3" concerning "Principles of Corporate Governance: Analysis and Recommendations." The draft, of course, does not represent the position of the ALI, but it does contain definitions and rules which we find helpful in resolving the main issue in this case. Section 5.12 of the draft, which contains the proposed general rule and definition, reads as follows:

"(a) *General Rule:* "A director or principal senior executive may not take a corporate opportunity for himself or an associate unless:

(1) The corporate opportunity has first been offered to the corporation, and disclosure has been made to the corporate decisionmaker of all material facts known to the director or principal senior executive concerning his conflict of interest and the corporate opportunity (unless the corporate decisionmaker is otherwise aware of such material facts); and

(2) The corporate opportunity has been rejected by the corporation in a manner that meets one of the following standards:

(A) In the case of a rejection of a corporate opportunity that was authorized by disinterested directors following such disclosure, the directors who authorized the rejection acted in a manner that meets the standards of the business judgment rule set forth in § 4.01(d);[8)]

(B) In the case of a rejection that was authorized or ratified by disinterested shareholders following such disclosure, the rejection was not equivalent to a waste of corporate assets; and

(C) In the case of a rejection that was not authorized or ratified in the manner contemplated in § 5.12(a)(2)(A) or (B) or permitted by the terms of a [validly adopted] standard of the corporation * * *, the taking of the opportunity was fair to the corporation.

"(b) *Definition of a Corporate Opportunity:* "A corporate opportunity means any opportunity to engage in a business activity (including acquisition or use of any *918 contract right or other tangible or intangible property) that:

(1) In the case of a principal senior executive or any director, is an opportunity that is communicated or otherwise made available to him either:

(A) in connection with the performance of his obligations as a principal senior executive or director or under circumstances that should reasonably lead him to believe that the person offering the opportunity expects him to offer it to the corporation, or

(B) through the use of corporate information or property, if the resulting opportunity is one that the principal senior executive or director should reasonably be expected to believe would be of interest to the corporation; or

(2) In the case of a principal senior executive or a director who is a fulltime employee of the corporation, is an opportunity that he knows or reasonably should know is closely related to the business in which the corporation is engaged or may reasonably be expected to engage." (Bracketed section references omitted.)

---

8) Section 4.01 provides in pertinent part:
"A director has a duty to his corporation to perform his functions in good faith, in a manner that he reasonably believes to be in the best interests of the corporation * * * and with the care that an ordinarily prudent person would reasonably be expected to exercise in a like profession and under similar circumstances." *See, Devlin v. Moore,* 64 Or. 433, 462, 130 P. 35, 45 (1913).

Section 5.12 presents an approach very similar to that suggested by Chief Judge Joseph in the Court of Appeals decision rendered in this case. Section 5.12 generally would require an opportunity that could be advantageous to the corporation to be offered to the corporation by a director or principal senior executive before he takes it for himself. Section 5.12 declines to adopt the rigid rule expressed in *Irving Trust Co. v. Deutsch, supra,* which precludes a person subject to the duty of loyalty from pursuing a rejected opportunity. The proposed rule permits a director or principal senior executive to deal with his corporation so long as he deals fairly with full disclosure and bears the burden of proving fairness unless the corporate opportunity was rejected by disinterested directors or shareholders. The comment to Section 5.12(a) reads:

"Section 5.12(a) sets forth the general rule requiring a director or principal senior executive to first offer an opportunity to the corporation before taking it for himself. If the opportunity is not offered to the corporation, the director or principal senior executive will have violated § 5.12(a).

"Section 5.12(a) contemplates that a corporate opportunity will be promptly offered to the corporation, and that the corporation will promptly accept or reject the opportunity. Failure to accept the opportunity promptly will be considered tantamount to a rejection. * * *"

and that

"* * * Rejection in the context of § 5.12(a)(2) may be based on one or more of a number of factors, such as lack of interest of the corporation in the opportunity, *its financial inability to acquire the opportunity,* legal restrictions on its ability to accept the opportunity, or unwillingness of a third party to deal with the corporation. * * *" (Emphasis added.)

The comment to Section 5.12(b) reads:

"Section 5.12(b) defines a corporate opportunity broadly as including any proposed acquisition of contract rights or other tangible or intangible property which falls into one of the categories set forth in §§ 5.12(b)(1) or 5.12(b)(2). * *"

Section 5.12(c) would allocate the burden of proof in corporate opportunity cases as follows:

"(c) *Burden of Proof:*

"In any proceeding in which there is a challenge under § 5.12(a), the challenging party has the burden of proof, except if the rejection of a corporate opportunity was not authorized or ratified in the manner contemplated in § 5.12(a)(2)(A) or (B) or permitted by the terms of a [validly adopted] standard of the corporation * * *, the director or principal senior executive has the burden of proving that his taking of the opportunity was fair to the corporation. If a good faith attempt has been made to achieve the disclosure contemplated by § 5.12(a)(1) in connection with rejection of a corporate opportunity, *919 the burden of proof remains on the challenging party even if the disclosure failed to so comply, so long as the rejection is ratified by disinterested directors or shareholders after complete disclosure has been made. *If the challenging party satisfies the burden of proving that a corporate opportunity was taken without being offered to the corporation, the challenging party will prevail.*" (Emphasis added.)

The comment to Section 5.12(c) reads in part:

"The burden of coming forward with evidence and the ultimate burden of proof will be upon the person attacking a director's or principal senior executive's conduct to prove that (1) the director of principal senior executive acquired a corporate opportunity * * *. The complainant will also have the burden of proof with respect to all other aspects of the transaction, including lack of disclosure to the corporate decisionmaker and establishing that the requisite number of directors or shareholders who approved or ratified the transaction were not disinterested. *However, if disinterested directors or shareholders have not approved or ratified the rejection of the opportunity, the director or principal senior executive will have the burden of proving that his taking of the opportunity was fair and that the rejection of the opportunity was fair to the corporation at the time of the rejection.* * *" (Emphasis added.)

Whether the rejection was fair or not includes consideration of whether the corporation was financially or otherwise incapacitated from undertaking the corporate opportunity. We agree with the proposed ALI Principles of Corporate Governance, *supra,* as to the following rules for application in close corporation corporate opportunity cases.[9)]

Where a director or principal senior executive of a close corporation wishes to take personal advantage of a "corporate opportunity," as defined by the proposed rule, the director or principal senior executive must comply strictly with the following procedure:

(1) the director or principal senior executive must promptly offer the opportunity and disclose all material facts known regarding the opportunity to the disinterested directors[10)] or, if there is no disinterested director, to the disinterested shareholders. [11)]If the director or principal senior *920 executive learns of other material facts after such disclosure, the director or principal senior executive must disclose these additional facts in a like manner before personally taking the opportunity.

(2) The director or principal senior executive may take advantage of the

---

9) We have approved other ALI Tentative Drafts. *See, Troutman v. Erlandson,* 287 Or. 187, 598 P.2d 1211 (1979).

10) The term "disinterested director" is not specifically defined in the tentative proposal for ALI's "Principles of Corporate Governance and Structure" (1984). Instead, an "interested director" is defined in Section 1.15(1) of the ALI's Principles of Corporate Governance and Structure (Tent.Draft No. 2 1984): "(1) a director or officer is `interested' in a transaction if: (a) the director or officer is a party to the transaction, or (b) the director or officer or an associate of the director or officer has a pecuniary interest in the transaction, or the director or officer has a financial or familial relationship to a party to the transaction, that is sufficiently substantial that it would reasonably be expected to affect the director's or officer's judgment with respect to the transaction in a manner adverse to the corporation." (Bracketed section references omitted.)
Section 5.04 of Tentative Draft No. 3 provides:
"A provision that gives a specified effect to action by disinterested directors requires the affirmative votes of a majority of the directors on the board or an appropriate committee who are not interested [§ 1.15] in the transaction in question." Thus we define a "disinterested director" as any director other than one "interested" as defined by Section 1.15(1).

11) The term "disinterested shareholder" is not specifically defined in the ALI tentative drafts. Section 1.09 reads:
"[This definition will be written in connection with Part V. On what constitutes a majority of disinterested shareholders, see [§ 1.27(2)].]" However, no definition of "disinterested shareholder" was written in Part V. Our definition of "disinterested shareholder" is derived from Section 1.15 of the ALI's Second Tentative Draft, *supra.* Subsection (2) of Section 1.15 provides: "A shareholder is interested in a transaction if either the shareholder or, to his knowledge, an associate of the shareholder, is a party to the transaction."
Section 5.05 of the Third Tentative Draft, *supra,* provides:
"A provision that gives a specified effect to action by disinterested shareholders requires approval of the proposal by a majority of the votes cast by shareholders who are not interested [§ 1.15] in the transaction in question." Thus, we define a "disinterested shareholder" as one who is not a party nor an associate of a party to the transaction in question.

corporate opportunity only after full disclosure and only if the opportunity is rejected by a majority of the disinterested directors or, if there are no disinterested directors, by a majority of the disinterested shareholders[12] If, after full disclosure, the disinterested directors or shareholders unreasonably fail to reject the offer,[13] the interested director or principal senior executive may proceed to take the opportunity if he can prove the taking was otherwise "fair" to the corporation. Full disclosure to the appropriate corporate body is, however, an absolute condition precedent to the validity of any forthcoming rejection as well as to the availability to the director or principal senior executive of the defense of fairness.

(3) An appropriation of a corporate opportunity may be ratified by rejection of the opportunity by a majority of disinterested directors or a majority of disinterested shareholders, after full disclosure subject to the same rules as set out above for prior offer, disclosure and rejection. Where a director or principal senior executive of a close corporation appropriates a corporate opportunity without first fully disclosing the opportunity and offering it to the corporation, absent ratification, that director or principal senior executive holds the opportunity in trust for the corporation.

Applying these rules to the facts in this case, we conclude:

(1) Lundgren, as director and principal executive officer of Berlinair, owed a fiduciary duty to Berlinair.

(2) The BFR contract was a "corporate opportunity" of Berlinair.

(3) Lundgren formed ABC for the purpose of usurping the opportunity presented to Berlinair by the BFR contract.

---

12) A simple majority of disinterested directors or shareholders is sufficient to authorize or ratify an appropriation of a corporate opportunity by a director or principal executive officer.

13) A valid acceptance of the offer by the disinterested directors or shareholders would bar the fiduciary from appropriating the opportunity. An acceptance of the offer by the disinterested directors which failed to meet the standards of the business judgment rule, or an acceptance by the disinterested shareholders which was the equivalent of a waste of corporate assets would have the same effect as an unreasonable failure to reject. The corporate fiduciary could appropriate the opportunity only upon a showing that the taking was fair to the corporation. *See* ALI, Principles of Corporate Governance and Structure § 5.12(a)(2) (Tent. Draft No. 3 1984).

(4) Lundgren did not offer Berlinair the BFR contract.

(5) Lundgren did not attempt to obtain the consent of Berlinair to his taking of the BFR corporate opportunity.

(6) Lundgren did not fully disclose to Berlinair his intent to appropriate the opportunity for himself and ABC.

(7) Berlinair never rejected the opportunity presented by the BFR contract.

(8) Berlinair never ratified the appropriation of the BFR contract.

(9) Lundgren, acting for ABC, misappropriated the BFR contract.

Because of the above, the defendant may not now contend that Berlinair did not have the financial ability to successfully pursue the BFR contract. As stated in proposed Section 5.12(c) of the Principles of Corporate Governance, *supra,* "If the challenging party satisfies the burden of proving that a corporate opportunity was taken without being offered to the corporation, the challenging party will prevail."

This specific conclusion is also backed by what some might call a legal platitude and others might call a legal classic. When *921 placing special burdens on those in positions of trust, it is worthwhile to recall the well-known admonition of Chief Justice Cardozo speaking for the New York Court of Appeals:

> "Joint adventurers, like copartners, owe to one another, while the enterprise continues, the duty of the finest loyalty. Many forms of conduct permissible in a workaday world for those acting at arm's length, are forbidden to those bound by fiduciary ties. A trustee is held to something stricter than the morals of the market place. Not honesty alone, but the punctilio of an honor the most sensitive, is then the standard of behavior. As to this there has developed a tradition that is unbending and inveterate. Uncompromising rigidity has been the attitude of courts of equity when petitioned to undermine the rule of undivided loyalty by the 'disintegrating erosion' of particular exceptions * * *. Only thus has the level of conduct for fiduciaries been kept at a level higher than that trodden by the crowd. It will not consciously be lowered by any judgment of this court." *Meinhard v. Salmon,* 249 N.Y. 458, 463-64, 164 N.E. 545, 546 (1928).

II. THE CROSS-APPEAL BY KLINICKI

We now turn to plaintiff's cross-appeal. In this case plaintiff brought equitable suits for a constructive trust, accounting and injunction against all defendants, and a personal claim against Lundgren. Plaintiff sought actual and punitive damages against Lundgren, but not against the other defendants. The court made no award of actual damages against Lundgren. The punitive damages issue was segregated and tried before a jury. The jury then returned a verdict for $750,000 punitive damages on February 19, 1979.

On May 6, 1980, some four months after the verdict of $750,000 punitive damages, the defendants moved under ORCP 21 A. to dismiss the fourth cause of action in its entirety upon the ground that it failed to state facts constituting a claim. Defendants' main contention in that motion was that Klinicki was not entitled to general damages and therefore could not recover punitive damages.

On July 7, 1980, further proceedings took place in which the trial judge announced his ruling setting aside the punitive damages verdict as a matter of law.[14] The trial judge ruled that (1) a corporate opportunity existed, (2) the opportunity was in the line of business of Berlinair, (3) defendants had not borne the burden of proving Berlinair was financially unable to undertake the opportunity, and (4) defendant Lundgren breached his fiduciary duty.

The trial court struck the punitive damages relying on *Pedah Company v. Hunt,* 265 Or. 433, 509 P.2d 1197 (1973). In *Pedah,* this court held that a court of equity cannot award punitive damages incident to the granting of injunctive relief. However, in *Rexnord, Inc. v. Ferris,* 294 Or. 392, 657 P.2d 673 (1983), decided after the trial in this case, this court overruled *Pedah*

---

14) ORCP 63 A. requires that a judgment now be granted "on motion": "* * * [T]he court may, *on motion,* render a judgment notwithstanding the verdict, or set aside any judgment which may have been entered and render another judgment, as the case may require." (Emphasis added.)
In this case Count IV of the complaint was stricken under a Rule 21 A.(8) motion (insufficient facts to constitute a claim), therefore rendering an ORCP 63 A. motion moot.

and held that a court may award actual and punitive damages as well as equitable relief in a single action if the plaintiff pleads and proves a claim which factually would permit an award of actual and punitive damages. In *Rexnord* actual and punitive damages were sought and obtained in addition to equitable relief against the same defendants flowing from the same defendants' tortious conduct. In this case no actual damages were awarded, but punitive damages were awarded against Lundgren personally and certain equitable relief was granted against Lundgren and ABC. We point out that the accounting and injunction *922 against transferring assets was directed against all defendants, but the constructive trust was only decreed against ABC and its officers, directors and their successors.

This case is similar to *Rexnord, Inc. v. Ferris, supra,* in that both claims were based on tortious conduct. In *Rexnord,* the complaint claimed defendants engaged in unfair competition, converted plaintiff's trade secrets, confidential information, plans, etc., and interfered with plaintiff's contractual relations. In this case, Lundgren was charged with a course of conduct in secretly diverting the BFR contract to his own company, ABC, constituting a breach of fiduciary duty.

We recently restated that in this state an award of punitive damages coupled with an award of only nominal damages is proper when the case involves special circumstances such as a breach of a fiduciary duty by a public officer. *Lane County v. Wood,* 298 Or. 191, 691 P.2d 473 (1984). We said in *Lane County* that there is no logical connection between actual damages and punitive damages because actual damages are to compensate the injured party, whereas punitive damages are "to give bad actors a legal spanking." 298 Or. at 203, 691 P.2d at 479. Nevertheless we feel, absent breach of public trust or cases in which damages are presumed,[15)] punitive damages claims cannot be awarded merely to punish; the plaintiff must also plead and

15) These include conduct involving invasion of the right of privacy, *Hinish v. Meier and Frank Co.,* 166 Or. 482, 113 P.2d 438 (1941); wrongful attachment of property, *Crouter v. United Adjusters, Inc.,* 259 Or. 348, 485 P.2d 1208 (1971); and trespass, *Rhodes v. Harwood,* 273 Or. 903, 544 P.2d 147 (1975)

prove he or she was somehow actually hurt and damaged by the defendant's conduct. In other words, a proven discrete, discernible harm must underlie any punitive damages award.

The question remains whether that proven harm may be manifested by a decree granting certain equitable remedies or whether actual damages must be awarded. In *Belleville v. Davis,* 262 Or. 387, 405, 498 P.2d 744, 752 (1972), the author of the opinion stated, "We have not previously decided whether an award of punitive damages is proper in an equity case." We have now resolved that issue in *Rexnord, Inc. v. Ferris, supra.* The author continued, "We have held, however, that an award of punitive damages is not proper in the absence of proof that plaintiff is entitled to an award of actual damages." 262 Or. at 405, 498 P.2d at 752. Citing *Crouter v. United Adjusters, Inc.,* 259 Or. 348, 364, 485 P.2d 1208 (1971), and *Carnation Lbr. Co. v. McKenney,* 224 Or. 541, 546-47, 356 P.2d 932 (1960), the court then concluded that under the record in *Belleville* plaintiff was not entitled to an award of actual damages in addition to the equitable relief of specific performance and, therefore, set aside an award of punitive damages.

This court, since ORCP 24 A. was adopted, has not had the opportunity to decide whether an award of punitive damages without an award of actual damages can be supported by a decree of affirmative equitable relief and, if so, what type of equitable remedy will support a claim for punitive damages.

ORCP 24 A. permits the joinder of legal and equitable claims. It provides:

> "A plaintiff may join in a complaint, either as independent or as alternate claims, as many claims, legal or equitable, as the plaintiff has against an opposing party."

We analyze this legal problem on this basis:

(1) Punitive damages cannot exist alone.

(2) Punitive damages cannot be awarded without proof of a harm.

(3) Harm may be presumed in cases of wrongful attachment of property, invasion of privacy and trespass, or when there is a certain type of breach of fiduciary duty by a public officer.

(4) The granting of certain types of equitable relief may or may not

demonstrate some harm to a person who does not have an adequate remedy at law.

*923 In this case plaintiff Klinicki was unable to prove actual dollar damages against Lundgren and the only equitable relief granted against Lundgren in Klinicki's favor was for an accounting and an injunction against transferring assets. The constructive trust was decreed solely in favor of Berlinair. Plaintiff's claim of actual damage against Lundgren was dismissed by the court. Klinicki's claim for punitive damages existed alone.

The fact that the court granted Klinicki equitable relief against Lundgren and ABC in the form of an accounting and an injunction under other counts in the complaint did not prove any independent harm or damage to Klinicki caused by Lundgren's conduct. A decree ordering an accounting does not prove damage or harm. The accounting may balance in favor of the defendant or the plaintiff, or may demonstrate nothing. An injunction or restraining order not to transfer assets also does not prove that Klinicki was personally harmed or damaged by Lundgren's breach of fiduciary duty. Such a decree is designed to prevent harm, not redress harm. Because the constructive trust was imposed only upon ABC, its officers and directors, and not Lundgren personally, and only in favor of Berlinair and not Klinicki, we do not reach the question whether a decree granting a constructive trust will support an award of punitive damages. The punitive damages award stood alone, and was not inextricably tied to proof by plaintiff that he had suffered an invasion of a legally protected interest. Under the circumstances of this case, the punitive damages claim was properly stricken by the court.

The Court of Appeals is affirmed.

U.S. Business Law Class

저 자 : 김 광 록
발행처 : 충북대학교 출판부
발행인 : 윤 여 표
주 소 : (361-763) 충북 청주시 서원구 충대로 1
전 화 : (043) 261-2952, 3014
팩 스 : (043) 274-1256
이메일 : presscbu@chungbuk.ac.kr
등 록 : 제1983-2001-7호
초판1쇄 : 2015. 1. 30.
인쇄처 : 삼성디자인기획(042-221-3111)
디자인 : 디자인오브(ofof.kr)

ISBN 978-89-7295-214-5 93360

이 저서는 2013학년도 충북대학교 학술도서지원사업에 의하여 발행되었음
(This work was supported by the academic books of the Chungbuk National University in 2013)

값 27,000 원